THE
KENNEDY
ASSASSINATION
TAPES

THE KENNEDY ASSASSINATION TAPES

Max Holland

ALFRED A. KNOPF   NEW YORK   2004

For Dora Holland,
who taught me the past always has a pattern

THIS IS A BORZOI BOOK
PUBLISHED BY ALFRED A. KNOPF

Library of Congress Cataloging-in-Publication Data
Johnson, Lyndon B. (Lyndon Baines), 1908–1973.
The Kennedy assassination tapes / [compiled by] Max Holland.—1st ed.
p.   cm.
Annotated compilation of Lyndon Johnson's recorded conversations on the subject during his two administrations.
Includes bibliographical references and index.
ISBN 1-4000-4238-0 (hc. : alk. paper)
1. Kennedy, John F. (John Fitzgerald), 1917–1963—Assassination—Sources.   2. Johnson, Lyndon B. (Lyndon Baines), 1908–1973—Archives.   3. United States—Politics and government—1961–1963—Sources.   4. United States—Politics and government—1963–1969—Sources.   I. Holland, Max.   II. Title.

E842.9.J6425 2004
364.152'4'097309046—dc22   2004048344

Manufactured in the United States of America

First Edition

Contents

Author's Note

This book emerged in part from work done by the author between 1999 and 2003 as a fellow of the Miller Center of Public Affairs, University of Virginia. The Miller Center is home to the Presidential Recordings Program (PRP), where the greatest concentration of scholars and resources has been marshaled to convey the rich history contained in the formerly secret recordings of twentieth-century Presidents, primarily Kennedy, Johnson, and Nixon. I benefited greatly from my affiliation with the PRP scholars, including Timothy Naftali, the Program's director, and Kent Germany, the coordinator of the Johnson project, who help insure high standards of accuracy and scholarship. David Shreve was always willing to share his unrivaled knowledge of the Johnson presidency, and much was learned from Pat Dunn about how to present presidential transcripts. David Coleman was a patient guide to knotty technological problems, and I also worked closely and fruitfully with Ashley High, especially on the difficult conversations of November 1963.

In addition to those individuals, the author would like to acknowledge the following for enhancing his understanding of the Johnson presidency and otherwise facilitating his work: Beppie Braswell; Margaret Edwards; George Eliades; Frank Gavin; Michael Greco; Ken Hughes; Rachel Kelly; Shirley Kohut; Christina Kopp; Robin Kuzen; Ted Kuzen; Fredrik Logevall; Erin Mahan; Tarek Masoud; Allen Matusow; William Miller; Jonathan Rosenberg; Patricia Schaub; Robert Schulzinger; Lorraine Settimo; Dan Stahl; Kenneth Thompson, director emeritus of the Miller Center; Garth Wermter; Matt Wood; and Don Zinman. The staff at the University of Virginia's Alderman Library, especially Lew Purifoy, and the archivists at the Lyndon B. Johnson Library also deserve thanks for their superb service. Without the help of these people and the resources of the Miller Center, this book would have been difficult to accomplish.

Finally, the author wishes to express his gratitude to Philip Zelikow, the director of the Miller Center and a general editor of the Presidential Recordings Series, whose own important work on the Kennedy tape recordings with Ernest May, also a general editor, inspired the creation of the Presidential Recordings Program. Philip welcomed me to the Center and championed my scholarship.

Anyone interested in presidential recordings, from scholars to lay readers, can find no better place to consult than the two websites maintained by the Miller Center: www.millercenter.virginia.edu/programs/prp/index.html

and www.whitehousetapes.org. Digital audio files of all of the conversations included in this book can be found at www.whitehousetapes.org, which is an online distribution point for presidential recordings and associated materials.

This volume takes a somewhat different approach to the presentation of transcripts. All the conversations from November 1963, however, will be presented verbatim and in their entirety in the first volume of the Presidential Recordings Program's chronological series of Johnson tape recordings, to be published by the Miller Center and W. W. Norton in 2005.

Editorial Note

On the surface, a book based upon transcripts of Lyndon Johnson's presidential recordings seems a straightforward proposition. As of this writing, the Lyndon Baines Johnson Library has processed tape recordings from November 1963 to March 1967, and they are available to anyone at a nominal cost. The Library has identified nearly all the participants in the conversations, as well as the dates and times of the recordings, and they are indexed by subject as well.

The processing of the recordings is a formidable task and often taken for granted. Yet, and as anyone who has produced a book based on the Johnson tapes (or for that matter, the Kennedy or Nixon recordings) will readily admit, the genuinely difficult part consists of the decisions that have to be made afterward: the criteria for selecting conversations to be transcribed, the nature of the transcripts, and to what extent the transcripts are annotated.

Selection

The President John F. Kennedy Records Collection Act of 1992 required every entity in the federal government, including federal/private partnerships like the presidential libraries, to search their holdings for any written, aural, or visual records pertaining to the November 1963 assassination of President Kennedy. In compliance with this act, the Johnson Library began processing "assassination-related" recordings and completed its initial release of the Kennedy or "K" series in April 1994. The Library employed a broad but defensible definition of assassination-related. It determined, for example, that all conversations from November 22 to December 31, 1963, fell under this heading because nearly every recording in that period had some bearing on the transition between the two administrations. In addition, the Library's definition included certain conversations from:

- January and February 1964, while the transition between the two administrations continued;
- September 1964, the month the Warren Commission's *Report* was published;
- December 1966, when the controversy over William Manchester's book *The Death of a President* was at its height; and
- January to March 1967, months in which the *Warren Report* became subject

to renewed scrutiny and the period when Jim Garrison instigated a new investigation of the assassination.

This book's definition of *assassination-related* is both very similar and different.

It does not include every recording from the first five weeks, and not only because the sheer number and length of these conversations make it prohibitive to do so. The focus here is on only one of the decisions facing President Johnson during his first days in office, namely, how to mount an investigation of the assassination that would both satisfy responsible opinion and keep the matter from being exploited for political or personal gain. November and December 1963 are thus reduced, more or less, to the decision to appoint what became known as the Warren Commission. Indeed, the Commission's formation and final report, and the subsequent controversies, constitute the backbone of this volume. As seen from the vantage point of Lyndon Johnson, it is a story that has never been told quite this way before.

If Johnson makes a pertinent comment during a conversation that is not presented in this book, every effort has been made to quote that remark in an accompanying annotation. A good example is the president's conversation with Senator George Smathers (D-Florida) on the day after the assassination. The greater part of the conversation is devoted to legislative strategizing and possible running mates for Johnson in 1964, and thus falls outside the scope of this book. Yet at one point, Johnson makes what is perhaps his most candid admission ever about the need to "keep the Kennedy aura" around him for the next eleven months. This revealing phrase is incorporated at an appropriate place in the annotations.

Besides the distillation of conversations from the first five weeks, one specific category of conversations deemed relevant by the Johnson Library is absent, both for reasons of space and also because it was not considered particularly illuminating. In the first few months of his administration, Johnson has several conversations with and about the Secret Service and its chief, James Rowley. During these recordings the president invariably complains about the suffocating presence of the Secret Service detail around him, especially on trips outside Washington. With no vice president in office, and having just lost a president, the Service is undoubtedly being overprotective. It is also worried about losing its protective function (and thus a large part of its budget) to the FBI. These conversations have been elided, though they are certainly assassination-related.

What is included in this volume is more significant than what has been left out. The book incorporates conversations recorded on November 22 prior to Johnson's arrival in Washington (which marks the beginning of the K series). While not technically part of Johnson's presidential recordings, these *Air Force One* conversations certainly fall under the rubric of assassination-related. They were captured during routine monitoring of radio traffic between the presidential entourage and other key parties, including officials at the State Department, in the White House Situation Room, in the surgeon general's office, and aboard a VIP airplane transporting most of President Kennedy's cabinet to Japan at the time of the assassination. Besides vividly illustrating the pain and confusion that resulted as the news of the assassination reached the highest levels of government, these *Air Force One* tapes provide unique information about some ad hoc (and subsequently controversial) decisions that had to be made, especially regarding the site for a postmortem on the president's body.[1]

This volume also incorporates conversations from 1964 and 1965 that initially escaped incorporation in the K series, albeit understandably. References to the Warren Commission can be so fleeting and vague that unless one is steeped in the subject, the import of what is being communicated is easy to miss. During a May 13, 1964, conversation, for example, Senator Richard Russell (D-Georgia) complains to Johnson that the panel is taking too much of his time because of allegations that a Communist sympathizer is a member of the Commission staff. Similarly, on July 23, 1964, press secretary George Reedy talks about a newspaper column that falsely alleges the president is putting pressure on the Warren Commission to submit its final report before the Democratic National Convention. Ideally, the Johnson Library should have released such conversations as part of the K series under its own definition of assassination-related; as it continues to process the tapes, the Library is so identifying them.

This book, in addition, has a somewhat more expansive definition than the Library as to what constitutes an assassination-related conversation. It is useful to understand, in light of the schism that develops between Johnson and Robert Kennedy, how the president views the years he spent as vice president. And Johnson is never more candid about his frustrations and the promises that were broken, than during a March 6, 1965, conversation with his vice president, Hubert Humphrey. The selection of conversations also includes all conversations that bear on the Warren Commission during the life of that panel, insofar as they shed light on attitudes toward one of Johnson's first and most important creations. Johnson was a political being, and the Commission was a political body; it could not be otherwise. Any conversations having to do with the *Warren Report*'s aftermath, of course, are incorporated. Among the more significant are recordings which illuminate the FBI's attack on the *Warren Report* in late 1964, and two conversations from 1966 that reveal how the bureau came to the Commission's defense.

This compilation also includes conversations that pertain to the obloquy and shame visited on the city of Dallas after the assassination. Presidents and leaders have been assassinated in Washington, Buffalo, Memphis, and Los

---

1. These tapes were first made publicly available by the Johnson Library in 1975. They are designated as SRT–969.1, SRT–969.2, and SRT–969.3.

Angeles, yet no city has suffered so from its identification with a political murder. Because they were an integral element of the politics of the assassination, such conversations are incorporated here. One of the better examples is Lyndon Johnson's call, at 3:25 a.m. on November 4, 1964, to the newly elected congressman from Dallas, Earle Cabell.

Lastly, this volume also endeavors to portray the vicissitudes in Lyndon Johnson's relationship with the two most important Kennedys following the assassination. The argument here, which will become explicit in the narrative accompanying the transcripts, is that President Kennedy's assassination, and the Warren Commission, cannot truly be understood without constant reference to these relationships. The struggle between Robert Kennedy and Lyndon Johnson for leadership of the Democratic Party, and presumably the nation, was remarkably similar to the schisms that sometimes follow the demise of an unrivaled religious leader. In both Mormonism and Islam, such a leader's death was followed by an epic struggle between those who believed in a succession by blood and those who supported the designated heir. The Johnson-Kennedy struggle certainly does not compare in import with schisms lasting centuries, but the intensity was reminiscent of religious fervor. Admittedly, there are more than enough conversations about this facet, and all its twists and turns, to make up an entirely separate book. Only a very small but representative selection can be included in these pages, such as Johnson's conversation with Attorney General Nicholas Katzenbach on March 17, 1966, when the president steps back and tries to put his troubled relationship with Robert Kennedy in perspective.

Transcripts

In the first few weeks of the Johnson administration, it was anticipated that the secretarial staff would keep pace with the president and churn out transcripts with only a few days' delay. The burden soon proved overwhelming, but even if it had not, the secretarial transcripts are not to be relied on. The quality varied considerably, as different secretaries understood the word *transcript* to mean different things. As the staff fell further and further behind, the secretaries increasingly resorted to conveying the gist of what was said rather than making a word-by-word rendering, and many nuances, if not the meaning itself, were often lost.

Fashioning a transcript is every bit as subjective as selecting which conversations to transcribe, if not more so. The instant one commits a spoken conversation to paper, it becomes a facsimile of that communication. One truth is clear from the outset: to get the most out of the conversations, there is no substitute for listening to them oneself.

The first question is how far one strays from presenting a verbatim transcript. If there is a guiding principle here, it is that these transcripts are meant to be read. They are accurate as to the substance of the conversations, but are not verbatim, as one might find in a reference work. Rendering the conversations in that manner would tend to make them harder and perhaps tedious to read. Thus, sounds like "ah" occur in these transcripts to be sure, but certainly not as frequently as they are uttered. They are rendered sparingly, most often to convey that the speaker is searching for the right word or thought, in my admittedly subjective opinion. The rule of thumb is akin to the one journalists follow when quoting a public figure. Similarly, in bilateral telephone conversations, the person at the other end of the line will often acknowledge what is being said by saying "yes," "yeah," "hmm," or "uh-huh." These are also not conveyed as often as they can be heard.

Making the transcripts readable still leaves a host of other issues, because there is no single right way to do them. Should Johnson be depicted as speaking the King's English even when he audibly does not? At the other extreme, if Johnson is rendered verbatim in his regional accent, does he begin to sound unfairly like a character out of a Mark Twain novel? Books derived from the John F. Kennedy tape recordings do not have the president saying "Cuber" for Cuba even when that's what it sounds like he is saying and *is* saying. Every tapes-based book seems to strike a somewhat different balance, and apart from accuracy, every approach seems defensible so long as the rules are made plain.

The primary aim here—apart from presenting readable conversations accurately—is to make them evoke the tone or mood of the president and/or the person at the other end of the telephone. This volume leans toward rendering Johnson as he is actually heard speaking, although the president would be the first to disagree with this approach. He made known his preferences in several conversations, but never more clearly than on August 15, 1964, when he told a White House operator, "Tell Juanita [Roberts] and everybody in there [the secretarial pool] to never type up 'yeah.' That's just their hearing. We never say that. We always say 'yes.' And everybody else says 'yes.' There's no such word as 'yeah' and 'uh.' Just say 'yes' and 'no.' "

To present Lyndon Johnson as he demanded to be heard, however, is to strip the conversations of too much color and immediacy. When the president actually says, "Don't y'all tear my foreign aid bill up now . . . you damned isolationists and you fortress America fellas," it loses flavor to transcribe this as "Don't you all tear my foreign aid bill up now . . . you damned isolationists and you fortress America fellows." One can easily go too far, of course, and turn a speaker into a caricature. Thus, not all of Johnson's distinctive dialect (or that of other southerners) is rendered. The intent here is to retain enough of the president's way of speaking so that the reader hears Johnson when reading his words. Discerning readers will note that when Johnson speaks to southern barons of the Senate like Richard Russell and James Eastland, his inflections and dialect become distinctly more southern. He was capable of turning it off and on.

The transcripts are all based on a fresh hearing of the available recordings on analog cassettes. In this regard I am indebted to Martel Electronics of Yorba

Linda, California, which made practical suggestions about how to achieve greater control over the sound on the tape recordings, chiefly via the use of a headphone volume control and frequency equalizer. During a visit to the Johnson Library in February 2004, several analog conversations were rechecked in the digital audio format available at the Library—specifically, critical conversations from November 23 and 29, 1963, and all the 1966 and 1967 conversations.

Other conventions used in transcribing the recordings are as follows:

- If a conversation is deemed assassination-related, the entire available conversation is transcribed or, at least, described. Nonrelevant portions that occur at the beginning, middle, or end are summarized briefly in italicized brackets, such as *[The conversation turns to discussion of an unrelated issue.]*. Whenever a conversation has not yet been released in full by the Johnson Library, it is so noted in a footnote at the beginning of the conversation.

- If a word, phrase, or sentence cannot be rendered with a high degree of certainty, it is identified as *[indistinct]*. The use of *[garbled]* means that not only are the words indistinct but the tape recording itself is flawed. The description *[inaudible]* is used for a section where the speaker's voice is not amplified enough to be heard.

- Italics are used whenever the speaker emphasizes a word, a phrase, or a sentence, and occasionally a particular syllable. If the speaker is reading, then the emphases should be understood to be added by the speaker unless otherwise indicated.

- The symbol ± is used whenever the time of a conversation can only be approximated because a precise time was neither noted when the tape recording itself was logged, nor in the president's Daily Diary.

- The word *sic* is used sparingly, and only to indicate when a speaker makes an obvious error (such as calling Robert Storey "Bill Storey").

- If the bracketed term *[excised]* appears in a transcript, that means that portion is still classified, or has been omitted in accordance with the president's deed of gift, which permits the Johnson Library to redact disparaging or off-color personal remarks.

- When the mood or tone of the person speaking is evident and seems meaningful, it is indicated in a bracketed, italicized description, such as *[anxious]* or *[playful]*. When a speaker is reading from a newspaper article, prepared statement, or memo, that is also indicated.

- If a speaker is not talking directly to the person at the other end of the telephone but is speaking to someone nearby, it is indicated in italicized brackets, such as *[to Bundy]*, or *[aside]*, if the person in the room with the speaker is unknown.

- Routine introductory or conclusionary remarks between participants who know each other well—the great bulk of the conversations, in other words—

have often been edited out. When President Johnson calls someone like Marie Tippit, the widow of the Dallas patrolman murdered on November 22 by Lee Harvey Oswald, the entire conversation is reproduced.

- The notifications by secretaries or White House operators that someone is on the line waiting to talk to the president are routinely eliminated, unless they convey something significant.
- The calls are listed as being "to" or "from" as noted in the president's Daily Diary; when brackets are also used, it denotes uncertainty over who initiated the call. If the call is being returned (having been initiated by the other party) it is so noted whenever possible.
- Ellipses (. . .) are used primarily to indicate faltering or interrupted speech "accompanied by confusion or insecurity," as suggested by the *Chicago Manual of Style*, fifteenth edition. They may also be used to indicate words trailing off, or a pause in the speaker's utterance, though pauses are not indicated unless they sound meaningful. Ellipses are not used in place of omitted words in the transcripts.
- For readability's sake, numbers are often rendered in numerals. For example, though SAM 26000 is often called "two-six thousand," the transcript will always read "26000."
- In a few instances, such as an important conversation between President Johnson and J. Edgar Hoover on November 23, 1963, there is no recording. In such cases the extant transcript is used, subject to only minor editing.
- Because pauses in speech, and even where sentences end or begin, can be quite arbitrary, punctuation marks (for example, commas) are used liberally and to make the spoken word read well.
- A dash (—) denotes an abrupt change in the direction of a speaker's thoughts. It is also used to mark off interruptions and/or overlapping speech.
- Letters, words, and names enclosed in brackets ([ ]) have been liberally inserted in the text to clarify the meaning of what was heard. In addition, in those gray instances where words are clearly audible but the degree of certitude is less than high—perhaps because both parties are talking at the same time—brackets are used to mark off somewhat uncertain words or phrases.

With respect to the *Air Force One (AF1)* conversations only, many audible transmissions have been redacted out. It is difficult to label any conversation from November 22 routine, and the confusion and urgency conveyed in nearly every transmission are testimony to the emotion of the day. Still, such topics as the parceling out of radio frequency assignments, reports from SAM 86972 about its unscheduled landing in Honolulu, and the reconfiguration of Secret Service assignments were judged to be of too little interest. None of the substantive conversations have been left out, though even here they have been edited to eliminate some of the coordination via Andrews Air Force Base that must occur before, say, McGeorge Bundy in the Situation Room can speak to a Secret Service agent aboard *AF1*. One other convention employed with respect to the *AF1* conversations is that individuals are identified as speaking only when their identity is known for certain. Otherwise, the location of the speaker is given. The times for the *AF1* conversations are often approximations, based upon known reference points. They are presented in the order they are heard on the tapes, which may differ.

Annotations

The rule of thumb was to provide enough context about a conversation, including the speaker's background, so that the full meaning could be extracted. Very few conversations are wholly self-evident, and even a conversation that sounds simple on the surface can take on a quite different meaning after being deciphered. Newspapers were often critical in this regard, as Johnson and his staffers are often reacting to articles published that very day. In each case, the precise article being referred to was consulted. The holdings of the Johnson Library were also vital in making sense of many passages that would otherwise be obscure. Particularly useful were basic collections like the president's Daily Diary and Daily Diary Back-up. Several secondary works—primarily biographies of leading figures like Johnson, Russell, Abe Fortas, and Robert Kennedy—also proved invaluable in fixing the conversations in their proper context.

It should be noted that many aspects of the assassination are never discussed by President Johnson in the extant tape recordings. No attempt has been made to incorporate information that is relevant to the assassination but beyond the ken of the president. This is a narrative of the issue as seen from a special perspective—that of President Johnson only—and does not purport to be a comprehensive history of the assassination and its aftermath.

Preface

Why prepare a volume dedicated solely to the assassination-related conversations secretly recorded by President Johnson?

That is a natural question, given that most of the recordings have been available for ten years; have been the subject of countless news articles and columns; and are aired repeatedly over C-SPAN. Such thorough exposure suggests there may not be much new to learn. In addition, of course, many of the assassination-related conversations have been featured in two well-received books, wholly organized around the Johnson tape recordings, by historian Michael Beschloss. Finally, at least a dozen new histories and biographies have appeared since the tape recordings were first released in 1993, and these books have exploited the same conversations as a primary source for their particular subject, whether it was Lyndon Johnson, Robert Kennedy, or the assassination itself. So what purpose is being served?

I have been a keen student of these conversations since 1995, when I began researching a history of the Warren Commission, the panel established in November 1963 to investigate the assassination of John F. Kennedy and the murder of Lee Harvey Oswald, the young man presumed to be the president's assassin. Being engaged in that endeavor, one soon realizes that virtually every primary source of information about the assassination has been distorted over the past forty years, often beyond recognition. Still, I thought, it would be very hard to twist Johnson's own words, and for that reason the tape recordings would somehow escape the fate of other primary sources pertaining to the assassination. That was naïve. The conversations have been misrepresented or misunderstood, purposely and otherwise, by authors seeking to advance one theory or another.

A recent example can be found in *Triangle of Death,* a book published to coincide with the fortieth anniversary of the assassination in November 2003. The authors claim that tape recordings from February 1966 corroborate the central premise of their book, which is that President Kennedy was killed in retaliation for his role in the November 1963 murder of the South Vietnamese president, Ngo Dinh Diem.[1] The corroboration consists of President Johnson

1. Brad O'Leary and L. E. Seymour, *Triangle of Death: The Shocking Truth About the Role of South Vietnam and the French Mafia in the Assassination of JFK* (Nashville, Tenn.: WND Books, 2003). WND Press Release, 23 September 2003.

exclaiming to, among others, Senator Eugene McCarthy (D-Minnesota) that the Kennedy administration "got together and got a goddamn bunch of thugs and assassinated" Diem.

Johnson certainly did say this, and he even expressed the belief privately that Kennedy's own assassination was "divine retribution" for the ill-advised decision to support Diem's forcible overthrow. But to turn this comment into a shocking piece of evidence about President Kennedy's murder is a stretch, to understate it. The interpretation ignores Johnson's well-known penchant to exaggerate and "speak for effect" in private conversations.[2]

Another example of distortion can be found in a 1998 book on the assassination, *Live by the Sword.* The author, Gus Russo, quotes from a conversation between Johnson and Richard Russell, a member of the Warren Commission, that occurred on September 18, 1964, the day the panel met for the last time. "Richard Russell phoned Johnson to say of the official conclusion, 'I don't believe it,' " writes Russo. "To that Johnson responded, 'I don't either.' "[3] Those very words were spoken, to be sure. But the two men were not referring to the official, overall conclusion that Oswald, acting alone, fired all the shots in Dealey Plaza. Rather, they were talking about the Commission's critical *forensic* finding, that one bullet fired from Oswald's rifle had penetrated both President Kennedy and Texas governor John Connally, who was riding in the front seat of the same car.

It would be one thing if misrepresentations of the tape recordings were confined to books by authors with an ax to grind or a theory to propagate. That is not the case. What has been truly surprising is the number of times assassination-related conversations have been misinterpreted in books that are justifiably considered reputable and lasting contributions to the historical literature about the 1960s.

One example can be found in Jeff Shesol's *Mutual Contempt,* a 1997 book about the rivalry between Johnson and Robert Kennedy, aptly described as the feud that defined a decade.[4] Shesol cites an exceptionally important November 29 conversation between President Johnson and FBI director J. Edgar Hoover in the wake of the assassination. The bureau was still uncertain about the significance of Lee Harvey Oswald's trip to Mexico City, where he visited Soviet and Cuban diplomats just six weeks prior to the assassination. In Shesol's rendering, the president wants to know "whether [Oswald] was con-

---

2. Another tendentious interpretation of the same remarks occurs in James Rosen, "What's Hidden in the LBJ Tapes: Johnson Thought JFK Was Responsible for the Murder of Ngo Dinh Diem," *The Weekly Standard,* 29 September 2003.

3. Gus Russo, *Live by the Sword: The Secret War Against Castro and the Death of JFK* (Baltimore, Md.: Bancroft Press, 1998), 378.

4. Jeff Shesol, *Mutual Contempt: Lyndon Johnson, Robert Kennedy, and the Feud That Defined a Decade* (New York: W. W. Norton, 1997).

nected with the Cuban operation [Mongoose] with money."[5] Mongoose, of course, was the CIA code name for the covert operation to overthrow Fidel Castro during the period November 1961 to November 1962 by any means possible, short of another invasion. The problem here is that Mongoose was not the "Cuban operation" Johnson meant. Rather, the president was alluding to the explosive but still secret allegation that Oswald had received $6,500 from Cuban officials during his visit to Mexico City. At no time did Johnson believe that Oswald was ever connected with an authorized CIA operation, and to suggest otherwise is quite mistaken.

An even more compelling example of the problems involved in presenting assassination-related conversations without sufficient attention to the background facts can be found in Michael Beschloss's *Taking Charge,* the first in his multivolume presentation of Johnson tape recordings. Again, it concerns the September 18, 1964, conversation between President Johnson and Senator Russell, the day the Commission met to iron out its last remaining differences over the language in its long-awaited report.

In his brief introduction to the conversation, Beschloss notes that Johnson is calling Russell "to ask about what [the report] contains."[6] That is the first mistake, because it attributes an intent that is not there. The president's call is in fact prompted by another reported clash between U.S. and North Vietnamese naval forces in the Gulf of Tonkin. Johnson is considering whether to respond with a show of force and wants Russell's counsel. The president has no idea that the Warren Commission has just concluded its deliberations, although he knows the report is imminent. Johnson is thus not calling long distance to get the gist in advance and firsthand.

This admittedly minor error would not be worth mentioning except that it is followed by a more substantive mistake. According to Beschloss's transcript, Russell tells the president that he had some profound points of disagreement with the final language of the report and tried to get his views registered. "I tried my best to get in a *dis*-sent," says Russell (according to Beschloss), "but they'd come 'round and trade me out of it by giving me a little old threat."[7] The suggestion is left that Chief Justice Earl Warren and the other members of the panel *threatened* the senior senator from Georgia, to a point where he dropped his objections and signed off on the final language against his better judgment, for the sole purpose of making the report unanimous.

This version of the conversation begs for an explanation. The antipathy between Russell and Warren was and is well known, yet it is unbelievable that

5. Ibid., 131.

6. Michael Beschloss, *Taking Charge: The Johnson White House Tapes, 1963–1964* (New York: Simon & Schuster, 1997), 559.

7. Ibid., 560.

Warren (or anyone else on the panel) would threaten Russell. The only aspect more incredible is that Russell, the most powerful man in Washington apart from the president himself, would *bow* to a threat from Warren on any issue. The inexplicable is resolved once the conversation is listened to carefully. What Russell actually says is that he tried to disagree but the other Commission members traded him out of each of his dissenting points "by giving me a little old *thread of it.*"

There is still a third problem with Beschloss's representation of this conversation, and it is an excellent example of the risk involved in presenting these conversations too literally and with insufficient context. As noted before, during the conversation Russell describes his disbelief in the Commission's so-called "single-bullet theory," that is, the conclusion that one of the missiles fired by Lee Harvey Oswald hit both President Kennedy and Governor Connally. It is the Commission's critical finding—indeed, it is the most important forensic fact that the Commission has added to the case in its entire ten-month investigation. After Russell says he doesn't believe the theory because of Connally's direct testimony to the contrary, Johnson chimes in immediately. "I don't either," says the president.

The problem here is an error of omission rather than commission, because without additional information it is too easy to misconstrue these firm-sounding convictions. While the president is vaguely familiar with the notion of the single bullet, he has no grounding whatsoever in the facts that led the Commission to this conclusion. Rather than truly disagreeing with a carefully arrived-at conclusion, Johnson is simply speaking for effect, in this case to show solidarity with his esteemed mentor. The president really doesn't know enough to register a meaningful opinion one way or another.

Russell's comment too is easily misunderstood absent sufficient context. While it is true that he refused to accept this forensic finding, as a matter of fact he had paid little or no attention to this aspect of the Warren Commission's investigation. To the degree that he participated in the panel's work, his attention was focused on whether Oswald was part of a domestic or foreign conspiracy, especially the latter. Russell, no less than Johnson, is stating an opinion rather than a considered judgment. His view of this particular issue, moreover, is bent by his determination not to let Earl Warren—a man he detests—contradict the sworn testimony of an honorable southern governor.

Because the proper context is lacking, the reader of Beschloss's book cannot arrive at an accurate understanding of the Russell and Johnson statements. And their exchange has been quoted to suggest that the president, along with a leading member of the Warren panel, did not believe in a vital fact that underpins the central finding of the *Warren Report,* that is, that Lee Harvey Oswald was solely responsible for all the wounds inflicted in Dealey Plaza. That suggestion is superficially correct but is also profoundly misleading.

The overall point here is not to highlight errors in other books. Every nonfiction book (including this one) contains them, try as authors might to eliminate them. Rather, the purpose of citing these examples is to show how difficult it is to construe history from the presidential recordings. They constitute a kind of microhistory that requires one to be steeped in contemporary minutiae and sometimes the events not just of a given day, but of a given hour. The recordings often demand a familiarity with heretofore unknown subtleties; certainly they require an understanding of personal foibles and prejudices, such as Johnson's proclivity to exaggerate and Russell's personal grudges.

This book then is conceived in the belief that because of the deserved fascination with the Johnson tapes, there should be a volume that collects all the assassination-relevant recordings in one place and seeks to present them fully and accurately, in their complete context. The conversations pertaining to the 1963 assassination and its aftermath deserve such considered treatment because of their integral role in the drama of Johnson's presidency. It is virtually an article of faith among historians that the war in Vietnam was the overwhelming reason the president left office in 1969 a worn, bitter, and disillusioned man. Yet the assassination-related tapes paint a more nuanced portrait, one in which Johnson's view of the assassination weighed as heavily on him as did the war.

1963

November 22

Friday

The day began on a note of keen anticipation. Friday, after all, would take the presidential entourage into Dallas, that unrivaled bank and bastion of anti-Kennedy sentiment. It wasn't simply the distinction of having been the only large American city to favor Richard Nixon over John Kennedy in the 1960 election that indelibly tagged Dallas. No, it was the sheer emotion and staggering wealth of its opposition in the three years since then that made the city synonymous with Kennedy's bitterest critics. Above and beyond its role as a wellspring for anti-Communism, and anti-Communist paranoia, Dallas was the fount of some of the ugliest anti-Kennedy vitriol in circulation.

Foremost in everyone's mind on the morning of November 22 was Adlai Stevenson's visit to Dallas on October 24. The U.S. ambassador to the United Nations, an experienced politician in his own right, had encountered hostility before on the campaign trail. But it was nothing compared with the mob that descended on him as he left the Dallas municipal auditorium after delivering a speech in favor of U.S. participation in the UN. One well-dressed woman hit him on the head with a placard, and a college student spat in his face. "Are these human beings or animals?" Stevenson muttered as he wiped off the spittle.[1] Afterward he pretended to treat the incident with aplomb, but privately he was shaken to the core. He had never encountered the kind of mindless, raw hate he saw on display in Dallas.

The Stevenson incident might have remained an isolated black eye but for a coincidental development. In a telling reflection of their growing influence and reach, the national news shows sponsored by CBS and NBC had recently expanded their nightly broadcasts from fifteen to thirty minutes. Just a few weeks before, the shoving and spitting would in all likelihood have remained a local story, filmed as it was by a local TV station. But the networks' suddenly larger appetite for graphic footage turned the story into a lead item, in the new way that many Americans were getting their news. Virtually overnight Dallas awoke to find itself stigmatized, its reputation for intolerance indelibly fixed in the national imagination. It was a revealing clue about the stunning power of a new medium.

1. Porter McKeever, *Adlai Stevenson: His Life and Legacy* (New York: William Morrow, 1989), 538–39.

The White House's script for the day called for a direct, ideological assault on the president's right-wing critics; in a sense, it was to be Kennedy's opening salvo against the clear front-runner for the Republican nomination in 1964, Arizona senator Barry Goldwater, easily the most conservative GOP candidate since Robert Taft. The White House press corps seemed poised to play its role in propagating the day's message, too. The advance text of the luncheon speech to be delivered at the Dallas Trade Mart pointedly criticized "voices preaching doctrines wholly unrelated to reality, wholly unsuited to the sixties," and was generating the desired buzz among the reporters.[2] There was every reason to believe they would take the bait and make the president's challenge the lead of every story datelined Dallas. Only one possible development threatened to intrude on this Daniel-walking-into-the-lion's-den theme, and that was a replay of the previous day's public feud between Texas Democrats.

Since the end of Reconstruction, Texas had been a one-party state, like much of the South, and therein lay the true origins of the Democrats' internecine sniping, even though it was often portrayed as a clash of personalities. The state Democratic Party's hegemony was unnatural and increasingly untenable; the Texas GOP, once a political oxymoron, was growing larger by the hour. (After Lyndon Johnson was elected vice president, a Republican won the special 1961 election to fill his Senate seat, the first GOP senator elected in Texas since the 1870s.) In the meantime, liberal and conservative Democrats were engaged in a tenacious, bitter brawl over the presumed soul of the state party, and this ferocious struggle had been bared for everyone to see during the first hours of President Kennedy's visit.

Texas senator Ralph Yarborough, a devout liberal, had quickly become furious about his treatment at the hands of Governor Connally, the conservative Democrat hosting the president's visit. They had already been feuding for weeks about such trivialities as who would stand where in receiving lines, and who would sit next to whom at banquet tables. With good reason, Yarborough believed that Connally was still scheming to diminish his visibility during the president's visit, to a point where Yarborough was not even being accorded the courtesies that a state senator from Amarillo would receive.[3] The lack of an invitation to a reception at the governor's mansion in Austin was particularly grating, and Nellie Connally, always fiercely loyal to her husband, didn't help matters with her own sharp comments.[4] Unable to take revenge against the gov-

2. "Remarks Prepared for Delivery at the Trade Mart in Dallas," 22 November 1963, *Public Papers of the Presidents of the United States, John F. Kennedy* (Washington, D.C.: U.S. Government Printing Office, 1964), 891.

3. Jeb Byrne, "The Hours Before Dallas: A Recollection by President Kennedy's Fort Worth Advance Man," *Prologue,* Summer 2000.

4. Felton West, "No Invitations Trigger Discord in JFK Party," *Houston Post,* 22 November 1963. According to Johnson, in remarks about the Texas trip that were recorded months later, Nellie Connally contributed to Yarborough's pique by joining her husband in saying that she would

ernor directly, Yarborough struck back at the nearest available target, Vice President Lyndon Johnson, Connally's political mentor and a witting conspirator in the humiliating treatment—or so Yarborough thought. In San Antonio and again in Houston, the first two stops on Kennedy's three-day, five-city Texas tour, Yarborough pointedly refused to ride in the same automobile as Johnson, and the headlines in the Friday morning papers were all about Yarborough's snub of the hapless vice president. The 1950s image of Johnson as the domineering majority leader who steered the U.S. Senate at will bore no resemblance to the shrunken politician who seemed to have no purpose other than to serve as Yarborough's scapegoat.

President Kennedy was determined that nothing get in the way of the message he wanted to get across, not even a Texas-sized political headache. On Friday morning Yarborough was informed in no uncertain terms that he had only two choices: "You will either ride in the same car with Lyndon Johnson in Dallas or you will walk."[5] Yarborough, though none too pleased, bowed to the president's request, and the way was cleared for the White House to dominate the news cycle on its terms.

Initially, Dallas seemed intent on playing into the White House's hands. The *Morning News* of November 22 carried a full-page advertisement on page 14, rimmed in black, underwritten by a group calling itself the "American Fact-Finding Committee." Under a sarcastic headline, "WELCOME MR. KENNEDY TO DALLAS," the committee listed twelve deliberately provocative questions, all couched to insinuate that the president (and his brother, the attorney general) were unbearably soft on Communism.[6] The advertisement complemented a handbill that had appeared mysteriously overnight under doors and on the windshields of countless Dallas cars. Featuring the president's image from the front and the left side, as if taken from a police mug shot, the broadside accused him of turning the United States over to the "communist controlled United Nations." In case the imagery or text was lost on anyone, the headline read, "WANTED FOR TREASON."[7]

After reading the paid advertisement, the president sought to prepare Jacqueline Kennedy for any unpleasantness that might occur in the afternoon. "Oh, you know," John Kennedy remarked to his wife, "we're heading into nut country today."[8] Intensely private, often diffident in public, the First Lady dis-

refuse to ride in a car with the senator. Johnson and Frank Erwin, conversation, 1 February 1964, 1:25 p.m., Lyndon Baines Johnson Library (hereafter LBJL).

5. Leslie Carpenter, memo to the president, 9 December 1963, Diary Back-up, Box 4, Special File on the Assassination of John F. Kennedy (hereafter Special File), LBJL.

6. William Manchester, *The Death of a President: November 20–November 25, 1963* (New York: Harper & Row, 1967), 109.

7. President's Commission on the Assassination of President John F. Kennedy [hereafter Warren Commission], *Hearings: Exhibits 392 to 884* (Washington, D.C.: U.S. Government Printing Office, 1964), 17:627.

8. Manchester, *Death,* 121.

liked retail politicking and the press. Campaigning combined the two and as such represented the ultimate invasion of her privacy and the control she cherished. Her disdain for the gestures expected of a politician's wife meant her presence was sometimes a mixed blessing when the president was electioneering. The state of being "on," the lot of political wives, exhausted her. The president would have to remind her not to wear large sunglasses, like some Hollywood movie star, and she almost never partook in behind-the-scenes bantering with staff. The most frequent adjectives applied to the First Lady were "aloof" and "regal," and the latter description was not necessarily intended as complimentary. Jacqueline Kennedy had a "formidable" temper in private, and to hardened pols she was "Jackie the Socialite."[9] She had nonetheless agreed to accompany her husband on his swing through Texas, her presence viewed as a drawing card because of her fluency in Spanish and because Dallas—home of the famed Neiman-Marcus department store—was such a fashion-conscious city that it would turn out just to see what "Jackie" would be wearing. And true to form, the November 7 news that Mrs. Kennedy would accompany the president had substantially increased demand for tickets to the Trade Mart luncheon as well as the other venues on the tour.

The *Morning News* advertisement was a perfect expression of Dallas's venom for the president. Passions, apparently, had not cooled in the wake of the Stevenson incident, and the prospect of a scuffle or some other unsightly incident along the motorcade route or at the Trade Mart appeared likely. But probably there would be nothing more than that, because Dallas law enforcement authorities had taken every precaution recommended by the Secret Service and then some. That morning the paid ad seemed destined only to make the laughs that much louder when Lyndon Johnson delivered his closing line at the gala fund-raising dinner scheduled for Friday evening in Austin. "And thank God, Mr. President," Johnson reportedly intended to say, before pausing for effect, "that you came out of Dallas alive."[10]

At 11:23 a.m. the president and Mrs. Kennedy board the specially designed Boeing 707 popularly known as *Air Force One* for the short hop from Fort Worth to Dallas.

12:29 p.m.[11]

Among the hundreds of people in Dealey Plaza, one of the eye- and ear-witnesses who will be closest to the assassination is Claudia "Lady Bird" Johnson, wife

9. Ibid., 347, 427.

10. Stanley Marcus, *Minding the Store: A Memoir* (Boston: Little, Brown, 1974), 255. This anecdote may be apocryphal.

11. All times for this day, unless otherwise noted, refer to central standard time until page 50.

of the vice president. She is riding, along with her husband and a tight-lipped Senator Yarborough, in a Lincoln Continental convertible just behind the "Queen Mary," an armored 1955 Cadillac convertible brimming with eight Secret Service agents and hidden automatic weapons. Just ahead of the Queen Mary, as the motorcade wends its way through downtown Dallas, is the president's limousine. Though Mrs. Johnson does not capture every detail, her account stands out because she tape-recorded it while her memory was still fresh and relatively untainted.[12]

It all began so beautifully. After a drizzle in the morning, the sun came out bright and beautiful. We were going into Dallas. In the lead car [were] President and Mrs. Kennedy, John and Nellie [Connally], and then a Secret Service car full of men, and then our car, with Lyndon and me, and Senator Yarborough. The streets were *lined* with people— lots and lots of children, all smiling—placards, confetti, people waving from windows. One last, happy moment I had was looking up and seeing Mary Griffith leaning out of a window, waving at me.[13]

Then almost at the edge of town, on our way to the Trade Mart, where we were going to have the luncheon, we were rounding a curve, going down a hill [when] *suddenly,* there was a *sharp,* loud report . . . a shot. It seemed to me to come from the right, above my shoulder, from a building. Then one moment [passed], and then two more shots in rapid succession.

There'd been such a gala air that I thought it must be firecrackers, or some sort of celebration. But then, in the lead car, the Secret Servicemen were suddenly down. I heard over the radio system, "Let's get out of here!" And our Secret Service man who was with us—Rufe Youngblood, I believe it was—*vaulted* over the front seat on top of Lyndon, threw him to the floor, and said, "Get down!"

Senator Yarborough and I ducked our heads. The cars accelerated terrifically fast—faster and faster. Then suddenly, they put on the brakes so hard that I wondered if they were gonna make it as they wheeled left around a corner. We pulled up to a building. I looked up and saw it said, "Hospital." Only then did I believe that this might be what it was. Yarborough kept on saying in an excited voice, "Have they

12. Mrs. Johnson's White House Diary Tapes, 22–24 November 1963, LBJL. The tape-recorded diary appears nearly verbatim in book form. See Lady Bird Johnson, *A White House Diary* (New York: Holt, Rinehart and Winston, 1970). Mrs. Johnson's recollection was apparently aided by notes she began taking in the hospital, at the behest of her husband. She was in the habit of carrying notebooks to record what she called her "never-to-be-forgotten moments." Manchester, *Death,* 231.

13. For many years Mary Griffith had been in charge of altering the clothes Mrs. Johnson purchased at the Neiman-Marcus store in downtown Dallas.

shot the president? Have they shot the president?" I said something like, "No . . . [it] can't be."

As we ground to a halt—we were still the third car—the Secret Servicemen began to pull, lead, guide . . . hustle us out. I cast one last look back over my shoulder and saw a bundle of pink, just like a drift of blossoms, lying in the back seat. I think it was Mrs. Kennedy . . . lying over the president's body.

They led us to the right, to the left, onward into a quiet room in the hospital, a very small room. It was lined with white sheets, I believe. People came and went: Kenny O'Donnell, Congressman [Homer] Thornberry, Congressman Jack Brooks. *Always* there was Rufe right there, [along with Secret Servicemen] Emory Roberts, Jerry Kivett, Lem Johns, [and] Woody Taylor.

It is standard practice for the *Air Force One* crew to monitor the signals that keep the traveling White House in contact with the real one in Washington at all times, courtesy of the White House Communications Agency (WHCA, or "Whakka") and the unrivaled virtuosity of Army Signal Corps operators. Secret Service headquarters, the State Department, and the Pentagon's National Military Command Center are also kept in this communications loop. As *Air Force One*'s pilot, Colonel James Swindal, eavesdrops on the Secret Service agents' chatter, he is pleased to hear that Dallas seems to be redeeming itself after the ugliness of the Stevenson visit. The crowds greeting the motorcade are unexpectedly large and friendly, with nary a hostile placard in sight.[14]

Seconds after 12:30 p.m. Swindal hears a shout explode on Charlie frequency—and then another. His body tenses up, and he recognizes the voice of Roy Kellerman, head of the Secret Service detail, who is riding in the front passenger seat of the president's limousine. Swindal can only make out one injunction from Kellerman—*DAGGER cover VOLUNTEER!*—before the radio becomes a cacophony of screeching voices. Then it falls silent.[15]

Something has clearly gone wrong, but Swindal has no idea what. DAGGER is the code name for Rufus Youngblood, and VOLUNTEER is Lyndon Johnson. Has someone thrown an egg at the vice president? Perhaps a riot has broken out along the motorcade route. While Swindal is mulling over the possibilities, WHCA patches a telephone call from Parkland Memorial Hospital into Special Air Missions (SAM) 26000 (the radio designation for *Air Force One* when it is not airborne). It is Brigadier General Godfrey McHugh, the president's air force aide, with new, cryptic orders. Refuel the airplane instantly and file a flight plan

14. J. F. terHorst and Ralph Albertazzie, *The Flying White House: The Story of Air Force One* (New York: Coward, McCann & Geoghegan, 1979), 210.

15. Ibid., 211.

to return to Andrews Air Force Base (AFB) near Washington immediately. General McHugh does not bother to explain, but since *Air Force One* is involved, Swindal now knows that whatever happened concerns the president. Minutes later the news is heard over the television set aboard SAM 26000. *The president has been shot!*[16]

The radio traffic is now anything but routine. While trained operators generally maintain a brisk demeanor betraying nothing, other voices quaver and speak haltingly, still reeling from the news. Tongues are tied, and there is an undertone of apprehension in nearly every conversation. The precaution of using code names instead of real names, and the protocol of distinguishing between *Air Force One* and SAM 26000, are cast aside more often than invoked.

±12:45 p.m.

The first substantive conversations preserved after the shots in Dealey Plaza involve press secretary Pierre Salinger, a passenger on board SAM 86972, which is en route to Tokyo from Honolulu, and Commander Oliver Hallett, a naval officer on routine duty in the Situation Room, the "nerve center" of the White House. Two hours out of Honolulu, the UPI teletype machine on SAM 86972 (whose passenger manifest includes Secretary of State Dean Rusk and Treasury Secretary C. Douglas Dillon) has come clattering to life with the first bulletin: "Dallas, Nov. 22 (UPI).—THREE SHOTS WERE FIRED AT PRESIDENT KENNEDY'S MOTORCADE IN DOWNTOWN DALLAS." Soon Secretary Rusk is huddling with all the administration officials onboard. The president may have been wounded; how seriously, no one knows. At least one cabinet secretary thinks the messages might be hopelessly garbled, so Rusk asks Salinger to get confirmation of the wire service reports from the Situation Room. If the president is indeed injured, Salinger is to notify Washington that the mission to Japan is being aborted. In the press secretary's haste to learn the truth from the White House, Salinger cannot remember any code name save his own (WAYSIDE).

SAM 86972: Roger. White House Situation Room, SAM—you got 86972. How [do you] read me? Over.

    [more deliberately] [This is] SAM 8-6-9-7-2. Do you read? Over. . . . White House?

White House: White House on.

SAM 86972: White House, this is SAM 8-6-9-7-2. How read? Over.

White House: 86972, I read you loud and clear. Loud and clear.

SAM 86972: Roger. Stand by one, please. We have another phone patch going

16. Ibid., 211–12; Manchester, *Death,* 236.

on with CINCPAC, but we do have traffic for you so hold on one moment, please.[17]

White House: Roger, Roger, 86972.

Salinger: *[sounding agitated]* White House Situation Room, this is WAYSIDE. Do you read me? Over.

White House: This is [the] White House. This is [the] White House. I read you loud and clear, WAYSIDE.

Salinger: Can you give me latest information on president? Over.

White House: Do you want the Situation Room? Is that a Roger?

Salinger: Repeat that transmission, please.

White House: This is *[indistinct],* this is CROWN, this is CROWN. Do you want Situation Room?

Salinger: I want the Situation Room. That's affirmative.

White House: Roger, Roger. Gettin' 'em now. Stand by, please.
    WAYSIDE, WAYSIDE, this is CROWN. Situation is room *[sic]* Room is on. Go ahead.

Salinger: Situation Room, this is WAYSIDE. Do you read me? Over.

Hallett: *[very somber, in contrast to Salinger's anxiety]* This is the Situation Room, I read you. Go ahead.

Salinger: Give me *all* available information on president. Over.

Hallett: All available information on president follows. Ah . . . Connally—John—he and Governor Connally of Texas have been hit in the car in which they were riding. We do not know how serious the situation is. We have no information. Mr. Bromley Smith is back here in the Situation Room now, we are getting our information over the [wire service] tickers.[18] Over.

Salinger: That is affirmative; affirmative. Please keep us advised out here. This plane, on which [the] secretary of state [and] other cabinet ministers headed for Japan, [is] turning around [and] returning to Honolulu. Will arrive there in approximately two hours. Over.

Hallett: This is WAYSIDE *[sic]*. Understand those departing Honolulu are turning around and will be back there in about two hours. Is that correct? Over.

Salinger: That is affirmative; affirmative. Will send you—will need all information to decide whether some of party should go directly to Dallas. Over.

Hallett: This is the Situation Room. Say again your last, please.

Salinger: Will need to be kept advised so [that we] can determine whether some members of this party should go directly to Dallas. Over.

17. Commander in chief, U.S. Pacific Command.
18. Smith is executive secretary to the National Security Council.

Hallett: Roger. You wish information as to whether some members of that party should go to Dallas. I [understand]—

Salinger: That is affirmative; affirmative.

Hallett: Do you have anything else, WAYSIDE?

Salinger: No. Any other information, get a hold of us [as] rapidly as possible.

Hallett: All right. The Associated Press is coming out now with a bulletin to the effect that they believe the president was hit in the head. That just came in. Over.

Salinger: *[emotionless]* The president was hit in the head. Over.

Hallett: Roger. We will pass on any additional information we get from here to you.

SAM 86972: That's a Roger. Will be standing by for your call.

Hallett: All right. *[suddenly puzzled]* Where are you, WAYSIDE?

SAM 86972: WAYSIDE is off the line. This is the radio operator, sir, and we are returning to Honolulu and should be back to Honolulu in about two hours. We will be in the air for about two hours into Honolulu, and you [may] contact us on the ground there then later.

Hallett: I understand. This is . . . *uh-oh.* Hold on the line there, WAYSIDE *[sic]*. We have some more information coming up.

SAM 86972: [WAYSIDE will] be right back.

Hallett: WAYSIDE, WAYSIDE, this is Situation Room. I read from the AP bulletin:

"Kennedy apparently shot in head. He fell face down in back seat of his car. *Blood was on his head.* Mrs. Kennedy cried, 'Oh no!' and tried to hold up his head. Connally remained half-seated, slumped to the left. There was blood on his face and forehead. The president and the governor were rushed to Parkland Hospital near the Dallas Trade Mart where Kennedy was to have made a speech."
Over.

Salinger: I read that. Over.

Hallett: This is Situation Room. I have nothing further for you now. I will contact you if we get more.

Salinger: WAYSIDE is Roger and out.

±12:55 p.m.

Unaware that Secretary Rusk is already heading back, George Ball, the acting secretary of state, asks Murray Jackson, a foreign service officer in the Executive Secretariat, to contact the VIP delegation aboard SAM 86972 via Andrews AFB, the home base for the SAM unit of the U.S. Air Force. Still unaware as to the severity of the president's wounds, the delegation is tentatively planning—

or hoping?—to split up in Honolulu. Most of the cabinet officers will proceed to Washington, while Rusk and Salinger intend to make a beeline for Dallas.

Andrews AFB: 86972, 86972, Andrews. I have a Mr. *Jackson,* a Mr. *Jackson,* on. Would you give him a call, sir?

SAM 86972: Mr. Jackson, this SAM 8-6-9-7-2. How read? Over.

Jackson: I read [you] very well, [869]72. I'd like to talk to Colonel Toomey or Colonel Ireland, please. Over.

SAM 86972: Mister, Colonel Toomey *[indistinct]* is coming on right now. Stand by one [moment], please.

Jackson: Okay.

Toomey: Roger. This is Colonel Toomey. Go ahead, please.

Jackson: Colonel Toomey, this is Murray Jackson. The president of the United States has been *shot* and seriously wounded in Dallas, Texas. The president of the United States, John F. Kennedy, has been *shot* and seriously wounded in Dallas, Texas. Governor Connally was also shot at the same time. Would you please get this message to Secretary of State Rusk? And I will stand by. Over.

Toomey: Roger, Murray. We have already received that news. We have UPI on. We have turned around; we are returning to Hawaii. We are estimating Hawaii in one hour and twenty minutes. Will be on the ground in Hawaii in one hour and twenty minutes, and returning to Washington or Dallas. The decision has not been made yet. We have one other aircraft alerted to take part of the party to Dallas, and we will return to Washington. Over.

Jackson: Thank you very much, Colonel Toomey. I'll relay this to Mr. Ball right away. Over and out.

±1:10 p.m.

Ensconced inside a booth at Parkland Hospital, neither Lyndon Johnson nor his Secret Service detail is certain about the scope or scale of the attack.[19] It might well be the work of Dallas zealots, yet it is almost as easy to conjure up an international conspiracy aimed at decapitating the U.S. government before a devastating nuclear strike is launched. In either case, it is critical to relocate the vice president to a safer location as soon as is humanly possible, which means in or around Washington. Until now Johnson has received token protection. Suddenly he cannot move an inch without a ring of agents surrounding him. Emory Roberts, the assistant agent in charge, and Rufus Youngblood, the agent most familiar to Johnson, are the key members of the Secret Service detail now guarding the vice president. They press him to leave Dallas irrespective of all

19. Jim Bishop, *The Day Kennedy Was Shot* (New York: Funk & Wagnalls, 1968), 199.

other considerations, emotional as well as political. Johnson is reluctant to leave the hospital premises, much less Dallas, as long as the president's life is supposedly hanging in the balance.[20] But having seen the president's head wound when he was removed from the limousine, Roberts insists "The president won't make it. . . . We've got to get in the air."[21] As Lady Bird Johnson recounts,

> There was talk about where would we *go*. Back to Washington? To the plane? To our house? People spoke of how widespread this may be. Throughout it all, Lyndon was remarkably calm and quiet. He said we'd better move the plane to another part of the [Love] Field. He spoke of going back out to the plane in black cars.
>
> Every face that came in, you searched for the answers that you must know. I think the face I kept on seeing it on was the face of Kenny O'Donnell, who loved him so much.[22]
>
> It was Lyndon, as usual, who thought of it . . . although I wasn't going to leave without doing it. He said, "You'd better try to see if you can see Jackie and Nellie."[23] We didn't know what had happened to John [Connally]. I asked the Secret Service if I could be taken to them. They began to lead me up one corridor, back stairs, down another . . .
>
> Suddenly I found myself face to face with Jackie . . . in a small hall I think it was, right outside the operating room. You always think of her, or somebody like her, as being *insulated, protected*—sort of on [Mount] Olympus. She was *quite* alone. I don't think I ever saw anybody so much alone in my life. I went up to her . . . put my arms around her, and said something—I'm sure it was *quite* banal, [something] like "God help us all"—because my feelings for her were too tumultuous to put into words.
>
> And then I went in to see Nellie. *There* it was different . . . because Nellie and I have gone through so many things together since about 1938. I hugged her tight and we both cried, and I said, "Nellie, it's going to be *all right*. There's been *enough* bad that's already hap-

20. Rufus Youngblood, *20 Years in the Secret Service: My Life with Five Presidents* (New York: Simon & Schuster, 1973), 116; Manchester, *Death,* 232–33. According to one nearly contemporaneous account, the first person to think of moving Johnson back to Washington immediately was Emory Roberts, a twenty-year veteran of the Secret Service. Roberts checked with his superiors in Washington, and they promptly agreed that Johnson had to be gotten back to Washington at once. Fletcher Knebel, "After the Shots: The Ordeal of Lyndon Johnson," *Look,* 10 March 1964.

21. Manchester, *Death,* 233.

22. O'Donnell was President Kennedy's appointments secretary and a member of the president's inner circle, the so-called Irish mafia.

23. In truth, Johnson also wanted to visit the wives of the stricken men, but the Secret Service agents guarding him would not permit it. Youngblood, *20 Years,* 117.

pened." It wasn't *only* the president I was thinking about. It was Kathleen, of course.[24] And Nellie said, "Yes, *John's going to be all right.*" Among her many other fine qualities, she is also tough.

   Then . . . I turned and went back to the small white room where Lyndon still was. Mr. [Malcolm] Kilduff and Kenny O'Donnell were coming and going.[25] I *think* it was from Kenny's face and from Kenny's *voice* that I first heard the words, "the president is dead." [Minutes later] Mr. Kilduff entered and said to Lyndon, "Mr. President."[26]

Soon after saying these words, but not immediately, Malcolm Kilduff will realize why the former vice president turns around and looks at him as if he is "Donald Duck."[27] Kilduff is the first person to so address Lyndon Johnson.

The assistant press secretary wants to issue an official announcement of the president's death as soon as possible. But Johnson, accepting the views of Secret Service agents Roberts and Youngblood, asks Kilduff to delay the announcement until the Johnsons have left Parkland Hospital and are safely aboard SAM 26000. "We don't know whether this is a worldwide conspiracy," reiterates Johnson, "[and] whether they are after me as well as they were after President Kennedy. . . . We just don't know."[28] Johnson is disturbed to learn that more than half the cabinet is five time zones away, somewhere over the vast Pacific Ocean. The coincidence heightens his fear that the attack might be a cleverly timed Communist conspiracy, and he orders Kilduff to get that VIP aircraft turned around instantly, unaware that it is already heading back.[29]

The task of recalling SAM 86972 yet again eventually falls to Major H. R. Patterson, a WHCA officer. Patterson wants to follow security protocols, especially during a crisis, but has no assigned code name. So he instantly devises one—STRANGER—in the hope that this self-admission will convey that he is

---

24. In March 1958 sixteen-year-old Kathleen Connally, the oldest of the Connallys' four children and the spitting image of the governor, secretly wed her high school sweetheart. With the disapproval of both families weighing on them, the young couple moved to Tallahassee, Florida. In mid-April, Kathleen learned she was pregnant. By late April, she was dead, killed (during a quarrel) by a shotgun blast that was ruled accidental. For the Connallys, Kathleen's death would always be the tragedy of their lives. "We yearned to make it less painful [for them], and there was no way to do it," recalled Mrs. Johnson. James Reston, Jr., *The Lone Star: The Life of John Connally* (New York: Harper & Row, 1989), 186.

25. Kilduff is an assistant press secretary.

26. Mrs. Johnson Diary Tapes, LBJL.

27. Manchester, *Death,* 219.

28. David Wise, "Revealed—Johnson's Delay of Death News," *New York Herald Tribune,* 24 December 1963. The first disclosure about Johnson's request for a delay—and his initial concern over the possibility of a plot to kill top U.S. leaders—occurs in December 1963 during a radio interview of Malcolm Kilduff.

29. SAM 86972 will eventually arrive at Andrews AFB after more than twelve consecutive hours in the air since departing from Honolulu at 12:03 p.m. EST on November 22.

nonetheless bona fide. It's only when Salinger repeats Patterson's order to Rusk that a sliver of doubt creeps in and leads to a subdued cabinet debate over whether to obey Patterson in lieu of independent confirmation from the Situation Room. "Who is STRANGER?" asks Rusk. "Who's in Washington?"[30]

Salinger: CROWN, this is WAYSIDE. Go ahead.

White House: Roger, stand by.

> *[to Patterson]* Go ahead, please.

Patterson: WAYSIDE, WAYSIDE, this is STRANGER. Do you read me? Over.

Salinger: STRANGER, this is WAYSIDE. Go ahead.

Patterson: Kilduff asks that *all cabinet* members return to Washington *immediately.* Over.

Salinger: Plane's already turned around and heading for Honolulu, where we have [KC-]135 plane [ready] as soon as [we] arrive [to take us] to Washington. Over.

Patterson: Roger, Roger. Will they notify us of time of arrival and location? Over.

Salinger: That is correct. Now I have one question, STRANGER. It still seems that, ah . . . for the staff *[indistinct]* goes to Dallas? Over.

Patterson: Roger, Roger. We do not have any *firm* word from down there as to the exact status, but I think—

White House: *[interrupting]* Pardon me. WAYSIDE, Situation Room *has* to have you. Go ahead.

Salinger: I read. Go ahead.

Patterson: WAYSIDE, this is STRANGER. Out. I'll get that information and ship it to Hawaii. Over.

Salinger: Affirmative.

White House: WAYSIDE, stand by for Situation Room. Go ahead, WAYSIDE.

Salinger: Situation Room go ahead. This is WAYSIDE.

Hallett: All right. This is—WAYSIDE, this is the Situation Room. I read you latest bulletin: "President Kennedy has been given blood transfusions today at Parkland Hospital in an effort to save his life after he and Governor John Connally of Texas were shot in an assassination attempt." Over the TV, we have the information that the governor has been moved to the operating room. The president is still in the emergency room at Parkland Hospital. Do you read me so far? Over.

Salinger: I read that loud and clear. Go ahead.

Hallett: WAYSIDE, this is the Situation Room. Are you getting the press coverage, or do you want us to continue to relay it to you? Over.

Salinger: Situation Room, this is WAYSIDE. We are getting very *garbled,* very *garbled,* transmissions. We'd appreciate [it if you kept us] informed. Over.

---

30. Manchester, *Death,* 224, 245.

Hallett: This is Situation Room. Roger. New subject. We will have information for you on whether to proceed to Dallas by the time you land at Honolulu. Over.

Salinger: Affirmative; affirmative. Also, [we need a] determination at that time, whether secretary of state, secretary of state, should also proceed Dallas. Over.

±1:25 p.m.

Murray Jackson is once again on the telephone to SAM headquarters at Andrews AFB, hoping to speak to SAM 86972. This time Jackson wants to convey a confirmation of an earlier request made by George Ball. The affirmation comes from McGeorge Bundy, the president's national security adviser. The VIP delegation is not to split up in Honolulu; everyone on board SAM 86972 is to return to Washington, though no explanation is proffered. The decision is not entirely unwelcome, though, because it might mean the president's wounds are *not* mortal and that he is stable enough to be evacuated to Washington.

Andrews AFB: Andrews sideband. Airman Gilmore [here].

Jackson: Airman Gilmer *[sic]*, this is Murray Jackson again at the State Department.

Andrews AFB: Yes *sir.*

Jackson: Well, the message I just gave you—about Mr. Ball wanting the secretary and all the passengers of the plane to return directly to Washington—has now been reconfirmed by McGeorge *Bundy,* who has called and asked that—and *also* said that he thinks the plane and all its passengers should return immediately to Washington, rather than Dallas.

Andrews AFB: Stand by one [moment], sir.

Jackson: Right.

[With some difficulty, Airman Gilmore arranges another patch to SAM 86972.]

Andrews AFB: 86972, 86972, Andrews.

SAM 86972: Loud and clear on our *[indistinct].*

Andrews AFB: Roger, loud and clear. I have a Mr. Jackson, a Mr. Jackson, on the line. Would you give him a call, sir?

SAM 86972: Jackson, [86]972. Go ahead, sir.

Jackson: [869]72, I read you well. I have a message from Undersecretary *Ball* and from McGeorge *Bundy* at the White House. They request that the secretary of state and *all passengers* aboard the aircraft return to Washington *immediately.* Over.

SAM 86972: Roger. The message is from Undersecretary Ball and Mr. Bundy:

advise that the secretary of state and *all passengers* return to Washington *immediately*. Over.

Jackson: This is correct. Over and out.

SAM 86972: Okay. Thank you, sir.

±1:35 p.m.

Shortly before 1:30 p.m., assistant press secretary Malcolm Kilduff begins making his way through the gaggle of agitated newsmen who have descended on Parkland Memorial Hospital. They are begging, demanding, imploring him to confirm or deny a report from a priest about the president's death. Kilduff doggedly fends them all off until he enters classrooms 101–102 and reaches the podium. After shouts of "Quiet!" the room falls unnaturally silent. Kilduff begins, "President John F. Kennedy—"

"Hold it!" yells a still photographer, as he clicks his lens.

"President John F. Kennedy died at approximately one o'clock central standard time today here in Dallas," intones Kilduff, as pandemonium breaks out.[31] The white lie goes unnoticed. For all intents and purposes, John Kennedy was dead on arrival at Parkland—indeed, he was dead in Dealey Plaza. If he had been just a prominent visitor to Dallas instead of the president, perhaps this would have been acknowledged.

Kilduff would like nothing more than to end the press conference, but the newsmen, of course, won't let him. Ironically, the Texas trip was supposed to be a going-away junket for Kilduff. Ken O'Donnell had recently decided that Kilduff was dispensable, and before the trip he was told to begin looking for another job. Kilduff makes a game effort at lighting a cigarette and the flame shakes violently. As the press secretary struggles to continue, at 1:50 p.m. the Johnsons reach the presumed sanctuary of SAM 26000 just 3.4 miles away.

As Lady Bird recalled the sequence of events, once Kennedy's life was not at issue,

> It was decided that we could go immediately to the airport. Quick plans were made about how to get to the car . . . who to ride in what. Getting out of that hospital . . . into the cars, was one of the *swiftest* walks I ever made. We got in. Lyndon said stop the sirens. We drove along as fast as we could. I looked up at a building . . . and there, already, there was a flag at half-mast. I think that was when the *enormity* of what had happened first struck me.
>
> When we got to the airplane, we entered airplane number one for

---

31. Ibid., 220–21.

the first time. There was a TV set on. The commendator *[sic]* was saying, ". . . Lyndon B. Johnson, now president of the United States."[32]

White House: *[urgently]* Start again, please. Your party is on.
*[In the background, NBC news anchorman Frank McGee is heard saying
   ". . . after having given the president the last rites [of the Roman Catholic
   Church."]*
Andrews AFB: Sir, be advised [that] we have another patch to WAYSIDE. Do you
   wish to break it? It's from SAM Command Post.
White House: Hmmm. . . . Yeah, break it.
Andrews AFB: Yes sir. *[aside]* Break it first.
     86972, 86972, Andrews.
SAM 86972: [86]972, go ahead.
Andrews AFB: Roger, sir. I have CROWN on; would you give him a call, sir?
SAM 86972: CROWN, [86]972. Go ahead.
Hallett: *[voice quavering]* Ahhh . . . this is Situation Room. Relay following
   to WAYSIDE. We have report quoting Mr. Kilduff in Dallas that the
   president . . . *is* . . . *dead.* That he died about thirty-five minutes ago. Do
   you have that? Over.
Salinger: *[quickly]* The president is dead; is that correct?
Hallett: That *is* . . . correct. That is correct. New subject. Front office desires
   plane return [to] Washington with no stop [in] Dallas. Over.
SAM 86972: That is copied. WAYSIDE copied all okay, and we return direct to
   Washington without stoppin' in Dallas. Roger, Roger.
Hallett: *[dejectedly]* All right. This is Situation Room, out.

Unbeknownst to Commander Hallett, he is about to become a member of
one of the world's most exclusive clubs. Back in October 1959, Hallett and his
wife were working for the U.S. mission in Moscow—Hallett as the naval
attaché, Joan as a receptionist—when a twenty-year-old ex-Marine walked in
the door and loudly announced his intention to renounce his U.S. citizenship.
The Halletts have never had a reason to remember the young man after that,
except that in some obnoxious way, the name and face of the ex-Marine were
unforgettable.[33] In about two hours Commander Hallett will be counted among
the tiny number of people who can say they have met both John F. Kennedy and
his accused assassin, Lee Harvey Oswald.

32. Mrs. Johnson Diary Tapes, LBJL.
33. Manchester, *Death,* 30–31.

±1:40 p.m.

As soon as Salinger delivers the confirmation to Dean Rusk, the secretary of state announces it over 86972's loudspeaker. With the unthinkable now realized, Rusk's thoughts turn to Lyndon Johnson's whereabouts and condition. At first he does not even recall that Johnson is in Texas, too, and now Rusk is alarmed about wire service reports that the vice president was either "wounded slightly" or clutching his chest as he was hustled into Parkland Hospital.[34] Johnson suffered a serious heart attack in 1955, but it turns out he was only rubbing his shoulder after being tackled in his seat by Rufus Youngblood. In the Situation Room, McGeorge Bundy makes the on-the-spot decision to release the sensitive information about the "vice president's" whereabouts.

Andrews AFB: It's Airman Gilmore [at Andrews] sideband; I have [86]972 for another patch, sir.
Situation Room: *[aside to Hallett]* [86]972 again.
Hallett: *[sounding depressed]* This is [the] Situation Room.
Andrews AFB: Stand by, sir.
SAM 86972: Situation Room, [86]972. I read.
Hallett: This is Situation Room. Over.
SAM 86972: Situation Room, SAM [86]972. WAYSIDE would like to know the whereabouts of, ah . . . the vice president. Over.
Hallett: Ah, yes. *[aside]* He's gotta have it now.
Bundy: *[in background]* Yes. All right. Give him *[indistinct]*.
Hallett: *[to Bundy]* Yes. All right. And he wants to know where the vice president *is* in Dallas.
  [to 86972] For WAYSIDE from Situation Room. The vice president is in the hospital *building*—Parkland Hospital in Dallas. He is *not* injured. I repeat: *not* injured. Over.
SAM 86972: Copied; copied. Call you right back.
Hallett: All right.

Whether intentionally or not, Hallett has conveyed some out-of-date information. By now the Johnsons—for the very first time—are aboard SAM 26000, which is fueled and ready for the flight back to Washington. It sits idly on the tarmac for two reasons. Although Johnson has bowed to the demands of the Secret Service and agreed to leave for Washington, he won't depart without Jacqueline Kennedy onboard, and Mrs. Kennedy will not leave without her husband's remains. Then, in the time it takes to get a suitable casket and whisk the

34. Ibid., 169.

presidential corpse from Parkland, and after discussions with the three Texas
congressmen who accompanied him from the hospital, Johnson reaches another
decision that will delay the flight from Dallas. It seems advisable to take the
oath of office before SAM 26000 is airborne, and he resolves to discuss the
issue with Attorney General Robert Kennedy, who will concur on administration of the oath.[35] Lady Bird Johnson recalled:

> The shades on the plane were lowered. We heard that we were
> going to wait for Mrs. Kennedy and for the coffin. There was discussion
> about when Lyndon should be sworn in as president.[36] There was a
> telephone call to Washington—I believe, to the attorney general. It
> was decided that he [Lyndon] should be sworn in *there,* in Dallas, as
> quickly as possible, because of international implications and be-
> cause we did not know how *wide*—whether this was an incident *there*
> [in Dallas] only, or whether it had a *wider spread* as to the intended
> victims.
>
> Judge Sarah Hughes, a federal judge in Dallas—and I am glad it
> was she—was called to come in a hurry. . . .[37]

In a matter of days, the issue of the Dallas swearing-in would become
freighted with undeserved significance. In point of fact, Johnson had become
president the instant John Kennedy died because Johnson had already sworn the
necessary oath of office in January 1961.[38] Retaking the oath was not even a
necessary formality and was important only symbolically, in that it reassured
the American people and the world that although Kennedy was dead, the presidency continued to function.

±2 p.m.

Transmissions from SAM 26000 while it is waiting on the airport tarmac are
periodic and routine—although nothing on this day is *truly* routine anymore.
The conversations that are preserved do not include the oath-of-office discussions known to have occurred between Johnson and Robert Kennedy shortly

35. There are two conversations within the space of six minutes. Johnson reaches the attorney
general at 1:56 p.m., and then Robert Kennedy, after consulting briefly with Deputy Attorney General Nicholas Katzenbach, calls the president back at 2:02 p.m. List of Telephone Calls, 28 December 1966, Current, Box 4, Special File, LBJL.

36. Mrs. Johnson is referring to her husband's discussion with Texas Representatives Jack
Brooks (D), Albert Thomas (D), and Homer Thornberry (D).

37. Mrs. Johnson Diary Tapes, LBJL.

38. Manchester, *Death,* 224–27.

before and after 2 p.m. They were not recorded apparently because no specific request was made to record them.[39]

±2:25 p.m.

At approximately 2:14 p.m., after another journey from Parkland Hospital to Love Field at breakneck speed, a snow-white Cadillac hearse edges up to SAM 26000 bearing Jacqueline Kennedy and a solid bronze casket containing her husband's corpse. With scarcely any room to maneuver, a bevy of presidential aides, Secret Service agents, and Dallas policemen begin straining and heaving to place the nearly half-ton load aboard the aircraft. A partition and four seats have been removed from the aircraft's tail end to accommodate the coffin.

As the time of departure draws nearer—hinging entirely now on Judge Hughes's arrival to readminister the oath of office—the logistics after landing at Andrews AFB become a primary topic of the radio traffic. Roy Kellerman (aka DIGEST), the agent in charge of the Secret Service in Dallas, first called the head of the White House Detail, Jerry Behn (aka DUPLEX), from Parkland Hospital. In that way Behn has been kept informed of every development, including the president's death approximately thirty minutes before it was officially announced.[40] Now, in Kellerman's first call from Love Field, they discuss the needs of both presidents aboard SAM 26000 and the wishes of LACE (Mrs. Kennedy).

Andrews AFB: 26000, Andrews. CROWN on; go ahead.
SAM 26000: Roger.
          CROWN, 26000. Would you get a patch with Jerry Behn, please?
White House: Roger, stand by.
          26000, DUPLEX is on. Go ahead.
SAM 26000: Thank you; stand by one [moment].
Behn: Hello?
Kellerman: Jerry? . . . Hello? . . . Just to give you the fill-in here now. We're at the airport . . . [SAM] 26,000 [sic] . . . with everybody aboard.

39. Ibid., 268–69. Although Manchester will write that conversations made from SAM 26000 were not recorded before the aircraft became airborne, that was not the case. Generally speaking, however, telephone calls were not taped unless requested; only radio traffic having to do with the flight was recorded. In addition, the calls from Johnson to Robert Kennedy may not have been recorded because they were placed from a telephone in the presidential quarters and routed through the White House national switchboard, which was separate from the WHCA switchboard. Memo re Telephone Conversation with General McHugh, 14 December 1963, President Johnson's Diary—November 22, 1963, Box 2, Special File, LBJL.

40. Manchester, *Death,* 254.

Behn: Okay; go ahead.

Kellerman: We're waiting for the swearing-in at the plane, before takeoff.

Behn: [Swearing-in] of the . . . ? That's of VOLUNTEER?

Kellerman: Roger.

Behn: Say again, Roy; say *again*.

Kellerman: They're waiting for a judge to appear for swearing-in.

Behn: That is for VOLUNTEER—is that right?

Kellerman: Yes, we are having one . . . getting one here to have it done before we take off, Jerry.

Behn: That's affirmative. Do you have any idea yet what LACE wants to do, and what VOLUNTEER wants to do on their arrival here?

Kellerman: No, but I will call you back with suggestions. We have a two-hour-fifteen-minute flight into Andrews. They have a full plane of at least forty [passengers].

Behn: Okay; go ahead.

Kellerman: I'll have to call you again as to the, ah . . . body. However, I'm sure the VOLUNTEER boys will call for his car and so forth. But we will need his and several others.

Behn: All right. Let me know what VOLUNTEER wants to do when they land— if they wanna come into CROWN by helicopter.

Kellerman: [That's] a Roger; I'll call you again.

Behn: Okay.

±2:30 p.m.

Under instructions to make the departure as swift as possible, pilot Swindal has ordered the ground air-conditioner disconnected in order to save a few seconds. Consequently the air inside the aluminum tube called 26000 is almost unbreathe-able, the aircraft dark and like a sweatbox. Lady Bird Johnson describes the moments leading up to the swearing-in ceremony.[41]

> I went in to see Mrs. Kennedy, and I don't—oh, it was a very, very hard thing to do. She made it as easy as possible. She said things like, "Oh, Lady Bird, it's always good . . . we've liked you two so much." She said—I remember other things she said. "Oh, *what* if I had not been there. I am so glad I *was* there." I remember things I said. I looked at her . . . *[Mrs. Johnson loses her composure]*
>
> Mrs. Kennedy's dress was stained with blood. One leg was almost entirely covered with it and her right glove was *caked*—that *immacu-*

---

41. For clarity's sake, Mrs. Johnson's recollections have been rearranged slightly to conform to the order of events established in Manchester's account.

late woman—it was caked with blood, her husband's blood. She always wore gloves like she was used to them; I never could. And that was somehow one of the most poignant sights . . . [Mrs. Kennedy] exquisitely dressed, and caked in blood.

I asked her if I couldn't get somebody to come in to help her change, and she says, "Oh no, that's all right. Perhaps later I'll ask for Mary Gallagher. But not right now."[42] And then with something—if with a person that gentle, that dignified, you can say [she] had an element of fierceness, she said, "I want them to see what they have *done* to Jack."

I tried to express . . . *something* of how we felt. I said, "Oh, Mrs. Kennedy, you *know,* we never even wanted to be *vice president.* And now, dear God, it's come to this." Well . . . I would have given anything to help her, and there was nothing I could do to help her. So rather quickly, I left and went back to the airplane to the main part of the room where everybody was seated.[43]

According to William Manchester in *The Death of a President,* before departing Mrs. Johnson also engages in a bit of inappropriate "Texas chauvinism." "What wounds me most of all is that this should happen in my beloved state of Texas," she says to Mrs. Kennedy.[44] As soon as it leaves her lips Mrs. Johnson instantly regrets the remark, and it is in neither the audio nor published versions of her White House diary.

At 2:30 p.m., approximately twelve minutes after President Kennedy's body is loaded onto the plane, Judge Sarah Hughes arrives at the ramp leading to SAM 26000. Once everyone is in place for the hastily choreographed ceremony, there is a moment of uncertainty. Jacqueline Kennedy's presence is desired, but no one knows if she can bear to appear. Finally she emerges from the private bedroom, her large, dark eyes bigger than ever, mirroring her shock and bewilderment. She is composed but ashen and quivering like an exposed nerve. A path opens in the crowded aircraft, and Johnson draws her gently to his left side. At precisely 2:38 p.m. Lyndon Johnson repeats the oath of office that symbolically elevates him, in the eyes of the nation and the world, to the presidency of the United States. He is flanked by his wife and Mrs. Kennedy in a hastily arranged tableau that takes place in the stateroom, the largest open space on the aircraft. White House staff photographer Cecil Stoughton has raced from Parkland to Love Field, knowing that history is about to be made. "While it seems tasteless,"

42. Gallagher is Mrs. Kennedy's personal secretary.
43. Mrs. Johnson Diary Tapes, LBJL.
44. Manchester, *Death,* 316.

he explains to Liz Carpenter, "I am here to make a picture if [Johnson] cares to have it and I think we should have it."[45] Acutely aware of his assignment, Stoughton carefully adjusts his Hasselblad camera so that it doesn't record the sickening bloodstains on Jacqueline Kennedy's pink suit. Virtually the only sound in the hushed, cramped cabin is the clacking of Stoughton's camera.

Of the two dozen people crammed into the stateroom, perhaps only one or two are conscious of the irony involved in having Judge Hughes officiate. As much as any single person possibly could, she once personified Johnson's utter powerlessness and deep frustration while vice president. Johnson did not wield enough clout inside the Kennedy administration to push her relatively minor patronage appointment through the Justice Department the year before, after Robert Kennedy rejected the sixty-four-year-old Dallas lawyer for being too old. Her nomination was stalled until Speaker of the House Sam Rayburn (D-Texas) finally intervened.[46] This evidence of Johnson's political emasculation was profoundly humiliating to him, a former Senate majority leader, once considered among the most skilled and powerful men in Washington. Now, in less than thirty seconds, Judge Hughes will affirm Johnson's ascension to the one office he has longed for with every fiber of his being for thirty years. If Lady Bird Johnson noticed the irony, she chose not to comment on it.

> It's odd at a time like that the very . . . the little things that come to you in the moment of deep compassion you have for people who are really not at the center of the tragedy. I heard a Secret Service man say, in the most *desolate* voice—and I *hurt* for him—"We've *never* lost a president in the Service."[47] And then, when police chief [Jesse] Curry of Dallas came on the plane and said to Mrs. Kennedy, "Mrs. Kennedy, *believe* me, we did *everything* we possibly could." God, that was a brave thing for that man to do.[48]

45. Liz Carpenter's Recollections of President Kennedy's Assassination, December 1963, Box 4, Special File, LBJL.

46. Rowland Evans and Robert Novak, *Lyndon B. Johnson: The Exercise of Power* (London: George Allen and Unwin, 1967), 314–15; Darwin Payne, *Indomitable Sarah: The Life of Sarah T. Hughes* (Dallas, Tex.: Southern Methodist University Press, 2004). In a January 1965 conversation, Johnson also refers to Rayburn's role in getting Hughes's nomination approved. Johnson and Edwin Weisl, conversation, 11 January 1965, 10:21 a.m., LBJL.

47. When William McKinley, the previous chief executive to die at the hands of an assassin, was shot in 1901, the Secret Service had neither the statutory authority nor the appropriations earmarked for presidential protection. Two Secret Service agents were standing within three feet of the president, however. Warren Commission, *Report* [hereafter *Warren Report*] (Washington, D.C.: U.S. Government Printing Office, 1964), 509; Philip Melanson and Peter Stevens, *The Secret Service: The Hidden History of an Enigmatic Agency* (New York: Carroll & Graf, 2002), 28–29.

48. In Manchester's account and in Mrs. Johnson's recorded diary, Curry's remark to Mrs. Kennedy was made before the swearing-in. But looking at the series of Stoughton's photographs, it is more likely to have occurred right afterward, just before Curry left SAM 26000. Richard Trask,

We borrowed a Bible. . . .[49] And there, in the very narrow confines of the plane—with Jackie on his [Lyndon's] left, her hair falling in her eyes, but very composed, and then Lyndon, and then I was on his right—Judge Hughes, with the Bible in front of [Lyndon], and a cluster of Secret Service people, and congressmen we'd known a long time— Lyndon took the oath of office.[50]

±2:46 p.m.

Colonel Swindal prides himself on the swiftness with which he can put SAM 26000 in the air, and drills constantly to shave off seconds. Getting airborne has never seemed more urgent. Moments before takeoff, as if he could not bear waiting an instant longer, Swindal utters the call sign everyone has been anxious to hear. Judge Hughes, Jesse Curry, and Cecil Stoughton disembark, and SAM 26000 becomes *Air Force One* as it lifts off from Love Field. It has been two relentlessly tense hours since the shots in Dealey Plaza, and being airborne beckons as some sort of sanctuary from the sordid events on the ground. "Darkness will be a blessing," and Swindal anticipates what he knows will be a rapidly darkening sky at this time of year, especially heading northeast at a speed well in excess of 500 miles per hour.[51] Apprehension regarding an international Communist plot has not evaporated entirely, as evinced by a Pentagon decision to put every air force base along the flight path on alert. Fighter pilots are literally strapped into their cockpits, ready to take off at the slightest indication that *Air Force One* is being targeted.[52]

±2:50 p.m.

Despite the *Air Force One* designation, confusion and chaos in Washington are so rampant that key command centers do not know if that means aircraft 26000 is carrying the new president, the old president, or both. The mere fact of the takeoff, and the passenger manifest, have to be confirmed repeatedly.

SAM Command Post: *Air Force One,* SAM Command Post. Go ahead.
AF1: Roger, Roger. You called me. Go ahead, please.

Pictures of the Pain: Photography and the Assassination of President Kennedy (Danvers, Mass.: Yeoman Press, 1994), 47; Manchester, *Death,* 323.

49. Actually it was a Catholic missal. Trask, *Pictures of the Pain,* 48.
50. Mrs. Johnson Diary Tapes, LBJL.
51. Manchester, *Death,* 340.
52. Ibid., 352.

SAM Command Post: Roger. This is Colonel Hornbuckle in operations. We have requests from the [Joint] Chiefs of Staff's office to know if you have, ah . . . Mr. Johnson and, ah . . . Mr. Kennedy's body aboard.

AF1: Stand by one [moment].

Okay, *Air Force One.* Affirmative on *all* of those questions. Go ahead.

SAM Command Post: Roger, thank you very much. Out.

±2:53 p.m.

Andrews AFB: *Air Force One,* Andrews. Give Command Post a call, sir.

AF1: Command Post, *Air Force One.*

SAM Command Post: Go ahead, *Air Force One.* This is Command Post.

AF1: Okay. Departure at 2047 [ZULU] and estimated cross to Andrews, 2305.[53] And we're climbing out to a flight level [of] two niner zero [29,000 feet]. Go ahead.

SAM Command Post: Roger, understand. Just stand by one [moment], please.

AF1: *[indistinct],* go ahead.

SAM Command Post: *Air Force One,* this is the Air Force Command Post. If possible, [we] request the names of the passengers on board, please.

AF1: We have forty *plus.* Go ahead.

SAM Command Post: Forty people? Is that affirmative?

AF1: That's *affirmative.*

SAM Command Post: Can you tell me, in regard to, ah . . . one and two, or, ah . . . [of] the top people?

AF1: Roger. The president . . . is on board. The body is on board. And, ah . . . Mrs. Kennedy is on board.

SAM Command Post: All right. Can you tell—affirm once again your takeoff time and your estimated time of arrival [at] Andrews?

AF1: 2047 [ZULU] takeoff time; [arrival at] Andrews 2305.

SAM Command Post: Roger, thank you. This is the Air Force Command Post. Out.

±2:54 p.m.

The "best evidence" in any violent death is the body of the decedent, and under Texas state law President Kennedy's corpse should have been subjected to an immediate autopsy by the Dallas County coroner. But the seeming emergency— along with an overwhelming impulse to get out of Dallas, that godforsaken city

53. ZULU is the radio call sign for the "Z" time zone, known then as Greenwich Mean Time.

that has allegedly struck down President Kennedy—proves superior to the law. Now one of the most urgent matters is to arrange for a postmortem examination in Washington. The federal government has no plan for such a contingency, however, and all the arrangements will be ad hoc.

AF1: CROWN, *Air Force One.*
White House: This is CROWN, go ahead.
AF1: [Loud and] clear. We need a patch with [the] surgeon general of the army, [Dr. Leonard] Heaton. Go ahead.
White House: Please repeat the message. Over.
AF1: Roger. We want a patch with General *Heaton.* H-E-A-T-O-N, the surgeon general. Go ahead.
White House: Roger, Roger. That's General Heaton, the surgeon general of the army. Over.
AF1: That is correct.
White House: Roger, Roger. Stand by.
    Air Force One, CROWN. Stand by please; we're reaching the [surgeon] general now. Over.
AF1: Standing by.

±2:59 p.m.

Air Force One cannot receive a weather forecast because it is preoccupied with a higher priority—trying to communicate with Dr. Leonard Heaton about arranging the autopsy. For security reasons the site will have to be a military hospital, and that means choosing between Walter Reed Army Hospital in Washington and the Naval Medical Center in nearby Bethesda, Maryland. But the surgeon general is proving difficult to locate.

White House: *Air Force One,* this is CROWN. Do you read? Over.
AF1: Roger; Roger, CROWN.
White House: *Air Force One.* . . . Hello?
    Air Force One, this is CROWN. You were cut out. General Heaton is at Walter Reed Hospital. You'll have to stand by just a moment, or else let me call you back when I get him on the line; it'll take about a minute to reach him.
    Air Force One, CROWN. Do you Roger? Over.
AF1: CROWN, Roger. If, ah . . . try to get General Heaton, and in the meantime, try to get the deputy surgeon general. We will talk to either one. Go ahead.
White House: This is CROWN, Roger. Will you stand by, or have me call you back? Over.

AF1: Roger. This is *very important.*

White House: Roger, I'll put an emergency on it. We'll get him as soon as possible.

AF1: Standing by.

White House: Roger, Roger.

±3:02 p.m.

Dr. George Burkley, the official White House physician, watched wordlessly while emergency room doctors tried in vain to resuscitate John Kennedy at Parkland Hospital. Then he was among those who intervened with Dr. Earl Rose, the Dallas County medical examiner, beseeching him to release the body regardless of what the law and sound practice dictated. Dr. Rose stood his ground, and Dr. Burkley was party to a virtual kidnapping of the president's corpse. Now the president's physician, aka MARKET, takes the lead in trying to see that an appropriate postmortem is conducted so that vital forensic findings can be presented during the presumed trial of the assassin(s).

AF1: CROWN, *Air Force One.* Go ahead.

White House: *Air Force One,* CROWN.

AF1: Roger. Stand by for a message.

Burkley: *Air Force [One],* this is Dr. Burkley—

White House: Roger—

Burkley: —is General [Heaton] here?

White House: Dr. Burkley—

Burkley: Did you ring him?

White House: Dr. Burkley, this is CROWN. You're cutting out, you're cutting out. You'll have to repeat. Over.

Burkley: This is Dr. Burkley. I want to get in touch with *General Heaton,* or *General Heaton's deputy.*

White House: Dr. Burkley, this is CROWN. We're working as fast as possible trying to get the call through for you. He is at Walter Reed. We're unable to locate [him]. We're still searching. Over.

Burkley: The deputy must be at the general's office, over in the main navy building.

White House: Roger, Roger. If you'll stand by, we'll try and reach him.
          MARKET, this is CROWN. You Roger? We're trying to reach each one of them if you'll stand by, please.

Burkley: All right. Roger.

±3:08 p.m.

Walter Reed Army Hospital is the premier government medical facility in Washington, and many of the presidential aides are instinctively inclined to have the autopsy performed there. But owing to President Kennedy's naval service, Mrs. Kennedy will ask for the postmortem to be done at the Naval Medical Center in Bethesda.[54] Her request adds to the already considerable confusion. Aboard *AF1,* Roy Kellerman (aka DIGEST) is under the impression that the Secret Service is arranging the postmortem logistics, yet he is vaguely aware that Dr. Burkley (also aboard *AF1*) is similarly engaged with General Heaton. At the same time, neither Kellerman nor Burkley is aware of Navy Captain Tazewell Shepard's parallel effort being organized from the White House, although Jerry Behn (DUPLEX) is familiar with it. It takes many conversations to sort everything out, as well as the mode of transportation. The difficulty of loading the casket onto SAM 26000 in Dallas has created doubt about relying on a helicopter to transport the president's body.

AF1: Get DUPLEX for us, please.
White House: Roger, Roger. DUPLEX is on the line, go ahead.
Kellerman: DIGEST to DUPLEX. Jerry?
Behn: Go ahead; go ahead. This is DUPLEX.
Kellerman: Jerry . . . arriving Andrews 1605 . . . 6:05 [p.m. EST] rather.
Behn: That's affirmative; I receive.
      This is DUPLEX. This is DUPLEX.
Kellerman: Six, ah . . . arrival Andrews 6:05, stand by. [Have] an ambulance
      from Walter Reed furnished to transport body. Over.
Behn: Arrangements have been made for a helicopter for the Bethesda Naval
      Medical Center. Over.
Kellerman: Stand by, Jerry . . . I'll have to get [Dr.] Burkley here.
Behn: Okay.

±3:11 p.m.

Aboard *AF1,* Kellerman brings Dr. Burkley into the conversation, and as the physician begins speaking, he refers to John Kennedy as the president. Jerry Behn, head of the White House Detail, is puzzled momentarily until he figures out that Burkley is not talking about Lyndon Johnson.

54. Manchester, *Death,* 349–50.

Behn: *Air Force One,* this is DUPLEX. Go ahead.

Andrews AFB: *Air Force One,* Andrews. DUPLEX is on; DUPLEX is on, sir.

Burkley: DUPLEX is on *[sic]*—this is Dr. Burkley. What arrangements have been made [with] regards to the reception of the president?

Behn: *[hesitantly]* The . . . everybody . . . aboard *Air Force One* . . . everyone aboard *Air Force One*—with the exception of the body—will be choppered into the [White House] south grounds. The body will be choppered to the Naval Medical Center at Bethesda. Over.

Burkley: [The] body will be choppered, or will go by *ambulance* to the [Naval] Medical Center?

Behn: Will be *choppered;* will be *choppered.*

Burkley: I have called General Heaton [and] asked him to call the Military District of Washington [with] regard to this. Would you call him and cancel the efforts to have it go to Walter Reed as . . . as we had spoken to him? I didn't know these arrangements were already made.

Behn: Say again; say again, doctor.

Burkley: [The] body is in a casket, you know, and it will have to be taken by *ambulance* and not by chopper.

Behn: All right, I'll tell Captain [Tazewell] Shepard that. Did you say—

Burkley: Jerry, would you be sure and get in contact with General Heaton?

±3:13 p.m.

As if the situation were not confused enough, Major General Chester Clifton, the army military aide to the president on board *AF1,* enters the fray and becomes involved in the contradictory instructions regarding the autopsy's location and mode of transport from Andrews AFB. Clifton is technically wrong about the legal aspect. With the Texas state statute having been violated, no matter how justifiably, there is no longer any effective law governing the autopsy.

Burkley: General Heaton, this is Admiral Burkley.

Heaton: Yes, Burkley.

Burkley: [I'm calling from] *Air Force One.*

Heaton: Yes . . . I read you Admiral Burkley.

Burkley: Hold for a minute, please. General Clifton is here.

Clifton: This is General Clifton.

Heaton: Yes, General Clifton.

Clifton: *[inaudible]* Two: We do not want a helicopter for the Bethesda Medical Center. We *do* want an ambulance and a *ground return* from Andrews to Walter Reed, and we want the regular postmortem that has to be done by law under guard performed at Walter Reed. Is that clear? Over.

Heaton: That is clear, General Clifton. You want an ambulance and another limousine at Andrews. And you want the regular postmortem by law done at Walter Reed.

Clifton: That is correct, *[indistinct]*. Hold on for a minute. Over.

Heaton: General, I'll hold on.

When Dr. Burkley comes back on the radio patch, he momentarily forgets he was talking with General Heaton rather than Jerry Behn.

Burkley: Hello, Jerry?

Heaton: General Heaton.

Burkley: What arrangements have you made?

Heaton: We have made no arrangements here but will follow through on what you [Clifton] just told me: an ambulance and a limousine at Andrews and in regards to the postmortem studies.

Burkley: Would you . . . General Heaton, would you kindly *hold*? There've been some arrangements already made. . . . I guess we'll have to clear that before we make any further [plans].

Heaton: *[muttering to himself]* A limousine and an ambulance at Andrews . . . *[indistinct]*.

Andrews AFB: *Air Force One,* Andrews. Say again your last transmission.

Heaton: *[talking to himself still] [indistinct]*

White House: Hello Andrews, this is CROWN.

Andrews AFB: CROWN, go ahead.

White House: We have Captain Shepard here who is also . . . evidently, who has made some arrangements on the funeral and so forth here in Washington, and the, ah . . . bringin' this body back, and so forth. He would like to get on and talk to *Air Force One* when General Heaton is finished. It might be possible for us to put him up on a conference [call], so that they could all make the arrangements together. I understand that Captain Shepard, the naval aide, has made some arrangements also.

Heaton: Yeah, I see.

White House: So you might explain this to *Air Force One* and tell 'em that we'll try and put 'em on a conference [call] *if they'd like.*

Heaton: Very well.

Burkley: Hello?

Andrews AFB: Okay, stand by. Will advise Admiral Burkley.

±3:15 p.m.

The contradictory arrangements having been resolved—Kennedy's body is to be transported in a hearse to the Naval Medical Center in Bethesda, some forty minutes from Andrews AFB—General Clifton turns his attention to the other logistics of the landing. Acutely aware of the difficulty they had loading the casket onto the aircraft, Clifton asks for a forklift to help accomplish this task at Andrews. Perhaps because a forklift seems undignified, or because at one point Clifton suggests a "platform" to walk onto, the ground crew at Andrews AFB will wheel out what they called a "catering bus," an ungainly steel/hydraulic contraption used to load meals onto aircraft. The bus will cause new problems unloading the casket and Mrs. Kennedy; it cannot be extended high enough to be flush with the rear door, and cannot be collapsed to be closer than five feet from the ground.[55]

Clifton also relays to Behn plans for media coverage, and Lyndon Johnson's desire to hold meetings in the White House that very evening with the congressional leadership, cabinet secretaries, and senior members of the president's staff. As of this conversation, no one has an inkling that dozens of senior officials from all three branches of government, close family friends, and representatives of the diplomatic corps intend to pay their respects at Andrews AFB, though Robert Kennedy has tried to make it clear he doesn't want a crowd of onlookers gawking at the arrival. Mindful of his sister-in-law's intense sense of privacy, Kennedy tells Supreme Court Justice Arthur Goldberg that the "last thing Jackie wants to see is a lot of people." Then Kennedy relents.[56]

Another notable aspect of the conversation is the gradual return of proper radio communications etiquette and security. There is no confusion over who is meant by the term "First Lady."

Clifton: DUPLEX, DUPLEX, this is WATCHMAN. Over.
Behn: Go ahead, WATCHMAN. This is DUPLEX. Over.
Clifton: DUPLEX, this is WATCHMAN. I understand that you have arranged for a [mortu]ary-type ambulance [to] take President Kennedy to *Bethesda.* Is this correct? Over.
Behn: WATCHMAN, ah . . . it has been arranged to helicopter—*helicopter*—the body to Bethesda.
Clifton: This is WATCHMAN. That's okay if it isn't after dark. And what about the First Lady? Over.
Behn: Everybody else aboard, [for] everybody else aboard, arrangements have been made to helicopter [them] into the [White House] south grounds.
Clifton: This is WATCHMAN. Are you sure that the helicopter operation will work when we have a very heavy casket? Over.
Behn: According to, ah . . . WITNESS [Tazewell Shepard], yes.
Clifton: This is WATCHMAN. *Don't* take a chance on that; *also* have a mortuary-type ambulance stand by in case the helicopter doesn't work.

55. Ibid., 387–90.
56. Ibid., 377.

Behn: That's affirmative.

Clifton: [I'll have more] instructions in a moment.

Behn: That's affirmative; I received.

Clifton: Now, some other instruction[s]. Listen carefully. We need a ramp, a normal ramp, put at the *front* of the aircraft on the *right-hand* side, just behind the pilot's cabin, in the galley. We are going to take the First Lady off by that route. Over. Do you understand?

Behn: I receive; affirmative.

Clifton: All right. *Also,* on the *right rear—*

Behn: Say again.

Clifton: No, no. [On] the *left* rear, the left rear of the aircraft, where we usually dismount—debark—we may need a forklift rather than a ramp, if there's such a thing that isn't too awkward. We may need a platform to walk out on and a forklift to put it [the casket] on. Is that possible? Over.

Behn: Say again; say again, WATCHMAN.

Clifton: I say again. The casket is in the rear compartment. And we *suggest,* 'cause it is so heavy, that we have a *forklift*—forklift—back there, to remove the casket. But if this is too awkward, we can go along with a normal ramp and several men. Over.

Behn: Affirmative. We will try for the forklift.

Clifton: Fine. Next item, DUPLEX, next item. The press—according to Lyndon Johnson—the press is to have its *normal* little fence[d-in space] at Andrews field, and he is going from there by helicopter to the White House. Over.

Behn: Say again, WATCHMAN; say again, please. WATCHMAN, this is DUPLEX. Say again.

Clifton: *[inaudible]* little fence, for the press; the normal, little *corral.* And it'll have to be [toward] the *front* of the aircraft, 'cause that's where the vice [president]—the—President Johnson will come off. Okay?

Behn: WATCHMAN, this is DUPLEX. Will you say that all over again please? You are breaking [up].

Clifton: DUPLEX, this is WATCHMAN. I say again. On the right front, a ramp for Mrs. Kennedy. On the left rear, if possible, a forklift for the casket. And on the *left front,* near the pilot, [a] normal ramp, and a normal *press* arrangement. Press—P-R-E-S-S. Over.

Behn: Say again, WATCHMAN. You are breaking—

White House: I got that. On the left front—

Behn: Yeah, I got *that—*

White House: —the normal press arrangements and a ramp for . . . President Johnson.

Behn: It's on the *left front.*

White House: The left front, near the . . . right behind the pilot.

Behn: All right.

Clifton: Did everybody get that clear? Over.

Behn: That is affirmative.

Clifton: Okay. Hold one [moment]. Roy Kellerman would like to talk to you. Over.

Behn: WATCHMAN, WATCHMAN, this is DUPLEX. Stand by one. Are you *there?* . . . WATCHMAN, WATCHMAN, this is DUPLEX.

Clifton: DUPLEX, this is WATCHMAN. Over. Go ahead.

Behn: WATCHMAN, should the secretary of defense and others be at Andrews on your arrival?

Clifton: No. I am about to—no; negative. I am about to call the White House. President Johnson wants to meet [with] the White House staff; the leadership of Congress; and as many of the cabinet members as possible, *at the White House,* [as] soon as we get there—approximately 1830, 1830 [EST]. Over.

Behn: Will you say that again please? I got the—

White House: Okay . . . I got it.

Behn: You got it?

White House: Right—

Behn: Okay; I'll get it from you.

White House: President Johnson's supposed to meet as many of the cabinet members [and] staff at the White House at 1830.

Behn: Okay.

Clifton: This is WATCHMAN. You didn't get it all. [President Johnson wants to meet with] White House staff, the key members of the White House staff; also, the leadership of Congress; also, all the cabinet members *available* . . . at the White House, from [1]830. Over.

Behn: That is affirmative, WATCHMAN. That is affirmative.

Clifton: Read that to me. Over.

Behn: *All* the leaders of Congress [and] as many cabinet members as *possible,* at the White House, at *1830.*

Clifton: And of the *key* members of the White House staff, that is, [Ted] Sorensen, [McGeorge] Bundy, *et cetera.*

Behn: That is correct.

Clifton: *[with tone of relief]* Okay.

±3:18 p.m.

As Jerry Behn and Roy Kellerman also plot out logistics of the landing and reconfigure Secret Service protection, one especially sensitive aspect concerns Mrs. Kennedy. As of yet, her stoicism and fierce determination have not yet registered back in Washington; indeed, "even the inner circle of Kennedy intimates

[are] slow to grasp the extent of [her] *volte-face.*"[57] The woman dubbed LACE by the Secret Service is still perceived as having a fragile temperament, more likely to wilt and wither, everyone imagines, after sitting next to her husband as he was murdered in cold blood. Accordingly, agent Kellerman conveys a request to usher her personal physician, Dr. John Walsh, to Andrews so that he can person-ally accompany her back to the White House, where it is presumed she will immediately retire (as was also suggested in the preceding conversation). It does not occur to Behn—or Kellerman, for that matter—that Mrs. Kennedy will have none of that and will not leave the body unattended until the moment it comes to rest at the White House. She has made a point of staying as close as is humanly possible to her husband's side.

Mrs. Kennedy is also unyielding about her appearance. *"No* . . . let them see what they've done," she would whisper fiercely, as she had done to Lady Bird Johnson, in response to repeated entreaties to change her blood-soaked suit.[58] Besides her literary appreciation of ritual, which would become evident in the next three days, Jacqueline Kennedy understands that consciousness is created by certain symbols, and in this realm, nothing exceeds blood's mystical and inflam-matory powers.[59] It is a necessary first step in investing her husband's assassina-tion with suggestions of martyrdom, irrespective of who killed him or why.

Kellerman: Do you have any questions? It's enough.

Behn: Ahh . . . not at the moment; if we do, we'll call back.

Kellerman: That's a Roger, but hold on. . . . Hold please.
      DIGEST to DUPLEX, go ahead.

Behn: Go ahead, DIGEST. This is DUPLEX.

Kellerman: Would you call Dr. John Walsh . . . in Washington and advise him of our arrival?

Behn: That is *affirmative.*

Kellerman: Okay?

Behn: Where does LACE want Dr. Walsh to meet her?

Kellerman: *[inaudible]* Dr. Walsh to meet her.

Behn: *Where?*

Andrews AFB: Say again, sir.

Behn: DIGEST, this is DUPLEX. Where does LACE wish Dr. Walsh to meet her? . . . DIGEST—

Kellerman: At the White House when we get there with her.

White House: *[to Behn]* At the White House.

Behn: Okay. Thank you. *[to Kellerman]* That's affirmative.

57. Ibid., 347.
58. Ibid., 348.
59. Thomas Mallon, "Sanctified by Blood," *Civilization,* January–February 1996.

±3:19 p.m.

On the dead president's final flight, Colonel Swindal is determined to fly the airplane as high as he possibly can, "higher than anyone ha[s] ever taken John F. Kennedy."[60] *Air Force One* reaches 41,000 feet, nearly eight miles straight up, before leveling off. At that altitude everything seems tranquil, but the weather on the ground is anything but. Behind *Air Force One* a cold front is moving rapidly into Texas, sending temperatures at Love Field plummeting. Ahead there is a line of violent weather along a 120-mile-long front from Arkansas to Mississippi, smack in the middle of *Air Force One*'s flight path. SAM Command Post Weather, which functions as *Air Force One*'s private forecaster, is anxious to communicate this information to the aircraft but cannot because the communication lines are so tied up. At the time of this conversation, *Air Force One* is less than fifteen minutes away from the weather front, which includes tornadoes.

Andrews AFB: Andrews sideband, Airman Gilmore [here], sir.

SAM Command Post: *[impatiently]* Sergeant Phillips [here], Air Force Command Post. Air Force Weather is still waiting to bring up *Air Force One*. We've been waitin' now for fifteen minutes; what's up?

Andrews AFB: *[evenly]* Right, sir. We're running *two* patches at *one* time to the White House, and they're real busy. We can't get through to 'em.

SAM Command Post: Would you—

Andrews AFB: They're makin', ah . . . arrangements to take the body off and everything else.

SAM Command Post: *[chastened]* Let me patch in with Air Force Weather, so you'll know—he'll know—

Andrews AFB: Right; I already told him that earlier.

SAM Command Post: Go ahead, sir.

SAM Command Post Weather: Weather's on.

Andrews AFB: Hello, sir?

SAM Command Post Weather: Yes, sir.

Andrews AFB: Right. We're running two patches at one time to *Air Force One* right now from the White House. And they're making arrangements about taking the casket and stuff off—

SAM Command Post Weather: Rog[er]—

Andrews AFB: —and we can't get through to you. As soon as we can, we'll give you a call.

SAM Command Post Weather: Okay. He *[Air Force One]* needs that temperature before he gets here.

60. Manchester, *Death,* 339.

Andrews AFB: Right, sir. We'll get—he should be done pretty soon. They been on it quite a while now.

SAM Command Post Weather: Okay, buddy.

Andrews AFB: Right—

SAM Command Post Weather: Thank you, sir.

Andrews AFB: Right.

±3:20 p.m.

From the moment the shots sounded in Dealey Plaza, Rufus Youngblood has been a dogged advocate of doing whatever is in the best interests of Lyndon Johnson's personal safety. Youngblood suggested leaving Parkland and Dallas altogether without regard for President or Mrs. Kennedy. Now, aboard *Air Force One,* he argues that Johnson (VOLUNTEER) should stay the night in the living quarters of the White House, along with Lady Bird (aka VICTORIA) and their younger daughter, Luci (aka VENUS), because "that's the best place to protect you, Mr. President."[61] Though he acts as if ice water were running through his veins, Youngblood is simply trying to live up to the commission that every Secret Service agent carries in his pocket: to protect the president of the United States. According to that instruction, agents had no choice but to shift their professional allegiance from John Kennedy to Lyndon Johnson while still in Dealey Plaza.[62] For his part, Johnson is receptive to Youngblood's exhortations save the last one. As Dallas and the perception of an imminent threat recede at the speed of 535 miles per hour, the president seems to be more and more comfortable following his own instincts. He views moving into the White House (CROWN) as an exceedingly delicate matter and flatly rejects the idea. "That would be presumptuous on my part," Johnson tells Youngblood. "I realize that [you have to think first of security], but you can protect the Elms, too, can't you?"[63] The Elms, aka VALLEY, is the Johnsons' home in the Spring Valley section of northwest Washington, as there is no official vice presidential residence.

White House: [DAGGER], DAGGER, DUPLEX is on. Go ahead.

Youngblood: DAGGER to DUPLEX, [I have] messages from VOLUNTEER and VICTORIA relative to activities tonight.

Behn: Go ahead, DAGGER. This is DUPLEX.

Youngblood: You are aware that we will go to CROWN for meetings?

Behn: That is affirmative . . . go ahead.

61. Knebel, "Ordeal."
62. Manchester, *Death,* 165.
63. Ibid., 346.

Youngblood: VOLUNTEER will reside at VALLEY for an indefinite time. I repeat: VOLUNTEER will *reside* at VALLEY for an indefinite time. VICTORIA requests that VENUS ought to [be escorted to] VALLEY with agents.

Behn: Will you say again? Will you say again?

White House: VENUS should go out to VALLEY with the agents.

Youngblood: That is Roger, that is a Roger. VENUS will go to VALLEY with agents [and] VICTORIA will go to VALLEY after first going to CROWN. Do you understand? Over.

White House: VICTORIA will go to VALLEY after first going to CROWN.

Behn: *[to White House]* Okay. *[to Behn]* That's affirmative.

Youngblood: Do you also understand that for *residential* purposes, VOLUNTEER [will] reside at VALLEY?

Behn: That is affirmative . . . that is affirmative.

Youngblood: All right. That is all the traffic I have. You will get *[inaudible]*

Behn: Okay, okay.

White House: Right, sir.

±3:21 p.m.

Air Force Brigadier General Godfrey McHugh (aka WING) wants to contact the official White House photographer, Captain Cecil Stoughton (aka SLUGGER), perhaps to make sure that Stoughton will be available at Andrews AFB to document the arrival of *Air Force One.* In the confusion, McHugh doesn't recall that Stoughton was part of the presidential entourage that went to Texas. Moreover, Stoughton has stayed behind in Dallas so that his pictures of the swearing-in can be processed as rapidly as possible. Though the White House photographer's presence is superfluous in the AP bureau's darkroom, until he actually sees the images develop he is holding his breath.[64] Stoughton is very aware that he alone is custodian of the visual proof that the government continues.[65]

Andrews AFB: *Air Force One,* Andrews. CROWN on.

AF1: CROWN, *Air Force One.* This is a message from WING going to SLUGGER. SLUGGER is to meet aircraft as soon as possible. If he cannot do this, he is to see WING as soon as possible; as soon as possible. Go ahead.

White House: Roger, Roger. WING to SLUGGER: meet aircraft as soon as possible. If this is impossible, see WING as soon as possible. Go ahead.

AF1: That is correct; or contact him any way feasible.

---

64. Trask, *Pictures of the Pain,* 50.
65. Stoughton's unforgettable photograph of the swearing-in will be broadcast by the television networks beginning at approximately 5:40 p.m. EST.

White House: Roger, Roger. CROWN understand[s]. Any[thing] further? Go
   ahead.
AF1: Negative. And I suspect that SLUGGER is back in Dallas.
White House: Roger, Roger.

±3:22 p.m.

White House: *Air Force One, Air Force One,* this is CROWN. Come in.
AF1: Request from VICTORIA to cancel or deaden her commercial telephone,
   that is, VOLUNTEER and VICTORIA's commercial telephone at VALLEY
   should be temporarily discontinued and [a] security line should be put in.
   Get WHCA personnel put on that [immediately. Do] you understand?
   Over.
White House: That's a Roger, Roger. Cancel commercial lines at VALLEY, at
   VALLEY, and install WHCA circuits, WHCA circuits. Is that a Roger?
AF1: That is a Roger.
White House: Roger, will do.

±3:30 p.m.

When Malcolm Kilduff (aka WARRIOR) finally gets an opening to talk to Andrew
Hatcher (aka WINNER), *Air Force One* is passing through the area of severe
weather, and the radio patch is a poor one. Hatcher, the number two man in the
press office under Salinger, seems more shaken and uncertain than the stolid
Kilduff, the assistant press secretary on his way out. Kilduff relays an important
message, namely that VOLUNTEER (Lyndon Johnson) will be making a statement upon arrival at Andrews.

For most Americans, this speech will be their first impression of Johnson in
years. As vice president, he suffered the usual indignities accorded the number-
two man. Just a few weeks before, the popular CBS television show *Candid
Camera* featured a segment wherein citizens on the street were covertly filmed
while answering the question, "Who is Lyndon Johnson?" Participants guessed
every occupation imaginable but the vice presidency of the United States. "No,
I don't know him," said one man. "I'm from New Jersey."[66]

Kilduff: WINNER, WINNER, this is WARRIOR. Do you read me? Over.
Hatcher: I hear you . . . over.

66. Robert Dallek, *Flawed Giant: Lyndon Johnson and His Times 1961–1973* (New York:
Oxford University Press, 1998), 44.

Kilduff: WINNER, WINNER, this is WARRIOR. Will you please advise press that normal press coverage, including *live TV,* will be allowed at the [Andrews Air Force] Base. VOLUNTEER, repeat, VOLUNTEER will make a statement on arrival; will make statement on arrival. Did you read that? Over.

Hatcher: I read you clearly. Will you listen to my question? Is Mrs. Kennedy aboard *Air Force One?*

Kilduff: WINNER, WINNER, this is WARRIOR. That is a Roger, that is a Roger. Over.

Hatcher: All right. The other thing is, I'm setting up the press section on the [White House's] South Lawn, about fifty yards from the position of helicopter number one. Would that meet Mrs. Kennedy's and the president's approval?

Kilduff: WINNER, they are not returning to the [White] House; they are not returning to the House. For your own information, ah . . . they're going someplace else, I don't want to, ah . . . go in on the radio on this one. So there will be an arrival there, but it will be VOLUNTEER; it will be VOLUNTEER [only]. Over.

Hatcher: Thank you. I will hold that information, and we can say something after you arrive. Let's see . . . hold it just a second, let me look through my list of questions.

Is it true that the body of President Kennedy will go to Bethesda Naval Hospital?

Kilduff: That is a Roger, that is a Roger. But we are not saying that yet. Over.

Hatcher: Well, we've already said it. I don't—I should have *checked* with you before doing it, but I don't think it makes too much difference. It takes a lot of, you know . . . we *should* know it. And it takes a lot [of pressure] off of us by doing it. I was in *error.* Over.

Kilduff: So far as that press area at—on the South Lawn—there is no objection to that. There is no objection to that.

Hatcher: Should that be live? Would we permit live [coverage]—yes, you [already] told me that. Okay . . . anything else?

Kilduff: Andy, would you repeat that?

Hatcher: Anything else that I should know?

Kilduff: Wait a minute, you're breaking [up]. But let me think about that for just a second, would you please?

Hatcher: Okay.

Kilduff: Yes. The [press] pool on this aircraft is Chuck Roberts [from *Newsweek*] and [Merriman] Smith [from UPI]. We lost [Jack] Bell [from AP] somewhere along the line. We don't have AP aboard, but I have given them the statement of VOLUNTEER on the death, which he will make at the airport. Over.

Hatcher: I understand you. Okay. Over and out.

Kilduff: No. Don't [go] out on me yet, because—are you still there, WINNER?

Hatcher: Yes, I am; I'm here.

Kilduff: I *think* that we're going to tell the press that on *arrival*—hold on just a second. Wait a minute. I've got [Chester] Clifton here, and he's trying to give me something. Hold on. . . .

WINNER , WINNER, this is WARRIOR. You can announce that on *arrival,* on *arrival,* he [President Johnson] will meet with, at the White House *[inaudible]* or *later,* he will meet with the [congressional] *leadership,* with the *leadership.* Did you read that? Over.

Hatcher: Yes. I did read that.

Kilduff: Wait a minute. You're breaking [up] badly. I cannot read.

Hatcher: Yes; yes. I understand, and I will announce.

Kilduff: Okay, very good, WINNER. Now there's . . . wait a minute, there's one other part I'm getting from Clifton now that I want to relay to you. Hold [on] one [moment]. They said that on arrival at the [White] House, the president will meet with *McNamara* and *Bundy.* Also, if Rusk is in *town,* he'll meet with Rusk. But I think he's in the Far East, so it'll probably be *Ball.* And after—about a half hour after *that* meeting is over—we will meet with the congressional *leadership* at eight—wait a minute, I'm getting a time on that now. That's eight o'clock. He will meet with the leadership at eight o'clock, at eight o'clock. Did you read that? Over.

Hatcher: I read it. Now is that bipartisan leadership or Democratic leadership?

Kilduff: That is *wholly* bipartisan, *wholly* bipartisan. Over.

Hatcher: I understand you.

Kilduff: Hold one [moment] and let me check any other information here. Is [that]—do you mind holding, Andy?

Hatcher: No; go right ahead.

Kilduff: [I] have nothing more at this time. I assume you'll be available so I can reach you if I have to get back and feed you more information as it develops, or whatever you call it. Over.

Hatcher: Yes. Over and out.

±3:35 p.m.

The radio patch to the White House is still beset by atmospheric interference when General Clifton converses with McGeorge Bundy about the presidential schedule for that evening. The requested meeting with congressional leaders on a bipartisan basis will serve two purposes: it will reassure the country, and it will be reassuring to Lyndon Johnson. Congress and its members are his natural habitat, after a quarter-century of service there. Because the meetings are in the White House, however, the delicate issue of appearing a bit *too* eager to assume power arises again. Bundy is of the opinion that Johnson should be seen as availing himself of the symbols of presidential power as soon as possible. But the politician, as opposed to the geopolitician, in Johnson tells him to move cautiously, and he is adamant about not yet trespassing into the spaces that are already his to use. The closest he will venture is the West Wing, a warren of offices and conference rooms appended to the original White House (the Executive Mansion) during a 1902 renovation; even then the Oval Office in the West Wing is deemed off limits. Ultimately, however, Johnson will hole up in EOB Room 274, his vice presidential office in the Executive Office Building adjacent to the White House.

One change of plans is also apparent: now there will be no meeting of the White House staff. McGeorge Bundy has advised against such a gathering, arguing that staffers personally appointed by the late president would be feeling too "bereft" for a meeting.[67] Johnson changes his earlier decision.

White House: *AF1,* this is CROWN.

Kilduff: This is WARRIOR to CROWN, WARRIOR to CROWN. CROWN, are you reading? Over.

White House: WARRIOR, WARRIOR, this is CROWN. Loud and clear; loud and clear.

Kilduff: CROWN, hold one [moment] for a transmission from WITNESS, [Tazewell Shepard], for a transmission from WITNESS. Over.

White House: Roger, Roger. Would also like to confirm at this time, would also like to confirm at this time, the request from *AF1.*

Clifton: CROWN, this is WATCHMAN. Over.

White House: This is CROWN. Go ahead, WATCHMAN.

Clifton: This is WATCHMAN. Get Mr. Bundy up [on the radio].

White House: *AF1* from CROWN. You were broken, you were broken. Say again.

Clifton: CROWN, this is WATCHMAN. Please get Mr. Bundy on the line. Over.

White House: Roger, Roger, Roger. Stand by; stand by.

Andrews AFB: CROWN, your party on this end is on. Go ahead and transmit to him.

Clifton: This is WATCHMAN. CROWN, please monitor.

Mac, ah . . . [Mr.] Johnson wants to meet with *only* you and Secretary *McNamara* at 6:30 [p.m. EST] at the White House. If Mr. Rusk is in town, fine for Mr. Rusk. If he is *not* in town, then we *do* not—*negative*—*do not* want an acting secretary [of state to attend]. Over.

Bundy: Correct. We are . . . will you tell him [Johnson] that the acting cabinet will be at the airport to greet him. He can bring McNamara and me in his chopper to the White House. Over.

Clifton: *That is correct.* That is *all* right. We will do *that.* Now take another message. Over.

67. Manchester, *Death,* 345.

Bundy: Yeah.

Clifton: Secondly, I told Jerry Behn about a White House staff meeting.

Bundy: Yeah.

Clifton: There will be *no—negative*—there will be no White House staff meeting tonight—

Bundy: All right.

Clifton: —it'll be tomorrow. Over.

Bundy: Correct. I have you . . . I have it. Let me repeat your message. Right, ah . . . over.

Clifton: Go ahead.

Bundy: First, that the, ah . . . president wishes to meet with [the] sec[retary of] def[ense] and me at the White House on return from Andrews. Second, that there will be no *other* meeting this evening; there will be a White House staff meeting on call tomorrow. Over.

Clifton: No, that is *not* correct. He wants to meet with the [congressional] *leadership* about 7:30 [p.m. EST], leadership about 7:30. Over.

Bundy: Right. Does he wish us to arrange that? Over.

Clifton: He wants you to arrange that. Two meetings tonight: [first, with] McNamara and Bundy [at 6:30]—

Bundy: Yeah.

Clifton: —and the leadership about 7:30. Over.

Bundy: Does he mean the Democratic leadership only? Over.

Clifton: Bipartisan leadership, and I'll give you some names. Over.

Bundy: All right. Over.

Clifton: The Speaker of the House [John McCormack (D-Massachusetts)].

Bundy: Yeah.

Clifton: Carl Albert [D-Oklahoma].

Bundy: Carl Albert.

Clifton: Hale Boggs [D-Louisiana].

Bundy: Yeah.

Clifton: Charles Halleck [R-Indiana].

Bundy: Wait a moment; say that one again.

Clifton: *[apparently not hearing Bundy]* Leslie Arends [R-Illinois].

Bundy: Arends? Yeah.

Clifton: [Now from the] Senate. Are you listening? Over.

Bundy: I have . . . will you take what I have from me? Over. And then we can go on.

Clifton: I'll listen to you. Over.

Bundy: I have the Speaker; Carl Albert; Hale Boggs; Leslie Arends. Over.

Clifton: This is WATCHMAN and that is correct.[68] I will now continue with the Senate. Over.

---

68. Bundy did not catch Charles Halleck's name, and Clifton does not realize it is missing.

Bundy: All right. Over.

Clifton: [Mike] Mansfield [D-Montana].

Bundy: All right.

Clifton: [Hubert] Humphrey [D-Minnesota].

Bundy: Yeah.

Clifton: [George] Smathers [D-Florida].

Bundy: Yeah.

Clifton: And [Everett] Dirksen [R-Illinois].

Bundy: Wait—

Clifton: [Thomas] Kuchel [R-California]—

Bundy: —a moment. Wait a moment, wait a moment. I have the first *three*. Over. . . . Repeat. Over.

Clifton: This is WATCHMAN. Out.

White House: Hello, sir? Stand by, please.

Bundy: Yeah.

Andrews AFB: WATCHMAN, Andrews. We're still standing by for orders to carry out, sir.

Clifton: CROWN, this is ANGEL [*Air Force One*]. CROWN, this is ANGEL. Out.

White House: CROWN, ANGEL.

Clifton: This is ANGEL. Would you—I broke down with Mr. Bundy. Would you check his *Senate* list for me? Over.

Bundy: I have Mansfield, Humphrey, Smathers. Over.

Clifton: This is WATCHMAN. In addition to Mansfield, Humphrey, and Smathers, we want Dirksen—

Bundy: Yeah.

Clifton: —Kuchel and [Bourke] Hickenlooper [R-Iowa]. Over.

Bundy: Dirksen, Kuchel, Hickenlooper. Over.

Clifton: That is correct. For about 7:30. Over.

Bundy: 7:30 at the White House? Over.

Clifton: 7:30 in the Cabinet Room. Over.

Bundy: Tell the vice president [*sic*] the Cabinet Room is under rearrangement, but the Oval Room will be ready.[69] Over.

Clifton: The Oval Room it will be . . . you mean the *Fish Room*?[70]

Bundy: The president—I mean—*both* the Fish Room and the president's study, and we will *try* to have the Cabinet Room. But that's a detail. We can work that out. Over.

Clifton: This is WATCHMAN. He [Johnson] does *not* want to go in the

---

69. During the president's trip to Texas, both the Oval Office and the Cabinet Room in the West Wing were being redecorated, with all the appointments selected by Jacqueline Kennedy.

70. The Fish Room served as the president's office in the West Wing until the Oval Office was built in 1909. It is called the Fish Room because Franklin Roosevelt used it to display an aquarium and fishing mementos.

[Executive] Mansion, or in the Oval Room, or the president's study, or the president's office.

Bundy: Correct.

Clifton: If the Cabinet Room isn't *ready,* then put it in the Fish Room. Over.

Bundy: I have you . . . I understand. Always in the [White House's] *West Wing.* Over.

Clifton: This is correct. Over.

Bundy: I have nothing further. Over.

Clifton: This is WATCHMAN. Now please [inform] DUPLEX about the changes, so we don't confuse it. DUPLEX is Jerry Behn. Over.

Bundy: All right; I will.

Clifton: See you in a little while. Over.

Bundy: Okay.

±3:15 p.m.

Halfway to Washington, somewhere in the airspace over Arkansas, Lyndon Johnson orders that a call be placed to Rose Kennedy, the seventy-three-year-old mother of the deceased president. Although the mass media have slipped easily into calling Johnson by his new title, the appellation comes with difficulty to those who served under President Kennedy. As the connection is established, *AF1* radio operator Joseph Ayres falters; he cannot bring himself to say, *President Johnson* wishes to speak with you. The matriarch of the Kennedy clan, however, has no trouble addressing Johnson in his new role. The conversation, in fact, seems harder on the president than on Rose Kennedy. After just one sentence he thrusts the telephone at Lady Bird "as if it were a hot potato."[71]

Andrews AFB: *Air Force One,* Andrews. Give CROWN a call.

AF1: Break. CROWN, *Air Force One.* VOLUNTEER requesting a patch with Mrs. Rose Kennedy as soon as possible. Go ahead.

White House: Understand VOLUNTEER wants a patch with Mrs. Rose *[sic]* as soon as possible.

AF1: Mrs. Rose *Kennedy.* Roger.

White House: Roger, Roger. I'll work on that right away. And also, while I'm working on that, could we have a confirmation, a confirmation, on [an] earlier transmission from *AF1,* stating that the commercial telephone service—I say again, commercial telephone service—for the Johnson

71. Johnson was overcome with emotion, according to the nearly contemporaneous account in Knebel, "Ordeal." Manchester will write that "it was the most difficult call of his life." Manchester, *Death,* 371.

residence should be discontinued with the direct lines [routed] through our White House's? Do you Roger that?

AF1: Stand by, and we'll have to check it out.

White House: Roger, Roger. While you're checking on that, I'll work on the call to Mrs. Rose Kennedy for VOLUNTEER. Stand by.

[AF1 confirms that WHCA is to take control of the Johnsons' telephone lines as the patch is being arranged.]

White House: *AF1, AF1, AF1* from CROWN. Come in.

AF1: CROWN, this is *Air Force One.* Do you read us? Over.

White House: I'm reading you loud and clear. I have Mrs. Kennedy standing by. Are you ready with VOLUNTEER? Go ahead.

AF1: Yes, we are ready. Can you put her on and I'll turn her over to him? Over.

White House: Roger, Roger. She's coming on now.

   AF1 from CROWN. Mrs. Kennedy [is] on. Go ahead, please.

AF1: Hello, Mrs. Kennedy. Hello, Mrs. Kennedy.

Mrs. Kennedy: Hello.

AF1: We're talking from the airplane.

Mrs. Kennedy: Yes.

AF1: Can you hear us all right? Over.

Mrs. Kennedy: Yes, thank you. Thank you . . . hello?

AF1: Yes, Mrs. Kennedy. I have, ah . . . Mr. Johnson for you here.

Mrs. Kennedy: Yes, thank you . . . hello?

Johnson: Mrs. Kennedy?

Mrs. Kennedy: Yes. *Yes,* yes, yes, Mr. President. Yes *[indistinct]*—

Johnson: I wish to God there was something that I could do, and I wanted to tell you that we were grieving with you.

Mrs. Kennedy: Yes. Well, thanks a—thank you very much.

Johnson: *[unable to continue]* Here's [Lady] Bird.

Mrs. Kennedy: Thank you very much. I know . . . I know you loved Jack, and he loved you.

Mrs. Johnson: Mrs. Kennedy, we feel like we've just had [our hearts cut out]—[72]

Mrs. Kennedy: Yes, all right.

Mrs. Johnson: *[her voice trembling]* We're glad that the nation had your son—

Mrs. Kennedy: Yes . . . yes.

Mrs. Johnson: —as long as it did.

Mrs. Kennedy: Yes. Well, thank you, Lady Bird. Thank you very much. Good-bye.

Mrs. Johnson: Love—

Mrs. Kennedy: Yes.

Mrs. Johnson: Love and prayers to all of you.

---

72. The portion in brackets is inaudible; the words are taken from the quote that appears in Knebel, "Ordeal."

Mrs. Kennedy: Yes . . . thank you very much. Good-bye . . . good-bye . . . good-bye.

Kilduff: CROWN, CROWN, this is WARRIOR. I think that [transmission] is over. Is that a Roger? Over.

White House: That is a Roger, WARRIOR. That is a Roger. Mrs. Kennedy has hung up. Go ahead.

Kilduff: CROWN, now would you give me that patch to [chief of staff] Walter Jenkins in President, ah, Johnson's office? Over.

White House: Roger. Stand by one.

±3:30 p.m.

When the presidential limousine arrived at Parkland Hospital three hours ago, Nellie Connally was all but sure that it carried two casualties: President Kennedy and her husband, the governor of Texas. John Connally had lapsed into unconsciousness after suffering his wounds, and though Mrs. Connally whispered in his ear, "It's going to be all right . . . be still," she didn't believe her own words. The exit wound in his chest was as big as a baseball.[73] But in fact his injuries were less serious than they looked, provided that he received prompt care. The bullet had fortuitously missed all his major arteries, despite the profuse bleeding. Indeed, the hair-raising, screeching stop at the emergency entrance helped rouse Connally back to consciousness. He was even able to cooperate actively with the stretcher bearers as they lifted him out of the limousine.[74] Still, one of the trauma-room nurses ventured a dire prediction. "The governor's not expected to live," she told Cliff Carter, a longtime aide who ran Johnson's Texas office.[75]

Thus, the news that Connally is in very serious but not critical condition following emergency surgery comes as an enormous relief to the Johnsons, who regret having had to abandon their friends.

AF1: CROWN, *Air Force One.* VOLUNTEER would like a patch to the governor colony *[sic]*—correction, Governor *Connally* of Texas, *Mrs.* Connally. That's the governor's wife. Go ahead.

White House: VOLUNTEER would like a patch with Mrs. Connally, Governor Connally's wife. Is that a Roger?

AF1: That is a Roger.

White House: Roger, Roger. Stand by one.

73. Nellie Connally, *From Love Field: Our Final Hours with President John F. Kennedy* (New York: Rugged Land, 2003), 43.

74. Manchester, *Death,* 170–71.

75. Ibid., 239.

AF1: Still standing by for the Connally call.

White House: Roger, Roger. We have Dallas on the line, and they are trying to contact her now. Stand by, please.

AF1: Roger, Roger. Standing by.

[The patch is arranged with relative ease.]

White House: *Air Force One* from CROWN. The Connally residence *[sic]* in Dallas is *on* the line, is on the line, and Mrs. Connally is available to speak with Mr. Johnson if he can get to the phone patch.[76] Go ahead.

AF1: Roger. He wants *specifically* to speak with her. Go ahead.

White House: Roger. Stand by just a moment.

AF1, AF1 from CROWN. Would you put VOLUNTEER on please? Mrs. Connally is *on* the line standing by for his call.

AF1: Stand by one [moment].

Mrs. Johnson: Nellie? Can you hear me?

Mrs. Connally: Yes, Bird.

Mrs. Johnson: There is some reassuring news, over the TV. We are up in the plane. But they . . . the surgeon, speaking about John, sounded *so* reassuring. How about it?

Mrs. Connally: The report he gave was true. That was the surgeon that had just [got] done operating on him. Yes, John is going to be all right . . . we are almost *certain,* unless [something] unforeseen happens.

Mrs. Johnson: Just a minute, Nellie. I can't hear you too well.

Johnson: Nellie, do you hear me?

Mrs. Connally: Yes.

Johnson: *[with emotion]* [I love you,] darling, and I know that . . . that everything's going to be all right . . . isn't it?

Mrs. Connally: Yes, it *is* . . . going to be all right.

Johnson: God bless you, darlin'.

Mrs. Connally: *[earnestly]* The same to you.

Johnson: Give John a hug and a kiss for me.

Mrs. Connally: Good luck.

Johnson: Good-bye.

Mrs. Connally: 'Bye.

±3:51 p.m.

Besides 26000, two other SAM aircraft are returning to Andrews AFB from Love Field. SAM 86970, normally the plane reserved for the vice president (and thus *Air Force Two* in SAM parlance), carries Senator Yarborough, five Texas

---

76. Nellie Connally, of course, was at her husband's bedside at Parkland Hospital.

congressmen, and Kennedy staffers evicted from 26000 in order to accommodate the Johnsons' entourage. In the confusion and grief, few appreciate the irony of Yarborough's position. That morning the question of the day was whether he would deign to sit in the same automobile as Lyndon Johnson; now Yarborough is the outcast, relegated to the backup aircraft.[77] SAM 86373, meanwhile, is a C-130 cargo jet carrying all the accoutrements of a presidential visit: the president's seal, a special American flag, the Secret Service's "Queen Mary," and the Lincoln Continental SS 100 X that is the president's limousine.[78] The automobile had been driven from Parkland to Love Field when the Johnsons made their getaway from the hospital. The Lincoln is material evidence in the felony that has been committed in Dallas County, and that crime can be prosecuted to the fullest extent only there. To their endless chagrin, federal law enforcement authorities have discovered that killing a president is not a felony prosecutable under federal statutes unless there is a conspiracy. Under normal circumstances, Dallas police would impound the limousine. But there is about as much chance of that as there was of having the president's autopsy performed in accordance with state law.

SAM Command Post: Air Force Command Post.

AF1: Go ahead, Command Post. *Air Force One.*

SAM Command Post: [86]373 departed at 2141 ZULU.

AF1: Roger. What is the complete plane number?

SAM Command Post: *Air Force One,* did you copy?

AF1: Roger. And who is this information to go to? Go ahead.

SAM Command Post: Say again?

AF1: Roger. [Who do you] wish this information passed to? Go ahead.

SAM Command Post: *Air Force One, Air Force One.* This is Air Force Command Post. Over.

AF1: Command Post, *Air Force One.* I read you loud and clear. I understand [86]373 departed at 2141. *Who* do you wish *notified* about this? Go ahead.

SAM Command Post: Didn't you request the time of departure on this aircraft? This is the one with the presidential cars on board.

AF1: Roger. Will pass that. I know where it goes now. Thank you.

SAM Command Post: Roger.

---

77. Yarborough is so nervous about his standing that upon arriving in Washington he immediately sends President Johnson a telegram pledging his undivided loyalty. The next day he will call Johnson and eagerly offer to "close ranks." Knebel, "Ordeal"; Johnson and Yarborough, conversation, 23 November 1963, 1:44 p.m., LBJL.

78. Manchester, *Death,* 329.

±5:06 p.m.[79]

Air Force One is now less than one hour from Andrews AFB and has crossed into the eastern standard time zone. Like the logistics of the postmortem, the plans for the arrival at Andrews AFB are subject to more than one confirmation because of conflicting information. Here, Air Force Major Michael Cook (aka TANKER) attempts to reconcile conflicting instructions with Colonel Swindal (aka TIGER), the pilot of *Air Force One*.

White House: Roger, Roger. *AF1, AF1* from CROWN. *AF1, AF1, AF1* from CROWN. Come in.

AF1: Hello, CROWN to *AF1*. Go ahead.

White House: Roger, Roger. Stand by for a patch from TANKER, TANKER.

AF1: Roger.

White House: *AF1, AF1,* TANKER on the line. Go ahead, TANKER.

Cook: Hello ANGEL, hello ANGEL. May I speak with WATCHMAN [General Clifton] or TIGER, WATCHMAN or TIGER? Over.

AF1: Roger. WATCHMAN is busy at the present time on another circuit. Stand by for TIGER.

Cook: Standing by for TIGER.

Swindal: TIGER. How do you read? Over.

Cook: Five by five, TIGER, five by five. I have been informed from Dallas that it was desired that the aircraft be parked in an isolated spot when you arrive here. However, WATCHMAN had a *long* discussion with [Jerry] Behn and nothing about that was mentioned. And the present plan on the ground here is to spot you in the regular place, unless WATCHMAN says *now* that this is not desired. Over.

Swindal: I believe they want to park us at the regular place, TANKER. Where did you get that information down in Dallas? Over.

Cook: It was from the USAF Command Post agent there, and I understood from him that you had told him to do this. Over.

Swindal: Well, we told him to look into that, and in the excitement there I guess he assumed that we wanted it done. We were going to discuss it in flight.

Cook: I see.

Swindal: We should go ahead with the present plan and park in the regular place. Now I asked [Colonel] Hornbuckle [at SAM Command Post] to get in touch with you, I passed some instructions to him.

---

79. All times in the book from this point onward are eastern standard or eastern daylight, depending on the date, or unless otherwise noted.

We need steps on the *right front* of the aircraft. The press box will be on the *left front* of the aircraft. The . . . President Johnson will deplane at the front of the aircraft . . . and we need a forklift at the *rear* of the aircraft. LACE will deplane on the *right front.* Over.

Cook: Understand, TIGER. Understand those instructions, and they have all been carried out. We will continue with the plan to spot you in the regular place. There will be a ramp left front, a ramp right front, a forklift left rear, the press area left front. Over.

Swindal: Mighty fine and will keep in touch.

Cook: Roger. Thank you and out.

±5:45 p.m.

By the time *Air Force One* crosses into Virginia from West Virginia, the manic pace of radio communications has slowed to a trickle, the conversations indistinguishable from what would routinely occur.

AF1: [Andrews,] *Air Force One.* Would you give me the Command Post, please?

Andrews AFB: Roger, sir.

SAM Command Post: Air Force Command Post, Sergeant Phillips here.

Andrews AFB: Rog[er]. Andrews sideband. I have *Air Force One* for a patch.

SAM Command Post: Roger. Yes, sir.

Andrews AFB: *Air Force One,* Andrews. Command Post on. Go ahead.

AF1: Roger, Command Post to *Air Force One.* We checked Front Royal, [Virginia] at 2242 [ZULU]. We're presently descending. Estimated block time remains 2305. Go ahead.

SAM Command Post: Roger, *Air Force One.* Command Post copy.

±6:05 p.m.

Colonel Swindal's landing is so gentle that most of the passengers aboard *Air Force One* are not even aware of the aircraft touching down.[80]

AF1: Air Force Command Post, please.

SAM Command Post: Air Force Command Post. Sergeant Phillips here.

Andrews AFB: Roger. Andrews sideband. I have *Air Force One* for a patch.

SAM Command Post: Uh-hmm.

Andrews AFB: Roger. Stand by for *Air Force One.*

80. Manchester, *Death,* 387.

SAM Command Post: Go ahead, Andrews. Air Force [Command Post].
Andrews AFB: *Air Force One,* Andrews. Command Post is [on]. Go ahead.
AF1: Roger, Command Post. *Air Force One* landed [at] Andrews at 2300 [ZULU].[81]
SAM Command Post: Roger, *Air Force One.* Command Post copy.

Solemnly, and with minimal comment, television news anchors describe the arrival of *Air Force One* as it slowly taxis toward the dreary Military Air Transport Service (MATS) terminal at Andrews. The television klieg lights are turned off so that Colonel Swindal will not be blinded, which only adds to the visual drama. Because of the helicopters warming up in the background, SAM 26000 cannot be heard before it is seen, and with only a dim November moon for illumination, it seems to appear out of nowhere. Then the floodlights come on. A small crowd of about fifty dignitaries—senior foreign diplomats, and representatives from all three branches of the federal government—is on hand to meet the aircraft. They are huddled in little knots in the chilly night. Beyond the fence, unnoticed, stand almost three thousand uninvited guests, a harbinger of the huge crowds that will pay their respects to President Kennedy over the next three days.

Robert Kennedy, crouching inside a service truck parked on the apron, is the first to board the aircraft, running up a ramp as it is being rolled into place. He slips inside so quickly that moments later some officials on the ground and passengers in the aircraft are astonished to see him; they hadn't known he too was in Dallas! Rushing through the length of the plane, he makes his way to the tail compartment with nary a glance at nor word for anyone—including Lyndon Johnson. "Where's Jackie? I want to see Jackie," he murmurs, his face stricken and streaked with tears. "Excuse me."[82]

Then the casket appears, carried primarily by the Secret Service agents responsible for President Kennedy's security in Dallas. It is a thoughtful gesture by Mrs. Kennedy because the agents are downcast, particularly Bill Greer, the driver of the limousine in Dealey Plaza. Greer cannot help but feel that if he had taken evasive action instantly, Kennedy might still be alive.[83] Despite a few awkward moments, the casket is lowered via the catering bus without incident, and then an honor guard of enlisted men from all the armed services loads it into a waiting gray ambulance. Seeing the casket has a mesmerizing effect on the crowd and, undoubtedly, the national TV audience. Until this moment, despite

81. Later corrected to 2304 ZULU.
82. Manchester, *Death,* 387; Jack Valenti, *A Very Human President* (New York: W. W. Norton, 1975), 55; Liz Carpenter's Recollections of President Kennedy's Assassination, December 1963, Box 4, Special File, LBJL.
83. Manchester, *Death,* 290.

five uninterrupted hours of television coverage, it still seems unbelievable; now it is undeniably true. As William Manchester will later observe, the casket's appearance is what finally makes the assassination "irrevocable."[84]

Jacqueline Kennedy and Robert Kennedy promptly get in the ambulance, along with Secret Service agents and Dr. Burkley. Three other cars swiftly line up behind it, and even before a ramp is attached to SAM 26000 to allow President and Mrs. Johnson to disembark, the motorcade begins its forty-minute drive to the Naval Medical Center in Bethesda.[85]

The second act is Lyndon Johnson's. Four minutes after the ambulance's departure, he and Mrs. Johnson emerge and slowly descend down a rear ramp. Johnson searches the crowd of dignitaries for one face in particular—that of Richard Russell (D-Georgia), his Senate mentor. But Russell is not in the crowd.[86] After briefly acknowledging a few people, the Johnsons make their way to a cluster of microphones placed in front of the press corral. It is 6:14 p.m., and Johnson has been president for less than five hours. As Lady Bird Johnson will later recall, "Lyndon made a very simple, very brief, and I *think,* appealing and strong talk . . . only about four sentences, I believe."[87] It runs more than four sentences in actuality, but it is brief, only fifty-seven words. Standing bareheaded before the glaring lights, Johnson is finished just as he seems to begin. The remarks are intended as a heartfelt expression of grief but simultaneously reintroduce Johnson to the American people.

> This is a sad time for all people. We have suffered a loss that cannot be weighed. For me, it is a deep personal tragedy. I know that the world shares the sorrow that Mrs. Kennedy and her family bear. I will do my best. That is all I can do. I ask for your help—and God's.

Within the drama that is on display for the world to see, the seeds of a conflict within the administration and the Democratic Party are sprouting. While it was not unheard of for brothers to hold influential jobs in the same administration— viz. the Dulles brothers under President Eisenhower—or to have a sibling serve directly under a president—viz. Dr. Milton Eisenhower, again under Eisenhower—the Kennedy administration took blood ties to an unprecedented level of power. The attorney generalship is one of the premier positions in the cabinet, the federal government's highest law enforcement office in a nation that

84. Ibid., 388.
85. Ibid., 391.
86. John Goldsmith, *Colleagues: Richard B. Russell and His Apprentice, Lyndon B. Johnson* (Macon, Ga.: Mercer University Press, 1998), 99.
87. Mrs. Johnson Diary Tapes, LBJL.

prides itself on having a government of laws, not men. Never before has a president's brother served as attorney general and wielded so much influence over the domestic and foreign policies of the government.

The appointment of Robert Kennedy in January 1961 was a shrewd move, made in the recognition that historically the cabinet officer capable of creating the greatest problems for a sitting president has been the attorney general. Notwithstanding his important statutory responsibilities, most of Robert Kennedy's pervasive influence stemmed from the president's desires and RFK's own inexhaustible drive and impatience with bureaucracy. After the Bay of Pigs debacle in April 1961, Robert Kennedy's brief within the administration expanded dramatically at the president's discretion. Robert Kennedy became a member of the panel investigating why the invasion of Cuba had failed so miserably, and the attorney general's role in foreign policy decisions of any moment became taken for granted, including deep involvement in the CIA's most sensitive covert operations. Even that enlarged portfolio failed to convey the degree to which Robert Kennedy made his presence felt throughout—some would say threw his weight around—the federal government. With one exception, he was the most powerful official in the executive branch, the president by proxy, because everyone in government knew that crossing the attorney general was likely to incur John Kennedy's displeasure.

This peculiar distribution of power would have made any abrupt transition awkward. But the situation now will be greatly complicated by the poor relationship between the vice president and the attorney general, which dates back years. Johnson and Kennedy are like oil and water; their personalities just don't mesh, and each one's behavior incites the other. The antagonism traces back at least to the 1960 convention in Los Angeles, when Johnson, the Senate Democratic majority leader, lost the nomination to John Kennedy, an unaccomplished senator by comparison. In the dying days of the race, Johnson campaigners attempted to raise questions about Senator Kennedy's health (in response to suggestions that Johnson's health was questionable after a 1955 heart attack), and recalled the isolationist views of Ambassador Joseph Kennedy, the family patriarch, prior to the attack on Pearl Harbor.[88]

John Kennedy regarded Johnson's tactics as forgettable, merely evidence of his desperation, but Robert Kennedy would never forgive the Texan. When John Kennedy won the nomination and shockingly offered Johnson a place on the Democratic ticket, which he accepted, Robert Kennedy was inconsolable and his opposition one of the biggest obstacles John Kennedy had to overcome.[89]

88. Robert Dallek, *Lone Star Rising: Lyndon Johnson and His Times, 1908–1960* (New York: Oxford University Press, 1991), 572–73.

89. Knowing that he faced a tough contest against Vice President Nixon, Kennedy wanted a running mate who would not only appeal to southern Democrats but bring to the ticket a large electoral prize. The politician who best fit that description was Johnson. An insightful account of

Robert Kennedy even went to Johnson and tried to get him to turn the offer down, not understanding why Johnson accepted in the first place. Losing the 1960 race for the nomination had proved Johnson was a regional candidate; in Johnson's words, "A fellow from my part of the country probably couldn't be anything more than another John Nance Garner," a reference to the House Speaker, and fellow Texan, who ran for the Democratic nomination in 1932 but had to settle for being Franklin Roosevelt's vice president. Johnson's reference was both prophetic and apt.[90] And the only way to transcend that label was to campaign on a winning—or *losing*—national Democratic ticket. If the former, Johnson agreed to defer his dream of being president until 1968. If the latter, Johnson would still be Senate majority leader and, more important, the front-runner for the 1964 nomination.

As the Kennedy presidency took shape, Johnson used his still-considerable influence in the Senate to secure Robert Kennedy's highly controversial appointment as attorney general. But neither that act, nor the certain knowledge that his brother would have been defeated in 1960 without Johnson on the ticket (Texas went Democratic for the first time since 1948), was sufficient to temper Robert Kennedy's dislike of and disdain for the vice president. Over the next three years Lyndon Johnson—or "Uncle Cornpone," as the administration's Ivy Leaguers called him—was repeatedly humbled and humiliated, while the assurances he thought he had won about having a significant role in the administration turned to dust. John Kennedy's actual vice president—if that term means *one who acts in place of*—was Robert Kennedy, and his extraordinary role left Johnson bereft of things to do, his prodigious political talents unemployed.[91]

As unhappy as Johnson was, he nonetheless abided by the deal he had made, though by 1963 it looked like a Faustian bargain. In return for nursing his faint hope of running for president in 1968—though he would be sixty years old by that time—Johnson consigned himself to being politically neutered and, worse, forgotten or dismissed. Stories by journalists close to the Kennedys began to appear about how Johnson was an "unwanted fifth wheel . . . a gawky, uncouth Texan" who simply didn't fit.[92] Hardened Washington columnists were nonetheless amazed at Johnson's self-discipline and their inability to gather political dirt from the vice president. All his differences of opinion with the president (and Johnson had some) were aired privately with John Kennedy. In

Robert Kennedy's opposition to Johnson's nomination in 1960 is James Hilty, *Robert Kennedy: Brother Protector* (Philadelphia: Temple University Press, 1997), 155–65.

90. Evans and Novak, *Exercise of Power,* 275. Johnson reportedly made this observation in March 1960, five months before the Democrats' convention.

91. According to Ken O'Donnell, Johnson felt Robert Kennedy "had taken over his rightful position as the number two man in the government." Arthur Schlesinger, Jr., *Robert Kennedy and His Times* (Boston: Houghton Mifflin, 1978), 624.

92. Drew Pearson, "Manchester Reopens Old Wounds," *Washington Post,* 22 December 1966.

appearance and deed, Johnson was completely loyal, and he gave every indication (when asked) of being content, although being number two in name and being heir apparent were very different things.[93]

Johnson's real problem began when his titular status got shaky. In the fall of 1963 he became deeply distressed over the amount of attention being directed his way once the Bobby Baker scandal exploded. Johnson was not even the majority leader when Baker allegedly misused his position as secretary of the Senate majority. So Johnson, rightly or wrongly, regarded the scandal as the handiwork of conservative Republicans eager to tarnish Democrats, and of Robert Kennedy, who was hell-bent on getting Johnson removed from the ticket in 1964, thus effectively ending the Texan's political career.[94]

As *Air Force One* comes to a halt at the MATS terminal, his troubled relationship with Robert Kennedy may not be foremost on Lyndon Johnson's mind, but it is not far from it. While not yet fully comfortable with the mantle of the presidency, the ever-sensitive Johnson is quite familiar with the deference accorded the president—which he now is, regardless of the brutality and suddenness of the assassination. Thus, he will be astounded at his treatment by the Kennedy family at Andrews, particularly by Robert Kennedy.

Johnson has been operating under the assumption that after a forklift gently removes the coffin, he will disembark the aircraft along with Mrs. Kennedy, essentially as one of her escorts. This does not happen. Instead, as Robert Kennedy forces his way through the jammed aisle, Johnson is pressed against the cabin wall. It is impossible for him to move. Nor does the attorney general pay the slightest attention or any courtesy to the president as he squeezes by; he acts as if Johnson does not exist. By the time Johnson gets to the aft doorway, Jacqueline Kennedy and the attorney general are already driving away. Disembarking ahead of the president is unheard of, an "unbelievable" breach of protocol.[95] Yet Johnson feels he has no choice but to turn the other cheek.[96] Being treated as a usurper is not an auspicious start to what is already the "most painful assumption of power in American history."[97]

After arriving on the White House grounds, the Johnsons go their separate ways. Mrs. Johnson, accompanied by Elizabeth "Liz" Carpenter, her husband's executive assistant, is driven directly to the Elms. Along the way they share some thoughts that only two Texans dare express. "It's a terrible thing to say," observes Carpenter. "But the salvation of Texas is that the governor was hit." Perhaps recalling her gaffe while speaking to Jacqueline Kennedy, Mrs.

93. Cabell Phillips, "Johnson Is Found Contented in Job," *New York Times,* 31 May 1963.
94. Evans and Novak, *Exercise of Power,* 332–33.
95. Valenti, *Human President,* 56.
96. Manchester, *Death,* 387.
97. Ibid., 403.

Johnson replies, "Don't think I haven't thought of that. I only wish it could have been me."[98]

President Johnson, meanwhile, continues with meetings that began during the seven-minute helicopter ride to the White House from Andrews. He discusses the overseas implications of the assassination with McGeorge Bundy, Robert McNamara, and George Ball, acting secretary of state in Rusk's absence. There is still no sign of any effort by America's Communist adversaries to exploit the assassination, though U.S. military forces remain on a high state of alert. With every passing minute it seems more and more likely that the heinous act was the work of one man, though it is an open question whether he was aided or abetted by others. In a building on the northeast corner of Dealey Plaza, Dallas police have found what they believe to be the assassin's weapon, a rifle of foreign manufacture fitted with a telescopic sight. And an old police rule of thumb is that one weapon means one shooter. For his part, Johnson suppresses for the time being his disappointment over having been slighted at Andrews AFB. He speaks only with wonder, if not awe, about the unexpected behavior of Jacqueline Kennedy. "I have never seen anyone so brave," Johnson tells George Ball.[99]

EOB Room 274, the vice presidential office, is actually a three-room suite of tastefully decorated, high-ceilinged offices, and Johnson settles in comfortably after arriving there. He will spend almost three hours in the Executive Office Building that evening, making telephone calls, receiving visitors, and taking some time to write two special letters by hand. After Bundy's review of the world situation concludes, Johnson is briefed by Navy Captain Tazewell Shepard, who brings the president up-to-date on the arrangements being made for President Kennedy.[100] Sargent Shriver, one of President Kennedy's brothers-in-law, is organizing the funeral. After the postmortem the president's body will be brought back to the White House's East Room, where he will lie in state on Saturday. The rest is still being decided. At 6:55 p.m. Johnson has a ten-minute meeting with Senator J. William Fulbright (D-Arkansas) and diplomat W. Averell Harriman to discuss possible foreign involvement in the assassination, especially in light of the two-and-a-half-year Soviet sojourn of Lee Harvey Oswald, a twenty-four-year-old man apprehended by Dallas police who is now considered the chief suspect. Harriman, a U.S. ambassador to Moscow during World War II, is an experienced interpreter of Soviet machinations and offers the president the unanimous view of the U.S. government's top Kremlinologists. None of them believe the Soviets have a hand in the assassination, despite the Oswald association.

98. Lyndon Johnson, *The Vantage Point: Perspectives of the Presidency, 1963–1969* (New York: Holt, Rinehart and Winston, 1971), 26; Liz Carpenter's Recollections of President Kennedy's Assassination, December 1963, Box 4, Special File, LBJL.

99. Manchester, *Death,* 402.

100. Ibid., 413.

Beginning with a call to former President Truman at 7:05 p.m., Johnson endeavors to talk with each of the three living U.S. presidents. Herbert Hoover cannot come to the telephone, but Dwight Eisenhower, having already conferred with former secretary of state Dean Acheson, is planning to be in Washington the next morning to pay his respects. The two presidents promptly arrange to meet. Eisenhower, though a Republican, is more than willing to let Johnson exploit his presence to emphasize the government's continuity, stability, and legitimacy. Then, having contacted his predecessors, Johnson writes two separate letters on engraved White House stationery, though it will be years, if not decades, before the intended recipients are able to appreciate them. The first is addressed to John F. Kennedy, Jr., who will be three years old on Monday, and the second to Caroline Kennedy, who will be six in a week. In between, the president has a brief unrecorded discussion with FBI director J. Edgar Hoover. Although the bureau has no jurisdiction over the Dallas murders, Johnson tells Hoover he knows the FBI is doing everything it can "to find out who killed the president" and hopes that every available agent is in Dallas.[101] Hoover summarily dispatches thirty agents to augment the FBI's Dallas field office.[102]

At 7:40 p.m. Johnson meets with congressional leaders in the anteroom to his office for about twenty minutes. Everyone who was asked to come is there, save for two Republicans who could not make it: Representative Les Arends, and Senator Bourke Hickenlooper, whose place is taken by Senator Thruston Morton (R-Kentucky). After a bowl of soup—Johnson's first food since breakfast in Fort Worth—a meeting is held with the president's ad hoc press office: Malcolm Kilduff, George Reedy, and Bill Moyers. Either at this meeting or later, with Kilduff alone, Johnson makes known his displeasure about his treatment at Andrews AFB. He is brooding over the disrespect and holds Kilduff responsible.[103]

Johnson makes only a few more telephone calls before heading to the Elms. Although he canceled the meeting with White House staffers, the president still feels compelled to contact Ted Sorensen, a speechwriter and counsel to John Kennedy. Sorensen is widely perceived to be the man closest in outlook, intellect, and temperament to the late president, if not his alter ego. At the end of their conversation, Sorensen routinely says, "Yes, Mr. President." A moment later, after hanging up, the implications of addressing Lyndon Johnson with those words fall on him like a ton. Sorensen collapses into grief, unbeknownst to Johnson.[104] Then the president calls his mentor, Richard Russell, the Georgia senator most responsible for Johnson's rise to power. Only two conversations from the dramatic evening of November 22 are actually preserved, however, although a transcript exists for Johnson's conversation with former president

101. George Reedy, handwritten note, undated, Diary Back-up, Box 4, Special File, LBJL.
102. Manchester, *Death*, 405.
103. Ibid., 386–87.
104. Ibid., 412.

Eisenhower. The vice presidential office was not well outfitted to record telephone conversations—it had only an IBM dictating machine available for such a task, which could double as a crude recording device in an emergency. Certainly Room 274 was not as expertly equipped as the Oval Office will be.

To Justice Arthur Goldberg / 9:06 p.m.

Arthur Goldberg and his wife, Dorothy, were among the fifty or so dignitaries who made the trek to Andrews AFB out of respect for President Kennedy. Indeed, it was Goldberg who, after learning that Robert Kennedy didn't want anyone to show up, called the attorney general to protest. "Bob, this is not right," Goldberg said. ". . . We owe this gesture to the president—and even to [Mrs. Kennedy]. It can't be private."[105]

The new president's call to Goldberg's home, when he might have called dozens of other, closer friends instead, or more likely no one at all, reveals that Johnson, in the earliest hours of his administration, is acutely conscious of the need to reach out to that segment of the Democratic Party that denied him the nomination in 1960 and is the only obstacle to his renomination in 1964. His vulnerability among liberals is no secret. As recently as February 1963 several were still attacking Johnson for allegedly demonstrating that his "first loyalty is to the Southern racists" in the party.[106] The new president needs an emissary to liberals, and few people fit that bill better than Goldberg. As a lawyer for organized labor, Goldberg, along with UAW president Walter Reuther, was one of the most vigorous opponents of putting Johnson on the Democratic ticket in Los Angeles. But then, as secretary of labor until his appointment to the Supreme Court in 1962, Goldberg got to know Johnson well while both men served on the President's Committee on Equal Employment Opportunity. His prejudices about Johnson were soon dissipated by the efforts he saw Johnson make, as committee chairman, to prevent racial discrimination in hiring by the federal government or government contractors. The two men became warm friends, and Goldberg is now perhaps Johnson's best contact with the liberal components of the New Deal coalition.[107] Indeed, in talking with Goldberg, Johnson is effectively reaching out to labor, Jewish, and black constituencies simultaneously.

One of Johnson's specific requests is for Goldberg to think about the speech the president is hoping to make before a joint session of Congress within the next few days. Harry Truman made such an address soon after taking office in 1945, and Johnson is going to propose a similar appearance to the Republican

---

105. Ibid., 377.

106. "The Vice President's Chances in '64," *U.S. News & World Report,* 25 February 1963.

107. Michael Amrine, *This Awesome Challenge: The Hundred Days of Lyndon Johnson* (New York: G. P. Putnam's Sons, 1964), 225.

leadership. The stakes will be high, as it will be Johnson's maiden speech to the American people as president. The first impression he makes is going to be a powerful one and likely to stick.

Johnson: Arthur, I just . . . you've been such a wonderful friend. You and that great wife of yours have been such a comfort and strength to me in this administration that I just didn't want to leave my desk tonight without telling you that you're going to have to do some heavy thinkin' for me, and. . . .

Goldberg: Dorothy and I came out to see you at the airport, [but] there were so many people around.

Johnson: No, I didn't [see you] . . . I didn't.[108] There's no one that I would have rather seen in the world than you, and I—

Goldberg: The most—all we can say is . . . we pray, [and] we have *confidence* in you.

Johnson: Well, don't be so damn modest and *shy.* I want you to come in and out [of the White House] now. I don't know what's proper and ethical, but [if] you're at the airport, you let me know it. Because I need all the strength that you can give me.

Goldberg: We came out because we wanted to wish you well and also express our grief. But . . . look, if there's anything that I can do, just . . . I'm at your service.

Johnson: I want you to be thinkin' about what I ought to do to try to bring all of these elements together and unite the country . . . and the main thing, preserve our system in the world. Because if it starts fallin' to pieces, and some of the extremes go to gettin' a—proceeding on the wrong assumption, why we could deteriorate pretty [quick].

Goldberg: No, it won't. I have no doubt about that.

Johnson: I want you to think . . . just . . . think [in] capitals . . . *think, think, think.* And then talk to me tomorrow or [the] next day.

Goldberg: I will, any time.

Johnson: Now, I want to give some thought to whether we oughta have a joint session [of Congress]. Truman did after [Roosevelt died].

Goldberg: I think you ought to.

Johnson: Well, what would we say to 'em? Think about it.

Goldberg: Well, I will.

Johnson: And I want you to think about who I [should] talk to on the delivery

108. Both William Manchester and Michael Beschloss, in their respective books on the transition, suggest that Johnson called Goldberg after having spotted him in the crowd at Andrews. But according to the conversation, Johnson did not see Goldberg during the brief time he spent acknowledging dignitaries. Manchester, *Death,* 401, 412, and Michael Beschloss, *Taking Charge: The Johnson White House Tapes, 1963–1964* (New York: Simon & Schuster, 1997), 20.

side, and *how* I oughta do it, without . . . with dignity and reserve, and without being down on my knees, but [at] the same time, [as] a man who'll respect my confidence in 'em.

Goldberg: I will.

Johnson: And I just . . . there's nobody in town that I believe in more than you and I've just *got* to have your help.

Goldberg: Well, it's there for the asking, and we wish you every . . . good fortune in the world. You'll do well and we have complete confidence.

Johnson: Well, I'm—

Goldberg: Dorothy's here, she wants to say hello to you.

Johnson: I'm totally inadequate to it, but I'll do my best.

Goldberg: No, no—not at all. And I'm at your service!

Johnson: Thank you, Arthur.

Goldberg: But here she is. *[aside to Mrs. Goldberg]* The vice president.

Mrs. Goldberg: *[perhaps realizing her husband's faux pas]* Mr. President!

Johnson: Hi, beloved. How are you?

[Johnson exchanges best wishes with Dorothy Goldberg, then talks to Justice Goldberg again before the conversation ends.]

To Richard Maguire / 9:10 p.m.

A Harvard-trained lawyer, Dick Maguire was one of the charter members of John Kennedy's inner circle of political advisers, the so-called Irish mafia. His association with JFK dated back to 1946, when Kennedy first ran for political office. Maguire, a World War II veteran like the candidate, was treasurer of Kennedy's successful campaign for a seat in the House of Representatives. Though lesser known than other, more publicized members of the Irish mafia like Larry O'Brien and Ken O'Donnell, Maguire is a force in his own right. In 1962 President Kennedy appointed him treasurer of the Democratic National Committee, eventually leading Washington columnists Rowland Evans and Robert Novak to label Maguire "easily the most powerful man in the national party structure."[109]

Johnson's call to Maguire now is the last conversation he has before leaving for home. He has already spoken with Ted Sorensen, the man closest to the president, and O'Brien and O'Donnell were with the presidential entourage in Dallas, so there is nothing to say to them that has not already been said. Maguire is contacted in all probability because Johnson is acutely aware of Maguire's long and intense relationship with John Kennedy.[110] And knowing that the presi-

109. Associated Press, "Richard Maguire, Close Aide to President Kennedy, Dies," *New York Times,* 21 February 1983.

110. Beschloss states that Johnson calls Maguire because the president "is already thinking about the 1964 campaign." Beschloss, *Taking Charge,* 21.

dent's trip to Texas was primarily a fund-raising trip, Johnson wants to console Maguire. Besides, unlike most other political men within the administration whose primary loyalty was to Kennedy, Maguire always treated Johnson with due respect and courtesy.

Johnson: Dick?
Maguire: Yes, sir.
Johnson: I know what a great personal tragedy this is to you, but it is to me too. And you have been so wonderful to the president, that I want you to know that . . . that I've got to rely on you more than he did.
Maguire: Mr. President . . . just tell me what you want, sir.
Johnson: Well, I just . . . I want the same kind of relationship tomorrow as we had yesterday.
Maguire: *[emphatically]* You will have it.
Johnson: I've been on your team ever since I got here, and I just want you to know that . . . I want you to be candid and frank, and come in and tell me what we need to do, and how we need to do it. And . . . I know how suffering you must be tonight, but so am I.
Maguire: I know it.
Johnson: And we're the same family, and . . . well, the one thing I know he'd want us to do is just carry on and be effective, and that's what we're going to do. And you be givin' some thought to what needs to be done, and when we get these things behind us [in] the next day or two, then we'll get together.
Maguire: Whenever you're ready, sir.
Johnson: Thank you, Dick.
Maguire: Good night, sir.
Johnson: 'Bye.

At 9:25 p.m. Johnson leaves the White House grounds for his home in northwest Washington. He has invited over four men he depended on during his rise to power: Horace Busby, Cliff Carter, Bill Moyers, and, to a lesser extent, Jack Valenti. With the exception of Carter, Johnson's chief political agent, who runs the office in Austin, Texas, all have drifted away from Johnson's orbit while he was a political cipher. Busby, Johnson's favorite speechwriter, has been putting out his own Washington newsletter to corporate clients; Valenti has been managing a prosperous advertising/public relations agency in Houston; and Moyers is deputy director of the Peace Corps, the only Johnson man to gain genuine acceptance as a "New Frontiersman."[111] There was no point in forgoing a lucrative income or better position in order to be on the staff of a vice president

111. Recognizing that presidents often benefited from having a catch-all phrase for their myriad programs, Kennedy's wordsmiths had come up with the "New Frontier."

with little to do. It was better to wait until (or if) Johnson emerged from political limbo to make the total sacrifice that would be required of anyone working for him. Johnson is known as one of the most exacting, demanding, and tireless politicians in Washington, that is, when he's at full throttle. Now the time for rededicating themselves to Lyndon is here, even though there is considerable uncertainty over how they are going to fit into a White House that is already fully staffed.

Among these advisers, perhaps only Horace Busby is aware of the full extent of the turnabout in Johnson's political fortune. On the surface, Johnson has gone from being forgotten to being the most powerful man in the world. But in fact the change is even more dramatic than that. Busby alone knows that just before leaving for Texas, Johnson was very near the end of his rope. The vice presidency was worth having only if it paved the way for his own candidacy in 1968, but he wasn't going to be humiliated. He believed that Robert Kennedy's Justice Department was out to get him via the Bobby Baker scandal, and that it would not cease until Johnson was forced off the ticket. Rumors to that effect were rampant in Washington, and the fact that the Republican front-runner was Senator Barry Goldwater did not help Johnson one whit. Running against such a conservative ideologue would almost surely give President Kennedy more leeway than he had in 1960 with respect to his running mate.

To close friends, Johnson ruminated about becoming a college president, or buying a major Texas newspaper that was reportedly on the market. Then, just before the trip to Texas, Johnson told Busby, "I'm going to buy the newspaper. You be the editor and I'll be the publisher. You'll let me write at least one column a week and we are going to run all the [special] interests out of Texas. We are going to run them across the Red River and let the people in at the State House."[112] Busby is acutely aware that Johnson has a deep streak of self-pity and that he often speaks for effect and doesn't genuinely mean what he says. But negotiations for the newspaper did take place, and until the motorcade in Dallas, Busby fully expected Johnson to use President Kennedy's visit to the LBJ Ranch to express disinterest in the 1964 campaign. It was to have been the perfect time for a private and frank discussion.[113] Unless Kennedy's appeals to Johnson were coupled with a promise to contain Bobby, Johnson was likely to have quit the ticket on his own, and before he was forced to.

During the ride to the Elms, the Secret Service agents are in a state of hair-trigger readiness. After the motorcade arrives, agents toting shotguns patrol the grounds while Johnson begins to relive the incredible day with his close aides. Also present, as inconspicuously as possible, is Dr. J. Willis Hurst of Atlanta,

112. Kenneth Thompson, ed., *The Johnson Presidency: Twenty Intimate Perspectives of Lyndon B. Johnson* (Lanham, Md.: University Press of America, 1986), 253.

113. Felton West, "Lady Bird Preparing Ranch for JFK Visit," *Houston Post,* 18 November 1963.

the heart specialist who saved the president's life in 1955. Hurst, who just happens to be in Washington, became very concerned after hearing the (erroneous) reports about Johnson's condition at Parkland Hospital. He runs his practiced eye over Johnson and is relieved to find that the president shows no visible signs of laboring under his new burden.[114] If anything, Johnson seems more at peace with himself than he has in years. Finally, he has the perfect outlet for his prodigious energies; his desire to wield power now corresponds with the power at his disposal. His first act, upon his arrival at the Elms, is a spontaneous toast to his original political mentor, Sam Rayburn. An official portrait of the late Speaker hangs in the library, with Rayburn in a Churchillian pose. The moment Johnson notices the picture he raises his drink and says softly, "I salute you, Mr. Speaker, and how I wish you were here now, when I need you."[115]

Well after midnight the president finally announces he is ready to retire. But in typical Johnson style, after he gets into his pajamas, the president turns on the bedroom television and invites Busby, Carter, Moyers, and Valenti to join him. Johnson's close aides are quite accustomed to this behavior; Johnson needs the same kind of "gentling down" that a groom might provide to a thoroughbred.[116] The networks are rebroadcasting worldwide reactions to the assassination and memorable scenes from the Kennedy presidency: his inaugural address, the Berlin Wall speech, and of course the October 1962 address to the nation announcing the discovery of Soviet missiles in Cuba. There is also footage from the trip to Texas and Dallas, including President and Mrs. Kennedy's now-poignant welcome at Love Field. There is some footage about the new president, but it is subordinated to clips of his predecessor. Johnson watches the television silently, interrupting only occasionally. His most frequent interjection concerns Jacqueline Kennedy, over whose courage and fortitude he continues to marvel. "At a time when we showed the world our ugly, seamy side," Johnson observes, "she revealed and symbolized our nobler side. We should always be grateful to her for it."[117]

Gradually, as the television coverage grows repetitive, Johnson begins talking about his ideas, large and small, for the days ahead, along with people to see and meetings to hold. Valenti begins taking notes on a pad, and in effect Johnson holds his first staff meeting. All the outstanding issues, he observes, are identical to the ones that were "on his desk" when he came to Washington as a congressman in 1937.[118] He begins thinking aloud about programs and a legislative agenda, and the meeting lasts until 3:30 a.m. Years later Valenti will claim that the "Great Society" had its genesis during the small hours of that Saturday morning.

114. Horace Busby, "At the Side of Power," *Washingtonian,* November 2003.
115. Valenti, *Human President,* 7.
116. Busby, "Power."
117. Knebel, "Ordeal."
118. Thompson, *Johnson Presidency,* 257.

November 23–30

November 23

Saturday

The weather front that was on the heels of *Air Force One* arrives in Washington on Saturday. The cold, gray day complements the prevailing mood, and a steady, eight-hour downpour suggests even the sky is weeping. It feels colder than it really is.

November 22 was Jacqueline Kennedy's longest day in every sense. The postmortem at the Bethesda Naval Hospital lasted almost four hours, until well past midnight, and morticians spent another three hours trying to make the corpse presentable for viewing. The cosmetic effort will go for naught. Mrs. Kennedy is adamantly opposed to an open casket because she wants Jack remembered alive, and ultimately Robert Kennedy agrees. The corpse looks too waxen, too made up.[1]

The waiting area at the hospital was initially crammed with the Kennedys' personal friends, close aides, and family members. Nearly everyone present, at one time or another, urged Jacqueline Kennedy to change her clothes. She steadfastly refused, though her point—let them see what they have done—had been made at Andrews. Instead, as she did with Robert Kennedy during the ride to Bethesda, she relived the day in minute, bloody detail. In her own way she was manic; her personal physician, Dr. John Walsh, called it a "talkathon" and decided to let her talk herself into exhaustion since she adamantly refused to take a sedative. "It's the best way," he observed. "Let her get rid of it if she can."[2] Eventually she did stop speaking about Dallas and, to general amazement, began trying to entertain her guests, all the while fending off renewed offers of a sedative and her mother's suggestion that she change her clothes.[3]

---

1. William Manchester, *The Death of a President: November 20–November 25, 1963* (New York: Harper & Row, 1967), 443.

2. Ibid., 415–16.

3. Ibid., 428.

Martha Bartlett, wife of Washington columnist Charles Bartlett, finally realized that Mrs. Kennedy was acting *as though she didn't want the day to end.* As if on cue, friends began drifting to the door. "Suddenly," *Newsweek* reporter Ben Bradlee would later recall, "we'd been there too long."[4]

Now it becomes a matter of just waiting. When Dr. Walsh senses Mrs. Kennedy is near exhaustion, he prepares to inject her with a sedative, 100 milligrams of Visatril. He is sure she will nod off in less than a minute. But he is the one who falls asleep, only to be awakened ten minutes later by Mrs. Kennedy as she searches for a cigarette. He might as well have injected her with Coca-Cola, Walsh thinks, as he stares at her.[5]

At 3:56 a.m. Kennedy's coffin is swiftly loaded into a waiting hearse for a stately thirty-five-minute drive to the White House. Since the events in Dealey Plaza, every trip by automobile carrying Kennedy's remains has exceeded speed limits by tens of miles per hour. Now there is no further purpose in racing from point A to point B. Kennedy's body will be transported three more times before it reaches its final resting place at Arlington National Cemetery, and each trip will be slower than the last, until the coffin is literally walked to the gravesite. When it reaches the East Room of the White House, the largest room in the mansion, originally called the Public Audience Chamber, the African mahogany casket is placed atop a catafalque draped in black. A priest says a brief blessing, after which Mrs. Kennedy buries her face in the flag unfurled atop the casket.

Once Jacqueline Kennedy retreats to the mansion's private quarters, she finally sheds her stained clothes and bathes. Still, she cannot fall asleep. Dr. Walsh is now determined to knock her out and prepares enough Amytal to sedate a prizefighter.[6] By this time the sun is up, though it will make no appearance on this dreary Saturday.

During these same wee hours, FBI agents in Chicago, having roused executives from Klein's Sporting Goods when it was still Friday, finally find what they are looking for. After poring through microfilmed mail orders for six hours, the executives find a coupon from *American Rifleman* filled out by an "A. Hidell" the previous March. Via postal money order, "Hidell" bought a surplus carbine of Italian manufacture, serial number C2766, and had it shipped to a Dallas post office box rented by Lee Harvey Oswald. C2766 is also the serial number of the Mannlicher-Carcano rifle found on the sixth floor of the Texas School Book Depository, where Oswald works.

The notion that another shoe is about to drop, that another event almost as horrific as the assassination itself might still happen, is beyond anyone's ken on

4. Ibid.
5. Ibid., 430.
6. Ibid., 451.

Saturday. It is "virtually impossible to think beyond yesterday's death and the coming funeral," William Manchester would write.[7]

President Johnson sleeps for only three and a half hours before rising for breakfast. If, the evening before, he was "honing skills grown rusty from disuse," today he is fully alive again.[8] With almost every meeting, briefing, or conference he will gain power and momentum—save for his deflating encounters with Robert Kennedy.

Though last night Johnson was careful to avoid the West Wing, this morning he is prepared to wrap himself in some of the most powerful symbols of the presidency, including use of the Oval Office. Encouraged by George Ball, Robert McNamara, and McGeorge Bundy, Johnson believes the need to prove the government's continuity—especially to America's adversaries overseas—must take precedence over any sentimental feelings. There is to be no gap in administrations, only an "unsightly scar."[9] Bundy goes so far as to assure the president the West Wing will be ready for him to occupy. Upon arriving at 9 a.m., Johnson takes Evelyn Lincoln, the late president's personal secretary since 1953, into the Oval Office and again expresses his condolences to her. Then Johnson asks if he can have his secretaries working in Lincoln's office by 9:30 a.m., in time for a meeting with Secretary of State Rusk, the day's first appointment. "Yes, Mr. President," says Mrs. Lincoln quietly.[10]

She returns to her own office to find Robert Kennedy. "Do you know he asked me to be out by 9:30?" she sobs.[11] The attorney general is appalled by Johnson's behavior, reinforcing resentments Kennedy is already nursing. The previous evening he spoke to Jacqueline Kennedy and Ken O'Donnell about the events in Dallas. In the midst of his grief, he learned to his fury that Lyndon Johnson was suggesting to one and all that the attorney general had *urged* Johnson to take the oath, saying that Johnson had to be sworn in before leaving Dallas. Kennedy felt he had done nothing of the kind, but it was behavior of precisely this kind that embittered him toward Lyndon Johnson.

Minutes later there is an awkward, brief encounter between Johnson and Kennedy in the hall outside Ken O'Donnell's office. "I want to talk to you," says Johnson. "Fine," answers Kennedy. They dart into a little anteroom, and Johnson immediately launches into a version of the line he has already used with a half-dozen White House staffers: "I need you more than your brother needed

7. Ibid., 471.
8. Ibid., 472.
9. Ibid., 454.
10. Ibid., 453.
11. Ibid., 391, 415, 453–54.

you." Having already heard about this plea, Robert Kennedy is singularly unimpressed. He then makes a suggestion that only he can make, for no other person in America would have dared utter it. "Can you wait [to move in]?" asks Kennedy.[12] The merest hint that Johnson is overstepping, is moving with unseemly haste in donning the trappings of presidential power, is like a punch to the solar plexus. When he recovers his breath, Johnson hastens to assure the attorney general that it wasn't *his* idea to occupy the Oval Office. President Kennedy's advisers were insisting on it to reassure the nation and the world.

In one fell swoop, the harsh feelings between Johnson and Robert Kennedy, percolating since their unforgettable 1960 clash, move perilously close to the surface. Johnson, who has been trying to ascribe Kennedy's rudeness at Andrews to the overwhelming emotion of the moment, no longer feels it was accidental. Despite his fealty to JFK after their political bargain was struck in Los Angeles, Johnson fears he is to be treated as an unworthy successor if not a pretender. When he arrives for an intelligence briefing in the basement of the West Wing, Johnson looks "massive, rumpled, and worried," according to one of the CIA officers accompanying John McCone, the director of Central Intelligence (DCI). Johnson exhibits little interest in his first briefing as president, and after the fifteen-minute discussion he retreats to his vice presidential suite.[13] For the rest of Saturday—indeed, for the next three days, until John F. Kennedy is safely buried—Johnson will conduct his official business out of the EOB.

Johnson believes the oval room is first of all the president's office; Robert Kennedy feels it is Jack's.

From J. Edgar Hoover / 10:01 a.m.

The most significant telephone conversation of the day pertaining to the assassination is the first one. Shortly after Johnson arrives in his office, J. Edgar Hoover calls to update the president on the Dallas crimes. The FBI director wants Johnson to know about the overnight discovery of the order coupon in Chicago, which all but clinches the evidence tying Lee Harvey Oswald to the Italian carbine found in the Texas School Book Depository. Buying the weapon presumably used to kill President Kennedy, not including ammunition, cost Oswald only $21.45, including postage and handling.

What makes this conversation problematic is that while a transcript exists, a recording does not. After the tape was transcribed by a member of the secretarial staff, the conversation with Hoover was erased, although other conversations

12. Ibid., 454.
13. Russell Jack Smith, *The Unknown CIA: My Three Decades with the Agency* (McLean, Va.: Pergamon-Brassey's, 1989), 163.

from November 23 are extant.[14] Perhaps the Hoover recording was regarded as exceptionally sensitive, as it is the first conversation to touch directly on the question of foreign involvement in the assassination. The National Archives and the Johnson Library later went to exceptional lengths to have the magnetic recording belt reprocessed to see if this significant conversation could be retrieved. But in the opinion of acoustic experts, the erasure was most likely intentional and is irreversible.[15]

The conversation's importance is twofold. First, it reveals what Johnson has gleaned from the media's saturation coverage of the assassination and elsewhere, along with the questions that are uppermost in his mind. During the morning briefing with McCone, Johnson learned some information from the Central Intelligence Agency that is not yet public knowledge—namely, that six weeks prior to the assassination, the CIA station in Mexico City observed Oswald visiting the Soviet embassy in the Mexican capital. This worrisome information is regarded as explosive, as it comes on top of the fact that Oswald lived in the Soviet Union from October 1959 until May 1962. Johnson has asked McCone to bring anything of import regarding the assassination to his personal attention at any time of the day or night, without going through an intermediary.[16]

The conversation is no less important for what it reveals about Hoover.[17] The director, and the bureau as a whole, are notorious in law enforcement circles for grabbing the lion's share of credit in high-profile criminal cases regardless of whether it is merited. Another oft-heard criticism is that working with the FBI is a one-way street. The bureau wants information from police sources but never shares what it knows with local departments. Several large metropolitan police forces (such as the Los Angeles Police Department) have very tense relationships with their local FBI field office, although until November 22 the

14. On November 22 and 23 Johnson recorded his EOB conversations on an IBM machine primarily designed to take dictation. The audio quality of the IBM belt recordings was so poor that by November 24 he switched to using recording equipment manufactured by the Dictaphone Corporation. John Powers, "The History of Presidential Audio Recordings and the Archival Issues Surrounding Their Use," 12 July 1996, 32–33, LBJL.

15. In October 1998 the Johnson Library and the National Archives and Records Administration hired a private contractor, the Cutting Corporation of Maryland, to try to recover an audible version of this conversation. After three months' work, the Cutting Corporation reported that the IBM magnetic belt had been erased and an audible recording could not be retrieved. "Notes Related to LBJ Recordings," Cutting Corporation, 21 January 1999, LBJL. The transcript here is taken nearly verbatim from the one prepared by Johnson's secretarial staff, probably within two or three days of the recording. Minor changes in punctuation have been made to clarify the conversation.

16. John McCone, memorandum for the record, 25 November 1963, CIA Box 1/14, JFK Assassination Records Collection (hereafter JFK), National Archives and Records Administration (hereafter NARA).

17. Since the accuracy of the secretarial transcript cannot be checked against a recording, this critique of Hoover might be considered misplaced. Yet the tendencies criticized here are also abundantly evident in an extant recording from November 25.

Dallas Police Department's (DPD) relationship with the bureau was fairly good, all things considered, and certainly not among the worst.

Normally, in situations like this where the FBI has no formal jurisdiction, submission of forensic evidence is entirely at the discretion of the local law enforcement agency. Will Fritz, captain of the Homicide and Robbery Bureau, maintained most of Friday that the DPD's own experts were quite capable of processing the Italian carbine found on the sixth floor, and the .38 caliber Smith & Wesson revolver in Oswald's possession. Yet the reputation of the FBI's crime lab is such that it was widely if erroneously believed that crucial ballistics and fingerprint evidence would be mishandled unless these items were sent to Washington immediately for examination. The DPD yielded custody of these weapons to the FBI temporarily and unenthusiastically, and only after considerable pressure was exerted on Henry Wade, the Dallas County district attorney, late Friday night.

Hoover's tendency to disparage local police is manifest here. Captain Fritz would have objected vigorously to Hoover's claim that the evidence against Oswald "is not very, very strong" and the insinuation that the DPD does not really have a case against Oswald without the bureau's information. In point of fact, the case is fairly damning already and is mounting by the hour; by Saturday afternoon, Fritz (along with other Dallas law enforcement officials) will be making statements on television such as "This man Oswald killed the president. We have a cinch case against him."[18] While ill-advised in terms of preserving Oswald's right to a fair trial in Dallas, the assertions are not objectively inaccurate.

Hoover's greatest sin, however, is that he is apparently unwilling to admit to a president that he doesn't know everything and doesn't have all the answers at his fingertips. Keeping up this false omniscience means that Hoover conveys a lot of bad information, or misinformation, while briefing the president. Hoover's biggest gaffe in this regard is telling the president that "we have the tape and the photograph of the man who was at the Soviet embassy using Oswald's name." As a matter of routine counterintelligence, the CIA tries to keep Communist bloc embassies in Mexico City under photographic surveillance and also taps their telephones. Before it knew what Oswald looked like but after word of his arrest was announced, the CIA station in Mexico City sent the FBI a picture of an unidentified heavyset white male with Slavic features who was photographed on the Soviet embassy grounds around the time Oswald was known to be visiting. But the picture was not that of Oswald, and the unidentified man never used Oswald's name. Photographic coverage of the embassy is not foolproof, and it will turn out that the CIA station has no pictures of Oswald visiting any Communist bloc embassy. The agency succeeded only in intercepting some of Oswald's telephone calls in Mexico City.

18. National Broadcasting Company, *Seventy Hours and Thirty Minutes* (New York: Random House, 1966), 67.

Ultimately, Hoover's propagation of half-facts and half-truths leaves Johnson with the impression that at least one other man may have been involved, and therefore that the assassination was the result of men "breathing together," the original meaning of "conspiracy."

Hoover: I just wanted to let you know of a development which I think is very important in connection with this case. This man [Oswald] in Dallas: we, of course, charged him with the murder of the president. The evidence that they have at the present time is not very, very strong.[19] We have just discovered the place where the gun was purchased, and the shipment of the gun from Chicago to Dallas—to a post office box in Dallas—to a man—no, to a woman—by the name of "A. Hidell."[20] It was purchased in March of this year. That gun is now in our possession here in Washington; we had it flown up last night, and our laboratory here is making an examination of it.

Johnson: Yes, I told the Secret Service to see that that got taken care of.

Hoover: That's right. We have the gun and we have the bullet. There was only one full bullet that was found—that was on the stretcher that the president was on. It apparently had fallen out when they massaged his heart, and we have that one.[21] We have what we call slivers, which are not very valuable in the identification. As soon as we finish the testing of the gun for fingerprints—and there are some latent fingerprints on it—we will then be able to test the one bullet we have with the gun.

But the important thing is that this gun was bought in Chicago on a money order—cost $21—and it seems almost impossible to think that for $21 you could kill the president of the United States.[22] Now, no one knows this.

Johnson: Now, who is "A. Hidell"?

Hoover: "A. Hidell" is an alias that this man has used on other occasions, and according to the information we have from the home in which he was living—his mother—he kept a rifle like this wrapped up in a blanket which he kept in the house.[23] On the morning that this incident occurred down

19. Hoover's use of "we" and "they" is typically self-serving, and incorrect. The Dallas police charged Oswald. *Warren Report,* 16.

20. "A. Hidell" is not a woman, of course, but an alias concocted by Lee Harvey Oswald. Ibid., 121.

21. Hoover is correct in that a seemingly "full" bullet was found on a stretcher in Parkland Hospital. But it was the stretcher used to transport Governor Connally, not the president. That the president's heart was massaged, causing a bullet to fall out, is another piece of misinformation imparted by Hoover. In truth, President Kennedy had been hit by two missiles, the first of which passed through his neck cleanly. The second missile burst open his head. Ibid., 18–19.

22. The total cost was $21.45 ($12.78 for the rifle, $7.17 for a telescopic sight, and $1.50 postage and handling). Ibid., 119. In 2004 dollars, the cost would be $131.

23. Oswald was not living in a house with his mother. During the workweek, he lived in a boardinghouse in the Oak Cliff section of Dallas. On most weekends, he would visit his wife,

there—yesterday—the man who drove him to the building where they work—the building from where the shots came—said that he [Oswald] had a package wrapped up in paper, not [wrapped in] a blanket. The blanket we found in the garage at the home. But the paper in which the gun was wrapped—that has also been sent up to us and [an inspection] will be made of that. He did carry some kind of package down there, which could have been the gun, yesterday morning in the car.[24] None of us can swear to that.

But the important thing at [this] time is the location of the purchase of the gun—by a money order apparently—to the Klein gun company in Chicago.[25] We were able to establish that last night.

Johnson: Have you established any more about the visit to the Soviet embassy in Mexico in September?

Hoover: No, that's one angle that's very confusing for this reason: we have up here the tape and the photograph of the man who was at the Soviet embassy using Oswald's name.[26] That picture and the tape do not correspond to this man's voice, nor to his appearance. In other words, it appears that there is a second person who was at the Soviet embassy down there. We do have a copy of a letter which was written by Oswald to the Soviet embassy here in Washington, inquiring—as well as complaining—about the harassment of his wife and the questioning of his wife by the FBI. Now, of course, that letter information—we process all mail that goes to the Soviet embassy— it's a *very* secret operation. No mail is delivered to the embassy without being examined and opened by us, so that we know what they receive. Such a letter was sent to the embassy by this fellow Oswald, making a complaint about his wife being harassed and being questioned.[27]

Marina, and their two daughters in Irving, a nearby suburb, where they were living temporarily with Ruth Paine, a Quaker interested in learning Russian, and her children. Oswald's rifle, wrapped inside a blanket, was in Paine's garage until the morning of November 22. Ibid., 128–29.

24. Buell Wesley Frazier, a fellow employee at the Texas School Book Depository, gave Oswald a ride to work whenever he visited his family in Irving. Frazier has already told police that on the morning of November 22 he gave Oswald a lift to work, and that Oswald was carrying a long package wrapped in paper. He told Frazier the package contained "curtain rods" for the room he was renting in Oak Cliff. Ibid., 129–30.

25. Hoover means Klein's Sporting Goods Company. Ibid., 118.

26. Hoover is in error, as he will admit during a conversation with DCI John McCone on November 26. See footnote 101, and also Gerald Posner, *Case Closed: Lee Harvey Oswald and the Assassination of JFK* (New York: Random House, 1993), 186–88.

27. Hoover is disclosing to the new president one of the key counterintelligence tactics used against the Soviet embassy in Washington. Under a highly classified arrangement with the U.S. Postal Service, every piece of mail to and from the embassy is intercepted by the FBI and subject to being read before it is delivered. The specific reference here is to a letter Oswald sent to the Soviet embassy dated November 9, in which he requested entrance visas and complained of renewed "interest" in him by the "notorious" FBI. *Warren Report,* 311; U.S. Senate Select Com-

The case as it stands now isn't strong enough to be able to get a conviction.[28] Then there is angle *[sic]* . . . I think we have a very, very close plan *[sic]*. Now, if we can identify this man who [was] at the Mexican embassy—at the Soviet embassy in Mexico City, the embassy in Mexico City . . . this man Oswald has still denied everything.[29] He doesn't know *anything* about *anything*. But the gun thing, of course, is a definite trend.

Johnson: It [the gun] definitely established that he . . . the same gun killed the policeman?

Hoover: That is an entirely different gun. We also have that gun. That was a revolver.

Johnson: You think he might have two?

Hoover: Yes, yes; he had two guns. And the one that killed the policeman was a [side]arm revolver, [while] the one that killed the president was found on the sixth floor in the building from which it had been fired. I think that the bullets were fired from the fifth floor, and the three shells that were [found] were found on the fifth floor. But he apparently went upstairs to the sixth floor [after having] fired the gun and to throw the gun away, and then went out. He went down to this [movie] theater—there, at the theater, was where he had the gun battle with the police officer.[30]

Johnson: I wonder if you will get me a little synopsis . . . and [also] let me have what developments come your way during the day, and try to get to me before we close up for the day.

Hoover: I certainly will do that.

A five-page synopsis arrives at the White House later in the day, summarizing the bureau's state of knowledge. In decided contrast to all the errors contained in Hoover's oral report, the FBI synopsis is terse and accurate. The only

---

mittee to Study Governmental Operations with Respect to Intelligence Activities (hereafter Church Committee), *Hearings: Mail Opening*, 94th Cong., 1st Sess. (Washington, D.C.: U.S. Government Printing Office, 1976), 4: 147–73.

28. If this statement were being made in the presence of DPD officials, they would beg to differ. They are gaining confidence by the hour in their case against Oswald as being solely responsible for firing the weapon that killed President Kennedy and wounded Governor Connally. What they are mostly uncertain about is whether Oswald received any assistance, or was acting on behalf of others. For the DPD's perception of the case against Oswald, see Judy Bonner, *Investigation of a Homicide: The Murder of John F. Kennedy* (Anderson, S.C.: Droke House, 1969).

29. Hoover is referring to the fact that Oswald, during his interrogations, is not admitting to anything. *Warren Report,* 180.

30. Hoover is incorrect about several facts here. The rifle and shell casings were found on the sixth floor of the Texas School Book Depository, the same floor from which Oswald fired the weapon. In addition, there was no "gun battle" with police at the movie theater where Oswald was finally apprehended. As he was surrounded, Oswald drew his revolver and there was a violent struggle as he resisted arrest. But no shots were fired either by him or by police officers. Ibid., 8–9.

mistake it makes is to repeat the error that the FBI has a CIA-provided picture of a man entering the Soviet embassy in Mexico City who identified himself as Oswald.[31]

Just past 11 a.m., the Johnsons, accompanied by the Kennedys, family friends, congressional leaders, and assorted dignitaries, attend a Mass in the East Room for the deceased president's. Lady Bird Johnson, once again, is among the best eyewitnesses to the events of the day.

> This is the day the president lay in state at the White House. It was a gray day, fitting the occasion. I went down to the EOB to meet Lyndon; we went over to the White House and met the [Kennedy] family in the Green Room. Lyndon marched past the president's body in the East Room. There was a catafalque in the center of the room and on it, the casket, draped with the American flag. At each corner, [there was] a large candle and a very rigid military man, representing each one of the services. There was some[thing] in the Catholic image at one end. I don't know quite what it was; it wasn't just a cross. . . .
>
> The people there—besides the family of the president—[were] the cabinet, the congressional leaders, [members of the] Supreme Court, [and] the White House staff. There was . . . that aura of quiet prevailed, that utter, complete quiet that seemed to grip . . . well, the country I suppose, certainly the surroundings where I was for three entire days.
>
> The cabinet had been called back from halfway around the world. They were on a plane, on their way to Japan, at least—oh, I don't [recall], four or five members of them were. And they had come back, [having] heard the news in mid-air, reversed the plane, returned, landed. And there they were, standing shocked and sad-faced, and filing past. All of us filed past, somewhat like automatons. There was black crêpe on the chandelier.
>
> After we left the White House, we went to brief services at St. John's Episcopal Church, right across Lafayette Square . . . a sort of a very "high church," a stern, rigid church, but most fitting for the day. And then we went home, and what we did the rest of the day, I don't know. I'm sure Lyndon worked terribly hard. I just sort of collapsed with Luci.[32]

After the Mass Jacqueline Kennedy briefly visits the West Wing, wanting to catch a glimpse of the rooms that were refurbished during the trip to Texas, at her

31. Hoover to Johnson, letter with attachment, 23 November 1963, Oswald, Box 2, Special File, LBJL.

32. Luci is the Johnsons' younger daughter. Mrs. Johnson White House Diary Tapes, 22–24 November 1963, LBJL.

painstaking instructions. She had sought to get rid of the Victorian feeling of the rooms and make them grand and worthy of the modern presidency. Now they are Lyndon Johnson's to use. Because of her "highly developed visual sense," seeing the new rooms, and all the packing that is going on all around her, makes her grasp the transition between presidents in a way she has not yet done.[33]

President Johnson, after a private twenty-minute meeting with the widowed First Lady, goes back to work in his EOB office, interrupted only by the services at St. John's. Former president Eisenhower is the first important visitor, and he chortles over the familiarity of the room. During World War I the EOB housed the War Department, and Eisenhower worked in this very room as a young aide to General John Pershing.[34] The meeting between presidents lasts an expectedly long time—well over an hour—as the two men discuss nearly every foreign and domestic issue of any moment. Johnson bluntly asks Eisenhower what he would do if he were in Johnson's shoes, and the former president proceeds to dictate a long memo.

One important subject the two presidents discuss is not written down. Probably as a result of his regular briefings by DCI McCone, Eisenhower is acutely aware of the unprecedented role played by Robert Kennedy while his brother was president, particularly with respect to foreign policy. Eisenhower warns Johnson that Kennedy's power is going to cause the new administration problems.[35] That there will be questions of divided loyalty, because of the wrenching transition, is a given. But Robert Kennedy will also provide loyalists with a dynamic figure and evocative symbol to coalesce around, if he is willing, and Eisenhower thinks he will be. He warns Johnson about relying on Kennedy appointees, but Johnson disagrees.

Instead, the president begins to regard "retirement from the government [now] as tantamount to desertion."[36] Dean Rusk will remind Johnson, later in the afternoon, that it is traditional for cabinet secretaries to submit their resignations when a new president takes office. Johnson still refuses to listen. It is almost as if Johnson is determined to prove to Robert Kennedy that as president he can now command the loyalties of the men who served John Kennedy.

It is a stance that Johnson will come to regret deeply, and he will rue the day he did not take Eisenhower's sound advice.

33. Manchester, *Death,* 465–66.

34. Horace Busby, memo, undated, Miscellaneous Material, Box 2, Special File, LBJL.

35. This early warning is recalled in Johnson's conversation with the ex-president nearly two years later. Johnson and Eisenhower, conversation, 27 August 1965, 11:30 a.m., LBJL.

36. Manchester, *Death,* 473.

To Edwin Weisl / 1:35 p.m.

Prior to the first meeting of his cabinet, scheduled for 2:30 p.m., President Johnson has some free time to catch up on a score of telephone calls. One of the first is to Edwin Weisl, an influential Wall Street lawyer with excellent contacts in the worlds of corporate business and high finance. Johnson has known Weisl as a friend and adviser for almost thirty years, going back to the days when Johnson was an up-and-coming congressman. He esteems no outside counsel more than Weisl's, save for that of Abe Fortas, another prominent Jewish lawyer. Weisl and Johnson last worked closely together in the late 1950s, when then-Senator Johnson headed the Armed Services Preparedness subcommittee. In the wake of the 1957 *Sputnik* launch, the subcommittee was investigating U.S. ballistic missile and satellite programs that were allegedly lagging behind those of the Soviet Union. The subcommittee provided a vehicle for Johnson to burnish his defense credentials prior to running for the presidency in 1960, and Weisl (ably assisted by a young lawyer from his firm named Cyrus Vance) was Johnson's trusted chief counsel. The Texan wanted to make headlines but knew better than to challenge President Eisenhower head-on on defense issues, as some other Democrats were inclined to do. As a result of Weisl's careful spadework, Johnson's critique was viewed as constructive and won the Texan many plaudits in the nation's press.

Weisl had advised Johnson against going on the ticket with Kennedy in July 1960, largely because Weisl detested the nominee's father. Years before, Weisl had fought Joseph Kennedy during a bitter battle for corporate control of Paramount Pictures, and the Kennedy patriarch allegedly made derogatory, anti-Semitic remarks about Weisl in return. Weisl did not believe Johnson could trust the Kennedys to keep their part of the proposed political bargain, which was to make the vice president a vital part of the administration should the Democrats win in 1960. And when Johnson accepted the offer against Weisl's advice, the Wall Street lawyer was devastated, heartbroken to see his friend allied with the "hated Kennedys."[37] He left Los Angeles (site of the 1960 Democratic convention) without seeing Johnson again, and their relations were never cooler than during Johnson's years as vice president.

Johnson is calling Weisl in part because he knows the Simpson Thacher & Bartlett lawyer has many excellent contacts in New York's financial markets, which were closed soon after news of the assassination broke. In particular, Weisl is a close friend of Robert Lehman, the senior partner at the venerable investment banking firm of Lehman Brothers, one of the most prestigious on Wall Street. With only the figurative lift of an eyebrow, "Bobbie" Lehman can

---

37. Rowland Evans and Robert Novak, *Lyndon B. Johnson: The Exercise of Power* (London: George Allen and Unwin, 1967), 287, 346.

move millions of dollars if not entire markets, and Johnson knows this. He wants Weisl to enlist the seventy-two-year-old Lehman in spreading the word, in anticipation of the markets' reopening, that a Johnson administration will be good for business and investors. Weisl is only too glad to oblige. In a further indication of just how much Johnson trusts Weisl, the president makes a veiled reference to the CIA's secret information about Oswald's visit to Mexico City. During the meeting with former president Eisenhower, DCI McCone had interrupted them at 12:30 p.m. to bring Johnson the latest information from Mexico City, thus underscoring the seriousness of the news. It turns out that Oswald visited not only the Soviet embassy in Mexico City but the Cuban consulate as well. The CIA knows this through its routine and tedious, but highly secret, surveillance of the Communist bloc outposts.

In none of his other recorded calls to private citizens or elected officials does Johnson so much as hint that there may be more to the assassination than meets the eye.

Johnson: [I] had a moment here, and I['ve] been visiting [with] President Eisenhower and [I'm] going to the Cabinet Room in 'bout fifteen minutes, but I wanted to tell you I was thinkin' of you, and [that] I never needed you as much as I do now. And I wish you'd . . . put on your skullcap and do some heavy thinkin' and give me a memo now and then, tell[ing] me what you think the situation is, and giv[ing] me the benefit of your wisdom.

Weisl: I'll do it right away, Lyndon; *anything* you want me to do.

Johnson: Well, I know that.

[There is a brief discussion about a new birth in Weisl's family.]

Johnson: Probably we'll have a joint session on Wednesday, and [if] you got any thoughts on what we oughta say in uniting the country, I'd like to have it.

Weisl: Well, tell me, where shall I send it, Lyndon?

Johnson: I'd just send it to, perhaps, President Lyndon Johnson, the White House—and that'll get it over here—attention: Walter Jenkins.

Weisl: Okay.

Johnson: What's your exchange doing? What's your stock market? What are your folks sayin' [and] talkin'?

Weisl: Well, of course, it came so suddenly and it created quite a panic. But I think that with you in there, there's great confidence on the part of business in this administration. And it's felt that if legislation could be pushed a little bit, you know . . . [if] we could get the foreign aid bill through, [and] the tax bill through in a hurry, it would be the greatest restoration of confidence—not restoration, but the *preservation* of confidence—that we could have.

Johnson: Hmm. Well, maybe you can get some of 'em to say that. You try to do that . . . talk to Bobbie [Lehman].

Weisl: Shall they say *that*?

Johnson: Well, I'd certainly indicate what you said their feeling is—

Weisl: *Yes.*

Johnson: —that confidence. We don't want this group . . . [we] don't want anybody to panic.

Weisl: That's right. Well, they won't, Lyndon, not with *you* there. You don't need to have any concern about that.

Johnson: Well, you just see that some of 'em say that.

Weisl: I'll do that; I'll see that they *do.*

Johnson: You go with *[indistinct]* and talk to 'em, and . . . I don't think you need [to] tell 'em what I indicated.

Weisl: No, I won't.

Johnson: But I think before the special session it'd be very good to show that we['re] goin' to preserve the system.

Weisl: I certainly will. I'll see who can pass it down.

Johnson: This thing on the . . . this assassin [Oswald] . . . may have a lot more complications than you know about.

Weisl: Well . . .

Johnson: So, ah . . . it may lay deeper than you think. So I think that this would be very good. . . . Okay.

Weisl: Okay, Lyndon, you just—anything that I can do.

Johnson: Yes, and tell Bobbie and some of his brethren—you just say that [it's] very tragic, but you have great confidence [in me] and [my] experience, and so on [and] so forth.

Weisl: I'll take care of it right away.

To Marie Tippit / 2 p.m.

The assassination has left two young widows, both with children to raise on their own. One widow, Jacqueline Kennedy, has the eyes of the world on her. The other is thirty-nine-year-old Marie Tippit, wife of the Dallas patrolman slain by Lee Harvey Oswald forty-five minutes after the assassination in Dealey Plaza.

Marie Gasway married J. D. Tippit, her high school sweetheart and a World War II paratrooper, on the day after Christmas in 1946. After an unsuccessful attempt at farming, the couple moved to Dallas in 1952 so that Tippit could join the police force. It was a familiar story. Most of the DPD's rank and file consisted of "country boys" who had tired of trying to eke out a living in rural Texas. With families to feed, they came to the big city for the job security and steady paycheck ($490 a month) that were a policeman's lot. While Dallas had the policing problems associated with any large municipality, being an officer there was not considered an especially dangerous occupation. In the prosperous postwar years, violent resistance to Dallas officers was rare; only one officer had been murdered during Tippit's eleven years on the force.

Marie Tippit is far from being forgotten, though the nation's attention is directed elsewhere. Immediately after the murder, relatives and friends converged on her modest home in the Oak Cliff section of Dallas, the same neighborhood where her husband was murdered. Donations to take care of the widow and her three children—ages thirteen, ten, and four—will reach more than $600,000 in a matter of weeks. But when President Johnson calls her, less than twenty-four hours after her husband's death, Marie Tippit is doubtless wondering how she will cope. Only one thing is certain. With the forensic evidence steadily mounting against Lee Harvey Oswald, her deceased husband is being recognized universally as a hero who did not die in vain. If J. D. Tippit had not interfered with Oswald's flight and precipitated his rapid capture, there is no telling what kind of manhunt would have been mounted in Dallas, and what pitch the level of national insecurity would have reached. Instead, as William Manchester will later write, Oswald's rapid apprehension meant that "almost as soon as conclusions had been drawn, they were . . . confounded, and instead of hysteria the national attitude became one of pervasive sadness."[38]

Robert Kennedy has already offered his condolences to Marie Tippit by the time President Johnson calls. The attorney general telephoned her Friday night from Bethesda Naval Hospital while waiting for the autopsy to be conducted. Interestingly, the one person Mrs. Tippit expresses concern about—the other woman made a widow by Lee Oswald—has no interest in commiserating jointly. When Robert Kennedy suggested to Jacqueline on Friday that she call the officer's widow, Mrs. Kennedy declined. Perhaps Mrs. Tippit's loss was as great as hers, "but she couldn't think so" that evening.[39] She would send the Dallas widow a note of condolence instead.

Mrs. Tippit: Hello?

Johnson: Mrs. Tippit?

Mrs. Tippit: Yes.

Johnson: This is Lyndon Johnson . . . in Washington.

Mrs. Tippit: Yes, sir.

Johnson: *[reading from prepared statement]* I know that words are not very useful at a time when your grief . . . is so great. But Mrs. Johnson and I wanted you to know that you and your children—[Charles] Allen, and Brenda Kay, and Curtis Ray—are not only in our thoughts, but in our

---

38. Hugh Aynesworth, "Slain Officer 'Gave His All,' " *Dallas Morning News,* 23 November 1963; Dale Myers, *With Malice: Lee Harvey Oswald and the Murder of Officer J. D. Tippit* (Milford, Mich.: Oak Cliff Press, 1998), 26–31; Manchester, *Death,* 251. The donations to the Tippitt family total $3.7 million in 2004 dollars.

39. Manchester, *Death,* 415, 435, 482.

prayers.[40] I hope that in the years to come that your husband's bravery, and his dedication to his country and his president, will be a great inspiration to law enforcement officers everywhere in the world. I just want to say God bless you, and I know you're a brave and a great lady.

Mrs. Tippit: *[earnestly]* Thank you so much . . . [we] certainly appreciate your praisin' him. It's . . . quite a consolation.

Johnson: Could I get your address there? I wanna drop you a little note, too.

[Mrs. Tippit spells out her home address.]

Mrs. Tippit: And would you . . . would you, ah . . . could you pass, ah . . . *[indistinct]* to . . . Mrs. Kennedy? 'Cause I can *certainly* [understand how she] feels at this time.

Johnson: I know you can. God bless you, my dear lady. Good-bye.

Mrs. Tippit: Thank you. Good luck.

Much of the rest of Johnson's day is consumed with small, brief meetings and more telephone calls. The exception is the 2:30 p.m. meeting with his cabinet secretaries. It is the first time that Johnson and Robert Kennedy must function in their new capacities, and the session is underwhelming. Johnson presides with uncharacteristic uncertainty, seemingly unable to shed the fact that in all previous meetings he attended as a subordinate. Meanwhile, the attorney general is a person who sounds and looks like the former president. And as everyone around the table knows—some *too* well—Robert Kennedy effectively exercised presidential power by proxy.

McGeorge Bundy virtually has to "drag Bobby into the cabinet meeting." Even then he arrives late and gives every indication of not wanting to be there. "Bobby hopes there can be *no* pictures," Bundy writes on a note slipped to the president.[41] Johnson feels he has no choice but to comply, even though the president is depending on photo opportunities to persuade the world outside that the government continues to function. Kennedy sits wordlessly throughout the twenty-five-minute meeting, brooding and listless. Afterward Bundy confides to a colleague that he is "worried about Bobby . . . [and his reluctance] to face the new reality."[42]

Despite eloquent statements in praise of Johnson from Adlai Stevenson and Rusk, the "drab little meeting" (in Bundy's phrase) ends unsatisfactorily; some in attendance consider it a disaster.[43] Secretary of Agriculture Orville Freeman is so concerned that he asks to meet Johnson privately in Room 274. For the first time to a relative outsider, Johnson speaks frankly about his prob-

---

40. The Tippits' youngest son is named Curtis Glenn.

41. Manchester, *Death,* 476; McGeorge Bundy, handwritten note, undated [23 November 1963], Warren Commission, Box 2, Special File, LBJL.

42. Manchester, *Death,* 476.

43. Ibid., 477.

lem. "Jackie has been just great," says Johnson. "She said she'd move out as soon as she could, and I told her 'Honey . . . I'm in no hurry.' " His "real problems" are with the attorney general. Johnson tells Freeman about the attorney general's unconscionable behavior at Andrews the previous evening. He is also convinced that Kennedy intentionally arrived in the middle of his remarks to the cabinet, so as to undermine their effect. "There [is] real bitterness in Lyndon's voice" as he speaks of these events, Freeman observes in his diary.[44] Johnson ends on a plaintive note. "What can I do?" he asks the agriculture secretary. "I do not want to get into a fight with the Kennedy family . . . the aura of Kennedy is important to all of us."[45]

Before he leaves, Secretary Freeman urges Johnson to speak before the Congress in a session that would be broadcast nationally, and as soon as possible. It is important to show the nation and the world that a Johnson administration is taking over. The first possible day for such an address is Tuesday, as John Kennedy is to be buried Monday. Yet Johnson is leery; a speech made that soon "might be resented by the family."[46] Two emissaries, McGeorge Bundy and Sargent Shriver, are sent in succession to obtain Robert Kennedy's assent. "I don't like [Tuesday]," Kennedy replies crisply. "I think you should wait at least one day after the funeral."[47] When Shriver reports back to Johnson, the president feels thwarted again but is not surprised.

To the world outside, the transition appears seamless, and no one accuses Johnson of overreaching or moving too slowly, or of acting without due regard for the Kennedy family's feelings. The dissension and resentments are known only to a tiny group of people. They recognize, even if the public at large is unaware, that just beneath the pomp and circumstance are severe strains.

In an odd way, it might have been an easier, certainly a cleaner, break if Richard Nixon, the loser of the 1960 election, could by some quirk have been elevated to the Oval Office instead of Lyndon Johnson.

November 24

Sunday

Johnson's second full day in office begins, somewhat deceptively, like the first, with an intelligence briefing by John McCone and McGeorge Bundy. Again, the

44. Ibid., 477–78.
45. Ibid., 387.
46. Ibid., 478.
47. Ibid., 480.

day's schedule pivots around whatever services are planned for the late president. At 1 p.m. the casket will begin a slow procession from the White House to the Capitol Rotunda, where John Kennedy will lie in state for another full day so that members of the public can pay their respects. Until now the closest average citizens could get to the proceedings was via a television screen, or by standing silent vigil outside the White House.

Sunday also marks Jacqueline Kennedy's first appearance in public since the assassination, after a day of seclusion. The wall-to-wall television coverage— or perhaps just Cecil Stoughton's searing photograph of the swearing-in—has instantly and fundamentally changed the public's perception of the former First Lady, as Jacqueline Kennedy's successor is among the first to realize.

> To me, one of the saddest things in the whole tragedy is that Mrs. Kennedy achieved on this desperate day something she had never quite achieved in the years she'd been in the White House—a state of love, a state of rapport between herself and the people of this country. Her behavior from the moment of the shot until I last saw her was, to me, one of the most memorable things of all. Maybe it was a combination of great breeding, great discipline, great character. I only know it was great. Her composure is one of the things that keeps on coming back to me.[48]

During the twenty-minute briefing of President Johnson, McCone covers a number of topics, including ongoing efforts via the CIA to overthrow Fidel Castro's dictatorial regime. With respect to Mexico City there is nothing new and significant to report though the issue remains very much on Johnson's mind. The news of Oswald's trip to Mexico is now public, having been the subject of a UPI wire service story from Laredo, Texas, where Oswald had crossed the border.[49] The public still does not know, however, that Oswald visited Communist diplomatic missions in Mexico City. Just before leaving the EOB Saturday night, during a long meeting with Ted Sorensen, Johnson asked John Kennedy's closest adviser about the possibility of a foreign government being involved. "Do you have any evidence?" asked Sorensen instantly.[50] Johnson had to admit the only information available was still too hazy, and nothing McCone has to say Sunday morning clarifies matters.

For anyone who does not see it live, the conjunction of the somber parade to the Capitol Rotunda with another terrible bulletin from Dallas defies belief. In accordance with standard procedure, Lee Harvey Oswald is being transferred from the DPD's custody to that of the Dallas County sheriff's department just as

48. Mrs. Johnson Diary Tapes, LBJL.
49. United Press International, "Oswald Made a Visit in September to Mexico," *New York Times*, 25 November 1963.
50. Manchester, *Death*, 481.

the Washington procession is getting under way. Having been the object of merciless criticism, Dallas authorities are intent on showing that Oswald was not mistreated physically while in police custody. Thus the transfer is to be transparent and hordes of reporters and photographers are permitted in the police headquarters basement to witness the event. Only one television network, NBC, is in place for live coverage of what is expected to be a very brief sighting of Oswald. The network shifts back and forth between pictures of the monumental preparations being made in Washington, solemn ceremonies elsewhere in the country, and the DPD's dingy basement. At 12:20 p.m. the network abruptly switches from a Catholic mass in Hyannis Port, Massachusetts, to the basement garage, where NBC's Tom Pettit is waiting, along with a scrum of other journalists, for Oswald to appear. Suddenly the accused assassin is seen being escorted to a waiting, unmarked squad car. The bright TV lights momentarily blind two policemen on either side of Oswald, or at least long enough so that they do not see a stout man in a dark suit lunge out of the crowd, holding a revolver. A loud bang is heard, and America has witnessed a murder on live television.

Every newsman's instinct is to abandon the funeral coverage and switch to the assault on—soon it would be murder of—President Kennedy's alleged assassin. But the networks remain fixated on coverage of the procession up Pennsylvania Avenue. It is the most bizarre, schizoid juxtaposition in television's admittedly short history. Long, uninterrupted sequences of the catafalque inching its way to the Capitol are punctuated by sotto voce reports about the pandemonium that has broken out in Dallas.

The schism between duty and disbelief is captured in Mrs. Johnson's audio diary for Sunday.

> This was the day the president lay in state at the Capitol. It is a day I will never forget—[n]or will the other people of America.
>
> In contrast to the day before, it was a bright, clear day of sparkling sun. We began by going to St. Mark's to church, with Luci and Congressman Thornberry. There was a line in Bill Baxter's sermon—something about every man who had fostered, or permitted to be fostered around him, the atmosphere of hate had his hand on the gun barrel that day.
>
> After church we went to the White House and waited in the Green Room for the [Kennedy] family. As they came in, Mrs. [Eunice] Shriver turned to me and said, "I hear Oswald has been killed," in that clipped, clinical manner that . . . some of the Kennedy ladies have.[51] That was the first news I had about Oswald.

51. This passage is one of the most significant differences between the tape-recorded diary and the published version. The latter omits Mrs. Johnson's description of Mrs. Shriver's reaction. Lady Bird Johnson, *A White House Diary* (New York: Holt, Rinehart and Winston, 1970), 8.

We were told by protocol that we were to ride with Mrs. Kennedy and the attorney general. Suddenly, Mrs. Kennedy came walking in, leading John-John by one hand and Caroline in the other, in two darling blue coats. And then I realized there would be six of us in the car, and I wondered if we shouldn't offer to change and get in another one. But it turned out that we all got into the same limousine: Mrs. Kennedy and Lyndon in the back seat, the attorney general and I in the jumper seats, Caroline next to her mother, and John-John, being absolutely peripatetic, jumping from [the] back seat to his uncle's lap, to the front seat, and back again.

As soon as we emerged from the gates of the White House, the first thing I was aware of was that *sea of faces* stretching away on every side . . . silent, watching faces. *[Mrs. Johnson is almost overcome with emotion.]* I wanted to cry for them and with them, but it was impossible to permit the catharsis of tears. I don't know quite why, except that perhaps one reason is that the continuity of strength demands it, and another reason was [that] the dignity of Mrs. Kennedy and the members of the family themselves demanded it.

In front of us, there was a handsome, black, riderless horse, with his boots reversed. I recognized it at once as the symbol of a fallen leader, but I didn't really know much about it. I asked Lynda Bird [her daughter] later, and she said it went a long [ways] back into history, in fact, back to Genghis Khan—and *then* the horse was sacrificed at the grave. A few centuries ago, they abolished that part of the custom.

In front of this horse there was the caisson . . . drawn by six white horses, the caisson itself draped with the flag. Soldiers marching . . . *always,* the whole time, this sound of muffled drums in the background . . . flags at half-mast. But most of all, the sea of faces *all* around us and that *curious* sense of silence, broken only by an occasional sob. I kept on comparing it in my mind with the time [Franklin Roosevelt] died. But that was so different . . . because *then* everybody could be as emotional as they felt like.

The feeling continued in me that I was stalking, step by step, through a Greek tragedy. I remembered a definition of it back in college some time—that a Greek tragedy is a noble protagonist being overtaken by an inevitable doom. But then there is a third ingredient and I can't remember it. Some time I must look it up.

The only note of levity was John-John, who bounced from the back to his uncle's lap, to the front, until finally, the attorney general said, "John-John, you be good. [If] you'll be good, we'll give you a flag afterwards. You can march with [Kennedy aide] Dave Powers."

We were a pretty silent group as we rode along, each wrapped in his own thoughts. The only time the attorney general said anything was when we passed a big building on the left, and he looked over there and said—and I think as much to himself, perhaps to the children—"That was where it all began. That was where he ran for the presidency."[52] He has a granite-like sort of a face, and there was a flinching of the jaw at that moment that almost made . . . oh, it . . . well . . . it made your soul flinch for him.

After that *interminable* drive we got to the Capitol, went into the Rotunda. There in the center, right underneath the dome, was the flag-draped coffin with the honor guard around it. One of them, I noticed, had on the green beret. There were eulogies by Chief Justice Warren, by Speaker McCormack, [and] by Mike Mansfield. An odd thing about Mike Mansfield's [eulogy]—that he, that [most] modest of men, repeated over and over the phrase, "and she took a ring from her finger and placed it on his hand."

Then Lyndon advanced and laid a wreath at the foot of the casket, and Mrs. Kennedy went over and knelt. I value all the little things, but I remember how gracefully she knelt and kissed the casket, with Caroline by her side . . . [Caroline] simply put her little hand on the flag, sort of underneath the flag. John-John had disappeared; I think maybe it was high time that he started his marching. And then we left, in separate cars.[53]

From Eugene Rostow to Bill Moyers / ±2:50 p.m.

President Johnson, no less than Lady Bird, is a captive of the funeral schedule. Moments before his wife hears that Oswald is dying, Secretary Rusk calls the president to say Oswald has just been shot "on television." When Johnson greets Robert Kennedy, who still knows nothing of the new shooting, the president blurts out, "We've got to get involved. It's giving the United States a bad name around the world."[54] Yet as much as Johnson wants to put federal authorities in command of the situation, he cannot allow that impulse to intrude on his participation in the memorial ceremonies. Before joining the procession, he has only a moment to sneak away and order, via telephone, the FBI and Secret Service into action. Within a day, more than fifty bureau agents would be on the scene and working the case.

Ninety minutes later, as the Johnsons are driven back to the White House, the networks announce the death of Lee Oswald. The identity of his murderer is

52. The attorney general was referring to the Caucus Room in the old Senate Office Building, where John Kennedy announced his candidacy for the Democratic nomination on January 2, 1960.
53. Mrs. Johnson Diary Tapes, LBJL.
54. Manchester, *Death,* 518.

common knowledge now too: Jack Ruby, the Chicago-born owner of a cheap burlesque joint in Dallas. Ruby's apparent motive is already surfacing. He appointed himself vigilante because he wanted to rub that smirk off of Oswald's face. "Well, you guys couldn't do it," Ruby proudly explained to Dallas's finest, after they asked him the expletive-laced question, "Why the **** did you do it, Jack?" Ruby's crime, coming on top of Oswald's crimes, gives Justice Department lawyers the opening they need to sweep aside Dallas authorities and take full, albeit temporary, control of the case. The pretext is that Oswald's civil rights have been violated by his death at the hands of Ruby, and while in police custody.

Johnson's afternoon schedule is such that he barely has time to confirm, in an unrecorded telephone call with Deputy Attorney General Nicholas Katzenbach, that Herbert "Jack" Miller, the head of the Criminal Division, is already heading to Texas and that the FBI has formally entered the case.[55] The rest of the president's day is taken up by a variety of prearranged meetings, including, most importantly, a long meeting on the rapidly deteriorating situation in South Vietnam. There is only one opportunity to discuss the new crisis, and that occurs when Johnson meets for almost twenty-five minutes with the Texas delegation to the state funeral, during what was supposed to be a routine meeting at 3:45 p.m. Johnson will ask the group, which includes state attorney general Waggoner Carr, to help him find a way through a legal and political thicket. Otherwise, the president will not be able to focus on Dallas again until late in the evening.

Some influential legal minds, in the meantime, wrestle with the problem for him. These men realize that due process is one of the most cherished constitutional rights, dear to the heart of every American. Their concern is not so much that Oswald's right to due process has been forever denied; rather, they are worried because the American public has been denied the purgative effect of a trial and punishment. The problem is to devise a process by which approximately the same end can be achieved—but only approximately, because everyone now recognizes that Jack Ruby's senseless act has planted a virulent notion that will be virtually impossible to disprove. It is eminently reasonable to speculate that Oswald was killed before he could talk, or prove his innocence; therefore, the assassination has to have been a conspiracy.

The first legal intellectual to take the initiative is Eugene Rostow, the politically minded dean of Yale Law School and a staunch, influential Democrat. Rostow calls a former Yale colleague who works in the Justice Department, Nicholas Katzenbach, to discuss the idea of a special commission to report on the assassination. The deputy attorney general, it seems, is already thinking along the same or very similar lines. Either at Katzenbach's suggestion or on his own initiative, Rostow then calls Bill Moyers at the White House to float the idea there while Katzenbach broaches it with J. Edgar Hoover. Rostow's idea is modeled in some respects on the special commission President Roosevelt appointed in the wake

55. Ibid., 543.

of the December 7, 1941, attack, the Commission to Investigate the Attack Upon Pearl Harbor. Headed by Supreme Court Justice Owen Roberts, a Herbert Hoover appointee, the five-man commission issued its report in January 1942 after a month's investigation. Rostow neglects to mention the Roberts Commission, though, perhaps for good reason: its findings satisfied virtually no one.[56]

One interesting difference between Rostow and Moyers emerges during the telephone conversation. Rostow views the problem created by Oswald's murder primarily through a legal, even sociological lens. He fears that Ruby's act has denied Americans the "catharsis, and the emotional protection," that a public trial of Oswald would have provided. Now there will be no way to "discharge intense feelings" through safe channels. Rumors and theories of conspiracies are likely to become rampant, "disturbing public opinion" and perhaps even the authority of the state.[57] Rostow's greatest concern is the pressing need to find a substitute for a purgative trial. By contrast, Moyers, who is an ordained Baptist minister in addition to being a shrewd adviser, seems more interested in thinking about how the assassination might be exploited for political advantage. From Moyers's viewpoint, even though the alleged assassin was a self-styled Marxist, right-wing purveyors of hate and vitriol are the ones responsible for creating the climate in which Oswald acted, and the assassination represents an opportunity to marginalize these political foes. Moyers's inclination is virtually identical to the message uttered in pulpits all across America that Sunday morning, as Mrs. Johnson noted, well before Oswald was gunned down.

Moyers: *[inaudible]* talk to you.
Rostow: Thank you, boy. I'm *[sighs audibly]* . . . if I can help in any way, I
    will. I'm calling with a suggestion. I've just talked to Nick Katzenbach.
Moyers: Yes.
Rostow: And the poor fella, *he* has so much of a burden on him. I've talked to
    him about three times today, and . . . he just sounded so groggy, that I
    thought I'd pass this thought along to you. And of course, I realize how
    tough it must be now for the president.
       In this situation, with this bastard killed, my suggestion is that a
    presidential commission be appointed of very distinguished citizens in the
    very near future, bipartisan and above politics—no Supreme Court
    justices, but people like Tom Dewey and, you know, Bill *[sic]* Storey from
    Texas, and so on, a commission of seven or nine people—maybe [even]
    [Richard] Nixon, I don't know—[58]

56. Martin Melosi, *The Shadow of Pearl Harbor: Political Controversy Over the Surprise Attack, 1941–1946* (College Station: Texas A&M University Press, 1977).

57. Eugene Rostow, "The Warren Report: The Legacy of Grief," *Yale Law Report* 11, no. 2 (Winter 1965).

58. Dewey is a former governor of New York who was twice the GOP nominee for president; Robert Storey is an internationally recognized lawyer and former law school dean from Dallas.

Moyers: Right.

Rostow: —to look into the whole affair of the murder of the president. Because world opinion—and *American* opinion—is just now so shaken by the behavior of the Dallas police, that they're not *believing* anything.

Moyers: That's . . . I can understand that.

Rostow: Now, I've got a party here. I've been pursuing the policy, you know, that people need to come together at this time.

Moyers: You know what you could do that would be very helpful? And this is a good suggestion, and I'll pass it on. Just a minute . . . the president's calling.

[After a few moments, Moyers comes back on the line.]

Rostow: What can I do that will help?

Moyers: Well, I was just thinking, coming in a few minutes ago after hearing the news of Oswald's shooting, that this is symptomatic of what has been happening into *[sic]* this country in the last few years, and the breakdown of respect for law and order, you know, [like] the signs "Impeach the Supreme Court," et cetera, et cetera, et cetera.[59]

If I could have a memorandum to give to the president along these lines, that one of his great tasks is to help, you know, continue the institutions that seem to be at least—if not in doubt right now—at least weakened by some kind of *sickness* that has taken hold of some parts of our population. I'd like him to have that to consider in some private talks he's having with newsmen and with, perhaps, for his joint session [address] next Wednesday night. He needs to make some point, you know, that America is known as a land of public order, a land of civility, a land of—in which the public safety is guaranteed. And there's a very serious question right now, in the mind of the world, about these institutions that undergird us so tremendously.

Rostow: Of course, his Gettysburg speech last spring was just terrific; it couldn't have been better.[60]

Moyers: Yes.

Rostow: I'll be glad to send any memo you think's helpful right away.

Moyers: All right. Now, your suggestion is that he [President Johnson] appoint

---

59. In the early 1960s the right-wing John Birch Society achieved notoriety for erecting billboards all over the country calling for the impeachment of Chief Justice Earl Warren.

60. Rostow is referring to a Memorial Day address (written by Horace Busby) that Johnson delivered in Gettysburg, Pennsylvania, in anticipation of the famous Civil War battle's centenary. Johnson's speech, in which he observed that "the Negro remains in bondage to the color of his skin," was widely noticed and considered the best address the vice president had made since entering politics. A *Washington Post* editorial hailed Johnson for his eloquence, political courage, and vision, and the *New York Times* ran a wire service story about Johnson's speech on its front page. "A Voice from the South," *Washington Post,* 1 June 1963, and United Press International, "Johnson Asks Cooperation Between White and Negro," *New York Times,* 31 May 1963.

a special commission of distinguished Americans, primarily in the field of law I presume, to look into the whole question of the assassination.

Rostow: That's right . . . and [make a] report on it.

Moyers: All right, I'll get that to him. Also, I wish you would keep me informed about how Nick is doing. We don't want to put any greater strain on him than is necessary—

Rostow: Yeah, that's true . . . well, he's a great boy.

Moyers: But he's an able man—

Rostow: I have utmost faith in him. But he's fighting back . . . [he's under] terrific strain.

Moyers: Thanks for calling; I'll follow through.

Rostow: Right.

After dinner at the Elms, Johnson receives three distinct proposals about what to do in the wake of Oswald's murder. On one point everyone is in agreement: some kind of report and process must take place that will convince the American public that Oswald was the actual assassin. Already TV commentators such as ABC's Howard K. Smith are suggesting that "we don't know if Oswald really committed the crime and perhaps we will never know."[61] After that, there is no consensus. Rostow and Katzenbach think that the president should appoint a commission of at least three outstanding citizens to make a determination and issue a report. Katzenbach even proposes specific candidates for such a panel: retired U.S. Supreme Court justice Charles Whittaker; Judge E. Barrett Prettyman, recently retired from the U.S. Court of Appeals for the District of Columbia; and Thomas Dewey.[62] The unspoken presumption, which they dare not repeat to J. Edgar Hoover directly, is that an FBI report in and of itself will carry insufficient weight, especially on the left wing of the American political spectrum. Desperate to get his proposal made known to a president he barely knows, Katzenbach shrewdly channels the idea through the one Johnson crony that he is on any terms with, Texas representative Homer Thornberry. The Democrat who filled Johnson's House seat when he was elevated to the Senate in 1948, Thornberry is about to resign from Congress in order to accept an appointment from President Kennedy to a federal judgeship.

J. Edgar Hoover's ideas on the matter are conveyed by Walter Jenkins, Johnson's administrative assistant who spoke with the FBI director at 4 p.m.[63] Hoover believes that the bureau should deliver an investigative report to the attorney general, leaving the president to decide what part of a Justice Department report to make public. Part of Hoover's argument against an outside com-

61. Walter Jenkins to Johnson, memo, 24 November 1963, Box 1, Special File, LBJL.

62. Ibid.

63. "J. Edgar Hoover Said As Follows," 24 November 1963, Kissinger/Scowcroft Files, Gerald R. Ford Library [hereafter GRFL].

mission is that some of the bureau's information about Oswald comes from sensitive "sources and methods," namely, CIA telephone intercepts in Mexico City and FBI mail openings in Washington. Another reason is that the FBI realizes that one of the Soviet officials Oswald met with in Mexico City, Valery Kostikov, is not really an embassy vice consul. In truth Kostikov is an officer in the KGB's First Chief Directorate; worse, he is assigned to "Department 13," the infamous KGB section that carries out such "active measures" as terrorism, sabotage, and assassination.[64]

Finally, Texas attorney general Waggoner Carr is proposing a third process, namely, deployment of an obscure institution peculiar to his state. Carr is empowered to convene a Court of Inquiry whenever he has good cause to believe that "offenses ha[ve] been committed against the laws of Texas."[65] In practice, the court resembles a congressional investigation more than anything; it cannot try or even indict anyone, and any report it issues will carry no legal significance. Nonetheless, witnesses can be subpoenaed, forensic evidence introduced, and in this manner Oswald's guilt in the murders of President Kennedy and Officer J. D. Tippit could conceivably be established beyond a reasonable doubt. Viewed in its most favorable light, a Court of Inquiry represents a forum for exposing the facts in a quasi-legalistic manner. Carr calls Johnson aide Cliff Carter just before 8:30 p.m. on Sunday to submit this idea for the president's consideration.

Coincidentally, Abe Fortas is over for dinner and Johnson promptly delves into a discussion of the proposals with his friend, a name partner in one of the most prominent law firms in Washington. Fortas has been a valued politico-legal counselor ever since 1948, when he represented Johnson in a legal tussle over a disputed primary election in Texas. With Fortas acting as his principal attorney in Washington, Johnson survived the challenge, thus assuring his election to the U.S. Senate for the first time. Fortas thinks poorly of Katzenbach's suggestion for a presidential commission, primarily because there is no legal precedent, and also because he is leery of getting Johnson involved in an investigation of his predecessor's murder. Fortas's assessment is a very legalistic one, since the assassination is a "local killing" only in the sense that there is a gaping hole in federal criminal statutes. Nonetheless, Fortas's considered legal judgment settles the matter for Johnson, carrying greater weight than Homer Thornberry's advocacy.[66] Just before 9 p.m., the president calls Katzenbach, who is really acting attorney general with Robert Kennedy all but disabled, to say he wants the matter left to ordinary legal processes, namely, an FBI report to the attorney general

64. James Hosty, *Assignment Oswald* (New York: Arcade, 1996), 175. "Active measures" is Soviet parlance for what the CIA calls "covert action."

65. Carter to Johnson, memo, 24 November 1963, 8:25 p.m., Appointment File, 24 November 1963, Box 1, Diary Back-up, LBJL.

66. Jenkins to Johnson, 24 November 1963, Box 1, Special File, LBJL.

and simultaneously a Court of Inquiry in Texas. Word is also passed back to Waggoner Carr: "Good idea, but purely a state matter. Can't say president asked for it."[67]

Precisely why Johnson is slow to appreciate the enormity of the problem caused by Oswald's death never becomes clear. He is not shy about injecting the federal government, via the FBI and Secret Service, into the situation. But he balks at the idea of a special investigating commission, most likely because as a native son, he doesn't quite view "Texas justice" as an oxymoron. Subconsciously, he may not want to treat Texas as he believes he is being treated by the attorney general. Or perhaps Johnson is just suspicious of any suggestion emanating from what is, after all, Robert Kennedy's Justice Department.

One of the clearest indicators of how heavily Kennedy's behavior is weighing on Johnson is the decision on Sunday, amid everything else, to promote LBJ's preferred version of the November 22 swearing-in. With both Dallas dailies obviously out of the running, the vehicle for this disclosure is another leading Texas newspaper, the *Houston Post*.[68] Jack Valenti, a member of Johnson's de facto presidential staff, has excellent contacts with the *Post,* having run a thriving public relations/advertising agency in Houston for years. The copyrighted story—"LBJ Was Decisive, Calm in First Hours as Chief"—will appear on Monday's front page and be picked up by hundreds of newspapers across the country. Written by William Hobby, Jr., son of the publisher, it claims to be the first well-sourced account of "hitherto unpublished details" about what took place aboard SAM 26000. The *Post* article might be regarded by the Kennedys as a harmless piece of puffery save for one thing. It presents as fact Lyndon Johnson's preferred version of his conversations with Robert Kennedy that afternoon, namely, that "the two [men] agreed that Mr. Johnson should immediately take the oath."[69]

Weeks later Valenti will encounter Robert Kennedy for the first time in the White House. Before a smiling Valenti can introduce himself to the attorney general, Kennedy bites off a few choice words about leaks coming from the White House—and from Valenti specifically. "There was no expression on [Kennedy's] face, only flint and gray smoke in his eyes and a straight, hard line across his mouth," a stunned Valenti will later write. ". . . [But] I could not for the life of me pinpoint any specific story Bobby was referring to."[70]

67. Carter to Johnson, 24 November 1963, Special File, LBJL.

· 68. There is no indication that Johnson approved the leak. It may be the case that Valenti was simply being responsive to his hometown newspaper.

69. William Hobby, "LBJ Was Decisive, Calm in First Hours as Chief," *Houston Post,* 25 November 1963.

70. Jack Valenti, *A Very Human President* (New York: W. W. Norton, 1975), 124–25.

November 25

Monday

Today is the official day of mourning for John Kennedy, and an estimated 105 million Americans will watch the late president being laid to rest in Arlington National Cemetery. President Kennedy's elaborate service is actually but one of three funerals scheduled for Monday that can be traced to the shots in Dealey Plaza. The services for J. D. Tippit attract only a tiny fraction of the attention being lavished on the solemn ceremony in Washington. Meanwhile, the Secret Service agents present almost outnumber the mourners in attendance at the mercifully brief service for Lee Harvey Oswald in Fort Worth.

All through the night the networks have fixated on the crowds passing by the casket in the Capitol Rotunda, the only break in the coverage coming every thirty minutes when there is a changing of the guard. Thousands of people make the pilgrimage to Washington, often traveling for hours, only to wait in line for an additional nine to ten hours in the freezing weather before being allowed past the bier. At 2 a.m. the queue is three miles long. By the time the Capitol doors are closed at 9 a.m., an estimated 250,000 citizens will have filed past. Nearly 12,000 still waiting in line are cut off.

At 11 a.m. the procession will leave Capitol Hill for St. Matthew's Cathedral, stopping briefly at the White House to rendezvous with the largest group of world leaders ever assembled in one place and time. Following the Mass, the president is to be buried in Arlington with full military honors. The state funeral will end with three volleys from twenty-one guns and the playing of "Taps" by an expert bugler whose first note cracks. In the words of McGeorge Bundy, "The end of the service at Arlington [is] like the fall of a curtain, or the snapping of taut strings."[71] The longest four days in American history will be over, and the normal rhythms of life will begin to reassert themselves remorselessly. Yet nothing will be quite the same anymore. Old certainties and verities will seem unreliable, as if the ground has shifted below the entire nation. And it has.

To J. Edgar Hoover / 10:30 a.m.

After going to bed Sunday believing the matter settled, Johnson wakes up to find the proposal for a presidential commission is alive and kicking. He learns from

71. Manchester, *Death*, 603.

aides that the *Washington Post* intends to run an editorial on Tuesday calling for just such a panel, and that is bad news. The *Post* is not yet considered one of the nation's great newspapers. Nonetheless, its editorials carry an influence far out of proportion to the paper's circulation because of its readership and privileged access to Washington sources. Every correspondent based in the nation's capital reads the *Post,* and Johnson fears that an editorial drumbeat in the newspaper will push him into the awkward position of publicly defending his decision.

Simultaneously, Nicholas Katzenbach has prepared a memorandum for Bill Moyers on the question of a presidential commission. For the time being, the deputy attorney general seems to be backing off the idea. He notes that it would have "advantages and disadvantages," but now believes that it can probably wait until after publication of the FBI report.[72] Public reaction to the FBI's findings will be the best indicator of whether it is needed or not, observes Katzenbach, perhaps realizing that nothing he can say will change the president's mind. For now, the only thing that is absolutely necessary, concludes Katzenbach, is for the president to assure the public that the facts will be made known in such a way as to eliminate any doubt about Oswald's guilt, and lingering questions about whether he had any confederates.

President Johnson has very little time in the morning to do anything before he must leave the EOB to participate in the state funeral. But he does make two telephone calls hoping to blunt the *Washington Post*. The first is to J. Edgar Hoover, and the president is completely candid about wanting Hoover's help in thwarting the *Post*. He informs Hoover about the news conference Waggoner Carr plans to hold in Washington just after the funeral, at which time the Texas attorney general will reveal his intention to convene a Court of Inquiry.[73]

Johnson's jaundiced view about appointing a presidential panel will be reflected in his remark about how sometimes a commmmission "hurts more than it helps." He is referring to a panel President Herbert Hoover created in 1929: the National Commission on Law Observance and Enforcement, also known as the Wickersham Commission, after its chairman, former attorney general George Wickersham. In an effort to court both the "wet" and the "dry" vote in 1928, Hoover had promised to create an unprejudiced panel that would study whether the Volstead Act (i.e., Prohibition) was the cause of an alarming increase in criminal activity. When the Wickersham Commission's report was published in 1931, the public became more befuddled than ever. Six of the eleven members condemned Prohibition—the "noble experiment"—because of

72. "Memorandum for Mr. Moyers," 25 November 1963, reproduced in U.S. House of Representatives Select Committee on Assassinations, *Investigation of the Assassination of President John F. Kennedy: Hearings,* 95th Cong., 2nd Sess. (Washington, D.C.: U.S. Government Printing Office, 1979), 3:567.

73. The White House, probably Abe Fortas, helps Carr draft his statement. "Statement of the Attorney General of Texas," Oswald, Box 2, Special File, LBJL.

its contribution to lawlessness. But Hoover (who favored the alcohol ban) nonetheless concluded the commission did not favor repeal. Ultimately, the Wickersham panel was regarded as an "unmitigated failure" and as a direct result presidential commissions labored in disrepute for decades afterward.[74] The Wickersham Commission's history may well have been one of the precedents cited by Abe Fortas in support of his argument against bringing the assassination investigation into the White House.

The conversation starkly reveals Johnson's tendency to speak for effect when he wants to make a point. Besides the reference to the Wickersham Commission, he ridicules such panels by invoking the name of Tom Dewey, the crusading New York prosecutor who has a reputation for being the most stilted politician in the country.[75] Dewey is a metaphor for a commission of prosecutorial-minded outsiders who would, as Johnson sees it, raise hackles in Texas. Johnson also dismissively refers to the Dallas crimes as a "shootin' scrape." If this characterization were uttered in public on Monday, resolutions calling for Johnson's impeachment would have doubtlessly been introduced in Congress on Tuesday.

Johnson: Two things: apparently some lawyer in [the] Justice [Department] is lobbying with the *[Washington] Post* because that's where the suggestion came from for this presidential commission, which we think would be very *bad.*[76]

Hoover: I do, too.

Johnson: [Such a commission would] put it right in the White House, and we can't be checkin' up on every . . . shootin' scrape in the country.

Hoover: *Certainly.*

Johnson: They've gone to the *Post* now to get 'em an editorial, and the *Post* is callin' up and sayin' they're gonna run an editorial if we don't do things. Now, we're going to do two things, and I wanted you to know about it. One: we believe that the way to handle this is, as we said yesterday—at your suggestion—that you put every facility at your command in making a full report to the attorney general, and then they'll make it available to the country in whatever form may seem desirable—

Hoover: *Right.*

Johnson: —as far as the president [is concerned]. Second: the state—it's a state matter too, and the [Texas] state attorney general is young, and able, and prudent, and very cooperative with you—he's gonna run a Court of

74. Carl Marcy, *Presidential Commissions* (New York: King's Crown Press, 1945), 39.

75. Dewey is unforgettably known as the politician who resembles "a groom on a wedding cake." "Thomas E. Dewey Is Dead at 68," *New York Times,* 17 March 1971.

76. Johnson is referring presumably to Katzenbach, who was in contact with *Post* editor Russell Wiggins. Paul Valentine, "FBI Tried to Avert Post Editorials," *Washington Post,* 8 December 1977.

Inquiry which is provided for by state law and he's gonna have associated with him the most *outstanding* jurists in the country. But he's a good, conservative fella—

Hoover: *Yeah.*

Johnson: —and we don't start invading local jurisdictions that way, and he understands what *you're* doing and he's for it. I wanted you to understand what *he* was doing, and he's very strong for it, [and] he's gonna announce it today. Now if you get too many cooks messin' with the broth, they'd mess it up.

Hoover: Yeah.

Johnson: And I think that these two are trained organizations. . . . The attorney general of the state holds courts of inquiries every time a law is violated, and the FBI makes these investigations.[77] So I wanted you to know that, and you oughta tell your press man that that's what's happening. And they can expect Waggoner Carr, the attorney general of Texas, to make an announcement this mornin' of a state inquiry, and that you can offer 'em your full cooperation and vice versa. He'll do it with you.

Hoover: Right. We'll both work together on it.

Johnson: And any influence you got with the *Post,* point out to 'em that you don't want too many things [simultaneous investigations], and that just pickin' out a Tom Dewey–lawyer from New York and sendin' him down on new facts—this commission thing, Mr. Herbert Hoover tried that and sometimes a commission that's not trained *hurts* more than it *helps.*[78]

Hoover: It's a regular circus then—

Johnson: That's right!

Hoover: —because it'll be covered by TV and everything else.

Johnson: Just like a [congressional] investigating committee.[79]

Hoover: *Exactly.* I don't have much influence with the *Post* because I frankly—

Johnson: I know *[chuckling]*—

Hoover: —don't read it.

Johnson: *[still chuckling]* I know that, I know that.

Hoover: I view it like the *Daily Worker.*[80]

77. In point of fact, the FBI has little experience conducting murder investigations per se. While the bureau's lab is a national leader in the examination of individual pieces of forensic evidence, murder investigations are generally the province of local authorities.

78. In his book, Michael Beschloss erroneously interprets this reference to mean commissions chaired by former President Herbert Hoover. Johnson is talking about a commission Hoover appointed while president, i.e., the Wickersham panel. Michael Beschloss, *Taking Charge: The Johnson White House Tapes, 1963–1964* (New York: Simon & Schuster, 1997), 32.

79. This ignores the fact that a Court of Inquiry, conducted as it would be in public, is bound to be a "regular circus" too.

80. The *Daily Worker* is the official newspaper of the U.S. Communist Party.

Johnson: *[laughing harder]* You told me that once before. . . . But I just want your people to know the facts, and your people can say that, and that kind of negates it, you see?

Hoover: Yes.

Johnson: Thank you.

Hoover: We'll take care of that.

The FBI director, unlike Johnson, is not talking for effect. Famous for ingratiating himself with presidents by implementing their wishes instantly, Hoover immediately orders assistant director Cartha "Deke" DeLoach to contact *Post* editors and explain the bureau's position, i.e., the risk of exposing sensitive sources and methods. DeLoach tells managing editor Al Friendly that Hoover is personally supervising the investigation in Dallas, and that it will be "swift and intensive." Friendly sounds receptive and promises to see that an editorial advocating a presidential commission is killed. Some forty minutes later, though, Friendly calls DeLoach back and retracts the commitment. DeLoach believes that Friendly reneges after checking with his superior, *Post* editor Russell Wiggins, who ultimately decides the newspaper's editorial stances.[81]

To Joseph Alsop / 10:40 a.m.

Leave no stone unturned until the votes are counted—that was Johnson's motto during his years as Senate majority leader, and he is applying that same principle until he is certain the idea of a presidential commission is stopped in its tracks. His first call after talking to Hoover is to Joe Alsop, one of the most powerful columnists in Washington and certainly the leading reporter among such journalists. An early backer of John Kennedy for president in 1960, Alsop's stock, influence, and social standing have never been higher. The columnist's ability "to lure the president [Kennedy] to his [dinner] table conferred upon him a professional stature unmatched in Washington journalism," as one biographer later put it.[82] Johnson knows that if anyone is able and willing to stop a *Post* editorial, it is Alsop, who never shies from exercising his influence. The president has known Alsop for almost twenty-five years, going back to the days when Johnson was an ambitious young congressman and Alsop an aspiring young journalist.

Johnson's discussion with Alsop is one of those conversations that are hard to render with an accurate transcript alone. Much of the color and flavor is lost by reducing it to mere words. Alsop speaks with an aristocratic, faux British

81. Valentine, "FBI Tried to Avert Post Editorials."

82. Robert Merry, *Taking on the World: Joseph and Stewart Alsop, Guardians of the American Century* (New York: Viking, 1996), 397.

accent that cannot be captured except at the risk of making him sound like a caricature. His inflection is so pronounced that every other word could be italicized. Though he is not disrespectful to Johnson, there is the tone of condescension, much as a tutor would speak to a rebellious pupil, and Alsop thinks nothing of interrupting the president. Few if any people talk to Johnson in such a manner, or fail to back down in the face of the president's obvious anger.

And make no mistake, Johnson is livid about being second-guessed on an important decision so early, if not furious about being lobbied and pressured through the *Washington Post*. At the outset of the conversation, he is practically yelling into the telephone receiver. Johnson is quite frank with Alsop about his concern over how Texas would respond to a bunch of "carpetbagger" investigators, alluding to despised northern politicians who flooded into the defeated South after the Civil War. He tries to impress Alsop with the quality of the Texas lawyers whom Waggoner Carr hopes to corral into working with the Court of Inquiry, renowned attorneys such as Leon Jaworski, Robert Storey, and Wilmer St. John Garwood. They are among the most esteemed men of law Texas has to offer; both Jaworski and Storey, for example, served as prosecutors at the Nuremberg war crimes tribunal after World War II, and Garwood served with great distinction for ten years on the state supreme court. Johnson goes so far as to suggest the Court of Inquiry will be the equivalent of a presidential commission.

Wisely, Alsop lets Johnson vent, then attempts to counter the president's argument by invoking the name of Dean Acheson, Harry Truman's secretary of state and one of the most venerated statesmen in Washington. Cagily, the archbishop of Washington columnists acts as if he could not possibly exert influence over what the *Washington Post* says on its editorial page. Gradually, Alsop persuades the president that he has only Johnson's best interests in mind and is not acting out of any other interest—least of all out of concern for Robert Kennedy. In contrast to Eugene Rostow, Alsop doesn't seem to view the presidential commission as a needed substitute for a purgative trial that can no longer take place. Rather, Alsop seems to regard the whole problem as primarily one of public relations.

Indeed, Alsop's recommendation is distinct from the one Katzenbach and Rostow are advocating. The columnist argues only for a three-man panel that will review the FBI report, not an independent body that will conduct an investigation of its own. The commission envisioned by Alsop is an added layer, intended only to complement the machinery Johnson has already set in motion. Alsop believes that the machinery cannot be exclusively Texan, nor will the FBI suffice because of the widespread distrust the bureau engenders on the liberal/ left of the political spectrum. Besides, as Alsop puts it in a typically acid observation, the FBI "doesn't write well."

Johnson: He [Waggoner Carr] will order during the day, probably right after the funeral, a state Court of Inquiry headed by the attorney general, in

which he will have associated with him one or two of the outstanding civil
liberties jurists in the country, perhaps [Leon] Jaworski, who represented
the attorney general in the Fifth Circuit Negro case, and [who was] head of
the trial lawyers of America, or Dean [Robert] Storey, or—[83]

Alsop: You mean somebody from outside Texas?

Johnson: No.

Alsop: Somebody from outside Texas?

Johnson: No, no; no. We're gonna have the FBI from outside Texas. But this is
under Texas law, and they take all the involvements, and we don't send in a
bunch of . . . carpetbaggers. That's the worst thing you could do right now.

Alsop: You think so.

Johnson: *[increasingly agitated]* Well, we got the FBI doing *anything* that—
if there's any question about Texas's operation, they got an FBI that's
going to the bottom of it and direct with the [U.S.] attorney general. But
paralleling that is a blue-ribbon state Court of Inquiry headed by the
brilliant [state] attorney general and associated with him, somebody like
[Wilmer] St. John Garwood, Will Clayton's son-in-law, who was a brilliant
[Texas] supreme court justice, that's retired [now] . . . somebody [who will
act] like [Justice Owen] Roberts did at Pearl Harbor.[84] And that's what the
attorney general's doin'.

   Now, if we have *another* commission—hell, you gonna have people
runnin' over each other, and *everybody* agrees. Now, I know that some of
the lawyers, they thought of the blue-ribbon commission first, at [the]
Justice [Department], and we just can't have them lobbying against the
president when he makes these decisions.[85] We decided that the best thing
to do—

Alsop: Nobody . . . nobody . . . nobody—

Johnson: —is to counterattack. Number one, to put a FBI in full force;
number two, to put the state [of Texas] in full force. Now—

Alsop: Nobody, Mr. President . . . nobody lobbied *me.* I lay awake all night—

Johnson: [I'm] not talking about you! They lobbied *me last night!*

Alsop: Did they?

Johnson: *[still exasperated, and speaking quickly]* Yeah, I spent the day on it.
I had to leave *Mrs. Kennedy's* side at the White House, and call and ask the
Secret Service and FBI to proceed immediately. I spent most of my day on

---

83. Johnson is referring to *Meredith v. Fair,* a case decided by the U.S. Court of Appeals for
the Fifth Circuit on June 25, 1962. The appeals court ordered the University of Mississippi to admit
James Meredith, a Negro, as a student, and the U.S. Supreme Court refused to hear the case on
appeal.

84. Will Clayton was an assistant secretary of state during the Truman administration, as
Alsop knows. Johnson is equating a Texas Court of Inquiry with the Roberts Commission that
investigated the Pearl Harbor attack.

85. Johnson is again referring to Katzenbach.

this thing yesterday. I had the attorney general from Texas fly in here. I spent an hour and a half with him late yesterday evening.[86] I talked to the Justice Department lawyers and to the FBI. The FBI is of the opinion that the *wisest, quickest, ablest, most effective* way to go about it is for them to thoroughly study it and bring in a written report to the attorney general at the—

Alsop: Yes, Mr. President.

Johnson: —earliest possible date, which they've been working on since 12:30 [p.m.] yesterday . . . [that's] number one. And they have information that's available to *no one,* that has not been presented thus far and so forth. Number two: to parallel that, we're having a blue-ribbon Court of Inquiry—

Alsop: In Texas.

Johnson: In Texas . . . where this thing *occurred.*

Alsop: *[evenly, trying to calm Johnson down]* Mr. President, just let me give you my political judgment on the thing. I think you've done *everything* that can properly be done.

Johnson: We just don't want to be in a position—I'll make this one statement and then I'm through . . . I want to hear you—we don't want to be in a position of saying that we have come into a state—other than the FBI, that they pretty well accept—with some outsiders, and have told them that their integrity is no good and that we're going to have some carpetbag *trials.* We can't haul off people from New York and try 'em in Jackson, Mississippi, and we can't haul off people from Dallas and try 'em in New York!

Alsop: I see that, Mr. President, but let me—

Johnson: *[calming down]* [It'd be a violation of] their constitutional right[s]. Go ahead now.

Alsop: Just let me make one suggestion, because I think this covers, I think . . . I think this *bridges* the gap which I believe, and Dean Acheson believes, still exists.

Dean and Bill Moyers are the only people I've talked to about it. And [Alfred] Friendly is going to come out tomorrow morning with a big thing about a blue-ribbon commission which he thought of independently. It isn't Justice Department lawyers who are carrying on this. It's just things happened to . . . [were] thought of [by] a lot people, and you've thought of more of the details than anyone else.

Johnson: *Justice—*

Alsop: *And I'm sure you're right,* except there's one missing piece.

I suggest that you announce, that as you do not want the attorney general to have the *painful* responsibility of reporting on his *own* brother's

86. The president is exaggerating to make a point with Alsop, and several statements here stretch the truth. Waggoner Carr, for example, flew to Washington as an official member of the Texas delegation to President Kennedy's funeral, not for the purpose of meeting Johnson.

assassination, that you have authorized three jurists—and I would suggest a Texas jurist and *two* non-Texas jurists—to review *all* the evidence [collected] by the FBI and produce a report to the nation for the *nation* . . . and *after* the investigation is completed . . . so that the country will have the story judicially reviewed *outside* Texas. And if you tell Bill Moyers to call up Friendly, and if you get out such an announcement this afternoon, you're going to make a *marvelous*—well, you've already made a marvelous start, you haven't put a damned foot *one-quarter* of an inch wrong. And I've never seen anything like it. You've been *simply marvelous* in the most *painful* circumstances. But I *do* feel that there is *that* much of a gap. And I'm sure that if Moyers calls Friendly, you'll have *terrific* support from the *Washington Post,* and from the whole of the rest of the press *instantly.*

Johnson: I'll ruin both procedures we've got, though.

Alsop: No, you won't. No, you won't. Just *use* the procedures you've got, and add to those procedures a statement saying that, when the FBI has completed its work, as you do not wish to inflict on the attorney general the painful task of reviewing the evidence concerning his *own* brother's assassination, you have asked two or three—I would include the best judge on the Texas bench—American jurists beyond [reproach] . . . or individuals—Dean Acheson, for example—two or three individuals beyond any possible suspicion as to their independence and impartiality, to draw up a written report giving to the public everything of the FBI evidence that is relevant. And then you will have this written report which is *not* Texas . . . which tells the whole story, which is based on the FBI evidence, which doesn't need to use the things that the FBI says can't be used . . . and yet will carry *absolute* conviction . . . and will just be that little *extra* added to the *admirable* machinery you've already got, that will carry complete conviction.

Johnson: *[no longer agitated]* My lawyers, Joe, tell me that the White House *must* not—the president *must* not—inject himself into, ah . . . local killings.[87]

Alsop: I agree with that. But in this case it does happen to be the killing of the president—

Johnson: *Right.*

Alsop: —and the thing is, I'm not suggesting—mind you, Mr. President . . . I'm not talking about an *investigative* body. I'm talking about a body which will take *all* the evidence that the FBI has amassed, when they have completed their inquiry, and produce a public report on the death of the president.

Johnson: That's right. Well, I—

Alsop: *That,* I think, you see . . . that is *not* an interference in Texas.

---

87. By "my lawyers," Johnson is referring to Abe Fortas.

Johnson: No, but it's—

Alsop: That is—wait a second now—that is a *way* to transmit to the public, without breach of confidence, and in a way that will carry absolute conviction, what the FBI has turned up.

Johnson: Why can't the FBI transmit it?

Alsop: Because no one—again, on the left, they won't believe the FBI . . . and the FBI doesn't *write* very well.

Johnson: They'd believe Nick Katzenbach?

Alsop: Well, I just wouldn't put it on Bobby and Nick Katzenbach. I'd have it outside. I think it's *unfair* to put it on Bobby. It's his own brother's death.

Johnson: *[irritated by Alsop's suggestion that he's being insensitive]* We're not going to push it on Bobby. We got—we put this on the finest jurists in the land, [including Jaworski,] the former head of the American Bar Association. That's number one that we're puttin' it on. *[garbled]*

Alsop: I'm not suggesting that you appoint an additional investigating commission. I'm just suggesting that if you want to carry *absolute* conviction, this very small addition to the *admirable* machinery that you've already set up will help you, and I believe that it will strike the imagination of the country and be a very useful, happy thing. Ask—if you have *two* seconds this afternoon, for example—ask Dean Acheson.

Johnson: Be glad to. I'll be—

Alsop: He's the man to ask. I see all the arguments you make, and you're dead right and my conception was *completely* wrong. But I *do* think that that *additional* feature is needed.

Johnson: I've talked to—I guess, after midnight last night, with the—

Alsop: Well, I *know* how you must have been concerned.

Johnson: —*ablest* . . . the *truest* civil liberties lawyer in this town in my judgment . . . the man that's made the *best* arguments before the Supreme Court.[88] And it was his judgment the *worst* mistake we could make was gettin' trapped!

Alsop: Well . . . and I now see exactly how right you are, and how wrong I was about this idea of a blue-ribbon commission.

Johnson: Now you see, Katzenbach suggested that. And that provoked . . . the lawyers that [were] counselin' me just hit the ceiling, [they] said, My God almighty—

Alsop: I see that you're right and that he was wrong. What I do—

Johnson: Then I called back to Katzenbach, and I thought he accepted [my decision].

88. This is another reference to Fortas, who had argued *Gideon v. Wainwright* before the Supreme Court in 1963. The decision in that famous constitutional case guaranteed indigent defendants the right to legal counsel, and Fortas's brief and oral argument were regarded as models of legal craftsmanship.

Alsop: Well, I don't know anything about Katzenbach because I haven't talked to him for three weeks. But—

Johnson: Well, you see, this is—

Alsop: —what I am suggesting is *not at all* what Katzenbach suggested. I'm suggesting *simply* a device—

Johnson: Let me talk to Acheson and—

Alsop: —for summing up the result of the FBI inquiry in a way that will be completely coherent, detailed, and will carry unchallengeable conviction. And this carrying conviction is just as important as carrying on the investigation in the right way. And I worry about this *Post* editorial . . . I'd like you to get *ahead* of them.

Johnson: Well, I worry about the *Post,* period. *[laughs]*

Alsop: Well, I do *too.* But I'd like you to get *ahead* of them. And if you make this decision, and have Moyers call Friendly or [publisher] Kay [Graham], instead of being . . . well, you know, this is what ought to be done and then what you do being denounced as inadequate—they'll be flattered, and will do you a tremendous piece, and I'm *sure* . . . that you will have the *strongest* possible support. It'll be thought that *everything* has been done that needs doing. But I *do* think . . . my own judgment is that there *is* that little missing piece. And Dean may disagree, and you talk to him.

Johnson: I'll talk to him, and—

Alsop: And I *hate* to interfere, sir. I only dare to do so because I care *so* much about you.

Johnson: [I] know that, Joe.

Alsop: And I have the *deepest* faith in you, and I think . . . you've been right and I've been wrong, as to the general conception.

Johnson: [It's] not a question—it's not *really* my thinkin'. I'm not enough experienced—

Alsop: What I'm really, *honestly* giving you is public relations advice and not legal advice.

Johnson: Well, I'm not grounded . . . I don't have the depth in the civil liberties picture that some of the folks that have worked on this with me [have]. I had a lawyer [who] left my house last night after midnight, and spent, I guess, three or four hours going over this thing from A to Z . . . who—after the attorney general was called in here yesterday afternoon, after the FBI was put on it, after we told [the] Secret Service to make available everything *they* had . . . and *we* thought that this was the best way to handle it.

Alsop: Well, I think your—

Johnson: And I thought we had [all] agreed. Now I—

Alsop: Mr. President, I *repeat* . . . I must not keep you because you'll be late getting into your trousers. But I *repeat.* I think your decisions have been 200 percent right, and I was *wrong.* But from a public relations standpoint . . . from the standpoint of *carrying* conviction, there *is* that missing piece which is *easy* to supply *without* infringing upon Texas feelings or sovereignty.

Johnson: All right. Thank you, my friend.

Alsop: Thank you, sir.

Right after he hangs up the telephone, Johnson contacts Abe Fortas to tell him about the conversations with Hoover and Alsop, and presumably, efforts to get the *Washington Post* editorial dropped. The conversation with Fortas is not recorded, but it appears that Fortas enlists in the attempt too, by promising to talk directly to the *Post*'s editors, or Kay Graham if need be. The president doesn't consider the *Post* editorial to be anything but a "deliberate plant" by Justice Department lawyers opposed to his decision.[89]

November 26

Tuesday

President Johnson's decision on the investigation of the assassination is still afloat but listing badly. In the morning a *Post* editorial appears, despite the combined efforts of Johnson, J. Edgar Hoover, and Abe Fortas. It isn't as adverse as it might be, because it doesn't specifically call for a presidential panel. The president credits Fortas's intervention for having "killed" that specific recommendation.[90] Instead, the *Post* only emphasizes the need for an approach that will satisfy both national and international concerns, and leaves the specifics up to the White House. It also calls for the federal government to "prosecute this inquiry by means that assure the most objective, the most thorough and the most speedy analysis and canvass of every scrap of relevant information."[91] This editorial position coincides with the suggestion Katzenbach has made to *Post* editor Russell Wiggins, namely that the *Post* not be precise as to how the federal government might investigate the assassination. Presumably, Katzenbach thought a specific suggestion would lead Johnson to believe the Justice Department was using the *Post* to lobby him; Katzenbach didn't realize that Johnson

89. John McCone, memorandum for the record, 26 November 1963, CIA Box 1/14, JFK, NARA.

90. The president tells McCone that he "personally intervened," but there is no record of the calls, and given Johnson's schedule, it is likely that Fortas made the telephone calls. Ibid.

91. "Full Inquiry," *Washington Post,* 26 November 1963.

already suspects as much. Advocacy also creeps into the *Post*'s news coverage of the issue. "In cases where [a] domestic event touches high government policy or top officials," says a story by Chalmers Roberts, the newspaper's top diplomatic correspondent, "most Western nations set up a special inquiry of some sort to obtain and publish the facts and kill the rumors."[92]

Adding to the president's difficulties, Oswald's visits to the Soviet and Cuban missions in Mexico City have ceased being a secret. The day before, *Excelsior,* a Mexican newspaper with excellent contacts inside the government, became the first to publish specific details about Oswald's trip.[93] The *New York Times* correspondent in Mexico City promptly confirmed the story with Interior Ministry officials, and the revelation is a major story in today's *Times.* There is also the pregnant suggestion, in the *Times* story, that Oswald's movements in Mexico City were reportedly tracked "by an unidentified United States agency."[94] To CIA officials, concerned about protecting intelligence sources and methods, this reference comes uncomfortably close to the truth.

Another adverse, albeit predictable, development is that by Tuesday, Congress seems to be stirring itself into action. The White House released a statement early Monday evening reiterating that the Justice Department and FBI would conduct a "prompt and thorough investigation of all the circumstances surrounding the brutal assassination of President Kennedy and the murder of his alleged assassin," and that "all the facts would be made public."[95] But that affirmation is not proving to be a deterrent to congressional kibitzing. Although some members, most prominently Louisiana representative Hale Boggs, have suggested a single bipartisan "blue-ribbon" congressional inquiry, there are rumors that more than one standing committee is anxious to start its own investigation.[96] The Senate Judiciary Committee is a natural venue, given that legislation will soon be introduced to make assassination of a president a federal crime. That means the House Judiciary Committee will probably get into the act

92. Chalmers Roberts, "U.S. Inquiry Is Ordered by Johnson," *Washington Post,* 26 November 1963.

93. "El Presunto Asesino de Kennedy Solicitó Visas Aquí Para ir a Moscú vía La Habana" (Presumed Assassin of Kennedy Sought Visas Here to Go to Moscow via Havana), *Excelsior,* 25 November 1963.

94. Paul Kennedy, "Oswald Visited Mexico Seeking Visas," *New York Times,* 26 November 1963.

95. "White House Statement Concerning Investigation of the Assassination of President Kennedy," 25 November 1963, *Public Papers of the Presidents of the United States, Lyndon B. Johnson* (Washington, D.C.: U.S. Government Printing Office, 1965), 4; Roberts, "U.S. Inquiry Is Ordered by Johnson." Interestingly, an early draft of this statement sought to characterize Jack Ruby's action as the act of a "private individual . . . [who] has taken the law into his own hands and thwarted the orderly processes of justice." But the version issued makes no attempt to define Ruby's act. "Memorandum, 25 November 1963," Appointment File, 25 November 1963, Box 1, Diary Back-up, LBJL.

96. Roberts, "U.S. Inquiry Is Ordered by Johnson."

too. And the House Committee on Un-American Activities is all but certain to enter the fray, on the basis of Oswald's links to such groups as the Fair Play for Cuba Committee and the U.S. Communist Party. The specter of competing congressional investigations is looming, with each committee trying to outdo the other.[97]

Even more worrisome are the press reports about the news conference held by Waggoner Carr to announce the Court of Inquiry on Monday afternoon. "All the venom against Texas" came pouring down on Carr while he steadfastly denied having coordinated anything with the White House.[98] At first Carr refused to take any queries; then he cut off reporters after being pummeled with such questions as whether the state of Texas, as one reporter asked, "has a sense of guilt."[99] Even in Texas itself, editorial comment is not very positive because Courts of Inquiry have a poor reputation. Often they are thinly disguised political vendettas, when not freewheeling fishing expeditions. There is a widespread belief that Carr is jumping into the fray in order to gain statewide publicity for himself, his political ambitions being no secret. Carr is aching to tell the press that he is convening the Court of Inquiry at the request of the White House, but Johnson does not want to create the impression of orchestrating the Texas investigation. In fact, the coordination between Abe Fortas and Carr could not be closer.

Save for a 10:30 a.m. briefing with John McCone, President Johnson's entire day—his first in the Oval Office—is taken up with meeting the dozens of foreign dignitaries who came to Washington to attend the state funeral. During the twenty-minute conversation with McCone, Johnson speaks contemptuously of the Justice Department's effort to overturn his decision and asks McCone to make sure that all the CIA's resources are at the disposal of the FBI. McCone replies that they are.

From John McCone to J. Edgar Hoover / 11:20 a.m.[100]

Minutes after arriving at CIA headquarters, McCone endeavors to make sure that his affirmative response to the president is accurate. He calls the FBI director, and they discuss coordination of their intelligence-gathering assets, especially in Mexico City. The two agencies are often at odds at the working level, although Sam Papich, the bureau's official liaison to the CIA, is highly

---

97. Miriam Ottenberg, "U.S. and Texas Push Probes," *Washington Star,* 26 November 1963.

98. Manchester, *Death,* 568.

99. Ibid.; Roberts, "U.S. Inquiry Is Ordered by Johnson."

100. This conversation is not part of the Johnson presidential tapes, and there is no recording. It is taken from a transcript apparently prepared by McCone's secretarial staff. DCI and J. Edgar Hoover, conversation, CIA 8/14, JFK, NARA.

regarded by everyone within the agency. But Hoover has never quite forgiven the CIA for supplanting the FBI in Latin America in 1947, and he is often prickly and difficult. In this instance, the agency is just as happy to have the bureau take the lead—that is, so long as the information it provides the FBI is kept absolutely secret. The CIA's counterintelligence efforts in Mexico City are tolerated (and sometimes supported) by Mexico's intelligence and internal security services. If that cooperation ever became open knowledge in Mexico, where every government pretends to disdain Washington's cold war practices, the public there would be scandalized.

McCone: I just want to be sure that you are satisfied that this agency is giving you all the help that we possibly can in connection with your investigation of the situation in Dallas. I know the importance the president places on this investigation you are making. He asked me personally whether CIA was giving you full support. I said that they were, but I just wanted to be sure from you that you felt so.

Hoover: We have had the very best support that we could possibly expect from you.

McCone: Good. Well, you can call on us for anything we have.

Hoover: We will feel free to do that.

McCone: I think it is an exceedingly important investigation and report, and I am delighted that the president has called on you to make it.

Hoover: We are trying to do it as fast as we can so we can dispel various wild rumors that have been circulating as to whether this man [Oswald] was the right man, etc., that fired the gun. But there is no question that he is the right man. There are a lot of aspects that we have dug up, for instance, with regards to the matter [of Oswald's visit] in Mexico City. We have now found that the photograph that was taken was not that of Oswald.[101] We do find from our informant down there that Oswald did call at the [Soviet] embassy that day, and the informant has given us the conversation that he had. He wanted to get a permit to go back to Russia, and the Cuban embassy couldn't give him the permit. The Soviet embassy stated that it would take three weeks. [Oswald] had, I think, a visitor's permit for about a week or ten days, so that is why he came back to the United States.

McCone: Well, all of that ties in importantly into the story, and we have those operational sources down there.[102] We want to handle them very carefully.

101. During his November 23 conversation with the president, Hoover erroneously said that the photograph was not of Oswald but of a man "using Oswald's name." Belatedly, he now understands there is no connection between the photograph and Oswald.

102. McCone is referring to intelligence sources and methods such as telephone taps, photo surveillance, and human agents.

It involves some very high-level people down there. Sam Papich and I have talked about that a couple of times.

Hoover: Mr. Katzenbach, who is handling it for the [Justice] Department—it is our intention when the bureau finishes the report, he will, of course, go over it very carefully because it will be a report that will be released to the public, probably through the White House. But it is the intention, after it is in final form, to [have it] be checked with each of the government agencies that are mentioned in it. [The] State Department is involved in regard to the issuing of the passport to [Oswald] to come back to this country, and that has got to be explained . . . why it was done, the law requires it, etc., all of which, of course, we are gathering. The aspects of the Mexico City thing . . . it [Oswald's visit] will have to be mentioned. It is his [Katzenbach's] intention to check with the agencies, Secret Service, etc., to be sure that whatever is said in the report is conferred in and it is agreed to by the various agencies mentioned. So you will have that opportunity to go over it and see exactly what is said, and I know he will welcome any suggestion that you care to make.

McCone: Well, that will be fine. Thank you.

Hoover: Good-bye.

What the *Washington Post* could not do—namely, change Johnson's mind—Senator Richard Russell begins to accomplish during a long lunch with the president. There is no one in Washington whom Johnson respects more, and owes more to, than the senior senator from Georgia. Russell schooled Johnson in the ways of the Senate when he arrived in 1949; nominated him to be majority leader in 1953; and provided politically adroit advice over the next seven years that played no small role in making Johnson one of the most powerful leaders the Senate had ever seen.[103]

Even that relationship does not fully describe the depth of their political alliance. A political prodigy, Russell had always accomplished what he set out to do—until 1952. Because Russell's position on civil rights anchored him to the South's past, he was rejected the one time he ran for the presidential nomination even though in most estimates he was the best candidate. That bitter experience was a watershed in Russell's life, and he would never seek national office again.[104] But in Johnson he sees a surrogate who shares and can achieve his thwarted ambition: to be the first politician from a state in the old Confederacy to be nominated, and then elected, president. When Russell talks,

103. When Johnson agreed to run for the Senate leadership post, he extracted a promise from Russell: the Georgian had to move his seat in the Senate to the desk directly behind Johnson, so that Russell's advice would be available momentarily. Evans and Novak, *Exercise of Power,* 51.

104. John Goldsmith, *Colleagues: Richard B. Russell and His Apprentice, Lyndon B. Johnson* (Macon, Ga.: Mercer University Press, 1998), 30.

Johnson not only hangs on every word but takes the austere, patrician senator's shrewd counsel to heart.

Their seventy-five-minute private lunch on Tuesday is the first opportunity both men have had to sit down at leisure and talk about Johnson's sudden accession to the presidency. Although there is no record of their discussion, educated speculation suggests the two friends broach a wide range of perennial and pressing issues.

Undoubtedly, they speak about not only the power that is now Johnson's to wield, but of making sure that Johnson is elected in his own right in 1964, thereby eliminating one of the last political vestiges of America's Civil War. Johnson freely discusses all the problems he is encountering with respect to investigating Kennedy's assassination, for there is no need for the president to be discreet. Russell, as a member of a tiny Senate subcommittee that oversees CIA activities, is familiar with even the most sensitive counterintelligence operations in Mexico City. To Johnson's surprise, apparently, the Georgian does not dismiss the idea of a presidential commission out of hand. Johnson thought Russell was going to agree that sending "carpetbaggers" from Washington violated Texas's sovereign right to investigate the Dallas murders as it sees fit. But for Russell, the geopolitical struggle with the Soviet Union trumps the ideology of states' rights. He has worked assiduously to build up U.S. intelligence capabilities, protecting them vigorously against all kinds of curious and meddlesome senators. The idea that a Texas Court of Inquiry might possibly be a venue for investigating any aspect of Oswald's trip to Mexico City—thereby posing a threat to CIA sources and methods—is appalling to Russell. He would much rather see the matter confined to one investigative body that is fully cognizant of the stakes involved.

Johnson begins to reconsider: perhaps the Rostow/Katzenbach idea isn't such a bad solution after all. His rethinking accelerates after he hears the news late Tuesday night that the Senate Judiciary Committee has announced that it will make a full investigation of the assassination as it considers a bill to make the killing of a president a federal crime. The prospect of a full-blown investigation headed by Mississippi senator James Eastland (D) is unappetizing to the president, to say the least. Eastland is a stern foe of Communists, which is fine by Johnson. But Eastland sees them everywhere.

November 27

Wednesday

The day is dominated by Johnson's address before a joint session of Congress, scheduled for 12:30 p.m. The first impression Johnson makes is bound to be lasting, and although the president has been in the public eye visually, he has been figuratively speechless since arriving at Andrews AFB Friday night. Those who know Johnson best have their fingers crossed, because oratory has never been considered his strong suit as a politician, notwithstanding his acclaimed May 1963 speech at Gettysburg. He has a tendency to shout rather than speak, while flailing his arms aimlessly. When he is too conscious of controlling himself, though, he often appears stilted and ill at ease. Will Johnson reflect the mood of the nation, while giving the public the sense that his shoulders are broad enough to bear the "full tonnage" of the presidency?[105]

The twenty-seven-minute address is an unmitigated success. The first line, written by Kennedy speechwriter Ted Sorensen, strikes just the right note. "All I have ever possessed I would have gladly given *not* to be here today," begins Johnson, and the speech takes off from there. Perhaps it is the familiarity of the surroundings; after all, Capitol Hill was his home for thirty-two years, as he notes in his address. Or maybe it is the serenity of having achieved his lifelong ambition. Probably it is a mixture of both. Even friends and advisers who wish Johnson nothing but the best are genuinely bowled over by his performance. It is a desperately needed tonic for a nation shaken to its core by the events of the past five days.

Interestingly, the line that receives the loudest and longest applause is the one in which Johnson calls for "an end to the teaching and the preaching of hate and evil and violence."[106] Every politician watching knew in advance that Johnson would try to wrap himself in the Kennedy mantle, at least until he can win the presidency in his own right. But this phrase portends that the president will use the assassination, whenever possible, as a political cudgel against the right even though Lee Harvey Oswald was a self-described leftist. If Johnson has his say, the 1964 election will amount to a referendum on whether a right-winger can be trusted with the presidency—that is, if Barry Goldwater is the GOP nominee.

105. Manchester, *Death,* 612.
106. *Public Papers of Lyndon Johnson,* 10.

To Nellie Connally / 1:35 p.m.

After the address to Congress, the first telephone call Johnson makes upon arriving back at the Oval Office is to Nellie Connally. The Johnsons, especially Lady Bird, still regret having to leave the Connallys' side after the governor was so seriously wounded.[107] If John Connally had not looked back over his right shoulder after hearing the first shot, to see if the president was hurt, he probably would have been shot through the heart. By turning, he saved himself in all likelihood.[108]

The Johnsons thought that one way to counter the antipathy toward Dallas, if not everything Texas, was for Nellie to have attended President Kennedy's funeral. Her presence, sure to be noticed by the television cameras, would have reminded everyone that a Texan had been wounded in the motorcade too. But the thought of leaving her husband's side so soon after his near death was unacceptable. Save for her husband's heroic service in the navy during World War II, the Connallys have been inseparable since Nellie Connally, née Idanell Brill, was the Texas University Sweetheart in 1938, the same year John Connally was president of the Students Association. In her stead went seventeen-year-old John Connally III. His presence didn't provide the same effect, as he looked like just another serious, albeit young, Secret Service agent guarding the president.

The telephone conversation with Nellie Connally, touching though it is, would be unremarkable except for one aspect. It provides a rare clue as to the Connallys' feelings about being treated as an afterthought. During the interminable ride from Dealey Plaza to Parkland, Nellie knew the president was already dead, as did Mrs. Kennedy and Clint Hill, the Secret Service agent who had leapt aboard the limousine. Nellie "had seen the gore."[109] No one could possibly be alive after that. And given the copious amount of blood spilling from her unconscious husband, Mrs. Connally was certain for a moment she was a widow too. Her husband's face was turning a yellowish-gray. Then the governor's hand trembled a little.

When the limousine arrived at Parkland, Secret Service agents instantly converged on the car, crying "Mr. President!" and begging Mrs. Kennedy to let go of her husband, whom she was cradling in her arms, while moaning softly. *"Mrs. Kennedy, you've got to get out!"* She would not, consumed by the thought that she could not let anyone see her husband's exposed brain. The longer Mrs. Kennedy refused to budge, the more Nellie Connally became agitated, even resentful of all the attention focused on a man she knew to be dead. How long would she have to wait before she could insist that someone tend to her beloved

107. Connally, *From Love Field,* 38.
108. "Turn May Have Saved Connally," 23 November 1963, *Houston Post.*
109. Manchester, *Death,* 163, 170; Connally, *From Love Field,* 146.

dying husband? Every agonizing second that passed because of Jacqueline Kennedy's obstinate desire for privacy and protection from prying eyes was from Nellie's perspective, reducing the odds that her husband might still live.[110]

Believing that no one could reach the president until the jump seats were cleared, Connally, now conscious, tried to lift himself up. His selflessness despite his injury caused something inside Nellie Connally to snap. To her, the situation was obvious. The president was dead and there was no use fussing over *him;* meanwhile, her husband was near death, and no one seemed to be doing anything about it. As William Manchester would later write, "They were just letting the governor of Texas lie there, leaving him to bleed while they poked and fooled around, *and it was outrageous.*"[111]

Minutes later, as physicians labored over the president and the governor in opposing trauma rooms, Nellie Connally was still fixated by the thought that her husband was being shortchanged. She wondered if "adequate and good doctors" were tending John, or if all the "A-list doctors" were across the hall, trying to resurrect a dead man.[112] Nellie's bitterness was unabated even as she and Jacqueline Kennedy stood just a few feet apart, each awaiting news about her husband. Rather than be drawn together and seek mutual comfort, they stood silently. Finally, the First Lady spoke, even though the proper protocol probably called for Mrs. Connally to console Mrs. Kennedy. The First Lady gently inquired about the governor. After a few awkward moments, Mrs. Connally abruptly replied, "He'll be all right," and allegedly said nothing else in return.[113]

The response of the Connallys to having the governor gravely, almost mortally, wounded and simultaneously being treated as an incidental casualty will have profound repercussions in the months and years to come. For psychological reasons, the Connallys, suffering as they are from post-traumatic stress, will demand to be recognized as victims too.[114] For the moment, though, this phenomenon is reflected only in passing. When Mrs. Johnson observes that she finally got a glimpse of Mrs. Connally on television amidst the wall-to-wall Kennedy coverage, the governor's wife makes a revealing comment, calling it a "pittance." The assassination of a president and the ascension of a new president

110. In her private account of the assassination, written on December 4, 1963, Mrs. Connally writes that Secret Service agents "were crawling all around us, but no one was taking John [Connally] out of the car. I knew he was alive and, in my heart, I knew the president was dead. I wondered how long I must wait before I could insist that someone tend to my dying husband." Connally, *From Love Field,* 147.

111. Manchester, *Death,* 170. The emphasis is added.

112. Connally, *From Love Field,* 14–15, 50, 149, 153. Within a few days, however, Mrs. Connally would realize the governor had "the very best doctors to be had anywhere."

113. Manchester, *Death,* 180.

114. Another manifestation of this is Mrs. Connally's statement in her private diary that following the assassination, "For the first time in my life, I was afraid for my family!" While understandable, there never was anything close to a threat posed to the Connallys. Connally, *From Love Field,* 52–53, 114, 154.

leaves "little air time" for news of her gravely wounded husband, Nellie Connally will note in her personal diary. And what news there is, is often incorrect, thus embittering her even more.[115]

Johnson: [I was] so proud of your boy when he was up here, and I'm sittin' here in my office with Lady Bird, and Luci, and Lynda, and we wanted to find out how our boy [the governor] was gettin' along.

Mrs. Connally: Well, wait a minute . . . I know this is irreverent—to tell the president to *hush*—but I want to tell you, I have *never* been prouder of *anybody* than I was of you a while ago. . . . Can you hear me?

Johnson: I sure can, and I've always been mighty proud of you, darlin', and I appreciate it. I'd rather hear that from you than nearly anybody.

Mrs. Connally: And I [was] just tryin' to decide whether to try to get in touch with you or not, but I . . . Lyndon, you just made me feel so wonderful.[116]

Johnson: Well, you're a wonderful girl. How's my boy?

Mrs. Connally: He's doin' real well.

Johnson: Is he in much pain?

Mrs. Connally: Considerable, but not *too* much. He's doin' real good. He's not talkin' on the phone yet or anything, 'cause as soon as he is, he'll talk to you.

Johnson: Here's three little chubblies [who] want to say a word to you.[117]

Mrs. Connally: All right. Well, don't you forget how proud we all were of you today.

Johnson: Give him a hug for me, and tell him I'll call you every day or so. I want to keep up with him.

Mrs. Connally: Well, you tend to your big business and we want to help, whenever we can.

Johnson: You woulda been proud of little Johnny. He's a chip off the old block, and the little blonde block too. He had all the grace and charm of Nellie, and all the wisdom of John, and the . . . poise. He made the nicest statement to Mrs. Kennedy that any seventeen-year-old could have.

Mrs. Connally: Oh, that makes me feel wonderful. You were wonderful to tend to him.

Johnson: Well, he didn't need any tending to. He can be on his own, honey. You can turn him out to pasture.

Mrs. Connally: Okay, I'll send him to *you.*

Johnson: Here's Lady Bird.

Mrs. Johnson: Nellie, I *finally* got to see you on television.

---

115. Ibid., 15, 150.

116. Reflecting the emotion of the moment. Nellie Connally almost never called Johnson by his first name. Ibid., 35.

117. Johnson is referring to Mrs. Johnson and his two daughters.

Mrs. Connally: Ohhh . . . well, that was a pitiful little pittance, wasn't it?

Mrs. Johnson: We ran a clip back again, and oh, I was so *glad* I got to see you.[118] And you looked beautiful and so feminine, and you looked so . . . distraught and full of compassion for everybody that was hurt. Well, you just couldn't have been better.

Mrs. Connally: I just finished listenin' to Lyndon. And I just *couldn't* have been prouder of him. I know you are.

Mrs. Johnson: Yes, ma'am. I sure am. And thank you.

Mrs. Connally: [He] was really wonderful, wonderful. I know you're havin' hard times yourself right now.

[The Johnsons' daughters come to the telephone and exchange greetings with Mrs. Connally before the conversation ends.]

After Johnson takes a long series of congratulatory telephone calls, Jacqueline Kennedy comes over to the business end of the White House at 2:50 p.m. Her first visit to the new chief executive occupying the Oval Office will also be her last, though neither Mrs. Kennedy nor President Johnson foresee this. The former First Lady is on the cusp of an emotional sea change. Until today she has been "giving more than she receives," guiding conversations without succumbing to wrenching emotion, her quiet composure a revelation to everyone who thought they knew Jackie.[119] But with the long weekend over, she is suddenly seized by an irrational thought.

To a hardened politician like Johnson, who realizes the name Kennedy is now magic, it comes as something of a surprise to learn that the president's widow is preoccupied with the fear that her husband will promptly be forgotten. Protected as she is from the public, Mrs. Kennedy is blissfully unaware of the "state of love" that now exists between her and the American people. She asks Johnson for two favors in the hope that they will extend the public's memory. One request is to change the geographical name of the space launch site in Florida from Cape Canaveral to "Cape Kennedy." The other favor is to affirm that JFK's commitment to the renovation of Washington, D.C., will not be sidelined. President Johnson cannot act fast enough in granting her wishes. The next day he will declare that the Florida landmark "shall be known hereafter as Cape Kennedy," and on November 30 Johnson will issue a special statement reiterating President Kennedy's promise to make Washington a world-class capital.[120]

118. Mrs. Johnson is probably referring to a clip from the news conference Mrs. Connally held on Sunday at Parkland.

119. Maxine Cheshire, "Mrs. Kennedy Begins Complex Ordeal of Moving," *Washington Post,* 24 November 1963.

120. Changing the name to Cape Kennedy does not sit well with Florida residents from the outset. The geographical area, one of the oldest named landmarks on America's Atlantic coast, has been known as Cape Canaveral for 450 years, since the days of the Spanish exploration. In 1973, just before the tenth anniversary of the assassination and after years of controversy, the name will

Just after 4 p.m. Robert Kennedy comes by the Oval Office for his first private meeting with the president. The encounter occurs at the instigation of Peace Corps director Sargent Shriver who, as RFK's brother-in-law, is privy to Kennedy's most recent complaints about Johnson.[121] Shriver brokered the meeting with help from his now former deputy, Bill Moyers, and based on Shriver's information, Moyers prepared a memo for the president on the "points of misunderstanding" that have arisen between the attorney general and the five-day-old Johnson administration. The first three points concern the swearing-in, the delay in leaving Dallas, and Johnson's abortive effort to use the Oval Office on Saturday.[122]

Johnson goes right down the list with Kennedy, trying to explain each misunderstanding in turn. The president says that Dean Rusk and Robert McNamara, among others, urged him to move into the Oval Office without delay to demonstrate the continuity of government, which is true. Regarding the swearing-in, Johnson insists that *Air Force One* took off "as soon as Jackie got there," which is not quite accurate. The flight was delayed about fifteen minutes. "People around you are saying things about me," Johnson observes. "I won't let people around me say anything about your people, and don't let any of your people say anything about me."[123] Kennedy is not in the same conciliatory mood, though he does not dare bring up one of the things grating on him most: the leak to the *Houston Post*. Indeed, he acts as if he does not want to be there, with an indifference bordering on hostility. The meeting is over after just twelve minutes. The two men will not see each other again privately for almost two months.

In all likelihood, Johnson also uses the occasion to inform Kennedy that he is rethinking his opposition to an independent panel to investigate the assassination. It probably comes as welcome news to the attorney general. Kennedy has tangled repeatedly, and often bitterly, with Senator Eastland on civil rights issues, and RFK would be as anxious as Johnson to derail any investigation by the Judiciary Committee. And there is no time to lose if Eastland is to be headed off. Minority Leader Everett Dirksen, the ranking Republican on the Judiciary Committee, has already indicated that hearings will begin right after the Thanksgiving holiday weekend. Another cause for concern is the fact that Eastland has reportedly assigned all responsibility for the investigation to the Communist-

---

be officially changed back to Canaveral. "Floridians Urge Cape Kennedy Be Renamed Cape Canaveral," *New York Times,* 25 November 1969; Tim O'Brien, "It's Cape Canaveral Again," *Washington Post,* 10 October 1973.

121. Edwin Guthman and Jeffrey Shulman, eds., *Robert Kennedy: In His Own Words* (New York: Bantam, 1988), 406.

122. Memo of conversation, 27 November 1963, 3:30 p.m., Manchester File, Box 1, Special File, LBJL.

123. Manchester, *Death,* 639; Arthur Schlesinger, Jr., *Robert Kennedy and His Times* (Boston: Houghton Mifflin, 1978), 628; Jeff Shesol, *Mutual Contempt: Lyndon Johnson, Robert Kennedy, and the Feud That Defined a Decade* (New York: W. W. Norton, 1997), 122–23.

hunting Internal Security subcommittee and Jay Sourwine, its notorious (at least in liberal circles) chief counsel.[124]

November 28

Thanksgiving Day
Thursday

John McCone's morning briefing of the president is conducted at the president's home (the Johnsons have yet to move into the Executive Mansion) because of the holiday. There are so many items in the PICKL—the President's Intelligence Checklist—that McCone doesn't have enough time to go over the latest developments from Mexico City before Johnson has to leave.[125]

After working feverishly for days, the CIA can report with more specificity on Oswald's contacts with the Cuban and Soviet missions in Mexico City, thanks to routine intercepts of telephone calls. Apparently Oswald was in Mexico from September 26 to October 3 seeking visas to go to Havana first and then supposedly back to the Soviet Union with his wife, Marina. The visas were not granted.

A related development concerns a Mexican national, Sylvia Duran, who works at the Cuban consulate and saw Oswald during his visit. The Mexican government has arrested Duran for questioning, a move that has agitated Cuban authorities. Communications between the Cuban embassy in Mexico City and Havana intercepted by U.S. intelligence do not reveal, however, whether Castro's regime is upset about the arrest itself (Duran has no diplomatic immunity) or is worried about what she knows and might disclose.

The genuinely troubling news from Mexico, however, concerns a Nicaraguan national named Gilberto Alvarado. A former informant for the Nicaraguan intelligence service who posed as a Communist—Mexico City is teeming with dissidents, exiles, and intrigue—Alvarado claims to have been inside the Cuban consulate when Oswald visited, and says he personally saw a Cuban official give Oswald $6,500 in cash on September 18.[126] Alvarado is being held at a CIA safe house in Mexico City, where he is undergoing intensive interrogation in

124. Associated Press, "Senators Launch Full Probe into Kennedy Assassination," *Washington Star,* 27 November 1963; James Clayton, "2 Senate Leaders Urge Assassination Inquiry," *Washington Post,* 28 November 1963.

125. McCone to Bundy, 28 November 1963, Oswald, Box 2, Special File, LBJL.

126. $6,500 is equivalent to $39,600 in 2004 dollars.

collaboration with the FBI. There is considerable doubt about his allegation, because the FBI can prove Oswald was in New Orleans on September 18. Still, Alvarado's information is not being dismissed out of hand. Perhaps he just got the dates mixed up.[127]

If Johnson has any residual doubts about appointing a presidential commission, these latest developments, and others, are enough to erase them. He is now convinced it is the right course, perhaps the only course of action open to him. For one, unless Johnson can consign the investigation to a responsible body, it appears the issue will continue to demand his attention at a time when he is anxious to get the wheels of government, and the presidency, moving forward again. Secretary of State Rusk has also weighed in on the matter and is strongly recommending a superior investigative panel based in Washington because of the foreign policy considerations involved. Finally, as an inveterate reader of the *Congressional Record,* Johnson is alarmed by the real prospect of competing and overlapping investigations. Members of Congress simply cannot resist thrusting themselves into the spotlight.

To James Eastland / 3:21 p.m.

Thanksgiving Day is not ordinarily a day for conducting business, but Johnson is now concentrating on establishing a presidential commission with all the fervor of a belated convert. "The idea of a national commission was first mentioned to me by Eugene Rostow of the Yale Law School," Johnson will write in his 1971 memoir. ". . . Out of the nation's suspicions, out of the nation's need for facts, the Warren Commission was born."[128] He would never let on that he initially—and vehemently—opposed the idea.

Before he begins stocking the commission with members, and because one of his primary purposes is to shut down any and all congressional probes, Johnson wants to make sure that key committee chairmen will bow to his wishes. Eastland is the most critical by far. One of the most conservative members of the Senate, Eastland is a "living symbol of Southern intransigence" on civil rights issues and is relentless in his efforts to identify and root out Communist subversion.[129] He is never happier than when he is able to conjoin these two issues, such as when he suggests the civil rights movement would not exist save for the "procommunist agitators" in its ranks.[130] With an omnipresent cigar in his hand

127. McCone, "Memorandum for the President," 28 November 1963, CIA Box 1/14, JFK, NARA.

128. Lyndon Johnson, *The Vantage Point: Perspectives of the Presidency, 1963–1969* (New York: Holt, Rinehart and Winston, 1971), 26.

129. Bart Barnes, "Former Senator James Eastland of Mississippi Dies," *Washington Post,* 20 February 1986.

130. Ibid.

and a thick Mississippi drawl, Eastland is almost a caricature of the publicity-shy southern senator who nonetheless wields great power behind the scenes.[131]

He is also quite accustomed to conducting investigations that make Republican and Democratic administrations alike squirm in discomfort. To the chagrin especially of the State Department, not even the presence of a Democrat in the White House has put a damper on the Internal Security subcommittee's search for Communists, Communist influence, or "aid and comfort to the Communists" from inside the U.S. government.[132] More to the point, Eastland's Judiciary panel has already announced a full-scale investigation into the assassination, scheduled to begin as early as this coming Monday, or Tuesday at the latest. "No time will be lost," noted Senator Everett Dirksen, the ranking minority member on the Judiciary Committee, when he endorsed the probe.[133] There are rumors that all the hearings will be open to the public and perhaps even televised, and because 1964 is an election year, the temptation to play to the crowd will be worse than normal. The Judiciary Committee has some members up for reelection who are particularly practiced in the art of self-promotion, such as Senator Kenneth Keating (R-New York).[134] If Eastland insists on going ahead, on the grounds that his committee needs to justify making assassination a federal crime, Johnson's desire to contain congressional investigations of the assassination will be thwarted.

Yet Eastland is also still discharging a very large political debt he owes to Lyndon Johnson. Back in 1956, when Eastland was next in line for the chairmanship of the Judiciary Committee, Senate liberals, led by New York's Herbert Lehman (D), were poised to oppose him because of his position on civil rights. Only three times in the Senate's history had seniority been overridden, but liberals felt that strongly about Eastland and showed every indication of going forward. It was only the handiwork of then–majority leader Lyndon Johnson that prevented Eastland from becoming the fourth senator in history to be denied a chairmanship.[135]

Eastland does not like Washington's social life and nearly every weekend retires to his 5,800-acre cotton plantation in tiny Doddsville, Mississippi. That is where he is spending the long Thanksgiving weekend. In the process of contacting Eastland, President Johnson's secretary somehow learns that today is the senator's fifty-ninth birthday and also the birthday of Eastland's wife, Elizabeth. Over the phone Johnson effortlessly switches gears and acts as if he is purposely calling to wish Eastland a happy birthday and other pleasantries of the day.

131. Ibid.

132. "Rusk Again Faces Issue of Security," *New York Times*, 13 October 1963.

133. "Senators Launch Full Probe into Kennedy Assassination," *Washington Star*; Willard Edwards, "Clash Hinted Over Warren Probe Role," *Chicago Tribune*, 3 December 1963.

134. Keating became nationally famous in October 1962 for claiming there were Soviet missiles in Cuba before President Kennedy revealed their presence.

135. James Eastland, Oral History, 19 February 1971, LBJL.

After waiting a decent interval—about fifteen minutes—and in the presence of Dean Rusk and McGeorge Bundy, who have entered the Oval Office, Johnson places another call to Mississippi and gets down to the real business at hand. Johnson, whose "Texas twang" has its roots in the traditional southern dialect, speaks in the most southern-inflected manner he can muster.

Johnson: On this investigation . . . [the Dallas] situation. What's your committee plan to do on it? I didn't ask you that and I intended to—had it in my mind—and I got to talkin' to [Elizabeth] and didn't do it.

Eastland: Well, we plan to hold hearings and just make a record of what the proof is, that's all.

Johnson: Uh-huh.

Eastland: . . . to show that this man [Oswald] was the assassin. To begin with, we've had a great number of senators that have come to us to request it, beginnin' with [Wayne] Morse [D-Oregon] . . . that it be done.

Johnson: Hmm.

Eastland: Now, if you want it dropped, we can drop it.

Johnson: I had this feeling—I don't know, this is very confidential and I haven't proposed it to anybody and I don't know that I would—but we've got a pretty strong states' rights question here, and I've had some hesitancy to just start havin' a bunch of congressional inquiries into violation of a state statute. And it might—

Eastland: Well, you see, we've got a bill in[troduced] to make it [presidential assassination] a federal [crime]—[136]

Johnson: Yeah, I know it. But you haven't got any law, and it might set a precedent that you wouldn't wanna *have*.[137] I talked to some of the fellas about it [the] day before yesterday. [Senator Richard] Russell was down here for lunch, and we—

Eastland: Well now, [he's] one of 'em that's urged it.[138]

Johnson: Now . . . *my* thought would be this, if we could do it. We might get two members from each body . . . you see, we're gonna have three inquiries runnin' as it is.[139]

Eastland: Well, I wouldn't want that. That wouldn't do.

136. Several bills making assault on a president a federal crime, including one by Eastland, were introduced on November 26. James Clayton, "Dozens of Questions Remain Unanswered," *Washington Post,* 27 November 1963.

137. Johnson seems to be hinting that if a particularly heinous racial crime were to occur in Mississippi, Eastland might come to regret holding congressional hearings about violation of a state statute. In effect, Johnson is turning the tables on Eastland, who frequently attributes racial unrest to "outside agitators."

138. Russell has urged introduction of a bill, but his support for Eastland's probe is doubtful.

139. Johnson is presumably referring to the FBI investigation, the Texas Court of Inquiry, and the Dallas trial of Jack Ruby.

Johnson: And . . . if we could have two congressmen, and two senators, and maybe a justice of the Supreme Court [to] take the FBI report and review it, and *write* a report . . . and do anything they felt like needed to be done, I *think* it would. . . . This is [a] very explosive thing and could be [a] very dangerous thing to the country.[140]

Eastland: *Well . . .*

Johnson: And a little publicity could just fan the flames. What would you think about—

Eastland: The whole thing wasn't my idea!

Johnson: What would you think about . . . if we could work it out, of getting somebody from the [Supreme] Court, and somebody from the House, and somebody from the Senate, and have a real high-level, judicial study of all the facts?

Eastland: Well, it would suit me all right. Now you'd have—there's gonna be some opposition on the committee from [Kenneth] Keating, and . . . I think [Everett] Dirksen [would] be all right. I don't know, he's very strong for it. You see—

Johnson: No, well he—

Eastland: —they've all done the *talkin'*. I've—

Johnson: If it's all right with you, I'm not worried about your committee; I know what you can handle.

Eastland: Why . . . we can work it out.

Johnson: You can handle your committee. Okay. Much obliged.

Eastland: Okay.

November 29

Friday

Exactly one week after the assassination, the president meets with his top national security advisers to discuss the latest reports from Mexico City. The interrogation of Sylvia Duran, the Mexican national who works in the Cuban consulate, has not revealed anything beyond what the CIA believes it already knows regarding Oswald's visit there. Meanwhile, the CIA has turned over to

---

140. There has already been one demonstration in front of the White House, though it was tiny. A dozen right-wing marchers picketed on Wednesday, carrying an effigy of Fidel Castro hanging from a gallows alongside signs reading "Invade Cuba Now!" and "Clean Out the Red Cuban Killers." "White House Pickets Carry Castro Effigy," *Washington Star,* 28 November 1963.

Mexican authorities the Nicaraguan informant, Gilberto Alvarado, who is the source of the allegation that Oswald received $6,500 from unidentified Cubans. His story is being treated with increasing skepticism but has not yet been ruled out.[141]

The absence of a dramatic break is less significant than the fact that the issue is taking up an inordinate amount of the president's time. The Oval Office cannot function like a homicide bureau, watching, waiting, and reacting to the latest piece of information gleaned from the field. A mechanism is needed to gather the facts so that the president can act on them, without getting bogged down in the minutiae of day-to-day changes. Consequently, the morning intelligence briefing serves to affirm the decision Johnson has made already: to appoint a presidential commission to determine, insofar as humanly possible, who killed President Kennedy. Almost the entire day after Thanksgiving will be given over to drawing up the requisite documents and selecting men for this task.

The first decision, regarding the commission's size and composition, is reached after consultation with the attorney general's office. Abe Fortas, who will function in effect (though not in name) as the president's White House counsel, contacts Nicholas Katzenbach, who clears this question, in turn, with Robert Kennedy. Because of the need to incorporate members of Congress, Katzenbach's original conception of a three-man panel has been enlarged to seven members: two from the House of Representatives, two from the Senate, two private citizens, and to chair the panel, not a retired Supreme Court justice (as originally proposed) but the sitting chief justice, Earl Warren.[142]

The president will rely on his own judgment to choose the congressional members. But in the course of the day Johnson will make sure Robert Kennedy has had an opportunity to submit suggestions with respect to the civilian appointments. Having become deeply involved in CIA matters during his brother's administration, Robert Kennedy is not unfamiliar with the sensitive sources and methods used in Mexico City and elsewhere, and recognizes the need to keep any investigation into the assassination tightly controlled. Consequently the first man Kennedy recommends is Allen Dulles, the longest-serving director in the CIA's admittedly short history and DCI under President Kennedy until November 1961.[143] While Dulles's management of the agency left much to be desired, his grasp of intelligence operations is unquestioned.

A retired military man (general or admiral) is initially considered for the

141. John McCone, "Late Developments on the Mexico City Investigation of Oswald's Activities," memo, 29 November 1963, CIA Box 1/14, JFK, NARA.

142. Walter Jenkins to Johnson, memo, 29 November 1963, Box 2, Special File, LBJL.

143. According to a Dulles biographer, "there was no evidence that the younger Kennedy played any role in the composition of the commission." Peter Grose, *Gentleman Spy: The Life of Allen Dulles* (Boston: Houghton Mifflin, 1994), 541. But the memo cited in footnote 142 states, "Abe [Fortas] has talked with Katzenbach and Katzenbach has talked with the attorney general.

other slot. But ultimately Robert Kennedy decides to recommend another pillar of the foreign policy establishment, entrusted with countless state secrets of the highest sensitivity during World War II and the cold war. That man is John McCloy, a Wall Street lawyer who originally achieved renown in the 1930s for cracking a case of German sabotage in 1917. More recently, McCloy negotiated the mechanics of the withdrawal of Soviet missiles from Cuba for the Kennedy administration, and the attorney general has come to admire McCloy's balanced judgment and complete discretion. Johnson pledges to get these men to serve if they are available, and the stage is now set.[144]

Johnson's recordings seldom provide such a revealing glimpse into his decision-making. In part, the bird's-eye view stems from the haste with which the commission must be cobbled together. Not only does the president want to get the matter off his desk, but there is a threat of imminent and competing congressional investigations unless the White House acts swiftly. The other mundane circumstance that contributes to unusually candid telephone conversations is the coincidence of the Thanksgiving holiday weekend. So many congressional members are out of town that Johnson has no choice but to construct the commission over the telephone. Indeed, at one point he is so amused about finding so many missing senators in Florida that he jokes about changing the name of Cape Canaveral not to "Cape Kennedy" but to "Cape Senate."[145]

One important aspect of the commission's establishment concerns the scope of the probe. As is clear from Johnson's sales pitch to J. Edgar Hoover, Richard Russell, and others, the commission as initially envisioned is only to review the FBI's imminent report on the assassination. There is no prohibition against mounting a separate investigation—in fact, that is expressly permitted—but no one frankly contemplates that a new inquiry will be necessary. That is why Johnson, in all honesty, will tell reluctant appointees like Senator Russell and Chief Justice Earl Warren that the commission will not be a great imposition on their already overburdened schedules, and in any event, the task will be over within a matter of two, or at most three, months. "All you're gonna do is evaluate a Hoover report that he's already *made*," asserts the president more than once. Through no fault of Johnson's, such will not be the case. The panel, officially named "The President's Commission on the Assassination of President John F. Kennedy," will gather evidence and deliberate for ten arduous months. Chief Justice Warren will come to consider it the single worst year of his life.

They recommend . . ." That Robert Kennedy suggested nominees is also confirmed during a subsequent discussion between Johnson and Abe Fortas. Johnson and Fortas, conversation, 17 December 1966, 10:45 a.m., LBJL.

144. Johnson, *Vantage Point,* 27.

145. The president will make this remark during his 8:25 p.m. conversation with California senator Tom Kuchel, one of the last telephone calls during a long day.

Establishment of the commission is arguably Johnson's first critical decision as chief executive, as important to his presidency as his comportment during his first weeks in office. The recordings from this day fully reveal the president who will slowly become known to the public over the next few years. Here is Johnson the superlative congressional tactician, the shrewd judge of character and ego, the master manipulator of men to a good purpose. The two most important members of the commission will be the hardest to get.

To Mike Mansfield / 11:10 a.m.

After an hour-long meeting with the Joint Chiefs of Staff, and with Secretary of State Rusk at arm's length, the president begins assembling his commission by contacting Mike Mansfield, who is in Florida during the Thanksgiving weekend. Taciturn and self-effacing, Mansfield served as the Senate Democratic whip from 1957 to 1961 before succeeding Johnson as majority leader, so the conversation is between two men who know and understand each other very well—so much so that Mansfield calls the president "Lyndon." Mansfield does not hesitate to lend his full support to a proposal that will take the Senate, as a body, entirely out of the business of investigating the assassination. When Johnson calls Rusk to the phone to chime in about the risks of letting rumors be played out in public, it is a superfluous gesture. Mansfield is already on board. Perhaps Johnson invokes Rusk because the president is still a bit tentative about the true extent of his own newfound power. In any case, Johnson is careful not to tip his hand about who he is considering for appointment to the panel, even though he has one and only one candidate in mind for chairman, Earl Warren. Although he barely knows the chief justice, the president is determined to draft the man who Johnson believes personifies "justice and fairness" to millions of Americans.[146]

[The recording starts abruptly.]
Johnson: . . . several investigations, and it could have some very dangerous implications. Secretary of state's here with me now, and he's quite concerned about it.
Mansfield: Yes, Lyndon.
Johnson: We have given a good deal of thought—at least I have—on the suggestion of [Nicholas] Katzenbach over at [the] Justice [Department] to having a high-level commission . . . try to get someone from the [Supreme] Court, and maybe two or three members from each side, in the House and Senate—

146. Johnson, *Vantage Point,* 26.

Mansfield: Yes.

Johnson: —and let them review the investigation [that's already] bein' made by the [Texas] Court of Inquiry and the thorough one by the FBI, and let them staff it.

Now . . . I have talked to [House Speaker John] McCormack and he said that would be agreeable to *him.*[147] I have talked to [Jim] Eastland, who started the investigation, and he said that that would be agreeable to *him.* I thought I better talk to you and anybody else you've suggested, see what your reaction to it might be, and maybe I oughta talk to some other people . . . I haven't talked to any of the justices or anything like that *yet.* But we think that's the best way to avoid a lot of television show, and our co[ncern is]—I'd like the secretary of state to just spend a minute with you, telling you some of his concern.

[Johnson hands the telephone receiver to Rusk.]

Mansfield: Well first, Mr. President, I think it's a good idea, and it's—

Rusk: Mike.

Mansfield: —okay with me, and then you ought to talk to [Everett] Dirksen.

Rusk: *[realizes Mansfield thinks he's still talking with Johnson]* Oh, excuse me.

[Rusk hands receiver back to Johnson.]

Mansfield: Hello? Yes, Dean.

Johnson: Go ahead, Mike. . . . Here's the secretary.

[Johnson hands receiver back to Rusk.]

Mansfield: Yeah; okay.

Rusk: . . . possible implications of this, that *if* they were—the rumors were—to leak out as *fact,* and if there were anything in this that had not been *fully* substantiated, it could cause a tremendous storm. And it's very important that we work on the basis of the *hardest* possible information on the situation—

Mansfield: Yes, it is.

Rusk: —[while] meanwhile, [we're] trying to get at the absolute *truth* on it.

Mansfield: Yes.

Rusk: So . . . I think that is very much in my mind. This has—this is already been commented on and picked up right around the world. And if we're not careful here, we could really blow up quite a storm.

Mansfield: That's right.

Rusk: So . . . may I put you back to the president?

147. There is no recording or transcript of such a conversation, though McCormack's prior agreement is referred to more than once. During his conversation with McCormack at 4:55 p.m., moreover, the president does not ask the Speaker for his assent to a commission but informs McCormack about the progress he has made in forming one. In all likelihood, Johnson called Speaker McCormack from the Elms on Thursday, and because it was a holiday the conversation went unnoted.

Mansfield: Okay.

Rusk: All right.

[Rusk hands back receiver to Johnson.]

Johnson: Yes, Mike.

Mansfield: Mr. President, I think the idea is a solid one. I would suggest that you contact Dirksen. As far as I'm concerned, you have my full support all the way, as always.

Johnson: Thank you. Now Mike, we have another thing that I—just let me step to my desk and get the memo I wanna ask you about.

[The discussion turns to the Kennedy family's request for $50,000 in federal funds to help Jacqueline Kennedy answer the unprecedented amount of condolence mail pouring into the White House.]

To Hale Boggs / 11:30 a.m.

Johnson's next call is to Louisiana congressman Hale Boggs, who is in Washington despite the holiday weekend because the House is holding a rare session on the day after Thanksgiving.

Boggs is one of a handful of men in Washington equally close to the late president and his successor. Boggs held a special affinity for Kennedy, as he shared the president's religion and was very proud of the first Catholic ever to be elected to the White House. But as a Louisianan Boggs identifies with Johnson, too, especially when it comes to such volatile issues as civil rights, where southern moderates have had to temper their private views in order to survive in elective office.

Boggs's devotion to both Kennedy and Johnson was never more evident than in 1960, during the Democratic convention in Los Angeles. The New Orleans congressman was the only politician advising Johnson to declare himself immediately in favor of Kennedy's offer. In fact, it was Boggs who persuaded Johnson's House mentor, Sam Rayburn, to hear Kennedy out at a time when the Speaker was absolutely dead-set against Johnson's acceptance of the number-two spot on the ticket. Rayburn relented after his meeting with John Kennedy, thus paving the way for the deal.[148] An influential strategist in Democratic backrooms, Boggs may even have known such a deal was in the offing. Three weeks before the convention opened, he made a wager with an incredulous friend that the ticket coming out of Los Angeles would be Kennedy-Johnson.[149]

148. Stanley Meisler, "Boggs Had Role in Footnote," *Washington Star,* 5 December 1963; Evans and Novak, *Exercise of Power,* 282.

149. Evans and Novak, *Exercise of Power,* 275.

Boggs's close ties to both presidents may have prompted him to be one of the first members of Congress calling for a bipartisan and noncompetitive investigation, days before Johnson decided on that course. As the two old friends discuss the panel-in-the-making, one significant difference emerges. Boggs's conception is that of an investigatory body established by a congressional resolution and chosen, at least in part, by Congress. But Johnson is intent now on creating the panel via an executive order and controlling all the appointments, thus making it a truly presidential commission.

Johnson: We are havin' some serious things present themselves in connection [with] all these investigations going on—

Boggs: Yes, yes.

Johnson: —on the Dallas thing. Now we think perhaps the best way to approach this is [to] try to get a couple members of the House, [and] a couple of the Senate, and maybe somebody from the [Supreme] Court— we don't want to say anything about that to anyone. But I've talked to the Speaker [of the House] and I've talked to the [majority] leader of the Senate, and the Justice Department, and that seems to be the consensus, the best thing to do. I wanted to—

Boggs: That's what I have intended to put in a resolution. But I had no intentions of doin' it until I had talked with you.

Johnson: Fine. Well, let's . . . hold back. Let me clear that . . . see how it goes, and I got to talk to some other people about it. But I wanted you to know what we were thinkin' and—

Boggs: My thought was that you might put a couple of people on that from the public, too, Mr. President.

Johnson: Well, ah . . . we might do that.[130]

Boggs: I just . . . that was exactly what I had in the [proposed] resolution that I'd asked Lew Deschler to draft, but which I've not put in [yet]: two from the House, two from the Senate, two from the judiciary, and two from the public.[131]

Johnson: Hmm . . . well that gives you eight.

Boggs: Yeah . . . the two, of course, from the public to be appointed by *you.*

Johnson: Well, wouldn't they all be appointed [by me]? Their thought was to have a presidential commission.

Boggs: Right—*all* of 'em appointed by you.

Johnson: Yeah.

[The discussion turns to the president's Thanksgiving Day address Thursday evening before ending.]

130. Johnson is obviously being coy here, as he has already decided to appoint two private citizens.

131. Deschler is the House parliamentarian.

To Everett Dirksen / 11:40 a.m.

Richard Russell once called Everett Dirksen "the most accomplished thespian who ever trod [the Senate] floor."[152] Beneath Dirksen's theatrical and florid persona, however, lurks a shrewd and effective politician, always seeking ways to alter the GOP's seemingly permanent status as the minority party. Dirksen became minority leader in 1959, after sweeping Republican losses in the 1958 election, and was arguably the most formidable GOP leader Johnson had to contend with in the Senate during his tenure as majority leader. Many observers, in fact, consider him to be Johnson's equal in the political arts. The president has known Dirksen since their days together as congressmen in the 1930s and 1940s, and insofar as Johnson has friendships that cross party lines, the relationship with Dirksen is one of his warmest and closest.[153]

After the Democrats reclaimed the White House in 1961, Dirksen began employing tactics identical to the ones Johnson used during the Eisenhower presidency. Chief among them was to make congressional Republicans appear nonpartisan whenever possible. The Illinois senator played a pivotal role in helping the White House defeat an attempted filibuster of the nuclear test ban treaty just two months before the assassination, thus helping President Kennedy to a rare congressional achievement. Johnson is acutely aware of Dirksen's strategy and knows that he will be a crucial ally in the months ahead, particularly on civil rights legislation. Consequently, consulting the minority leader prior to establishing the commission is not a pro forma exercise. The fact that Dirksen is also the ranking minority member on the Judiciary Committee makes his consent doubly important.

White House operators track down Senator Dirksen in Illinois, where he is spending the long holiday weekend. Johnson, as he had with Mansfield, engages in a bit of political overkill with Dirksen, this time by invoking J. Edgar Hoover's name. While the FBI director is hardly in favor of congressional investigations clamoring for attention, he has expressed no concern that the FBI's reputation will be hurt by any such probes—nor would such a concern be warranted. Congress in general is intimidated by Hoover's FBI, in marked contrast to its attitude toward almost every other federal agency. There has not been any vigorous oversight of the bureau's internal workings by either house for more than twenty years.

Johnson: Everett.
Dirksen: Yes.

152. Robert Jensen, "Sen. Everett Dirksen Is Dead," *Washington Post,* 8 September 1969.
153. Ibid.

Johnson: Two things. These investigations in the House and Senate on this Dallas affair . . . Hoover's a little concerned about [them] reflecting on him. He's making a very full report on it. The [Texas] attorney general's gettin' an inquiry—a state inquiry [going, on] he's a very young, and able, and effective man. And we don't wanna . . . we got some international complications that could come up to us if we are not very careful.

Dirksen: Yes.

Johnson: So we've been tryin' to figure out how we could best handle this thing, and seems to us we might ask a member of the [Supreme] Court, might even ask Allen Dulles, might ask a couple of members of the House, and a couple of the Senate, and wrap up the three divisions of government so we'd have a very *high-caliber, top-flight,* blue-ribbon group that the whole world would have absolute confidence in.[154]

Dirksen: Yeah.

Johnson: I've talked to [Mike] Mansfield and to the Speaker, and that appeals to them. Now . . . I think that appeals to Hoover [also]. I think it appeals to the Justice Department, and the secretary of state. I wanted to see what, ah . . . reaction you have.

Dirksen: See, this started when [Jim] Eastland came over to my office the other afternoon, and he wanted to get this thing [going].

Johnson: Incidentally, I've talked to him, too, and he said that he'd—

Dirksen: Did you talk to him?

Johnson: Yeah, and he said it's agreeable to him.

Dirksen: Okay.

Johnson: He's got a states' rights problem there. If he goes to sendin' investigations down into Texas, they're maybe going into Jackson, [Mississippi, next time] you know—

Dirksen: Yeah.

Johnson: —and vice versa.

Dirksen: Yeah. I undertook this only because Jim [Eastland] initiated it, and I talked to [John] McClellan [D-Arkansas], and Sam Ervin [D-North Carolina] and others.[155]

Johnson: I had occasion [to talk to] Dick Russell, too, and he kinda thought it would be bad for just [the] Senate committee and the House—

Dirksen: Yeah.

154. This early mention of Dulles is further evidence that Robert Kennedy's recommendation is being followed.

155. Since Dirksen is the ranking Republican on the Judiciary Committee, Eastland would have to seek his cooperation for any large-scale undertaking. Senators McClellan and Ervin are two of the most influential Democrats on the Judiciary Committee.

Johnson: —committee and all of 'em [to] be runnin' [all] over the lot.[156] So if
it's all right by you. . . .

Dirksen: [It would be] much better if it could be buttoned up in. . . .

*[The conversation shifts abruptly to the Kennedy family's request for
additional funds, and then to discussion of tax cut legislation pending in
the Senate.]*

From Hale Boggs / 1:11 p.m.

Shortly before the president breaks for lunch, he receives a telephone call from
a deeply chagrined Hale Boggs. To be sure, Boggs didn't *intend* to break the
news about a presidential commission before the White House formally issued
the announcement. Yet he did just that while responding to some remarks
uttered on the House floor after he had talked to the president in the morning.

Representative Charles Goodell, a moderate Republican from western New
York state, had risen to express his opposition to competing investigations, amid
rumors that the House Judiciary and Un-American Activities committees were
not about to cede the entire stage to the Senate.[157] Without thinking, Boggs let
his colleagues in on the president's still-secret decision. "I can state on the highest authority that this matter is going to be the subject of an inquiry," said Boggs,
"and that it will be a very high-level inquiry and that it will bear no resemblance
to partisanship."[158] Now Boggs's office on Capitol Hill is being besieged by
reporters seeking more information.

Boggs realizes he had better talk to Johnson and explain, insofar as he can
and as soon as possible, for he knows acutely how much Johnson hates being
scooped. Johnson is meeting with Roy Wilkins, executive secretary of the
NAACP, in the Oval Office when Boggs places his call. The congressman,
uncharacteristically, waits on the line for a tense six minutes because he dares
not get off. The only factor that might mitigate the president's anger will be
hearing the news directly from Boggs before he hears it from someone else.

Boggs's tone is matter-of-fact as he describes what happened. Johnson, surprisingly, doesn't sound too annoyed, though he does try to make the congressman squirm a bit by suggesting the commission might not be as imminent

156. Johnson is referring to his lunch with Russell on Tuesday.

157. On November 27 Goodell introduced a resolution to create a joint committee of seven
senators and seven representatives to investigate the assassination. Thus he looked upon Judiciary
and/or HUAC hearings as a threat to a joint and bipartisan investigation. A resolution authorizing
a HUAC probe into the Fair Play for Cuba Committee had been introduced on November 26.
Congressional Record, 26 and 29 November 1963, 22831, 22945; John Morris, "Johnson Names
a 7-Man Panel to Investigate Assassination; Chief Justice Warren Heads It," *New York Times,*
30 November 1963.

158. *Congressional Record,* 29 November 1963, 22954.

as Boggs claimed on the House floor. The president knows that he needs no authorizing legislation from Congress to create the commission but pretends otherwise.

Johnson saves his harsh criticism for later conversations with other advisers. If he could have delayed announcement of the commission, solely for the purpose of embarrassing Boggs and teaching him a lesson, the president probably would have. In the near future Johnson will become notorious for delaying planned announcements and appointments, even to the point of rescinding them, whenever word leaks out prematurely.

Johnson: Yes?

Boggs: Mr. President.

Johnson: Yes.

Boggs: Hale.

Johnson: Yeah.

Boggs: When the House convened today, Goodell of New York took the floor and started talkin' about a resolution he had for an investigation, and complainin' about both bodies investigatin', and the Senate Judiciary Committee and the House Un-American Activities Committee, and so forth. I was in the chair at the time, so I got [Representative] George Mahon [D-Texas] to take the gavel and I got the well of the floor, and said that there would be an investigation, that it would *not* be a congressional investigation, [and] that I thought I could say on the highest authority that there would be a high-level, *objective,* fact-finding investigation. 'Course since that time, I've had a lot of people call me, and they're talking now about it.

Johnson: Well, we've gotta touch these bases with everybody, and we haven't got 'em touched with the [Supreme] Court, of course—

Boggs: Right.

Johnson: —and we haven't got 'em touched with some others.

Boggs: So I have said absolutely *nothin'* about who might be on such a—

Johnson: *[disapprovingly]* All right.

Boggs: —commission, but I've said there *is* gonna be a commission.

Johnson: Yeah, well . . . I hope there is. I guess I've got authority to do it without any legislation, I don't know.

Boggs: I understand that you can issue an executive order and do it.

Johnson: All right. Well—

Boggs: You can appoint anybody you want.

Johnson: I've got my lawyers checkin' it now, and I just haven't got back [to working on it].[159] I've had to check it with Dirksen and Mansfield and Rayburn—I mean, and McCormack—and you. And then I've had [the]

159. By "lawyers," Johnson is referring to Abe Fortas.

Joint Chiefs of Staff, [the] secretary of state, [and the] secretary of defense all in all mornin', and I got Roy Wilkins with me now.

Boggs: Right.

Johnson: So . . . I'll get 'round to it and get a report soon as I can, and I'll be back to you.

Boggs: Right. All I wanted to tell you was what *happened,* Mr. President.

Johnson: Okay. All right.

To Abe Fortas / 1:15 p.m.

The president's most trusted legal counselor is drafting the press statement that will accompany the executive order establishing the commission. Fortas, at Johnson's behest, is also in charge of the effort to draft Chief Justice Earl Warren as chairman of the commission. Rather than approach Warren directly, Fortas has arranged for a delegation, comprised of Nicholas Katzenbach and Archibald Cox, the U.S. solicitor general, to make the case before the chief justice. Cox, as the U.S. government's lawyer in all cases before the Supreme Court, appears before Warren more than any other single member of the bar. The two-man delegation is scheduled to meet with the chief justice in his chambers at 2:30 p.m., a little more than one hour away.

Johnson is calling Fortas immediately after his conversation with Boggs to let Fortas know the cat is out of the bag. It takes a moment for Fortas to understand what the president is saying, and that everything must be speeded up. Now it is urgent to release the news just as soon as possible, certainly by the close of business Friday.

This conversation is the first of many in which Johnson will reveal his thinking about the commission appointments. Because he is talking to such a trusted adviser, the conversation is much more candid than comparable ones later in the day. The chief justice's chairmanship, of course, is a given; Johnson never seriously contemplates anyone else for the task. For one of the two civilian slots, some consideration is briefly given to Air Force General Lauris Norstad, who retired in early 1963 as supreme commander of NATO forces in Europe. Presumably Norstad's participation would be reassuring to America's most important (and shaken) allies in Western Europe. But in fairly short order Norstad is dropped in favor of John McCloy, who, as the U.S. High Commissioner for Occupied Germany from 1949 to 1952, is very well known and respected in European capitals.

Regarding the members from Congress, Fortas presumes that the president will not be able to avoid placing the respective chairmen of the judiciary committees, James Eastland and Representative Emanuel Celler (D-New York), on the panel. But neither man appeals to Johnson, in part because neither Eastland's nor Celler's judgment is held in very high esteem by the people who know them best—their respective colleagues. Celler, a liberal, is as much a political ideologue as Eastland. Johnson is intent on drafting men renowned, at least internally, for their probity and integrity.

In fact, if the president truly intends to appoint the chief justice, then he almost has to find a way around putting Eastland on the commission. The antagonism between Eastland and Warren is such that the commission will be congenitally deformed with both men on it. Even if they were willing to serve with each other—a *big* if—they probably would not be able to agree on the same set of findings. In 1962, on the seventh day of a southern filibuster against a civil rights measure, Eastland charged that the Warren Court "decides for the Communists" whenever it adjudicates a case pitting the security of the United States against the rights of Communists. Despite ample opportunity and widespread condemnation from Senate colleagues, Eastland refused to back down from calling the justices "Communists almost in so many words." Eastland insisted, "The speech speaks for itself."[160]

Thus it is with the utmost calculation that Johnson chooses, from the Senate, his own mentor, Richard Russell, and a Republican from Kentucky named John Sherman Cooper. Both senators' reputations are impeccable. Insofar as the House goes, the president is less familiar with members of that body since he last served there fifteen years ago. He is peeved with Hale Boggs for prematurely breaking the news, but it would be awkward not to appoint Boggs since he was one of the first congressmen to advance the commission idea. For Boggs's House counterpart, Johnson initially leans toward William McCulloch, a moderate and respected Republican from Ohio. But McCulloch is also the ranking minority member on the Judiciary Committee, and that makes his selection problematic, because it would raise questions about why Celler is being passed over. Eventually Johnson abandons McCulloch and settles instead on Gerald Ford, a fast-rising, hardworking conservative congressman who represents Grand Rapids, Michigan. Ford's name is first suggested by Secretary McNamara, who has worked closely with the congressman because of Ford's influence over Defense Department appropriations.[161]

As Fortas and Johnson toss around names of possible appointees, one thing becomes apparent. Johnson begins to enjoy his newfound power to decide the workload of very important men. That power is not absolute, of course. But as the day progresses, it will become evident just how hard it is to turn down a determined president.

160. Warren Duffee, "Kuchel Raps Eastland for Attacks on Court," *Washington Post,* 4 May 1962; Associated Press, "Eastland Charge on Court Scored," *New York Times,* 4 May 1962.

161. James Cannon, *Time and Chance: Gerald Ford's Appointment with History* (New York: HarperCollins, 1994), 76.

Johnson: [Any] progress on the [Supreme] Court?

Fortas: Yes, sir. And . . . I['ve] been trying to handle this with the greatest tact, and so [the] way we worked out is that Nick [Katzenbach] and the solicitor general are going to call on the chief justice . . . see, instead of my doing it.

Johnson: Well, we need it right quick though, because—

Fortas: I know that.

Johnson: —they already announcin' it in the House and Senate, and all over the damned place. And [whenever] you talk to the [congressional] leaders, it's just like talkin' into a big microphone.

Fortas: I know, and that's why I asked Nick to get over there right away.

Johnson: All right.

Fortas: I talked to him this morning, and he's going to take the—

Johnson: Now who—

Fortas: —solicitor general and do it.

Johnson: How many men on the commission we gonna have?

Fortas: Well, if you had [Allen] Dulles and a general, and two from the House, two from the Senate, and the chief justice—

Johnson: Who do you think of as the general?

Fortas: The only one I can think of, and I don't know many of those fellas, is [Lauris] Norstad, who's always—

Johnson: . . . if I had any idea who we wanted. . . .

Fortas: Oh, I thought we'd probably have to take the . . . Eastland and the ranking minority member on the Judiciary Committee, and similarly on the House [side]. But maybe not. Isn't this—wouldn't this ordinarily be [under the jurisdiction of the] Judiciary Committee?

Johnson: Yeah, but Celler . . . God, I hate to . . . Celler and Eastland, I hate to have them on it.

Fortas: [chuckles] They couldn't stand to be [together].

Johnson: Wait a minute.

[aside] Huh?

[to Fortas] What would you think about John McCloy instead of General Norstad?[162]

Fortas: I think that'd be great. He's a wonderful man and a very dear friend of mine. I'm devoted to him.

Johnson: Well, let's think along that line. Now, can we do this by executive order?

Fortas: Yes, sir.

Johnson: Do we infringe upon the Congress any way in doin' it?

Fortas: No, sir.

162. From the flow of the conversation, it seems possible that McGeorge Bundy (who is present in the Oval Office) reminds the president that McCloy is Robert Kennedy's preferred choice.

Johnson: Reflect on 'em in any way?

Fortas: No, sir. I think on the contrary—you know, all these editorials saying this would be a *shame,* to have all these investigations. I think the country will think that Congress has started acting wisely for a change. I think it'd be a *great* thing, Mr. President, for them and for . . . the country.

Johnson: Who'd you think about in the Senate?

Fortas: *[sighs]*

Johnson: [There's] a whole lot [of] men I would [rather] have, if I had to have somebody *[sighs audibly]* that's chairman of a lot of things.[163] I'd a whole lot rather have Russell than Eastland.

Fortas: Oh, I would, too. Yes, *sir* . . . for anything, I'd rather have him than most anybody for anything. That'd be *wonderful* if that could be arranged. I didn't think about that because I thought it [Eastland's selection] would be foreordained.

Johnson: I'd like to have Russell and Cooper, . . . that'd be my two.

Fortas: That'd be *marvelous* . . . simply *marvelous.* On the House side, if we could get Hale Boggs . . . he's a well—

Johnson: Aw, he's talkin' *all the goddamned time.* He's [a] good fella, but he's done announced it in the House.

Fortas: Yeah, that's what I mean. And I thought maybe this would help to get it through.

Johnson: What do you have to get through?

Fortas: Well, I mean just their agreement that they'll do this *in lieu of* a Senate and House investigation.

Johnson: Well, he's agreed to that.

Fortas: Well, that's wonderful.

Johnson: And McCormack's agreed to it.

Fortas: Yes, sir.

Johnson: I would get—what's that fella that . . . McCulloch—he's the ranking Republican. He's pretty good, or Jerry Ford. . . . I would think Jerry Ford would be good from the Republicans.

Fortas: Uh-huh. Well, that would be fine. How about . . . is little old Carl Albert [available?] What about him?

Johnson: I think he's—

Fortas: He's the majority floor leader; I don't know whether he'd want it.

Johnson: Yeah, well . . . [I] don't know whether he'd take it or not.

Fortas: Uh-huh.

Johnson: *[as if contemplating his handiwork]* Yeah, I'd think that'd be pretty good.

Fortas: Uh-huh.

---

163. Johnson is referring to the fact that any senior senator is likely to be chairman of at least two important committees/subcommittees.

Johnson: I'd rather get away with—it might be a slap at Hale if we did that [i.e., appointed Albert].

Fortas: That's what I'm afraid of. I don't . . . wonder if we [aren't] stuck—

Johnson: [It] might be [that it] oughta [be] Hale and McCulloch.

Fortas: Yes, I wonder if we aren't stuck with Hale.

Johnson: All right.

[aside] Mac [Bundy], write those names down for me so I won't forget 'em. We'll have the chief justice . . . and John McCloy and Allen Dulles; that's three. We'll try to get Jerry Ford as the Republican and Hale Boggs as the Democrat in the House. [And] we'll try to get Russell and, ah . . . Cooper.

Fortas: Yes, sir. Now I don't know, the chief justice may, ah . . . not want to do this, but I'll call Nick immediately and see if he's got a report yet. He shoulda gone over there right away; I really gave him the hotfoot this [morning].

Johnson: Well, they already announced it. You call him back and see what the hell's happened.

Fortas: Who's announced it?

Johnson: Hale Boggs got down [in the House well and] told 'em. You see, I had to tell him what I was contemplatin'.

Fortas: [dismayed] Oy!

Johnson: So he got down on the floor of the House—some *jerk* [Goodell] got up and said something—so he thought he had *to show his knowledge.*

Fortas: *Oh, Lord.* Yeah, I thought you meant he'd just announced that the House was going to investigate the whole thing.

Johnson: Well, he's now—no, he announced there's gonna be a high-level commission.

Fortas: I see.

Johnson: That's why I'm waitin' on it [the meeting with Warren].

Fortas: I'll be damned.

Johnson: [teasingly] And I don't know . . . I guess we have [to] talk to these fellas before we announce we're gonna appoint 'em, don't we?

Fortas: Yes, sir.

Johnson: All right. By God, I'm not much . . . I think we oughta *order* 'em to do it, and then let 'em bellyache.

Fortas: [laughs] All right.

Johnson: [aside] Hmmm?

Fortas: I think that's great.

Johnson: [aside] Yeah, we'll have to get him.

[to Fortas] Yeah; okay.

Fortas: Thank you, sir.

Johnson: You call me now.

Fortas: Yes, sir!

From J. Edgar Hoover / 1:40 p.m.

One of the most difficult calls of the day—at least Johnson *thinks* it will be difficult—is to the FBI director, a master bureaucrat. Virtually everyone in Washington has to address Hoover gingerly and as a supplicant, with the exception of the person who happens to occupy the Oval Office. But after barely a week in office, Johnson is behaving as if his old relationship with Hoover still obtains, instead of acting now like that one exception.

Johnson's trepidation is evident in his opening words. He presents the commission as if some unknown "they" were responsible for its establishment. Soon Johnson shifts to "we," but only after assuring Hoover that if it had been left up to him alone, there would be no commission. Hoover's quick assent to the idea seems to come as something of a surprise to Johnson; listening to the recording, the president's relief is almost palpable. He then shifts to asking Hoover his opinion about the potential appointees. To show how reasonable he's being, Johnson throws out the name of Jacob Javits, knowing that Hoover will recoil at the mere mention of the liberal Republican senator. With the possible exception of Kenneth Keating, his voluble colleague from New York, no one is more adept than Javits at getting his name into newspapers, especially the *New York Times*.[164]

Johnson's purpose here is not to discuss the pros and cons of each appointee, as it was with Fortas. The president simply wants to make sure Hoover is not rigidly opposed to any of the nominees. He names them one by one but neglects to say that the chairman will most likely be Earl Warren if the president gets his way. The chief justice used to be on exceptionally good terms with the FBI director when he was attorney general and then governor of California. Since Warren's appointment to the Supreme Court in 1953, however, relations between the two men have cooled dramatically. Hoover cannot forget such days as June 17, 1957, "Red Monday," when the Warren Court effectively halted prosecutions of Communist Party members under the Smith Act and essentially terminated the activities of congressional committees that had specialized in pillorying suspected Communists in public and jailing them for contempt.[165]

The conversation then turns to a discussion of the FBI's investigation of the assassination. Hoover makes, to the president, his most unambiguous declara-

---

164. True to form, Javits has spoken out and been widely quoted on the issue of investigating the assassination. Clayton, "2 Senate Leaders Urge Assassination Inquiry"; *Congressional Record,* 27 November 1963, 22904.

165. Hoover probably learns about Warren's chairmanship of the panel during a later, and very brief, telephone conversation with the president. There is no recording or transcript of this 5:41 p.m. conversation, however. Daily Diary, 29 November 1963, LBJL.

tion about the assassination to date. Echoing what the DPD said six days earlier, Hoover avers that Lee Harvey Oswald *is the man* who killed President Kennedy. However, the FBI director is not nearly as definitive about the other outstanding questions, namely: Did Oswald act at the behest of the Castro regime? Is Jack Ruby a vigilante or a co-conspirator?

Notwithstanding his assertion that Oswald was the lone shooter, Hoover's summary of the ballistic evidence is again studded with errors. For every correct statement—such as the finding that three shots were fired in Dealey Plaza, all aimed at the president—there is a misstatement of the facts. Some of Hoover's statements border on the absurd, such as his confident declaration that a nearly intact missile rolled out of the president's head as his heart was being massaged. How Hoover arrives at these observations is a mystery. As imperfect as some of the interim FBI reports are, they do not convey such bad information. Perhaps time (Hoover is sixty-eight years old) has dulled the director's once renowned ability to recite a battery of facts from memory.

Hoover's tendency to denigrate the Dallas Police Department at every opportunity remains manifest. Every failure is attributable to the DPD and the DPD alone; every accomplishment involves the bureau, even when it doesn't. Yet the ultimate source of failure is traceable to Washington. Assassination of a president should have been a federal crime in the first place, and Dallas police should never have been saddled with the enormous and unfair burden of solving a national crime that just happened to occur in their city.

Johnson: Are you familiar with this proposed group that they tryin' to put together on . . . this study of your report and other things—two from the House, two from the Senate, somebody from the [Supreme] Court . . . [and] a couple of outsiders?

Hoover: No, I haven't heard of that. I've seen the reports on the *Senate* investigating committee that they've been talking about.[166]

Johnson: Yeah. Well, we think if we don't have . . . I wanted to get by just with your file and your report. But—

Hoover: I think it'd be very, very bad to have a *rash* of investigations on this thing.

Johnson: Well, the only way we can stop 'em is probably to appoint a high-level one to evaluate your report—

Hoover: Yeah.

Johnson: —and put somebody that's pretty good on it from . . . that I can select, out of the government, and tell the House and Senate not to go ahead with an investigation.

Hoover: Yes.

---

166. Hoover is undoubtedly referring to the Senate Judiciary Committee's announcement of hearings.

Johnson: 'Cause [otherwise] we get up there and get a bunch of . . . television going, and I thought it'd be bad.

Hoover: It'd be a three-ring circus.

Johnson: *[sotto voce]* All right.

[to Hoover] What do you think about Allen Dulles?

Hoover: Ah . . . I think he would be a good man.

Johnson: What do you think about John McCloy?

Hoover: Ah . . . I'm not as enthusiastic about McCloy. I knew him back in the [Robert] Patterson [days], when Patterson was down here as secretary [of war] then.[167] He's a good man. But I'm not so *certain* as to the matter of the publicity that he might seek on it.

Johnson: What about General [Lauris] Norstad?

Hoover: A good man.

Johnson: All right. I guess [Hale] Boggs has started it in the House. I thought maybe I might try to get Boggs and Jerry Ford in the House, and maybe try to get Dick Russell and maybe Cooper in the Senate.

Hoover: Yes, I think so.

Johnson: I don't know—you know anything, any reason . . . I was just talkin'—me and you gonna talk like brothers, you know.

Hoover: Yes.

Johnson: By the way, is there any reason . . . I thought Russell could kinda look after the general situation . . . see that the states and their relations—

Hoover: Russell would be an excellent man.

Johnson: And I thought Cooper might look after the liberal group.

Hoover: Who's that?

Johnson: Cooper, from Kentucky.

Hoover: Oh, yeah. Cooper.

Johnson: So they wouldn't think that . . . he's a pretty judicious fella, but he's a pretty liberal fella.

Hoover: Yeah.

Johnson: I wouldn't want [Jacob] Javits—

Hoover: No, no!

Johnson: —or some of those fellas on it.

Hoover: Javits plays to the front page all the time.

Johnson: But Cooper's kinda [from a] border state—

Hoover: Yes.

Johnson: —it's not the South, and it's not North.

Hoover: That's right.

Johnson: Do you know Ford from Michigan?

---

167. Hoover is confused. McCloy served as assistant secretary of war from 1940 to 1945, but under then–Secretary of War Henry Stimson. Patterson was undersecretary during this same period, then succeeded Stimson.

Hoover: I know *of* him, but I don't know him.

Johnson: All right.

Hoover: I saw him on TV the other night for the first time. He handled himself well on that.

Johnson: You know Boggs?

Hoover: Oh yes, I know Boggs.

Johnson: He's kinda [the] author of the resolution, that's what I understand.

Hoover: Yes, yes. I know him.

Johnson: Now, Walter [Jenkins] tells me that you've designated "Deke" [DeLoach] to work with us like you did on the Hill.[168]

Hoover: I have, yes.

Johnson: And I wanted to tell you, I sure appreciate that. I didn't ask for it 'cause I knew you knew how to run your business better than anybody else. And I just want to tell you, though, that we consider him as high-class as you do, and it's [a] mighty gracious thing to do, and we['ll] be mighty happy, and we salute you for knowin' how to pick good men!

Hoover: Well, that's mighty nice of you, Mr. President, indeed. . . . We hoped to have this thing [the assassination investigation] wrapped up today. But we're being—we probably won't get it [finished] before the first of the week.[169] This angle in Mexico is giving us a great deal of trouble.

Johnson: Uh-huh.

Hoover: Because the story's there of this man, Oswald, getting $6,500 from the Cuban embassy—

Johnson: Hmm.

Hoover: —and then coming back to this country with it. We're not able to *prove* that fact. But the information was that he was there on the *eighteenth* of September in Mexico City, and we are able to prove *conclusively* he was in New Orleans that day.

Now, then they've moved—they [Gilberto Alvarado] changed the date. the story came in changing the date to the *twenty-eighth* of September, and he [Oswald] *was* in Mexico City on the twenty-eighth.[170]

Now the Mexican police have again arrested this woman, [Sylvia] Duran, who's a member of the Cuban embassy . . . and will hold her for two [or] three more days. And we're going to confront her with the original informant [Alvarado]—who saw the money pass, [or] so he

---

168. DeLoach served as the bureau's liaison to Johnson when he was Senate majority leader. Cartha DeLoach, *Hoover's FBI: The Inside Story by Hoover's Trusted Lieutenant* (Washington, D.C.: Regnery Publishing, 1995), 376.

169. Hoover means the bureau's report on the assassination requested by President Johnson.

170. The fact that Alvarado abruptly switched his story when confronted with the information that Oswald could not have been in Mexico City on the day Alvarado first alleged is the first crack in the Nicaraguan informant's fabrication. Within a few hours, he will admit to having concocted the entire allegation. *Warren Report,* 307–08.

says—and we're also going to put the lie detector test on him. [In the] meantime, of course, [Fidel] Castro's hollering his head off.[171]

Johnson: Can you pay any attention to those lie detector tests?

Hoover: I would not pay 100 percent attention to them. *All* that they are is a *psychological* asset in an investigation. I wouldn't want to be a party to sending a man to the [electric] chair on a lie detector. For instance, we have found many cases where we've used 'em, and—in a bank, [for example], where there's been embezzlement—and a person will *confess* before the lie detector test is finished . . . more or less *fearful* of the fact that the lie detector test will show them *guilty.*

Johnson: Hmmm.

Hoover: Psychologically, there's that advantage. Of course, it's a *misnomer* to call it a "lie detector" because what it really is, it's the *evaluation* of the chart that is made by this machine . . . and that evaluation is made by a human being. And any human being can be apt to make a wrong interpretation. So I would not *myself* go on that alone.

   If, on the other hand, if this fella Oswald had lived and had taken the lie detector test, and it had shown definitely that he had done these various things . . . together with the evidence that we very *definitely* have, it would've just added up that much more *strength* to it. There's no question but that *he is the man,* now with the fingerprints and things that we have.

   This feller Rubenstein [Jack Ruby] down there . . . he has offered to take the lie detector test, but his lawyer [has] gotta be, 'course, consulted first. And I doubt whether the lawyer will allow him. He's one of these criminal lawyers from the West Coast, and somewhat like an Edward Bennett Williams type . . . and almost as much of a *shyster.*[172]

Johnson: Hmmm . . . *[chuckles].* Have you got any . . . any relationship between the two yet?

Hoover: Between Rubenstein [and Oswald]?

Johnson: Yeah.

Hoover: No. At the present time, we have not. There was a story down there that—

Johnson: Was he ever in his bar and stuff like that?

Hoover: There was a story that this fella [Oswald] had been in this nightclub, that is, a striptease joint that he [Rubenstein] had. But that has not been

---

171. Hoover is either referring to the protest lodged by the Cuban government over Sylvia Duran's detention, or to Castro's public remarks on the assassination, in which he tried to pin responsibility for the murder on "ultrarightist and ultrareactionary sectors" in U.S. society.

172. Hoover is referring to Melvin Belli, a flamboyant attorney from San Francisco, who will officially join Ruby's legal defense team on December 10. The seeming impossibility of winning an acquittal for Ruby, after millions have seen him gun down Oswald, is a challenge Belli cannot resist. Williams, a Washington criminal lawyer, is also renowned for winning favorable verdicts in the face of seemingly insurmountable odds for clients with less-than-savory reputations.

able to be confirmed.[173] Now, this fellow Rubenstein is a very shady character, has a bad record [as a] street brawler, fighter, and that sort of thing. And in the [striptease] place in Dallas, if a fella came in there and couldn't pay his bill completely, Rubenstein would beat the very devil out of him and throw him out of the place. He was that kind of a fella. He didn't drink, didn't smoke . . . boasted about that. He's what I would put in the category "one of the ego-maniacs." He likes to be in the limelight. He knew all the police . . . in that white-light [sic] district where the joints are down there. And he also let 'em come in, see the show, get food, and get liquor, and so forth. That's how I think he got into police headquarters . . . because they accepted him as kind of a police character hangin' around police headquarters, and for that reason raised no question.[174]

Of course, they never made any moves, as the pictures show, even when they saw him [Rubenstein] approaching this fella [Oswald], and got up right to him [Oswald] and pressed his pistol against Oswald's stomach. Neither of the police officers on either side made any move to push him away or to grab him. [It] wasn't till after the gun was fired that they then moved. Now, of course, that is not the highest degree of efficiency, certainly it is to say.[175]

Secondly, the chief of police [Jesse Curry] admits that he moved him [Oswald] in the morning as a convenience and at the request of the motion-picture people, who wanted to have daylight.[176] He shoulda moved him at *night* . . . but he didn't. And . . . I mean . . . those derelictions in that phase—but so far as tying Rubenstein and Oswald together, we haven't as yet done so. There've been a number of stories [that have] come in—we've tied Oswald into the [American] Civil Liberties Union in New York— membership into that—and [of] course, into this Cuban Fair Play

173. Oswald was a prude, and the idea of his visiting a striptease joint is risible. In contrast, Hoover's thumbnail description of Ruby is insightful. The outstanding work on the self-appointed vigilante is Garry Wills and Ovid Demaris, *Jack Ruby: The Man Who Killed the Man Who Killed Kennedy* (New York: New American Library, 1967).

174. Hoover is correct in depicting Ruby as a police "hanger-on," and a brawler who is always trying to curry favor with the police. But his friendly relations with some officers played no role in his slipping unnoticed into the basement garage of DPD headquarters just minutes before shooting Oswald. *Warren Report*, 224.

175. Hoover is being unfair. Though at least one DPD officer, the detective on Oswald's right, saw Ruby dart out of the crowd, the officer had only about a second and a half to react before the shot was fired. The officers' vision was also adversely affected by the television and other camera lights in the basement. Larry Sneed, *No More Silence: An Oral History of the Assassination of President Kennedy* (Dallas, Tex.: Three Forks Press, 1998), 396; *Warren Report*, 230.

176. Curry, who wanted the news media to testify that Oswald had not been physically mistreated while in DPD custody, did not time the transfer "at the request of the motion-picture people" (actually, television newsmen). *Warren Report*, 229.

Committee, which is pro-Castro and dominated by Communism, and financed to some extent by the Castro government.[177]

Johnson: How many shots were fired? Three?

Hoover: Three.

Johnson: Any of 'em fired at me?

Hoover: No. There were—

Johnson: All three at the president?

Hoover: All three at the president, and we have 'em. Two of the shots fired at the president were splintered, but they have characteristics on 'em so that our ballistic[s] expert was able to prove that they were fired by this gun.[178]

Johnson: God.

Hoover: The third shot, which hit the president—he was hit by the first and the third [shots], the second shot hit the governor.[179] The third shot is a complete bullet that wasn't shattered, and that rolled out of the president's head . . . tore a large part of the president's head off. And in trying to massage his heart at the hospital, on the way to the hospital, they apparently loosened that and that fell onto the stretcher.[180] And we recovered that; and we have that. And we have the gun here also.

Johnson: Was they aimin' at the president?

Hoover: They were aiming directly at the president. There's no question about that. This telescopic lens, which I've looked through, it brings a person as

177. Oswald's application to join the ACLU was processed on November 4, 1963. Priscilla Johnson McMillan, *Marina and Lee* (New York: Harper & Row, 1977), 393. Regarding the Fair Play for Cuba Committee (FPCC), which Oswald first contacted in the spring of 1963, Senator Eastland's Internal Security subcommittee revealed at a January 1961 hearing that the ostensibly independent and indigenous FPCC received funds from the Cuban government. U.S. Senate, Committee on the Judiciary, *Fair Play for Cuba Committee,* Hearings before the Subcommittee on Internal Security, 10 January 1961, 87th Cong., 1st Sess. (Washington, D.C.: U.S. Government Printing Office, 1961), 80.

178. Hoover is still wrong about the ballistics evidence. Of the three shots aimed at President Kennedy, the missile from the first shot has not been recovered in whole or part; the missile from the second shot has been recovered from Governor Connally's hospital stretcher; and remnants of the missile from the third shot, which fragmented upon striking the president's head, have been recovered. Regarding the sequence of Oswald's rifle shots, and the condition of the recovered missiles, see *Warren Report,* 18–19, 97–117, and U.S. House of Representatives, *Report of the Select Committee on Assassinations* (hereafter *HSCA Report*), 95th Cong., 2nd Sess. (Washington, D.C.: U.S. Government Printing Office, 1979), 41–52.

179. Again, Hoover is imparting misinformation to Johnson. The first shot missed the occupants in the presidential limousine; the second shot hit President Kennedy and then plowed into Governor Connally; the third and final shot hit Kennedy in the head. *HSCA Report,* 41–52.

180. The missile found on the stretcher (i.e., the second shot) had fallen out of Governor Connally's thigh where it superficially lodged after all its energy was spent. The third shot split into fragments after striking the president's head; the suggestion that a "complete bullet . . . rolled out of the president's head" while his heart was being massaged is preposterous. *Warren Report,* 19, 86–87.

close to you as if they were sittin' right beside you. And we also have tested the fact that you could fire . . . those three shots were fired within three seconds.[181] There'd been some stories going around in the papers and so forth that there must have been more than one man, because no one man could fire those shots in the time that they were fired. We've just proved that by the actual test that we've made—

Johnson: How'd it happen they hit Connally if [he was] two feet ahead of him?

Hoover: Connally turned . . . Connally turned to the president when the first shot was fired, and I think in that turning, it was where he got hit.

Johnson: [If] he hadn't turned, he probably wouldn't [have] got hit.

Hoover: I think that's very likely.[182]

Johnson: Would the president got hit [by] the second one?

Hoover: No, the president wasn't hit with the second one.[183] At the—

Johnson: I say, if Connally hadn't been in his way?[184]

Hoover: Oh yes! Yes. The president no doubt woulda been hit.

Johnson: He'd been hit *three* times.

Hoover: He would've been hit *three* times.[185] On the fifth floor of that building, where we found the gun—and the wrapping paper in which the gun was wrapped, had been wrapped, and upon which we find the full fingerprints of this man Oswald—on that floor we found the three empty shells that had been fired, and one shell that had *not* been fired.[186] In other words,

181. This is another piece of incorrect information conveyed by Hoover, misstating the bureau's own ballistics tests. On November 27 three FBI marksmen each fired the Mannlicher-Carcano three times. It required more than two seconds just to work the bolt *once* on Oswald's rifle, making it impossible to fire three shots within three seconds. No FBI expert will ever be able to fire the rifle three times in less than 4.6 seconds, and that speed will be achieved only by firing at a stationary target (while Oswald fired at a slowly moving one). *Warren Report,* 194; Warren Commission, *Hearings,* 3:403–4.

182. Connally did hear the first shot (which missed), and it prompted him to turn around to see if the president had been hit. Nonetheless, the act of turning did not put Connally in the line of fire; *any* missile that passed through the president was likely to hit the governor. If anything, as suggested earlier, turning might have saved Connally's life because the missile that did hit him thereby missed his heart and arteries. "Turn May Have Saved Connally," *Houston Post,* 23 November 1963; *HSCA Report,* 40.

183. In point of fact, the first missile to strike the president *was* Oswald's second shot. *HSCA Report,* 41.

184. Connally was never in President Kennedy's way; quite the opposite. The governor was seated in front of the president, and Oswald was firing from a position above and behind the presidential limousine.

185. As noted earlier, Oswald's first shot missed. In all likelihood it was deflected from its intended target by a branch of the oak tree that partially obscured Oswald's view from the Texas School Book Depository's (TSBD) sixth floor. *Warren Report,* 98.

186. Hoover continues to repeat the mistake he first made during his November 23 conversation with Johnson. The rifle was found on the sixth floor, the same floor from which Oswald fired

there were four shells apparently, and he had fired three, but [he] didn't fire the fourth one.[187] He then threw the gun aside and came down, and at the entrance of the building he was stopped by a police officer. And some manager in the building told the police officer, "Well, he's all right. He works here. He can . . . you needn't hold him." So they let him go. That's how he got out.[188]

Johnson: Hmmm.

Hoover: And then he got on a bus—the bus driver has identified him—and went out to his home.[189] And . . . got hold of a jacket that he wanted for some purpose, and came *back* downtown, walking downtown.[190] And the police officer who was killed stopped him not knowing who he was, and not knowing whether he was *the* man. But they were . . . [Oswald was stopped] just on suspicion, and he fired, of course, and killed the police officer.[191] Then he [Oswald] walked about—

Johnson: And you can prove that?

Hoover: Oh, yes . . . oh yes, we can prove that. Then he walked about another two blocks and went to the theater. And the woman at the theater window selling the tickets . . . she was so suspicious [because of] the way he was acting, and she said he was carrying a gun.[192] He had a revolver at that time, with which he had killed the police officer. He [Oswald] went into the theater, and then she notified the police, and the police and our man down there went in there and located this particular man.[193] They had quite a struggle with him—he fought like a regular lion—and he had to be subdued, of course, but was then brought out and, of course, taken to the police headquarters.

---

the weapon. Moreover, Hoover's use of "we" is misleading. The weapon, sniper's nest, and spent shells were found by two Dallas County deputy sheriffs. Ibid., 8–9, 18.

187. When the Mannlicher-Carcano was found on the sixth floor, it contained one unspent cartridge. Ibid., 9.

188. To be fair to the police officer, he naturally assumed the gunman was someone who did not work at the TSBD. On the other hand, the officer should have sealed off the building and not allowed anyone to leave or enter. Ibid., 149–52.

189. Oswald went not to his home but to the Oak Cliff rooming house where he typically slept during the work week. Ibid., 163–65.

190. Oswald did not go back downtown and was in fact walking in the Oak Cliff neighborhood away from downtown Dallas; besides a jacket, he also retrieved a revolver from his room, which he used to kill Officer J. D. Tippit. Ibid., 165–76.

191. Tippit had received the APB (all points bulletin) giving a vague description of the slender white male seen on the TSBD's sixth floor. What probably caught Tippit's eye, however, was Oswald's furtive behavior when he caught sight of Tippit's police cruiser. Myers, *With Malice,* 65.

192. The ticket seller did not see Oswald's revolver, and she called police only because a shoe salesman noticed Oswald behaving suspiciously. Ibid., 178.

193. While an FBI agent was present at the Texas Theater, he played no direct role in locating and apprehending Oswald. Ibid., 178–79.

But he apparently had come down the five flights of steps—[down the] stairway—from the fifth floor.[194] So far as we've found out, the elevator was not used, although he *could* have used it. But nobody remembers whether it was or whether it wasn't.

Johnson: Well, your conclusion is that (a) he's the one that did it; (b) the man he's after was the president; and (c) he woulda hit him three times except the governor turned—[195]

Hoover: I think that's correct.

Johnson: —(4) that there's no connection between he and Ruby that you can detect now; and (5) whether he was connected with the Cuban operation . . . with money, you're [still] tryin' to—[196]

Hoover: That's what we're trying to nail down now. Because, of course, he [Oswald] was *strongly* pro-Castro . . . he was strongly anti-American. And he had been in correspondence, which we have, with the Soviet embassy here in Washington, and with the American Civil Liberties Union, and with this committee for fair play to Cuba.[197] We have copies of the correspondence . . . so that we've got him nailed down in his contact with them. *None of those letters,* however, dealt with any indication of violence, or contemplated assassination.[198] They were dealing with the matter of a visa for his wife [Marina Oswald] to go back to Russia. Now there's one angle to this thing that I'm hopeful to get some word on today. This woman—his wife—has been very hostile. She would not cooperate . . . she speaks Russian and Russian only. She did say to us yesterday down there that if we could give her assurance that she would be allowed to remain in this country, she might cooperate. I told our agents down there to *give* her that assurance . . . that she could stay in this country, and I sent a Russian-speakin' agent into Dallas last night to interview her. So that . . . we've got her now, and whether she knows anything or talks anything, I, [of] course, don't know and won't know—

Johnson: Where did he work in the [TSBD] building? On this same floor?

Hoover: He had access on all floors.

Johnson: But where was his office?

194. Oswald fired his rifle from the sixth floor. Ibid., 18.

195. The first two inferences Johnson draws are correct, but (c) is not.

196. The "Cuban operation" Johnson is referring to is the allegation that Oswald received $6,500 while visiting the Cuban consulate. He is not referring to Operation Mongoose, code word for the governmentwide effort in 1961–62 to overthrow Fidel Castro, as asserted in Shesol, *Mutual Contempt,* 131.

197. Hoover is again drawing Johnson's attention to the FBI's routine interception of letters sent via the postal system to the Soviet embassy, a highly secret operation Hoover first revealed to the president during their November 23 telephone conversation.

198. Hoover is very anxious that Johnson not believe for a moment that the bureau had any inkling of Oswald's proclivity for violence prior to November 22.

Hoover: Well, he didn't have any particular office. He would . . . orders came in for certain books, and some books would be on the first floor, second floor, third floor, and so forth.

Johnson: But he didn't have any particular place he was stationed?

Hoover: No, he had no particular place where he was stationed at all. He was just a general packer of the requisitions that came in for the schoolbooks from the Dallas schools there.[199] And therefore he had access, perfectly proper access, to the fifth floor and to the sixth floor. Usually most of the employees were down on lower floors.

Johnson: Did anybody hear . . . anybody see him on the fifth floor?

Hoover: Yes, he was seen on the fifth floor by one of the workmen there before the assassination took place.[200] He was seen there . . . so that we got—

Johnson: Have you got a . . . did you get a picture of him . . . shootin'?

Hoover: Oh, no. There was no picture taken of him shooting.

Johnson: Well, what was this picture that [that] fella sold for $25,000?[201] Have you—

Hoover: That was a [moving] picture taken of the parade, and showing Mrs. Kennedy climbing out of the backseat. You see, there was no Secret Service man standing on the back of the car. Usually the presidential car in the past has had steps on the back next to the bumpers, and there's usually been one [agent] on either side standing on those steps at the back bumper.[202]

Johnson: Hmm.

Hoover: Whether the president asked that that not be done, we don't know . . . and the bubble-top was not up. But the bubble-top wasn't worth a damn anyway, 'cause they're made entirely of plastic.[203] And much to my surprise, the Secret Service do not have any armored cars.

Johnson: Do you have a bulletproof car?

199. Actually, the TSBD serviced school districts throughout Texas. B. Drummond Ayres, "Building from Which Oswald Fired Brings $650,000," *New York Times,* 17 April 1970.

200. The last known TSBD employee to see Oswald prior to the assassination placed him on the sixth floor, the same floor from which the shots were fired. *Warren Report,* 143.

201. Johnson is referring to the twenty-six-second amateur movie taken by Abraham Zapruder, a Dallas manufacturer of ladies' clothing. According to press reports, Zapruder sold the three-dollar roll of film to the Time-Life media company for $25,000. In fact, that was only the first installment in a contract that called for a $150,000 guaranteed advance, and 50 percent of all royalties after the advance ($915,000 in 2004 dollars) had been earned back via subsidiary sales. Richard Trask, *Pictures of the Pain: Photography and the Assassination of President Kennedy* (Danvers, Mass.: Yeoman Press, 1994), 91.

202. President Kennedy had repeatedly instructed the Secret Service not to have agents stand on the steps unless it was absolutely necessary. He wanted to maximize his and Mrs. Kennedy's visibility to the public whenever possible. *Warren Report,* 45.

203. The bubble-top was designed to protect against stormy weather only and was neither bulletproof nor bullet-resistant. Ibid., 43.

Hoover: Oh yes, I do! It's a—

Johnson: Do you think I oughta have one?

Hoover: I think you most *certainly* should have one . . . most certainly should.
Because . . . I have one here [and] we have one in New York . . . we use it
for different purposes. I use it here for myself, and if we have any raids to
make, or have to surround a place where anybody's hidden, we use the
bulletproof car on that. Because you can bulletproof the entire car
including the glass. But it means that the top has to remain up, you could
never let the top down. It's a regular limousine-type . . . and looks exactly
like any other car, but I do think you oughta have a bulletproof car. But I
was surprised the other day when I made [an] inquiry. All that I understand
the Secret Service has had [is] two cars with metal plates *underneath* the
car to take care of a hand grenade or a bomb that might be thrown out and
rolled along the street.

Well, of course, we don't do those things in this country. In Europe that's
the way they assassinate the heads of state . . . with bombs. They've been
after General [Charles] de Gaulle, you know, with that sort of thing.[204]

Johnson: Yeah.

Hoover: But in this country all of our assassinations have been with guns. And
for that reason, I think very definitely . . . I was *very* much surprised when
I learned that this bubble-top thing was *not* bulletproofed in any respect,
and that the plastic top to it—that was down, of course . . . the president
had insisted upon that so that he could stand up and wave to the crowd.
Now it seems to me that the president oughta *always* be in a bulletproof
car. It certainly would prevent anything like this *ever* happening again. It
doesn't mean—you could have a thousand Secret Service men on guard,
and still a sniper can snipe you from up in the window if you are exposed,
like the president was. But he can't do it if you have a solid top,
bulletproof top to it, as it should be.

Johnson: You mean [whenever] I ride around in my ranch, I oughta be in a
bulletproof car?

Hoover: Well, I would certainly think so, Mr. President. It seems to me that
that car down at your ranch there . . . the little car that we rode around in
when I was down there, I think that oughta be bulletproof. I think it oughta
be done very quietly. There's a concern that is out, I think, in Cincinnati,
where we have our cars bulletproofed.[205] And I think we've got four

---

204. In the early 1960s de Gaulle was the target of several assassination attempts because of
his efforts to negotiate an end to the revolution against French sovereignty in Algeria.

205. Hoover is referring to Cincinnati's Hess & Eisenhardt Company, which is famed for
modifying assembly-line automobiles to make them bullet- and bombproof. Hess & Eisenhardt
outfitted President Kennedy's limousine in 1961, but the Secret Service specifications did not
include a permanent, bulletproof roof over the passenger compartment. United Press International,
"Kennedy Car Built for Security," *New York Times,* 23 November 1963.

[sic] . . . we've got one on the West Coast, one in New York, and one here. And I think it can be done *quietly* without any publicity being given to it, or any pictures being taken of it, if it's handled *properly*. But I think you oughta have [one], because on that ranch there, it's perfectly easy for somebody to get onto the ranch.

Johnson: You think those entrances all oughta be guarded, though, don't you?

Hoover: Oh, I think by *all* means. I think by all means. I think you've got to recognize . . . you've gotta really, almost, be in the capacity of a so-called prisoner . . . because without that security, anything can be done. Now we've gotten a lot of letters and phone calls over the last three or four, five days . . . we got one about this parade the other day . . . that they were gonna try to kill you then. And I talked with the attorney general about it. I was very much opposed to that marching . . . to the White House.[206]

Johnson: Well, we'd—[the] Secret Service told 'em not to, but the family felt otherwise.

Hoover: Well, yeah, that's what Bobby told me. But when I heard of it, I talked with the Secret Service and they were very much opposed to it. I was very much opposed to it, because it was even *worse* than down there at Dallas.[207]

Johnson: Yes.

Hoover: You were walking down the center of the street—

Johnson: Yes, I think that's right.

Hoover: —and somebody on the sidewalk could dash out. I noticed even on Pennsylvania Avenue here . . . I viewed the procession coming back from the Capitol, and while they had police assigned along the curbstone, lookin' at the crowd, when the parade came along, the police turned around and *looked at the parade*—

Johnson: *[chuckles]*

Hoover: —which was the worst thing to do. They also had a line of soldiers . . . but they were lookin' at the parade [too].

Johnson: Well, I'm gonna take every precaution I can, and I—

Hoover: I think you've got to—

Johnson: —want to talk to you [about it]. And I wish you'd put down your thoughts on that a little bit, 'cause—

Hoover: I will.

Johnson: You're more than the head of the Federal Bureau [of Investigation] far as I'm concerned. You're my brother and personal friend—

206. Hoover is referring to the walking procession from the White House to St. Matthew's Cathedral in downtown Washington on November 25.

207. The eight blocks from the White House to St. Matthew's were among the most densely built-up in the capital, and threats had been made against de Gaulle, Johnson, Robert Kennedy, Earl Warren, and Anastas Mikoyan, the top Soviet official in attendance at the state funeral. "If [an assassin] missed one celebrity, his chances of hitting another [in the procession] were excellent." Manchester, *Death,* 573–75.

Hoover: Well, I certainly—

Johnson: —and you have been for twenty-five [or] thirty years, so . . . *[garbled]*

Hoover: Absolutely not.

Johnson: I got more confidence in your judgment than anybody in town, so you just put down some of the things you think oughta happen. And I won't involve you, or quote you, or get you in jurisdictional disputes or anything, but I'd like to at least advocate 'em as *my* opinion.[208]

Hoover: I'll be very glad to, indeed . . . I certainly appreciate your confidence. I do.

Johnson: Well, thank you . . . thank you, Edgar.

Hoover: Fine, Mr. President.

Sometime after 3 p.m. Johnson learns the outcome of the Katzenbach-Cox meeting with Earl Warren at 2:30 p.m., probably from Abe Fortas. Notwithstanding the formidable persuasive skills of a U.S. solicitor general and a deputy attorney general acting in tandem, the chief justice was immovable. Warren stubbornly maintained that the history of justices' extracurricular involvements is a very sorry one. Whenever justices become embroiled in an outside dispute, their effort seldom achieves the lofty goal set and inevitably brings grief, division, or disrepute to the justice involved and the Court itself. Warren harked all the way back to the involvement of five justices on the Hayes-Tilden Electoral Commission, established to help settle the bitterly contested presidential election of 1876. The commission ended up voting strictly along party lines, and the Court's reputation for meting out justice evenhandedly was greatly tarnished. Warren also mentioned the divisiveness and stalemate caused by Justice Robert Jackson's seventeen-month leave of absence to be chief prosecutor at the 1945–46 Nuremberg war crimes tribunal, and the price Justice Owen Roberts paid for getting involved in the controversial 1941 panel on the Pearl Harbor surprise attack.[209] Despite their best efforts, Katzenbach and Cox left Warren's chambers empty-handed. The chief justice will not participate in a presidential commission on the assassination, though he recognizes the importance of identifying the party or parties responsible for the assassination.

In the meantime, at 3:17 p.m., the president receives a previously scheduled twenty-minute briefing from Dr. Glenn Seaborg, chairman of the Atomic Energy Commission, the federal agency charged with building and maintaining

208. By "jurisdictional disputes," Johnson means getting the FBI involved in presidential protection, which is the exclusive domain of the Secret Service. Whether the president appreciates it or not, Hoover has no intention of trying to usurp one of the Secret Service's two main functions (the other being counterfeiting). Hoover believes presidential protection receives attention only when it fails, and he is not interested in getting the bureau entangled in a thankless chore.

209. Lewis Wood, "Jackson's Absence Raises Court Issue," *New York Times,* 20 January 1946.

Washington's nuclear arsenal. With chilling precision, Dr. Seaborg tells Johnson about the consequences of an all-out nuclear exchange with Moscow. The cost in American lives from a first strike alone is breathtaking: 39 to 40 million American casualties, not to mention untold dislocation and devastation that will take decades to overcome. As much as Johnson is taken aback, he immediately zeroes in on the figure of estimated casualties, realizing it might prove useful in overcoming the chief justice's recalcitrance. As the briefing with Seaborg breaks up, Johnson asks an aide to call Warren's chambers and request that the justice come to the Oval Office to discuss an urgent matter. Warren agrees to be at the White House at 4:30 p.m., less than an hour away.[210]

Johnson is far from willing to give up. As he would later remark in connection with Warren's initial, and seemingly adamant, refusal, "Early in my life I learned that doing the impossible frequently was necessary to get the job done."[211] The president intends to administer a healthy dose of what is well known on Capitol Hill as the "Johnson treatment." Much harder men have succumbed, against their better judgment, to Johnson's inimitable style of cajoling, pleading, and manipulation. Earl Warren has no inkling of what he is in for.

To Richard Russell / 4:05 p.m.

By the time he places this call, the president fully expected to have corralled Chief Justice Warren into heading the commission. The fact that Warren is still not on board will make this conversation problematic. On the one hand, Johnson probably does not want to wait much longer before telling Russell about the appointment he has in mind for the sixty-six-year-old senator, who is spending the holiday weekend at his home in Winder, Georgia. Yet with Warren's participation still undecided, Johnson dares not reveal his entire hand just yet. Johnson apparently wants to use the involvement of Warren to sell Russell on serving, and vice versa.[212]

The president's need to camouflage his intentions leads to a rambling (and, as Russell will later realize, deceptive) conversation about which judges Johnson might consider appointing to the commission. The two men discuss a variety of possible candidates from federal courts in New York, Washington, and Georgia in an illuminating look at how politicians evaluate sitting judges. It is certainly not on the basis of the beauty of their abstract legal reasoning. Almost as an afterthought—although it is hard to be certain, because Johnson may have intended to ask this all along—Johnson turns to Russell for advice on how to

210. Earl Warren, *The Memoirs of Earl Warren* (Garden City, N.Y.: Doubleday, 1977), 356.
211. Johnson, *Vantage Point*, 27.
212. In his meeting with Warren, Johnson will in fact tell the chief justice that Russell has agreed to serve on the commission provided Warren does so.

overcome Warren's objections to serving on the commission. Russell is unwitting because Johnson carefully avoids mentioning his strong preference for Warren. The senator, of course, would be beside himself if he knew Johnson intends to invoke not only his argument but his name in the upcoming meeting with the chief justice.

Johnson wants Russell on the panel for a variety of reasons. The most obvious one was mentioned already to Abe Fortas: enlisting Russell will allow Johnson to avoid appointing Jim Eastland to the commission. The president has little confidence in Eastland's judgment or in his ability to arrive at a tempered verdict as opposed to an ideological one (namely, that Oswald was somehow a tool of international Communism), irrespective of the evidence. A closely related reason is that Russell's presence will assuage any anxiety in Texas, and the rest of the old Confederacy, over Washington's insertion of itself into what is still, after all, a violation of state statutes. Russell is the unrivaled leader of states' rights in the Senate, and no one could possibly take issue with the commission on these grounds if the Georgian commits his prestige to the task. If anything, respect for Russell inside the small exclusive club that is the U.S. Senate is higher than in the general public. Russell, as Johnson will tell Rusk on another occasion, has more influence in the Senate than any other single member—that is, when he chooses to exercise it.[213]

Johnson also believes—and probably quite rightly—that a commission featuring Warren and Russell will make an enormous political statement from the outset. Each man is viewed as a hero by his respective constituency; together they represent the best arguments that can be mustered on the great divide in American domestic politics. The notion of them agreeing to serve together, in and of itself, is a powerful symbol. If they can arrive at a consensus on the party or parties responsible for the assassination, virtually the entire gamut of respectable opinion in the United States ought to be satisfied.

Another aspect of Russell's selection is his familiarity with the CIA's secret operations. In its sixteen-year history, the agency has seldom been subject to searching congressional scrutiny in public.[214] That relative immunity is by design, of course, and even the 1961 Bay of Pigs postmortem was conducted entirely behind closed doors. Any probe into the assassination will necessarily pry into CIA sources and methods because of Oswald's visit to Mexico City. Consequently, Johnson wants to have congressional members who have demonstrated their trustworthiness on such sensitive matters. By virtue of his interests, committee assignments, and seniority, there is no more vigorous guardian of the

213. Johnson and Rusk, conversation, 2 August 1965, 10:33 a.m., LBJL.
214. One rare exception occurred in 1948, when the CIA became the target of congressional critics for failing to predict unrest in Colombia. David Barrett, "Glimpses of a Hidden History: Sen. Richard Russell, Congress, and Oversight of the CIA," *International Journal of Intelligence and Counterintelligence* 11, no. 3 (Fall 1998).

CIA in Congress than Russell. Only two tiny Senate subcommittees have any oversight responsibility with respect to the CIA. The Georgia senator is chairman of both of them.[215]

Russell's selection in this regard also demonstrates a bit of cunning on Johnson's part. The president is congenitally suspicious, especially of an agency practiced in the black arts of deception and so-called plausible deniability. He is acutely aware of the agency's role in such events as the coup d'état in South Vietnam, which culminated in President Ngo Dinh Diem's murder.[216] Putting Russell on the panel simultaneously puts the agency on notice. Any effort that falls short of maximum cooperation with the commission puts at great risk the CIA's relationship with its most powerful congressional patron.[217]

But even if Russell had none of these credentials, Johnson would still be determined to put him on the commission, for a simple reason: there is no one in Washington who enjoys more of the president's trust and respect than Russell. Johnson realizes he has to be prepared, at this juncture, for the possibility that the commission's findings may spark a profound crisis. He wants Russell completely conversant with the facts in such a situation, so that Russell's advice and counsel will be fully grounded. Because in all likelihood, what Russell suggests after the commission's work is done is what President Johnson will end up doing. As Johnson will observe to Russell later in the day, "You're *my man* on [that commission] . . . *period.*"[218]

Johnson can never forget how Russell defused a crisis that was rocking the nation in the spring of 1951. Then the issue was civilian control of the military. President Harry Truman had relieved General Douglas MacArthur of his command in Korea because of rank insubordination. And the image of a failed haberdasher, and unpopular president, firing a "war hero" created a political firestorm the likes of which the country had seldom seen—fueled, as it was, by Senator Joe McCarthy's sensational claims regarding Communist infiltration of ruling circles. Far from being disgraced by the abrupt dismissal, MacArthur

215. The Senate Armed Services Committee (chaired by Russell) has a Subcommittee on Central Intelligence Agency also chaired by Russell. Its three other members are Senator Harry Byrd (D-Virginia), John Stennis (D-Mississippi), and Leverett Saltonstall (R-Massachusetts). The other Senate panel with CIA oversight responsibility is the Appropriations Subcommittee on the Department of Defense. This subcommittee is also chaired by Russell, and CIA oversight is restricted, moreover, to a subset of this panel, namely, Senators Russell, Stennis, Saltonstall, and Carl Hayden (D-Arizona), three of whom also sit on the Armed Services CIA subcommittee already! Thus, only five senators in total are normally privy to CIA secrets, and Russell's voice is unusually influential because of the authorization and appropriations power concentrated in his hands.

216. The CIA station chief in Saigon and DCI McCone were opposed to the coup. Once President Kennedy decided to go forward, however, agency officers played a vital role, with U.S. ambassador Henry Cabot Lodge acting in effect as the case officer for the operation.

217. Barrett, "Glimpses of a Hidden History."

218. Johnson and Russell, conversation, 29 November 1963, 8:55 p.m., LBJL.

received "an almost hysterical" welcome upon arriving in Washington, as an estimated seven and a half million New Yorkers turned out to greet him during a tickertape parade, or nearly twice the crowd that cheered Dwight Eisenhower's emotional return from Europe in 1945.[219] Russell chaired the Senate's inquiry into MacArthur's firing, and in the course of six weeks adroitly managed to first contain, and then slowly defuse, the crisis. It was one of the most masterful performances ever seen in the upper chamber. MacArthur emerged with his political pretensions shattered, while Russell's "fair, impartial and dignified conduct" of that investigation won universal praise and became an oft cited model for constructive congressional probes.[220] In fact, Democratic liberals no longer viewed Russell as a southern "evil genius" after his handling of MacArthur, although the Georgian remained anathema with respect to the 1952 nomination for the presidency.[221] Clearly Johnson is hoping for a reprise of Russell's performance, although the aftermath of Kennedy's assassination is not quite comparable. Nonetheless, a full-fledged foreign policy crisis, much less a war, is simply not part of the ambitious agenda that Johnson has in mind for his presidency.

The commission is not the only serious piece of business that Johnson will discuss with Russell. At his intelligence briefing on Thanksgiving Day, the president asked John McCone about the state of the CIA's relations with Congress. Overall, everything is "excellent," replied McCone. "The only problem [is] a continual harangue for a Joint Committee on Intelligence."[222] McCone then suggested that if Russell and Carl Vinson, the respective chairmen of the Senate and House Armed Services committees, could be persuaded to expand their CIA oversight subcommittees by a modest number, the pressure from Congress might abate.

Johnson thinks McCone has a good idea, especially now that the agency will be briefing the CIA subcommittees on the possibility of foreign involvement in the assassination for weeks if not months to come. The president knows that Russell is fiercely protective of his CIA oversight responsibilities. Nor-

219. Robert Dallek, *Lone Star Rising: Lyndon Johnson and His Times, 1908–1960* (New York: Oxford University Press, 1991), 398.

220. Richard Henschel, "The Committee on Armed Services," *Washington World* 4, no. 7 (24 February 1964), 14. After the four-month investigation in 1951, the controversy ended with a whimper, not a bang. Eight Republicans signed a minority report, but a majority of the committee voted not to issue any formal findings.

221. Goldsmith, *Colleagues,* 26.

222. Before the Senate and House established permanent select committees to monitor the U.S. intelligence community in the mid-1970s, congressional oversight was carried out by four subcommittees in name. See footnote 215 for the arrangement in the Senate. In the House, two subcommittees carried out the task: the Special Subcommittee on Central Intelligence Agency of the Armed Services Committee, chaired by Representative Carl Vinson (D-Georgia), and the Subcommittee on Defense of the Appropriations Committee (limited to the most senior members, usually five in number), led by Representative George Mahon.

mally a subcommittee hearing is automatically open to any member of the full committee, but Russell does not permit that practice with respect to the CIA. The Georgian is intent on keeping a record he is proud of: during his watch, CIA testimony before the Senate has never leaked out, which is nothing short of remarkable for Congress.[223] In light of the circumstances, Russell quickly agrees with Johnson's proposal to expand temporarily the Armed Services CIA subcommittee by two senators, J. William Fulbright and Bourke Hickenlooper, the respective chairman and ranking minority member of the Committee on Foreign Relations.

Johnson: . . . it concerns [J. Edgar] Hoover, and [the] secretary of state, and some others. We're trying to avoid having all the House committee[s] . . . Hale Boggs and a bunch have got some things started over there, and Jim Eastland and [Everett] Dirksen and a bunch have got 'em started in the Senate, and Bobby Kennedy's got his ideas, and Hoover's got his report. They want to have [Thomas] Dewey in for a while.[224]

So . . . I've about concluded upon—that I can get people pretty well together, and I've talked to the leadership—on trying to have the three branches . . . have two congressmen and two senators, and maybe two [or] three outsiders, and maybe somebody from the [Supreme] Court—or at least some person of a judicial background—that are absolutely top-flight folks, on about a seven-man board to evaluate Hoover's report. And it'll be largely done by staff . . . but they can work on it.[225]

[aside to Moyers] Bill, gimme that list of the people.

[to Russell] And I wanted to get your reaction to it. I think that'd be *better* than [the Senate] Judiciary [Committee] runnin' one investigation, the House [Judiciary Committee] runnin' another investigation, and havin' four [or] five going in opposite directions because—

Russell: Well, I agree with *that.* But I don't think that Hoover oughta make his report too soon.

Johnson: He's ready with it now, and he wants to get it off just as quick as he can.

Russell: *[sounding alarmed]* Uh-oh.

223. Henschel, "Armed Services Subcommittees Report to Unit." Even by the standards of the Senate Armed Services Committee, one of the most secretive in Congress, the CIA subcommittee is extraordinarily hush-hush. Few people even realize it exists. Information it gathers is rarely disclosed to the public and never printed. The visits to Capitol Hill by the director of Central Intelligence, usually three times a year, are secret and not recorded.

224. Johnson is harking back to Eugene Rostow's November 25 proposal to Bill Moyers, which mentioned Dewey, an experienced prosecutor, as a plausible candidate for appointment to a commission. Johnson may be trying to impress Russell with his effort to bring order out of the cacophony of alternatives.

225. Johnson is being disingenuous when he says "maybe somebody" from the Supreme Court, as he is dead set on getting Earl Warren.

Johnson: And he'd probably have it out today . . . at most on Monday.

Russell: *[in disbelief]* Well, he ain't gonna *publish* the damned thing, is he?

Johnson: He's gonna turn it over to this group . . . and there's some things about it I can't talk about, but—[226]

Russell: Yeah, I understand that. But I think it'd be mighty well if that thing was kept quiet another week or ten days. . . . I just *do.*

Johnson: Well, I think it would be turned over . . . they're takin' this Court of Inquiry in Texas, and I think the results of that Court of Inquiry, and Hoover's report, and all of 'em, would go to this group and they would evaluate it, and then maybe evaluate it for the general public.

Russell: Uh-huh.

Johnson: Now here's who I'm going to try to get on it. I don't know . . . I don't think I can get any member of the [Supreme] Court, but I'm going to try to.[227] Gonna try to get Allen Dulles . . . I'm gonna try to get Senator Russell and Senator [John Sherman] Cooper from the Senate.

Russell: Oh, no, no. Get somebody else, now.

Johnson: Yeah, I know. Wait a minute now. I'm gonna try—

Russell: I haven't got *time.*

Johnson: —[to] get Jerry Ford. It's not gonna take much time. But we got to have a states' rights man and somebody that the country has confidence in, and I'm gonna have—[Hale] Boggs has entered a resolution over there, and I haven't talked to anybody about the membership but you.[228] But I would think that Ford and Boggs would be pretty good, they're both pretty young men, and—

Russell: They're both solid citizens.

Johnson: And I think that Cooper's a Republican and you're a good states' rights man. I think [we] might get John McCloy and Allen Dulles, and maybe somebody from the [Supreme] Court.

Russell: [If] you don't get somebody from [the] Supreme Court . . . I don't know him personally, but this Judge [Harold] Medina, up there that tried all those Communists, is known all over the United States.[229] I don't know what kind of man he is—he might not do—but Judge Medina—

Johnson: Uh-huh.

226. Johnson is almost certainly referring to the allegation that Oswald received $6,500 in the Cuban consulate.

227. Now Johnson is being a little more candid but is still concealing his preference for Warren, who will be arriving for a meeting in the Oval Office in twenty-five minutes.

228. Johnson, of course, has already discussed his nominees with Abe Fortas and with J. Edgar Hoover (save for Warren). He may have meant that Russell is the first prospective member he is talking to about the commission's makeup.

229. Judge Medina achieved lasting fame after presiding over the 1948 trial in New York of eleven U.S. Communist Party leaders charged under the Smith Act. Political conservatives consider Medina a champion of anti-Communism in the legal sphere.

Russell: I think he's on the Circuit Court of Appeals up in New York now.

Johnson: Who would be the best one if I didn't get the chief [justice]?[230] I understand none of the Court—

Russell: Oh, no, no. You wouldn't want [Justice Tom] Clark hardly.

Johnson: I understand none of the Court . . . no, we can't have a Texan.[231]

Russell: No, that's what I said. That'd disqualify him.

Johnson: Hoover tells me all three of these shots were aimed for the president. And that this telescopic sight [would] bring this thing up to where you could shoot a man with it as easy as you'd get a man sittin' talkin' to you.

Russell: I thought it was just a seven-dollar-and-a-half thing.[232]

Johnson: Well, it was a twenty-one-dollar gun. But he said he looked through the telescopic sight himself, and he said, "Mr. President I could hit a man on that street going twenty miles an hour as easy as I could hit you sittin' talkin' to you." That's his language. Okay, now I . . .

Russell: Well, I . . . really, Mr. President, unless you—

Johnson: Well, I'm—

Russell: Unless you really think it'd be of some benefit—

Johnson: I know it would be.

Russell: —[I don't know] why you need me . . . it'd save my *life*. I declare, I don't want to serve on that commission.

Johnson: I know you don't wanna do anything, but I *want* you to. And I think that this is important enough, and you'll see why. Now, the next thing . . . I know how you feel 'bout this CIA, but they're worried about havin' to go into a lot of this stuff with [the Senate] Foreign Relations Committee. How much of a problem would it give you to just quietly let [J. William] Fulbright and [Bourke] Hickenlooper come into your CIA [sub]committee?

Russell: [So] long it's confined to those two, it wouldn't present any problem at all.

Johnson: Well, that's all we'd make it now.

Russell: But there'll be changes made up there, and I don't want some of those fellas . . . some of those fellas got no business *there* . . . gotta lot of bad talkers on that [Foreign Relations] committee.

Johnson: Why don't you do it by invitation then?

Russell: And we've had a splendid record up to now. There never [has] been *one thing* leaked.

230. In light of Johnson's mind-set, this seems a tricky construction. Russell probably misunderstood Johnson's question to mean, "I'm not going to ask Chief Justice Warren, so who's the best Supreme Court justice left?" Later Johnson would aver that he told Russell during this conversation that he would try to get the chief justice.

231. Clark is not only from Texas but is a native of Dallas.

232. Russell probably has in mind the price of the telescopic sight, which cost Oswald about seven dollars.

Johnson: You got a perfect one, you got a perfect one. And they . . . that's what . . . they know that. But they're worried about . . . they can't do it with—

Russell: See, I've been very careful. I've even kept Margaret Chase Smith [R-Maine] off that [sub]committee though I've got a lot of faith in *her.* But I've kept her off.

Johnson: Yeah.

Russell: 'Cause I just wanted to be *sure* that I *knew* what I was doin'.

Johnson: *[aside]* That's right.

   [to Russell] Couldn't you do it quietly by invitation?

Russell: Yes, I could.

Johnson: Just on a personal basis, and then that invitation to end anytime you wanted it to, and I'd say that to 'em?

Russell: Yes, I'll be glad to do that; invite 'em over there.[233]

Johnson: Okay. When you comin' back?

Russell: Well, I just got down here. I'm comin' in there Sunday afternoon.

[Johnson and Russell discuss Governor Carl Sanders (D), head of Georgia's delegation to the state funeral, who sat beside Lady Bird Johnson during the president's speech to the Congress. Then they return to the subject of the commission.]

Russell: Mr. President, can't you get someone else [for that job]?

Johnson: Well, if I can, I will. But I'm not gonna . . . this country's gotta lot of confidence in you, and if I had my way, you'd be in my place and I'd trade with *you!*

Russell: *[chuckles]* Oh no, that would never do.[234]

Johnson: Well, it would too.

Russell: I'd go crazy in six weeks in that job, and you—

Johnson: [The] country [would] be in a helluva lot better shape.

Russell: And you'll go run it the next nine years; I'll be dead in another two [or] three years.[235] You can have it.

Johnson: You get your rest. I don't wanna bother you anymore, but I'm gonna have to be callin' you every once in a while, so . . .

Russell: Well, you know I'm always available, but I—

Johnson: Okay. All right. Good-bye.

Russell: Well . . . *[indistinct].*

Johnson: You think about anybody else now, besides [Judge] Medina.

---

233. Later in the day, after membership on the commission is settled, Johnson will place calls to Fulbright (at 7:11 p.m.) and Hickenlooper (7:20 p.m.) to inform them of Russell's invitation to participate in CIA subcommittee hearings on an ad hoc basis.

234. Johnson is playing to Russell's now-dormant ambition to be the first southern president.

235. Having succeeded to the presidency in the third year of Kennedy's first term, Johnson is eligible to serve out the term and be elected to the office twice. Potentially he could be the longest-serving president save for his political hero, Franklin Roosevelt.

Russell: Well, I don't know him.

Johnson: What about that old man [who] died, that's on that circuit court down there that I liked?

Russell: Oh, he would have been ideal, but he's dead.

Johnson: Uh-huh. That other fella—

Russell: [Judge Samuel "Ned"] Sibley . . . he's a magnificent man, he'd been perfect.[236]

Johnson: That fella you got on there now, though, is not too good . . . is he?

Russell: [Judge Elbert] Tuttle? No.[237]

Johnson: Yeah, Tuttle. He's an Eisenhower appointee?

Russell: Yeah . . . he's a pretty good man, but. . . .

Johnson: They tell me he gives 'em some problems, but that's—

Russell: He's gonna give 'em more problems. He's the kinda fella that thinks he's the last word.

Johnson: Uh-huh.

Russell: Thinks he's the last word. Is there someone there?

Johnson: You know [Judge E. Barrett] Prettyman?

Russell: Yeah.

Johnson: What do you think about him?

Russell: Pretty good man. He's gettin' a little old, isn't he?[238]

Johnson: Yeah.

Russell: Prettyman's a good man.

236. Sibley died in 1958. In 1946 he upheld Georgia's "county unit voting system," which no doubt endeared him to Russell, as it gave added weight to rural, more conservative counties. Georgia's county unit rule endured until the Warren Court ruled it unconstitutional in March 1963, on the grounds that it violated the Constitution's equal protection clause. Harold Hinton, "Georgia Defends County-Unit Vote," *New York Times,* 16 August 1946; "Unit-Vote System Upheld by Court," *New York Times,* 27 August 1946; "High Court Voids County Unit Vote," *New York Times,* 19 March 1963.

237. Russell frowns upon Tuttle for the same reasons he holds Sibley in high regard. The U.S. Court of Appeals for the Fifth Circuit, where Tuttle has been chief judge since 1961, comprises six southern states from the old Confederacy (Alabama, Florida, Georgia, Louisiana, Mississippi, and Texas) and has been the chief legal battleground for the civil rights movement since the late 1950s. Tuttle is one of several Eisenhower appointees whose rulings are systematically dismantling the legal underpinnings of segregation and discrimination in the South. Johnson is only pretending to share Russell's view of Judge Tuttle. Jack Bass, "Elbert P. Tuttle, 98, Federal Appeals Judge Who Sought Racial Justice in South, Dies," *New York Times,* 25 June 1996.

238. Russell looks favorably on Judge Prettyman no doubt because of his rulings on internal security issues. In 1952 Prettyman wrote the majority opinion upholding the Subversive Activities Control Act of 1950 (the McCarran Act), requiring the U.S. Communist Party to register as a subversive organization controlled by the Soviet Union. Similarly, in 1959 he wrote the decision permitting the State Department to bar U.S. citizens from traveling to Communist-ruled countries. But the seventy-two-year-old Prettyman retired from regular active service in 1962. Ellen Hoffman, "Judge E. Barrett Prettyman Dies at 79," *Washington Post,* 5 August 1971; "E. Barrett Prettyman Dies at 79; Former Chief of Appeals Court," *New York Times,* 5 August 1971.

Johnson: But I don't think he's *known*.

Russell: Well, he's not, but . . . he don't have to be. He doesn't have to be. Now you gonna let the attorney general nominate someone, aren't you?

Johnson: No. . . .[239]

Russell: Well, you gonna have [J. Edgar] Hoover on there?

Johnson: No. It's his report.

Russell: Oh, that's right . . . that's right. It wouldn't do.

Johnson: But he's agreeable to folks like Dulles, and . . .

Russell: Well, Dulles is a good man; that was a happy thought.

Johnson: McCloy.

Russell: McCloy, I guess, is a good man. I don't think . . . I don't hold him in near as high regard as I do Dulles, but he's all right. He's got a big reputation. Let me see . . . if I think of a judge in the next thirty [or] forty minutes, I'll call you.

Johnson: Thank you.

Russell: But you can get plenty of 'em . . . some of these circuit court judges . . . some right there in the District [of Columbia] . . . one or two of 'em are pretty good.

Johnson: What do you think about a [Supreme Court] justice sittin' on it?[240]

Russell: I don't . . . I think it'd be all right.

Johnson: Why shouldn't you [have a justice on the commission]? How many assassinations . . . you don't have a president assassinated but every fifty years.[241]

Russell: Well, they put 'em on the Pearl Harbor inquiry, you know.

Johnson: I know it, but he's . . . that's why [Warren's] against it now.[242]

Russell: They're afraid it might get into the courts?

Johnson: I guess so, I don't know.

Russell: That's probably the theory of it . . . I'm not very good on thinkin' 'bout things like that.[243]

239. Johnson is apparently not comfortable about disclosing to Russell that the two private citizens being appointed to the panel, John McCloy and Allen Dulles, are Robert Kennedy's choices.

240. Johnson is dissembling.

241. Actually, the last assassination attempt to succeed had occurred more than sixty years ago, in 1901.

242. Johnson is referring to the fact that the five-man Roberts Commission—which assigned principal blame for the surprise attack to the two ranking officers in command at Pearl Harbor—did not put an end to the controversy over who was negligent when it issued its 1942 report; quite the contrary. Presumably, Johnson is also conveying Warren's belief that Justice Owen Roberts's involvement sullied the Court's reputation. In light of their later argument about who said what during this conversation, this is the point where Russell, if he had carefully parsed Johnson's sentence, might have come to understand that the president is asking Warren to lead the commission.

243. Russell is speculating that some aspect of the Dallas crimes is bound to reach the Supreme Court; in that case, of course, a justice could always recuse himself.

Johnson: Well, give me the arguments . . . why they ought to.[244]

Russell: Well, [the basic argument is that in a] matter of this magnitude . . . the American people would feel reassured to have a member of the highest court [on the commission], that's the only [argument] you've got. You have many more circuit court judges who are far abler than some of your Supreme Court justices, but that is the argument. [That is the] only argument you can make for it. If you had some top-flight state supreme court justice . . . if you knew [someone like that] . . . but they're not known all over the country, I don't care *how* able they are. This thing of television and radio has *narrowed* the group of celebrities to just those in the very highest positions. I don't know. You've got some smart boys 'round you [there] that can give you the name of some outstanding circuit court judge.

Johnson: Okay. You be thinkin'.

Russell: All right.

Johnson: 'Bye.

Russell: 'Bye, Mr. President.

Earl Warren / 4:30 p.m.

Two hours after turning Archibald Cox and Nicholas Katzenbach down, the seventy-two-year-old chief justice is ushered into the Oval Office by McGeorge Bundy, who then departs. Warren is alone with the president, which is just the way Johnson wants it. The moment Warren sits down, Johnson launches into his full court press. He starts by telling Warren he is aware of the chief justice's views, as they were communicated to him by some very fine men. But he doesn't care who delivered the message. The country has been rocked to its very foundations, and faces the prospect of threatening divisions and suspicions unless the facts are explored objectively and in a manner that will be respected by the public.

The president then turns to the dangers posed by the congressional committees planning highly publicized investigations, in addition to those of the Dallas and Texas authorities. (Johnson neglects to mention that he has been instrumental in prodding the investigation by the Texas state attorney general.) All these probes will inevitably compete for attention, the president argues, leaving the public more emotional and confused than ever. A bipartisan presidential commission is the only way to defuse an ominous situation, Johnson concludes, and he has pledges from Senator Eastland and Speaker McCormack that all congressional efforts will be aborted if such a body is appointed. Finally, Johnson maintains that Warren's "personal integrity" is the key element in ensuring that

---

244. In effect, Johnson is asking an unwitting Russell for the best argument to use when Warren comes to the Oval Office in twenty minutes.

the commission will unearth all the facts and issue credible conclusions.[245] The president says he has already decided on the other members and ticks their names off, one by one, for the chief justice. Johnson then says, in a bold misrepresentation of the facts, that he has already contacted these men and all have agreed to serve *if Warren accepts the chairmanship.*[246] The chief justice cannot help but be impressed by the stature of his prospective colleagues. Warren is probably flattered by the notion that their participation is contingent upon his and, in particular, that Richard Russell is willing to serve under him.

Warren attempts to get a word in edgewise. He refers to Justice Robert Jackson's absence from the Supreme Court to serve as chief prosecutor at the Nuremberg war crimes tribunal, and to President Kennedy's ill-advised effort to have Justice Arthur Goldberg mediate a railroad labor dispute in July 1963.[247] Before Warren can finish his point, Johnson declares his agreement with Warren's reasoning—except that this situation is not like the Nuremberg trial, or the railroad strike. "Let me read you one report," says Johnson, as he reaches for a document describing the allegation that Lee Harvey Oswald received $6,500 in the Cuban consulate, presumably as a down payment, in order to kill the president of the United States.[248]

Without skipping a beat Johnson concludes his pitch. He impresses Warren with Dr. Seaborg's classified estimate of 40 million casualties should Washington and Moscow ever come to nuclear loggerheads. "You were a soldier in World War I, but there was nothing you could do in that uniform comparable to what you can do for your country in this hour of trouble," Johnson observes.[249] "When the president of the United States says that you are the only man who can handle the matter, you won't say 'no,' will you?"[250]

Warren does not stand a chance. Tears well in his eyes. He swallows hard and says, "Mr. President, if the situation is that serious, my personal views do not count. I will do it."[251]

245. Johnson, *Vantage Point,* 27.

246. Warren, *Memoirs,* 357.

247. Cabell Phillips, "Kennedy's Choice of Goldberg Has 9 Precedents," *New York Times,* 10 July 1963. The chief justice was aghast at the idea of turning a sitting justice into the arbitrator of a labor dispute; in any event, the unions rejected President Kennedy's proposed role for Goldberg.

248. Johnson and Russell, conversation, 29 November 1963, 8:55 p.m., LBJL.

249. Warren, *Memoirs,* 358.

250. Johnson, *Vantage Point,* 27.

251. Warren, *Memoirs,* 358. The exact words spoken between Warren and Johnson are rendered differently in their respective memoirs and also differ from more contemporaneous accounts. But the gist is consistent. See also Manchester, *Death,* 630, and Marquis Childs, "Mr. Warren Tries His Hardest Case," *Washington Post,* 15 January 1964.

To John McCormack / 4:55 p.m.

Like the late president, McCormack is Irish, Catholic, and hails from Massa-chusetts, but the similarities end there. The entirely self-made McCormack grew up in South Boston, the other side of the tracks from the Kennedys, and speaks the language of a politician who most certainly did not go to Harvard. Indeed, there is no love lost between McCormack, whose brand of Irish machine politics emphasizes "paying your dues," and the Kennedys. In 1962 McCormack's favorite nephew, the highest Democratic officeholder in Massachusetts and the logical nominee for an open Senate seat, lost a bitter race for the Demo-cratic nomination to President Kennedy's inexperienced thirty-year-old brother Ted.

McCormack was known for his partisan belligerence while serving as majority whip for twenty-one years under Sam Rayburn. But he has undergone a seemingly remarkable transformation since becoming Speaker in 1961. The seventy-one-year-old McCormack is now more like a kindly, elder gentleman struggling hard to control an "unruly brood."[252] He exhibits little of Rayburn's famed knack for knowing how to make the House behave. Consequently, John-son is particularly concerned about McCormack's ability to keep all House committees at bay, now that a commission has been organized.

McCormack is the first person Johnson calls after winning Earl Warren's agreement to serve. During the conversation with the Speaker, there is an unmis-takable note of satisfaction in Johnson's voice, almost as if he is admiring his own handiwork, while reveling in the power of the presidency to bring together such disparate political souls. Although McCormack is the first legislator to be privy to the news that the chief justice will chair the commission, Johnson does not emphasize Warren's role, presumably because he is still concerned word will leak out before the White House can issue the actual announcement. The presi-dent also entrusts McCormack with the "real" reason why he selected Richard Russell: he wants to keep Jim Eastland off the commission, though he neglects to mention his disdain for Manny Celler too, Eastland's House counterpart.

McCormack's reaction to the appointments is parochial. As he mulls over the commission, he is concerned primarily about the geographic spread of its congressional members. Three of the four members—Russell, Boggs, and Cooper—hail from the South, though Johnson insists Cooper is not truly from the region but represents a border state.

[The tape recording begins abruptly.]
Johnson: . . . evaluate this [FBI] report. It's not gonna be like the Nuremberg

252. Richard Lyons, "Ex–House Speaker McCormack Dies," *Washington Post,* 23 November 1980.

trial, or the railroad strike, or anything like that. But this is a . . . wait just a second.

[Johnson talks with aides in the Oval Office.]

Now Edgar Hoover thinks he'll be ready [with the FBI report] tomorrow maybe, and maybe then Monday . . . we think we oughta announce this thing as quickly as we can because Rusk is rather concerned about it. And—

McCormack: You mean announce the—

Johnson: The Commission . . . say they gonna evaluate the [FBI] report.

McCormack: I sent you down—if you haven't got it yet—a complete memorandum on the Pearl Harbor [Roberts Commission], so you'd have it. You know, on the executive order—

Johnson: Yeah, yeah.

McCormack: —and the other things that happened. I just sent it down for information, in case you'd want to get it for sort of guidance and background.[253]

Johnson: Now here's who I would think—who we think would be—would make pretty good ones. And I wanted to tell it to you, and I don't want you to repeat to a human bein', 'cause I haven't talked to any of 'em.

McCormack: Yeah.

Johnson: *[correcting himself]* I've talked to Russell, talked to Dick Russell.[254] *[aside to Walter Jenkins, his chief of staff]* Close this door, Walter.

Got to have some outstanding states' rights man, and [James] Eastland was kinda head of the resolution investigatin' it over there . . . I've got to get him to call off his investigation.

McCormack: Yeah.

Johnson: I thought I'd take the chief justice and John McCloy . . . and Allen Dulles.[255]

McCormack: Wait a minute . . . John McCloy—

Johnson: Allen Dulles . . . Richard Russell.

McCormack: Yes.

Johnson: Senator Cooper.

McCormack: Yeah.

Johnson: And I was considerin' Representative Boggs, who has been talkin' about this stuff all the time.

253. Earlier in the day McCormack sent Johnson a copy of the executive order creating the Roberts Commission and a copy of its findings. Report of the Commission, *Attack Upon Pearl Harbor by Japanese Armed Forces,* 77th Cong., 2nd Sess. (Washington, D.C.: U.S. Government Printing Office, 1942).

254. The president does not tell McCormack that he has already talked to Earl Warren, too, presumably so that the Speaker will keep that news confidential.

255. Although McCormack is the first congressional leader to learn that Warren will be on the commission, it does not seem to register.

McCormack: What Boggs?[256]

Johnson: Hale Boggs . . . and Congressman Ford.

McCormack: Uh-hmm . . . good men.

Johnson: Can I get any better ones that you [can] think of? I've talked to nobody but Russell about it. Now, I've got to be sure that we've . . . [the] House and Senate don't mess with 'em, and that I've got to have someone that can work with the Justice [Department], the administration, with Hoover, and that has been interested in it, so it's kinda like the author of a resolution. I really . . . just between us, I don't want Eastland, so that's why I got Russell.

McCormack: On the Republican member, I'd have to consult with . . . in the House, you know, the procedure [is that] you consult with [Charles] Halleck.[257]

Johnson: Well, that's on your appointments up there. But this is going to be appointed by the president.

McCormack: Oh, you're going to appoint it.

Johnson: Yeah.

McCormack: Yes . . . well [then,] what do we do up here?

Johnson: Well, I just . . . you give me *advice.* I'm just askin' you, do you think there's anybody better that I could get? What's your judgment?

McCormack: No.

Johnson: I just . . . do you know of an abler or better, more patriotic fellow than . . . a Republican that would suit this mission, if you were president, than Ford?

McCormack: No . . . no. He's a top-rate man . . . a man who would rise to the consciousness of responsibility, too.

Johnson: And Boggs . . . you feel all right too about, I guess?

McCormack: Yes . . . yes.

Johnson: Is [there] anybody that's shown more interest in it?

McCormack: He's a good man. You couldn't have . . . those are two good men.

Johnson: All right. Now what do you [think about]—yeah, I always want to make a Mr. [Sam] Rayburn out of you—Dick Russell and John Cooper?[258]

McCormack: Yes . . . Cooper is . . . Dick Russell, yes. Cooper, of course, is a strong man.

Johnson: Now Hoover doesn't much like McCloy.[259]

---

256. There is a Republican senator from Delaware named J. Caleb Boggs.

257. Halleck is the minority leader. McCormack is initially under the same misimpression as Boggs was over the nature of the commission.

258. Johnson seems to be suggesting that he is now looking to McCormack for the advice and counsel he once received from his House mentor, Sam Rayburn.

259. Inadvertently Johnson is suggesting he may have talked over the candidates with Hoover, though the president has insisted to McCormack he has talked only with Russell thus far.

McCormack: [Let] me see . . . 'course you'd have Cooper and Russell from more—

Johnson: The Senate.

McCormack: —more or less from the South.

Johnson: Well now, they would be the . . . Cooper's [from] a border state. Russell would be [from] the South.

McCormack: Yeah.

Johnson: Boggs would be [from] the South.

McCormack: You wouldn't have anyone here really from the North.

Johnson: Well, I got McCloy . . . [and] I got Dulles.

McCormack: Yeah, [but] I mean on the legislative level.

Johnson: No . . . no . . . no. I have Cooper [from a] border state. Ford from Michigan . . . and they consider that pretty North. . . . But I'd have a chief from California and McCloy from New York, [and] Dulles from New York.

McCormack: *You* are the one to make the decision.

Johnson: Yeah, but I'm just . . . I just wanna get the best judgment. I'm gonna make it. Do you know anything about McCloy yourself?

McCormack: *Not* myself . . . no.

Johnson: My impressions are very good of him.

McCormack: I don't . . . everything I've heard about him . . . has been very favorable, that is, about the man *personally.*

Johnson: Now I've told the chief [justice] that Eastland promised me in the Senate that he wouldn't go on . . . [and] that I'd talk to you about it in the House. I don't want to appoint a commission if they're gonna start a whole bunch of investigations [in Congress], so. . . .

McCormack: Well, as far as the House is concerned, I'll stop . . . I'll do anything that I can to stop investigations.

Johnson: *[aside]* Yeah . . . I know it.

[to McCormack] Well, I think we . . . ought to. We don't wanna be testifyin', [having] some fella comin' up from Dallas, sayin' "I think [Nikita] Khrushchev planned this whole thing, and that he got our president assassinated." Then news television sayin' that assistant chief said today, that he believes Khrushchev did so-and-so. You can see what that'll lead us to right quick.

McCormack: Who said that?

Johnson: Nobody said it, but if they *do,* you know.

McCormack: When you gonna make the appointments?

Johnson: Just [as] quick as I can talk to 'em, and get an executive order drafted, and so forth. I better get on with it, I just thought I'd want to talk to you before I did it, my friend. You think it's all right?

McCormack: The theory of the commission is *absolutely* correct.

Johnson: All right. Do you think—

McCormack: I know of nothing on the legislative level . . . you see, the only thought was on the legislative level, with . . . Russell, Cooper, and Boggs, you'll have three from the South.

Johnson: No. Russell . . . Cooper's not a southerner—

McCormack: He's from a border state, but they—

Johnson: —and Boggs is not much of a—

McCormack: No, I agree with you that. But Louisiana—

Johnson: He's been kinda authorin' the resolution, you know. He's been wantin' to investigate it over there.

McCormack: Who?

Johnson: Boggs.

McCormack: Hale Boggs?

Johnson: Yeah . . . hell, he made a speech about it today.[260]

McCormack: Well, he was just answering some questions.

Johnson: Yeah, but he's been gettin' . . . he's been on television three or four times about there oughta be a congressional investigation.

McCormack: Well, I hadn't heard of that.

Johnson: Yeah.

McCormack: If I did . . . I'd spoken to him . . . toned *him* down.

Johnson: But . . . Cooper's considered a pretty liberal fella, you know.

McCormack: There's no question about that, Mr. President.

Johnson: And Ford is from the North.

McCormack: Yes.

Johnson: And Cooper's from a border state. And you got two southerners, but you got two northerners that are civilians—you see what I mean—to offset 'em.

McCormack: Yes, I'm not . . . I wasn't undertaking to *argue* with you. I wouldn't do that under any circumstances.

Johnson: Well, I sure want you to if you disagree with me . . . you just tell me.

McCormack: But . . . *you couldn't have better men!*

Johnson: Yeah.

McCormack: But I['m] just thinkin' of the geographical location on the . . . legislative level, and that's something I just simply call to your conscious mind for *you* to consider. That you would have . . . that Cooper's— Kentucky up north is considered *South.* I agree it's a border state.

Johnson: Well, you see from the public, though, I wouldn't have *any* southerner.

McCormack: What's that?

Johnson: There're *three* men that [are] appointed to represent the public.

McCormack: Yes.

---

260. Johnson is referring to Boggs's statement of four hours ago in the well of the House, in which he leaked word of the president's decision to appoint a commission.

Johnson: And *none* of them are southerners.

McCormack: No, that's true. Well, . . . listen, you go ahead.

Johnson: Will you take care of the House of Representatives for me?

McCormack: Well, now . . . how am I going to take care of them?

Johnson: Well, just keep 'em from investigatin'!

McCormack: *Oh, well!* From that angle I've been *doing* it!

[The conversation then turns to a discussion of foreign aid appropriations.]

To Allen Dulles / 5:41 p.m.

The White House switchboard has been informed that the president needs to make some urgent calls. If the announcement is going to be carried in full in the Saturday papers, the president has only about forty-five minutes or so to round up the rest of the commissioners. The conversation with Allen Dulles will commence Johnson's effort to secure commitments from the five men he wants to appoint to the commission besides Warren and Russell. The only prospective appointee Johnson will not speak personally with is Hale Boggs, perhaps out of pique. The president probably instructs an aide to inform Boggs he is a member of the commission he has been talking so much about, whether he has time for it or not.

Johnson is not unfamiliar with Dulles, but the two men do not know each other particularly well, either. Since leaving the CIA in November 1961 after having served as DCI for nine years, longer than any other man, the seventy-year-old Dulles has been leading a quiet life in retirement, lecturing and writing about intelligence. His first book on the subject, *The Craft of Intelligence,* has just been published to mild praise. Dulles is too discreet to write a genuinely gripping memoir.

Dulles is spending a quiet afternoon at his Georgetown home when his wife calls him to the telephone. As soon as he picks up the receiver, a harried White House operator says the president wants to speak with him and will be calling Dulles back shortly. This gives Dulles a few moments to ponder why Johnson is calling. Dulles thinks it may have something to do with the assassination. Five minutes later the telephone rings again.[261]

Their conversation has two notable aspects. In marked contrast to the conversations with Richard Russell and Earl Warren, Johnson does not bother Dulles with the names of his soon-to-be colleagues. The president recognizes that Dulles will serve regardless of whom he has to serve with. The other interesting detail is that Dulles makes a point of raising his prior occupation as director of Central Intelligence as possible grounds for exclusion from the panel. Though he doesn't specify why, Dulles is undoubtedly thinking of the vigor-

---

261. Grose, *Gentleman Spy,* 540.

ous Communist propaganda and disinformation efforts directed against him in the late 1950s and early 1960s, when Dulles was the KGB's chief target in its relentless psychological warfare against the CIA.[262] The international media controlled directly and indirectly by the Soviet Union will surely exploit Dulles's presence on the commission if the panel arrives at findings the Kremlin does not find congenial—and maybe irrespective of the findings. Yet the prospect that Dulles's participation might be used to discredit the commission internationally is apparently of no concern to the president or his advisers. Presumably, the need to apply Dulles's expertise to get to the bottom of Oswald's years in the Soviet Union, and his murky visit to Mexico City, overrides this consideration.[263]

Johnson: [I] got a little unpleasantness . . . news for you.
Dulles: Yes.
Johnson: We're going to name very shortly a presidential commission made up of seven people: two from the House, two from the Senate, and two from the public, and one from the [Supreme] Court—
Dulles: Yes, sir.
Johnson: —as a study group to go into this FBI report, and this [Texas] Court of Inquiry, and all the incidents—
Dulles: Yes, sir.
Johnson: —[in] connection with the assassination of our beloved friend.
Dulles: Yes, sir.
Johnson: And you've got to go on that for me.
Dulles: You think I can really serve you?
Johnson: I know you can; I know you can. There's not any doubt about it. Just get ready now to go in there and do a good job. We've got to have a . . . America's got to be united in this hour.
Dulles: If I can be of any help . . . and you've considered the effect of my previous work and my previous job?
Johnson: I sure have . . . we want you to do it . . . that's that. You always do what's best [for your country]. I found that out about you a long time ago. Thank you very much.

262. Lester Hajek, "Target: CIA," *Studies in Intelligence,* Winter 1962; Vladislav Zubok, "Spy vs. Spy: The KGB vs. the CIA, 1960–1962," *Cold War International History Project Bulletin,* no. 4 (Fall 1994).

263. Dulles will prove to be a valuable asset in evaluating Oswald's visit to Mexico City, as well as his sojourn in the Soviet Union. But over time he is proved right. Dulles's participation will be twisted into proof of CIA involvement in a "cover-up" of the assassination, if not complicity in the assassination itself. See Max Holland, "The Key to the *Warren Report*," *American Heritage,* November 1995; Armand Moss, *Disinformation, Misinformation, and the "Conspiracy" to Kill JFK Exposed* (Hamden, Conn.: Archon Books, 1987); Max Holland, "How Moscow Undermined the Warren Commission," *Washington Post,* 22 November 2003.

Dulles: *[indistinct]* . . . [in the] years that I have left.

Johnson: Thank you. I'll be talking to you further.

Dulles: Right. And I'll keep this entirely quiet for—

Johnson: Please do, please do, till it's announced.

Dulles: I'll certainly do [that]—

Johnson: 'Cause I haven't cleared it with but one other man.

Dulles: I understand.

Johnson: 'Bye. *[hands telephone receiver to aide]*

Dulles: *[unaware that Johnson is no longer on the line]* I'll be at your orders if you want me.

Aide: Thank you, sir.

Dulles: If you've taken into account [my previous job] . . . I think of nothing else that would recuse me unless that other . . . the old job did.

Johnson: *[gets back on the line]* No, no. Thank you.

Dulles: Thank you.

Johnson: 'Bye.

Immediately after talking with Dulles, Johnson takes a telephone call from J. Edgar Hoover that is not recorded. Presumably Johnson chooses this occasion to inform Hoover that the "somebody from the [Supreme] Court" Johnson mentioned earlier in the day is Earl Warren. If Hoover is less than pleased about Johnson's sleight of hand, there is no evidence that he indicates as much to the president.

[From] Abe Fortas / ±5:43 p.m.

Johnson is racing the clock to contact the rest of the commission's prospective members by 6:30 p.m., when most newspaper reporters will be leaving the White House. In between those calls he must finish consulting congressional leaders. Fortas, meanwhile, is busy putting the finishing touches on the press statement that will accompany Executive Order No. 11130, the directive establishing the presidential panel. Fortas's draft will be nearly identical to the statement actually issued, save for the last paragraph and some minor changes in verb tenses and punctuation. These changes are probably suggested by aides who are working closely with the president throughout this long day, such as Bill Moyers and McGeorge Bundy.

During this conversation Fortas brings up an awkward point. Following the president's abrupt change in position, and in the rush to get the commission established, Johnson and Fortas have neglected Waggoner Carr, the Texas attorney general. He willingly climbed out on a limb when he announced a state Court of Inquiry at the White House's urging, and now that limb is about to be sawed off. Carr has already been chastised in Texas for grandstanding, and

Johnson's appointment of a presidential commission just four days after Carr's announcement will tend to confirm that criticism—or suggest that Washington has no confidence in Texans investigating anything.[264] Fortas tells the president he took the liberty of breaking the news after Carr asked about Boggs's leak. As it turned out, the state attorney general seemed genuinely relieved to have some of the burden lifted, though the Court of Inquiry's role and purpose will be uncertain now.[265]

Fortas: . . . have one, Mr. President, and it isn't any good, and I rewrote it, and I told him I was going to.

Johnson: That's good. Okay, go ahead.

Fortas: All right. You ready?

Johnson: Yeah. You got anything else to say to me?

[Marie Fehmer, one of Johnson's secretaries, is also on the line, ready for Fortas's dictation.]

Fortas: Yes, sir.

Johnson: *[aside to Fehmer]* Wait a minute, Marie. Let him—

Fortas: After [Hale] Boggs made his announcement—

Johnson: Yeah.

Fortas: Carr called me, the attorney general of Texas.

Johnson: Yeah.

Fortas: And he was going on and on, and I thought he oughta be told about the plans for the commission, and I swore him to secrecy—

Johnson: Yeah.

Fortas: —because Boggs had already said it.

Johnson: Yeah.

Fortas: I didn't tell him anything. And he was very appreciative and said, "That's a wonderful idea and all to the good." So I think we got that under way. *[laughs nervously]*

Johnson: Okay.

Fortas: I just wanted to cover that base with him.

Johnson: You think I oughta tell him . . . talk to him, 'fore it's over?

Fortas: No—

Johnson: I imagine so—

264. Waggoner Carr, *Texas Politics in My Rearview Mirror* (Plano, Tex.: Republic of Texas Press, 1993), 92.

265. By this time Carr has secured two outstanding Texas attorneys to assist him as special counsel: Robert Storey, former dean of the Southern Methodist University Law School, and Leon Jaworski, a Houston lawyer who will become nationally famous in the 1970s as a special prosecutor in the Watergate scandal. After the commission's announcement, Johnson will ask Carr to combine the Court of Inquiry's effort with that of the Warren Commission. And eventually Carr will agree to stand down almost entirely, pending the final report of the presidential panel, though he will retain the right to reconvene the court if the commission proves not to be "fair to Texas." Ibid., 95.

Fortas: —I can do it. Don't you bother with him. I've been talkin' to that guy every day . . . practically every hour.

Johnson: Well, somebody better call him because he'll think I've broken faith with him.

Fortas: I called him and already told him I'll call him again.

Johnson: You tell him as soon as it's done. Put that first on your list, soon as I get some clearances.

Fortas: All right.

Johnson: Okay. You on, Marie?

Fehmer: Yes, sir.

Johnson: Go ahead.

[Johnson hangs up, leaving Fehmer to take Fortas's dictation.]

Fortas: *[reading]* "The president today announced that he was appointing a Special Commission"—capital S, capital C—"to study and report upon all facts and circumstances relating to the assassination of the late President John F. Kennedy and the subsequent murder of the man charged with the assassination."[266]

Fehmer: Uh-hmm.

Fortas: [New] paragraph. "The president stated that the majority and minority leaders of the Senate and the House of Representatives have been consulted with respect to the proposed Special Commission." Marie, you have to make a note there for me on the side. Will you?

Fehmer: Uh-hmm.

Fortas: I do not know the facts—

Fehmer: Now, this is your note.

Fortas: Yeah . . . within, you know, in relating to this paragraph I just dictated. I do not know the facts, and this has to be conformed. That's—

Fehmer: Conformed.

Fortas: —correct. Now we continue [the dictation], right?

Fehmer: All right.

Fortas: [New] paragraph. "The members of the Special Commission are," colon . . . then leave space, 'cause I don't know who they are.[267]

Fehmer: All right.

Fortas: Then [new] paragraph. "The president stated that the Special Commission would be instructed to evaluate all available information concerning the subject of the inquiry. The Federal Bureau of Investigation," comma, "pursuant to an earlier directive of the president," comma, "is

---

266. The actual statement will substitute the words "violent death" for "murder." *Warren Report,* 472.

267. Fortas, of course, knows who Johnson intends to recruit, but not all of them have agreed yet.

making a complete investigation of the facts," period. "An inquiry is also scheduled by the Texas Court of Inquiry"—that's capital C and I—

Fehmer: Thank you.

Fortas: —"convened"—well, you're welcome, ma'am.

Fehmer: *[laughs]*

Fortas: —"convened by the attorney general of Texas under Texas law." [New] paragraph. "The Special Commission"—

Fehmer: The Special Commission. . . .

Fortas: —"will have before it all evidence uncovered by the FBI and all information available to any agency of the federal government. The attorney general of Texas has also offered his cooperation," period. "All federal agencies and offices are being directed to furnish services and cooperation to the Special Commission," period. "The Commission will also be empowered to conduct any further investigation that it deems desirable." [New] paragraph. "The president stated that the investigations now under way by the FBI and others, together with the report of the Special Commission, will make certain that all aspects of the assassination and murder are *known,* and that the public is fully informed."[268]

Fehmer: All right, sir.

Fortas: Thank you very much.

Fehmer: Thank *you.*

To John Sherman Cooper / 5:45 p.m.

On the surface, there is no obvious, compelling reason for Johnson to appoint the sixty-two-year-old Kentucky senator to the commission. A member of the Agriculture and Public Works committees, Cooper is not involved in overseeing intelligence activities, U.S. foreign relations, or anything having to do with the administration of justice. He is not in the GOP leadership (having lost out to Everett Dirksen in 1959), and he would be the first to admit he is a "truly terrible public speaker," probably the worst in the Senate.[269] On those rare occasions when he takes the floor, his heavy eastern Kentucky accent and a tendency to swallow words combine to make him nearly incomprehensible. Yet apart from these considerations, Cooper is one of the most valued and respected senators in the entire chamber, as Johnson well knows from his years as majority leader.

268. The actual statement will read, "The president is instructing the Special Commission to satisfy itself that the truth is known as far as it can be discovered, and to report its findings and conclusions to him, to the American people, and to the world." *Warren Report,* 472.

269. Albin Krebs, "John Sherman Cooper Dies at 89; Longtime Senator from Kentucky," *New York Times,* 23 February 1991.

Cooper's electoral road to the Senate was an unusually bumpy one, befitting his persuasion in the 1950s as a member of that virtually unknown political species: a Republican from south of the Mason-Dixon line, representing a state with a Democratic majority of two to one.[270] Elected three times to fill out unexpired Senate terms, he did not win a normal contest until 1960, and then only with the help of five professional campaign consultants ordered to Kentucky by President Eisenhower.[271] Cooper, a former county judge, is famed for his integrity, decency, and principled stands even when the political winds are blowing hard the other way. He was one of the first Republicans in the Senate to denounce the reckless tactics of his GOP colleague Senator Joe McCarthy, and he did so well before McCarthy's fall from political grace. Cooper also firmly opposed legislation diminishing the right of witnesses to invoke the Fifth Amendment against self-incrimination when anti-Communist hysteria was at its height in the 1950s. And in a position that Lyndon Johnson appreciates above all, Cooper, for all his mumbling, is one of the most outspoken voices in the Republican Party in favor of civil rights legislation.

Two other factors in Johnson's mind argue for Cooper's inclusion. One is that Cooper, a former U.S. ambassador to India (having served there after he lost his Senate seat for the second time), will be useful to the commission because of his understanding of State Department procedures. Clearly the department is going to be subject to intense scrutiny for facilitating Lee Harvey Oswald's return to the United States in 1962. The other factor is that Cooper, among all the commission members, is the only one justified in calling the late president a close friend. Although they were an unlikely pair on the surface, when Cooper and Kennedy both served in the Senate a bond existed between the two men, facilitated by the coincidence that they both lived on the same fashionable street in Georgetown. The first dinner invitation Kennedy accepted after entering the White House was to Cooper's N Street home.[272]

As in the call to Dulles, the president does not bother mentioning the other commission members. He knows Cooper will serve if asked.

Johnson: *[reading quickly]*

"... today establishing a presidential commission composed of seven distinguished Americans, headed by the chief justice [of the] Supreme Court of the United States. I've acted after full consultation with leaders of Congress and with members of my own cabinet. This commission will be established before the end of the day by executive

---

270. Glenn Finch, "The Election of United States Senators in Kentucky: The Cooper Period," *Filson Club History Quarterly* 46, no. 2 (April 1972), 161.

271. Nelson Lichtenstein, ed., *Political Profiles: The Kennedy Years* (New York: Facts on File, 1976), 98.

272. Finch, "Election of United States Senators in Kentucky," 170.

order. Its functions will be to receive and to evaluate information obtained by *all* sources in [the] executive branch; to satisfy itself that the truth is known as far as we can know it; and to report its findings and conclusions to me, to the American people, and to the world."

Cooper: I think that's fine.

Johnson: Now, I want you to go on that commission.

Cooper: *[in astonishment]* What!

Johnson: Yes.

Cooper: Well . . . [if] you want me to go on it, I'll do it, [of] course.

Johnson: Thank you, my friend.

Cooper: *[sounding stunned]* Yes, sir.

Johnson: 'Bye. Don't say a word 'bout it now!

Cooper: *[as if accustomed to Johnson's penchant for secrecy]* I won't say a thing.

Johnson: 'Bye.

To John McCloy / 5:55 p.m.

John McCloy is a sixty-eight-year-old Wall Street lawyer, banker, and diplomat who personifies the versatile statesmen who serve Democratic and Republican presidents alike. He has worn so many hats in and out of the federal government—none of them absolutely defining—that his name always sounds familiar, but he is constantly confused with other men, such as John McCone. McCloy, as noted earlier, is best known at home and in Europe for his service as U.S. High Commissioner to Occupied Germany from 1949 to 1952, and more recently for helping to negotiate an end to the 1962 Cuban missile crisis. Previously, he served as assistant secretary of war from 1941 to 1945 and as president of the World Bank from 1947 to 1949. After 1953 McCloy became, simultaneously, chairman of the nation's second largest bank (Chase Manhattan), its largest foundation (Ford), and its most influential think tank (the Council on Foreign Relations). McCloy is so ubiquitous yet behind-the-scenes that one journalist dubbed him "chairman of the Eastern Establishment" in a 1961 tongue-in-cheek *Esquire* essay.[273] It is a moniker that McCloy, who is actually modest and low-key, though hardworking and tenacious, instantly disdains. But it sticks.

McCloy is one of at least two members—Richard Russell being another—who comes to the commission all but convinced that the assassination must have been the bitter fruit of a conspiracy. Oswald's death in Dallas police custody, two days after his capture, is just too suspicious. In no small part, this belief

273. Richard Rovere, *The American Establishment and Other Reports, Opinions and Speculations* (New York: Harcourt, Brace & World, 1962); Max Holland, "Citizen McCloy," *Wilson Quarterly*, Autumn 1991.

stems from McCloy's own experience in cracking a famed international sabotage case in the late 1930s. The so-called Black Tom case involved German sabotage of a U.S. munitions factory in New York harbor prior to America's entry into World War I. Before it was over, McCloy ventured to Baltimore, Vienna, Warsaw, London, Munich, and Dublin in his search for clues proving that the kaiser's agents were responsible for the explosion. His own law firm deemed the case utterly hopeless in the early 1930s. But McCloy persisted and, in a twist worthy of a spy novel, eventually discovered a secret message that clinched the case. His public career actually started when Secretary of War Henry Stimson brought McCloy into the War Department in 1940 because of renewed fears over sabotage, this time by Nazi agents. McCloy is thus no stranger to international intrigue and conspiracy.

During World War II McCloy had sporadic contacts with then-Congressman Johnson, who served on the House Committee on Military Affairs (as the Armed Services Committee was then called). More recently McCloy carried on informal conversations with Vice President Johnson during National Security Council meetings on the 1962 missile crisis. When Johnson calls him late Friday afternoon, McCloy is probably less surprised than any other member, accustomed as he is to receiving urgent appeals to serve directly from presidents. Their conversation is not recorded, but in an oral history interview six years later, McCloy will recall that he did not hesitate for a moment. "It was a very emotional period, and it was so obvious that something like this had to be done. [President Johnson] made it appear to me over the telephone . . . that we should go into the thing with absolutely no holds barred, and to come out with all the facts . . . [though he] told me that he had quite a difficulty in getting Warren to agree to act."[274]

From Leslie Arends / 6:15 p.m.

After a brief conversation with Senator Mike Mansfield, presumably to inform him about the actual appointments to the commission, Johnson turns his attention to the House GOP leadership.[275] He needs to talk with minority leader Charlie Halleck, if at all possible, so that the White House press office can release a statement that says the president consulted with the entire congressional leadership prior to naming the commission. In addition, Johnson wants to gain the assent of the GOP's senior House leadership to his selection of Gerald Ford. This is not as easy as it sounds, because of tensions simmering just below the surface of the minority party. Both Halleck and his minority whip, Leslie

274. John McCloy Oral History, 8 July 1969, LBJL.
275. Johnson informed Senate GOP leader Dirksen about the commission's makeup during a brief conversation at 5:10 p.m.

Arends, have been in Congress since 1935, and their "Old Guard" is facing a rising challenge from the "Young Turk" faction of the party. Many of the latter are war veterans, around fifty years old, and have served in Congress fewer than ten years. Their chief argument is that the Republican leadership consists of aging, uninspired political warhorses who make the party appear antediluvian when compared with the dynamic young Kennedy administration. And their undisputed leader is Gerald Ford—the very congressman Johnson is now proposing to elevate to national prominence.

Because White House operators are having a difficult time locating Halleck, who is away from Washington, despite the House being in session today, Johnson calls upon Arends for help. In this conversation the president will stress the need to have members from Congress on the commission who are well versed in CIA matters. That encompasses Ford, of course, who sits on the relevant House Appropriations subcommittee. But it also includes Arends, who is the ranking member of the House Armed Services Committee and also ranking minority on its CIA subcommittee. In fact, as the GOP's minority whip, Arends is the genuine Republican counterpart to Hale Boggs, Johnson's choice to represent House Democrats. This passing over of Arends, which goes unremarked but could not go unnoticed, suggests that Johnson believes the GOP's Young Turk faction will be more inclined to support his legislative agenda than those midwestern, isolationist-minded Old Guard Republicans who have been steadfastly opposing Democratic programs since the New Deal. Thus, Johnson is willing to bolster the fortunes of one GOP faction, even at the risk of putting a younger face on the Republican leadership.

Johnson: Most of these [newspaper] boys are gonna be leaving here not later than 6:30, and I've tried to get [Halleck for] over an hour.

Arends: Yeah. You want to put this . . . you wanna make this release tonight?

Johnson: Yeah; oh, yeah. I'm gonna make the announcement tonight. It's just a question . . . I'd just *like* to be able to say that I'd consulted with the leadership.

Arends: Well, that was my problem.

Johnson: It's a presidential commission, you see—

Arends: I know it is.

Johnson: And I don't [have to], I just want to . . . I want to work with my friends.

Arends: That's right, and that's why I called you back, Mr. President.

Johnson: What I want to do is, I want to try to get someone that's pretty familiar with the defense picture and the foreign relations picture, and also the CIA picture, you see, the Hoover picture. And that's why I'm tryin' to get [a] man [Gerald Ford] that handled the . . . [who's] kinda high up on military over in the House, but [like] Russell on Armed Services in the Senate.

Arends: Yeah. Well, I tell you, the reason I—

Johnson: Cooper's a former ambassador to India, you see, and McCloy's a former ambassador, and Dulles is former CIA.[276]

Arends: Sounds good, yeah.

Johnson: And I don't know . . . I have no particular reason for interest in the Republicans. But the hell of it is, you can't clear these things! You can't even *talk* to 'em, you can't *get* 'em!

Arends: Well, let me—

Johnson: Mike Mansfield's in Florida, Dirksen's in Illinois, and—

Arends: Well, let me see if I can't get him [Halleck]. But in the meantime, I didn't want to be put in a position where I put an okay on something and then find out that Charlie [Halleck] was jumpin' or something.[277]

Johnson: Well—

Arends: *[indistinct]*

Johnson: I haven't . . . no. What I was just gonna do, I was gonna try to get him for another fifteen minutes, and then have to decide what to do about it because—

Arends: Yeah . . . I'll do likewise. I'll work on it, too. And I'll try to call you back within *[indistinct]*.

Johnson: Fine. Just tell him what we'd like to do is to have men with the military background, the CIA background, the appropriations background . . . see, we're doin' a good deal in this field, Les, that . . . I think you're on the committee, aren't you?

Arends: I'm on the [House] Armed Services Committee.

Johnson: You're on the [CIA] subcommittee there, and—

Arends: Yeah . . . CIA, yes; oh yes.

Johnson: And so we're tryin' to spread it out, and we're gettin' the chairman of [the Senate] Armed Services [Committee], [that's] one group you see, and we're tryin' to go to [the] Appropriations [Committee] with the other—[someone from the House subcommittee] that handles the [CIA] appropriations—and we're tryin' to go to somebody that has a good deal of foreign service, like John Cooper, [a former] ambassador.

Arends: Yeah, that's good. Fine.

Johnson: And Dulles, you see, [is from] the CIA, and—

Arends: That's fine . . . that's real good.

Johnson: Hale's [Boggs] been talkin' about this thing, and he talked a little *too* much today.[278]

---

276. McCloy was not technically an ambassador when he was U.S. High Commissioner to Occupied Germany because the Bonn government was not a fully sovereign state.

277. This remark is probably as close as Arends can come to admitting that the appointment of Ford—"a jowlless, articulate football hero"—is a sensitive issue for the senior GOP leadership. Richard Lyons, "Party Elders Yield Some Ground After GOP 'Young Turk' Rebellion," *Washington Post,* 28 November 1963.

278. Johnson, of course, is referring to Boggs's leak.

Arends: *[chuckles in amusement]* You know members of Congress!

Johnson: Well, that's the trouble. They all talk, you know, when you tell 'em. Now he called down here and said, "This fellow's talkin'." And I said, "Well, I'm tryin' to work out things like that."

Arends: Yeah . . . that's right. Well, you're doing the right thing on this *[indistinct]*.

Johnson: But if I talk to 'em, they talk to the press. So you try to get back to me in fifteen [minutes].

Arends: I'll try to get in touch with him just as quick as I can.

Johnson: Fine.

Arends: 'Bye.

To Charles Halleck / 6:30 p.m.

White House operators finally track down Minority Leader Halleck minutes after the president sends Arends out looking for him. Halleck is familiar to millions of Americans as the combative half of "the Ev and Charlie show," a regularly scheduled news conference that also features Everett Dirksen. The Illinois senator is often described as the star of the "soft-shoe numbers," while Halleck energetically wields the partisan stiletto, as he did in 1962, just after Ted Kennedy overcame a meager résumé to win a Senate seat. Halleck was one of the first politicians to openly accuse the Massachusetts family of trying to create a political dynasty.[279]

As the GOP's shrewd leader in the House since 1958, Halleck has been able to form effective alliances with conservative southerners to block or curtail much of President Kennedy's legislative agenda, despite the Democrats' overwhelming numerical majority in the lower chamber. Halleck nonetheless is facing a rising tide of disaffection in his own ranks.

As in previous conversations, Johnson is vague to the point of being disingenuous when he talks to Halleck about the actual commitments regarding membership on the commission. By this time all the members have been contacted save for Jerry Ford. Halleck promptly accepts Ford's appointment on the basis of his familiarity with the CIA, though he probably understands the political calculus involved. But the commission, after all, is a presidential one, and Johnson is free to appoint whomever he wants. The president tries to soften the blow by bringing up Representative George Mahon's name. Yet the Texas Democrat, who is chairman of the Appropriations subcommittee on the CIA, was never under serious consideration precisely because he is from Texas and a Democrat.

279. Ben Franklin, "Charles Halleck, a G.O.P. House Leader, Dies," *New York Times,* 4 March 1986.

What surprises the president is Halleck's fairly stiff attitude to Earl Warren's appointment. The minority leader is opposed in principle to drafting justices for extracurricular duties, even on momentous occasions. In addition, though, Halleck has a particular reservation about Warren because the chief justice—*of all people*—engaged in a rush to judgment. After the announcement of the president's death, but before it was revealed that a self-styled Marxist had been apprehended, Warren issued a statement declaring, "A great and good president has suffered martyrdom as a result of hatred and bitterness that has been injected into the life of our nation by bigots."[280] In the parlance of the time, "bigot" is almost exclusively a code word for southerners opposed to civil rights. Warren then compounded his mistake, at least in Halleck's eyes, when he delivered a eulogy in the Capitol Rotunda two days later that referred to the "forces of hatred and malevolence . . . eating their way into the bloodstream of American life."[281]

Halleck is the first person to direct Johnson's attention to Warren's utterly injudicious remarks, but he will not be the last.

[The conversation opens with remarks about the Thanksgiving holiday.]

Johnson: Charlie, I hate to bother you, but all you damn fellas abdicated. I talked to Les Arends and told him I was gonna keep tryin' to reach you till 6:30, when I . . . I've got to appoint a commission and issue an executive order tonight on an investigation of the assassination of the president, because this thing is gettin' pretty serious and our folks are worried about it.

Halleck: Yeah.

Johnson: It's got some foreign complications, CIA and other things. And I'm gonna try to get the chief justice to go on it. He declined earlier in the day, but I *think* I'm gonna try to get him to head it. I'm gonna try to get John—

Halleck: Earl Warren?

Johnson: Yeah. I'm—

Halleck: I think that's a mistake.

Johnson: I'm gonna try to get John McCloy . . . well, we've just got to—

Halleck: I'll tell you . . . I think this use—well, look. You didn't ask me to say.

Johnson: Well, what I wanna talk to you about . . . I'd be glad to hear you, but I want to talk to you about—he [Warren] thought it was a mistake, until I told him everything we knew. And we just can't have [the] House and Senate, and FBI, and other people going around testifyin' that [Nikita] Khrushchev killed Kennedy, or [Fidel] Castro killed him. We've gotta have

280. "Stunned Eisenhower Calls Slaying 'Despicable Act,' " *Washington Post,* 23 November 1963.

281. Warren, *Memoirs,* 353–54.

the facts, and you don't have a president assassinated [but] once every fifty years. And this thing is so *touchy* from an international standpoint that every man we've got over there is concerned about it. And we think we've gotta have somebody that can not only be judicious and assure America, but somebody that's had some experience with these CIA matters and other things.

   So we're gonna try to get John McCloy from an international standpoint [and] Allen Dulles. We want to get Jerry Ford from the [House] Appropriations Committee. We want to get Dick Russell from the [Senate] Armed Services Committee. We wanna get John Sherman Cooper because he's had some international background and ambassadorial experience. And Allen Dulles and John McCloy, and we wanna ask the chief justice to preside. And we *hope* that . . . we've talked to the leadership in both houses, and asked them to cooperate with the commission, and—

Halleck: I'll cooperate, my friend. I'll tell you one thing, Lyndon—[I mean] Mr. President.

Johnson: Yes, sir.

Halleck: I think to call on Supreme Court guys for these jobs is kind of a mistake. I thought so *[indistinct]*—

Johnson: It *is* on *all* these other things. I agree with you on Pearl Harbor, and I agree with you on [the] railroad strike. But this is a question that *could* involve our losing 39 million people. This is a judicial question.

Halleck: I don't want *that* to happen. Of course, I was a *little* disappointed in the speech the chief justice made, and I'm talkin' real plainly [here].

Johnson: Yeah . . . yeah.

Halleck: He jumped at the gun, and of course, I don't know whether the right wing was in this or *not.* You've been *very* discreet. You have said . . . you mentioned the left *and* the right.[282]

Johnson: That's right.

Halleck: And I am *for* that. Well, *look* . . . Jerry Ford is a *top-drawer* guy on our side.

Johnson: You can't name George—just between us . . . I don't want you to repeat this to a human—but I can't name George Mahon. Because he's from *Texas* . . . and it *happened* in Texas.

Halleck: Of course, the guy that *I'd* prefer on there would be Tom Clark.[283] But I guess maybe that's *[inappropriate].*

Johnson: No, you can't . . . you can't do it. I wanted Tom Clark. You can't do

---

282. In contrast to Warren's injudicious statement, Johnson decried "fanatics" on the far left and the far right who "pour venom into our nation's bloodstream," during his joint session address on November 27.

283. Interestingly, if Johnson is determined to appoint a Supreme Court justice, Halleck's preference is identical to Russell's. Justice Clark's opinions generally support the federal govern-

it. He's [from] *Texas,* Charlie, and there might [be] somebody say a *Texan* did it, you know.

Halleck: Yeah.

Johnson: You see what I mean?

Halleck: Yeah. Well, if you're set on that, as far as—

Johnson: Well, I'm not set. I want to talk to you about it [and] discuss it. This is my best judgment. I think I can get Dick Russell . . . I haven't talked to most of these people, but I did talk to Russell. Russell doesn't want to do it, but he thinks it *oughta* be done. He thinks I've *got* to have some top justice.[284]

Halleck: I'll buy Jerry Ford.

Johnson: All right. Okay.

Halleck: *[indistinct]*

Johnson: All right. Thank you, my friend.

Halleck: Okay.

Johnson: Now you help us [and] protect my *flanks* there, because I don't want a bunch of television cameras runnin' on this thing.

Halleck: Well, I don't *want* any television cameras.

Johnson: I don't want the House and Senate committees . . . I've talked to [James] Eastland, and he said he's not gonna run his, and [John] McCormack—

Halleck: I don't think we've started one on this.

Johnson: No, no, you haven't, and McCormack said he wouldn't, and I just want . . . you're my leader, *too.*

Halleck: Well . . . you're *damned* right, Mr. President.

Johnson: All right. I noticed the other night the man that spoke up, [and] the first man in line . . . and I haven't forgotten it.[285] Thank you, my friend.

Halleck: Okay, Mr. President.

---

ment's powers in the areas of loyalty and internal security, especially in comparison with his colleagues on the Warren Court. In addition, the controversial Smith Act prosecutions against the U.S. Communist Party were brought during Clark's tenure as attorney general. Martin Weil, "Former Supreme Court Justice Clark Dies at 77," *Washington Post,* 14 June 1977, and "Tom C. Clark, Former Justice, Dies; On the Supreme Court for 18 Years," *New York Times,* 14 June 1977.

284. Johnson is bending the truth here, as Russell is not that keen about getting a justice from the Supreme Court.

285. Johnson is referring to Halleck's public statement of "deep affection" for the new president, and the fact that the GOP leader was one of the first congressmen to shake his hand after the joint session address. Richard Lyons, "2 Major Bills May Be Delayed Until January," *Washington Post,* 28 November 1963.

To Carl Albert / 6:37 p.m.

Johnson's conversation with the House majority leader, Carl Albert, has a delicate facet to it. Earlier in the day, when the president was candidly discussing commission membership with Abe Fortas, they discussed the possibility of appointing Albert, diminutive in stature but not in reputation, to represent House Democrats. But eventually Johnson and Fortas agreed that choosing the "Little Giant" from rural Oklahoma might be interpreted as a slap at Hale Boggs because of the latter's outspokenness in favor of a commission. Now the time has come to inform the majority leader. The president is not quite sure how Albert will react to being excluded, although he is known for his self-effacing, yet scrappy, nature.[286]

This is Johnson's first direct conversation of the day with Albert. Nonetheless the House majority leader seems fully informed about the commission's genesis, probably having learned about it from McCormack or Boggs. True to form, Albert makes no issue of having been passed over. His endorsement of the president's handiwork is wholehearted and complete, from Johnson's choice of Earl Warren down to their shared disdain for the "headline-hunters" on Capitol Hill.

Johnson: We think tonight, after talkin' to the Justice Department and the secretary of state, we think we oughta have the highest-level commission we can have to study these reports relating to the assassination of the president.[287]

Albert: Right.

Johnson: And the FBI will be in[volved], and we don't want anything going in the House [or] Senate . . . just a bunch of television cameras or a lot of loose testimony around [James] Eastland's committee and otherwise . . . sayin' that—

Albert: We've got it *all* under control, all right.

Johnson: —[Nikita] Khrushchev's done this or [Fidel] Castro's done this or somethin' else—

Albert: Right.

Johnson: —'cause it could be very dangerous. I'm gonna try to get the chief justice to serve as chairman of it.

Albert: Yes.

Johnson: Senator Russell . . . Senator Cooper . . . Congressman Boggs—he['s]

286. "Carl Bert Albert, a Powerful Democrat for Three Decades, Is Dead at 91," *New York Times,* 6 February 2000.

287. Minutes before calling Albert, Johnson informed Secretary Rusk about the appointments to the commission. Johnson and Rusk, conversation, 29 November 1963, 6:34 p.m., LBJL.

been talkin' a good deal about it—and Representative Ford . . . and Allen Dulles, [representing the] public, and John McCloy. Now that's who I'm thinkin' of. Have you got any suggestions or any better ones?

Albert: No, those are fine . . . nothing wrong with those.

Johnson: There may be a good many Republicans, but I think that this oughtn't to be a partisan thing, and I think nobody that looks upon McCloy or at [the] chief justice either [looks at them primarily] as a Republican.

Albert: That's right.

Johnson: Ford, I guess . . . is he a pretty vicious Republican?

Albert: Well . . . he's fairly level-headed, you know, and he's respected on his side.

Johnson: Pretty judicious?

Albert: Yes . . . yes, he is.

Johnson: Is he a lawyer?

Albert: I don't know whether he's a lawyer or not, but I *assume* he is.[288] But I've never checked it . . . never had occasion to know. But I assume he is.

Johnson: The reason I was suggesting Hale was because he'd been talkin' about it, and relating to it. Now, if it didn't take your time and it wouldn't work you to death, I'd be glad to put *you* on there.

Albert: No, I don't . . . I really don't want it.

Johnson: I don't think you oughta ask the Speaker [of the House] to go on it, and I thought that you . . . I'd rather have *you* than anybody in the House of Representatives. And I talked to 'em about that, but then . . . I don't know how you're gonna mess around with this thing and be a leader.

Albert: No, I agree with you, and . . . I think Hale is a good man for it. He's been interested in having [it] done, I think it *should* be done. Since we're not gonna have a jury verdict on that man [Oswald, who's] dead, it's important that some commission say something about it, I think.

You know . . . since Oswald was *killed* before he was *tried,* I think it's *very* important that you have somebody, and I think you better take it away from the headline-hunters out on the [Capitol] Hill. And I think you have, by this. I'm *all* for it, and I like your committee. Now the Speaker didn't like . . . his first impression was that there shouldn't be anybody from the judiciary on it since they might have to pass on the issue.[289]

Johnson: He's not going to pass on Oswald; he's deader than *hell.*

Albert: That's right. I think Warren should be chairman of it, just between you and me. Yes, sir . . . I think it's *perfect.*

288. Ford, a 1941 graduate of the Yale Law School, was a practicing attorney for three years before winning a congressional seat in 1948. Gerald Ford, *A Time to Heal: The Autobiography of Gerald R. Ford* (New York: Harper & Row, 1979), 57, 62, 65. All the commissioners, in fact, are lawyers.

289. McCormack did not express such a reservation to Johnson when they talked at 4:55 p.m. He only questioned the number of southerners appointed.

Johnson: Well, I haven't done it. I'm drafting the executive order and I don't need to, but I believe it's better to do it than not to do it.

Albert: I do too, and I think you oughta do it before everybody starts moving in. Now, I had a letter from Dante Fascell [D-Florida], and the Speaker and I talked it over. He [Fascell] thought his committee had jurisdiction.[290] Other committees thought they had jurisdiction, and they were all gonna start puttin' in resolutions. And of course, a few *have* put them in. We've buried them in the [House] Rules Committee, and I think this will shut it up! And I think that's what you should do.

Johnson: And you'll protect my flank on it.

Albert: Yes, *sir.* And I want to tell you one other thing. I'll *never bother* you. But whenever you need me, I'm there.

[The conversation turns to discussion of favorable reaction to Johnson's joint session address.]

To Leslie Arends / 6:43 p.m.

Johnson calls Arends to let him know that Ford's nomination has been cleared with Halleck. While Johnson mentions Halleck's dim view of having anyone from the Supreme Court serve on the commission, the president neglects to add that Halleck objected to Earl Warren in particular. Arends probably knows this anyway because he too managed to reach the House minority leader on the telephone.

Johnson: [Charlie Halleck] said he'd buy Ford fine. He doesn't like much for a Supreme Court justice to go on it. But when I told him that there were plenty of foreign implications to it, and we had to have the highest judicial officer we could get, why . . . we just don't want to leave any doubt that any foreign nation had anything to do with this, you see—

Arends: *[indistinct]*

Johnson: And we want the *facts,* [and] Hoover's gonna have the facts, and this commission can go over 'em. He [Halleck] said he'd protect the flank, and go all the way and buy Jerry Ford—

Arends: Yeah . . . I've talked to him [Halleck]. Either right after [you]—and it was good that you called—I was talkin' to him.

---

290. Fascell is chairman of the Legal and Monetary Affairs subcommittee of the House Committee on Government Operations. As such, he has asserted jurisdiction because the assassination involves the Secret Service and FBI, as well as liaison between the two agencies and their parent departments (Treasury and Justice). Though Fascell has not announced hearings yet, he has given every indication of doing so in the near future, bringing the total number of separate House investigations to at least three and still counting. *Congressional Record,* 27 November 1963, 22845.

Johnson: Well, I'll be darned.

Arends: So it was all right.

Johnson: Okay. Well, now—

Arends: I'm glad it's been cleared . . . with him.

[The conversation ends after Johnson expresses appreciation for Republican leaders' support.]

To Gerald Ford / 6:52 p.m.

"Jerry" Ford is tall, athletic, and good-looking, a World War II Navy veteran with an attractive family. Prior to November 22 many Republicans believed he represented the party's best answer to John Kennedy's youthful appeal, someone who might sell a modern brand of Republicanism to the public.[291] Abruptly that fixation no longer seems quite so crucial, but Ford clearly remains a politician on the rise.

The fifty-year-old congressman from Michigan, whose greatest ambition is to be Speaker of a Republican-controlled House, is the last prospective commissioner Johnson must contact. A staunch conservative on domestic issues, Ford is a strong internationalist and vigorous anti-Communist who has fashioned himself into an expert on defense and intelligence matters. He works hard to win passage of foreign aid bills, a prime target for conservative Democrats and isolationist-minded Republicans. More to the point, in 1961 Ford was elected chairman of the House Republican Conference, marking him as the undisputed leader of the GOP's Young Turk faction.

Appointing Ford to the commission carries with it several ramifications. His presence will help mollify the Turks, one of whom is Charles Goodell, the New York congressman whose outspokenness on the House floor prompted Hale Boggs to leak word of the commission prematurely. Ford's participation will also help ensure the intelligence community's full cooperation with the commission, as the CIA will likely think twice before crossing anyone who holds the power of the purse over it. Most of all, by plucking Ford out from a number of candidates, Lyndon Johnson is handing the Grand Rapids congressman a political plum that will add immeasurably to his stature in Washington and that of his Republican faction. Ford is the only commissioner whose future lies mostly ahead of him.[292] Everyone else on the panel has already reached, or is even a little past, his absolute peak. Little wonder that when Johnson asks Ford to serve, the Michigan congressman does not hesitate for an instant—though

291. Paul Duke, "GOP Leader Halleck Acts to Mollify Young Republicans in House," *Wall Street Journal,* 19 February 1963.

292. The forty-nine-year-old Boggs is a year younger than Ford but more advanced in his career. The commission appointment is not the boost to Boggs's career that it represents for Ford.

he too is no fan of Earl Warren, seeing the chief justice as someone who coddles America's Communist adversaries.

Ford and Johnson don't know each other very well, though Ford remembers the president from the time in 1957 when they served on a bipartisan House-Senate committee to draft space legislation after the *Sputnik* launch. "Johnson elected himself chairman," Ford will later recall, "[and] knew exactly what he wanted. . . . He knew how far he could push, how to cajole, how to threaten. . . . I knew I was seeing a master in action."[293]

Ford: Yes, Mr. President. How are you, sir?

Johnson: Happy Thanksgivin'. Where are you?

Ford: I'm home, sir.

Johnson: You mean Michigan?

Ford: No . . . no, I'm here in Washington.[294]

Johnson: You're in Washington? Well, thank God, there's somebody in town!

Ford: *[chuckles]*

Johnson: I was gettin' ready to tell [James] MacGregor Burns [that] he's right about the Congress . . . they couldn't function.[295]

Ford: I thought your speech was *excellent* the other day.

Johnson: Why, thank you, Jerry. Jerry, I got somethin' I want you to do for me.

Ford: Well, we'll do the best we can, sir.

Johnson: I've got to have a top, blue-ribbon presidential commission to investigate the assassination. And I'm gonna ask the chief justice to head it, and then I'm gonna ask John McCloy and Allen Dulles.

Ford: Right.

Johnson: And I want it nonpartisan. I'm not gonna point out I got five Republicans and [only] two Democrats. But I'm gonna *do* that, and I'm just . . . then you forget what party you belong to and just serve as an American, and I want Dick Russell and Sherman Cooper of the Senate.

Ford: Right.

Johnson: Dick's on [the] Armed Services [Committee] over there, and I want

293. Cannon, *Time and Chance,* 67.

294. The Fords live in Alexandria, Virginia, a Washington suburb. Brian Krebs, "My Jerry Built Home," *Washington Post,* 13 October 1996.

295. In January 1963 Burns published a book that blamed an unholy alliance of southern Democrats and Republican conservatives for blocking President Kennedy's programs. Johnson does not think much of the book, as it is emblematic of liberals' typical complaints. Rather than criticize such congressional traditions as the seniority system, as Burns does, Johnson sees deadlock stemming from a lack of presidential leadership, interest, and willingness to exercise political muscle. James MacGregor Burns, *The Deadlock of Democracy: Four-Party Politics in America* (Englewood Cliffs, N.J.: Prentice-Hall, 1963); Jean White, "Burns Calls Congress Chief Drag on Democracy," *Washington Post,* 3 February 1963.

somebody on [the] Appropriations [Committee] who knows CIA over in your shop—

Ford: Right.

Johnson: —from the appropriation angle, 'cause I'm coverin' the Armed Services angle with Russell.

Ford: Right.

Johnson: [I] want to ask Hale Boggs and you to serve from the House . . . *[pauses awaiting Ford's reaction]*

Ford: Well, Mr. President. . . .

Johnson: It'll be McCloy, and Dulles, and Ford, and Boggs, and Cooper, and Russell, and Chief Justice Warren as chairman.

Ford: Well, you know very well I would be honored to do it, and I'll do the very best I can, sir.

Johnson: You do that, and . . . keep me up to date and I'll be seein' you.

Ford: All right. Thank you very much, and I'm—

Johnson: Thank you.

Ford: —delighted to help out.

Johnson: Thank you, Jerry.

Ford: Thank you.

The political calculus that prompts Johnson to name Ford to the Warren Commission will ultimately prove flawed, at least from the president's perspective. As expected, the appointment to the Commission elevates Ford's standing, and in the Republican bloodletting that follows the 1964 election, Ford will narrowly depose Charlie Halleck as the House minority leader. But an empowered Jerry Ford will soon prove to be a far tougher political opponent in the clinches than Halleck ever was. The president will attempt to remind Ford from time to time of the debt he ostensibly owes Johnson for having been plucked from the GOP ranks and placed on the Warren Commission. Nonetheless, Johnson will never enjoy a relationship with Ford akin to the one Johnson had with Eisenhower, especially on foreign policy issues. Far from engaging in what Johnson likes to call the "politics of responsibility," Ford will invariably find a way to bloody Johnson's nose even when the Michigan congressman agrees with a basic policy, such as prosecution of the war in Vietnam.[296] He will seek a partisan edge when- and wherever possible.

Within two years, Johnson will be openly yearning for the relatively tranquil days of "the Ev and Charlie Show." Halleck was more or less permanently resigned to political inferiority after twenty years in Congress, all but four of

296. Johnson will publicly accuse the minority leader of leaking and distorting foreign policy decisions told to him in confidence, as Ford proves unwilling to practice bipartisanship in Johnson's definition of that term. Julius Duscha, "Ford Declines to Argue Over LBJ's Charge," *Washington Post,* 3 August 1965.

which were spent in the minority. Ford is not, and Johnson will rue the day he contributed one whit to Ford's rise to power.[297]

But these events lie well in the future. For now, having secured Ford's participation, President Johnson releases the press statement and text of the executive order prepared by Abe Fortas. Coming thirty minutes later than planned, the news just barely manages to make the Saturday morning editions of several major East Coast newspapers. Although a *Washington Post* reporter has been working on the story since Boggs's inadvertent leak, the *Post* has no choice but to insert the late-breaking AP bulletin at the beginning of its much softer, front-page story on the prospective commission.[298]

To Joseph Alsop / 7 p.m.

Having confirmed all the appointments to the commission, Johnson is eager to share his achievement with Alsop. Four days ago Johnson reacted angrily when Alsop suggested that the White House's approach to the assassination fell short of being adequate. Now, with all the pride of a student who solves a difficult problem in front of his professor, Johnson briefs Alsop on his accomplishment. Johnson reads the final press release almost verbatim. Alsop, who is spending the holiday weekend in a "nest" of Connecticut Republicans, responds positively, even though only two of the seven members (Russell and Boggs) are Democrats. Alsop realizes that ideology trumps party affiliation here. The commission is dominated by trusted moderates; only Russell and Ford are considered politically conservative by 1963 standards. And two of the commissioners—Dulles and Cooper—are neighbors of Alsop's in Georgetown, while McCloy used to be.

Johnson: *[reading quickly]*
> ". . . is he's appointin' a Special Commission to study and report certain facts and circumstances relating to the assassination of the late President John F. Kennedy. The president stated that he consulted with the Democratic and Republican leaders of the Senate and the House with respect to the proposed Special Commission. The members of

297. For an example of Johnson's exasperation with Ford as early as 1965, see Johnson and Ford, conversation, 19 January 1965, 2:29 p.m., LBJL. In July 1966, as Johnson faces the prospect of shipping 100,000 more troops to Vietnam, the president will converse with Dwight Eisenhower and pine for the days when Charlie Halleck was the minority leader instead of the "modern boy" Ford. Halleck was the best leader House Republicans ever had, Johnson will assert, as he complains bitterly to Eisenhower. Johnson and Eisenhower, conversation, 23 July 1965, 11:45 a.m., LBJL.

298. Robert Albright, "7-Man Quiz Will Study JFK Killing," *Washington Post,* 30 November 1963.

the Special Commission are: Chief Justice Earl Warren, chairman; Senator Richard Russell, Georgia; Senator John Sherman Cooper, Kentucky; Representative Hale Boggs, Louisiana; Representative Gerald Ford, Michigan; Honorable Allen Dulles; and Honorable John J. McCloy."

Alsop: I think that's very good.

Johnson: I believe that covers every [geographic] section, and there're a good many Republicans on it, but I guess there oughta be.

Alsop: Yes, I think—

Johnson: *[reading rapidly]*

"The president stated the Special Commission's being instructed to evaluate all available information concerning the subject of inquiry. The Federal Bureau of Investigation, pursuant to an earlier directive of the president, [is] making a complete investigation of [the] facts. [An] inquiry is also scheduled by a Texas Court of Inquiry convened by the attorney general of Texas under Texas law. The Special Commission will have before it all evidence uncovered [by] the Federal Bureau of Investigation, [and] all information available to any of the federal agencies. The attorney general of Texas offered his cooperation. All federal agencies [and] offices are being directed to furnish services and cooperation to the Special Commission. The commission will be empowered to conduct any further investigation it deems desirable. The president [is] instructin' the Special Commission to satisfy itself that the truth is known as far as it *can* be known, and to report its findings and conclusions to him, to the American people, and to the world."

Alsop: That's *just* fine, sir. I think that's just fine.

Johnson: Well, thank you very much . . . [I] hope you write as good—

Alsop: I'm glad you put Dulles and McCloy on, and Warren. I think just to have a *congressional* one would have been . . . but it's just the right *mix,* I think.

Johnson: Well, we got two and two from each place. I hope you continue in your old age to write as good a column as you do these days when you're a young man.[299]

Alsop: Oh, the hell with that.

Johnson: And good-bye . . . good-bye.

Alsop: Mr. President, good luck to you.

Johnson: Give your bride my love.

Alsop: We're all praying for you. But I'll [be] secretly pleased . . . I'm in a *nest*

299. Johnson is referring to two very complimentary columns Alsop has penned about the new president's first week in office. Joseph Alsop, "President Johnson," *Washington Post,* 27 November 1963, and "Johnson's Next Bridge," *Washington Post,* 29 November 1963.

of Republicans [here in] Connecticut. They even think that you've
knocked the ball beyond the bleachers in every damned town so far.

Johnson: Well, this is a nest of Republicans here I got. Warren and Cooper's
two, and Ford's three, and Dulles is four, and McCloy is five out of a
seven-man commission. You reckon I can trust that many?

Alsop: *[chuckles]* Those are rather more trustworthy than usual.

Johnson: You think they're trustworthy enough?

Alsop: *Yes,* sir.

Johnson: All right. Good-bye.

Alsop: Good-bye, sir.

To James Eastland / 7:03 p.m.

Calling James Eastland to inform him about the commission appointees turns
out to be one of Johnson's easier conversations of the day, though the Mississippi senator initially posed the greatest obstacle to a presidential panel. Eastland protests only mildly when he learns that Johnson's "maybe a justice from
the Supreme Court" turns out to be none other than Earl Warren. Eastland points
to (as Halleck did) the injudicious remarks Warren uttered after the assassination. Johnson, however, is in no mood for such reservations.

The most delicate problem involving Eastland now has to do with leaving
the Judiciary Committee chairman off the commission. Johnson explains this
away by emphasizing the need for men familiar with the CIA's intelligence
sources and methods, rather than commissioners versed in the intricacies of
internal security. Eastland readily accepts being passed over for Richard Russell. And as Johnson well knows, it would be exceedingly hard for him to do
otherwise, given Russell's stature and reputation.

Eastland: Ah-ha! I wouldn't have it![300]

Johnson: Here's what I'm gonna announce in a few minutes, and I want . . .
[reading rapidly]
"The president announced he's appointing a Special Commission to
study all facts and circumstances relating to the assassination of the
late president, and the subsequent violent death of the man charged
with the assassination. The president stated the majority and the
minority leaders of the Senate and House have been consulted with
respect to the proposed Special Commission. The members of the
Special Commission are: Chief Justice Warren; Senator Richard
Russell; Senator John [Sherman] Cooper; Representative Hale Boggs;

300. The recording begins after the conversation has already started, so Eastland's reference
is unclear. But he may have been expressing relief at not having been asked to serve.

Representative Gerald Ford; Honorable Allen Dulles; Honorable John J. McCloy."

Now we had—

Eastland: [That sounds] all right!

Johnson: —we had to have a justice, and then I wanted to have the head of the CIA [sub]committee in the Senate that controls all their money, and that they report to—

Eastland: Sure . . . I think that's all right.

Johnson: I thought I'd get Cooper because he'd had international experience, 'cause this Russian thing's gettin' in it. And I got Boggs—he's been talkin' over there [in the House]—and Ford handles the [CIA] money on [the House] Appropriations [Committee], and then Dulles is ex-CIA, and John McCloy [will] help it from an international standpoint a little bit. It gives us—

Eastland: I think it would improve it if you'd put [Justice John Marshall] Harlan on there instead of Warren.[301]

Johnson: Well—

Eastland: See, Warren made a political [statement] . . . he was *[indistinct]* of Kennedy was political.[302]

Johnson: Yeah, but I've got to get the top one, and he's the chief [justice].

Eastland: Well . . . that's true.

Johnson: That's true. And he . . . none of 'em want to do it, but I've gotta do it, and you've got to protect my flank over in the Senate now.

Eastland: I'll do that.

Johnson: Thank you, Jim.

Eastland: Yeah.

Johnson: 'Bye.

Immediately following the conversation with Eastland, Johnson places calls to Senators J. William Fulbright, Bourke Hickenlooper, and Thomas Dodd (D-Connecticut).[303] In the conversations with Fulbright and Hickenlooper,

301. Patrician in manner and appearance, Harlan is widely viewed as a principled dissenter and the "conservative conscience" on the Supreme Court. His 1955 appointment was opposed by several conservative senators, but he turned out to be an articulate spokesman for their complaints about Warren's brand of judicial activism and a restraining influence. Some of Harlan's most pointed dissents are against applying the Warren Court's "one man, one vote" approach to states' legislative apportionment schemes, a most sensitive issue for Eastland and other southerners. Lesley Oelsner, "Harlan Dies at 72; On Court 16 Years," *New York Times,* 30 December 1971.

302. It is not clear whether Eastland is referring to Warren's statement right after the assassination (in which he ascribed the crime to "bigots") or to the chief justice's November 24 eulogy.

303. Johnson and Fulbright, conversation, 29 November 1963, 7:11 p.m.; Johnson and Dodd, conversation, 29 November 1963, 7:15 p.m.; Johnson and Hickenlooper, conversation, 29 November 1963, 7:20 p.m., all LBJL.

Johnson informs them of Richard Russell's invitation to join his CIA subcommittee temporarily, and for the sole purpose of getting intelligence briefings on foreign involvement in the assassination. Given the allegation from Mexico City, Johnson is all but sure that he will have to address this issue in the weeks to come, and he wants the chairman and ranking member of the Senate Foreign Relations Committee fully informed and on board.

The brief conversation with Tom Dodd concerns the commission. Johnson and the senator are old friends, going back to their days together at the National Youth Administration (NYA), a quintessential New Deal agency. Dodd had left the FBI in 1935 to be state NYA director for Connecticut, while Johnson ran the NYA program in Texas from 1935 until he left to run for Congress in 1937. Though the presidential commission has already been cleared with Jim Eastland, giving Dodd a heads-up provides Johnson with added insurance on Capitol Hill. Dodd, the second-ranking Democrat on the Judiciary Committee and vice chairman of its Internal Security subcommittee, is intensely anti-Communist and has excellent relations with J. Edgar Hoover, dating back to Dodd's two years as an FBI agent. Johnson probably believes it will be useful for Dodd to help spread the word in the Senate that Hoover assented to the commission.

To Thomas Kuchel / 8:30 p.m.

After disposing of some unrelated matters, Johnson returns to the subject of the commission in a conversation with Republican senator Kuchel of California. The telephone call to Kuchel, like the one to Dodd, is something of an afterthought. The announcement is already ninety minutes old, and Johnson has already cleared the commission with the GOP's Senate leadership in the person of Everett Dirksen. But there is something to be gained from giving Kuchel, the minority whip, the courtesy of a personal call before he hears the news.

Johnson is not wrong in thinking that Kuchel, one of the most liberal Republicans in the Senate, will welcome the announcement. The Californian owes his Senate career to Earl Warren in the first place, then–Governor Warren having appointed Kuchel to fill the vacancy created by Richard Nixon's election as vice president in 1952. More pointedly, Johnson fully expects that Kuchel will be thrilled about the deft end run around Jim Eastland. In May 1962, after Eastland's attacked the Warren Court for siding "with the Communists," Senator Kuchel was the first Republican to take the Senate floor and denounce the criticism as "shocking and evil . . . a pitiful, puny, and highly regrettable attempt to slur" the Court.[304] Kuchel's response to the neutering of Eastland will not disappoint Johnson.

304. Warren Duffee, "Kuchel Raps Eastland for Attacks on Court," *Washington Post,* 4 May 1962.

Yet the more important reason for stroking Kuchel has to do with Johnson's own legislative program in the near future. If he successfully cultivates Kuchel, the president will surely gain a pivotal vote on divisive legislative proposals in the months ahead. Johnson knows Kuchel is as close to him in ideology as almost anyone in the Senate, notwithstanding their party affiliations. Kuchel refused to endorse Nixon during the 1962 governor's race in California and is almost a lock to withhold support from Senator Barry Goldwater, should he win the 1964 GOP presidential nomination.

Making this courtesy call is a shrewd way of drawing Kuchel closer and will soon pay dividends. In 1964 Kuchel will be the floor comanager of the successful effort to break a southern filibuster on the Civil Rights Act, and in 1965, Kuchel's vote will be critical in passing the Medicare program.[305]

[Johnson initially chides Kuchel, a southern Californian, for being in Florida during the Thanksgiving weekend, along with so many other congressional leaders.]

Johnson: What I called you about, Tommy, was . . . I was namin' a commission on the assassination of the president to make a full study for the world and [for] the United States.

Kuchel: *[abruptly somber]* Yes, sir.

Johnson: And I wanted to discuss with you who I was namin'. But I got Dirksen and I got Mansfield, and . . . I'm sure that you'll think it's all right, but I wanted you to know who it was.

Kuchel: Yes, sir.

Johnson: I got the chief justice to be chairman of it.

Kuchel: Magnificent.

Johnson: I got Dick Russell.

Kuchel: Fine.

Johnson: I got John Sherman Cooper . . . your manager.[306]

Kuchel: That's great!

Johnson: I got Hale Boggs and Jerry Ford of Michigan . . . from the House.

Kuchel: [I] think both of 'em are good.

Johnson: Got Allen Dulles and John McCloy. That's five Republicans and two Democrats. So I just wanted you to know . . . *[begins reading]*
 "The President announced today that he's appointin' a Special Commission to study and report upon the facts and circumstances relatin' to the assassination of the late president, and the subsequent

---

305. David Binder, "Thomas H. Kuchel Dies at 84; Ex–Republican Whip in Senate," *New York Times,* 24 November 1994.

306. Displaying his encyclopedic command of Senate political minutiae, Johnson recalls that Cooper was Kuchel's campaign manager when he ran for the job of minority whip in 1959.

violent death of the man charged with the assassination. The president stated that the majority and minority leadership of the Senate and the House had been *consulted* with respect to the proposed Special Commission. The members of the commission *are*: Chief Justice Earl Warren; Senator Richard Russell; Senator John Sherman Cooper; Representative Hale Boggs; Representative Jerry Ford; Honorable Allen Dulles; Honorable John McCloy."

Now Warren and Cooper and Ford and Dulles and McCloy are *Republicans.*

Kuchel: And they've accepted, Mr. President?

Johnson: Yes, sir, all of 'em. I called each of 'em *myself,* and in addition to that I called every congressional *leader* myself. And I'm still at the office and I'm catchin' hell, and I'd like to trade jobs with you and, if you don't mind, bring Betty on back here and find a good constitutional lawyer to tell us how to make the transition.[307]

Kuchel: No, sir . . . no, no, Mr. President, I would not do that. But . . . ah, Mr. President, that *ought to* eliminate the necessity for the Senate Judiciary Committee, shouldn't it?

Johnson: Yes, and Eastland agreed that he wouldn't go ahead with it if I do this, and the House agreed the same way.

Kuchel: *[enthusiastically]* Oh, *that's just excellent,* Mr. President . . . I'm not kidding you, *that's great!*

Johnson: Well, I know how you . . . what a good American you are, and how you want to support [the president] every time you could, and that's why I called you early in the day to just . . . before this went out, to tell you. But it has gone out . . . it went out about fifteen, twenty minutes ago.

Kuchel: Well, I'm grateful and honored that you would call me. Incidentally, I think you should take considerable pride in what the Senate did the other night on that [Karl] Mundt thing.[308]

Johnson: Well, I'm glad it did. I don't know what's going to come, but I'm going to do the best I can as long as I'm here, and that's all I want to do. And you and Betty know how I feel about y'all, and please . . . I don't expect you to abandon your party, but our principles are about the same,

307. Betty is the senator's wife.

308. In what Johnson, rightly or wrongly, regarded as the first legislative test of his presidency, on November 26 the Senate easily defeated legislation that would have forbidden the use of U.S. government credits to finance trade with Communist nations. The first casualty of the ban would have been a proposed sale of surplus wheat to the Soviet Union. The bill's sponsor was Senator Karl Mundt (R-South Dakota), who is such an ardent anti-Communist that he is willing to act against the interests of the state he represents. Associated Press, "Senate Roll-Call Vote Tabling Wheat Curb," *New York Times,* 27 November 1963.

and I told Otis Chandler that last week.[309] He went hunting with me down there in Texas, and I said this is an American first, and that's *my* philosophy. And that's the way I won the Senate away from Eisenhower, is 'cause I didn't play politics. I was responsible and supported him.

Kuchel: Yes, sir.

Johnson: Bill Knowland fought him, and by God, I got a majority [after] the first two years.[310]

Kuchel: You sure did, and I tell you that was—

Johnson: And if they followed *you,* they [would] do the same thing with *us.*

Kuchel: Yes, sir.

Johnson: But anyway . . . I just wanted you to know, and I thought that you wouldn't object to [the appointment of] Cooper, your manager, [to the commission]. *[chuckles]*

Kuchel: I think he's great . . . and I think that chairman [Warren], Mr. President, is the *greatest.*

Johnson: He turned it down today, and Bobby [Kennedy] and them went to him.[311] So I just called and sat him down here, and I said, Now listen, you'd get in a World War I uniform, and you'd go and fight if you thought you could save one American life. Now these wild people are chargin' [Nikita] Khrushchev killed Kennedy, and [Fidel] Castro killed Kennedy, and everybody else killed Kennedy. Now we've had sixty FBI agents working for seven days, and they've got the story, and they've got the fingerprints, and they've got everything else. But the American people and the world have *got to know* who *killed* Kennedy and *why,* and somebody's got to evaluate that report. And if they don't, why [if] Khrushchev moved on us, he could kill 39 million in an hour. And we could kill 100 million [in] his country in an hour. But here I'm askin' you [Warren] to do somethin', and you're saying "no" to everybody, when you could be speakin' for 39 million people. Now I just don't think you wanna do that. Tears just

309. As Kuchel is acutely aware, the Chandler family owns the Times-Mirror media company based in southern California, and Chandler is the publisher of its flagship newspaper, the *Los Angeles Times.*

310. Johnson is referring to the first two years of the Eisenhower presidency, when the Republicans controlled the Senate by a paper-thin margin. While Senator Knowland (R-California), the majority leader, fought with the president from his own party, Johnson engaged in what he called the "politics of responsibility." Johnson often marshaled just enough Democrats to provide critical support to Eisenhower's legislative proposals when they came under assault from GOP conservatives like Knowland. All the while Johnson suggested that the popular Eisenhower would be better off with a Democratic-controlled Senate. In November 1954 voters agreed and reinstalled a Democratic majority in the Senate. Johnson does not really believe the same tactic will work for Kuchel; he merely wants to maximize GOP support for his legislative agenda. Dallek, *Lone Star Rising,* 441; Goldsmith, *Colleagues,* 35–36.

311. The attorney general, of course, did not speak directly to the chief justice.

came to his eyes . . . they just came up, just . . . you never saw anything
like it, and he said, "I can't say no."

Kuchel: Oh, Mr. President, I think *that's just fine.*

Johnson: He's a patriot . . . he's a patriot, that fella. By God, you'd better
breed some more like him. You'd better just—

Kuchel: *You* ought to, Mr. President.

Johnson: You just better breed 'em. Well, I'm gonna be [breeding them as]
long as I'm here. There's nothin' I want . . . I got more than I deserve, and
it's too frightening for me to even think of . . . but I'm gonna do my best,
and I'm gonna be fair, and I'm gonna be just, and I'm gonna be as
nonpartisan as a man can be and still hold the office.

Kuchel: Yes, sir.

Johnson: And I'm gonna expect your help, and I'm gonna give you mine.

Kuchel: Thank you, Mr. President. You have it, and God bless you, and we
pray for you.

To Richard Russell / 8:55 p.m.

After nearly twelve hours at his Oval Office desk, Johnson calls the man whose
opinion and approval he seeks above all others. The president probably suspects
it is going to be a difficult conversation. Certainly it was reasonable for Johnson
to come away believing, after their four p.m. conversation, that Russell had
agreed in principle to serve on the commission, albeit reluctantly. But Johnson
was disingenuous, too, and now he has to make explicit what he purposefully
obscured. The consequence will be one of the most argumentative conversations
ever between Johnson and Russell.

The president sounds unprepared for the depth of Russell's genuine resentment over having been misled earlier. Russell is bitter and will sound disconso-
late at several points during the conversation. When he realizes he has been
sandbagged, too, he is incensed. Russell never changes his mind regarding the
wisdom of a commission. But on judicial rulings that range from national security to civil rights to states' rights, to the very concept of federalism and the
separation of powers, Russell cannot abide the Warren Court and the man who
leads it. The Georgian believes Warren has destroyed the integrity of the
nation's highest court. And now he faces not only serving with, but effectively
under, the chief justice whose results-oriented jurisprudence he detests. Russell
is only partly mollified when he learns, contrary to his prejudice, that the president figuratively had to draft Warren before the chief justice would agree to
serve on the commission. Russell's opinion of Warren is so low that he believes
the chief justice will grab any opportunity for more publicity.

Of course, if Russell knew that Johnson misleadingly invoked *his* name to persuade Warren to serve, the Georgian would be apoplectic. But the release of the announcement by the White House two hours ago has left Russell trapped, as Johnson may have intended. The senator cannot force a retraction of the press release without delivering a stunning rebuke to his protégé. In the end, he cannot bring himself to deliver such a political blow to Johnson, who needs more than anything to prove that confidence in his leadership is warranted rather than a constitutional technicality.

Though Russell talks about President Kennedy's assassination with almost clinical detachment now, his reaction to the news a week ago was anything but. The Senate was in session at the time, and when it instantly recessed, everyone converged on the "marble room," a lobby behind the Senate chamber where UPI and AP teletype machines are located. Roger Mudd, a young reporter covering the Congress for CBS News, would never forget the sight of the Senate's most powerful man, bent over the UPI machine, reading aloud to a group huddled around him. Tears streamed down Russell's face.[312]

Johnson: Dick?
Russell: Yes?
Johnson: I hate to bother you *again,* but . . .
Russell: [That's] all right, Mr. President.
Johnson: I wanted you to know that I'd made that announcement.
Russell: *[puzzled]* Announcement of *what*?
Johnson: Of this special commission.
Russell: Oh, you have already?
Johnson: Yes.
Russell: All right.
Johnson: And I got you . . . may I read it to you?
Russell: Yes.
Johnson: *[reading, but not quickly]*

> "The president announced that he's appointing a Special Commission
> to study and report upon all the facts and circumstances relating to the
> assassination of the late president, John F. Kennedy, and the
> subsequent violent death of the man charged with the assassination.
> The president stated that the majority and minority leadership of the
> Senate and the House had been consulted with respect to the proposed
> Special Commission. The members of the Special Commission *are,*
> colon: Chief Justice Earl Warren, chairman; Senator Richard Russell,
> Georgia; Senator John [Sherman] Cooper, Kentucky; Representative
> Hale Boggs, Louisiana; Representative Gerald Ford, Michigan;
> Honorable Allen Dulles, Washington; Honorable John J. McCloy,
> New York.

312. Goldsmith, *Colleagues,* 99.

The president stated the Special Commission is to be instructed to evaluate all available information concerning the subject [of] the inquiry. The Federal Bureau of Investigation, pursuant to an earlier directive of the president, is making a complete investigation of the facts. An inquiry is scheduled by a Texas Court of Inquiry convened by the attorney general of Texas under Texas law. The Special Commission will have before it *all* the evidence uncovered by the Federal Bureau of Investigation and all the information available to any agency of the federal government. The attorney general of Texas has also offered his cooperation. All federal agencies and offices are being directed to furnish services in cooperation to the Special Commission. The commission will *also* be empowered to conduct *any further* investigation that it deems desirable. The president is instructing the Special Commission to satisfy itself that the truth is known as far as it can be *discovered,* and to report its findings and conclusions to him, to the American people, and to the world."

Russell: Well now, Mr. President . . . I know I don't have to tell you of my devotion to *you,* but I just can't serve on that commission. I'm highly honored you'd think about me in connection with it. But I couldn't serve there with Chief Justice Warren. I don't like that man, and . . . I don't have any confidence in him, [even] though I realize *[Russell is speaking facetiously]* he's a much greater man in the United States nearly . . . today [than] near almost *anyone.* And so you get John Stennis.[313] He's a—

Johnson: Dick, it's already been announced, and you can serve with anybody for the good of America. This is a question that has a good many more ramifications than's on the surface, and . . . we got to take this out of the arena where they're testifyin' that [Nikita] Khrushchev and [Fidel] Castro did this and did that, and that [could end up] kickin' us into a war that can kill 40 million Americans in an hour, and . . . you'd put on your uniform in a minute [to stop that from happening].

Now the reason I asked Warren is because he's the chief justice of this country, and we've got to have the highest judicial people we can have.[314] The reason I ask you is because you have that same kind of temperament, and you can do anything for your country. And don't go to givin' me that kinda stuff about you can't serve with anybody. You can do *anything*.

Russell: Well see, it's not only that. I don't think the chief justice should have *served* on it.

Johnson: Well . . . [the] chief justice oughta do anything he can to save

---

313. Stennis is regarded as Russell's apprentice in the Senate; the Mississippi Democrat is also privy to CIA operational secrets as a member of the Armed Services CIA subcommittee.

314. Whether Russell recalls it or not, Johnson is throwing back a refined version of the argument Russell fashioned for the president when they talked five hours ago.

America, and right now we've got a *very touchy* thing, and you wait till you look at this evidence. And you wait till you look at this report.[315] Now don't just . . . I'm not gonna lead you wrong, and you're not gonna be in *Old Dog Tray*—[316]

Russell: You know that I—

Johnson: You're not gonna be in *Old Dog Tray* company, but—

Russell: I have never—

Johnson: You never turned your country down—

Russell: *[indistinct]* knew that I could, when I could.

Johnson: Well, this is not *me*. This is your country, and . . . "the members of the Special Commission are Chief Justice Warren, Senator Richard Russell," and I go right down the list. Now I've got Allen Dulles and John McCloy [also], but you're *my man on that commission. And you gonna to do it!* And don't tell me what you can do and what you *can't*, because . . . I can't arrest you. And I'm not gonna put the FBI on you, but you're *goddamned sure gonna serve,* I'll tell you *that*! And A. W. [Moursund's] here and he wants to tell you how much all of us *love* you.[317] Wait a minute.

Russell: Well, I know, but Mr. President, you oughta told me you were gonna *name* [Warren].

Johnson: *I told you!* I told you *today* I was gonna name the chief justice, when I called you.

Russell: *No, you did not.*

Johnson: I did.

Russell: You talked about gettin' somebody on the Supreme Court—

Johnson: That's right.

Russell: —and who do you think you oughta *get*. You didn't tell me you was gonna name *him*.

Johnson: I told you I was gonna name Warren, and you said it'd be *better* to name [John Marshall] *Harlan*![318]

315. Johnson is once again referring to the allegation that Oswald received $6,500 in the Cuban consulate.

316. An expression taken from the song "Old Dog Tray," an 1853 work by the American composer Stephen C. Foster. Tray embodies an unquestioning friend.

317. Since 1949 Russell has been a frequent guest at the Johnsons' ranch in Texas, where days are spent hunting and nights spent talking politics. Through these at least annual visits Russell has become well acquainted with Albert W. Moursund, a local attorney and banker and one of the Johnsons' closest advisers on personal and business matters. Johnson and Moursund have known each other since boyhood. Moursund is often referred to by his initials only, or as Judge Moursund, in recognition of his seven years as a Blanco County, Texas, judge.

318. Russell's recollection of the conversation is more accurate than Johnson's, though to be fair to the president, at the end of a long day, he seems genuinely confused about who told him what. During the 4 p.m. conversation with Russell, Johnson mentioned Warren's name but once in passing, and in a deliberately vague manner hardly calculated to impress upon Russell that the

Russell: No, *no.* We talked, and I said [Tom] Clark wouldn't do cause he's [from Texas]—

Johnson: No, that's *right* . . . that's right. And I've got to get the highest justice I can *get.* He [Warren] turned Bobby Kennedy *down!*[319] They talked to him [Warren], and he just said he wouldn't serve under any circumstances. I called him down here and I spent an *hour* with him.[320] And I begged him as much as I'm beggin' *you.* I just said, Now here's the situation. I wanna tell you what mister—

Russell: You never have had to beg me. You've always *told* me, all right?

Johnson: *No,* I haven't.

Russell: Yes, you *have.*

Johnson: No, I haven't.

Russell: I don't . . . Mr. President, *please* now.

Johnson: No. It's already *done!* It's been announced . . . *hell.*

Russell: *[in disbelief]* You mean you've given out that—

Johnson: Yes, sir. I mean I gave it . . . I gave [out] the announcement, and it's already in the papers, and you're on it, and you're gonna be my man *on* it. And you just forget that. Now wait a minute. A. W. [Moursund] wants to say a word to you, and then I'll be back.

Moursund: Hello, Senator?

Russell: *[sounding glum]* Yeah.

Moursund: We're just sittin' here talkin', and he [Johnson] said, "I got *one man* on there that's smarter than all the rest of 'em put together."

Russell: *[not amused]* Oh . . . [it's no use you] trying to butter me up.

Moursund: I ain't buttering you up, Senator—

Russell: You know just like I do he ought not [to] be puttin' me on this [commission]—

Moursund: Well, goddammit, you know I'm not that kind of *feller.* And I just heard that, and I just wanted you to know that. 'Cause hell, he['s] *dependin'* on you, you know that. And he just got through sayin', he said, "I got one man on there that's smarter than all the rest of 'em put together."

Russell: *[laughing skeptically]* Yeah.

Moursund: That's the *truth,* and you know it. *You know I know it,* Senator.

Russell: Well, A.W., . . . I don't know when I've been as *unhappy* about a thing as I am this. This is *awful.*

Moursund: Well, I know, but you can take 'em. God almighty, you've took 'em

---

chief justice was Johnson's first and only choice. The suggestion of Justice Harlan occurred during the president's 7 p.m. conversation with James Eastland, when the Mississippi senator mentioned Harlan after learning that Warren's selection was a fait accompli.

319. Johnson says this emphatically, as if it's more stunning that Warren turned down the brother of the deceased president than the sitting president.

320. A typical Johnsonian exaggeration, calculated to make a point. The president's meeting with Warren lasted twenty-five minutes at most.

for years . . . and the hard ones, and the tough ones. And you can take care of it, and you take care of yourself.

Russell: Well, how's everything down in Texas? Kill any deer down there this season?

Moursund: Well, you come see us.

Russell: Well . . .

Moursund: But *don't* say you can't do anything, 'cause you the best can-do man there *is.*

Russell: Oh, no . . . oh, no.

[The president gets back on the line.]

Johnson:*:* Dick?

Russell: *[no longer sounding so glum]* Yeah.

Johnson: Now . . . we're goin' into a lot of problems. We had lunch together [on Wednesday], and I saw [Carl] Sanders [afterward], and I saw . . . I've seen a good many people since then [Wednesday], and even saw [Roy] Wilkins today. Had a long talk with him. Now, these things are gonna be developing . . . and I know you're gonna have your reservations, and your modesty, and you're gonna have a—

Russell: *[indistinct, but clearly disagreeing]*

Johnson: *Wait a minute!* Now wait a minute! I understand that. But now your president [is] askin' you to do these things, and there're some things that I want you in besides civil rights. And by God, you gonna be *in* 'em 'cause—

Russell: Well—

Johnson: *I can't run this country by myself!*

Russell: You know damn well my future's behind me, and that's not enterin' into it at all. *[indistinct]*

Johnson: Well, your future is . . . your future's your *country.* And you gonna do everything you can to serve *America.* And I—

Russell: I just haven't . . . I can't *do* it. I haven't got the *time—*

Johnson: Oh well, now . . . well, all right. We'll just—

Russell: *[struggling to be heard] [indistinct]—*

Johnson: We'll just make the time—

Russell: All my Georgia items in there—

Johnson: Well, we'll just make the time. There's not gonna be any time to begin with. All you're gonna do is evaluate a [J. Edgar] Hoover report that he's already *made.*

Russell: Well, I don't think we oughta move that fast on it.

Johnson: Well, okay. Well then, we won't move any faster than you wanna move. But you're gonna lend your name to this thing because you're head of the CIA [sub]committee in the Senate. And you're gonna have [J. William] Fulbright and [Bourke] Hickenlooper on it, because this thing is breakin' faster than you think.[321] And I've already talked to Hickenlooper and Fulbright and asked them to go with you, [to] sit [in] on your [sub]committee, because I don't want these things torn up.

The secretary of state came over here this afternoon.[322] He's *deeply* concerned, Dick, about the idea that they're spreading throughout the Communist world that Khrushchev killed Kennedy![323] Now he *didn't*. He didn't have a *damn thing to do with it*!

Russell: Well, I don't think he did di-*rectly*.

Johnson: Well—

Russell: I know Khrushchev didn't, 'cause he thought he's gettin' along better with Kennedy in there—

Johnson: All right.

Russell: —better than anybody else *[indistinct]*.

Johnson: All right. But we got to have some people—

Russell: [But] I wouldn't be surprised if Castro had something to do with it.

Johnson: All right . . . then okay. That's what we want to know. And people got *confidence* in you. And you can just be surprised, or *not* surprised. They want to know what *you think*. And if my . . . A. W. Moursund's one [that] wants to *know* what you think. And you—

Russell: I think you're sorta takin' advantage of me, Mr. President—

Johnson: No.

Russell: —but of course, I can't turn it down.

Johnson: No, you're not . . . I'm not takin' advantage of you. I'm gonna take *helluva* lot of advantage of you, my friend, 'cause you *made* me and I know it, and I don't ever *forget*. And if you think . . . I'll be takin' advantage of you a good deal. But you gonna serve your country, and you gonna do what's right, and if you can't do it, you get that damn little Bobby [Russell] up there, and let him twist your tail and put a cocklebur under it.[324]

Russell: Well, he's . . .

Johnson: *Where is he?*

Russell: I don't know. He's in Atlanta tonight, I don't *[indistinct]*—

321. Johnson has in mind the Gilberto Alvarado allegation. The unconfirmed information is so sensitive that it has not yet been disclosed to the Armed Services CIA subcommittee chaired by Russell.

322. Rusk was with Johnson late in the morning, of course, and participated in the day's first call regarding the commission to Senator Mansfield.

323. Johnson is so agitated he mangles the sentence, and conveys the opposite of what the State Department's Kremlinologists believe.

324. "Little Bobby" Russell, a Georgia appeals court judge, is the senator's favorite nephew, a confidant, and (Russell hopes) his eventual successor in the U.S. Senate. Johnson knows Bobby Russell well, as he managed the 1960 Kennedy-Johnson campaign in Georgia. Bringing Bobby Russell's name into the conversation is akin to asking Russell (a lifelong bachelor) about his son.

Johnson: Well, you just tell him to get ready, 'cause I'm gonna need him. And . . . you just tell him that.

Russell: I saw he *[sic]* and [Ernest] Vandiver this afternoon for about thirty minutes, they came by here.[325]

Johnson: Well, just tell either one of 'em that I'd just like to use 'em any place, because I'm a *Russell* protégé, and I don't forget my friends. And I want you to stand up and be counted, and I don't want to beg you, by God, to serve on these things that *amount* to somethin'.

Russell: [I know, but this is a] sort of rough one. Now you—

Johnson: No, it's not rough! What's rough about this? I talked to Jim Eastland . . . Jim Eastland said [this is] the best thing that's ever happened!

Russell: *[unimpressed]* Yeah.

Johnson: I talked to Tom Dodd. I talked to *everybody.* Not a damned one of them that *[indistinct].* All these folks are gonna be for it!

Russell: *[still sounding unimpressed]* Yes sir, I'm sure they will [be].

Johnson: They had a full-scale investigation going, Dick, with the TV up there. They had the House Un-American Activities Committee in it.[326]

Russell: Well, all of that was a lot of crap, and they shouldn't have done it.

Johnson: Well of course, but *how do I stop it?* How do I *stop* it, Dick? Now don't tell me that I've worked all day and *done wrong.*

Russell: I didn't say you'd done wrong! I said that they ought not to have had that kind of a hearing, and it oughta have been stopped. And it *could* have been stopped some other way. But I just—

Johnson: Well now, what do you think—

Russell: I could have stopped it in the Senate.

Johnson: What do you think I've done wrong now, by appointin' you on a commission?

Russell: *[dismissively]* Hell, I just don't like Warren. I don't like—

Johnson: Well, of course you don't like Warren, but you'll like him 'fore it's over with.

Russell: I haven't got any confidence in him.

Johnson: Well . . . you can *give* him some confidence. *Goddammit! Associate* with him! Now you're not, *you've* got nothing to—I'm not afraid to put your intelligence against Warren's. Now by God, *I* want a man on that commission . . . and *I've got one!*

Russell: I don't know about the intelligence, of course. And I feel like I'm bein' kidded. But if you think—

Johnson: Well, if you think . . . now Dick, do you think I'd kid you?

325. Vandiver, husband of one of Russell's nieces, was Georgia's Democratic governor from 1959 until earlier in the year.

326. Johnson is referring to the House resolution authorizing a HUAC investigation into the Fair Play for Cuba Committee, and the Senate Judiciary Committee's intention to televise its hearings.

Russell: If it is for the good of the country, you know damned well I'll *do* it, and I'll do it for *you,* for that matter. I still feel like I'm sort of getting wrapped up.

Johnson: Dick, do you remember when you met me at the Carlton [Hotel, and we] had breakfast in 1952 . . . one mornin', [when] I became leader?

Russell: Yes, I think I do.

Johnson: All right. Do you think I'm kiddin' you?[327]

Russell: No, I don't think you're kiddin' me *[chuckles]*—

Johnson: All right.

Russell: But I think I'm . . . well, I'm not gonna say any more, Mr. President, [because]—

Johnson: Well, you ought—

Russell: I'm at your command, and—

Johnson: All right.

Russell: I'll do anything you want me to do—

Johnson: Well, you're damn sure gonna be at my command—

Russell: —*[indistinct]* where the country's involved.

Johnson: You're gonna be at my command [as] long as I'm here.

Russell: I hope to God you'll be just a *little bit* more deliberate and considerate next time about it. But *this* time, of course, if you've done this, I'm gonna do it and go through with it and say I think it's a wonderful idea *[unenthusiastically]*.

Johnson: Well, I'm not gonna be any more deliberate than I been about this, 'cause I been pretty deliberate. But I'm gonna have you on a good *goddamned* many things that I have to decide, and you gonna be America's representative. And I don't want any *special* obligation. I just know you gonna call 'em as you see 'em, and I served under you . . . and I don't give a damn if you have to serve with a *Republican*; if you have to serve with a *Communist*; if you have to serve with a *Negro*; if you have to serve with a *thug*; if you have to serve with A. W. Moursund.

Russell: I can serve with a Communist, and I can serve with a Negro. I can serve with a Chinaman, and—

Johnson: *Well, you may have to serve with A. W. Moursund!*

Russell: And if I can serve with A. W. Moursund, I would say, Mr. Chairman, I am pleased to serve under *you,* Judge Moursund. But . . . well, we won't discuss this [anymore].

Johnson: No . . . no.

327. Johnson is probably referring to a meeting on November 10, 1952, the day when the Georgia senator "buttoned up the [Senate Democratic] leadership for [Johnson]," as Russell put it at the time. This was also the moment when Johnson asked Russell to move his desk so that they would be sitting next to each other on the Senate floor. Winder Materials, Calendars, 1952, Richard B. Russell Library (hereafter RBRL); Robert Caro, *The Years of Lyndon Johnson: Master of the Senate* (New York: Alfred A. Knopf, 2002), 475.

Russell: Of course, Mr. President. I'll serve.

Johnson: Okay, Dick.

Russell: All right.

Johnson: And give Bobby my love, and tell him he'd better get ready to give up that fruitful law practice he's got.

Russell: He's a judge [on the] Court of Appeals of Georgia now.

Johnson: Oh, God almighty.

Russell: *[indistinct],* you see. I got him on there . . . he's makin' as much money as I am.

Johnson: Oh, yeah?

Russell: His salary's exactly the same.

Johnson: What about Vandiver?

Russell: Well, he's runnin' for governor next time and will be elected.[328]

Johnson: Hmmm . . . well, who the hell's gonna help me, besides you?

Russell: Well, *those* boys will help you if you need 'em!

Johnson: Well, I need 'em!

Russell: Damn it, they're harder for you at one time than I was, don't you remember?[329]

Johnson: No . . . no. I never did. Nobody [has] ever been more to me than *you* have, Dick . . . except my mother.

Russell: *[chuckles]* Oh . . .

Johnson: No . . . no, that's true. I never . . . I've bothered you *more,* and made you spend *more* hours with me tellin' me what was right and wrong, than anybody except my mother.

Russell: [You get me] to do more things I didn't wanna *do* than anybody!

Johnson: No . . . I've never made you do anything that was wrong.

Russell: *[indistinct]*

Johnson: I've never made you do anything wrong.

Russell: I didn't say *wrong.* I said more things I *didn't want to do!* But Bobby and Ernie are two of the most loyal friends you've got on earth.

Johnson: I know that.

Russell: They both called me up and said, *[mimicking their voices] You've just got to do whatever Mr. Johnson says.*

Johnson: No, I don't want you to do that. I just want to counsel with—

Russell: I'm not talkin' right on this [commission thing] now, I'm talkin'—

Johnson: I just want to counsel with you, and I just want your judgment, and your wisdom, and I don't expect us to agree on—

---

328. Vandiver is considered the front-runner for the 1966 Democratic nomination.

329. Then-Governor Vandiver supported the 1960 Kennedy-Johnson campaign vigorously, too, but only after extracting a pledge from nominee Kennedy that federal troops would never be sent to Georgia to enforce school desegregation. Associated Press, "Vandiver Tells of Pledge," *New York Times,* 10 May 1961.

Russell: For whatever it's worth, you've *got* it, but—

Johnson: I'm gonna have it 'cause I haven't got any daddy, and you gonna be it . . . now just forget that.

Russell: *[chuckles]* Well, Mr. President, you know . . . I think you know me.

Johnson: I do . . . I do. And I know you['re] for your country and period. Now, you just get ready to do this. You're *my man* on there, and *period.*

Russell: If you hadn't announced it, I would absolutely—

Johnson: *No* . . . you wouldn't. No, you wouldn't.

Russell: I would . . . yes, I would.

Johnson: No. I told Warren—

Russell: *Yes, I would have.*

Johnson: Warren told me he wouldn't do it under any circumstances. [He] didn't think a Supreme Court justice oughta go on it; he wouldn't have anything to do with it. He said a man that had criticized this fella that went on the Nuremberg trial—[Justice Robert] Jackson—[could hardly go on the commission].[330] He told me what he thought about [Arthur] Goldberg; he [Warren] thought it was terrible that he's arbitratin' the track.[331] And I said, "Let me read you one report." And I just picked up one report and read it to him. And I said, "Okay. Now . . . [there are] forty million Americans involved here"—

Russell: Well . . . I may be wholly wrong. But I think Mr. Warren would serve on anything that'd give him any publicity, unfortunately.

Johnson: Well, [do] you want me to tell you the truth?

Russell: I ain't [looking for] publicity. *[chuckles]*

Johnson: You know what happened? Do you know what happened? Bobby [Kennedy] and 'em went up to see him today, and he turned 'em down cold and said, *"No."*[332]

Russell: *[listening intently]* Yeah.

Johnson: Two hours later I called him and ordered him down here, and he didn't want to come.[333] I insisted he come, he came down here and *he told me no twice.* Then I just pulled out what Hoover told me about a little incident in Mexico City, and I said, Now, I don't want Mr. Khrushchev to be told tomorrow, and [to] be testifyin' before a camera, that he killed this

330. Johnson is referring, of course, to Warren's opposition to extrajudicial activity by sitting justices. Justice Robert Jackson's decision to serve as chief prosecutor at the International Military Tribunal in 1945–46, according to Warren, resulted in "divisiveness and internal bitterness" on the Court. Warren, *Memoirs,* 356.

331. This is another reference to President Kennedy's attempt to get Justice Goldberg involved in settling a threatened railroad strike in July 1963.

332. Again, Johnson seems to be taking inordinate pleasure in having succeeded where Robert Kennedy supposedly failed.

333. Johnson is exaggerating. Warren came down willingly to the White House, confident he could withstand the famed "Johnson treatment," which he had never been subjected to before.

fella, and that *Castro* killed him.[334] And all I want you to do is look at the *facts,* and bring any other facts you want in here and determine who *killed* the president. And I think you'd put on your uniform [from] World War I—[as] *fat* as you are—and do anything you could to save one American life.[335] Now I'm surprised that *you*—the chief justice [of the] United States—would turn *me* down. And he started cryin', and he said, "Well, I won't *turn* you down. I'll just do whatever you say." But he turned the *attorney general* down.

Russell: Well . . . you ought not to be so persuasive.

Johnson: Well, I think I ought to.

Russell: I think you did wrong gettin' Warren, and I know *damn* well you got it wrong gettin' me, but—

Johnson: No.

Russell: —we'll both do the best we can.

Johnson: I think that's what you'll do. That's the kind of Americans both of you are. Good night.

Russell: *[resignedly]* Good night.

Russell's agreement, though reluctant, marks the second time he has come to Johnson's aid because of something that happened in Dallas. Back in November 1960, the Johnsons were on the campaign trail when they stumbled into a downtown Dallas crowd of several hundred people who had just finished attending a posh rally for the GOP ticket. It took Johnson almost thirty minutes to shepherd Lady Bird through the upscale crowd, which grew increasingly abusive, shouting and swearing at the couple.

Russell, at the time, was in Europe, having consciously avoided campaigning for the national ticket. But when he heard that the Johnsons had been endangered by a mob of "unruly, rich, and profane" Republicans—Russell was particularly fond of Lady Bird—he cut short his trip and traveled on Johnson's chartered plane during the campaign's waning days. His formal endorsement made headlines in Georgia and helped the Kennedy-Johnson ticket in the "increasingly unsolid" South.[336]

334. The "little incident," of course, is the allegation that Oswald received $6,500 in the Cuban consulate.

335. Calling Warren "fat" is Johnson's typical way of cutting someone down to size—in this case the chief justice, for Russell's benefit.

336. Goldsmith, *Colleagues,* 81; Mark Hatfield, *Vice Presidents of the United States, 1789–1993* (Washington, D.C.: U.S. Government Printing Office, 1997), 458.

November 30

Saturday

For the first time as president, Johnson has no postfuneral obligation, address, or duty to perform today. Perhaps as a result, his morning intelligence briefing is the longest to date, lasting more than one hour. Much of the briefing concerns Cuba and continuing U.S. surveillance of Soviet forces stationed on the island. With reference to the Oswald matter, John McCone has nothing new to report. The latest cable from the CIA station in Mexico City about Gilbert Alvarado's allegation is that it remains neither proved nor disproved, though now he is being interrogated by Mexican authorities. McCone briefly discusses the composition of the presidential Commission announced by Johnson the previous evening. The story dominates the Saturday newspapers, and editorial comment will be almost universal in its praise.

Throughout the conversation, McGeorge Bundy is in attendance. Perhaps because he believes both Bundy and McCone are close to Robert Kennedy, Johnson raises this very difficult relationship with the two men and asks for their help in resolving it. The president is acutely aware of the unprecedented role that Kennedy played in intelligence matters, including covert operations that are normally far removed from an attorney general's portfolio. The president "indicated that there must be some cabinet changes," notes McCone in his "eyes only" memo for the record. "By inference [Johnson] made reference to the attorney general, but not by direct statement. Apparently, he is waiting for the attorney general to decide what role, if any, he wishes to play in the Johnson administration."[337] Johnson will soon ask McCone to talk to Robert Kennedy and explain to him the obvious: Kennedy cannot expect the same kind of access to secrets in a Johnson White House.[338]

From John McCone / 3:14 p.m.

In keeping with his pledge to inform the president personally of every significant development, McCone calls with important news about the Alvarado allegation. He has just received a telephone call from the CIA station in Mexico

337. McCone, memorandum for the record, 2 December 1963, CIA Box 1/14, JFK, NARA.
338. McCone, memorandum for the record, 13 December 1963, CIA Box 1/14, JFK, NARA.

City. Alvarado has signed a confession in which he admits to lying all along. Soon he will be deported to his native Nicaragua by Mexican authorities.[339]

One of the most significant factors in prompting Johnson to change his mind about a "Special Commission" has melted away. Nonetheless, the president's apprehensions about Cuban involvement have been aroused. And once having been aroused, over time, and in conjuction with some new information, these suspicions will prove indelible.

Johnson: *[sounding preoccupied]* Yeah.

McCone: Mr. President?

Johnson: Yeah.

McCone: We had a phone call from Mexico City that this fellow Alvarado, that I was telling you about this morning, signed a statement that all the statements he'd made in connection with that matter had been false.

Johnson: *[chuckles]*

McCone: So apparently there's no substance in it at all.

Johnson: Hmmm.

McCone: He explained that he was—[he] wanted to ingratiate himself to the United States' interests in order to gain admission to the United States and to work with the security forces here. So . . . we're sending down a whole series of questions to be sure this isn't misleading. But this is the opinion of our [CIA] station [in Mexico City], and I guess, the FBI. Why this [latest statement] looks to be like it's probably [true] . . . and washes that out [the $6,500 allegation] entirely.

Johnson: Okay, my friend.

McCone: All right, sir.

Johnson: Thank you.

McCone: Okay.

339. "Information Developed by CIA on the Activity of Lee Harvey Oswald in Mexico City," 28 September–3 October 1963, 31 January 1964, Warren Commission Document 347, CIA Box 1/14, JFK, NARA.

December

News and commentary about the establishment of the Warren Commission (as it is immediately dubbed) dominate the media; nearly all the coverage is favorable. Only a few outlets express reservations in the days after November 29, either by harking back to the Roberts Commission's unfortunate history or raising questions about the chief justice's participation. The conservative *Chicago Tribune,* for instance, claims that a half-dozen senators and many more representatives are disgruntled over Earl Warren's selection because of the remarks he made prior to Oswald's arrest and/or during his Capitol eulogy. "The chief justice has already prejudged the case," the *Tribune* reports, by blaming "right-wing extremists." But none of the congressmen will go on record making such a charge "in this period of regard for a new president's burden."[1] The closest thing to dissent with a name on it is uttered by unidentified "friends" of Senator James Eastland. The Mississippi senator earlier told AP that he was in "favor [of] what the president is doing."[2] But according to the *Tribune,* when Eastland told his friends about the president's telephone call, he explained that he "could see no alternative to a reluctant assent."[3]

For Lyndon Johnson, one of the desired consequences of the Commission's establishment becomes manifest in December. Aside from occasional scattered references, neither the assassination nor the Commission will be a major topic of his telephone conversations, as they were during his first week in office. His schedule ceases to be cluttered with meetings and tasks directly related to investigation of the assassination. It begins to resemble a president's regular schedule, that is, if a man of Johnson's prodigious energies can be said to have a normal schedule. Even with the assassination successfully compartmentalized, of course, Johnson still has to grapple with the political legacy of a slain president who has suddenly taken on aspects of martyrdom. The situation is all the more complicated by the fact that there are two living Kennedys to whom Johnson must attend: the president's widow and Robert. Johnson is intent on staying

1. Willard Edwards, "Clash Hinted over Warren Probe Role," *Chicago Tribune,* 3 December 1963. In all likelihood, one of the main sources for Edwards's article was Jay Sourwine, chief counsel to Eastland's Internal Security subcommittee.

2. John Morris, "Johnson Names a 7-Man Panel to Investigate Assassination; Chief Justice Warren Heads It," *New York Times,* 30 November 1963.

3. Edwards, "Clash Hinted over Warren Probe Role."

within the "Kennedy aura," as he terms it, until at least the November 1964 election, when he can win the presidency in his own right.[4] His efforts to do so will appear almost desperate at times.

December 2

Monday

To Katherine Graham / 11:10 a.m.

Mrs. Graham is calling to invite President Johnson to speak at the annual meeting in April of the newspaper publishers' association. In the course of their conversation, Johnson flirts, speaks wistfully about Graham's recently deceased husband, Philip, and discusses his first week in office, as befits their friendly relationship. Prior to 1961 Philip Graham, the publisher of the *Washington Post* until his August 1963 suicide, served as a sounding board and occasional speechwriter for then-Senator Johnson, in addition to being an early advocate of a Kennedy-Johnson ticket in 1960. Now Johnson is intent on cultivating Kay Graham. Although he's running thirty minutes behind schedule, nothing is more important than talking to the *Post*'s publisher. Mrs. Graham is quite willing to be treated as a confidante, though she was just calling to ask a favor.

Among the other items on his agenda, Johnson talks about his strategy for forcing the Rules Committee to permit a vote on civil rights legislation that is stalled in the House. It is a revealing example of Johnson's willingness to exploit the assassination, as he makes a facile comparison between the silencing of Lee Harvey Oswald and Representative Howard Smith's (D-Virginia) refusal to allow a vote in the Rules Committee, which he chairs. Johnson's goal is to pique Graham's interest in this important procedural issue and thereby provoke a rash of favorable news stories and editorials in the *Post*. A concerted campaign by the newspaper might also have the side benefit of taking up column inches that might otherwise be devoted to the still-simmering Bobby Baker scandal.

When the subject of the Warren Commission comes up, Johnson instantly renames it the "Kay Graham Commission"—a playful reference to the *Post* editorial that advocated creation of an independent panel. "The *Post* proposes and Lyndon Johnson disposes," or so suggests the president. He conveys some heretofore unpublished details about the Commission's formation, most notably

4. Johnson and Smathers, conversation, 23 November 1963, 2:10 p.m., LBJL.

the fact that neither Chief Justice Warren nor Senator Russell wanted to serve. (In about six weeks *Post* columnist Marquis Childs will break the story about Warren's reluctance, perhaps having heard the story from Mrs. Graham.)[5] That Johnson railed against the newspaper for trying to pressure him, was angry about being second-guessed, and even sought to block the *Post* from publishing its first editorial on the matter goes unremarked.

[Johnson is describing his joint session address to Congress on November 27. Kennedy speechwriter Ted Sorensen was upset at the extensive alterations to his first draft made by others, and was still arguing about the changes with Johnson during the drive up to Capitol Hill, a piece of inside gossip that has already made the rounds in Georgetown.][6]

Johnson: Now the speech that came in [from Sorensen] was a great tribute to a great man. But the Congress expected a little somethin' else. They wanted to know how I was gonna *stand* on these things. And I had to *say* so. And I had to say, "action now" because . . . I've got to talk to you about it, [and there's] no better time than right this minute, although I'm thirty minutes behind in my appointments and I got the cabinet waitin' out here.

Mrs. Graham: Mr. President, go on.

Johnson: But I've got to ask you this: Howard Smith said to the Speaker of the House—that I quietly and judiciously asked to go talk to him [Smith] about civil rights—that you'll have to come back and talk next year, [in] January . . . and we'll all be late comin' back [in] January, [because] they want to have their holidays. And we won't even give you a *hearing* on a bill that's been up there since May . . . that they've had hearings on from May till November . . . that's [been] reported, several days ago, that they don't *need* any more hearings on . . . but that we'd be willing to spend all the year on hearings if they'd give 'em. But he [Smith] won't even *give* 'em a hearing. He won't even call a meetin'. He just said, "I'm out at my farm, and I can't have any *hearings.*"

   Now I don't want him lectured on account of it. I want to give you my *factual* situation. So we have no alternative, when you won't give a man a hearing. We thought *Oswald* oughta have a hearing. We are upset—that's why we got a commission, because we thought even *Oswald* oughta have a hearing. In this country, that's not in keepin'. So they're gonna try to sign a petition that will give 'em a hearing in the House, and so they can discharge the Rules Committee and bring it out.

Mrs. Graham: Right.

5. Marquis Childs, "Mr. Warren Tries His Hardest Case," *Washington Post,* 15 January 1964.

6. According to Manchester, "If you were literate, informed and empathic, you were being drafted" to help craft Johnson's speech. William Manchester, *The Death of a President: November 20–November 25, 1963* (New York: Harper & Row, 1967), 474, 605–6.

Johnson: Now every person that doesn't sign that petition has got to be fairly regarded as being *anti–civil rights* because he is even against a hearing! I don't care if he votes against the bill after he gets [a] chance to vote on it. [If] he says it goes too far, if he says that public accommodations oughta do this or do that . . . we [still] got the votes to *pass* it. But I don't think *any American* can say that he won't let 'em have a hearing *either* in the committee or on the floor. That is worse than [what] Hitler did.[7] So we've got to get ready for that. And we got to get ready *every* day, front page, in and out, individuals, [asking Smith] *"Why are you against a hearing?"* And point 'em up, and have their pictures, and have editorials, and have everything else that is in a dignified way, *for a hearing on the floor.*

[Johnson continues discussing ways to pressure the Congress.]

Johnson: So you can tell your editorial board—

Mrs. Graham: I sure will.

Johnson: —that this Rules Committee has quietly said they're not gonna do *anything.* And somebody oughta be askin' these [congressional] leaders . . . I can't do it.

But do you know what I tried to do in appointin' your commission the other day, the Kay Graham Commission?

Mrs. Graham: Yeah?

Johnson: I talked *all day long* and into the night on that . . . includin' talkin' to you. But they . . . Justice Warren turned the Justice [Department] down! Nick Katzenbach and 'em went to him. He wouldn't do it. I had to come in here and plead with him and . . . finally got him to do it. Everybody *else* wanted to turn it down. Dick Russell—I had to talk to him *four times!*[8]

Mrs. Graham: *[sympathetically] Oh.*

Johnson: But . . . we went through . . . with all that thing. Now . . . you know where I had to talk to 'em? Russell was in *Winder.* Dirksen was in *Illinois.* Humphrey was on the *beach.* Mansfield was on the *beach* in Miami, in houses that people—it's become popular to lend [vacation homes] to 'em [congressional leaders].

Mrs. Graham: Yeah.

Johnson: Charlie Halleck was . . . out hunting—*turkey!*

Mrs. Graham: Gosh!

Johnson: There wasn't a human *here*! And they're not here *now*! And they're not *workin'* now! And they're not passin' *anything*! And they're not going to! Now somebody has got to . . . instead of just writing those stories about how the [congressional] pages live . . . or about . . . Bobby Baker's *girl*— whether he had a girl or whether he *didn't* . . . is not a matter that's going

---

7. Invoking Hitler is the ultimate example of Johnson talking for effect.

8. Again, Johnson is exaggerating. He spoke to Russell only twice, and the other five commissioners readily agreed to serve.

to settle this country. But whether we have *justice* and *equality* is pretty damned important!

[Johnson continues to talk about the need for Congress to act on the civil rights bill with dispatch.]

To Jacqueline Kennedy / 2:42 p.m.

As William Manchester will later observe, Jacqueline Kennedy, at the age of thirty-four, has become a "national institution."[9] Everyone wants to honor her, including President Johnson. She is still living in the Executive Mansion, that part of the White House complex that constitutes the presidential living quarters. But although they have exchanged letters, Johnson has not seen her in person since November 27, when she stopped by the Oval Office after the joint session address to ask that Cape Canaveral be renamed for her husband.

This is their first recorded conversation, one of several during the month of December. It typifies the president's desire to provide whatever comfort and solace he can offer, whenever Mrs. Kennedy wants it. She has an open invitation to walk over to the Oval Office. The tenderness in his voice is impossible to convey in a transcript, and this is a side of Johnson the public will never glimpse. Somehow he manages to leave her laughing as the conversation ends.

Mrs. Kennedy: Mr. President?

Johnson: I just wanted you to know you are *loved* . . . and by so *many*, and so much—

Mrs. Kennedy: *Oh, Mr. President!*

Johnson: —[and] I'm one of 'em.

Mrs. Kennedy: I tried—I didn't *dare* bother you again, but I got Kenny O'Donnell over here to give you a message, if he ever saw you. Did he give it to you yet?

Johnson: No.

Mrs. Kennedy: About my letter?

Johnson: No.

Mrs. Kennedy: That was waiting for me last night?

Johnson: *[gently]* Listen, sweetie . . . now [the] first thing you got to learn . . . you got some things to learn, and one of 'em is that you don't *bother* me. You give me *strength*.

Mrs. Kennedy: But I wasn't going to send you in one *more* letter—

Johnson: Don't send me anything!

Mrs. Kennedy: —I was just scared you'd answered.

Johnson: Don't send me anything! You just come over [and] put your arm

9. Manchester, *Death,* 644.

around me, that's all you do. When you haven't got anything else [to] do, let's take a walk. Let's walk around the *backyard,* and—

Mrs. Kennedy: *Oh!*

Johnson: —just let me tell you how much you *mean* to all of us, and how we can carry on if you give us a little strength.

Mrs. Kennedy: But you know what I want to say to you about that letter?[10] *I know* how rare a letter is in a president's handwriting. *[voice trembling]* Do you know that I've got more [letters] in your handwriting than I do in Jack's now?

Johnson: *[groping for words]* Oh . . . well. . . .

Mrs. Kennedy: And for you to write it at this time and then to send me that thing today of, you know, your Cape [Kennedy] announcement and everything.

Johnson: I want you to just know this, [something] that I told my mama a *long* time ago, when everybody else gave up about my election in '48.[11]

Mrs. Kennedy: Yes?

Johnson: My mother, and my wife, and my sisters [never lost faith]. And you females got a *lot* of courage that we men don't have. So we have to rely on you and depend on you, and you got something to do.

Mrs. Kennedy: *[sobs]*

Johnson: You got's a president [who's] *relyin'* on you, and this is not the *first* one you had, so . . . so there're not many women, you know, runnin' around with a good many presidents.

Mrs. Kennedy: *[laughs]*

Johnson: So you just bear that in mind, and you got the *biggest* job of your *life*!

Mrs. Kennedy: She ran around with two presidents. That's what they'll say about me.

Johnson: *[chuckles]*

Mrs. Kennedy: Okay, anytime.

Johnson: *[kissing sound]* Good-bye, darlin'.

Mrs. Kennedy: Thank you for calling, Mr. President.

Johnson: 'Bye, sweetie.

Mrs. Kennedy: Good-bye.

Johnson: Do come by.

Mrs. Kennedy: I will.

10. She is referring to a handwritten letter Johnson sent her on December 1, in which he thanked her for calling him on Thursday evening, after his Thanksgiving Day message was broadcast nationally.

11. The 1948 race for the Democratic nomination ranked among the most bitterly contested in Texas history. Johnson finally prevailed by an eighty-seven-vote margin, which led to him being dubbed "Landslide Lyndon." Robert Dallek, *Lone Star Rising: Lyndon Johnson and His Times, 1908–1960* (New York: Oxford University Press, 1991), 346.

December 4

Wednesday
From Clark Clifford / 6:25 p.m.

The president has known Clifford since 1946, and the quintessential Washington lawyer is on equal or even better terms with the Kennedys, having led the transition team in 1960. Clifford could have had any of a number of jobs in the administration but preferred to profit handsomely from his connections to the first Democratic White House in eight years. As President-elect Kennedy observed, Clifford wanted nothing for his services during the transition "except for the right to advertise the Clifford law firm on the back of the one-dollar bill."[12] Now, Clifford's familiarity with both sides, along with the fact that he had participated in and observed the last wrenching transition in the White House and the Democratic Party—from Roosevelt to Truman in 1945—makes him the ideal counselor on the "appropriate mixture of continuity and change."[13]

The president, along with Abe Fortas, Paul Porter (Fortas's law partner), and Clifford, first meet on the afternoon of November 30 to discuss the transition, and also the organization of the White House staff to best accommodate Johnson's working style. Clifford describes the problems of the Roosevelt-to-Truman transition from his vantage point. He urges Johnson to allow Kennedy people to leave "at their own pace," retaining for as long as possible those persons deemed the most able.[14] The president's inclination, at this point, is still to turn every departure into a loyalty test.

Robert Kennedy, naturally, represents a profound and special problem. Johnson asks Clifford to become the first of what will be several intermediaries shuttling between Johnson and Kennedy in the coming years. Their relationship, terrible to begin with, has gotten worse since Johnson became president, primarily because of the swearing-in issue, which was exacerbated by Valenti's

12. Robert Dallek, *Unfinished Life: John F. Kennedy, 1917–1963* (Boston: Little, Brown, 2003), *306*. Clifford's only official post in the Kennedy administration was a part-time job, albeit a prestigious one. After the 1961 Bay of Pigs debacle, Kennedy appointed Clifford to one of the least-known but most sensitive panels in the government, the President's Foreign Intelligence Advisory Board (PFIAB). Two years later Clifford became the PFIAB's chairman.

13. Clark Clifford, *Counsel to the President: A Memoir* (New York: Random House, 1991), 390–91.

14. Ibid.; Daily Diary, 30 November 1963, LBJL.

suspected leak to the *Houston Post.* The only thing preventing more real and imagined slights between the two men is the fact that over Thanksgiving Kennedy sequestered himself in Treasury Secretary Dillon's Hobe Sound, Florida, compound, and has been literally incommunicado since. But today he is due back in Washington, and Clifford has been tasked with finding out what the attorney general has in mind to do. Robert Kennedy's adult life has been largely devoted to furthering the career of his older brother, and now that frame of reference is missing.[15] In addition, the attorney general has tasted the kind of power that normally only presidents become accustomed to wielding. Johnson does not know which possibility to be more concerned about: that the thirty-eight-year-old attorney general will quit in a huff and spark a wave of resignations, or that he will decide to stay.

Interestingly, in Clifford's 1991 memoir he will write at some length about his advisory role at precisely this time. During the November 30 meeting, according to Clifford, "President Johnson took my arm and said, 'Clark, you're *my* transition expert now.' " But Clifford also asserts that he did not discuss the "special problem" of the attorney general until late February 1964. Possibly, Clifford may have forgotten this earlier intervention, although he never shies from placing himself at the center of events in his memoir. A more plausible explanation is that the hope he held in December 1963, as expressed in this conversation, does not pan out, so he will later gloss over it. "I had known from the beginning that there was simply no way that Lyndon Johnson and Bobby Kennedy could ever get along with each other," Clifford observes in his memoir.[16] In 1963, however, he obviously thinks the possibility exists for a modus vivendi between the two men.

Johnson: Yes, Clark.
Clifford: Mr. President?
Johnson: Yeah.
Clifford: I have just finished a *two-hour* session with Bobby.
Johnson: Yeah.
Clifford: And, ah . . . first I want to say, he's going to *stay*.
Johnson: *[unenthusiastically]* Yeah.
Clifford: And, ah . . . I have the feeling that when it's convenient for you, and you can afford about ten or fifteen minutes, I had better report in some detail about it—
Johnson: All right.
Clifford: —so that you get the *feel* of it and all. Ah . . . we really had it *out* . . .

15. James Clayton, "Robert Kennedy Expected to Stay in Cabinet Until After '64 Election," *Washington Post,* 26 December 1963.
    16. Clifford, *Counsel,* 391, 395.

and we covered it *all,* and . . . I think there're some arguments that he found *unanswerable.*[17]

Johnson: Hmm.

Clifford: And, ah . . . I'm just authorized to say now that he's going to *stay.* He's going to have a *talk* with *you,* and I oughta have a *talk* with you *first.* It's a relationship that I think is exceedingly *important,* and it's one that we oughta look at together.

Johnson: All right. Let me see right now what my schedule is here. Just a second.

[They agree to meet the next day at 12:30 p.m.]

The discussion with Clifford will take place as scheduled; a subsequent meeting with Kennedy will not. Although Johnson readily extends an invitation, saying he'd like to meet the attorney general whenever it is convenient, Kennedy doesn't feel like seeing the president anytime soon. "I'm not mentally equipped for it, or physically," Kennedy explains to Richard Goodwin.[18]

The attorney general is still steaming over the suggestion that he encouraged the oath-taking. In mid-December General Godfrey McHugh, presumably at Kennedy's request, contacts WHCA to see if the telephone calls between the president and attorney general were recorded along with the precise times they occurred. And he wants the information within thirty minutes.[19]

December 7

Saturday

To Jacqueline Kennedy / 5:20 p.m.

President Johnson makes a special point of calling the former First Lady today, the first day the Johnsons will actually reside in the Executive Mansion.[20] Mrs.

17. Presumably Robert Kennedy expressed some of the reasons behind his behavior, and Clifford, in his firm but even manner, tried to impress on him the new political facts of life.

18. Edwin Guthman and Jeffrey Shulman, eds., *Robert Kennedy: In His Own Words* (New York: Bantam, 1988), 406; Richard Goodwin, *Remembering America: A Voice from the Sixties* (Boston: Little, Brown, 1988), 295.

19. Memo re Telephone Conversation with General McHugh, 14 December 1963, President's Diary—November 22, 1963, Box 2, Special File, LBJL.

20. Johnson also called Mrs. Kennedy at 1:20 p.m. on December 6, the day the move began. That call was not recorded.

Kennedy and her children finished moving out in the morning and are now living temporarily in the spacious, elegant Georgetown home of diplomat Averell Harriman. Within a matter of weeks she will move again, this time across the street to the house at 3017 N Street, just a block away from the home she shared in the 1950s with then-Senator Kennedy.

She feels "like a wounded animal," Mrs. Kennedy confides to Nicole Alphand, wife of the French ambassador to the United States, and what she really wants to do "is crawl into a corner and hide."[21] The fragile, temperamental woman whom the Secret Service calls LACE will finally emerge, now that a brave visage is no longer required. In the days ahead Mrs. Kennedy's self-control will desert her as she spirals into a deep depression, dependent on sedatives to get through the night lest she wake up screaming. Having postponed her grief until after the funeral, now she is in its unyielding grip. Most days she rarely leaves her bedroom on the second floor, and when she does, it is to visit the president's gravesite in Arlington National Cemetery or to pray at St. Matthew's Cathedral.[22] She alludes to her gathering depression when she mentions in passing to Johnson that she hasn't gotten out of bed all day.

Although Johnson's warmth and tenderness are again manifest, it is also clear that he does not know Mrs. Kennedy's mentality very well, especially her almost religious sense of privacy. He thinks he is being flattering when he congratulates her and the children for looking so attractive when they were photographed the other day, never realizing she is mortified by the constant, prying attention. He is trying so hard to be comforting that she cannot bring herself to contradict him, as she surely would do to anyone else. Nor does she even draw back when Johnson seems to mock the opening line from his joint session address, in an incredible, if momentary, lapse of taste. Until this moment he has been careful to hide the exhilaration he feels about being president from Jacqueline Kennedy, though he often freely expresses it to others. Mrs. Kennedy will later recall, "I almost felt sorry for him because I knew he felt sorry for me. There wasn't anything anyone could do about it, but I think the situation gave him pain and he tried to do the best he could."[23]

Anxious to be photographed with the former First Lady, or to at least let it be known that he has seen her, Johnson implores Mrs. Kennedy to stop in the next time she drops Caroline off at school. Though the Kennedy family has moved out, the Johnsons have readily agreed to let the White House's exclusive first-grade class continue until the end of the year. Six-year-old Caroline and about twenty of her playmates attend the makeshift school on the third-floor

21. Manchester, *Death,* 628.
22. Sarah Bradford, *America's Queen: The Life of Jacqueline Kennedy Onassis* (New York: Viking, 2000), 287.
23. Jacqueline Kennedy Oral History, 11 January 1974, LBJL.

Solarium of the Executive Mansion. Permitting the class to operate was a delightful thing to say yes to, Lady Bird Johnson noted in her diary. "The way [Mrs. Kennedy] asked this, if it had been a request to chop off one's right hand, one would have said, 'Sure.' "[24]

Mrs. Kennedy: . . . tonight, will it be in the news?[25]

Johnson: [It] might be, I don't know.

Mrs. Kennedy: The press [conference] . . . is it—

Johnson: No, I just had 'em come in the office, and they just sat around while I was drinkin' coffee. And I don't know whether [they] even took TV of it [or] not. I guess they did. They had some shinin' stuff in my eyes, but I don't imagine it's worth bein' on.

Mrs. Kennedy: *Oh good,* 'cause I thought it might have been one of those things that went on while you were doing it.

Johnson: Do they keep you busy all day?

Mrs. Kennedy: Oh listen, I'm just *collapsed.* I haven't gotten out of bed.

Johnson: Your picture was *gorgeous.* And you had that chin up, and that chest out, and you looked *so pretty* marching in the front page of the *New York Daily News* today, and I think they had the same picture in Washington.[26]

Mrs. Kennedy: *[disapprovingly]* [On] Friday—

Johnson: And little John-John and Caroline, and they're wonderful, too.

Mrs. Kennedy: I really—

Johnson: Have you seen the *Daily News*? The *New York Daily News*?

Mrs. Kennedy: *[hesitantly]* Ah, no . . . but I haven't seen anything today except the *[Washington] Post* 'cause I was just sort of collapsed. But they're all downstairs, *[indistinct]*.

Johnson: Well, you look at the *New York Daily News*. I'm lookin' at it now, and I just sat in my desk and started signin' a lot [of] long things, and I decided I wanted to flirt with you a little bit.

Mrs. Kennedy: How *sweet*! And I read . . . will you sleep in the White House tonight?

Johnson: *[chuckles]* I guess so. I'm paid to.

Mrs. Kennedy: *Oh! [laughs]* How can I—

24. Lady Bird Johnson, *A White House Diary* (New York: Holt, Rinehart and Winston, 1970), 11.

25. Mrs. Kennedy is referring to Johnson's first news conference, an informal Saturday afternoon affair to which only twenty-five reporters were invited after just two hours' notice. Johnson institutes these "sudden death" briefings because he does not want to be compared with his predecessor, an acknowledged master of large, formal news conferences that were often broadcast live. *The Johnson Presidential Press Conferences* (New York: Earl Coleman Enterprises, 1978), i–ii; "The President Keeps Press on Alert," *New York Times,* 19 December 1963.

26. The photograph showed Mrs. Kennedy walking out of the White House with her children.

Johnson: You don't know—

Mrs. Kennedy: You should all three sleep in the same room, 'cause it's the *worst thing* your first night.[27]

Johnson: Darlin', you know what I said to the Congress: I'd give anything in the world if I wasn't here today. *[laughs]*

Mrs. Kennedy: Well listen—oh, it's gonna be funny 'cause the rooms are all so *big*. You'll all get lost. But anyway. . . .

Johnson: Maybe you oughta come back [and] see me.

Mrs. Kennedy: *[laughs]*

Johnson: Hmm?

Mrs. Kennedy: N[o] *[overcome with laughter]* . . . someday I will.

Johnson: Someday.

Mrs. Kennedy: But anyway, take a big sleeping pill tonight.

Johnson: Aren't you gonna bring . . . you know what they do with me? They [sleeping pills] just keep my . . . [it's] like taking a hypo[dermic injection]. They just stimulate me, I just get [hyper] . . . every idea that I ever had in my life comes back and I start thinkin' new things and new roads to conquer.

Mrs. Kennedy: Yeah? *Great!*

Johnson: So I can't . . . a sleepin' pill won't put me to sleep. It just wakes me up.

Mrs. Kennedy: Aww. . . .

Johnson: But if I know that you gonna come back [to] see me some mornin' when you bring your—

Mrs. Kennedy: I will.

Johnson: —kid to school, then I'd . . . the first time you do, *please* come and let me walk down—

Mrs. Kennedy: Oh, yes.

Johnson: —to the seesaw with you, like old times.

Mrs. Kennedy: I *will*, Mr. President.

Johnson: Okay, darling. Give Caroline and John-John a hug for me.

Mrs. Kennedy: I will.

Johnson: Tell 'em I'd like to be their daddy.

Mrs. Kennedy: I will.

Johnson: Good-bye.

Mrs. Kennedy: Oh, thank you. Good-bye.

27. Lynda, the Johnsons' elder daughter and a sophomore at the Univeristy of Texas, has returned to Austin to finish the semester.

December 23

Monday
To Jacqueline Kennedy / 7:18 p.m.

Mrs. Kennedy and her children are spending the Christmas holiday in Palm Beach, Florida. Before leaving Washington, the former First Lady tried to drop in to see the president on December 17, as he has beseeched her to do so many times. But Johnson spends much of that day in New York, addressing the United Nations General Assembly, so they miss each other. It marks the last time Mrs. Kennedy will try to visit. With the closure of Caroline's White House classroom, Mrs. Kennedy begins ordering her Secret Service driver to avoid any route that will take her within sight of the White House. It is that painful.

This call to Mrs. Kennedy, the president's second in three days, springs out of a typical Johnsonian effort to impress some guests—in this instance, four women reporters who normally cover only social events at the White House, or the First Lady.[28] The president has been presiding over a hastily arranged holiday reception for the Congress and cabinet members, and his informal Texas style is in full throttle. At one point, in order to be heard above the din in the cavernous dining room, he pulls over a chair with gold damask upholstery, carries it to the middle of the room, and promptly stands on it, startling all two hundred guests. When the reception is over, Johnson is in no mood for the party to end. As the four female reporters don their coats and hats, he regales them with stories about today's vote on the foreign aid bill—all off the record, of course. Just as they are about to exit, Johnson suddenly decides they must have their picture taken with him and Mrs. Johnson on a curving marble staircase. After the picture taking is done, the president suddenly blurts out, "Hey, want to see the swimming pool?"[29] An impromptu one-hour tour of the White House commences, replete with a chatty, running commentary by the president.

By the time they reach the Oval Office, Johnson is exuberant, and the reporters can hardly believe their good luck. Intoxicated as he is by the holiday

28. The president called Mrs. Kennedy on December 21 at 6:55 p.m. to wish her and the children a Merry Christmas. Johnson and Mrs. Kennedy, conversation, 21 December 1963, 6:55 p.m., LBJL.

29. The president may have been slightly inebriated. The eggnog is spiked with alcohol, and Johnson tells the reporters that he had only one hour's sleep the night before, and his lunch consisted of a diet soda. Isabelle Shelton, "President, as 'Guide,' Drops News Nuggets," *Washington Star,* 24 December 1963.

cheer, Johnson drops the appearance of being subdued in the presidency. The official month of mourning, in fact, has just ended, and Johnson by nature can stand being glum for only so long. For the first time outsiders are allowed to glimpse his joy over being in the job he has long ached for. They are being shown offices and hideaways rarely seen, and how the new president has chosen to decorate them. Johnson deliberately begins dropping nuggets of newsworthy information, disclosing, for example, that he received advice and suggestions from former president Eisenhower on November 23. "You're as good as the men reporters, and I want your bosses to know it," says Johnson, as he hands out story suggestions. One claim he makes is that he telephones Mrs. Kennedy "every day or two."[30] And then, to prove just that, he dials up the president's widow in Florida and allows the reporters to eavesdrop on his half of their conversation over the phone.[31]

If Mrs. Kennedy thinks there is something odd about a second call from the president wishing her a happy holiday, she doesn't let on. And in the president's exuberance, he does not realize that it may look as if he is exploiting her for political gain.

Mrs. Kennedy: Hi, Mr. President.

Johnson: I hope that you're doin' all right.

Mrs. Kennedy: Oh, I'm doing *fine, thank* you.

Johnson: Well, this Congress is gettin' pretty rough up here, and I may have to send for you 'fore it gets through.[32]

Mrs. Kennedy: *[giggles]* I *hope* you get home for Christmas, will you?

Johnson: I don't know, honey.

Mrs. Kennedy: You're *so* nice to call me, Mr. President. You must be out of your *mind* with work piled up.

Johnson: I have a few things to do, but not anything that I enjoy more than what I am doin' *now.*

Mrs. Kennedy: Oh, you're *nice.*

Johnson: How's my little girl?

Mrs. Kennedy: She's *fine,* and John just set off this awful *jet* plane. It's the noise you hear in the background.

Johnson: *[chuckling]* Well, tell 'em hello, and I wish all of you a Merry Christmas, and I wished I could do something to *make* it happier for you.

Mrs. Kennedy: Oh no, you're *so* nice, and you've done *everything* you could. I thank you so much. A Merry Christmas to you.

Johnson: Do you know how much we love you?

Mrs. Kennedy: Oh, well . . . you're awfully nice.

30. Ibid.

31. Ibid. It does not sound as if the president is using his speaker phone.

32. The president is in the middle of the annual fight with Congress over the foreign aid bill.

Johnson: You don't know?

Mrs. Kennedy: *[giggles]* No, I don't. Well yes, I . . . you know.

Johnson: *You better know.* All the 180 million [Americans] love you, dear—

Mrs. Kennedy: Oh thanks, Mr. President.

Johnson: —and all the world, and I'll see you after Christmas, I hope. And if you ever come back here again [and] don't come to see me, why, there's gonna be *trouble.*

Mrs. Kennedy: All right, I—

Johnson: You don't realize I have the FBI at my disposal, do you?

Mrs. Kennedy: *[laughs]* No. I *promise* I will.

Johnson: Well, I'm gonna *send* for you if you don't come by!

Mrs. Kennedy: *Good.*

Johnson: Or someday they gonna create a traffic jam out there in Georgetown.

Mrs. Kennedy: Okay. Well, that would be great.

Johnson: You have a good Christmas, dear.

Mrs. Kennedy: Thank you. The same to you.

Johnson: Good night.

Mrs. Kennedy: Good night, Mr. President.

Following this conversation, Johnson signs family portraits for the women reporters, and they are finally excused. The president is still fixated on Jacqueline Kennedy, though, and is worried that she has nothing to do but brood. Suddenly Johnson has a brainstorm. He is elevating Tom Mann, the current U.S. ambassador to Mexico, to become assistant secretary of state for Latin America, and he is seized by the idea of making Mrs. Kennedy the new ambassador. In a telephone conversation with Pierre Salinger, he asks the press secretary about his inspiration, in his inimitable way. "God almighty, all she'd have to do is just walk out on her *balcony* about once a week," says Johnson. ". . . It would electrify the Western hemisphere. . . . She'd just walk out on that balcony and look down at 'em, and they'd just *pee all* over themselves *every* day."[33]

Johnson is disappointed when Salinger does not leap at the idea. "You think they'd think we're tryin' to *use* her or somethin'?" the president asks.[34] Salinger requests a day or so to think the idea over, knowing that in Mrs. Kennedy's current state, the idea is unthinkable. Deep into her suffering, she is barely able to function.[35] Johnson will try out the proposal on different people for several days, but nothing will come of it.

33. Johnson and Salinger, conversation, 23 December 1963, ±8:30 p.m., LBJL.
34. Ibid.
35. Bradford, *America's Queen,* 287.

From Pierre Salinger / 9:45 p.m.

Approximately one hour later, Johnson is again on the telephone with his press secretary. Representative William Green, a leader of Philadelphia's Democratic machine and a power in the national party, has died, and Johnson is making arrangements to attend the memorial service. The president wants to make a point of attending the services for Green because he is from that Democratic faction where Johnson's support is weakest, urban liberals. Owing to Green's political machine, John Kennedy carried Philadelphia by such a margin that he managed to win Pennsylvania in 1960 by 116,000 votes, and Johnson has his eye on doing the same in 1964.[36] Still in an expansive mood following the White House reception, Johnson makes clear his desire to be associated in the public eye with any Kennedy who will be attending the funeral, too.

Since the earlier conversation, the AP teletype machine in the press secretary's office has begun carrying an account of Johnson's impromptu White House tour, including details from his telephone conversation with Mrs. Kennedy. It is written by the AP's Frances Lewine, one of the four female journalists who overheard the conversation with Jacqueline Kennedy. Abruptly Johnson's celebratory mood evaporates. He is mortified at the obvious implications of his faux pas. Apart from how Robert Kennedy will react—he is fiercely protective of his brother's widow—if Jacqueline Kennedy feels violated, lets her feelings become known, or, worst of all, spurns Johnson, he may yet face a challenger for the Democratic nomination in 1964.

Salinger: We're taking some of Billy Green's friends, including some people who worked in the White House . . . Kenny O'Donnell, Ethel Kennedy, and people like that. I just wonder whether we want to put them on *our* plane.

Johnson: Sure. *Love* [them] to be on our plane. Any plane [that] I'm on, Kenny O'Donnell, Ethel Kennedy—anybody else that ever even *knew* the Kennedys can go with me, if you got room for 'em.

[They discuss the logistics of the presidential entourage to the funeral.]

Johnson: Whatever you want, you get. But *goddammit,* don't let Ken O'Donnell and Ethel Kennedy and anybody like that go without, 'cause they're members of the *team*!

Salinger: Well, the only thing I was thinking of is, I think it would [be]—it's better that they arrive with *you* than arrive on a separate plane.

Johnson: Damn sure *is* better to arrive with me than a separate plane!

Salinger: Mr. President, can I ask you another question?

Johnson: *[enthusiastically]* Yeah, we haven't *got* any separate planes. Just let

---

36. Stephen Rogers, "Party Leader William Green," *Washington Post,* 22 December 1963.

'em go with me. Wherever *I* go, Kenny O'Donnell and Ethel *Kennedy* go, and anybody *else* named Kennedy, or anybody else that's ever *smelled* the Kennedys. This is one *team*—period.

Salinger: Mr. President, when you had the conversation with Mrs. Kennedy, apparently there were some newspaperwomen present?

Johnson: Yes?

Salinger: Did you know they were gonna write stories about it?

Johnson: Yes. [I mean] I didn't *know* they were. I told 'em they couldn't say anything 'cept I *called* her.

Salinger: Well, apparently Frances Lewine has filed a very lengthy story about the conversation.

Johnson: *[warily]* Well, she shouldn't have . . . not anything wrong with it, though, is there?

Salinger: Well, I'd better find out. I'll get it read.

Johnson: I told 'em to write nothing except [that] I talked to her [Mrs. Kennedy], because I didn't want a *private conversation* to be *recorded.*

Salinger: Right.

Johnson: All I said to her [Mrs. Kennedy] was that I just wanted to wish her a Merry Christmas, [and] that we were thinkin' of her, and I wanted her to tell Caroline and John hello for me. And I'm *sure* that she [Lewine] didn't say anything *beyond* that. If she did, she violated a confidence. But anyway, that's all that was said *anyway.*

Salinger: All right, sir.

Johnson: I don't see nothin' wrong with the president—

Salinger: There was nothing wrong with that. I just—

Johnson: —callin' Mrs. Kennedy and the children, and wishin' 'em Merry Christmas.

Salinger: There's nothing wrong with that. It was given to me as much *more* than that.

Johnson: Well . . . I'll check it, and if it—

Salinger: No, let *me* check it for you, Mr. President.

Johnson: If there's anythin' *more* than that, why . . . it's *wrong,* but anyway, I want to be as *nice* and *affectionate* and *considerate* and *thoughtful* of Mrs. Kennedy as I can during these days. And I just think that's good *politics.*

Salinger: Right, sir.

Johnson: Okay.

Salinger: And I'll get on it. I'll get back to Jack [Valenti] on the number of people on this other plane.

Johnson: All right. Now, did you get anything that . . . any *stuff*. . . that there's anything *wrong* with my talkin' to Mrs. Kennedy?

Salinger: Not a *thing*!

Johnson: All right. Okay.

Salinger: Not a thing.

To Frances Lewine / 9:54 p.m.

Pierre Salinger is supposed to be handling it, but Johnson is so worried now that he immediately calls Frances Lewine at home, though it is late at night. Undoubtedly the AP reporter is taken aback to find the president on the line, though the recording does not catch this part of their conversation. After she gets over her astonishment, Lewine tries to assure Johnson that she did not report any details of the conversation itself other than its gist. Fortunately, the same will prove true of the other journalists present.[37] Thus, the only Johnsonian exaggeration that might upset the Kennedys is his assertion that he calls Jacqueline every day or two.

Johnson: You didn't say anything except that I *talked* to her, did you?
Lewine: That's all.
Johnson: Okay. They said there's [a] much longer story and a private conversation [is] revealed, and I got some *kickback* from the family, and I don't want to get *hurt,* honey, so. . . .
Lewine: I didn't reveal any of the conversation *at all.* [I] simply said, after the party you placed the call to Mrs. Kennedy.
Johnson: And, ah . . . I just wished her Merry Christmas.
Lewine: That's right. And [you] said that you'd been calling her, ah . . . every day or two . . . when you could.
Johnson: All right. That's *sweet* of you. Thank you, darlin'. I *appreciate* it, and I *knew* that was *true.* But, ah . . . I got a call from the news office, and they were upset.
Lewine: *Uh-huh.* Well, I haven't done anything.
Johnson: Well, I know it. But *I* have, and . . . I didn't *clear* it, and I'm not *gonna* clear things around here. I'm gonna do somethin' for y'all once in a while. So you help protect me.
Lewine: Well, we certainly appreciate it, and *I* certainly will protect you.
Johnson: Well, I just got this *kickback,* and I just wanted to find out. And I'm *protected,* so . . . I just don't want to be carryin' on my *private* conversations in public and have her think I'm *using* her or somethin'.
Lewine: Right.
Johnson: *All* I was doin' was just to be sweet, and [to] wish her a Merry Christmas, and I hope you didn't say any *more* than that.
Lewine: That's all I said, Mr. President.
Johnson: Thank you, Frances.
Lewine: Right. Good night.

37. The three other reporters are Isabelle Shelton of the *Washington Star,* Dorothy McCardle of the *Washington Post,* and Hazel Markel from NBC. McCardle does not write a story at all, and Shelton's account, which will appear the next day in the *Star,* is sufficiently discreet.

1964

Having compartmentalized the assassination, Johnson is free to concentrate all his considerable skills on a single goal: election to a full term in his own right. To the degree he thinks about the assassination at all, it is mostly privately, where he harbors his own doubts about who and what was involved. Johnson is a preternaturally suspicious man who tends to see a conspiracy whenever anything goes wrong.[1] And though he cannot put his finger on it, he believes President Kennedy died as the result of a conspiracy, and that he, Lyndon Johnson, may be the plotters' next victim rather than, say, Robert Kennedy.

In February 1964 Johnson will convene a meeting in the family quarters of the White House with several of the highest federal officials amid FBI reports that a Cuban "kamikaze" pilot might try to intercept *Air Force One* during an upcoming trip to Florida.[2] But for the most part Johnson's suspicions are focused on South Vietnam, an unlikely quarter insofar as most Americans are concerned. The president is acutely aware of the degree to which the Kennedy administration was responsible for the coup d'état that resulted in President Ngo Dinh Diem's death in November, and the proximity of the two political murders nags at him. More often than not he will link them metaphorically, but on one occasion he makes the connection explicit. On December 19, the president's top advisers from the Pentagon, CIA, State Department, and NSC gather to reevaluate the Kennedy policy of overthrowing Castro's regime. Johnson tells this small group, which includes the CIA's Richard Helms, that he believes Kennedy's assassination was an act of retribution "by unnamed persons seeking vengeance for the murder . . . of . . . Diem."[3]

Meanwhile the Warren Commission will take much longer than anyone expects to deliver its report to the president and the American people. And when those findings are finally published in September, they are well received but somewhat anticlimactic. The perception will be that there is little in the long report that wasn't already understood, more or less, by December 1963. None-

---

1. Robert Dallek, *Flawed Giant; Lyndon Johnson and His Times 1961–1973* (New York: Oxford University Press, 1998), 654.

2. Ibid., 53. The "kamikaze" rumor is also the subject of telephone conversations with McNamara and Senator George Smathers. Johnson and McNamara, conversation, 26 February 1964, 3:39 p.m., and Johnson and Smathers, conversation, 29 February 1964, 9 p.m., both LBJL.

3. Thomas Powers, *The Man Who Kept the Secrets: Richard Helms and the CIA* (New York: Alfred A. Knopf, 1979), 121; U.S. Department of State, *Foreign Relations of the United States, 1961–1963: Cuban Missile Crisis and Aftermath* (Washington, D.C.: U.S. Government Printing Office, 1996), 11:904. According to Powers, Johnson expresses this belief to a group including Helms "not too long after he became president." The only day Helms sees the president during the administration's first six months is December 19.

theless the matter will seem at rest, as far as most Americans are concerned, and Johnson's decision to entrust the matter to a select group will appear fully vindicated. In retrospect, 1964 will mark only the beginning of a honeymoon for the *Warren Report,* one that does not last two years.

The perceived martyrdom of John F. Kennedy will always cast a shadow, but Johnson is intent on making the American people forget how he came into the White House and judge him solely for his deeds. In his first six months he will shepherd Kennedy's two major legislative initiatives, a tax cut and a civil rights bill, through the same Congress that previously stalled them. The president will also announce with fanfare a domestic "war on poverty." Johnson has in mind a progressive, heroic presidency on a Rooseveltian scale, either Theodore or Franklin, though the latter is his personal favorite. That is the long-range plan. For the time being, and until he can win election in his own right, Johnson recognizes that it is best to present himself as the man who can realize President Kennedy's unfinished agenda. As he has told Senator George Smathers, Kennedy "is a national hero . . . and we've got to keep this Kennedy aura around us through this election."[4]

To keep himself wrapped in the Kennedy mantle, Johnson will continually seek the benediction of the late president's widow, the most admired woman in the country. Jacqueline Kennedy will prove elusive, however, though it has nothing to do with her feelings about Johnson one way or another. She would probably act the same way regardless of who succeeded her husband in the Oval Office. It is Johnson who interprets her desire to be at arm's length as some kind of personal rebuff. After his entreaties to her to visit the White House are turned down, he will call on Mrs. Kennedy at her Georgetown home in February. The courtship fades quickly after that visit is not returned, and the two will grow still further apart once the former First Lady flees Washington in September for the anonymity of Manhattan's Fifth Avenue. The constant stream of "morbidly curious" sightseers made living in Washington unbearable.[5]

The other Kennedy who remains a fixation for Johnson is the attorney general. The schism between the two is irreparable though there are spasmodic efforts at reaching some kind of accommodation. Johnson understands the power Robert Kennedy has lost. Still, he cannot comprehend why Kennedy won't just concentrate on paying his dues if he wants to be president someday. Kennedy has never run for a single elective office on his own. "That upstart's come too far and too fast," Johnson remarks to an adviser. "He skipped the grades where you learn the rules of life. He never liked me, and that's nothing compared to what I think of him."[6]

4. Johnson and Smathers, conversation, 23 November 1963, 2:10 p.m., LBJL.

5. Thomas Maier, *The Kennedys: America's Emerald Kings* (New York: Basic Books, 2003), 475.

6. Dallek, *Flawed Giant,* 136.

The drama between the two men in 1964—or what Johnson aides call the "Bobby problem"—will pivot around the question of the vice presidency. Eventually Kennedy decides he wants it, and there is a noticeable thaw in their relationship early in the summer. But Johnson is categorically against the idea for a number of sound reasons. In late July, with the convention less than a month away, the president is forced into issuing a statement that no one in the cabinet will be considered as a running mate. The ploy is transparent, and Johnson smolders at not having Kennedy bow out gracefully on his own. Even when Kennedy resigns in September to run for the U.S. Senate from New York, the decision becomes the basis for new resentments between the two men following the 1964 election. Johnson believes that but for his long coattails, Kennedy would not have been able to overcome the telling criticism that he is an opportunistic carpetbagger. Yet Kennedy, in his victory statement, only grudgingly acknowledges the popular president who campaigned in New York on his behalf.

January 9

Thursday
To Jacqueline Kennedy / 11:30 a.m.

The president's December brainstorm—to make the former First Lady an ambassador—has been forgotten after being declined, though it is unclear whether Johnson fully appreciates the reason why. He cannot reconcile the brave woman of November 1963 with the lonely young widow whose suffering pervades her household. Although Mrs. Kennedy is still distraught and subject to violent mood swings, spending the holidays in Florida did help her emerge from her December "shell of grief."[7] She is beginning to function again, driven by two factors: an urge to glorify Jack Kennedy's presidency, so that he will not be forgotten, and a desire to raise her two children so that they grow up normally. She is determined that their father's death not define and darken their entire lives.[8]

During this conversation the president once again tries to lure Mrs. Kennedy back to the White House for a visit. She promised to do so after moving out in early December, but now that she is righting herself, she realizes that

7. Sarah Bradford, *America's Queen: The Life of Jacqueline Kennedy Onassis* (New York: Viking, 2000), 289; Jacqueline Kennedy Oral History, 11 January 1974, LBJL.

8. Bradford, *America's Queen,* 286.

returning is the last thing in the world she wants to do.[9] She makes this clear for the first time to Johnson, and means it. She will not set foot in the White House again until February 1971, when she receives a private viewing of the official portraits of President and Mrs. Kennedy just before they are unveiled.[10]

Johnson will not be able to stop himself from feeling bitter about his inability to get Mrs. Kennedy to visit the White House. According to Pierre Salinger, he cannot understand, "after all his kindnesses to her," why she won't come in.[11]

Mrs. Kennedy: *[laughing]*

Johnson: I'll *resign*! Yeah, listen, I don't like these ten o'clock lights still burnin' over here, and these early mornin' breakfast appointments. *[chuckles]*

Mrs. Kennedy: Will you *please* start to take a nap after lunch? It changed—

Johnson: I'm going to.

Mrs. Kennedy: —Jack's *whole* life. He was always sick, and when we got to the White House, he did it every day . . . even if you can't sleep. And you know, [Winston] Churchill did that. Now [that] you've got your State of the Union [address] over, you just *can't* tear around.

Johnson: I'll start it the day you come down here to see me. And if you don't, I'm gonna come out there to see *you*.

Mrs. Kennedy: Oh, Mr. President—

Johnson: And I'll just have all those motorcycle cops around your *house*, and it'll cause you all kinds of *trouble*, and—

Mrs. Kennedy: I *can't* come down there. I wanted to tell you. I've *really* gotten hold of myself.

Johnson: *[disappointedly]* Hmm.

Mrs. Kennedy: *[draws deep breath]* You know I'd do *anything* for you; I'll talk to you on the phone. I'm so scared I'll start to *cry* again.

Johnson: *Oh,* you never cried . . . honey, I never saw anyone as *brave* as you—

Mrs. Kennedy: But I mean it's . . . you know—

Johnson: —or as *great*.

Mrs. Kennedy: I just *can't* *[indistinct]* down there.

Johnson: You know how great we think you are?

Mrs. Kennedy: Well, you . . . you know—

Johnson: *[solemnly]* You sure?

9. As noted, the former First Lady tried to see Johnson on December 17, but the president was in New York for most of the day.

10. Mrs. Kennedy and her children will dine privately with the President and Mrs. Nixon and their children during this visit and return to New York the same day. Sarah Booth Conroy and Sally Quinn, "Jackie Returns," *Washington Post*, 4 February 1971; Sarah Booth Conroy, "Two Portraits," *Washington Post*, 5 February 1971.

11. Arthur Schlesinger, Jr., *Robert Kennedy and His Times* (Boston: Houghton Mifflin, 1978), 647.

Mrs. Kennedy: Plus, I'll *talk* to you, I'll do *anything* I can—
Johnson: Fine.
Mrs. Kennedy: *[firmly]*—for you, but *don't* make me come down there yet.
Johnson: Well, I got to see you before long.
Mrs. Kennedy: Any time you say is *great.*
Johnson: All right.
Mrs. Kennedy: Thanks, Mr. [President]—
Johnson: I'll call you sometime and come by.[12]
Mrs. Kennedy: Okay . . . thank you.
Johnson: 'Bye.
Mrs. Kennedy: 'Bye.

January 20

Monday
To Richard Russell / 7:20 p.m.

During his first months as president, Johnson frequently calls Russell to discuss any number of problems, foreign as well as domestic, that are on his desk. In sharp contrast to many of the recorded conversations, when Johnson is on the telephone with Russell the president listens as much as he talks, even when he doesn't agree. During this wide-ranging twenty-minute conversation, Johnson cautiously brings up his nominee to replace the ailing Edward R. Murrow as director of the U.S. Information Agency (USIA), the entity responsible for depicting the United States abroad. The man Johnson has in mind is a Negro journalist named Carl Rowan, and he is gauging Russell's reaction before sending up Rowan's name for confirmation. Notwithstanding Rowan's outspokenness, which is not limited to civil rights issues, Russell has no objection to the journalist personally.[13] But the senator cautions the president against letting Rowan use USIA "to give the South hell," as has happened in the past and again on November 22 most recently.[14]

---

12. The president will visit her on February 26 and present Mrs. Kennedy with one of the ceremonial pens used to sign the tax bill. Dorothy McCardle, "President and Cabinet Pay 'Spiritual' Visit," *Washington Post,* 28 February 1964.
   13. "Outspoken Spokesman," *New York Times,* 22 January 1964.
   14. The Voice of America (VOA), the USIA's worldwide radio broadcasting service, habitually put things into context for its foreign listening audience. Accordingly, when VOA broadcast its first bulletin about the assassination (at 1:59 p.m., before the president was declared dead), it noted

Russell reminds the president that in 1957, USIA propagated some reports on racial unrest that put the South in a "very bad light." Several southern senators took umbrage and "raised hell" over USIA for two days, and ever since then the agency has had trouble getting its annual appropriation through the Congress.[15] The latest incident from last November has stuck in Russell's craw, too, for one of the Georgian's most pronounced personal characteristics is his recall. As he puts it, "I've got a funny memory. Things stick in my mind."

Russell: He's [Carl Rowan] got a good deal on the ball, but if USIA goes tearing off [and says derogatory things about the South] . . . and you know they *did* that, to start with, on the Kennedy assassination. They started givin' the South hell on the *first* announcement of it. They [started out]—

Johnson: *[disbelieving]* No, that'd be—

Russell: —talkin' 'bout a southern *racist*.

Johnson: Not USIA!

Russell: Yes, it *did* . . . United States Information Service. Yes, said he [President Kennedy] was shot by a southern racist. And they *stopped* [broadcasting] it in about thirty minutes . . . but the first [message] they sent out *was* that. If you'll check it, you'll find out I'm right about it. And somethin' like that . . . if that fella [Rowan] is down there, it can really cause some trouble, and we got a mighty tranquil situation down there [in the South] at present. But he got enough sense to run it if he hasn't got some great ambition that he's gonna take over and be the spokesman for all the Negroes by denouncin' the South before the world. I don't know enough 'bout him to appraise him. But you won't have the slightest repercussion unless he does do *that*.

[The conversation turns to discussion of Murrow's tenure and a new USIA film on the August 1963 march for civil rights in Washington.]

---

that "Dallas is the scene of the extreme right-wing movement [in the United States]." This "gratuitous suggestion" about the identity of the assassin(s) was withdrawn eleven minutes later and not repeated. In truth, it was not markedly different from what the national networks were broadcasting domestically. But the fact that a *government* agency propagated this stigma is what rankles Senator Russell. The initial broadcast has also provided invaluable grist for Radio Moscow's propaganda. Arthur Krock, "The Modern Miracles and the Ancient Curse," *New York Times*, 26 November 1963; John Mashek, "Voice of America Chief Explains 'Far Right' Tag," *Dallas Morning News*, 28 November 1963.

15. Senator Allen Ellender (D-Louisiana) led the criticism in 1957, charging that USIA had "grown like a bad weed." But Ellender's attack, while couched in terms of wasting taxpayers' money, stemmed in truth from southern senators' anger over USIA's depiction of their region. Jack Bell, "Ellender Calls for USIA Cuts," *Washington Post*, 21 April 1957.

February 1

Saturday
From Sargent Shriver / 6:28 p.m.

The single greatest irony in the brutal presidential transition of November 1963 is the fact that it is Lyndon Johnson, rather than John Kennedy, who is saddled with the consequences of the decision to overthrow Ngo Dinh Diem. Barely three months after the Washington-backed coup, the decision is already regarded as a terrible mistake, the worst decision made by President Kennedy save for the Bay of Pigs debacle.

Johnson was so morose as vice president that as the administration wore on, he became less and less inclined to offer an opinion. Only a genuine turning point—say, over missiles in Cuba—was sufficient to rouse him out of his silence. In the last few months of the Kennedy presidency, there was one such crisis over Vietnam. Self-immolating Buddhist monks, and the bad press they engendered, caused Washington to lose its remaining confidence in the regime of South Vietnamese president Diem. President Kennedy, egged on by State Department officials and especially Henry Cabot Lodge, the U.S. ambassador to Saigon, approved U.S. support for a coup d'état that would remove the stubborn, troublesome Diem and install a presumably more malleable general.

At this prospect, Johnson spoke up. One of his missions abroad as vice president had taken him to Saigon in 1961, and somehow a curious affinity quickly developed between the gangly, expansive Texan and the trim, reserved Catholic leader of half the Vietnamese nation, which was overwhelmingly Buddhist. Diem is the "Churchill of Asia," the vice president averred in a typical display of Johnsonian hyperbole.[16] After the first coup attempt against Diem failed in late August 1963, the vice president was particularly forceful at a key State Department meeting of all the principals save the Kennedy brothers. Driving home his point, he compared Diem to one of the president's chief congressional antagonists, Representative Otto Passman (D-Louisiana).[17]

> [I] recognize the evils of Diem but [see] no alternative to him. Certainly we can't pull out. We must . . . stop playing cops and robbers

16. Powers, *Man Who Kept the Secrets*, 121.
17. Passman has a deserved reputation as one of the most skillful and obstreperous members of the House. Year after year he uses his position as chairman of the House Appropriations Sub-

[though]. . . . [C]ertainly there were bad situations in South Vietnam. However, there were bad situations in the United States. It was difficult to live with Otto Passman but we couldn't pull a coup on him.[18]

Now Johnson is gamely shouldering, for the most part, the burden of a decision he opposed as vigorously as any made by President Kennedy. He would not be human, of course, if he did not slip in a little reminder now and then that it was not *his* idea to overthrow, for the first time in the cold war era, an avowed U.S. ally, and usher in a series of revolving-door regimes that are turning South Vietnam into the world's laughingstock. Occasionally, and often in direct correlation with the temperature of his relationship with Robert Kennedy, Johnson invests the U.S.-backed coup that resulted in Diem's very bloody execution with another meaning—an interpretation that Johnson surely knows will incite the attorney general to anger.[19] In effect, Johnson repeats privately what Malcolm X dared to utter publicly. The controversial Black Muslim minister was heatedly and roundly condemned in December for mocking the assassination as an instance of the "chickens coming home to roost."[20]

The first known reference of this kind by Johnson occurred on November 26, the day after President Kennedy's state funeral, while Johnson was livid over real and perceived slights administered by Robert Kennedy. Hubert Humphrey was visiting the president at the Elms, and the two men passed by a portrait of Diem hanging prominently in the hallway, a token of Johnson's affection for the Vietnamese politician. "We had a hand in killing him," Johnson said, motioning to Diem. "Now it's happening here."[21] A day or so later Johnson made a more pointed version of his comment to Ralph Dungan, a special assistant in the White House. "I want to tell you why Kennedy died," Johnson said. "Divine retribution . . . divine retribution. He murdered Diem and then he got it himself."[22]

committee on Foreign Operations to give presidents, regardless of party affiliation, fits over the foreign aid bill.

18. U.S. Department of State, *Foreign Relations of the United States, 1961–1963: Vietnam, August–December 1963* (Washington, D.C.: U.S. Government Printing Office, 1991), 4:74.

19. This metaphorical link is in addition to a genuine connection between the two murders that Johnson believes is possible, as he made clear on December 19.

20. The remark was made on December 1, 1963, during a Black Muslim rally in New York. Malcolm X accused President Kennedy of "twiddling his thumbs" over the murder of President Diem and also said, "Being an old farm boy myself, chickens coming home to roost never did make me sad; they've always made me glad." The Nation of Islam, Malcolm X's own organization, instantly condemned the remark and suspended the minister. "Malcolm X Scores U.S. and Kennedy," *New York Times,* 2 December 1963; R. W. Apple, "Malcolm X Silenced for Remarks on Assassination of Kennedy," *New York Times,* 5 December 1963.

21. Ellen Hammer, *A Death in November: America in Vietnam, 1963* (New York: Dutton, 1987), 309.

22. Richard Mahoney, *Sons and Brothers: The Days of Jack and Bobby Kennedy* (New York: Arcade Publishing, 1999), 302–3.

Three weeks later, Johnson again makes the connection before the aforementioned audience of national security officials (including Richard Helms), several of whom have firsthand knowledge of the U.S. role.

At the time of this conversation with Sargent Shriver, director of the Peace Corps, Johnson has new reasons to be exercised over Robert Kennedy's behavior. Public opinion polls show Kennedy to be the leading choice among Democrats for the 1964 vice presidential nomination, and there is some evidence that Kennedy is quietly encouraging such talk via trusted political operatives.[23] Running with another Kennedy is anathema to Johnson, even if their ticket positions were to be reversed from those of 1960. The president is utterly determined to win the presidency without being any more beholden to the Kennedys than he already is. When Johnson raises the Diem issue in this conversation, his language is even sharper than before. He uses the word "assassinate" and suggests premeditation. The official U.S. explanation at this time, of course, is still the cover story that was propagated right after the November 1963 coup: the Kennedy administration monitored the event closely and with the greatest interest, but had no involvement in the plot.

The most provocative element in this reference to Diem, of course, is that Johnson is making it to Shriver, one of Robert Kennedy's brothers-in-law. The president wants to remind Shriver, who thinks the recent news from Saigon is very disheartening, that Johnson inherited a mess not of his own making. It is not clear whether the president knows it or not, but RFK, like Johnson, opposed U.S. support for the coup against Diem.[24]

Shriver: How is that Vietna[m] . . . that [Charles] de Gaulle thing? Isn't that a . . . that's really a pain in the neck.[25]
Johnson: No, that's all right . . . if we could neutralize all of it [Vietnam]. But hell, they don't want to neutralize anything but *South* Vietnam.
Shriver: Yeah.
Johnson: The goddamned Soviets are not going to let you neutralize *North* Vietnam, so you're just whistlin' through your hat. And the only way to neutralize it is to whup hell out of them.
Shriver: Yeah. Is it goin' really any better? It looks *terrible* in the paper.
Johnson: No, it's . . . we *think* it's going to go a little better.
Shriver: God, it's just terrible.

23. Edwin Guthman and Jeffrey Shulman, eds., *Robert Kennedy: In His Own Words* (Boston: Little, Brown, 1988), 406.

24. Johnson may not have known because he was not at the meeting where the final decision was taken. Afterward it would have been unlike Robert Kennedy to let the vice president know that he disagreed with the president's decision.

25. French president Charles de Gaulle has just proposed the political neutralization of the former French colonies in Indochina, in collaboration with China's Communist regime, a government not recognized by Washington.

Johnson: The last two weeks have been better.
Shriver: The Thais out there are—
Johnson: We weren't . . . we've assassinated a few people, you know—
Shriver: Right.
Johnson: —and that *always* gives us problems. That's not . . . we went in there and killed 'em off, and now you see what shape we're in.[26]
Shriver: You know, I've often wondered how smart that *was*.
Johnson: *That* wasn't smart at all . . . wasn't smart at all.
Shriver: It was . . . yeah, that's that CIA business [over there].[27]
Johnson: Well, it just wasn't smart at all, my friend.[28]
Shriver: 'Cause they're better off . . . they were better off [under Diem] than what you've got now.
Johnson: I attended one meetin', and they asked me my opinion.[29] And I said, If you boys want to play cops and robbers, why don't you get on television. But *goddammit,* let's don't go to doing it with allies, 'cause you—[it'll] take you six months to get back [to] where you are now.
Shriver: You're right.
Johnson: But . . . they wanted to play cops and robbers, and they have, so . . . anyway, that's water over the dam. . . .

Shortly after this remark to Shriver, Johnson also juxtaposes the two murders during a conversation with Pierre Salinger.[30] He isn't sure, Johnson tells Salinger, that the assassination of the president was not some sort of "divine retribution" for the political murders of Diem and Rafael Trujillo, the dictator of the Dominican Republic, who was also gunned down during the Kennedy administration.

There is absolutely no doubt that Johnson's linking of the two assassinations gets back to Robert Kennedy, perhaps multiple times. When Kennedy hears about the remark directly from Salinger in February or March 1964, he is newly embittered at Lyndon Johnson over what he considers an intentionally

26. Diem's notorious brother, Ngo Dinh Nhu, was also murdered during the coup.
27. Shriver was out of the policymaking loop, so he attributes the coup to the machinations of the CIA. In point of fact, the CIA station chief in Saigon, John Richardson, and DCI John McCone were united in opposition to U.S. backing for a coup. Once President Kennedy decided to go ahead anyway, the CIA followed the president's orders and facilitated communication between U.S. officials and rebellious Vietnamese generals. As mentioned earlier, the undisputed case officer for the coup was Henry Cabot Lodge. Hugh Tovar, "Vietnam Revisited: The United States and Diem's Death," *International Journal of Intelligence and Counterintelligence* 5, no. 3 (Fall 1991).
28. Johnson is not going to get involved in correcting Shriver's misunderstanding of who did what to whom.
29. Johnson is referring to the meeting he attended on August 31, when he compared Diem to Otto Passman.
30. The precise timing of Johnson's remark is unknown, but it probably occurs before Salinger resigns as press secretary on March 19 to run for an open U.S. Senate seat in California.

cruel observation. It is this "guileful" remark that makes the gulf between Johnson and Kennedy "ultimately impassable," according to the posthumous biography of RFK written by Kennedy intimate Arthur Schlesinger, Jr.[31] While contemporaneously denying in public any rancor between himself and President Johnson, the attorney general cannot help but convey this story in April to an interviewer who is compiling oral histories for the John F. Kennedy Presidential Library in Boston.[32] After he tells the story in detail, Kennedy takes a long pause.

"But otherwise it's a friendly relationship," he acidly observes.[33]

May 13

Wednesday
From Richard Russell / 5:17 p.m.

A week rarely goes by without a call from the president to his mentor or vice versa, even when they are engaged in combat on the Senate floor. In this instance, Johnson is on the verge of overcoming a fifty-five-day Senate filibuster (led by Russell) on a civil rights bill when Russell calls to deliver some unwelcome news. The Republicans are attempting to revive the all-but-dormant Bobby Baker scandal in an effort to embarrass Johnson before the fall election.

At the tail end of a long conversation, after Johnson dispenses some advice on how to abort an extended investigation, Russell refers to his unusually heavy workload, made all the worse because of his obligations to the Warren Commission. Although Russell is the one member who talks to the president on a regular basis, the two men seldom talk about the Commission, its deliberations, or the problems it encounters, at least on the telephone. This conversation is

---

31. Schlesinger, *Robert Kennedy,* 649.

32. Anthony Lewis, "Kennedy Denies a Johnson Feud: Says Relations Are Friendly—Discourages Write-ins," *New York Times,* 13 March 1964.

33. The president coupled his remark to Salinger with a warning about godforsaken people. "When I was young in Texas, I used to know a cross-eyed boy. His eyes were crossed, and so was his character. . . . That was God's retribution for people who were bad, and so you should be careful of cross-eyed people because God put his mark on them." It isn't clear whether Johnson was referring to John Kennedy, his brother, or both men. Schlesinger, *Robert Kennedy,* 649, and Robert Kennedy Oral History by John Bartlow Martin, 13 and 30 April 1964, John F. Kennedy Library (hereafter JFKL). The anecdote told to Martin in April was repeated by Kennedy to Schlesinger in July 1964.

one of those exceptions. It turns out that the panel is not only having to investigate the very complicated matter of the assassination; now the Commission *itself* is being investigated. Right-wing commentators and newsletters have picked up on the fact that one of the staff members, a New York attorney named Norman Redlich, has lent his name to left-wing causes in the recent past. Redlich has written critical articles about the abuse of the Constitution's Fifth Amendment by Communist-hunting congressional committees, and signed public advertisements calling for the abolition of the House Un-American Activities Committee.[34] A staff member with such credentials should not be allowed to participate in the Commission, say right-wing pundits, given that the possibility of a Communist conspiracy to kill President Kennedy has to be investigated thoroughly. It has gotten to the point where some members of Congress are even raising questions in the *Congressional Record* about the investigation's integrity.

Johnson: Well, you ought to tell [Everett] Dirksen that, too, Dick. You oughta take time to tell those two fellas, and I'll tell 'em—

Russell: Well, I have a helluva lot else to do, Mr. President. I'm doin' the best I can, but God knows I've got [a] helluva lot to *do*.

   I sat up last night till 11:30 readin' the FBI reports on some son-of-a-*bitch* that this fella [J. Lee] Rankin hired over here on the Warren Commission.[35] Everybody's raisin' hell about him [Redlich] bein' a Communist and all . . . a left-winger.[36] The FBI was investigating. [They] got *eight thousand* pages of all raw . . . material.

   I just . . . there ain't but twenty-four hours in a *day*. 'Course, I know I'm talkin' [to] a man [who's] got a helluva lot more to do than I have. *[chuckling]* But you're the only man in Washington that *does*.

34. Display Advertisement, "Petition to the House of Representatives of the 87th Congress of the United States," *New York Times,* 9 February 1961; Display Advertisement, "An Appeal to the House of Representatives: Abolish HUAC," *New York Times,* 22 February 1962.

35. Rankin is the Warren Commission's general counsel.

36. Michael Beschloss's transcript of this conversation is in error, and because of that he incorrectly identifies Rankin, rather than Redlich, as the Warren Commission lawyer who is coming under attack. Michael Beschloss, *Taking Charge: The Johnson White House Tapes, 1963–1964* (New York: Simon & Schuster, 1997), 351.

June 23

Tuesday
To Allen Dulles / 7:05 p.m.

Almost six months to the day after the president's last telephone call to Dulles, which resulted in Dulles joining the Warren Commission, Johnson is calling again with another request for Dulles's services. In November 1963 the president started out by saying, "I've got a little unpleasantness . . . news for you." This time his first words are even more colorful.

Three young civil rights workers engaged in registering blacks to vote have been missing for two days near Philadelphia, Mississippi. Racial tensions are rising because there is ample reason to believe they are in danger—or, worse, already dead. Philadelphia is near the heart of Klan country in Mississippi, and the workers' charred Ford station wagon was found in a swamp by FBI agents just hours ago. Initially, the agents cannot determine if the students' remains are in it. Despite Johnson's injunction to the bureau that it spare no effort in its search for the missing men, the president is concerned that friction between the FBI and local law enforcement officials will hamper the effort. Mississippi senator James Eastland, who thinks the three missing workers are engaged in a "publicity stunt," conveys a suggestion from the governor of his home state: Johnson should send an impartial observer to Mississippi. "You'll get the surprise of your life. . . ." says Eastland. "There's no violence, no friction of any kind."[37]

The conversation with Dulles about this emergency sheds light on Dulles's perception of the Warren Commission's significance and on the state of its investigation, seven months into the inquiry. And because Robert Kennedy also participates in the telephone call, it is revealing of the nature of the relationship between Kennedy and Dulles, who was fired as DCI by President Kennedy in 1961 after the Bay of Pigs fiasco. Critics of the Commission will, in time, assert that Dulles's participation tainted the panel because he supposedly harbored a grudge against the Kennedys. That claim is belied by this conversation.

---

37. Taylor Branch, *Pillar of Fire: America in the King Years, 1963–65* (New York: Simon & Schuster, 1998), 366–70. The three students, two white, one black, will be found dead more than six weeks later, buried in a newly erected earthen dam near Philadelphia.

Johnson: We got the ox in the ditch, and we need [a] little help.

Dulles: You have what?

Johnson: The ox [is] in the ditch, and—

Dulles: *[chuckles]* I didn't catch the first word.

Johnson: *[chuckles]* Ox, O-X.

Dulles: Oh! *[laughs, then becomes somber]* What can I do?

Johnson: The attorney general and I are sittin' here talkin' . . . and the governor of Mississippi this afternoon sent me word that he would like for me to pick some impartial, objective observer that'd represent the president and come down and talk to him. [That would] let him show my representative what he was doin' to try to prevent violence, and what the state police were doin', and what the local officials were doin' . . . and review what his problem was and what we were doin'. We wanted to get someone that we thought that all the country would respect, and I wanna be careful who represents me and [the] attorney general.

Now I've talked about it [with him, and] we concluded that you were about the best and only fella that we knew [who] could get that job done for me, and we want to talk to you about it.

Dulles: Well, I've certainly—any time I'm adjured [a] position . . . whether I'm the best man for this or not, I don't know.

Johnson: Oh yes, you are.

Dulles: *[laughs heartily]*

Johnson: I know you are. Now let the attorney general tell you what he thinks about it, and I'll be back on in a minute.

[Robert Kennedy takes the telephone.]

Kennedy: Allen?

Dulles: Bob?

Kennedy: How are you?

Dulles: [I'm] very well.

Kennedy: Good.

[There is a brief discussion of Senator Edward Kennedy's injuries from a plane accident.]

Kennedy: I think this could be awfully important. You know the situation is *extremely* explosive in Mississippi.

Dulles: Oh, I know it is.

Kennedy: And there's very little contact—and [it] has been [that way] for the last few years—between the authorities down there *and* the federal authorities. And the fact that the [Mississippi] governor said that this was a possibility that he'd *accept,* and have some impartial person go down there and *look* at the situation, I think could, you know, be a big help and give us some breathing space. And also, somebody with your reputation around the country and around the world, I think, could perform a real service. I think it would be a question [of] going down and talking to him, talking to some of these students, talking to some of the Negro people down there, talking to some of the FBI [agents]—

Dulles: Yes.

Kennedy: —and then coming in and talking quite frankly with the governor and talking quite frankly with President Johnson about what you think needs to be done.

Dulles: I'm not a great expert on this subject, though.

Kennedy: I don't think that's [a problem] . . . I think it's just a question of *decency,* really, and just looking at the facts, and we'd obviously give you a briefing of how we found the situation, and then you could talk to him and see what you think. But I think it'd be . . . you know, it's something that we don't have and *never* have had, and the fact that you have no communication in such an explosive situation is very, very dangerous for the country.

Dulles: Oh, I realize it is.

[There is discussion regarding Dulles's lack of civil rights expertise.]

Dulles: My job is *purely* advisory [then], I mean—

Kennedy: That's right . . . that's right. And I think you'd go down and report on what the facts are and make suggestions. . . .

[There is discussion of finding a young lawyer to assist Dulles.]

Kennedy: I think it could be . . . you know, we've worked together for a long time, so I know what you could do and I know you'd do this well. And I know that you *could* do it, Allen.

Dulles: You want to announce it right away?

Kennedy: Well, I think it'd be well if—

Dulles: What is the timing on this? I'm on this other [Warren] Commission, you know, and we're trying to finish up our work, and I wouldn't want—

Kennedy: No, but I think if you could—

Dulles: —the chief justice [to] think I'd run out on him.

Kennedy: What I think is that if you could go down there for a day or so, or a *couple* of days, and then come back up here—

Dulles: Yeah.

Kennedy: —I think just to be . . . go down and talk to the governor, and talk to some of the other people down there. And then you could come back up . . . but I think just to get it started, it would be helpful [to issue an announcement immediately].

Dulles: [I'd] go down pretty soon, you mean?

Kennedy: Yes.

Dulles: Something like [the] day after tomorrow, or tomorrow or something.

[There is discussion of whether the governor is acting in good faith.]

Kennedy: If President Johnson has to take some steps later on, you know . . . and these things have such an *effect* across the country. It's not just Mississippi, but [they] just have an effect across the country. I mean, this is not just a local [matter].

Dulles: *Why d'you pick me for this?*

Kennedy: *[sheepishly]* Because I . . . *know* you.

Dulles: *[laughs heartily] [teasingly]* I've been a little mad at you, you know, a little bit, on this Bay of Pigs book.[38]

Kennedy: Uh-huh.

Dulles: But I like . . . forget that very easily.

Kennedy: *[subdued]* Oh well, I'm glad.

Dulles: *[begins laughing again]*

Kennedy: But anyway . . . you know I—

Dulles: *[still laughing]* I don't stay angry long.

Kennedy: *[sounding uncomfortable]* Yeah . . . well, fine. But I think it [a visit by you] could be a . . . and I think [the] president feels [it] could be a big help.

Dulles: Well, I'd do anything for the nation, you know, [at] any time. I've never refused. I just have a *little* question of my [suitability]—

Kennedy: Well, I'm sure you could do it.

Dulles: —whether it's a wise . . . a wise thing to do.

[Johnson gets back on the telephone, says he will call the governor now.]

Johnson: You're the man for it. Now, we want to get you some . . . any assistants you want. I don't know who you may want. Anybody [that] I know that I can get, I will.

[There is a second discussion about getting a young lawyer from a private firm to assist Dulles.]

Dulles: You remember that I'm on . . . you put me on this [Warren] Commission that—

Johnson: Yes, yes.

Dulles: —I'm working on with the chief justice and the others.

Johnson: Yes, I know that.

Dulles: And that is now reaching a point—

Johnson: I know.

Dulles: —where I wouldn't want to neglect that work for *anything*.

Johnson: I understand that. But you [would have to] stay [in Mississippi only] a day or two, and then [you could] come right on back, and I'll put a plane at your disposal.

[There is further discussion of logistics.]

Johnson: Thank you so much, Mr. Dulles.

Dulles: Thank you, Mr. President, for your confidence.

---

38. Dulles is referring to Haynes Johnson's recently published book on the 1961 invasion, which places most of the blame for the debacle on the CIA. Haynes Johnson, with Manuel Artime, José Pérez San Román, Erneido Oliva, and Enrique Ruiz-Williams, *The Bay of Pigs: The Leaders' Story of Brigade 2506* (New York: W. W. Norton, 1964).

July 23

Thursday
From George Reedy / 10:50 a.m.

One of the most common misperceptions about the *Warren Report* that will arise in the years to come is that President Johnson exerted pressure on the Commission during the summer of 1964. Critics will charge that because the report was overdue and questions were being raised about what was taking so long, Johnson allegedly pushed the Commission into finishing its work prematurely and for selfish political reasons.

The allegation is untrue. Keeping in mind Fortas's injunction of the previous November, Johnson always regards preparation of the final report and its findings as matters solely for the Commission to decide.[39] Once the report takes much longer than anticipated, however, the White House begins to consider the report's timing—or what happens *after* the findings are submitted to the president in an election year—a very sensitive issue and matter of legitimate concern.

In mid-July McGeorge Bundy meets with J. Lee Rankin, the Commission's general counsel, to discuss publication of the panel's findings. Bundy expresses a clear desire not to have the report come out in the midst of the Democratic National Convention. It would get in the way of the news that the president wants to generate out of Atlantic City, and Johnson, presumably, is also anxious lest publication then stampede the delegates into putting Robert Kennedy on the ticket. Rankin tentatively agrees to publish the report in early August. But a week later he tells Bundy that that schedule is much too tight, both for the final drafting of the report and for the purpose of ensuring a dignified presentation of the principal findings. On July 22 Bundy submits a memo to Johnson proposing that publication be deferred until after the Democratic convention.[40]

In the meantime, however, news reports mischaracterizing the president's position have begun to appear. On this particular morning, Johnson picks up a newspaper that carries the syndicated column by Robert Allen and Paul Scott, two journalists of a conservative bent. It flatly asserts that President Johnson "is reportedly strongly urging the issuing of the Commission's report" before next month's convention, but that some commissioners are opposed to "slamming the door and rushing out a report."[41]

39. Fortas, of course, initially opposed a presidential commission precisely because it would make Johnson to some degree responsible for investigating his predecessor's murder.

40. Memo re Warren Report, 22 July 1964, Box 2, NSF Memos to the President, LBJL.

41. Robert Allen & Paul Scott, " 'Gaps' in JFK Death Data," *Philadelphia Daily News,* 22 July 1964.

The president is annoyed naturally and lets press secretary George Reedy, a frequent target of his ire, know it.

[There is discussion of unrelated press releases.]

Johnson: I've got a little note here this morning . . . it doesn't trouble *me* because it doesn't *bother* me. But it's not very complimentary to your profession.[42] I have seven items . . . and *six* of 'em are *absolutely* incorrect. And they['re] all quoting me, and they're all reliable newspapers. Now, if that's the kind of information the country's gettin' generally, we're gonna be in a helluva shape exercising judgment.

Allen and Scott say Johnson is *"strongly urging"* the report of the Warren Commission be made before the Democratic [convention] and is giving no reason for it.[43]

I haven't *heard* of it. Don't know a thing about *it.* [I] haven't seen either one of 'em. Haven't talked to any of their *stringers.* And [it] never entered my *mind.* And [Earl] Warren's gonna get it out whenever he *wants* to. That's *pure* makeup.

Reedy: I don't think *[indistinct]* about it—

[Johnson, obviously irritated, cites several other erroneous but unrelated stories appearing in the press.]

Johnson: I don't guess you'd want . . . I guess it would be terrible if you just pointed out that none of these [stories] are accurate.

Reedy: [I don't mind] pointing it out to the individuals. I think it would be a mistake for me to do it *publicly* because I would open up a controversy. None of them are people around the White House.

[There is discussion of a possible press conference the next day.]

To McGeorge Bundy / 11:05 a.m.

Release of the Warren Commission's findings will not only be a major domestic news event, as a State Department memo points out to Bundy in mid-July. Publication will have even greater import for the U.S. government, "particularly because of the aura of suspicion and mystery with which journalism overseas has shrouded the assassination."[44] President Kennedy has been overwhelmingly depicted abroad as the victim of a racist and/or rightist plot.[45]

42. Reedy, prior to joining Johnson's Senate staff in 1951, was a wire service reporter for many years.

43. The president is the one summarizing (accurately) the column as "giving no reason for it."

44. Memo for Bundy re Warren Report, 11 July 1964, Pre-Release Distribution (#1), Box 14, NSF Committee File, LBJL.

45. U.S. Information Agency analysis, cited in Michael Schuyler, "The Bitter Harvest: Lyn-

Accordingly, the president's assistant for national security affairs is already thinking about the logistics of dissemination, so as to ensure "widespread, dignified, and effective publication of the report and its principal findings."[46] The State Department is particularly concerned that foreign correspondents receive at least as much care and attention as domestic newsmen. In the same July 22 memo in which Bundy advises the president that the report will be delayed until after the Democratic convention, he proposes the steps that will eventually be taken, including the report's prompt publication by the U.S. Government Printing Office. While it will undoubtedly bring "renewed attention" to the entire tragedy, Bundy believes, the report will simultaneously redound to the president's political benefit because it will "provide a telling comment on the issue of extremism."[47] Bundy is fully aware this issue is the negative subtext of the campaign the president intends to wage against Barry Goldwater.

Bundy: Sorry to bother you. The chief justice is on holiday, and I sent you a memo about the timing of that [Warren] Commission report—
Johnson: I approved all of it.
Bundy: Oh, you did? Well, that's . . . all I need to know.
Johnson: Tell Jack [Valenti] to get those things [memos for his approval] back to you in the morning. I had 'em out at 3:30 this morning. I passed 'em all.
Bundy: I'm sorry to be pestering you, Mr. President. I should've asked him.
Johnson: That's all right.
Bundy: Thanks.
Johnson: 'Bye.

September 18

Friday

From Richard Russell / 7:54 p.m.

Shortly after nine a.m. the White House receives a disturbing new report from the Gulf of Tonkin, site of a clash between U.S. and North Vietnamese naval forces in early August. Four Vietnamese patrol boats allegedly displayed hostile

don B. Johnson and the Assassination of John F. Kennedy," *Journal of American Culture* 8, no. 3 (Fall 1985).
46. Memo, 22 July 1964, Box 2, NSF, LBJL.
47. Ibid.

intent toward two U.S. destroyers patrolling in international waters; the patrol boats were fired upon before withdrawing. If the report is true, the incident is disturbing because it suggests North Vietnam is not intimidated by U.S. power. After the August incident Johnson ordered a retaliatory bombing raid on Vietnamese bases, naval craft, and an oil-storage depot. Then the U.S. Congress ostensibly put North Vietnam on notice by passing the Gulf of Tonkin resolution by overwhelming margins in both houses.[48] The nonbinding but open-ended statement expressed congressional support for Johnson's efforts to "repel any armed attack against" U.S. forces and "prevent further aggression" by Communist North Vietnam.[49] In less than a year Johnson will claim the resolution sanctions and authorizes his deployment of U.S. armed forces, including ground troops.

The attack makes for a very tense afternoon, as Johnson meets with his national security team for forty-five mintues, beginning at 2:30 p.m., to consider whether to respond.[50] The election, less than six weeks away, obviously complicates the president's decision. He is campaigning as the candidate of peace and moderation yet cannot afford to appear soft in the face of seeming Communist aggression. As more reports are filed, evidence of hostile intent becomes dubious and the president decides not to respond with another retaliatory bombing raid, having already demonstrated his will and resolve in August.[51]

In the evening Johnson talks to Richard Russell, who is in Winder, Georgia, for the weekend, to run the politically sensitive decision by the senator. Unbeknownst to Johnson, the Warren Commission held its final deliberative meeting that morning to settle outstanding differences regarding some of the language in the final report. With that exhausting responsibility finally over, the forthcoming report is still on Russell's mind when he receives a message that the president wants to talk to him.[52]

The Commission's pivotal forensic finding is that three shots were fired, but contrary to the FBI's report of December 1963, not every one of them hit an occupant in the presidential limousine. The Commission staff has concluded that one of the three missiles missed entirely, and that another hit both President

48. The vote was 416–0 in the House and 98–2 in the Senate.

49. Max Frankel, "U.S. Destroyers Open Fire Again in Tonkin Gulf," *New York Times,* 19 September 1964; U.S. Senate, Committee on Foreign Relations, *The U.S. Government and the Vietnam War: Executive and Legislative Roles and Relationships, 1961–1964* (Washington, D.C.: U.S. Government Printing Office, 1984), 2:302, 342.

50. Daily Diary, 18 September 1964, LBJL.

51. Senate Foreign Relations Committee, *U.S. Government and the Vietnam War,* 354–57.

52. According to Michael Beschloss, Johnson is calling Russell to find out what the Warren Commission has concluded. But it is clear, given the day's events and the entire conversation, that Johnson is calling to consult about Vietnam, not to ask about the Commission. Beschloss, *Taking Charge,* 559; Daily Diary, 18 September 1964, LBJL.

Kennedy and Governor Connally in that order.[53] This conclusion is at odds with the direct testimonies of the governor and Mrs. Connally, both of whom adamantly maintain that the governor was hit by his own missile, not one that hit the president first. This unshakable belief is traceable to the anger Mrs. Connally felt at Parkland Hospital, when she perceived that her wounded but alive husband was being ignored at the expense of an already-dead president.

Russell has concentrated on the question of a foreign or domestic conspiracy, insofar as he has devoted himself to the work of the Commission, and is not conversant with the facts that led the staff to what will become known as the "single-bullet theory." He is displaying his ignorance, rather than his usual acumen, when he proclaims to the president that, in the end, "it don't *make* much difference." It does. To argue that a separate missile hit Governor Connally is tantamount to arguing that there were two riflemen in Dealey Plaza. That is the forensic/ballistic fact that led the staff to this conceptual breakthrough in the first place. But instead of taking the time to study the issue seriously, Russell insists upon protecting the honor and sworn testimony of a southern governor, especially from a panel headed by Earl Warren. And rather than have an official dissent registered, the chief justice and his colleagues willingly massage the language of the final report until Russell's view is incorporated to the senator's satisfaction.[54]

When Johnson proclaims that he doesn't believe in the single-bullet theory either, it is a blatant example of his tendency to speak for effect. He has not studied the issue; indeed, he doesn't understand what the issue is. He is just trying to agree with his old mentor and get to the subject he really wants to talk about: Vietnam.

Johnson: Well, you always leavin' *town*. You must not *like* it up here.
Russell: Well, *you* left.[55] I figured if you'd got out of town that [the] country could get along a whole lot better without me than it could you.
Johnson: I don't know.
Russell: So I got out. No, that dang Warren Commission business has whupped me down so. We got through today, and I just. . . . You know what I did? I went over, got on the plane, [and] came home. I didn't even have a toothbrush, I didn't bring a shirt. I got a few little things here.

53. The staff, while certain that one missile hit both the president and the governor, was less certain about whether this missile was the first or second shot fired by Oswald. *Warren Report,* III–17.

54. Russell is not the only commissioner who tends to accept Connally's testimony at face value. Senator Cooper and Representative Boggs are also swayed by the governor's dogged insistence.

55. The president has just returned from a campaign swing in California, Oregon, and Washington.

I didn't even have my antihistamine pills to take care of my em-*phy*-se-ma.[56]

Johnson: Why did you get in such a rush?

Russell: Well, I was just worn out, fightin' over that *damn* report.

Johnson: Well, you oughta [have] taken another hour and gone to get your clothes.

Russell: No . . . no.

Well, they were tryin' to prove that [the] same bullet that hit Kennedy first was the one that hit Connally . . . went through him and through his hand, [and] his bone, into his leg and everything else. Just a lot of stuff there . . . I hadn't . . . couldn't . . . didn't hear all the evidence, and cross-examine all of 'em.[57] But I did read the record. So I just, ah . . . I don't know, I was the only fella [commissioner] there that even . . . *practically,* that suggested any change whatever in what the staff had got up. This *staff* business always scares me. I like to put my *own* views down. But we got you a pretty good report.

Johnson: Well, what difference does it make which bullet got Connally?

Russell: Well, it don't *make* much difference. But they said that they believe . . . that the Commission believe[s] that the same bullet that hit Kennedy hit Connally. *Well, I don't believe it!*

Johnson: I don't either.

Russell: And so I couldn't sign it. And I said that Governor Connally testified di-*rectly* to the contrary, and I'm not gonna *approve* of that.[58] So I finally made 'em say there was a difference in the Commission, in that part of 'em [a few commissioners] believed that that wasn't so.[59] 'Course, if a fella [Lee Harvey Oswald] was accurate enough to hit Kennedy right in the neck on *one* shot, and knock his head off in the *next* one when he's leanin' up against his wife's head and not even wound *her* . . . why, he didn't miss *completely* with that *third* shot.[60] But according to *that* theory, he not only

56. Russell suffers from several ailments, including insomnia and emphysema. He takes so many medications of various kinds that he has to keep track of them in his personal journal. John Goldsmith, *Colleagues: Richard B. Russell and His Apprentice, Lyndon B. Johnson* (Macon, Ga.: Mercer University Press, 1998), 93.

57. Russell is frankly admitting that he is not completely familar with the evidentiary record on this very point. His main interest throughout has been whether Oswald was part of a foreign (Communist) conspiracy.

58. In their direct testimonies before the Commission, both the governor and Mrs. Connally rigidly stuck to their story, viz., the president appeared to be hit in the throat by the first shot; the second shot hit the governor in the back; and then the president was hit again, this time in the head, by the third shot. *Warren Report,* 112; *HSCA Report,* 40.

59. The final language will state that "Governor Connally's testimony and certain other factors have given rise to some difference of opinion" as to whether the same missile that hit the president in the upper back also wounded Connally. *Warren Report,* 19.

60. Oswald's marksmanship is not the issue. Initially, his view of the president was obscured

missed the whole automobile but he missed the *street!* Well, a man [who's] a good enough shot to put two bullets right into Kennedy, he didn't miss that whole automobile—

Johnson: Hmm.

Russell: —nor the street. But anyhow, that's just a little thing, but we—

Johnson: What's the net of the whole thing? What [does] it say? That Oswald did it, and he did it for any *reason*?[61]

Russell: Well, just that he was a general misanthropic fella . . . that he'd . . . had never been satisfied anywhere he was on earth, in Russia or here, and that he had a desire to get his name in history and all. I don't think you'll be displeased with the report. It's too long, but it's a . . . [it's a] whole volume.

Johnson: Unanimous?[62]

Russell: Yes, sir.

Johnson: Hmm.

Russell: I tried my best to get in a *dis*-sent, but they'd come 'round and trade me out of it by givin' me a little old thread of it.[63]

Johnson: Hmm.

[The president turns to the Gulf of Tonkin incident.]

September 19

Saturday

From George Reedy / 1:45 p.m.

Publication of the *Warren Report* is an unprecedented problem in the annals of public relations. Because of the vastly different production schedules of television news, news radio, and newspapers, it is difficult to conceive of a release schedule that gives everyone a fair shake. Even newspapers cannot quite agree on what is equitable. James Reston, Washington bureau chief of the *New York*

---

by a tree partially blocking his line of sight. As the presidential limousine proceeded down Elm Street, it emerged from being partially obscured, and Oswald's next two shots found their mark.

61. Johnson is expressing the same expectation and hope that the general public has: Will the Warren Commission, after nearly ten months, be able to answer the question *why?*

62. Johnson might be as anxious as the chief justice to have a unanimous final report.

63. As noted in the preface to this book, Michael Beschloss incorrectly transcribes this sentence as "I tried my best to get in a *dis*-sent, but they'd come 'round and trade me out of it by giving me a little old threat." That means something quite different from what Russell actually said. Beschloss, *Taking Charge,* 560.

Times, wants the report a week in advance, presumably so that a team of reporters can take a long and critical (if need be) look at the findings. Alfred Friendly, the *Washington Post* managing editor, says lock up all concerned in a room for six hours with copies of the report, then let the chips fall where they may.

Interestingly, Johnson's main concern is to keep the report out of the White House until just before its release. He doesn't want the findings coming out via a leak. He already knows the essence of the report, courtesy of Richard Russell, and wants to keep up the appearance and reality of a commission independent of the White House.

Reedy: Oh, one other thing: on the Warren Commission report for Monday. Should we—

Johnson: What do you mean *for* Monday?

Reedy: Well, [as of] yesterday, you're supposed to get it delivered to you [on] Monday. And the query is whether it should be put on the record or not.

Johnson: That I'm gettin' it Monday?

Reedy: Yeah.

Johnson: *No,* I wouldn't. I'd . . . take a little time. I don't think we need to rush in on that thing.

Reedy: [McGeorge] Bundy and I are meeting with bureau chiefs and Al Friendly, and. . . .

Johnson: Well, [you] oughta been meetin' a *week* ago. And I've asked 'em to do it *two* weeks ago. So please don't start your meetings after you get the report. Go on [and] get your folks in and decide what the hell you're gonna *do* with it [first].

Reedy: We've talked to all these people individually.

Johnson: All right. What do they say?

Reedy: They want—

Johnson: *[tersely]* What do they *say?*

Reedy: They think that it should be—you've got two points of view. Al Friendly believes that we should just lock people up in a room for about six hours . . . then have the report released at the end of the six hours. Scotty Reston, on the other hand, wants it about a week in *advance*. And my own judgment is that it should be an in-between point. That we put it out, let's say, Friday around noon, and that . . . with two embargoes on it. One, that it cannot be moved on the wire [services] until Saturday evening, and two, that it be released to the public for Monday morning.

Johnson: Well, won't you break it in all the radios and televisions that way, and a lot of folks?

Reedy: From 6:30 [p.m. onward on Saturday], yes sir. [But] that is the *fairest* time I can find.

Johnson: Huh.

Reedy: We have a lot of difficulties with fairness in this because of the different production problems.

Johnson: Why in the hell didn't they get it to you *this* Friday, then? Why do they make you wait a week?

Reedy: Well, they didn't have it ready, sir.

Johnson: Well then, I'd tell 'em to hold it a little bit. You want to put it out Friday and get it over here to you along the middle of the week, or latter part of it, so *we* won't be leakin' it.

Reedy: Okay.

Johnson: *[sarcastically]* Or do you want to sit on your ass with it for a week?

Reedy: I don't particularly, sir. It's just a question of formal presentation.

Johnson: All right [then], I'd tell [Lee] Rankin, "Now, we'd like to put it out Friday if you get it to us by next Thursday."

Reedy: Okay . . . I think that's wise. I think Bundy will agree with it.

Johnson: Tell Bundy to get a hold of 'em [and] try to work it out.

Reedy: Right, sir, and we just won't go into it Monday . . . *good*. Because I think the closer *you* get it to when they put it out, the better.

Johnson: All right. That's right.

Reedy: And now these people I'm getting together with today . . . I just want them to sort of talk themselves *into* certain things, so they're *all* together in this and nobody thinks that we're just bein' arbitrary here. On the other hand, I don't want us to lose *control* over it, either.

Johnson: Okay.

Reedy: You bet, sir.

A copy of the 296,000-word report, compiled at a cost of $1.2 million, will be hand-delivered to President Johnson by all the commissioners, along with general counsel Lee Rankin, in the Oval Office on September 24.[64] Because he was not expecting such a massive volume, the president's first reaction is unscripted. "It's pretty heavy," says Johnson.[65] A double embargo is then placed on the media. News services are banned from transmitting any part of the report until 3 a.m. on Sunday, September 27, and proscribed from actually publishing or broadcasting any news about its contents until 6:30 p.m. on Sunday.

The embargo doesn't work as planned, and by Sunday afternoon television and radio stations are all over the story.

64. The cost in 2004 dollars is $7.3 million, a quarter of which went for salaries. Earl Warren, *The Memoirs of Earl Warren* (Garden City, N.Y.: Doubleday, 1977), 362.

65. Leon Jaworski, *Confession and Avoidance: A Memoir* (Garden City, N.Y.: Anchor Press, 1979), 106.

September 27

Sunday
From McGeorge Bundy / 12:55 p.m., CST

After the president receives his copy of the *Warren Report* on Friday, he barely
glances at it before fobbing it off on Horace Busby to read and digest. Richard
Russell has already given Johnson the gist of the *Report,* and the president sees
no need to clutter his mind with details.

Before Busby apparently has time to submit an analysis, the press embargo
is broken and stories about the *Warren Report* dominate the wire services' tele-
types. AP and UPI zero in on the *Report's* criticisms of the Secret Service
and FBI.[66] McGeorge Bundy decides that Johnson needs to show movement in
response to the findings, and that he can get ahead of the curve by announcing
formation of a committee to study the Commission's recommendations. The
president hesitates, but only because he has been chafing under the watchful eye
of the Secret Service detail as it is presently constituted.[67] The last thing Johnson wants is somebody recommending that more agents surround his every
move.

The president will not commit until he's had a chance to talk it over with
Abe Fortas, the man who provides the first opinion to Johnson on nearly
everything.

Bundy: On the Warren Commission *Report* . . . there's a good deal coming on
  the tickers now, and it suggests that we may be well advised *not* to wait till

66. Jonathan Spivak, "Warren Panel Assails Secret Service, Urges Reforms; Says Oswald
Was Kennedy's Killer Beyond Any Question," *Wall Street Journal,* 28 September 1964. The *Journal's* headline and story are typical.

67. The 1964 recordings include numerous conversations between Johnson and Secret Service personnel like James Rowley, the Secret Service chief, in which the president complains,
repeatedly and vociferously, about the suffocating protection he is being afforded. In the wake of
the Kennedy assassination, the Service is doubtlessly mortified at the prospect of losing another
president and is probably overdoing it. See Johnson and Rowley, conversation, 6 January 1964,
7:50 p.m.; Johnson and Rufus Youngblood, conversation, 6 January 1964, 8:05 p.m.; Johnson and
Rowley, conversation, 2 March 1964, 11:25 a.m.; Johnson and Rowley, conversation, 4 March
1964, 7:56 p.m.; Johnson and Rowley, conversation, 13 May 1964, 3:32 p.m.; Johnson and Rowley,
conversation, 13 May 1964, 5:10 p.m.; and Johnson and Floyd Boring, conversation, 15 June 1964,
5:50 p.m., all LBJL.

tomorrow to get out a reaction from you. Because in addition to working on whether Oswald did it and Ruby did it—[and] on the whole, accepting those findings—they [the wire services] give a good deal of attention to the fact that the *Report raps* the Secret Service and the FBI, and says your doctor should be with you *always,* and that kind of thing. And goes on to say that some of it is directed . . . can be *read* as meaning that they're [the commissioners are] giving *you* warnings and [giving] you an indication that the Secret Service needs to be jacked up.

I think to get this away from *you,* and to get it into business, it may be worthwhile to appoint a committee *today,* and have George Reedy get it out with the 6:30 [p.m.] deadline which is on the *Report* itself. I've talked to Douglas Dillon about it, and he feels the same way.

Johnson: Hmm.

Bundy: Now what they recommend—I don't know how much time you've had to look at it—

Johnson: No, I haven't . . . I haven't looked at it.

Bundy: —is a committee of cabinet members including the secretary of the treasury and the attorney general, *or* the National Security Council. Now I don't think you ought to do [that], put the *whole* Council in charge, 'cause that brings in the secretary of state [and] the secretary of defense. But I think you can appoint a committee, and my own suggestion would be, after some reflection, the secretary of the treasury, the acting attorney general, the director of CIA, and someone from the White House. And as I said in my memo the other day, I think probably from the, sort of, official point of view, it oughta be me, although I think the *real* question of what the Secret Service does and how it goes about its business oughta be done by someone who's with you all the *time.*

So my recommendation would be that we get George to put out the fact that you are reviewing these recommendations, and have asked that . . . specific recommendations for their execution to be developed *for* you by a cabinet-level committee consisting of those four men. And get that [statement] out tonight. Because otherwise there'll be a half day, anyway, of people saying that these recommendations are aimed at *you,* and it'll look as if we weren't doing something about it.

And I think it also quite important that [Dr.] George Burkley be conspicuously near you, even at some risk of inconvenience to you, because it's not the kind of headline we want to fuss around with . . . that you don't let your doctor get near you.

It's an *irritating* kind of thing, because it does damage the processes the Secret Service are . . . are *not* as smart and up-to-date as they oughta be. And now to get 'em that way, it's going to be a real problem. Bromley Smith said that if he were Chief [James] Rowley, he'd just read this *Report* and *resign*.[68] But I'm afraid that's not about to happen, nor even that we *want* it to happen.

I played with the idea of adding to this committee people who've been in the office of secretary of the treasury and attorney general before, like [William] Rogers and [Robert] Anderson, but I think that maybe builds it up a little too much.[69] I think you might have trouble lining them all up anyway as fast as we need to act. Now this *can* wait until tomorrow, but as I say, I advise against it because I think there's real advantage in your picking it up *promptly* and *dumping* it in the lap of a few other people so that it doesn't come back to you directly for a while.

How do you feel about it?

Johnson: Well, I don't know *enough*. I don't know what it is they *say*. I haven't *read* it, and I didn't get the impression that it was as drastic as you indicate.

Bundy: Well, I didn't *either* until I began to see the take on the tickers, but. . . . There are quite a lot of things that are going to hit the headlines in terms of critical attention [that needs to be paid] to the Secret Service reporting, and. . . . Here's Merriman Smith's [UPI] lead, for example:

[reading]

> "The commission raps Secret Service, FBI, and State Department procedures which allowed Oswald to be in the right place at the right time. [The] bipartisan panel found no evidence of any conspiracy, but . . . in its trenchant *[indistinct]* criticism of the security given Kennedy, the commission said there was insufficient liaison and coordination between the FBI and the Secret Service. It called for an immediate and substantial increase in protection of the [vice] president and a complete overhaul of the Secret Service's ability to advance protection of potential threats. [It] urged appointment of a cabinet committee to oversee *all* presidential protection and legislation to make assassination a federal offense. The Commission . . ."

[It] goes on then about the specific events in the survey. . . .

[reading again]

> "In a lengthy set of conclusions the *Report* focused criticism more on sins of *omission* than of commission. The *Report* [is] highly critical of newspaper, radio, and television representatives for overcrowding the Dallas jail. The *Report* cited a breach in discipline by some members of the Secret Service. Recommendations . . . [the] first recommendation, the basic one, is assignment to a special cabinet committee *or* the National Security Council of responsibility for reviewing an overseas

68. Smith is the NSC's executive secretary.

69. During the Eisenhower administration William Rogers was attorney general (1957–61) and Robert Anderson was secretary of the treasury (1957–61).

protective activity for the Secret Service. [The] Commission thought that it was necessary to follow up on the suggestion it [presidential protection] be taken *from* the Secret Service and assigned *to* the FBI or another agency. [The] Commission thought this determination [should] be made by the president and the Congress . . . complete overhaul of Secret Service facilities, improve Secret Service protective measures. . . ."

Then they want to . . . incidentally, that recommendation is *not* for more people near *you,* but for more Secret Service people to be able to go out in the field and to follow up leads in suspicious cases, and generally, to *check* the *kind* of thing that would have led to people keeping an eye on Oswald, which they never do . . . never *had* done, really, in any serious way before.

So we *will* get sort of a, What's the president going to do about it? fairly fast. And as I say, I don't think the world comes to an end if we *wait* twenty-four hours, but I think we gain *something* by acting on it today.

Johnson: What do they recommend the cabinet committee *do*?

Bundy: *[reading]*

"[The cabinet committee] should be assigned the responsibility of reviewing and overseeing the protective activities of the Secret Service and the other federal agencies that assist in safeguarding the president. Once given this responsibility, such a committee would ensure that the maximum resources of the federal government are fully engaged in the task of *protecting* the president, and would provide guidance in defining the general nature of the foreign and domestic dangers to presidential security."

Now I don't myself now propose that you establish *that* formal committee. But rather that you *appoint* a committee to review the recommendations, and to ensure that those which are ready for ripe action are promptly brought to you *for* action, and generally speaking, to *act for you* in getting cracking on these recommendations. I don't think you want to be pinned into an approval of every recommendation. But I don't think you want to leave a hiatus in which it looks as if you weren't *acting* on it. And the device of appointing a committee today is simply a way of getting the thing *going* so that some of these things can be done fairly *quickly*.

The improvements in Secret Service procedures . . . some of those things are going on *now. One*—some of the people on the commission have thought there oughta be a supplemental appropriation right away.[70] I don't think the congressional leadership will want that or that you oughta want that, myself, although Jerry Ford is said to want it very much . . . to get some of these additional investigators going.

---

70. The way Bundy begins this sentence suggests he may have been keeping close tabs on the Commission by communicating directly with one or more of its members.

Johnson: He wants some for [Barry] Goldwater, that's what he wants.[71]

Bundy: Well, I don't know whether he . . . I don't see anything for Goldwater in *this,* do you?

Johnson: Yeah, if he can get enough agitation stirred up. They've got bills to extend it [presidential protection] to all of 'em.

Bundy: Get what?

Johnson: They have bills introduced to include 'em, you know.

Bundy: Include who?

Johnson: Goldwater.

Bundy: Oh. Guarding *them.*

Johnson: Yeah.

Bundy: Well, that's . . . there's no *hint* of that in this report . . . nothing whatever about guarding candidates in any way, shape, or form.

Johnson: Well, that's a. . . .

Bundy: You want me to check with Clark Clifford [to see] how he feels about it, or check with anybody else?

Johnson: No, [but] he might be a good one, though, to go on if we appointed somebody. He's been with the president a good deal, you know. What do you [think is the] political objective?

Bundy: Yes, and he's currently the head of your foreign intelligence advisory thing.[72] He gets a little bit of criticism for being, you know, a partisan adviser rather than a nonpartisan one. But *in fact,* he's a very sensible, longheaded, helpful fellow, as we all know.

I'd be a little inclined at this stage—you *had* an advisory commission, the Warren Commission, of distinguished citizens—I think there's some advantage to bringing the operation within the executive branch. If you were going to go outside, then I would think [of] Clifford, and I think of Anderson, and I think, in a sense, this fellow Rogers who—

Johnson: [The] trouble is, I'm afraid some of these fools will get a hold of it and just go to recommendin' more Secret Service. And my *own* judgment is they *endanger* me more than they protect me *now.*

Bundy: Well, I think that's . . . that's why I think it's terribly important to keep it under your own *control,* and to appoint people, really, that are . . . that's *one* reason. I don't believe, myself, that what you need is more Secret Service around *you.* I *do* think there's a need for more people who *pay attention* to this *problem* of what kind of people are dangerous and where

71. Johnson believes that Ford wants a Secret Service detail assigned to Goldwater, the GOP nominee. Presumably, the aura of protection will make candidate Goldwater look more presidential.

72. Clifford has been chairman of the President's Foreign Intelligence Advisory Board since 1963.

might there be danger. And what I *really* think, myself, is that the Secret Service needs an injection of brains at the *top,* and that they just don't *have* it. But how to get that in a tactful, diplomatic, and effective way is very much of a different question.

Johnson: Let me think about it, and I'll call you back. If you don't hear from me, we'll just let it go till I come in tomorrow night.

Bundy: All right, fine.

Johnson: If I do, why, I'll call you back.

September 28

Monday
To Mike Mansfield / 7:22 a.m.

Early in the morning—he is leaving on a quick campaign swing through New England—Johnson telephones Mansfield to inform the Senate majority leader about formation of the President's Committee on the *Warren Report,* informally known as the Dillon Committee, after its chairman, Treasury Secretary C. Douglas Dillon.[73] The panel was created so swiftly that Johnson did not consult with any congressional leaders, which is his preference in matters that might involve legislative action.

The president is now much better informed about the *Warren Report*'s contents, either because Horace Busby has given him a thorough rundown, or via the news stories about it, or maybe both. Johnson notes that the *Report* does not identify Oswald's motive, which is perhaps the single greatest disappointment. Above all, Americans wanted to know *why.* Despite the death of the assassin at the hands of a vigilante, the public was hoping that the Warren Commission would be able to discern an answer from all the information it accumulated. But the *Report* states that "the Commission could not make any definitive determination of Oswald's motives."[74]

With an election looming, even the composition of the Dillon Committee, and the recommendations it might make, are weighed in terms of their possible political consequences.

---

73. The other committee members are John McCone, director of Central Intelligence, McGeorge Bundy, the president's national security adviser, and Nicholas Katzenbach, the acting attorney general since Robert Kennedy's departure to run for the U.S. Senate from New York.

74. *Warren Report,* 22.

Johnson: I didn't have a chance to call you last night because it was too late. But we went over this *Warren Report* as carefully as we could in the time that we had—

Mansfield: Yes, sir.

Johnson: —and I will submit to the Congress recommendations just as soon as we're in a position to do so. I wouldn't think that that would be before the early part of January and my group gets through meeting.[75] First, we don't want to leave any impression if we can—unless the facts require it—that [John] Kennedy did anything that contributed to this, or was negligent in any way, by any of *his* arrangements, or conduct, or whatnot.

Second, we want to make as thorough a plan as we can to coordinate the Secret Service and the FBI, together with the White House staff, plus all this foreign intelligence. There's a good deal of feeling that . . . maybe the Cuban thing—they [the commissioners] don't quite understand why he [Lee Harvey Oswald] was messin' back and forth *with* Cuba and what connection they have with it. And they don't quite find the *motive* yet [that] this fella [Oswald] *had* for wantin' to kill him [Kennedy] . . . why he [Oswald] was goin' back and forth to Russia . . . [why] he was messin' around in Mexico with the Cubans.[76]

So for that reason, my advisers, and the best lawyers I have available to me, thought that the thing we oughta do was to set up a blue-ribbon group to take this report—[77]

Mansfield: [I'm] glad you did this [and hope you're glad] you did, too.

Johnson: —and try to pull it together and have that story and the same story as the other one—kind of like you say, as quick as we could.

Mansfield: Yeah.

Johnson: But they also thought—[and] I don't want to say this publicly, but I thought I could tell *you*—that we oughta have it preponderantly *Republican,* so that first of all, these people would be *fair* to Kennedy but they wouldn't be *vulnerable* to Kennedy, and [it] wouldn't just be a Democratic National Committee document.

Mansfield: Yes.

Johnson: So for that reason I put John McCone on it, who *loves* Kennedy—[78]

Mansfield: Yes.

Johnson: —[was] very close to him, but who's [an] *ultra* Republican; Bundy, who also loves Kennedy, but who is a Republican, too; and Dillon,

75. The "group" is the Dillon Committee.

76. The Commission "found no evidence that either Lee Harvey Oswald or Jack Ruby was part of any conspiracy, domestic or foreign, to assassinate President Kennedy." *Warren Report,* 21.

77. "Best lawyers" is Johnson's code word for Abe Fortas.

78. A previous conversation with Bundy that is not included here indicates that McCone was appointed primarily because of the CIA's equity in presidential protection. Johnson and Bundy, conversation, 27 September 1964, 2:55 p.m., LBJL.

[a] Republican; and Katzenbach, [Nicholas] Katzenbach, who's not *anything*. I mean, he's just a good civil servant and a dean of a law school.[79]

So I'm going to meet with them as soon as I get back here [in the] next two or three days . . . and try to set 'em up [as] a study group so that they can then pull [J. Edgar] Hoover in without creating a big *fight* within the administration, and try to get Hoover and the Secret Service together. Now, between *us,* the Secret Service that covers me [is a] fine, and devoted, and dedicated group. But just honestly, Mike—[and] I wouldn't have this repeated to anybody—my judgment is that they're more likely to get me killed than they are to protect me.

Mansfield: Yes, sir.

Johnson: They're just not heavy thinkers. They're just like the average cop . . . and they don't plan. Hoover's the one that's put me in an [armored limousine] . . . [and] he doesn't object to my shakin' hands with high school kids or people along a fence at Billings, Montana.[80]

Mansfield: Yes.

Johnson: But he does object to my riding down the street in a car that's not bulletproof, because that's where people *hide*. It's not likely that an *assassin* [is] gonna be in with a bunch of [kids in a] high school band. But it is [likely] that he gets in an upstairs window. Yet they [the FBI] had the stuff on Oswald, but didn't give it to [the] Secret Service.[81]

So what we're going to do, if y'all . . . if it's all right . . . [if it] works out, I'm gonna meet with them, I guess, Wednesday or Thursday, maybe Wednesday. I got to go to the SAC base with this NATO man tomorrow.[82] And [then] I'm gonna call Dillon and them in, and make Dillon the chairman of it.

Mansfield: Good.

Johnson: And then have him try to get McCone to see that everything that comes in, from any foreign country, is very carefully handled. [And] get Bundy [to try to] take that from the president's viewpoint, and kind of not be a *super* detective, but let him be the *intelligence* man for the White

79. Katzenbach was a professor at the University of Chicago Law School prior to joining the Justice Department in 1961, but not the dean.

80. Montana, of course, is the state Mansfield represents. In a conversation with House Majority Leader Carl Albert on October 2, Johnson makes the same argument even more colorfully. Johnson and Albert, conversation, 2 October 1964, 6:46 p.m., LBJL.

81. The FBI had the thickest file on Oswald of any government agency and thus knew more about his whereabouts and activities. But under then-existing criteria, only persons known to pose a direct threat to the president were referred to the Secret Service, and Oswald was not even known to be violent. *Warren Report,* 24.

82. Johnson is scheduled to visit the USAF Strategic Air Command Headquarters base near Omaha, Nebraska, with NATO secretary-general Manlio Brosio.

House's Secret Service [detail]. And then *pull* the Treasury [Department] and the attorney general together on how to coordinate those two groups of people.

Honestly, just between us, I'd whole lot rather have *you* protected, or my daughter protected, or my wife—somebody I love—by [the] FBI. They're sharp, fast, quick, and the [Secret Service] boys around me are just as good as any boys you ever saw. But the men at the top [of the Secret Service] . . . they don't have the facilities, and directors, and if you'll remember when I was vice president, the Republicans just denounced *hell* out of me because I had agents. And I didn't *want* 'em. But they're trying to *hide* now. So if they get you in a corner on why we didn't do more, you can always just say, Well, one reason [we] didn't do more was 'cause they just jumped up and raised *hell* about even the *vice president* bein' covered in the House Appropriations Committee. And I begged 'em to take the money *away*.

So that is the story, and I wanted to tell you why I appointed 'em and what they's gonna do. And I'll be glad, if the Congress wants to make any recommendations to 'em, or before I send up my message, I'll be glad to have anybody make any suggestions they want to because we *always* welcome 'em.

Mansfield: I don't think you should, Mr. President. When [I] was asked the question . . . well, I said, if the president sends up any recommendations needing consideration—

Johnson: That's good.

Mansfield: —you anticipated by appointin' this commission that's *[indistinct]*.

Johnson: That's right. You just tell 'em that the moment the president's recommendations get there, that you['re] gonna see that they're given full consideration.

[The conversation turns to an unrelated subject.]

The Dillon Committee will meet well into the fall, working on many administrative fixes that will implement the Warren Commission's recommendations. Its key decision will be to leave the investigative aspect of protecting the president, as well as the task of physically guarding him, with the Secret Service, rather than turning some part of that job over to the FBI. Of course, J. Edgar Hoover plays a significant, behind-the-scenes role in this decision. Hoover doesn't want the bureau to have any part of a thankless responsibility.[83]

As for Johnson's personal views, the public release of the *Report* on September 28 stills his own speculation about a conspiracy for the time being. He will not talk again about "divine" or any other kind of retribution for years.

83. Felix Belair, "Panel Opposes New FBI Role in Johnson Guard," *New York Times*, 22 November 1964.

October 2

Friday
To Myer Feldman / 5:25 p.m.

The *Warren Report* concludes that the FBI "took an unduly restrictive view of its role in preventive intelligence work prior to the assassination," and that "more carefully coordinated treatment of the Oswald case" might have resulted in bringing Oswald to the attention of the Secret Service.[84] Stung by this "unfair and unjust" criticism—to J. Edgar Hoover, any and all criticism of the bureau by outsiders is unwarranted—the FBI director strikes back in a time-honored Washington way: he leaks.[85]

One of the bureau's favorite reporters is Jerry O'Leary of the *Washington Star.* O'Leary is on such good terms with assistant director Cartha DeLoach that DeLoach is godfather to one of O'Leary's children.[86] Hoover—or more likely, DeLoach, with Hoover's blessing—gives O'Leary a copy of the FBI director's May 1964 testimony before the Commission, and O'Leary knows what is expected in return. He writes a copyrighted front-page story, replete with extensive excerpts from Hoover's testimony, that tends to absolve the bureau and contradict the Commission's criticism. Hoover's defense is that if any entity of the U.S. government is to blame, it is the State Department for not only allowing but facilitating Oswald's return to the United States in 1962. The lead paragraph in O'Leary's article states that Hoover testified about a State Department document that described Oswald as "a thoroughly safe security risk."[87]

Minutes after the *Washington Star,* an afternoon newspaper, hits the streets, Johnson is on the telephone to Myer "Mike" Feldman, a deputy legal counsel in the White House. It has not yet dawned on Johnson that Hoover is responsible for the leak.

Johnson: Mike?
Feldman: Yes, sir.

84. *Warren Report,* 24.

85. Ben Franklin, "Hoover Assails Warren Findings," *New York Times,* 19 November 1964.

86. Cartha DeLoach, *Hoover's FBI: The Inside Story by Hoover's Trusted Lieutenant* (Washington, D.C.: Regnery Publishing, 1995), 181.

87. Jerry O'Leary, "Oswald Labeled 'Safe Risk,' Hoover Told Warren Probers," *Washington Star,* 2 October 1964. The Warren Commission found little fault with the State Department's role, having determined that it was only following the law. *Warren Report,* 777–78.

Johnson: Two things you better get on top of: that's this Hoover leak to the . . . on his testimony [before] the Warren Commission to this *Washington Star* [reporter], Jerry O'Leary—

Feldman: All right.

Johnson: —and let's see what the *facts* are. Check with Katzenbach and Hoover, and see what we can say. They wanna know if we're gonna have the FBI investigatin' the leak.

Feldman: Yes.

[The conversation turns to an unrelated topic.]

Feldman: All right. I'll get on it right away, Mr. President.

From Myer Feldman / 5:38 p.m.

Little more than ten minutes later Feldman has an answer for the president, probably after having conferred with Attorney General Katzenbach. Eventually, Hoover's testimony (indeed, all direct testimony) will be published in supplemental volumes to the *Warren Report*.[88] So the *Washington Star* exclusive is only a premature revelation of what is going to be disclosed anyway. The leak is Hoover's way of striking back while the Commission's criticism is still ringing in the public's ears.

Feldman: Now on the leak: he has . . . they haven't done anything about the leak of the information because they're pretty sure that Jerry O'Leary got it *either* from Mr. Hoover or somebody *close* to Mr. Hoover. And *anyhow,* this information *is* going to be made public just as soon as it can be printed. There's nothing to hold back letting *everybody* have Mr. Hoover's testimony. So they just would make it available to anybody and say there's no reason why this should be secret. And they have *not* done anything . . . any *checking* of it.

Johnson: *[long pause, as if mulling over the implication]* All right . . . okay.

Feldman: But I'll get statements on both of these [issues you raised] and have it sent down to you?

Johnson: Okay.

Feldman: Yes, sir.

The next day a bureau spokesman is asked whether any FBI official is responsible for making Hoover's testimony exclusively available to the *Star.* "I

---

88. Ultimately the 888-page *Report* will be supplemented by twenty-six volumes of sworn testimony, depositions, and exhibits that are published on November 23, 1964. Associated Press, "Warren Panel Data Sold by U.S. for $76 a Set," *New York Times,* 24 November 1964.

don't think so," he responds. "I just don't know where it came from."[89] Simultaneously, the State Department lashes back at Hoover. "We have been unable to locate any Department of State document" that states or implies Oswald was a "thoroughly safe risk," notes a spokesman. It turns out that that phrase was Hoover's characterization of the State Department's position.[90]

October 14

Wednesday
To John Connally / 8:45 p.m.

Johnson, who is nursing a sore throat, and Connally are discussing Walter Jenkins's arrest in Washington on a morals charge a week ago.[91] The president is stunned, mortified, and fearful that the scandal involving his aide of twenty-five years will change the dynamics of the presidential election with little more than two weeks to go. The Texas governor momentarily changes the subject to a campaign dinner scheduled for Dallas. In response, Johnson makes some revealing comments about how sensitively he regards the city synonymous with the assassination.

Connally: Let me tell you what's happened down here on one problem . . . you perhaps have already made up your mind. I don't want to add to your troubles. I know you've got lots of 'em.

After my meeting in Dallas with these 225 business people, they got the word last weekend about a dinner in Dallas. They had a breakfast yesterday morning. . . . Tom Scruggs came to San Antonio last night and told me that they had a quota of 600 tickets up there.[92] Yesterday mornin' in thirty minutes they sold $113,000 worth of tickets at one meeting,

89. Anthony Lewis, "FBI Chief Sees a Limit to Protection of President," *New York Times,* 3 October 1964.

90. Bernard Gwertzman, "Didn't Call Oswald Safe, State Department Says," *Washington Star,* 3 October 1964; "Hoover Claim Oswald Was Called a Safe Risk Makes State Cry 'Foul,' " *Washington Post,* 4 October 1964.

91. On October 7 Jenkins was arrested in a YMCA men's room on a charge of indecent sexual behavior. Dallek, *Flawed Giant,* 179.

92. Scruggs is a politically active Texas businessman.

yesterday morning.[93] I understand [that] today they've sold 700 [tickets] in Dallas *alone*. But I under[stand] . . . and, of course, this is a statewide dinner which, you know, I won't go into all the details on it . . . but I understand you've just said you're not gonna *go*.

Johnson: *[speaking softly]* Well, I never heard a thing about it until yesterday afternoon. They came in and said, We're havin' a fund-raising dinner, in Fort Worth, or some kind of breakfast, and in Dallas. And I said, I just . . . we can't do that . . . [there're] two or three *reasons* why we can't. But the *important* one is, we cannot *look* like . . . that we killed Kennedy in Dallas, and [now] I'm goin' down [there] and they're gonna give me a lot of *money*.

Connally: *[somberly]* Um-hmm.

Johnson: I just think it . . . everybody I talked to thinks it would be *revolting*. Most of 'em think I've made a terrible mistake by goin' *back* to Dallas—

Connally: Naw.

Johnson: —but I think you got to go back *sometime*. And I think that you oughta go back and keep your chin up and march in. And show 'em that you don't believe that they['re] all *thugs*.

Connally: Uh-huh.

Johnson: But when I do it for a *consideration* . . . everybody thinks that it would just be the *end* of me.

Connally: Yeah.

Johnson: Now, when I got that word, I told Jack [Valenti] to call Hunter [McLean] and call him, and ask him *why in God's world* he would book me on a fund-raisin' dinner I never heard of.[94] Well, Hunter said, well . . . he'd mentioned that he was gonna have a reception or a dinner, and I [supposedly] said, Fine. Now what he said to me was that he wanted to arrange for our day . . . our plans up there, and I said, That's good. That's fine. You get a hold of Jack Valenti, and y'all work out what plans you want me to do.

And I say look it, "Now I never *heard* of a *fund-raisin'* dinner." Nobody mentioned that to me, and if I had . . . the first time I heard of it, I had the same reaction. I'm afraid people are gonna think that it's just a *payoff*, and I think it'll be looked upon . . . it'll be bad for Dallas and be bad for me—

Connally: Yeah.

Johnson: —in the light of this thing [Jenkins's arrest] because I've just caught hell all . . . the last two days for goin' to Dallas *at all*.

Connally: Hmm . . . yeah.

Johnson: And they think I'm bringing up *all* the memories, [and that] I'm

93. The amount cited by Connally would be $681,000 in 2004 dollars.
94. McLean is a politically active businessman from Fort Worth.

retracing the *same* steps. They had me goin' to Fort Worth first and then over to Dallas, just like Kennedy did.

Connally: Yeah.

Johnson: And I don't know, we'll talk about it though tomorrow, and I'll do anything you think that I oughta do, after you look at it.

Connally: Well, I assumed that that was *probably* your reason, and I don't want to argue with your judgment. All I want[ed] to tell you was that it *will* be a success. I can understand that reasoning. I have pretty much the *same* reaction, at least it *occurred* to me that you might feel that way about it, and I don't know—

Johnson: For two reasons really, I don't want to. One is [that] I think they will . . . that'll be the interpretation [that'll] be placed on it.

Connally: Yeah.

Johnson: Number two, I want to *do* some things if those people help me. And I want to do them in *December*. And I don't want to do 'em for a consideration.

Connally: Yeah . . . yeah. Well, they're willin' to help you. All I want to do . . . I suspect what I'll have to do if you call it off . . . I think I better go up there and *talk* to 'em, and explain, as best I can, *why* it's being called off. I'm not tryin' to assess any *blame* for it. I think, in fairness to Hunter and George [Reedy] and the rest of 'em, they thought it had been cleared because they're sure not as hell . . . they're sure not going to do anything that you don't want *done*, and they don't want to do anything that [would] cause you any trouble. But you've *got* . . . we've got a support in Dallas that you've *never* had in all your political history, and I don't want to see it go down the drain. And I don't *know* that it will. . . .

Johnson: *[plaintively]* Why don't you get on that plane tonight or tomorrow, and come on up here. You sure are *needed*, my friend.

[The conversation turns to Jenkins's arrest.]

Ultimately, Johnson does not attend the fund-raiser in Dallas. He will cancel his two-day campaign swing through Texas, claiming that "international developments" require his presence in Washington.[95]

---

95. Associated Press, "First Lady Takes Husband's Place," *New York Times,* 20 October 1964.

November 4

Wednesday
To Earle Cabell / 3:25 a.m., CST

Superficially, the 1964 election is a straightforward choice as to whether Lyndon Johnson is deserving of his own term in office. Following his resounding victory, the president will declare, "I believe we won that election the first ninety days we served, when we . . . showed [the American people] we could act . . . and gave 'em an atmosphere of confidence and respect. I just don't think [Barry Goldwater] could ever move 'em after that time."[96]

But underlying the simplicity, the election has been cast as a struggle between extremism (Goldwater) and moderation (Johnson), with the assassination always lurking in the background, though it is rarely mentioned. It doesn't need to be. It is like the elephant in the room that no one talks about. For want of a better explanation, political extremism and intolerance are seen as the cause of President Kennedy's shocking murder. The meaning that Johnson prefers carries the day, and to the Democrats' decided advantage. Goldwater is vanquished to such a degree that the GOP nominee carries only five states, the hardcore old Confederacy, besides his home state of Arizona.[97]

Many of the congratulatory telephone calls speak to the underlying contest. Tommy Corcoran, a New Deal lawyer who arrived in Washington to do good and stayed to do well, calls Johnson and exclaims that the returns prove that this was no simple election. Americans "really feel as if you *passed a shadow* from them. . . . This is a *happy* country . . . somehow, you drove the demon out for them. . . . People are *grateful* to you for winning the great victory."[98]

In Texas, Johnson has not only arrested GOP inroads into the Democrats' hegemony, he seems to be reversing Republican fortunes. There is an across-the-board defeat of GOP candidates; even Senator Ralph Yarborough wins

96. Johnson and Russell, conversation, 9 November 1964, 11:57 a.m., LBJL.

97. The five states were Louisiana, Alabama, Mississippi, Georgia, and South Carolina. In his election postmortem Richard Russell attributes Johnson's failure to carry these states to lingering resentment over Washington's role on civil rights issues since 1961. "They just got a mad on, and they've had to get it out of their system," says Russell. "And from their standpoint, 'course, they had some cause to be mad." Ibid.

98. Johnson and Corcoran, conversation, 4 November 1964, 10:51 p.m., LBJL.

reelection handily over a well-financed, "personable and dynamic" Republican oilman from Houston named George Bush.[99] Nowhere, of course, does this drama play out with more intensity than in Dallas itself. Outwardly, Dallasites remain proud and even defiant. The assassination "could have happened any-where" is the frequently heard refrain.[100] But it didn't, and the city carries the uncomfortable burden in an uneasy combination of grief, guilt, and resentment despite being exonerated in the *Warren Report*.[101] Even if the inhabitants want to forget, the constant stream of visitors to the assassination site won't let them. It will always be November 22, 1963, in Dealey Plaza, site of the city's founding and its once-proud gateway to the west.

Inexorably the election in Dallas is considered an opportunity for redemption. The *Dallas Morning News*, formerly the dependable bastion of anti-Kennedy sentiment, endorses the Democratic candidate for president, something that would have been unthinkable on November 21, 1963. No newspaper in Texas, in fact, "plugs" Johnson more consistently and in a more favorable light than the *Morning News*.[102]

The congressional race in Dallas is no less of a barometer. Since 1955 Dallas has been represented by Republican Bruce Alger, one of the most ultraconservative members in the U.S. House of Representatives. The forty-six-year-old Alger, a former real estate developer, opposed Kennedy's Peace Corps as socialistic and condemned the 1963 Nuclear Test Ban Treaty as appeasement. As much as an individual can, Alger embodies the pre–November 22 Dallas stereotype: bombastic, swaggering, raucous, and completely sure of himself. Until the assassination Alger was not going to face any serious opposition for reelection; no Democrat wanted to be the sacrificial lamb. But afterward city fathers prevailed on the city's popular mayor, Earle Cabell, a moderate Democrat, to run against Alger, arguing that Dallas could no longer afford to be represented by him. Both major newspapers endorse Cabell and run highly critical articles about Alger's shortcomings while in office, including his failure to get a badly needed new federal building erected in the city.[103]

99. Gladwin Hill, "Republican Loss in Texas Is Virtually Total," *New York Times*, 8 November 1964.

100. Marguerite Higgins, "Report from Dallas: City Troubled by Tarnished Image," *Washington Star*, 4 January 1964.

101. The Warren Commission found "no evidence that the extreme [right-wing] views expressed toward President Kennedy . . . had any connection with Oswald's actions on November 22, 1963." *Warren Report*, 415; United Press International, "Dallas Absolved, Civic Leaders Say," *New York Times*, 28 September 1964; Haynes Johnson, "Proud Dallas Is Unable to Forget," *Washington Star*, 4 October 1964.

102. Johnson and Rhea Howard, conversation, 31 August 1964, 8:42 a.m., LBJL.

103. Darwin Payne, *Big D: Triumphs and Troubles of an American Supercity in the 20th Century* (Dallas, Tex.: Three Forks Press, 1994), 322–24.

Still, in the weeks leading up to the election, Alger is expected to squeak through.[104]

The night of Johnson's landslide victory, the very last phone call the president makes before retiring is to Earle Cabell, and their conversation tells the story.

Johnson: Congratulations!

Cabell: Thank you, sir! It's good to hear from you.

Johnson: Well, I'm mighty proud of you. How did things go up there?

Cabell: Mighty proud of *you*. And it's gone *wonderfully* well up here. I did something that I didn't *think* I would do . . . 'course, with that big a majority. And we got our Texas Democratic legislators in, down to Austin, and so we feel awfully good here.

Johnson: What is your majority?

Cabell: Well, it looks about 50,000.

Johnson: *Good God almighty!*

Cabell: Oh, it fooled *me*! I'll tell you.

Johnson: I'm so *proud* of you.

Cabell: Well . . . I'm just . . . I just don't know how to express it.

Johnson: Did I carry the [Dallas] County?

Cabell: Yes sir, *you* did.

Johnson: That's wonderful.

Cabell: Now, I believe you're gonna be just a few votes behind *me*.

Johnson: *Well, I—*

Cabell: *But we won't argue about that!*

Johnson: *[amused]* I'd expect that. I['m] just lucky if I just carried the county.

Cabell: Well, you carried the county, there's no question. And that is something that I was awfully proud of.

Johnson: Well, we'll have to get goin'. You'll have to come up the next week or so, [as] soon as we get established, and we'll have to start gettin' some stuff [earmarked for Dallas] in this budget and start movin'.

Cabell: Yeah. Well, thank you, [and] unless I heard otherwise, I planned on being in Washington about the first of December.

Johnson: That's good.

Cabell: And we'll spend some time there and find a place to live and kind of get oriented there.

Johnson: *[in disbelief]* But you beat him [Alger] by *50,000*!

Cabell: About 50,000 votes *[indistinct]*.

Johnson: Out of 300[,000]?

Cabell: Sir? Out of about 300,000, yes.

104. Donald Janson, "Dallas Democrats Are Hoping to Unseat Alger," *New York Times*, 19 October 1964.

Johnson: God, I'm proud of you. Well, *congratulations,* my friend, and I sure worked with you, and I'll do anything I know to help you.

Cabell: Well, I know *that.* And you know, about two years ago he [Alger] beat his opponent by *20,000* votes. And I just had no idea that I'd beat him by that amount, frankly. It's just *beyond* what I thought was possible.

Johnson: How d'you [account] . . . what do you account for it?

Cabell: Well, I gave him a helluva *race.* You know, *you* didn't back down, did you?

Johnson: No.

Cabell: Well, all right! So I think we both ran that same kind of race.

Johnson: *[lost in thought for a moment]* I guess there's [a] little atonement there too that helped.

Cabell: I think there *was,* very definitely, yes. They've had *enough* of it [extremism]. And it was a wonderful gesture on the part of the people of Dallas.

Johnson: I'm mighty proud of you, and I wanted [you] to know 'fore I went to bed.

Cabell: Bless your heart, and I *do* appreciate it more than you know.

Asked to comment on the election, Bruce Alger says he foresees the United States "moving into a socialist dictatorship."[105] But in return for Dallas's mending of its ways, Johnson will see to it that funds are earmarked for a new federal building, appropriations that were somehow never available so long as Alger was Dallas's representative. The building will eventually be named after Earle Cabell.

November 11

Wednesday

To Richard Russell / 8:26 p.m., CST

Having won election in his own right, Johnson enjoys the most serene days of his presidency. The new, decidedly more liberal Congress will not be arriving for two months, so the president has ample time to contemplate the future. The *New York Times*'s James Reston interviews Johnson for more than two hours and

105. Payne, *Big D,* 324.

pronounces him quite different in an internal memo. "No frenetic monologue this time," writes Reston. "He was subdued and, for him, almost serene."[106]

Still, the president must contend with the Kennedy shadow as the first anniversary of the assassination approaches.[107] The president is conversing about a number of matters with Richard Russell when the subject of the senator's annual fall visit to the LBJ Ranch comes up. It happens to coincide with the anniversary.

Johnson: Now you're comin' the afternoon . . . the mornin' of the twenty-second?

Russell: I'm gonna try to get out there on the mornin' of the twenty-second.

Johnson: Now listen . . . I'll be goin' to church; I'll be back here at noon.[108] I got to put a wreath on Kennedy's grave. Now you want to think about whether we oughta be huntin' *that* afternoon or not.

Russell: I don't think we should.

Johnson: I think—

Russell: I never thought about that.

Johnson: All right. I think that what we might do is drive over and see 'em [the deer], and figure 'em out in A. W. [Moursund]'s field, and tell the press that we're just visitin' and talkin' about the future of the world, and things of that kind.

Russell: That's right. No, we won't hunt on that day. I didn't think about that, [to tell you the truth].

Johnson: Well, if we do, we'll keep it *quiet.*[109]

Russell: That's right.

Johnson: We'll just drive 'round. . . .

106. Reston to Catledge, memo, 19 December 1964, Lyndon Johnson, 1957–1966, Series II C/D Biographical, Turner Catledge Papers, Mississippi State University.

107. Another example of Johnson's sensitivity to the anniversary will occur on Friday, November 20. Press secretary George Reedy counsels the president not to do anything too news-worthy on November 21, lest it be seen as an effort to compete with anniversary coverage of the assassination. "I think we oughta be pretty quiet tomorrow," says Reedy, and Johnson agrees. Johnson and Reedy, conversation, 20 November 1964, 4:39 p.m., LBJL.

108. The Johnsons are scheduled to attend, along with the Connallys, a memorial service in Austin to mark the first anniversary. Daily Diary, 22 November 1964, LBJL.

109. Reedy will dutifully inform the press that neither Russell nor Johnson went hunting on November 22. Johnson and Reedy, conversation, 23 November 1964, 3:25 p.m., LBJL.

November 20

Friday
From Cartha DeLoach / 4:23 p.m., CST

On November 18, before a small group of female reporters, J. Edgar Hoover unexpectedly lashes out at the Reverend Martin Luther King, Jr., calling the civil rights leader "the most notorious liar in the country."[110] Hoover is usually taciturn in public; his outburst is a response to King's charge that FBI agents in Albany, Georgia, have been less than scrupulous about investigating civil rights violations because they are southerners themselves. Hoover's remark sparks a flurry of denunciations and counterdenunciations that will last for weeks.[111]

The King controversy tends to overwhelm another scornful remark made by Hoover during the extraordinary three-hour meeting with the press. He also charges the Warren Commission with "a classic case of Monday morning quarterbacking" for daring to criticize the FBI. The *Warren Report* is "unfair and unjust," insofar as the FBI is concerned, because it wrongly chastises the bureau for failing to notify the Secret Service about Lee Harvey Oswald's activities and presence in Dallas.[112]

Johnson first caught a glimpse of Hoover's deep anger toward the Warren Commission in early October, when the president belatedly came to understand that the FBI itself leaked the director's sworn testimony to the Commission. He is uneasy about this all-too-public spat just weeks after publication of the *Warren Report*. The president had sold the Commission to Hoover in November 1963 as merely a review of the FBI's investigation of the assassination. Warren's panel was not supposed to undertake an investigation of the FBI.

Cartha "Deke" DeLoach is calling Johnson to inform him personally about the results of several FBI background investigations that the president ordered back in October, after the Walter Jenkins scandal. Johnson did not want to be surprised again by the private lives of the men closest to him. The president takes the occasion to discuss the rare public tantrum by the only director the bureau has ever known.[113] Johnson believes Hoover is only drawing more attention to the *Warren Report*'s criticism, which would otherwise be quickly forgotten.

110. Franklin, "Hoover Assails Warren Findings."
111. "Hoover Criticism Draws King Retort," *Washington Star,* 19 November 1964.
112. Franklin, "Hoover Assails Warren Findings."
113. Inside the bureau, of course, Hoover's outbursts are both legendary and routine.

Johnson: Now how's the boss [Hoover] feel. I was kind of concerned about that statement and about his feeling that somebody was being "unfair" and, ah . . . trying to be *personally* critical to *him.* I don't think that's a very general opinion *at all.*

DeLoach: Yes, sir.

Johnson: And I didn't know what to say about it. I started to say that I thought that it [the *Warren Report*] demonstrated a very *exceptional* application, and diligence, and *concern* with the laws of the land and [has] done a very fine job in that field.

DeLoach: Yes, sir.

Johnson: I regretted to see these differences appear because everybody in retrospect can look back and see if somethin' might have been done that would change things. But there's no use in tryin' to divide America and *blame* anybody for somethin' that was unavoidable.

DeLoach: Yes, *sir.*

Johnson: Then I figured, well, that'll just make somebody else come back and answer back and forth. [And] what we need [is] to try and pull 'em together now, instead of divid[ing] 'em, and I would—if I were you—try to use your . . . whatever counseling they do with you—

DeLoach: Yes, sir.

Johnson: —to let him [Hoover] know that the only way that anybody gets any advertisement that he has made *any* mistake is for him to advertise it *himself.*

DeLoach: Yes, sir.

Johnson: 'Cause what they say don't . . . nobody pays any attention to it.

DeLoach: Right.

Johnson: What *he* [Hoover] says kind of draws *attention* to it.

DeLoach: Right.

Johnson: And that's *my* judgment. I don't think anybody . . . I don't think *two* people out of a hundred, in whatever groups they're in—outside of some of your *super-extreme, shadowy* groups—I don't believe that two out of a hundred would find anything to criticize about his operation. They all have great confidence in it.

DeLoach: Right.

Johnson: I think you oughta boost him up that way. We all get to feelin' sorry for ourselves once in a while, and feel like somebody is pickin' on us—

DeLoach: Yes, sir.

Johnson: —pickin' at us, and sometimes people *do.*

[The conversation turns to Martin Luther King, Jr.'s criticism of the FBI.]

Somewhat ironically, one of the organizations that rises to Hoover's defense is the American Civil Liberties Union, or at least its New York chapter. For all of Oswald's arrogance, aggressiveness, and political activity, writes the chapter's general counsel in a letter to the editor of the *New York Times,* there was no reasonable basis for the FBI to have believed Oswald posed a threat to President Kennedy. "Hoover's resentment is . . . justified."[114]

114. Nanette Dembitz, letter to the editor, "Hoover Stand on the Report," *New York Times,* 30 November 1964.

1965

Although Johnson takes great and justifiable pride in the 1964 election—he received the largest share of votes (61 percent) ever achieved by a nominee—the president views the overwhelming victory with some trepidation. Ever the student of presidential history, he knows that electoral landslides are never duplicated. All one has to do is think back to Roosevelt's triumph in 1936. It marked the high point of FDR's popularity, though no one thought so at the time. In all likelihood Johnson has passed his electoral peak, try as he may to defy history. Nonetheless he is going to try to do exactly that, for he views the election results as nothing less than a mandate for his ambitions, both for himself and for the nation.

For much of the year Johnson will command the political landscape just as thoroughly as he once dominated the Senate. He will use the Democratic majorities in the House and the Senate to maximum effect, passing a raft of "Great Society" legislation. While Democrats enjoy their largest numerical advantage since 1938, for Johnson's purposes, the fact that it is a liberal majority is far more significant. But imperceptibly the wheel is turning. In August the president will sign into law the Voting Rights Act, which promises to usher in dramatic changes more swiftly than any other piece of civil rights legislation. That same month a race riot breaks out in the Watts area of Los Angeles. For the rest of Johnson's term the civil rights issue will be framed primarily in terms of hot summers, "black power," and a white backlash nationwide, rather than the nonviolent protests confined to the South that characterized the early 1960s.

The war in Vietnam follows a similar adverse trajectory, as the magnitude of the blunder involved in overthrowing President Ngo Dinh Diem becomes painfully apparent. In 1964 Johnson ran as the candidate who would stand up to Communist aggression but not send "American boys . . . 10,000 miles away from home" to fight an Asian land war.[1] While that is truly the president's preference, because the situation continues to deteriorate he will make a fateful decision to enlarge the U.S. commitment, first via sustained bombing of North Vietnam, then by the creeping introduction of the very ground forces he seemingly pledged to avoid.

Lastly, the 1964 election was, in some sense, a national plebiscite on Johnson's assumption of the presidency, of which the Warren Commission was a most important part. Public confidence in the Commission's probity and the integrity of its findings will persist throughout 1965. But not much longer.

---

1. Robert Dallek, *Flawed Giant: Lyndon Johnson and His Times 1961–1973* (New York: Oxford University Press, 1998), 238.

January 13

Wednesday
To Robert McNamara / 3:07 p.m.

Two days before this conversation John McCone appeared before Richard Russell's Armed Services Committee to brief senators on various strategic matters, primarily developments in the military balance of power vis-à-vis the Soviet Union. During the strategic *tour d'horizon,* the worsening situation in Vietnam came up. When Russell emerged from the three-hour secret hearing, he warned that unless Saigon found some solution to its "changing-chair government," he foresaw a prolonged stalemate.[2]

Russell's dim view is nothing new. For the past year, if not longer, he has privately expressed deep reservations to Johnson about the will of the South Vietnamese to defend their regime, imperfect though it is.[3] But his comments are sufficient to merit a front-page story in the *New York Times* and set tongues wagging in Georgetown.[4]

Anyone experienced in the ways of Washington knows that the ratio of genuine versus calculated news stories is no better than two to one. That is, for every two stories stemming from a reporter's enterprise or based on an unexpected development, one article appears because of a calculated leak by someone in power. Because Russell is perceived (and correctly so) as being closer to President Johnson than anyone else in Congress, the suspicion arises among Georgetown pundits that McCone's testimony and Russell's statement have been orchestrated in order to prepare the public for a major shift in U.S. policy. Based on his 1964

2. Warren Unna, "Russell Lays Vietnam Impasse to Instability," *Washington Post,* 12 January 1965.

3. Russell first expressed his reservations publicly when President Eisenhower sent in a small number of U.S. military advisers after the 1954 French defeat in Vietnam. "We commit the flag, and I support the flag," said Russell. "But it is going to be a long, drawn-out affair, costly in both blood and treasure." E. W. Kenworthy, "Johnson's Policy in Vietnam—4 Positions in Congress," *New York Times,* 25 July 1965. The best expression of his private views occurred during a telephone conversation on May 27, 1964, after Johnson asked Russell to "talk a little bit" about this "Vietnam thing." Russell replied, "It's the damn worst mess I ever saw. . . . But I knew that we were going to get into this sort of mess when we went in there. . . . It appears that our position is deteriorating. And it looks like the more that we try to do for them, the less that they're willing to do for themselves." Johnson and Russell, conversation, 27 May 1964, 10:55 a.m., LBJL.

4. E. W. Kenworthy, "Russell Asserts Instability Bars a Saigon Victory," *New York Times,* 12 January 1965.

campaign, Johnson presumably has no taste for a war that might interfere with his ambitious domestic agenda. Thus, he is going to reduce U.S. involvement now that the Vietnamese situation is fast approaching a no-turning-back point.

Since the U.S.-supported overthrow of the Diem government in November 1963, the Communist insurgency has steadily gained momentum amid an almost comical number of military coups in Saigon. Unless Washington puts boots on the ground, few expect the current Saigon regime to be around in a year. Russell therefore must be the president's stalking horse, laying the ground-work for a diminished U.S. role. Under this scenario, some blame for the pend-ing withdrawal will be apportioned to President Kennedy. He got the United States involved with a regime that can't, or won't, fight the Communists because its fractious members are too busy fighting amongst themselves.

Johnson's tone during the conversation is surprisingly even, given the insin-uation. Vietnam is not quite yet the problem it will be in a year or even six months from now. The president is certainly not above the scheming being attributed to him; perhaps his relaxed attitude stems from the knowledge that the suspicion is sheer buncombe. In an effort to enlist McNamara in setting the Georgetown pundits straight, Johnson gives almost a soliloquy on his concept of loyalty to President Kennedy both before and after Dallas.

When he was vice president, Johnson longed to emulate the influential role Vice President John Nance Garner played during Franklin Roosevelt's first term. But Garner provided a negative role model, too, during Roosevelt's second term, once his relationship with the president soured over such issues as Roosevelt's "court-packing" plan to enlarge the Supreme Court. The fellow Texan became the favorite scapegoat of frustrated New Dealers, who accused Garner of a "trai-torous knifing in the back of the commander-in-chief."[5] Garner's experience shaped Johnson's view of how a vice president ought to behave.

Johnson: . . . They're out, and they don't get consulted, and they don't feel their great power.[6] And you could throw all three of them on the scales at once and it wouldn't be eighty-nine pounds. But they have these little parties out at Georgetown, and they discuss. Bill Moyers tells me—I just wanna be sure there's no basis for *this*—that they had a party last night, and Joe Alsop called up very excited today and said that he and Kraft and [Rowland] Evans—[7]

5. Mark Hatfield, *Vice Presidents of the United States, 1789–1993* (Washington, D.C.: U.S. Government Printing Office, 1997), 392. The breach between Roosevelt and Garner grew so wide that the vice president became the first man holding that office in the modern era to challenge his own chief executive for renomination.

6. Johnson is probably referring to newspaper pundits who were favored during the Kennedy administration.

7. Joseph Alsop, Joseph Kraft, and Rowland Evans are three of the most prominent syndi-cated columnists based in Washington.

McNamara: Was this at Evans's house?

Johnson: Yeah.

McNamara: I know I was invited to one [party], and I couldn't remember what night it was.

Johnson: Well, it was [at] Evans's house. And the Kennedy crowd *decided* that I had framed up to get [the] Armed Services [Committee] in the Senate to call McCone to put the Vietnam war on Kennedy's tomb. And that I had a conspiracy going on to show that it was Kennedy's immaturity and poor judgment that originally led us *into* this thing, that got us involved. And that his execution of it had brought havoc to the country [Vietnam]. And that McCone had gone up [to the Senate] and done it. And that this was my game: to lay Vietnam off onto Kennedy's inexperience and immaturity, and so forth. [There was] a good deal more, but that was the guts of it.

I explained by sayin' [to Moyers] that I knew nothin' about his [McCone] being called, that was Russell['s] doing. That McCone told me he was going. McCone told me he was distressed about some [strategic] weapons, but I told Bill not to tell 'em that. That's all he [McCone] talked to me about; he didn't *mention* Vietnam. *[Johnson conveys more details.]* But I subsequently checked with McNamara, and he told me that he thought things were all right, so I assumed, since McNamara was a part of the administration, that—

McNamara: *[amusedly]* And he was going to be tagged with the war in any case!

Johnson: What?

McNamara: And [he] is going to be tagged with the war in any case! *[laughing]*

Johnson: *[chuckles]* That since he was a part of the administration, I had assumed that he [McNamara] didn't resent very much what was said or he would have said to me that it didn't go well, or it wasn't true or somethin'. But he told me that the hearing went off all right, and I guess he'd be a good authority to tell 'em that. [I told Moyers] that I considered myself responsible for every decision made by Kennedy, beginning with the nomination of the vice president and the adoption of the platform, through the Bay of Pigs, through the Dominican Republic and Diem problems, and right down to that day in Dallas.

And that I had had an opinion on an occasion [or] two, including civil rights and one or two others. But I never discussed them with anybody but the president, and never discussed 'em with anyone since and didn't propose to. And that whatever he did, I supported. And if they can find a more loyal man in this town to him or to his memory, I'd like for 'em to *produce* him. And that I had a considerably bigger slice of the Kennedy presidential pie, [a role in] making him president, than either Rowland Evans or Joe Kraft, even though they wrote a few speeches.

Now, that's about the story. I don't want to . . . it's not worthy of a lot of your attention except I wanted you to know that that's what they were saying. And I *assume* it's an injustice to McCone, too, isn't it?

McNamara: I think so, Mr. President. . . . [It] was my impression that McCone did a good job. I do know this, that from everything you said, you would have been delighted if McCone hadn't gone *up* there.

Johnson: Sure.

McNamara: So to indicate that you *maneuvered* the appearance just is obviously *incorrect.* I can maybe do something about this. . . . I can get back into communication with some of those people and, I think, throw some light of realism onto whatever they're thinking about.

Did I understand that Alsop called to *report* this?

Johnson: [He] called to report it to Bill [Moyers].

McNamara: Because I think that Alsop *strongly* supported President Kennedy's decisions to engage in this war, if you want to call it that. So I can't imagine *now* he'd be going back and trying to accuse him of making some serious errors in getting mixed up with it.

Johnson: Well, no, *Alsop's* not. Alsop is sayin' that *I'm* doing it. Alsop's charging that I'm gettin' McCone to go up and lay the blame for Vietnam on Kennedy's tomb. Now, of course, I have never laid any blame on Kennedy. Have you ever heard me blame Kennedy for anything?

McNamara: None, none. Absolutely not.

Johnson: Even when you knew that I did not share opinions.[8]

McNamara: That's right. Now I've mentioned this to Jackie several times. I've been very impressed by your attitude on that [as well as when] the president was alive, as a matter of fact.

Johnson: I may not have anything *else* in my life, but I got loyalty. Well, anyway, I want you to know it, and I want you to straighten it out. If you—you might find out, though, to be sure that nothing like this happened—I can't believe it did or you'd known it—I think if they'd gone up there and said that we got into Vietnam . . . *I was told by someone* that Russell *purposely* came out and said we reviewed Vietnam as a *cover* [story] for the submarine and the missiles. Did you hear that? Did you tell me that?[9]

McNamara: No, I didn't tell you that, Mr. President. And I didn't *hear* that, but I did understand the bulk of the discussion was on the strategic weaponry and not on Vietnam.

Johnson: McCone didn't tell me, and so Russell didn't. I don't know who . . .

---

8. Johnson is probably referring to the fact that, as McNamara knows, he vigorously opposed U.S. support for the military coup that overthrew Diem.

9. At the end of the *Times* story, the reporter noted that "several senators said that Mr. McCone had not concentrated on South Vietnam, but had given them an intelligence picture 'around the world.' " Kenworthy, "Russell Asserts Instability."

[it] must have been some newspaperman that suspected. Somebody told me, though, that he came out and discussed that. But I think if any of this crowd is in your vicinity or in your associates' vicinity, I think what *you* oughta say to them is this. That I came into Vietnam, or I went out there in early 1961, [and] I was permitted to make any recommendation I wanted to at any time. That I assume *full responsibility* for *everything* and don't ask anybody else to take it, *includin'* President Kennedy. And during his lifetime, whatever he did I was *for*. And in his death, it's my *complete* responsibility. And I don't shove it off on *anybody* else.

And that's that.

McNamara: Sure. Well, I'll do that, and I think I can do something on this. . . .

March 6

Saturday
To Hubert Humphrey / 11:25 a.m.

As he prepared to depart Fort Worth for Dallas on the morning of November 22, 1963, President Kennedy called John Nance Garner in Uvalde, Texas, to wish him well on his ninety-fifth birthday, which happened to fall on that day. For most of the people in the presidential entourage it was simply a nice, thoughtful gesture. For Lyndon Johnson though, it was a poignant reminder of just how far his presidential hopes and political stock had fallen. Garner was the Texan who had come closer to the presidency than any southerner since Appomattox. It must have seemed to Johnson, on the morning of November 22, that he had little or no hope of surpassing Garner. Nor had Johnson come close to matching Garner, really.

To the extent he was still remembered in 1963, "Cactus Jack" Garner was most often thought of in connection with his blunt aphorism about the vice presidency. The office, volunteered Garner, wasn't "worth a bucket of warm piss." (Garner always complained when "pantywaist" journalists substituted the word *spit* for *piss*.)[10] But he did not always think so, and no one knew that better than Lyndon Johnson. During Roosevelt's first term, Garner was, without a doubt, one of the most powerful vice presidents to ever hold office.

Garner was the wheeling-and-dealing Speaker of the House when Roo-

10. O. C. Fisher, *Cactus Jack* (Waco, Tex.: Texian Press, 1978), 118.

sevelt invited him onto the 1932 Democratic ticket in a union that anticipated the Kennedy-Johnson political marriage twenty-eight years later.[11] At the time Garner's reputation was that of a "secretive backroom operator," a cantankerous, table-thumping whiskey-drinking Speaker whose most important activities took place out of the public eye, in a haze of cigar smoke.[12] As a rural populist with a taste for states' rights, Garner did not always agree with President Roosevelt's novel proposals to lift America out of the Great Depression. Yet the vice president proved invaluable to the innovative but inexperienced administration in its dealings with Congress. Roosevelt was sufficiently confident to make Garner his political general on Capitol Hill, and Garner responded by using his mastery of Congress to get the New Deal passed. As Johnson tells his vice president, "The last time a great program was put on the books in this country, [Garner] put it on, whatever else they say about him. . . . He damned sure passed the stock exchange and the holding company act[s], and the Agricultural Adjustment Act, and the NRA, and everything else."[13] During those exciting days days, no one observed Garner with greater admiration than a young, ambitious congressional secretary from Texas named Lyndon Johnson.[14]

Though Roosevelt's second term witnessed a complete breakdown in the working relationship between the president and Garner, Johnson never forgot what the Texan had been able to achieve during the years he enjoyed the president's trust. Thus, when Johnson accepted second place on the 1960 ticket, it was partly conditioned on the belief that should Kennedy win the election, the worst that could happen was that Johnson's skills as a legislative tactician would be utilized à la Garner.[15] And that too would enable Johnson to remove the millstone around his neck, the label of being a regional, rather than a national, politician. One of Johnson's most bitter disappointments after 1961 was his belated

---

11. Interestingly, according to a 1967 article, Garner predicted that Kennedy would win the 1960 nomination and ask Johnson to be his running mate; therefore he advised Johnson via Sam Rayburn that Lyndon "must be ready to accept." "Garner: 'He Couldn't Be Elected Without Our Lyndon,' " *U.S. News & World Report,* 16 January 1967.

12. Hatfield, *Vice Presidents,* 385.

13. Johnson is referring to landmark pieces of New Deal legislation: the 1934 Securities and Exchange Act; the 1935 Public Utility Holding Company Act; the 1933 Agricultural Adjustment Act; and the 1933 National Recovery Act. These comments occur in a portion of the conversation that is not transcribed.

14. Johnson served as secretary to Texas Representative Richard Kleberg (D) from 1931 to 1935.

15. The best outcome of the 1960 campaign, from Johnson's standpoint, was for him to run well but for Kennedy to lose. In that case, he would still be majority leader; he would have transcended his regional limitations; and he would be regarded as the odds-on favorite for the 1964 nomination. Perhaps that explains why those who spent the long election night with Johnson observed that he showed no signs of elation at Kennedy's narrow victory over Nixon. Hatfield, *Vice Presidents,* 458.

realization that President Kennedy had no intention of delegating so much power to the vice president—although to be fair, the Senate itself might have rebelled at any prolongation of Johnson's "benevolent dictatorship."[16]

In this conversation with his vice president, Hubert Humphrey, Johnson lays all this out in detail. This conversation is not prompted by reports that Johnson is "ignoring" Humphrey or that the vice president's morale is flagging.[17] Far from shunting him aside, Johnson is the vice president's exacting taskmaster. Humphrey has been deployed as a congressional troubleshooter and spokesman for the administration, and is "the busiest vice president in history during his first year in office."[18] Indeed, Humphrey's old liberal friends are somewhat irritated in that he speaks of Johnson in only adulatory tones now.[19]

Here the president specifies what he expects from his congressional "field marshal" during a discussion about a bill providing federal aid to education that is not moving fast enough through the Congress for Johnson's taste.[20] It is the first crucial piece in the package of social programs that make up Johnson's vision of a Great Society, the most sweeping and ambitious package of legislation since the New Deal.

The conversation is one of the very few times Johnson is candid about the precise reasons for his frustration during his years as vice president under John Kennedy (though he had made every effort to pretend otherwise).[21] Virtually the only aspect that Johnson does not disclose to Humphrey is the decision he was pondering in his own mind in Fort Worth on the morning of November 22. That weekend Johnson was either going to tell President Kennedy he did not want to be his running mate in 1964, thereby abandoning his residual hopes for the White House in 1968; or Johnson was going to complain but continue to endure

16. Dallek, *Flawed Giant,* 8–9. It is not at all clear that Senate Democrats would have accepted Johnson as the administration's legislative field marshal. One indication is the election of Mike Mansfield—the anti-Johnson—to succeed the Texan as majority leader. As Senator George Smathers will later recall, "There was a big sigh of relief when Johnson departed the Senate. Not that they didn't like Johnson . . . but he was so strong, and so difficult, and so tough, that it was a relief to get him over to the vice president's office." Hatfield, *Vice Presidents,* 453.

17. Michael Beschloss writes that "Humphrey has been suffering from renewed press reports that Johnson is ignoring him." Michael Beschloss, *Reaching for Glory: Lyndon Johnson's Secret White House Tapes, 1964–1965* (New York: Simon & Schuster, 2001), 206. But that is not supported by contemporaneous news articles. Robert Albright, "There's a New Lilt at Helm of Senate: Humphrey's Obviously Enjoying His Job and the Members Reflect His Élan," *Washington Post,* 7 February 1965; Alan Otten, "Humphrey's Helpers: Vice President's Advisers Influence His Many Projects," *Wall Street Journal,* 1 March 1965; Rowland Evans and Robert Novak, "Remaking the Vice Presidency," *Washington Post,* 9 March 1965.

18. Hatfield, *Vice Presidents,* 468.

19. Evans and Novak, "Remaking the Vice Presidency."

20. Hatfield, *Vice Presidents,* 469.

21. Cabell Phillips, "Johnson Is Found Contented in Job," *New York Times,* 31 May 1963.

the humiliations and investigations that Robert Kennedy was sure to visit on him, in hopes of forcing the Texan off the 1964 ticket.[22]

Johnson: Now, we are starting to work on our legislative program for next year, [to] build you a record to run on.[23] But I want to emphasize with you that [your participation on] the [National] Security Council, and Malcolm X's funeral, and [your leadership of the] space council, and presiding [over the Senate], and everything else, is *important.*[24] And we *believe* in that poverty and civil rights [programs] and particularly [helping] your mayors.[25] I've counted [them] up, to give to some of the reporters [who have] been askin' me [about the] assignments that you have. You have more than any man ever had except [John Nance] Garner, and *more than* Garner. But the one that Garner had—and the only vice president that I've ever looked at that had any influence *was* Garner. I had none, 'cause [John] Kennedy wouldn't gimme any. He didn't just *assign* it to me.

But I want to make it clear—*here and now,* and *once and for all,* and even if it made a *break* between us, where we split wide open—your number-one responsibility in my administration—it comes even ahead of [John] McCormack, [Mike] Mansfield, [or] anybody else.[26] I expect you to be my liaison with *both* of 'em, and to speak with *authority* with both of 'em, and get the line down here on what it is. And then, as you've said in your speeches, come back down *here* with a message, because I think the vice president is peculiarly equipped because (a) he has the legislative training, he has the contacts, he has the *power* to make a speech for them, he's on the ticket, he's only one of two elected. He's there [on Capitol Hill] with 'em. The president can't go see 'em. Hell, I'd *love* to! I don't even go to a dedication of a gymnasium, although I think I'm goin' to. But I want to go eat with Allen

22. At virtually the same moment Johnson assumed the presidency, Senate Rules Committee investigators were quizzing Don Reynolds, a Maryland insurance agent, in closed session. Reynolds allegedly had information linking Johnson to the Bobby Baker scandal. One staffer left the room for a moment, heard that President Kennedy was dead, and reentered the room without disclosing the news. The man Reynolds was talking about was now the president. Fletcher Knebel, "After the Shots: The Ordeal of Lyndon Johnson," *Look,* 10 March 1964.

23. Johnson is being sly here, hinting that he may not run for reelection in 1968, though he fully intends to.

24. The reference to Malcolm X's funeral is odd, since Humphrey did not attend the services in February for the controversial black leader, who was assassinated in New York. But Humphrey does go to a lot of funerals.

25. Humphrey was mayor of Minneapolis before becoming a senator in 1948 and firmly believes local officials deserve more attention and help from the federal government.

26. Johnson is saying Humphrey is his chief contact with Congress, ahead of the elected leadership.

Ellender![27] I want to go to Albert Thomas's![28] I want to go to the Texas delegation! That's where I want to be, every day.

Humphrey: Yes, sir.

Johnson: I don't want to be sittin' down here receiving the ambassador from Ghana and spending all day down here. But I can't do it. But the vice president *can.* Now some presidents get *jealous* of the vice president *participating* in these acts. I think that education bill is *51 percent* yours. I think that Appalachian bill next Tuesday is *49 percent* yours. It's Johnson/Humphrey, or Kennedy/Johnson, and it's split, half and half. Just as much as you and Muriel own that home.[29]

Humphrey: Yes, sir.

Johnson: And I want them to understand it, and I want *you* to understand it, and I want you to act accordingly. Because . . . you just get you a chart, and get those 104 bills, and just *watch 'em like a hawk,* 'cause if you're successful—even when we lose—of knowing that we *were* voting, and why we were voting, and who was wrong . . . even if we lose 'em all, you will be a successful vice president. 'Cause the only man that I ever knew that was, was *Garner. Garner could *run* the Senate. He had the *power* . . . why they would follow him and do what he wanted [them] to [do]. And he could talk to [Sam] Rayburn and run the House.[30] *And he did.* And [Franklin] Roosevelt passed *all* of his stuff . . . and Roosevelt and Tommy Corcoran got the [lion's share of the] credit.[31] And you never have heard of old man Garner, but I studied and watched him *every damn day.* And that's what I want you to do.

Now Kennedy felt [that] if I did it, then I would be . . . they'd say I was the "master craftsman," and so forth. So he told the Catholics, and Mike [Mansfield] and them, to pay no attention to me.[32] And [for congressional leaders] to come down *here* [to the White House]. Now they don't have to do that. You can negotiate with Mike [Mansfield]. You can negotiate with [Senator] Russell Long [D-Louisiana]. You can negotiate with McCormack . . . and [Carl] Albert and [Edith] Green [D-Oregon] and [Wayne] Morse and *all the rest of 'em.* And let 'em *know* that you're speaking for the president. And let 'em know that we work through the leaders—we're for 'em—but this [administration] is a *dual operation.* And

27. Ellender is chairman of the Senate Committee on Agriculture and Forestry.
28. Thomas is an influential member of the House Appropriations Committee.
29. Muriel is the vice president's wife.
30. Rayburn had been Garner's longtime apprentice in the House.
31. Before he became a Washington lobbyist and "fixer," Corcoran was one of the best-known members of Franklin Roosevelt's so-called Brain Trust, a group of lawyers who fashioned much New Deal legislation.
32. By "Catholics" Johnson seems to be referring to the many Catholics on the White House staff, Kennedy's so-called Irish mafia.

put that up there as the *highest* thing, because what we're going to . . .
we're not goin' to 'em on how well the Peace Corps did, or how well even
the poverty [program] did, or how well even the meetings we have over
there [went]. What we're goin' to the folks with four years from now—that
all you *young* men will be goin' with—[is] *did we pass Appalachia?*[33]
Humphrey: Yes, sir.

March 25

Thursday
To Jacqueline Kennedy / 4:56 p.m.

Johnson's telephone calls to the former First Lady have become infrequent, in
part a consequence of her move to New York City in September 1964. The
president has not seen her since October, when he visited her new home on Fifth
Avenue during a campaign swing.

Johnson no longer needs to wrap himself in the Kennedy mantle. If he
runs in 1968 and wins, it will be on the basis of the record he has built. Emo-
tionally, however, he still seeks the approbation that only Mrs. Kennedy can
confer. The president is exceptionally sensitive to the perception of the Johnsons' being slighted by the president's widow, who is now something akin to a
living saint.

The point of this call, the first conversation between them in months, seems
to concern the upcoming dedication of a seven-ton stone memorial in Runnymede, England, to the late president. Queen Elizabeth is going to preside over
the ceremony in the very meadow where the signing of the Magna Carta awoke
the world to the concept of limited government 750 years ago.[34] Yet, as usual,
Johnson has an ulterior purpose in mind. For more than a year, Lady Bird Johnson has been working to complete Mrs. Kennedy's plans for the White House
grounds.[35] Now that the East Garden is finished and will be in its full glory in a
manner of weeks, Lady Bird is planning to honor Mrs. Kennedy by naming that

33. Johnson is referring to legislation to alleviate poverty in Appalachia, one of the poorest
regions in the country.

34. Anthony Lewis, "British Shrine Honors Kennedy," *New York Times,* 15 May 1965.

35. Mrs. Johnson is working on the project with Mrs. Paul "Bunny" Mellon, a personal friend
of Jacqueline Kennedy and an authority on gardening. It is Mrs. Mellon's idea to put a little plaque
in the garden as a tribute to Mrs. Kennedy. Lady Bird Johnson, *A White House Diary* (New York:
Holt, Rinehart and Winston, 1970), 97–98.

section of the grounds after her in late April. By putting a USAF jet transport at the disposal of the Kennedys for the trip to Runnymede, Johnson hopes to lure the elusive former First Lady down for the Washington dedication.[36] Johnson knows that Lady Bird is quietly but anxiously anticipating her predecessor will attend, hoping that the lapse of time has been sufficient for Mrs. Kennedy to cope with the emotion a dedication will surely evoke.[37] President Kennedy's widow has been invited numerous times for all manner of events, but has invariably declined.[38] This time the president fears that if Mrs. Kennedy goes to Runnymede but doesn't come down to Washington for the naming of a garden she planted while First Lady, tongues will start wagging.

The tone of the conversation is warm as always. Despite Johnson's thoughtfulness, Mrs. Kennedy will send her mother and members of the Kennedy clan to represent her at the White House dedication on April 25. "It was just too painful for me to go back to that place," she will later recall.[39] And just as Johnson fears, her absence—particularly after the ceremony at Runnymede—is interpreted by the press as a snub of Lady Bird in particular and the Johnsons in general. Some will even call it a "boycott."[40]

[Jacqueline Kennedy is in Hobe Sound, Florida.]
Johnson: . . . you just started headin' south fast as you could.
Mrs. Kennedy: *[laughs]*
Johnson: *[chuckles]* Got any sunshine down there?
Mrs. Kennedy: Oh, it's *wonderful.* How are you?
Johnson: Oh, I'm harassed to death, and I don't know whether I'm gonna survive or not, but I may go till the weekend, anyway.
Mrs. Kennedy: Well, everything's been just wonderful. Your speech was beyond belief.[41]
Johnson: Thank you, dear. I wanted to . . . I just heard that you were going . . . probably [would] go to the memorial to the president . . . [on the 750th

36. Nan Robertson, "A White House Garden Is Named for Mrs. Kennedy," *New York Times,* 23 April 1965.

37. Maxine Cheshire, "Only Her Name Could Grace 'Glowing Greensward,' " *Washington Post,* 24 April 1965.

38. Johnson, *White House Diary,* 126.

39. Jacqueline Kennedy Oral History, 11 January 1974, LBJL. Mrs. Kennedy is also not keen on the idea of having a garden named after her and gives her approval reluctantly.

40. Drew Pearson, "Manchester Reopens Old Wounds," *Washington Post,* 22 December 1966. One indication of how Mrs. Kennedy's absence cuts may be found in the fact that there is no entry about the dedication in the published version of Mrs. Johnson's White House diary.

41. Mrs. Kennedy is referring to Johnson's March 15 address on voting rights to a joint session of Congress. It is being widely regarded as Johnson's greatest speech and "one of the most moving and memorable presidential addresses in the country's history." Dallek, *Flawed Giant,* 218.

anniversary celebration of the] Magna Carta [signing] at Runnymede.[42] And I wanted to suggest that if you cared to, that you and your party take one of the [Boeing] 707s [from the presidential fleet]. And I thought I might ask Bobby and Teddy [Kennedy] if they wanted to go to represent me, along with the secretary of state and chief justice—who [are] already gonna be over there—and you might wanna take any other members of the family or anybody in the party you wanted to, and if you would *care* to do that, the plane would be at your disposal and your direction any time you want it to [be]. I told Teddy, when I couldn't get you, and Bobby's not available, but I'll tell him when he comes back. In other words, the government would be represented by Bobby, and Teddy, and the chief justice, and [Dean] Rusk.

Mrs. Kennedy: *[approvingly] Oh.*

Johnson: They're gonna be over there anyway. The ones to go with you would be whoever you wanted to take in your own party. And if you'd like to do that, you just let me know and I'll have it all set up for you, and it'll be at your disposal whenever you want it, for whatever time you want it.

Mrs. Kennedy: Oh, that's *really* [being] so nice. *[kiddingly]* But that's *wasting taxpayers' money*!

Johnson: *[seriously]* No, no . . . it's not at all. It's very important to us, and very important to the country, and . . . you just let me know how you feel after you have a chance to think about it.

Mrs. Kennedy: Oh, *listen* . . . I just don't know what to *say*. How could you think of [doing] that!

Johnson: You don't say anything.

Mrs. Kennedy: That's the nicest thing I *ever* heard of.

Johnson: Just quit bein' so elusive . . . [it's] been too long since I saw you.[43] There [was] that horrible night, you know, [concerning] Walter Jenkins, when I was tryin' to think of *all* the terrible things there.[44] *[chuckles]*

Mrs. Kennedy: *Oh* . . . when I *think* of it *since* then . . . *I* don't see *how* you controlled yourself. Remember you sipping honey?[45]

Johnson: Well . . . I was sittin' there with one of the sweet, beautiful creatures

42. The announcement that Mrs. Kennedy would go to Runnymede was reported in leading newspapers on March 6, nearly three weeks earlier. Winzola McLendon, "Mrs. Kennedy to Attend British Memorial Ceremony," *Washington Post,* 6 March 1965.

43. This, and a remark about "maybe our paths will cross before long," is as close as Johnson will come to mentioning the upcoming garden dedication.

44. Johnson is referring to his visit to Mrs. Kennedy's Fifth Avenue apartment on October 14, 1964, the same day Jenkins resigned because of his arrest a week earlier. Johnson was in New York to campaign alongside Robert Kennedy, whose 1964 campaign against incumbent senator Kenneth Keating was flagging.

45. Johnson was nursing a sore throat at the time.

of my life, and all the time my mind was down here about who was going to jail that night.

Mrs. Kennedy: Ah . . . good. Well—

Johnson: But . . . maybe our paths will cross before long, and whenever [or] wherever I can do anything, you know I'm as close as the phone, dear.

Mrs. Kennedy: I know . . . *thank you,* Mr. President. Listen, that's the nicest thing I ever heard of—

Johnson: Well, you just—

Mrs. Kennedy: I don't think *[indistinct],* but I really am touched.

Johnson: You just let us know. Anything, dear.

Mrs. Kennedy: *[warmly]* Thank you.

Johnson: 'Bye. Give my love to your children.

Mrs. Kennedy: I will.

Three days later Mrs. Kennedy will send a handwritten letter to President Johnson saying she wants to accept the offer. But she is mortified at the thought of riding aboard SAM 26000, the aircraft that carried her back from Dallas, or SAM 86970, which looks fairly similar, and that is the reason why she did not agree instantly. "I did not know if I could steel myself to go on one of those planes again," she writes. So while she accepts in principle, "please do not let it be *Air Force One.* And please, let it be the 707 that looks least like *Air Force One* inside."[46] Johnson complies, and the USAF transport command supplies an ordinary jet transport.

The dedication at Runnymede receives front-page and adoring treatment in many influential newspapers, including the *New York Times,* and the Kennedys' standing continues to reach heights most mortal politicians don't dare dream of. In the media there is a growing recognition and some grumbling behind the scenes at the "constant effort of the Kennedys to keep JFK's wake going," as Turner Catledge, the *Times*'s executive editor, puts it in June. "However, as resentful as I am at their dragging his poor body around, I cannot say it's not news, and important news."[47] More than 9 million Americans have visited Kennedy's gravesite at Arlington National Cemetery in less than two years.

46. Mrs. Kennedy to Johnson, letter, 28 March 1965, Box 5, White House Famous Names, LBJL.

47. Catledge to Sulzberger, memo, 2 June 1965, John F. Kennedy, 1957–1962, Series II C/D Biographical, Turner Catledge Papers, Mississippi State University.

August 11

Wednesday
From Robert McNamara / 4:08 p.m.

At one time or another, Johnson will use everyone who has a foot in both camps to act as his intermediary with the Kennedys. Right now it is Robert McNamara's turn. Robert Kennedy has aligned himself with a group of senators who are "persistently and temperately criticizi[ng] the evolving policy" in Vietnam.[48] While Kennedy is not the most outspoken critic, he is the only senator whose rivalry Johnson genuinely fears. Meanwhile Johnson also feels he is growing more estranged from the former First Lady, primarily because of the perceived snub over the April dedication of the East Garden. Word of the Johnsons' hurt feelings has surfaced in the press, and the president's calls to the former First Lady have all but ceased.

McNamara: I'm carrying on my continuous campaign with the Kennedys . . . I
   don't know. I'm making a *little* progress with Bobby. I'm going to try and
   see Jackie tonight and I'll try and work on *her* some more . . . and stop off
   some of this wild talk. . . .
[There is a brief discussion about John Kenneth Galbraith.]
Johnson: I'm very fond of Mrs. Kennedy, and I don't know what to do. I used
   to call her, and I decided I might overdo it and I didn't do it. But Bobby, I
   jerked him out of their line the other day. He [was] way back in [the] back.
   [And I] gave him the third pen.[49] I gave the first one to the vice president,
   and the second one to a Republican—[Everett] Dirksen—and Bobby the
   third one.
      And he wrote me a nice note, and he really *was* touched and he was
   grateful. Nick Katzenbach told me about it.
*[Johnson refers to a letter from Kennedy, about cleaning up water pollution,
   that seems to have been delivered to him deliberately late.]*
      . . . He wrote a letter to me urging a lot of things that we were [already]

48. Kenworthy, "Johnson's Policy in Vietnam."
49. On August 6, in the President's Room of the Capitol, Johnson signed the 1965 Voting Rights Act in an elaborate ceremony that was broadcast live on the national networks. Traditionally, presidents sign bills into law with several pens, then bestow these pens, in order, to the legislators deemed most responsible for inspiring and/or shepherding the bill through Congress.

doing. . . . And I don't know whether my post office department is that inefficient . . . [and] then I thought *that'd* make a helluva big story.

McNamara: No. Mr. President, you've got so much power and position and prestige, you can afford to lean over *backward* to him—

Johnson: I didn't—

McNamara: —[and] settle him down.

Johnson: Teddy [Kennedy] . . . they both turned down the invitation, and I kept repeatin' it on these extra days. Teddy came yesterday.

McNamara: Well, as far as Jackie is concerned, Mr. President, she will *not* come to Washington for *anything*.

Johnson: Yeah, well, I don't want her to come—

McNamara: It's because—

Johnson: —I just want her—

McNamara: —it doesn't have anything to do with you, or—

Johnson: *[mutters disbelievingly]* Yeah.

McNamara: —or Lady Bird. She just won't come.

Johnson: I just don't want her to be against us—

McNamara: I realize—

Johnson: *[voice rising]*—and *this* stuff has never been said. They keep saying that we're *very* upset—

McNamara: Yeah.

Johnson: —about her not being here to dedicate the [White House East] Garden. We're not at all [upset]. We *understood* [why] she didn't. We don't blame her. I don't think *I'd* want to come around the White House and look at the room, and get in the bed where my husband was, and stuff like that. But these damn—

McNamara: Reporters—

Johnson: —*gossipmongers* say that. *Lady Bird* doesn't feel that way. *I* don't feel that way. When I went to New York, I went to see her.

McNamara: I know she feels very warm toward Lady Bird and, of course, you.

Johnson: Well, you don't let 'em—you don't let her feel any other way.

McNamara: I will not. I'll talk to her tonight, and I'll—

Johnson: Fine.

McNamara: —[be] back [to you] in the morning.

A year in politics, it is often said, is a lifetime. But even by that yardstick the precipitous decline in Lyndon Johnson's political fortunes in 1966 is remarkable.

At the moment of his inauguration in January 1965, Johnson seemed poised to be the dominant president of the 1960s. With the Democratic coalition seemingly as strong as ever, Johnson appears likely to occupy the Oval Office until January 1973. Yet by the autumn of 1966 the president will not even be the choice of most rank-and-file Democrats for renomination in 1968.

The primary reason for the fall in Johnson's approval rating is the widening war in Southeast Asia. Nearly 60 percent of Americans now regard Vietnam as the nation's most urgent problem. At the same time it has finally dawned on the president and his top advisers that (in McNamara's words) "we have been too optimistic" about the application of American military power.[1] There is no end in sight to the stalemate, which is increasingly claiming more lives and treasure. Still, Johnson approves plans to almost double the size of U.S. ground forces by the end of the year and, after a bombing pause, actually intensifies the air war.[2]

The unrest in America's inner cities is eroding Johnson's standing, too. It suddenly becomes apparent that while laws guaranteeing civil rights are fine and overdue, intractable problems of education, housing, and employment are immune to a quick legislative fix. Johnson must contend with the dilemma of unmet expectations after having raised hopes of an immediate change for the better. There will be riots in thirty-eight cities over the summer, including Chicago, Cleveland, Milwaukee, Philadelphia, and Minneapolis, all of which are far removed from the problem South. For the first time, too, the economy is not on the president's side. Some adverse trends, most notably inflation caused by huge government expenditures, compound the president's difficulties. He wants guns *and* butter.

There is, finally, an attack from a completely unexpected quarter. Beginning in the summer of 1966, the first significant decision of Johnson's presidency—his handling of the assassination of his predecessor—is no longer viewed as impeccable. A relentless controversy springs up over the "official version" of what happened, that is, the *Warren Report*.[3] Owing to the criticism, and some

1. Robert Dallek, *Flawed Giant: Lyndon Johnson and His Times 1961–1973* (New York: Oxford University Press, 1998), 340, 344.

2. Ibid., 345.

3. Four major books critical of the *Warren Report* will be published by October 1966; Edward Jay Epstein, *Inquest: The Warren Commission and the Establishment of Truth* (New York: Viking, June 1966); Mark Lane, *Rush to Judgment: A Critique of the Warren Commission's Inquiry into the Murder of President John F. Kennedy, Officer J. D. Tippit and Lee Harvey Oswald* (New York:

unfortunate remarks by Governor Connally, who is still angling for his own bullet, for the first time since the *Report*'s September 1964 publication a plurality of Americans now believe that the assassination was the culmination of a successful conspiracy.[4] With the appearance of *MacBird!* in the fall of 1966, the cultural attack on Johnson will be in full force. The play, a biting satire based on Shakespeare's *Macbeth,* casts Johnson as the king who ascends to the throne after arranging the assassination of his predecessor.[5] The allegation almost has to surface in the cultural sphere initially; it is too unspeakable a charge to be made elsewhere.

Despite calls to reopen the investigation, thoughtful aides to the president, like special assistant John Roche, strongly advise against reconvening the Warren Commission or appointing a new panel.[6] The Justice Department is tenacious in its refusal to revisit the matter, saying it will not reinvestigate unless important new evidence arises.[7] Congress, unusually, dodges the controversy, in large part because all the members who served on the Warren Commission remain staunchly behind the panel's findings. Fewer than six congressmen call for a reopening of the investigation, and none have real clout.[8] The net result, however, is to continually remind Americans of the violent and abrupt manner in which Lyndon Johnson became president, and aggravate nagging doubts about the painful transition. The assassination is a wound in the body politic that has not yet healed, nor is it being allowed to.

As if this situation were not bad enough, by September Washington and

---

Holt, Rinehart and Winston, September 1966); Leo Sauvage, *The Oswald Affair: An Examination of the Contradictions and Omissions of the Warren Report* (New York: World Publishing Company, September 1966); and Richard Popkin, *The Second Oswald* (New York: Avon Books, September 1966). Lane's book is a runaway best seller, and Epstein's best-selling book is considered a responsible and damaging critique of the Commission's probity.

4. "66% in Poll Accept Kennedy Plot View," *New York Times,* 30 May 1967.

5. Barbara Garson, *MacBird!* (Berkeley, Calif.: Grassy Knoll Press, 1966). Johnson is not the only leader who comes off badly in Garson's satire on the lust for power. Robert Kennedy is depicted as the unscrupulous avenger of his slain brother. Garson, a veteran of the 1964 "Free Speech Movement" at the University of California, originally conceives the play as an "entertainment" for an antiwar protest rally. It becomes an underground best seller and will open in an off-Broadway production in February 1967, despite criticisms that it is vulgar, cruel, and tasteless. Leroy Aarons, "Satiric Stab at U.S. Leaders," *Washington Post,* 27 November 1966.

6. Roche to Johnson, memo, 23 November 1966, Original Warren Commission Material, Box 3, Special File, LBJL.

7. Some influential members of the president's White House staff believe he ought to convene a "small (2–3) confidential task force" to reassess the Warren Commission's findings in light of the controversy. But Johnson declines, believing that such action would serve no purpose except to reopen old wounds for the Kennedy family. Joseph Califano, *The Triumph and Tragedy of Lyndon Johnson: The White House Years* (New York: Simon & Schuster, 1991), 295.

8. Peter Kihss, "Warren Panel Member Suggests Independent Group Study Kennedy X-Rays," *New York Times,* 28 November 1966.

New York will be awash in rumors about William Manchester's authorized and much-anticipated book about the assassination. It is said to be harshly and unrelentingly critical of President Johnson. The searing transition will no longer appear to be Johnson's "finest hour" as Manchester reveals the tensions just behind the façade during that fateful weekend in November 1963. Manchester will articulate, as no one has heretofore dared, the condescension and lack of acceptance that Johnson feels deep down. As he will later recall bitterly,

> I took the oath, I became president. But for millions of Americans I was still illegitimate, a naked man with no presidential covering, a pretender to the throne, an illegal usurper. And then there was Texas, my home, the home of both the murder and the murder of the murderer. And then there were the bigots and the dividers and the Eastern intellectuals, who were waiting to knock me down before I could even begin to stand up. The whole thing was almost unbearable.[9]

February 1

Tuesday
To Maxwell Taylor / 9:33 a.m.

Johnson asks Maxwell Taylor, the former ambassador to Saigon from 1964 to 1965, to go on a "little labor of love." He wants Taylor to brief Senator Eugene McCarthy (D-Minnesota), an "intellectual and one of our problems," so that McCarthy will accept resumption of the air war against North Vietnam after a thirty-eight-day bombing pause. In this call Johnson takes the opportunity to express his view on the origins of the problem he inherited. In so doing, he returns to a refrain he uttered during the first few months of his presidency, although the complementary facet of "divine retribution" is absent now. This may be the first time Taylor has ever heard Johnson attribute responsibility for Diem's assassination to President Kennedy, but Taylor is far from taken aback. He participated in the critical White House meeting just before the mutiny and aligned himself with the minority position, in opposition to the coup,

9. Doris Kearns, *Lyndon Johnson and the American Dream* (New York: Harper & Row, 1976), 170.

along with such advisers as Robert Kennedy and John McCone.[10] Indeed, Taylor agrees with Johnson's assessment of the Kennedy administration's "heavy responsibility" for Diem's death, and the terrible consequences that have flowed from that "autumn of disaster."[11]

[Johnson instructs Taylor on how to prepare for the briefing of McCarthy.]
Johnson: We oughtn't to be blamed now for being warmongers, because we *did* [try for peace, with the bombing pause]. We tried to extend the peace wand, and we know that the United Nations is not gonna resolve anything, at least we don't *think* so. But they [Senate liberals] raise hell about the United Nations, so we gonna do *that.*
　　Now their record of prophecy and success is just about as poor as ours. *[laughs bitterly]* They started out and said, We got to kill Diem, because he's no damn good, and let's knock him off—
Taylor: And, ah. . . .
Johnson: And we did.[12]
Taylor: That's where it all started.
Johnson: *[voice rising] That's exactly where it started!* And I just plead with 'em at the time, please don't do it. But *that's* where it started. And they knocked *him* off.[13]
[Johnson continues to discuss criticisms of his Vietnam policy leveled by liberals.]

10. U.S. Department of State, *Foreign Relations of the United States, 1961–1963: Vietnam, August–December 1963* (Washington, D.C.: U.S. Government Printing Office, 1991), 4: 470.

11. In his memoir Taylor will write, "there is no question but that President Kennedy and all of us who advised him bore a heavy responsibility" for Diem's murder. Taylor will also agree that Diem's overthrow prolonged the war and precipitated increased U.S. involvement. Maxwell Taylor, *Swords and Plowshares* (New York: W. W. Norton, 1972), 301–02.

12. Johnson is speaking for effect. He believes the Kennedy administration is responsible for Diem's murder, but not that it was intended, desired, or planned. Authors like James Rosen, who argue that Johnson believed Kennedy "organized and executed" Diem's murder, are misreading Johnson. James Rosen, "What's Hidden in the LBJ Tapes: Johnson Thought JFK Was Responsible for the Murder of Ngo Dinh Diem," *Weekly Standard,* 29 September 2003.

13. Just before the conversation with Taylor, Johnson talks to Senator McCarthy and says much the same thing. "We all got together and got a goddamn . . . bunch of thugs, and we went in and assassinated [Diem]." Johnson and McCarthy, conversation, 1 February 1966, 9:20 a.m., LBJL. And Johnson will have a very similar conversation with Labor Secretary Willard Wirtz on February 19. "Since November 1963 they [liberal opponents of the war] have suggested about twenty-five specific moves. And they have ranged from assassinatin' Diem to . . . [Johnson enumerates eight other decisions taken since 1963]." Johnson and Wirtz, conversation, 19 February 1966, 1:50 p.m., LBJL.

March 17

Thursday
To Nicholas Katzenbach / 10:02 p.m.

While Johnson constantly seeks emissaries to Robert Kennedy who might be able to negotiate a truce with the New York senator, it has become all the more pressing now that chinks are beginning to appear in Johnson's political armor. Katzenbach is an obvious choice, inasmuch as Kennedy recommended that Katzenbach succeed him as attorney general in 1964, and Johnson has come to trust and respect the former law professor, too. In this conversation Johnson asks Katzenbach why Kennedy seems bent on distancing himself from an administration that is still brimming with John Kennedy's appointees and following his policies. Johnson predicts that continued disharmony among the Democrats will lead to substantial losses in the off-year election, especially of congressional seats narrowly gained from the GOP in 1964.

Sounding weary, Katzenbach is as patient as he can be at this late hour. He pledges to talk to the senator upon Kennedy's return to Washington. From Katzenbach's tone, he believes the possibility of a détente between the two men is nonexistent.

[The conversation opens with a discussion of Kennedy's various and alleged complaints about the Johnson White House.]
Johnson: I'm not trying to shove [Hubert] Humphrey or shove anybody out in front of Bobby. *I* have no objections to Bobby becomin' president of this country. I just, by God, want to be a president *myself.* And I think it ill behooves the Kennedys, after all *I've* done for the Kennedys, to not reciprocate the treatment that I've given them. Everything they've ever asked—the father, the president, Bobby, and Teddy—I've done *except* put Bobby on the ticket for vice president! That's all.
[Johnson mentions two recent requests fulfilled at the behest of the Kennedys.]
     And I named you attorney general, and I've done every damn thing they asked. And I went to New York [in 1964], and every time he asked me I went, and I campaigned, and I traveled [from] one end of that state to the other. I think if I [had] just sent the word down the line that I thought [the incumbent, Kenneth] Keating would make [a] helluva lot better senator, and I think he oughta knock his [Kennedy's] ass off, I think they [would have] *beat him.*

302 THE KENNEDY ASSASSINATION TAPES

Katzenbach: I think so, yeah.

Johnson: And I think he oughta have a *little* bit of gratitude. And I don't ask for that. But he goes around and he stirs up all this trouble. Let me show you how cheap it is.

[Johnson tells an anecdote about the New York chairman of the state Democratic Party and also criticizes Joe Clark, a liberal Democratic senator from Pennsylvania.]

Now . . . Bobby oughtn't to be *doin'* that. And Teddy [Kennedy] oughtn't to be *findin' little ways* of bein' away from me. I found ways to embrace Jack Kennnedy's program. I leaned over *every way a human could,* and when I didn't agree, as I told him I didn't on the Bay of Pigs, I just stood up *like a man* and said he did the right thing, and I'm *for him.* I didn't run, or shimmy, or bellyache, or cry. In the Cuban missile crisis, I thought that we oughta do some other things, and still thought so. But I didn't differ [in public]. And nobody knew it but he and I, and the secretary of state!

But I've got a clear conscience. I don't know why they do this. But both of 'em do it, Bobby much more so than Teddy. Bobby is behind this revolt up there [in the Senate] on Vietnam. He's goin' around meetin' with 'em, and callin' 'em together, suggesting this and suggesting that. And when [Richard] Russell put him on the spot [on Vietnam], which I didn't know [about] . . . I called Russell and begged him *not* to. He said, Well, I want to show these guys up. I want to make a record and rub their nose in it, and then let the [American] Legion and everybody understand it.

[Johnson discusses Russell's antipathy to Senate critics of the administration's Vietnam policy.]

Now what these liberals are gonna do, they're not gonna hurt *me one damn bit,* 'cause I've already made my recommendations and I don't have to implement 'em. And my salary's gonna be paid. But they gonna clean out a bunch of *good liberal* freshmen here by all this disharmony and this division. And it's not gonna help them. And if they come along, the [1968 presidential] nomination [is] not gonna be *worth a damn* to 'em if they get it. And *that's* why I don't understand why they can't *see* that.

Katzenbach: Can I try that [line of reasoning] with Bobby when he gets back?

Johnson: I think you ought to!

Katzenbach: I'd like to.

Johnson: I don't say anything against him. I don't have any of my staff cussin' him. Ain't nobody out *tryin'* to defeat him. I'm tryin' to help! Hell, I've called him *five times* for every time he's called me. He came in [and] recommended the first [bombing] pause. I put it in effect, purely and simply because he thought [it] would do the job. I don't. I think he's *immature* on this thing. I think the [Arthur] Schlesingers and the boys that advise him . . . I don't *think* they're right. But that's not any reason why I haven't *tried* it.

Katzenbach: Well he never did, either, Mr. President, and this is one thing I could tell him. 'Cause, you know, Schlesinger was never . . . you know, Bobby would laugh at this [kind of advice] when he was really deciding *[indistinct].*[14]

Johnson: He's got an *idea,* though, that I'm an *evil,* [James] Eastland–[type character] that is tryin' [to] trip him up. Now if I were tryin' [to] trip him up, why in the livin' hell would I tell everybody including [Robert] *Wagner* to support him [in 1964]?[15] And I just told Wagner he had no choice. I not only did that, I told [Edwin] Weisl he had no choice, he had to get in there and help him.[16] Adlai Stevenson wanted to run [for the New York Senate seat] and told me if I would just *indicate* to him it's *all right,* he'd do it. And I told him not to do it. And Adlai Stevenson never liked me until his *dying* grave.[17] Well, [if] a fella did me that way, Nick, I'd never forget it as long as I live.

Katzenbach: Yeah, I agree with you. I'd like to—

Johnson: And I have no obligation to Humphrey. I just happened to think that Humphrey was the best thing that I could do as vice president of the whole thing. And I thought I had a *right* to do that!

Katzenbach: It was very clear that that was *right,* Mr. President. I'd like to really have something of a free hand to take a crack at Bobby, and just like to—

Johnson: Yeah, but not only a free hand . . . but you can *deliver* on this side of the fence.[18] You can *produce. Any comment* that he hears . . . he jumped on Jack Valenti out here one night. Just abused him somethin' terribly.[19] And Jack Valenti hadn't said a *word* against him, [it] wasn't true at all. Somebody had gone tellin'. He's [Kennedy] got the Rowland Evanses and the little guys, that want to suck up to him, by goin' around [and] tellin' him that *everybody* in the White House is gunnin' for him. Now Joe Califano is his friend.[20] He *likes* him. He admires him. Bill Moyers is his *friend.* I thought he [Kennedy] murdered Bill Moyers the other day, but Bill didn't cry a word. He [Kennedy] misrepresented him; he said he

14. Katzenbach probably means that prior to November 22, 1963, when Kennedy's voice carried great weight on foreign policy matters, the then attorney general did not think very highly of advice from liberals like Schlesinger.

15. Robert Wagner was mayor of New York City in 1964.

16. A Wall Street lawyer influential in Democratic Party circles, Weisl detests the Kennedy family.

17. Stevenson, twice the Democratic presidential nominee, died in July 1965.

18. Johnson means that Katzenbach can obligate the president if Kennedy is willing to negotiate a truce.

19. Kennedy bears a grudge against Valenti that dates back to the suspected leak to the *Houston Post* in November 1963.

20. Califano is a special assistant to the president.

[Moyers] said something he didn't *say*. He misquoted him, and everything else . . . and I thought he made *himself* look bad.

Katzenbach: I agree.

Johnson: But I didn't say so. And I never . . . nobody at this White House hit him. Now what happened was, he made this damn fool speech [on Vietnam in February] that Schlesinger wrote—they tell me—I don't know.

[Johnson criticizes Kennedy for ostensibly advocating negotiations with the South Vietnamese National Liberation Front, the "Vietcong."]

But he [Kennedy has] got a martyr complex. He thinks that this White House spends twenty-four hours a day tryin' to show him up. Now this White House [is] not tryin' [to] do anything. I'd like to show him *good*! I'd like to see him down here *walkin' down* the street with me! I'd like to go to Alexandria and make *speeches* with him. I'd like to hear him get up there and say, This administration is [a] damn good one, and mention Lyndon Johnson in his speeches. He *doesn't*.

He goes all over Latin America just givin' me hell by sayin' that he never would have gone in[to] the Dominican Republic.[21] And yet I got his brother's memo, as late as October 12, [1963,] askin' McNamara to tell him how many people he can put in Venezuela, and Haiti, and [the] Dominican Republic in twelve hours . . . in twenty-four hours, because we may have to move [U.S. armed forces that quickly].[22] And Rusk said that he [President Kennedy] would have moved in *naked by himself* after the Bay of Pigs, if he had thought the Communists were takin' over one of those countries.

Katzenbach: Yeah.

Johnson: *[chuckles at hypocrisy]* Anyway, the *memo is there*! And all I got to do is *release* this memo, and just show that his *own* brother was considerin' doin' it *three weeks* before he died. Before they had made the *move*![23] He [President Kennedy] directed a memo to the secretary of defense . . . and dictated [it] himself, [and] said you tell me how many men you can put in the Dominican Republic, in Venezuela, and some other place—Haiti, I think—in twelve hours, in twenty-four hours, in forty-eight hours. And it ran up [that] in forty-eight hours, McNamara said he could put in 30,000 men, which we did put in, in that period of time. And then when *I* was called on to put 'em in, the very men his brother had

21. In the spring of 1965 Johnson ordered U.S. Marines into Santo Domingo, allegedly to prevent a Castro-like takeover of the Caribbean nation. The decision was widely criticized by liberals in the Democratic Party.

22. Memo for the President, 12 October 1963, Kennedy, John F., Box 1375a, Office Files of Marvin Watson, LBJL.

23. Presumably Johnson means before Dominican leftists allegedly tried to seize power.

appointed—Bundy, McNamara, and Rusk—*all* recommended it to me. And we did it, then he [Robert Kennedy] *undercut* me, after it had happened. And I just don't *understand* that. I wouldn't do that to him.

[They discuss a judicial appointment Robert Kennedy wanted Johnson to make.]

    Well, what do you think? You think that *he* thinks the *Texas* establishment tried to keep him from bein' senator? Or doesn't want him to be senator?

Katzenbach: No, I don't think so, Mr. [President]. I think it's . . . well, I don't really know what I *do* think. That's the problem I have—

Johnson: I'll tell you what Bob McNamara thinks. Bob McNamara thinks that *he* [Kennedy] thinks that it's politically *wise* not to be identified with this administration . . . get away from it. Now my judgment is, if I'm president, I think I'm gonna have somethin' to do with [Democratic] conventions [in the future], I don't care how many things. . . .[24] I have things *every* day that I could move on them [the Kennedys] if I wanted to.

[Johnson discusses political fund-raising pressures allegedly being exerted by Ted Kennedy.]

Katzenbach: *[tone of resignation]* Well, let me take a short stab at this, Mr. President, see if I can help at all.[25] I agree with everything you've said about this, and it's something that I have. . . . My relationship with Bobby has never been particularly personal, it's mostly been professional, but maybe I can do *something* about it.

Johnson: It looks like to me that he could see that this administration is not against him. Every man I have named was either named by his brother, or I believe, with one exception . . . [Robert] Weaver was named by his brother.[26] [Henry] Fowler was named by his brother.[27] Katzenbach was named by his brother.[28] I think it's a rather unusual thing when a president doesn't have a single man . . . Larry O'Brien was named by his brother.[29] I think I have demonstrated that I am *not* a bigoted, biased, prejudiced, anti-Kennedy man. I've kept all that he had, and all the vacancies I've had, I've put in *unquestionable* Kennedy men. If Fowler wasn't a Kennedy man, I never saw one. He's [as] loyal as a *dog*. Larry O'Brien is loyal as a *dog*.

---

24. An ironic comment, in that Johnson will not be welcome at another Democratic convention for the rest of his life and beyond.

25. Katzenbach sounds none too optimistic.

26. Robert Weaver was appointed the first secretary of housing and urban development in 1966.

27. Henry Fowler succeeded C. Douglas Dillon as treasury secretary in 1965.

28. Johnson means that several of the men he has promoted to cabinet rank were originally selected by Kennedy in 1961.

29. O'Brien was appointed postmaster general, then a cabinet post, in 1965.

Katzenbach [is] loyal as a dog, and [so is] Weaver. The only man that's been brought in that wasn't a Kennedy man—and I don't know who he voted for—was [John] Connor.[30]

Katzenbach: He helped a lot.

Johnson: Yes he did; yes, he did. In Cuba.[31]

Katzenbach: Back in Cuba, yes sir.

Johnson: Now there're my five cabinet officers out of eleven. And there's not a one of that . . . if I [had] gone up and picked Henry Cabot Lodge, that ran against his brother, that'd be different. But *they* picked Lodge![32] And I can understand if I went up and picked Eddie McCormack, and brought *him* down here, and made *him* attorney general.[33] I can understand how they'd say somethin' and [if I] let him start investigatin' some of Teddy's election stuff up there. I can understand it [then]. But I don't play that way. . . . I don't want their support. I don't ask him to ever make a speech for me, or to ever go to a convention for me, or to ever cast a vote for me. I don't want anybody to do that. I'm not *runnin'*. I'm not appointin' people that way. I'm just tryin' to hold this country together and run a good government, from now till January 1969.[34] And I think I'm entitled to have a *just* deal on it.

Katzenbach: I do, too.

Johnson: Okay, pardner. God bless you.

30. Connor became secretary of commerce in 1965, replacing Luther Hodges.

31. Connor, then chief executive of Merck, was instrumental in providing medicines that were exchanged for Cuban exiles captured at the Bay of Pigs.

32. John Kennedy ran against (and beat) Lodge in the 1952 election for a Senate seat. As president, Kennedy appointed Lodge to be the U.S. ambassador to South Vietnam in 1963, and Johnson reappointed Lodge to that post in 1965.

33. There is no love lost in Massachusetts between the Kennedys and the McCormacks. In 1962, the state attorney general, Eddie McCormack, the nephew of Speaker McCormack, lost the Democratic nomination for a U.S. Senate seat to Ted Kennedy.

34. Johnson is being disingenuous, of course, as he has every intention of seeking a second full term.

August 29

Monday
With Abe Fortas et al. / 9:30 a.m., CST[35]

In December 1963, before Mrs. Kennedy had even moved out of the White House, Jim Bishop, author of *The Day Christ Died* and *The Day Lincoln Was Shot,* proclaimed his intention to address John Kennedy's death in the same manner. Reportedly, Bishop's "style, taste, standards, and personality" were abominations to Jacqueline Kennedy; Robert Kennedy was suspicious because Bishop had once written admiringly of Teamsters union president Jimmy Hoffa.[36] Consequently, she decided that perhaps it would be best to choose one trusted writer, and ask everyone to speak just to him, in the hope that this would dampen efforts to sensationalize and commercialize the tragedy.[37] Robert Kennedy agreed, and handled the negotiations.

In March 1964 a former *Baltimore Evening Sun* reporter named William Manchester entered into a contract with the Kennedy family to do an authorized book on the last days of President Kennedy and the assassination's aftermath. The agreement was an attempt not only to write history, but control it. The press release issued by the Justice Department explained that the project was being undertaken "in the interest of historical accuracy and to prevent distortion and sensationalism."[38] Manchester was asked to do the book with the Kennedys' preferred editor and publisher, Evan Thomas at Harper & Row. Thomas had edited John Kennedy's 1956 book, *Profiles in Courage,* and several others by members of the Kennedy inner circle.[39]

Manchester was reputedly selected because Mrs. Kennedy believed his 1962 book, *Portrait of a President: John F. Kennedy in Profile,* was the most insightful of many works about her husband's life in the White House. Ini-

35. While the subject matter has been identified, the tape recording of this conversation is still being processed as of the writing of this book and will be released as part of the WH series of Johnson tape recordings.

36. William Manchester, *Controversy and Other Essays in Journalism, 1950–1975* (Boston: Little, Brown, 1976), 11; Arthur Schlesinger, Jr., *Robert Kennedy and His Times* (Boston: Houghton Mifflin, 1978), 760.

37. Jacqueline Kennedy Oral History, 11 January 1974, LBJL.

38. John Corry, *The Manchester Affair* (New York: G. P. Putnam's Sons, 1967), 32.

39. Thomas had also edited Robert Kennedy's *The Enemy Within* (1960) and was working on Ted Sorensen's biography of the late president, *Kennedy* (1965).

tially, the author believed the research and writing would take him three to five years, so publication was tentatively scheduled to occur no earlier than the assassination's fifth anniversary, November 1968. Manchester also said he needed the time to gain some perspective. As of 1964, the forty-one-year-old author still awakened nights in his Washington apartment hearing the "stutter of drums" along Pennsylvania Avenue, where the Kennedy funeral cortège had walked by.[40] He worked in an office provided rent free in the National Archives, also along Pennsylvania Avenue.[41]

From the outset, it was clear that Manchester identified with the fallen president completely. That, along with his demonstrated willingness to submit a manuscript for review, were major factors in his selection.[42] Like Kennedy, Manchester had been born in Massachusetts and was stationed in the Pacific during World War II, fighting as a Marine on Guadalcanal while Lieutenant Kennedy was commanding a PT boat nearby. Manchester considered his selection a supreme honor, for he would be responsible for setting down "the single most electrifying story of his generation," as one writer puts it.[43] Manchester certainly wasn't doing it for the money, for his advance was but $36,000, and the author's royalties after the first printing were to be donated to the John F. Kennedy Library in Massachusetts.[44]

A compulsive, tenacious researcher, Manchester personally visits every physical location in Dallas and Washington that figures in the story, from the grimy basement of the Dallas police department to the soaring Capitol Rotunda. Despite the authorized nature of the project, however, Johnson refrains from cooperating with Manchester for two reasons. The president certainly does not want to tell the unvarnished truth about November 22–25, 1963, believing it is not in his interest or the country's. Nor does he want to contribute to a philo-Kennedy narrative. Consequently, while Manchester conducts more than a thousand interviews, Johnson is the only central figure (besides Marina Oswald) who declines to be interrogated, though the president (via Jack Valenti) does reluctantly answer fourteen questions submitted in writing in June 1965.[45]

40. " 'Profile' Set on Kennedy," *Baltimore Sun,* 27 March 1964.

41. Manchester occupied Suite B-11, according to the stationery he printed up, and was also probably given a free telephone.

42. According to Manchester, "Jackie picked me because she thought I would be manageable." He had voluntarily submitted his draft of *Portrait of a President* to John Kennedy prior to publication. Manchester, *Controversy,* 6.

43. Corry, *Manchester Affair,* 24.

44. The advance was $217,000 in 2004 dollars. Manchester retained royalties from English rights outside of North America and from any translations; 25 percent of any book club or paperback money; and 100 percent of first serial rights. Harper & Row limited its profit to $35,000. Manchester, *Controversy,* 8.

45. Initially McGeorge Bundy told Manchester the president would sit for an interview following the 1964 election. In April 1965 Johnson promised to see Manchester after a direct request

Manchester's capacity for work is bottomless, and he is renowned for his ability to write for days with little or no sleep.[46] After two years of careful preparation, he finishes a draft of the manuscript in a manic, grueling burst of energy. In March 1966 he submits it to Evan Thomas, years before anyone anticipated it would be ready. Manchester is intent on publishing before Jim Bishop, who steadfastly refused to drop his project despite direct pleas from Mrs. Kennedy. Publishing first will presumably please her to no end.

By mid-August, New York and Washington are buzzing with rumors about what is being titled *The Death of a President,* especially Manchester's unflattering portrayal of Johnson's behavior in the immediate aftermath of Dallas. Naturally, the president is angry. His effort to refrain from expressing *his* frustrations over the way he was treated in November 1963 appears to have been in vain. But he is not surprised by the rumors, for they only confirm his own worst thoughts and feelings about Robert Kennedy's overweening ambition. Just how big a publishing event the book promises to be becomes manifest in early August, when *Look* magazine announces it has purchased first serial rights to the 1,287-page manuscript. *Look* pays a record amount—$665,000—for the rights, and Manchester suddenly stands to earn a windfall from his labor of love.[47]

Johnson's initial response to the unflattering rumors about his behavior occurs on August 22. He asks secretary Juanita Roberts to collect everything in the files about his contacts with Jacqueline Kennedy following the assassination.[48] A week later, on August 29, the White House is really stirred into action by an article in that morning's *Washington Post.* There are going to be

---

from Eunice Shriver, sister of the late president. In anticipation, Manchester drew up a list of proposed questions, but ultimately Johnson declined and responded in writing only. Johnson also refused to let Manchester hear the radio traffic recordings between *Air Force One* and Andrews AFB and denied him access to notes from November 22 written by Cliff Carter and Homer Thornberry. "I'm not under any obligation to Manchester," scrawled the president on a memo from Valenti. Once the nature of Manchester's book becomes apparent, Johnson will bitterly criticize Valenti for getting him to cooperate at all. Manchester to Valenti, memo, 12 April 1965; Valenti to Johnson, memo, 31 August 1965; and Conversation Between "A" (President Johnson) and "B" (probably Jake Jacobsen), undated, all in Manchester File, Box 1, Special File, LBJL. See also Corry, *Manchester Affair,* 42. Marina Oswald has her own book arrangement, which probably explains why she refused to be interviewed by Manchester. Her account will appear in Priscilla Johnson McMillan, *Marina and Lee* (New York: Harper & Row, 1977).

46. Manchester, *Controversy,* 9; Dexter Filkins, "Ailing Churchill Biographer Says He Can't Finish Trilogy," *New York Times,* 14 August 2001.

47. Homer Bigart, "Big Bid Reported for Book on Kennedy," *New York Times,* 5 August 1966. Although Bigart states $650,000 in his article, the correct figure is $665,000, or $3.8 million in 2004 dollars. Ultimately, Manchester will voluntarily turn over a large portion of his first serial rights income to the Kennedy Library.

48. Johnson and Roberts, conversation, 22 August 1966. While the subject matter has been identified, the tape recording of this conversation is still being processed as of the writing of this book and will be released as part of the WH series of Johnson tape recordings.

"200 page-one stories" in the Manchester book, according to the AP article.[49] Insofar as Johnson is concerned the first pejorative disclosure seems to involve the Kennedy "family Bible."[50] Allegedly, after Judge Sarah Hughes used it to swear Johnson in aboard *Air Force One,* she gave it to a man she assumed was a Secret Service agent. The Bible has not been seen since and was presumably stolen. At 9:30 a.m., the president, who is at his ranch to celebrate his fifty-eighth birthday with family and friends, organizes an extraordinary and extended group conversation over the telephone in an effort to find out what happened to the Bible. Besides the president, the discussion involves Abe Fortas in Washington, as well as Mrs. Johnson, Bill Moyers, and secretary Marie Fehmer.

Following the conversation, Fortas will enlist Clark Clifford in an effort to get to the bottom of the matter. After interviewing Judge Hughes and JFK aide Lawrence O'Brien, Fortas and Clifford believe they have the true story.[51] Manchester has his facts wrong, at least in this instance. The "very personal" Bible belonging to President Kennedy—ostensibly his "most cherished personal possession"—was in fact a Catholic missal or prayer book.[52] To all appearances it had never been opened, and it is not missing. Mrs. Johnson carried it with her as a memento when she disembarked at Andrews AFB.[53]

Even if the Bible story is easily disproven, however, there are many signs of other ominous stories in the offing. According to a *Look* executive quoted in the *Post* article, the "kind of material in [this book] doesn't usually find its way into print. . . . It's extraordinarily strong. The president is going to have to read it and I don't think he's going to like it."[54]

Simultaneously, another kind of rumor is circulating about the book. Word is out that the "inner circle of the [Kennedy] clan" is quite concerned about political repercussions from Manchester's opus.[55] In late August the *New York Times* reports persistent rumors of efforts by the family to "delay, censor, or squelch" *Look* magazine's planned serialization of the book. The Kennedys, according to the *Times,* are concerned that "certain episodes printed outside

49. Associated Press, "Peace Letter by Mrs. JFK Is Revealed," *Washington Post,* 29 August 1966; "Controversies: The Best Kennedy Book?" *Newsweek,* 5 September 1966. The AP article is actually about the story that is going to appear in the September 5 *Newsweek.*

50. Ibid.

51. Johnson and Fortas, conversation, 17 December 1966.

52. William Manchester, *The Death of a President: November 20–November 25, 1963* (New York: Harper & Row, 1967), 324, 328.

53. Liz Carpenter's Recollections of President Kennedy's Assassination, December 1963, Box 4; Fortas to Johnson, memo re Bible, 29 August 1966, President's Diary—November 22, 1963, Box 2; both in Special File, LBJL.

54. "Peace Letter by Mrs. JFK Is Revealed."

55. Kintner to Johnson, letter, 31 August 1966, Copies of Material from Jake Jacobsen's File, Box 4, Special File, LBJL.

the total context of the drama, might present some important individuals in an unsympathetic . . . light."[56]

Still, as far as the Johnson White House and the world know, the manuscript is going to be serialized and published. *Look* announces as much in a full-page advertisement in the *New York Times* on September 1, waving off the rumors of trouble and touting *The Death of a President* as the "most important book of 1967" if not "one of the most important historical documents of our time."[57]

The end of the summer is a tense time at the White House. Until now it has been plausible, if barely so, to deny the bitterness of the president's rift with Robert Kennedy and write it off as newspaper gossip.[58] The Manchester book, having the Kennedys' imprimatur, promises to make that impossible.

October 3

Monday
To Abe Fortas / 8:16 a.m.

Later in the afternoon, Johnson is swearing in Nicholas Katzenbach as the new undersecretary of state, replacing George Ball. Ramsey Clark will become the acting attorney general, and if the president decides to make Clark's appointment permanent, that will probably force the retirement of Clark's father, Supreme Court Justice Tom Clark. Not that Johnson is dismayed by the prospect; in fact, Clark's nomination may be contingent upon his father's willingness to step down from the Court. The elder Clark's resignation would permit Johnson to replace a somewhat conservative, sixty-seven-year-old Truman appointee with a younger and more liberal man, perhaps even the first Negro on the bench. Johnson has been grooming Thurgood Marshall, the solicitor general and the great-grandson of a slave, for the next Supreme Court vacancy.

If everything works out, this chain reaction of appointments will be the political equivalent of Johnson having his cake and eating it, too. Abe Fortas, who now sits on the Supreme Court courtesy of Lyndon Johnson, is helping the president by quietly keeping him abreast of Tom Clark's intentions. At the out-

56. Homer Bigart, "Pressure Denied on Kennedy Book," *New York Times,* 27 August 1966.

57. Corry, *Manchester Affair,* 125–26, 139.

58. As recently as June 1966, for example, Johnson tells *Newsweek* "he isn't aware" of any feud. It's all a "ploy" by the press. "The White House: LBJ vs. RFK," *Newsweek,* 13 June 1966.

set of this conversation, Fortas informs the president that Clark will send a letter today to Earl Warren, informing the chief justice that he will step down should his son receive a permanent appointment as attorney general.[59]

Following that discussion, the two men talk about the Supreme Court's internal politics and how they might be shaped to the administration's advantage. Johnson lobbies Fortas to have the Court accept a case or two so as to stress that law and order will prevail over the rising tide of criminal black militancy, lest white backlash increase.[60] Then, about two-thirds of the way through the twenty-five-minute conversation, Johnson turns to another burgeoning political phenomenon: the growing controversy over President Kennedy's assassination, three years after it occurred and two years after the *Warren Report* supposedly put the matter to rest.

The most interesting aspect of their remarks, by far, is Johnson's genuine suspicion that Robert Kennedy is the reason why the *Warren Report* is newly mired in controversy. To the president's mind, the senator is responsible for every adverse trend or development. Johnson believes that Kennedy thinks it is in his political interest to suggest that the Warren Commission did not get to the bottom of the assassination. The Commission is thus the first, and a most conspicuous, failing of the Johnson administration.

Johnson could hardly be more wrong. His suspicion is revealing only of his fixation on the senator, and Johnson's proclivity to relate things that are not connected. Robert Kennedy, in truth, has absolutely no interest in stirring up controversy about the assassination.[61] He "refused to involve himself in the problem of who had murdered his brother," as Arthur Schlesinger will later put it.[62] Kennedy's unchanging answer, whenever aides dare (and infrequently) bring the subject up, is uncharacteristically—even curiously—passive. "What differ-

59. Clark will, in fact, announce his retirement on February 28 after Ramsey Clark's confirmation. And at the conclusion of the 1966–67 Supreme Court term, President Johnson will name the fifty-eight-year-old Marshall to the vacancy left by Clark. Fred Graham, "Justice Retiring," *New York Times,* 1 March 1967; Roy Reed, "Marshall Named for High Court, Its First Negro," *New York Times,* 14 June 1967.

60. Johnson goes so far as to suggest that it would be a good idea to "let our new justice" (Thurgood Marshall) write this future opinion, as Fortas is well aware of the president's intention to nominate Marshall. "If he can be mean enough about criminals" he will get approved by the Senate, observes Fortas.

61. The same cannot be said for others in the Kennedy camp. When Richard Goodwin reviews Edward Epstein's *Inquest* for the *Washington Post* in July, he becomes the first member of the late president's "inner circle" to suggest that a public reexamination of the assassination is warranted. Goodwin's review is instrumental in elevating Epstein's critique to an undeserved level of respectability. Edith Evans Asbury, "Former Kennedy Aide Suggests Panel to Check *Warren Report,*" *New York Times,* 24 July 1966. Later, Arthur Schlesinger, Jr., will suggest a new inquiry too because of the "residue of uncertainty." Peter Kihss, "House Chiefs Back Warren Commission as Criticism Grows," *New York Times,* 23 November 1966.

62. Schlesinger, *Robert Kennedy,* 614.

ence does it make?" says Kennedy. Jack's dead, and nothing will bring him back to life.[63]

Johnson: Say, Bobby [Kennedy] is makin' quite a show of this assassination thing. [They] got a big story in *U.S. News [& World Report]* this week, [entitled the] "Truth About Kennedy Assassination: Questions Raised and Answered."[64] I haven't read it, but it looks like it does a good job for the Warren Commission.[65] But he's got everybody raisin' questions about it, [and] they claim now [that] the [William] Manchester book [is] gonna raise a lot of questions.[66] He's got Lou Harris runnin' a poll—

Fortas: Yes.

Johnson: And a good [many]—the majority of 'em doubt that this is the whole story on Kennedy. Did you see that poll?[67]

Fortas: Yes, sir. Now—

Johnson: And two percent of 'em think that *I* did it![68]

Fortas: Yeah.

Johnson: According to Lou Harris.

Fortas: Yeah.

Johnson: Now, Lou Harris is just *owned* by Bobby.

Fortas: Sure.

Johnson: He's got him makin' polls all over the country. He got him to make this one showin' that he beat me [by] two points, which was a phony at the time, although I think it's true *now*.[69] Because I think that they've sold the poll all over the country.[70]

63. Ibid.; Evan Thomas, *Robert Kennedy: His Life* (New York: Simon & Schuster, 2000), 333.

64. "Truth About Kennedy Assassination: Questions Raised and Answered," *U.S. News & World Report,* 10 October 1966. The story is featured on the cover.

65. Johnson is pointing out that this story is an exception to a barrage of articles and books that are almost unanimously critical.

66. The president is suggesting that Manchester's forthcoming book will diverge from the findings in the *Warren Report.* In fact, Manchester will affirm the Commission's verdict.

67. Louis Harris, "The Harris Survey: Country, 3–2, Rejects Main Argument of Warren Report on Kennedy Slaying," *Washington Post,* 3 October 1966. According to the survey, 34 percent of Americans subscribe to the conclusions of the *Warren Report,* 46 percent believe in a conspiracy of some kind, and 20 percent don't know. Johnson is adding the latter two percentages together.

68. Ibid. According to the Harris poll, about as many Americans think Johnson was behind the president's assassination (2 percent) as believe Fidel Castro was responsible (1 percent). This is the first time Johnson has been so linked to the assassination in a Harris poll. He is insulted by the insinuation, and indignant that Harris listed his name.

69. A Lou Harris poll published in late September showed that 51 percent of voters interviewed favor Robert Kennedy as the Democratic nominee in 1968, while 49 percent prefer Lyndon Johnson. Andrew Glass, "Robert Kennedy Bars Race in 1968 for Either President or the No. 2 Spot," *Washington Post,* 6 October 1966.

70. Johnson is suggesting that the Harris poll is actually contributing to his decline in public opinion surveys.

Fortas: Yeah.

Johnson: And I think everybody says, Oh, God. And I read *seven stories* [in various newspapers] this weekend where nobody wanted me, and the very people that [supposedly] weren't wantin' me [in] North Carolina were up here the day before yesterday, *beggin'* me to come.[71] The governor came up himself . . . but Bobby puts out that stuff, and all of 'em write it! [The] *Baltimore Sun* wrote it; *New York Time[s]* wrote it; [and the] *Washington Post* wrote it.[72] He had one backgrounder up on the [Capitol] Hill. . . .

Fortas: Yes.

Johnson: I don't how to deal with that.

Fortas: Well, on the Warren Commission thing itself . . . I . . . you know, [Jake] Jacobsen called—[73]

Johnson: Yeah.

Fortas: —the chief [justice], and then the chief called me in, and asked me if I can handle it for him. He didn't think he oughta handle it direct. And I called Jake, and told him [that] the chief wouldn't reply to his inquiry, but . . . [he] oughta get in touch with me, keep me informed.
Now, I . . . there is one thing—

Johnson: Well, I didn't have—he didn't make any *inquiry* of him, did he?

Fortas: Sir?

Johnson: He [Jacobsen] didn't make any inquiry of the chief, did he?

Fortas: Ah—

Johnson: I thought he just told him to . . . call this to his attention and see that his general counsel *knew* that this effort was goin' on, so that they wouldn't overlook it.[74]

Fortas: Oh, well, ah. . . .

Johnson: That's what I told him [to do].

Fortas: [The chief] thought he wanted some comment back. But it [doesn't] matter].

71. On Thursday, Johnson had lunch with eleven governors, one of whom was Dan K. Moore (D) from North Carolina. Carroll Kilpatrick, "11 Governors Meet LBJ at Lunch Today," *Washington Post,* 29 September 1966.

72. Laurie Holder, "Carolina Loath to Invite LBJ," *Washington Post,* 2 October 1966. The *Post* story alleges that "Moore's administration opposes a presidential appearance" in the weeks just before the November elections.

73. Jacobsen, a Texas lawyer, carries the title of special counsel to the president, and probably spends more time with Johnson than any other single person on the staff. He has contacted the chief justice at the president's request.

74. The president seems to be hoping that the chief justice and J. Lee Rankin, the Commission's general counsel, will be stirred into action by the attacks and speak out publicly thereby putting an end to Robert Kennedy's alleged effort to impugn the *Warren Report*. The chief justice has stubbornly taken the position that everything he has to say about the matter is within the pages of the *Report.* Peter Kihss, "Warren Panel, Under Attacks, Stands Firm on Its Findings in Kennedy Death 3 Years Ago," *New York Times,* 22 November 1966.

Johnson: No, no. No, all I wanted him [Jacobsen] to do is [to] tell his [Warren's] law clerk, if he knew him, that he oughta remind—*tell* the chief, that this was headin' up, up here in the Senate building—[75]

Fortas: Yes.

Johnson: —he oughta watch it, and [that he] oughta have [J. Lee] Rankin and whoever he *had*—

Fortas: Yeah.

Johnson: —to kinda *look* at these things. I'd clip this poll of Harris's, for instance—

Fortas: Hmm.

Johnson: —and I'd put it on top of my file. I'd take these interviews, and put 'em on. I would keep a little eye on each one of these guys that writes an article.

Fortas: Well, I—there's some—[there's] a couple of things that I'm doing, that [are] . . . not quite ready. But number one, the chief and I talked about this. I told him I thought somebody oughta write a book on his side, [and] do it right away. And he thinks the best man to do that is Lee Rankin, who was counsel to the committee [*sic*], you know, who was [also] Eisenhower's solicitor general.

Johnson: Yeah.

Fortas: And he was counsel to the Warren committee [*sic*].

Johnson: Yeah.

Fortas: I think that's a fine idea. I don't think it'll *work,* because Rankin is counselor up in the city of New York to [John] Lindsay.[76] But in any event, the chief's gonna ask him [in] the next day or two.

Johnson: I see.

Fortas: That's number one. Number two [is]—

Johnson: Why won't he? You just don't think he'll have time to do it?

Fortas: That's right. Yes . . . otherwise, he'd do it. He's a fine man.
Number two: Mr. President, you know that—

Johnson: Would he [Rankin] be a good man for us to have as solicitor general?[77]

Fortas: Well, he *was* solicitor general.[78]

Johnson: I say, would he've been—

Fortas: He'd be grand but he . . . I doubt if he'd want to come back and do it.

Johnson: Why would he want to be counselor in New York then?

---

75. Johnson is suggesting that criticism of the *Warren Report* is ultimately traceable to the machinations of Senator Kennedy.

76. Rankin was appointed the New York City corporation counsel (in effect, the lawyer for New York City) in December 1965 by John Lindsay, then the mayor-elect.

77. Johnson is suggesting that Rankin might replace Thurgood Marshall.

78. Rankin was solicitor general from 1956 to 1961.

Fortas: Oh, I don't know. Politics, I guess, get in [the] political swing [of things] . . . he's a first-rate man.[79]

Johnson: Well, maybe he oughta be deputy [attorney general].[80]

Fortas: That's a place where you make all your poli[tical]—all your appointments.

Johnson: Yeah.

Fortas: [And] he's a *Republican.*

Johnson: Hmm.

Fortas: Why that could be kinda rough.

Johnson: Okay.

Fortas: Mr. President, there are two things I wanna mention to you about this. Number one, were you *aware* that . . . about this testimony of [Lee Harvey] Oswald's wife, saying that there came a *day* when he put on his pistol [and] was going down [to] shoot the vice president?[81]

Johnson: No, uh . . . Jake told me that.

Fortas: Oh, I told Jake; that's right.[82]

Johnson: Yeah.

Fortas: Well, I've got that all buttoned down now. And it's a day when you were in Dallas, and [Richard] Nixon was not; she meant *you,* and not Nixon. Now that's . . . that he's gonna shoot, you see?[83]

Johnson: Uh-huh.

Fortas: Now, number two—

Johnson: Why didn't that ever come out?[84]

Fortas: Heh . . . I don't know. I don't think our publicity's very good. *[chuckles]* Number two . . . and this I don't know whether I'm at liberty to use, and I'm trying to find out more about it. There is, in the vault of the Federal Bureau of Investigation—this is [what] the chief told me—President Kennedy's clothes. Those clothes quite clearly refute the main charge that's been made, and that is, that one of the bullets came from the *front.*

79. Rankin and Lindsay were old friends, having served together in the Justice Department during the 1950s. Lindsay, a former congressman with Kennedyesque good looks and breeding, is considered a rising star in the Republican Party's moderate to liberal wing, which Rankin supports. Lindsay "has hopes and dreams that must be accomplished," explained Rankin in 1965. Ibid.

80. The number two post at Justice will be vacant if Clark remains attorney general.

81. Marina Oswald testified before the Warren Commission in June 1964 that her husband had threatened to shoot the vice president in April 1963. She believed Oswald meant Nixon, but the only vice president in Dallas around that time was Johnson. *Warren Report,* 188.

82. Fortas may have had the story pointed out to him by Warren himself.

83. Fortas seems to think that if Johnson is widely accepted as Oswald's target, too, then rumors about the president's involvement might diminish.

84. This fact did come out, but only as a sidebar during newspapers' extensive coverage of the Warren Commission's findings in September 1964. That Johnson is unaware of it reveals his general lack of familiarity with the *Warren Report.* "Shot at Walker Laid to Oswald," *New York Times,* 28 September 1964.

Because the fabric on those clothes show that the bullet came from behind, [because of] the way that fabric [was] pressed out.

Now, I'm checking into that more extensively. I've got one of my law clerks, whom I have total confidence [in], checking into that. And if it checks out, I'm gonna . . . I'd like to talk with you about it and see whether we can't get it [out and use it] some way . . . get some publicity, or maybe you could get those clothes released. It was never talked about, and the clothes were put in the FBI vault just because of Mrs. Kennedy's feelings.[85]

Johnson: I would doubt that. I'll bet ten dollars they're in the archives of the Kennedys.[86] I saw a story last night somewhere, where Bobby had . . . no, it's this *morning,* in the *U.S. News* that's out today, that he had seized all the pictures . . . *[as if reading]* "missing X-ray pictures that provide the major remaining mystery about the facts in the assassination of President Kennedy are reported . . . some officials [are] concerned, had been taken over soon after the assassination by Robert Kennedy, then attorney general, [and] placed in the Kennedy archive."

Fortas: [That's odd].

Johnson: *[as if still reading]* "They reportedly were never offered to the Warren Commission investigatin' the assassination, because this would have involved publication in the *Report* of the gory, death pictures [of the president]."[87]

Fortas: Oh, good Lord. Well, the chief thinks they're . . . I'll find out about that. The chief thinks that the clothing's over in the FBI vault, and he also [says] there's also a picture . . . of the . . . President Kennedy's brains from the autopsy, that's very important, Mr. President. But I'm gonna follow all this through and get you a report just as fast as possible, and then maybe we can figure out something to do with it.

Johnson: Okay. I sure think we ought to, and I think you oughta point this . . . these little things up. Each week, they hit 'em. Now they got an agency up there . . . they tell me they got forty-one men workin'—

85. Fortas is wrong to suggest the clothes were "never talked about." The clothes' evidentiary value is summarized in the *Warren Report,* discussed at length in direct, expert testimony, and pictures of the clothes appear in supplementary volume 17 as Commission Exhibits 393–395. *Warren Report,* 92.

86. Johnson probably means the clothes are under the Kennedys' complete control but physically housed at the National Archives, along with other sensitive and vital evidence like the postmortem X-rays and photographs. "Truth About Kennedy Assassination."

87. The withholding of the X-rays and photographs from the Warren Commission, along with the fact that they are not among the Commission's records at the National Archives, the supposed repository for all evidentiary materials on the assassination, first became public knowledge in July. Jacob Cohen, "What the *Warren Report* Omits: The Vital Documents," *The Nation,* 11 July 1966. Under pressure, the Kennedy family will turn these materials over to the custody of the National Archives in November. Fred Graham, "Autopsy Photos Put in Archives by the Kennedys," *New York Times,* 2 November 1966.

Fortas: Yes, sir.

Johnson: —[at] the Kennedy foundation.[88]

Fortas: Yes.

Johnson: And they just busy at this stuff *all* day long.

Fortas: Yeah.

Johnson: Just all day . . . okay.

Fortas: Right, sir. Right.

October 6

Thursday
From Abe Fortas / 6:02 p.m.

Just as the president desires, the press is reporting that Johnson is thinking about making Ramsey Clark's appointment permanent. Justice Fortas begins the conversation by reading Johnson the text of Tom Clark's letter to Earl Warren in light of these press reports. The elder Clark promises the chief justice he will retire should his son be nominated as attorney general, and then confirmed by the Senate. Fortas says the letter is "just exactly right . . . [we] worked it out together." The president is satisfied too. "That's it," says Johnson. "That's it."

Fortas turns next to the matter of the Warren Commission, and Johnson's angst over the wave of attacks on the Commission's findings. Johnson fears that if criticism of the *Warren Report* is not met head-on, the relatively new insinuation that he had something to do with his predecessor's violent death will only grow. As revealed in the previous conversation, Johnson would like the chief justice and J. Lee Rankin to speak out against the critics. Toward the end of this conversation, however, Fortas suggests that it might be better for the FBI to come to the Warren Commission's defense.

Johnson again traces the attacks on the Commission to Robert Kennedy's invisible hand and influence over the media. Indeed, the president attributes virtually *every* adverse story of the past four years, going back to the Billie Sol Estes scandal, to Kennedy's ostensible ability to plant stories in the press. It is a sinister, powerful tactic "Bobby" learned from his father, or so Johnson believes.

88. It is not clear whether Johnson means the Kennedys' family foundation, the Joseph P. Kennedy, Jr., Foundation, or the organization that is working to establish the John F. Kennedy Library in Massachusetts. Jack Star, "The Kennedy Legend," *Look,* 30 June 1964.

Fortas: Now, more on this . . . terrible stuff about the Warren Commission. The chief [justice] told me yesterday . . . and he's developing a slow *burn* on this thing . . . and he's taken himself to attend today . . . to it. He [Warren] thinks what he ought to do is to get Lee Rankin to come down here, who was the chief counsel to the committee *[sic],* you know—

Johnson: Yes.

Fortas: —and then work some way out for the committee, including himself, [and me], et cetera, [to] take a good hard look at this thing.

Johnson: I just sure think that's indicated more than *anything I know.* 'Cause this man [Robert Kennedy] has these forty folks, and they just go around and plant things [in the press]. And it's the *damnedest* thing you ever saw.

Fortas: Yes.

Johnson: And you know, poor little Eddie [Weisl], he cried one time when I went on the [Democratic] ticket in '60.[89] And [he] just said to me, if you do it, [he] said, you'll be destroyed. You just don't have *any idea* what I [Weisl] went through, and what's happenin'.[90]

One time I was down in Palm Beach, [Florida], and the old man [Joseph Kennedy] said to me, That *sonofabitch* [Weisl] . . . [and] what he [Kennedy] said about his [Weisl's Jewish] ancestry and everything else, is the worst you ever *heard* about Eddie Weisl.[91]

Fortas: Uh-huh.

Johnson: But I have just been *watching* this thing. And I know I don't have an obsession. And I know I'm not a *mean man.* And I know I'm not after *anybody.*

Fortas: Uh-huh.

Johnson: But I look into this whole picture, and I'm *convinced* that's where [Thomas] Dodd got all [of] his problems. I'm *convinced* that's where *every* bit of the problem—[and] I wouldn't tell anybody but you—I'm convinced that's where *all* the problem of Bobby Baker started.

Fortas: Uh-huh.

Johnson: I'm convinced that that's the . . . *all* the problem with [J. William] Fulbright.

Fortas: Uh-huh.

Johnson: It's headed up right there. He [Kennedy] supplied Fulbright these reports on Dodd and on Julius Klein.[92] He brought 'em all up and gave

89. Weisl urged Johnson not to become Kennedy's running mate in Los Angeles.

90. Weisl was speaking about the Kennedys' ability to influence the press.

91. As noted earlier, Weisl engaged in a bitter corporate battle with Joseph Kennedy in the mid-1930s, during which the family patriarch was accused of making vicious, anti-Semitic remarks about Weisl. Rowland Evans and Robert Novak, *Lyndon B. Johnson: The Exercise of Power* (London: George Allen and Unwin, 1967), 281. Fortas, of course, is also Jewish.

92. Since early 1963, Fulbright, chairman of the Foreign Relations Committee, has been conducting a probe of lobbyists registered with the Justice Department as agents of foreign govern-

'em to Fulbright. He's got the whole thing stirred. Somebody . . . comes in the other day and tells me that on the Billie Sol Estes thing, he [Kennedy] did all the Billie Sol thing and wouldn't let 'em give 'em to [J. Edgar] Hoover—the agricultural reports—because *anything* he wanted to be sure [if] . . . if he couldn't find some way [of it] pertaining to Johnson—[93]

Fortas: Uh-huh.

Johnson: —even back there, when I was just been *[sic]* vice president a year or so . . . all of that went on. Do you remember the *real* battle on that?

He has [Drew] Pearson, now, that he's givin' regular leaks to, besides [columnist Rowland] Evan[s]. He's had at least a half a dozen books written that go out and *suggest* the books.[94] He's infiltrated the press in Nashville, Los Angeles, [and] Detroit . . . each place with one of his men, and then this *man* works feverishly to get these things done.[95] He takes about six [or] eight [or] ten columnists up . . . *regularly*. And they come back, then they spew out. [And] it'll be the Warren Commission this week; the next week, it'll be the cities. The next week it'll be poverty, and how we're spendin' money on beautification and not on poverty. And *all* the time he's *way* in the background, and never seen. But these things are *movin'*.

And I would just think of the folks that have been subjected to great difficulties connected with me [like] Walter Jenkins. I don't *where* that came from, but I know somewhere that . . . that thing's there.[96] I know that Tom Dodd . . . I know that the *Fulbright* thing . . . he's been *feeding* that with *[indistinct]*. He brought him the reports on the foreign agents, you remember—[97]

Fortas: I know.

---

ments. One of the most controversial relationships has turned out to be the one between Senator Thomas Dodd and Julius Klein, a Chicago public relations executive and registered foreign agent for West Germany. Dodd, who is staunchly anti-Communist and a close Senate ally of the president, is now undergoing an ethics investigation because of his alleged efforts on Klein's behalf. Ben Franklin, "Aide Says Dodd Talked with Adenauer for Klein," *New York Times,* 25 June 1966. Johnson is wrong to believe that Kennedy is the source of Dodd's problem. Former aides disgruntled with Dodd photocopied documents from the senator's files, and have been leaking them to muckraking columnists Drew Pearson and Jack Anderson since 1965. Jack Anderson, *Peace, War, and Politics* (New York: Forge, 1999), 126–28.

93. An FBI investigation of the Agriculture Department's dealings with Estes led to his 1963 conviction on mail fraud and conspiracy charges. Dallek, *Flawed Giant,* 39–40.

94. What Johnson means by this assertion is unclear.

95. Johnson is apparently referring to former Kennedy aides who are now in prominent newspaper jobs. John Seigenthaler, RFK's former administrative assistant, is editor of the *Nashville Tennessean;* Edwin Guthman, a former press secretary, is the national editor for the *Los Angeles Times.* The reference to Detroit is unknown.

96. Johnson means Kennedy's invisible hand.

97. At the outset of Fulbright's investigation in 1963, then attorney general Robert Kennedy naturally made available Justice Department documents on registered foreign agents.

Johnson: —and the John Connally thing.[98] And *now* he's creating great doubt about whether or not I . . . I really, uh, killed the president![99]

Fortas: Yeah.

Johnson: And I *know* he's got Lou Harris, *body and soul*.[100]

Fortas: Yeah.

Johnson: I know he . . . he suggests these things. Ah . . . a *month* before they ever conducted the survey, Harris was tellin' our boy that he had great *pressure* to run a survey, but he didn't see how they could hang it on. Looks like the people couldn't understand a survey on '68 when neither of us were runnin' and it was three years *[sic]* [be]fore '68. But by God, they ran it. And it came out right [for Kennedy]: 51 [to] 49 [percent].[101]

Fortas: *[chuckling]* Yeah.

Johnson: And nobody ever asked a question why it was run.

Fortas: It was a real phony, too.[102]

Johnson: I think the whole *thing* is that, and that's what they build toward. But I don't know what to *do* about it.

Fortas: I, ah . . . did Marvin [Watson]—

Johnson: And if you'd listen to [J.] Edgar [Hoover], *hmm*!

Fortas: Did Marvin tell you on the . . . that I suggested that . . . *really*, the outfit that's under attack on this Warren [Commission] thing is a, ah, basically . . . an FBI—

Johnson: Well, if we had somebody with enough sense for the statements, and the *reasoning* behind it. But you just did like a . . . steer: you've lost your social standing in the community where you reside.

Fortas: *[chuckles]*

Johnson: You're *cut* up there on that damn [Supreme] Court.

Fortas: I did what?

Johnson: I say, you're like the . . . somebody asked me, he said, What's the difference between a steer and a bull?

Fortas: Yeah.

Johnson: The fella said, Well he's one that's lost his social standing in the community where he resides.

Fortas: *[breaks into hearty laughter]*

98. The meaning of the reference to Connally is unknown.

99. Johnson is speaking for effect. What he really means is that Kennedy, by allegedly helping to impugn the *Warren Report,* is lending credence to the innuendo that Johnson was complicit in the assassination.

100. See footnotes 67 and 68.

101. See footnote 69.

102. Fortas may be referring to the fact that the survey polled all voters rather than voters who identified themselves as Democrats. Glass, "Robert Kennedy Bars Race in 1968 for Either President or the No. 2 Spot."

Johnson: And you've just been *cut* when I put you on that damned Supreme Court. I wish Carol never had talked me into it.[103]

Fortas: *[still laughing]*

Johnson: *[joins in the laughter]*

Fortas: Yeah . . . I'll tell her that . . . I'll tell her that.

Well, I've got a very elaborate memorandum on . . . from which I think J. Edgar [Hoover] could draw a statement. You know, you've got a very close friend down there [at the FBI] in [Deke] DeLoach.

Johnson: I would sure tell him to do it. And I'd get him in it . . . hard.

[Discussion turns to a case pending before the Supreme Court that involves FBI electronic surveillance during Kennedy's years as attorney general; Johnson reiterates his adamant opposition to unfettered eavesdropping. The "whole republic revolves" on the right to be protected from such intrusive tactics].[104]

Fortas: Well, uh . . . [do] you think I oughta talk to Deke about [the Warren Commission]—

Johnson: *Yes, sir, yes, sir, yes sir.* Strong as a human can.

Fortas: You know, he's sorta . . . his relations with his boss [Hoover] aren't always very good.

Johnson: *[sounding surprised]* They're not?

Fortas: No. Sometimes the . . . you know, the boss thinks he's gettin' too uppity.

Johnson: I didn't know that.

Fortas: Yeah.

Johnson: They tell me that documents about . . . whether these [wiretaps and bugs] were authorized are now declassified.[105]

Fortas: Oh, really?

Johnson: Uh-huh.

Fortas: *[chuckles]*

Johnson: *[aside]* Who declassified them?

[to Fortas] Edgar did.

Fortas: *[laughs]*

Johnson: Hmm?

Fortas: That's great, and he'll go get him [Kennedy]. All right, sir, well then, I'll follow through on this Warren [Commission business]—

103. Carol Agger is the justice's wife, and the two men are laughing because Mrs. Fortas was dead set against her husband's 1965 appointment to the Supreme Court. She refused to speak to Johnson for two months after it was announced. Laura Kalman, *Abe Fortas: A Biography* (New Haven, Conn.: Yale University Press, 1990), 242–45.

104. On the impropriety of discussing this case, see ibid., 313–17, and Athan Theoharis, ed., *From the Secret Files of J. Edgar Hoover* (Chicago: Elephant, 1993), 267–75.

105. In a dramatic escalation of their feud, Hoover will release internal documents allegedly proving that Robert Kennedy knew and approved of the FBI's electronic surveillance during his tenure as attorney general. Victor Navasky, *Kennedy Justice* (New York: Atheneum, 1971), 76–78.

Johnson: I can't talk to that fellow that . . . leader, but *you* sure can.

Fortas: All right. *[indistinct]*

Johnson: And I just . . . I'll leave here tomorrow and go to be a poor peasant and wear a wooden shoe, and have a purple vine growin' around my door. I'd rather have *all that* than be that personification of *murder* known as Napoleon the Great. [You] know what old [Robert] Ingersoll said?[106] Well then, that's the way I'd be. I'd rather be a poor peasant and wear a wooden shoe and have a purple vine *around my door* than to let this thing go on.[107]

Fortas: Yes . . . exactly.

Johnson: All *right.* 'Bye.

The Warren Commission will never convene again to consider the criticisms of its findings, or issue a rebuttal as a body. But three days after the assassination's third anniversary, J. Edgar Hoover will release a statement on the *Warren Report,* ostensibly in response to a request from the *Washington Star.* It will be the first comment the FBI has made in two years on the adequacy of the Warren Commission's probe and on alleged discrepancies between the Commission's findings and the bureau's initial claims. Hoover notes that while there are some differences between the two, ultimately "there is no conflict." "All available evidence and facts point to one conclusion—that Oswald acted alone," concludes Hoover.[108] The flatness of the director's statement puts a damper on calls for a reinvestigation of the assassination.

106. Colonel Robert G. Ingersoll, 1833–1899, was an American original. The son of a Congregationalist minister, a lawyer by profession, and a decorated Civil War veteran, he was made famous by his gift for oratory and known as the "Great Agnostic" for his deep antipathy to organized religion. "Robert G. Ingersoll Dead," *New York Times,* 22 July 1899.

107. While Johnson often recites stories or anecdotes, this is one of the rare instances where he attempts to make a point by quoting a famous saying. Ingersoll's exact words, after visiting Napoleon's tomb, were, "I would rather have been a French peasant and worn wooden shoes. I would rather have lived in a hut with a vine growing over the door and the grapes growing purple in the kisses of the autumn sun. I would rather have been that poor peasant with my loving wife by my side, knitting as the day died out of the sky, with my children upon my knee and their arms about me. I would rather have been that man and gone down to the tongueless silence of the dreamless dust than to have been that imperial impersonation of force and murder known as Napoleon the Great." Johnson is searching for the most powerful words he knows so as to convey just how contemptible he finds the insinuation that he had anything to do with the assassination. He almost certainly learned this peroration from his mother, Rebekah Baines Johnson, who once taught public speaking, or, as it was called at the turn of the century, "elocution." Robert Dallek, *Lone Star Rising: Lyndon Johnson and His Times, 1908–1960* (New York: Oxford University Press, 1991), 37.

108. UPI, "Text of Statement by Hoover on the *Warren Report,*" and Fred Graham, "Hoover Says Facts Show Oswald Alone Was Kennedy Killer," both in *New York Times,* 26 November 1966. The temperate and reasoned tone of the statement—so unlike Hoover—indicates that Fortas may have played some role in drafting it, as is suggested by the October 6 conversation.

December 5

Monday
From Nicholas Katzenbach / 10:46 a.m., CST[109]

While the crisis in confidence over the *Warren Report* shows signs of ebbing by early December, the controversy over Manchester's book is escalating. Currently, only a miniscule percentage of Americans believe the president was complicit in the assassination, as the Harris poll published in October indicated for the first time. But as the *Wall Street Journal* accurately observes on November 25, the White House fears that Manchester's portrayal of Johnson's "beastly" behavior "will subtly fan the nasty whispers of far-right and far-left crackpots: that Lyndon himself had some hand in the assassination."[110] The depth of the president's anger over this insinuation may explain a lingering mystery about an event that occurred while Johnson was spending the Thanksgiving holiday at his ranch. After engaging in what was an undoubtedly frank conversation with trusted counselor Abe Fortas, Johnson ordered the Dictabelt recording of their conversation destroyed. It is the only known, documented instance during the Johnson years when a recording was "destroyed on [the] president's instruction."[111]

During the course of this long conversation with Katzenbach, Johnson expresses his exasperation over the stories that are leaking out about Manchester's forthcoming book. Reportedly, Manchester alleges that on the evening of November 21, in a Houston hotel room, John Kennedy and Lyndon Johnson got into a heated argument during their last one-on-one meeting. The Manchester manuscript is also said to open with the claim that President Kennedy felt his trip to Texas was unnecessary, even an "imposition." Lyndon ought to be able to heal the breach in his state's Democratic Party on his own, or so Kennedy allegedly thought.[112]

Johnson will not just talk about published leaks here, because he raises several allegations about his behavior that have not yet appeared in print. The

---

109. As of the writing of this book, the Johnson Library has released only the assassination-related portion of this conversation.

110. "Washington Wire," *Wall Street Journal,* 25 November 1966.

111. Daily Diary, 24 November 1966, LBJL. The ten- to fifteen-minute call, which occurred at 1:47 p.m., was from the president to Fortas, returning the justice's call.

112. Homer Bigart, "Pressure Denied on Kennedy Book," *New York Times,* 27 August 1966; William Manchester, *Death,* 3.

president has not, and will not, read the manuscript himself. But he is hearing about it directly in great detail. Without inordinate difficulty, press secretary Bill Moyers has managed to get a copy of the *Look* galley proofs from Richard Goodwin, the chief speechwriter in the White House from mid-1964 to late 1965 and Moyers's close friend during the Kennedy/Johnson years.[113] The 139-page photocopy of the *Look* galleys is the hottest underground publication in existence, next to the entire manuscript.[114]

Hayes Redmon, an assistant to Moyers, has been compiling a list of derogatory comments concerning Johnson as gleaned from the galleys. The list stands at thirty-eight as of December 2, and Redmon is still counting.[115]

Johnson: It's just like this Manchester stuff about [John] Kennedy and I havin' an *argument*. I never had an argument with him in my *life* . . . and incidentally, Nick, that thing is full of *forty-six mean, vicious errors,* and they comin' *[approximately five seconds excised].*

[I mean] it's just so *unfair,* like my callin' him up and makin' him put a deer head in his outer room, [as if] he didn't want to.[116] *[dismissively]* I never called him in my *life* on it. He had his fish up there, that he caught at his honeymoon, and he *put* his deer head up there. And my forcin' him to go to Texas . . . I never *heard* of it. Matter of fact I tried to *postpone it,* and told him our popularity's too low.[117] But *all* that kind of stuff, it's just gonna [be] really raucous when it comes out. I want to talk to you about it *sometime* to see if there's *anything* that we can do to at least *moderate* their charges.

My yellin' around that John Connally had three-hundred-dollar suits . . . I never did it in my *life,* he never *had* one! He buys 'em off the rack; he's got a good figure, he doesn't have to do like *I* do.

113. Moyers has been press secretary since George Reedy resigned in July 1965. The characterization of his friendship with Goodwin is from Richard Goodwin, *Remembering America: A Voice from the Sixties* (Boston: Little, Brown, 1988), 267.

114. Copies of the manuscript were distributed to six separate magazines to stimulate serialization bids. Rumors abound that office boys are running off copies on Xerox machines and selling them privately. James Reston, "Washington: Farewell to Camelot," *New York Times,* 18 December 1966; Corry, *Manchester Affair,* 73; "The Assassination: 'Death of Lancer,'" *Newsweek,* 17 July 1967.

115. Redmon to Moyers, memo, 2 December 1966, Manchester File, Box 1, Special File, LBJL.

116. President-elect Kennedy had visited the Johnson ranch and gone deer hunting on November 17, 1960. Johnson then had the deer heads mounted, and presented them as gifts to his guests.

117. Johnson's claim will be confirmed by an article in a Texas newspaper the following month. Margaret Mayer, "Memo Gives New Insight into JFK Trip Background," *Dallas Times Herald,* 13 January 1967. Mayer will divulge the contents of an internal memo from the *Times Herald*'s Austin bureau dated 11 September 1963, which confirms that JFK insisted on going to Texas to raise money.

But . . . just *pure* stuff . . . *all* of it makes Bobby [Kennedy] look like a great hero and makes me look like a *son-of-a-bitch,* and *95 percent* of it is completely fabricated.

Katzenbach: Hmm.

Johnson: Visionary . . . he [Manchester] doesn't even remember that I *talked* to Bobby [from aboard *Air Force One*]. *[bitter laugh]* Yet he's got you callin' at his [Kennedy's] instructions, and readin' the oath. Just *all kinds* of stuff. And *that* thing is gonna *require* a book or two to *answer* it, you see.[118] And when it does, they gonna hit back the other way, and it's not gonna do the *country* any good.

December 16

Friday
From Abe Fortas / 4 p.m.

Manchester was exhausted, yet euphoric, after submitting his manuscript in March. The first private indication that something might be seriously amiss came in early May, during a Connecticut cocktail party. While the author was talking to a man who still worked for President Johnson, Richard Goodwin sauntered over. Having read the manuscript at Manchester's request, he said, "Manchester has written a great book, but your boss and my ex-boss may not think so."[119] Goodwin is destined to play a Rasputin-like role in the Manchester affair.

The first public hint that the Kennedys were less than enthusiastic about Manchester's work surfaced in late August, when the *New York Times* reported efforts to "delay, censor, or squelch" *Look* magazine's planned serialization of the book.[120] But the Kennedys were said to have no problem with the book as a whole, which was scheduled to be published by Harper & Row early in 1967. In truth, the serialization issue was only the tip of an iceberg.

Once Evan Thomas read the manuscript, he became deeply troubled. *The Death of a President* has the makings of a "really considerable piece of work,"

118. The excerpt of this conversation as printed in Jeff Shesol's dual biography is incorrect. Johnson clearly says "require a book or two to answer it," not "gonna require a look or two [before] answer[ing] it." Jeff Shesol, *Mutual Contempt: Lyndon Johnson, Robert Kennedy, and the Feud That Defined a Decade* (New York: W. W. Norton, 1997), 357.

119. Manchester, *Controversy,* 17.

120. Bigart, "Pressure Denied on Kennedy Book."

he wrote in May, "one might almost say a great book." Yet Thomas was also astounded by Manchester's violation of the norms by which reputable publishing houses treat a sitting president of the United States. The book is "gratuitously and tastelessly insulting to [President] Johnson," Thomas told journalists Edwin Guthman and John Seigenthaler, the two associates of Robert Kennedy charged with vetting the manuscript.[121] Thomas was concerned less about Johnson's reputation than with the potential for harm to Robert Kennedy's. The book will be an association Kennedy cannot escape, and publication of the manuscript in its current form, Thomas feared, will damage the senator politically.

Years later Manchester will caustically describe Thomas as "a highly complex man . . . [whose] air of crusty independence was misleading. Under it he was eager to be accommodating toward celebrated men and women, a trait which won him many famous friends."[122] Thomas was not alone in his thinking, however. Kennedy intimates predisposed to cast Johnson in the worst possible light, such as Arthur Schlesinger, Jr., told Manchester that his portrait of Johnson "too often acquires an exaggerated symbolism." Critics will say Manchester treats Johnson as the embodiment of the "forces of violence and irrationality which ran rampant through his native state and were responsible for the tragedy of Dallas."[123] Another unidentified reader noted that the manuscript's main proposition seems to be that "Lyndon Johnson had a heavy personal responsibility for the Dallas climate that . . . made the assassination possible."[124] In a less guarded moment Manchester even admitted to his hostility: "though I tried desperately to suppress my bias against a certain eminent statesman who always reminds me of somebody in a Grade D movie on the late show," Manchester wrote Jacqueline Kennedy in July, "the prejudice showed through."[125]

Throughout the summer five gifted writers and Kennedy men—Thomas, Seigenthaler, and Guthman, joined by Schlesinger and Goodwin—labored over the manuscript and made editorial suggestions, many of which were incorporated by Manchester.[126] For a two-week period in late July, the author believed he had won from Robert Kennedy a release to publish, for the agreement gave the family the right to approve the manuscript. But on August 10 the senator reneged, and asked Harper & Row to neither publish the book nor allow it to be

121. Corry, *Manchester Affair,* 61.

122. Manchester, *Controversy,* 7.

123. Schlesinger, *Robert Kennedy,* 761.

124. Richard Rovere, "A Question of Taste and Something More," *The New Yorker,* 8 April 1967.

125. Corry, *Manchester Affair,* 87. Manchester will later deny, in a letter to Liz Carpenter, that he was referring to Lyndon Johnson. But the only "eminent statesman" who comes off badly is the president. Manchester to Carpenter, letter, 14 June 1967, Vice President Johnson's Diary Back-up, Box 4, Special File, LBJL.

126. Thomas is considered a Kennedy man by virtue of Harper & Row's standing as the family's preferred publisher.

serialized. In the meantime, Jacqueline Kennedy has become appalled by the whole idea.

Mrs. Kennedy once told Manchester that she conceived of his book as a slender volume, "bound in black and put away on dark library shelves."[127] Once *Look* agreed to pay an unprecedented sum for first serial rights, though, she realized her most private moments were going to be shared with at least 8.5 million readers.[128] In his August 10 letter to Evan Thomas, Senator Kennedy concluded that the family "should take [its] chances with Jim Bishop."[129] Having brought Manchester in to stop Bishop, now the Kennedys want to stop Manchester.[130]

Over the next four months, increasingly bitter negotiations occur behind the scenes and amid rumbling that Mrs. Kennedy is very unhappy.[131] Robert Kennedy, during a newspaper interview, tries to open up some distance between the family and the book. He states he hasn't read it, and won't, but people whose judgment he respects have led him to believe the book is not "entirely sound."[132] At one juncture Harper & Row also turns against Manchester and threatens not to publish the book unless the author makes *all* the changes requested by the Kennedys, regardless of whether the redactions are for personal or political reasons.[133] Manchester refuses to depict the first cabinet meeting on November 23 as "completely amicable," however, and make other changes he deems to be politically motivated falsifications of a record painstakingly assembled.[134]

127. Manchester, *Controversy*, 25.

128. In the mid-sixties, *Look* has a larger circulation than its arch-rival, *Life*. "Gardner Cowles Jr. Is Dead at 82; Helped Build Publishing Empire," *New York Times*, 9 July 1985.

129. Corry, *Manchester Affair*, 97. It is never clear whether Mrs. Kennedy is upset by the unprecedented amount of money Manchester (as opposed to the Kennedy Library) stands to receive from the first serial rights, or by the manuscript's contents, or both. She shared very intimate details with Manchester during ten hours of interviews in 1964, and now that her thoughts and feelings are actually going to appear in print, she seems to regard her recorded recollections an invasion of privacy. It may also be that now that she realizes JFK will not be forgotten any time soon, Jacqueline Kennedy feels quite differently about conveying the story. In 1964, her privacy was a small price to pay for the martyrdom of Jack. Now it will be breached needlessly.

130. Not entirely ironically, the Johnsons will endeavor to help Bishop with his book on the assassination. The president will give Bishop a thirty-minute interview on May 2, 1968, and both the president and Mrs. Johnson will read his manuscript in July 1968 prior to publication (as will several other Johnson aides, along with Deke DeLoach and James Rowley). Bishop's book will present Johnson's version of such events as the swearing-in, and Robert Kennedy's first snub of the new president at Andrews AFB. The book will achieve little of Manchester's success. Jim Bishop, *The Day Kennedy Was Shot* (New York: Funk & Wagnalls, 1968), 270–71, 406, 683–84.

131. Following Homer Bigart's August story in the *Times*, a literary monthly entitled *Books* reported that Mrs. Kennedy wanted Harper & Row to cancel publication. Corry, *Manchester Affair*, 169.

132. Richard Starnes, "A Dark Night with Robert Kennedy," *Washington Daily News*, 30 November 1966.

133. Corry, *Manchester Affair*, 163–64.

134. Manchester, *Controversy*, 30.

Interestingly, press coverage of the affair will later point to changes demanded of Manchester on the grounds that he was being unfair to President Johnson. But Robert Kennedy's agents are equally intent on scrubbing the manuscript for worrisome portrayals of the senator. It was his behavior at the November 23 cabinet meeting that is, in retrospect, unflattering.

After weeks of denials that anything is amiss, on December 14 Mrs. Kennedy petitions a state supreme court justice in New York to block publication of *The Death of a President* and its serialization, to the shock of the publishing world. What will be called "the battle of the book" is joined, and a court hearing is scheduled for December 27. The former First Lady is confident about prevailing, fully cognizant of her iconic status. "Anybody who is against me will look like a rat," she observes to Manchester, in one of their last meetings.[135] In truth, the Kennedys' case is fatally flawed in legal terms.

Shortly before the papers are filed in court, Johnson handwrites a note to Mrs. Kennedy drafted for him by Abe Fortas.[136]

Lady Bird and I have been distressed to read the news accounts of your unhappines about the Manchester book. Some of these accounts attribute your concern to passages in the book which are critical or defamatory of us.

If this is so, I want you to know while we deeply appreciate your characteristic kindness and sensitivity, we hope you will not subject yourself to any discomfort or distress on our account. One never becomes inured to slander but we have learned to live with it.[137]

Hours after the lawsuit is actually filed on December 16, Johnson again confers with Abe Fortas, the president's de facto counsel regardless of the portfolio he happens to hold. The two men are as surprised as anyone at the turn of events, but Fortas is justifiably dubious about the likelihood of the Kennedys' winning a permanent injunction against publication. He advises Johnson to prepare a rebuttal. They discuss the possibility of utilizing journalist Theodore White, author of the celebrated 1960 book *The Making of the President,* to challenge Manchester's account on some key points. James Rowe, a Washington lawyer and Democratic Party mover and shaker, ran into White the previous evening, and White reminded Rowe that he had an exclusive interview with Jacqueline Kennedy on the Thanksgiving holiday weekend after the assas-

135. Ibid., 34.

136. Apparently, in an earlier conversation, possibly on December 15 at 9:27 a.m., Abe Fortas and the president discussed sending Jacqueline Kennedy a note about the Manchester controversy, and Fortas agreed to draft it. Daily Diary, 15 December 1966, LBJL.

137. Johnson to Jacqueline Kennedy, note, from 11:20 a.m., 16 December 1966, Manchester File, Box 1, Special File, LBJL.

sination. White has a copy of his interview notes, according to Rowe, and is prepared to state publicly that at no point in her long and troubled outpouring of grief did Mrs. Kennedy in any way criticize the president or Mrs. Johnson.[138] If so, that nearly contemporaneous recollection would powerfully contradict Manchester's blistering account. But the president does not trust Teddy White because his 1960 best seller was notable for its pro-Kennedy slant. Then, too, it was White who fashioned that 1963 interview with Mrs. Kennedy into the over-wrought "Camelot" metaphor for *Life* magazine.[139]

One interesting detail that neither Johnson nor Fortas knows is that Bill Moyers advocates the very legal step the Kennedys have now taken. In a letter to Goodwin on December 10, just after he finished reading the *Look* galleys, Moyers wrote, "the book is permeated by a malignancy I find dishonest, disgraceful, and distorted. . . . I would sue the magazine to prevent publication of the serialization, and I would withhold publication of the book for many years to come . . . I believe both of these proposals are feasible."[140]

Fortas: It's Abe.

Johnson: Yeah. *[television blaring in the background, drowning out Fortas]*

Fortas: Jack [Valenti] is down here with me. We've been trying to get hold of the lawyers, but haven't yet succeeded.

I wanted to check something with you before we propose this to Bill [Moyers]. The question is whether some statement oughta be mapped out that . . . [and] *who* oughta get it out. And I think the best way to handle this thing is to get it down . . . and to have Bill Moyers do it . . . to get out a statement that was prepared in advance, if [everyone could agree] to it . . . covering all of these points based first, [on] personal knowledge, and second on research [of the files].

For example, on that Bible business . . . we've got that blanketed as you will remember.[141] And so on . . . every one of these points that needs to be, gets covered *[indistinct]*. I didn't want to propose this to Bill without checking it with you [first].

Johnson: Yes, I think that'd be all right. I talked to him about getting the thirty-nine or forty things and straightenin' 'em out and doin' research, but after he got off on this other tack, I haven't discussed it with him anymore.

Fortas: Yeah.

138. Rowe to Johnson, memo, 15 December 1966, Manchester File, Box 1, Special File, LBJL.

139. The Camelot analogy first appeared in a thousand-word essay by Theodore White, "For President Kennedy: An Epilogue," published in a December 6, 1963, special memorial issue of *Life*.

140. Moyers to Goodwin, letter, personal and confidential, 10 December 1966, Moyers, 1966–1967, Office of the President File, LBJL.

141. Fortas is referring to the August investigation he conducted on the allegedly missing "Bible" used at the swearing-in. See the August 29, 1966 conversation.

Johnson: And I don't know what his disposition would be about [doing] it. Jim Rowe has a letter in here today, two pages [long], that Teddy White had talked to her [Jacqueline Kennedy] six days afterwards, [on] Thanksgiving Day, after this trouble. Have you seen that?[142]

Fortas: No, [but] I heard about it . . . [supposedly] that is directly contrary [to Manchester's account].

Johnson: Yes . . . but *I* didn't tell you. I just got the letter. You get me mixed up with some people, Mr. Justice! *[breaks into laughter]*

Fortas: Now that would be a fine *[indistinct] [joins in laughter]*

Johnson: Well now, I sure didn't! I just *read* the letter, and he just sent it to me. So I know *I* didn't. I haven't seen him. I *refused* to see White.

Fortas: No, I know that *[indistinct]*.

Johnson: Well, Teddy White—according to Rowe—told *Rowe* this. Now *[indistinct]* puts it in a letter . . . but I don't know . . . I just *saw* it just a little bit ago. So I haven't talked to you, so I know *I* didn't [tell you about it]. But I think it's something you oughta look at *before* . . . and that *they* [Moyers] oughta look at before too, 'cause it may be that *that's* the way to do it.

Fortas: Yeah.

Johnson: I don't *think* so. I don't have any confidence in him [White] at all. And he's . . . but *I* think *we* probably. . . . Don't you think we oughta [wait to] see what they do with the book?

Fortas: Well, it's gonna be too late. They're going to get out the *Life [sic]* articles.

Johnson: Wait just a minute.

[The president listens to a TV news report about Vietnam.]

So that's what. . . .

Fortas: I think that's the basis for keeping *[indistinct]* . . . whether we oughta do somethin' *before* the *Look* articles come out—

Johnson: Well, I say . . . isn't it possible that the book would be restrained? [The Kennedys would obtain] a restraining order in the court, [like the one] that they asked for today?

Fortas: Oh, no. I think if it is restrained by the trial judge, it'd be set aside on appeal. *[indistinct]* You know, Si Rifkind knows *that*.[143] They may be able to get a temporary order from a willing judge, but he can't ban it. That's not *[indistinct]*.

So I think we have to *assume* that that would just come out. In any

---

142. Rowe to Johnson, memo, 15 December 1966; and Roche to Johnson, memo, 15 December 1966; both in Manchester File, Box 1, Special File, LBJL. John Roche, a special assistant to the president, has also just spoken to White about his 1963 interview with Mrs. Kennedy.

143. Simon Rifkind, a federal district court judge from 1941 to 1950, is Mrs. Kennedy's lawyer.

event, we certainly . . . the press is calling Jack and undoubtedly calling Bill . . . so there'll be a lot of articles coming out on this thing.

It looks like they're going to have . . . I don't know. I haven't heard anything. It's not at all certain. We sure need . . . from a [factual basis] what has been said so far. And if Bill will do it . . . Bill's the only one that can do it, in my opinion. If he'll be willing to is another matter.

Johnson: Well, why don't you see.

Fortas: All right, sir.

December 17

Saturday
From Abe Fortas / 10:45 a.m., CST

The president has left Washington to spend Christmas at his Texas ranch. By now Justice Fortas has read the *Look* excerpts in Bill Moyers's possession. The galleys are being kept away from the president, and not just so that he can honestly claim not to have read them. If Johnson were ever to read the actual articles, as opposed to reports about their contents, he might not be able to turn the other cheek.

Moyers and Jack Valenti are with the justice as he discusses the matter with the president. It is certain now that a point-by-point rebuttal will be prepared for some future purpose, because Fortas has not changed his estimate of the Kennedys' lawsuit against Manchester, Harper & Row, and *Look* magazine. The Kennedys will not prevail, if by "prevail" one means the manuscript will never be published in any form. Consequently, most of the discussion concerns who can be trusted to prepare such a sensitive document. Candidates include Jake Jacobsen, special counsel to the president, and H. Barefoot Sanders, the U.S. attorney in Dallas in November 1963, who has since taken a job in the Justice Department. Ultimately, it falls to Jacobsen to prepare the seventy-three-page compilation of mistakes, misrepresentations, and falsehoods in the Manchester book. In Johnson's inner circle Jacobsen's analysis will be known as the "black book."[144]

In 1965, when Manchester was pressing the White House for an interview, Fortas advised Johnson to give one but dissemble. Fortas had heard all the stories and knew about the tensions with Robert Kennedy, and suggested that the

144. "Jacobsen Analysis Manchester Book," Box 1, Special File, LBJL.

president plead "lapses of memory or respond vaguely" to any sensitive questions from Manchester.[145] The president subsequently declined to be interviewed by Manchester except in writing, and right now that looks to have been the wiser course.

Because of his familiarity with the issues, and owing to his penetrating intelligence, Fortas is able to cut through a lot of the confusion and get to the heart of the matter. As he tells the president, there is some truth to Jacqueline Kennedy's protestations over sensitive or intimate details that now stand to be made public. But the genuine problem is that the book is tantamount to a "plain declaration of war" by the Kennedys on Johnson. It depicts the president as a power-hungry usurper, another expression of the climate of intolerance and violence that stoked Oswald into action.

Fortas is mostly right, but he is wrong to believe that the Kennedys intended for the book to come out this way. While the manuscript perfectly replicates Robert Kennedy's dislike of Lyndon Johnson, which is never far below the surface, it was supposed to stay below. Instead, Manchester has unexpectedly produced what Arthur Schlesinger, Jr., calls a "romantic mythodrama."[146] The author is so inculcated with the "Camelot" metaphor that he profoundly believes in Norman Mailer's comment, uttered the day after the assassination: "It was our country for a while. Now it's theirs again."[147]

Fortas: . . . material, subject by subject. And make a very careful analysis of what the version is as *we* know it, what the facts are as *we* know them, and the premises on which *we* relied, with [the] material we relied [on], subject by subject. And then have that *available* for whatever use we might want to make of it to answer specific questions, or to do something affirmatively in the future. But that in view of the fact that the lawsuit *was* filed today *[sic]*, it's our judgment that we can't make a statement or have a statement made on our *behalf,* without getting in a . . . [involved in the] fallout [or] flak from that lawsuit. So that we all feel that [we] just oughta *get ready* and not *do* anything.

The next question is, what the fellas oughta do with respect [to] *specific* questions that are asked [of] them by the press. And when you got a good answer for it, Jack and Bill will make the good answers [if there are any very] specific questions asked by the press.

Is that all right with you?

Johnson: Yes; sure.

Fortas: Now the next thing is that I read this manuscript . . . that['s] in hand.

145. Kalman, *Fortas,* 223. The written replies to Manchester were deliberately uninformative, per Fortas's suggestion.

146. Schlesinger, *Robert Kennedy,* 761.

147. Manchester, *Controversy,* 4.

It's *[indistinct]* fantastic thing. I can see how there might be some objections to things [involving] the widow, in matters of taste, by and large *[indistinct]*. I think that there are enough *specific things* here so that . . . we can kind of chip [away at Manchester's] credibility. For example, you remember that we worked out a series of answers to questions . . . questions that the author [had submitted?]

Johnson: Yeah.

Fortas: One of those questions was, was there a violent disagreement between you and JFK in the [Houston] hotel?

Johnson: Yes.

Fortas: And we sent back the answer saying that there was a discussion but no disagreement. And he [Manchester] *precisely* misquoted that. [He writes that] there [was] a "discussion *and violent* disagreement."[148]

Johnson: I didn't read it that way. I thought he said there was a discussion but *no* violent disagreement.[149]

Fortas: No, and then he says, "*and* violent disagreement." He says *both*. And Bill has agreed that we shouldn't advise him of that in advance because this is one—unless it's *changed* before publication—it's one in which there's a cold, black-and-white discrepancy.

Johnson: Well, tell him to be careful not to advise *anybody,* dammit.

Fortas: Yeah, I said that yesterday. He [Moyers] has written a letter, he tells me, to [Richard] Goodwin.

Johnson: Who is "he"?

Fortas: [He] said—

Johnson: *Who is "he"?*

Fortas: Bill.

Johnson: Yes.

Fortas: In which he said the book is so terrible that . . . the fact that the book's so terrible that he can't comment on *[indistinct]*.[150] And that's *good,* and I don't think we oughta try to get them to *improve* the book . . . particularly in an appendix to this lawsuit.

The lawsuit *itself* is about as *brazen* an attack on freedom of the press as I've seen in a hundred years. And I was very amused that the *Washington Post,* which usually has an editorial on things before they happen, did not

---

148. The manuscript may have alleged this, but the published book will say only that Kennedy and Johnson "had words." Manchester, *Death,* 82.

149. This suggests that Johnson is getting his information secondhand, i.e., from press accounts about the *Look* excerpts.

150. While Moyers has told Fortas about his December 10 letter to Goodwin, apparently Moyers has not mentioned his suggestion to Goodwin that the Kennedys take legal action to prevent publication. Moyers to Goodwin, letter, 10 December 1966, Office of the President File, LBJL.

have an editorial on *this*.[151] There is a wonderful column by Bill White, [which] you probably have seen. You didn't see Bill White's column?

Johnson: No; no.

Fortas: 'Cause it's just marvelous. [He] calls this thing . . . and calls the shots for what they *are*.[152]

Johnson: Abe, while I can remember it: *all* that *I* remember was Mrs. Kennedy was practicin' talkin' about her Spanish, and about going to appear—and whether she would go or not—appear to this Spanish thing.[153]

Fortas: Uh-huh.

Johnson: The president called me down there [to the hotel room in Houston] and told me that he just thought that it was an *outrage* . . . that he had heard what [Ralph] Yarborough had done, and that he had told them that Yarborough had to ride with us or get out of the party.

Fortas: Uh-huh.

Johnson: And there was no disagreement of *any* kind, and no *violence* of any kind, and a very friendly thing, and he and I had a drink together. And he sat there with his shirt off, and [then I] left. And we had no *debate* or no *argument* or no report, and I had not asked to see him or *anything*. And if she [Jacqueline Kennedy] *heard* anybody having a disagreement of any kind, it was the *president* talking about *Yarborough*.

Fortas: Yeah. Well, that's certainly . . . seems to me a clear, then, [example]—

Johnson: Now what are the *damaging* things from *our* standpoint with the country and the public in here . . . about this plane that they're talkin' about? Who is the perpetrator of the fraud on us, Kenny O'Donnell, or General [Godfrey] McHugh, or who?[154]

---

151. Fortas is referring to the *Washington Post* editorial page, which is famed for its nearly absolutist defense of freedom of the press. But Fortas is wrong. The *Post* did publish an editorial on December 15, stating that it "is impossible to agree with the legal steps [Mrs. Kennedy] has taken" against Manchester and his publishers. "They Belong to the Ages," *Washington Post,* 15 December 1966.

152. White, the president's closest friend in the world of syndicated columnists, writes that "President Johnson has had to bear a frightful burden in the unremitting hostility of the Kennedy cult and its common attitude that the man who now sits in the White House is . . . only a crude usurper." William White, "Manchester's Book . . . Comment Becomes a Duty," *Washington Post,* 17 December 1966.

153. Mrs. Kennedy briefly addressed, in Spanish, the League of United Latin American Citizens in Houston on the evening of November 21. Johnson recalls her rehearsing in the next room during his last private meeting with President Kennedy. Manchester, *Death,* 67, 82.

154. Brigadier General McHugh was the air force aide to John Kennedy and part of the presidential entourage in Dallas. In the stories that are leaking out about the Manchester book, it is alleged that McHugh argued with Johnson about the departure of *Air Force One* from Dallas. In fact, it was Malcolm Kilduff who exchanged words with McHugh. Manchester, *Death,* 315–16; Robert Dallos, "Johnson Termed Unhappy on Book," *New York Times,* 26 December 1966.

Fortas: *Both.* Those two . . . it's pretty obvious that those are the two villains *[indistinct]*—

Johnson: Now what about [Malcolm] Kilduff?[155] Is he against us?

Fortas: I think Kilduff, by and large, comes out on our side.

[aside to Moyers] Wouldn't you think so, Bill?

Moyers: Yes.

Johnson: What about Larry O'Brien?

Fortas: There's very little about Larry O'Brien in there, and I would not say that it was hostile.

Johnson: I wonder if the—

Fortas: Kilduff is affirmatively friendly, I would say, yes. So is *[indistinct]*. And that O'Brien is neither one way or the other.

[aside to Moyers] How 'bout you, Bill?

Moyers: Yes, I would agree with you [on that].

Johnson: Could we find out from O'Brien if he, O'Brien, thought that we did anything improper?

Fortas: You know . . . Clark Clifford and I had a talk with him.

Johnson: Yeah.

Fortas: You remember that, in connection with that Bible . . . situation, we got the story on that taken down very well.[156] But you never released it at the time [that] there was all that flak about the late Kennedy family Bible. And it's *not* the Kennedy family Bible *[indistinct]*.

Johnson: It's not one that [had] ever been *opened.*

Fortas: That's right. It's a Catholic prayer book that was in pristine condition in a white box. And [it] had never been . . . never been opened. And certainly, based on *that* conversation, O'Brien is okay.[157]

But now the thought here is that after we get up this analysis, that there will be a recheck with everybody. The time to do that is after the analysis is gotten [down].

Bill thinks that the best way to go about it is to have Juanita [Roberts] give him the material. . . . He points out that she just kind of holds [on to] the material.[158]

Johnson: *[agitated]* She has to because we have so damn many *spies* around us!

Fortas: Yeah . . . and then have Jake Jacobsen make [the] analytical job. I'll be glad to help him [in] such time as I have available. But it really . . . somebody really oughta be put on this full time, day and night. Of course,

155. Kilduff was the acting press secretary in Dallas with Salinger en route to Tokyo.

155. Kilduff was the acting press secretary in Dallas with Salinger en route to Tokyo.

156. See conversation on August 29, 1966, with regard to the erroneous "Bible" story.

157. Fortas is suggesting that O'Brien is not among those spreading negative stories about Johnson because he leveled with Clifford and Fortas when they asked him about the allegedly missing Kennedy family Bible, which turned out to be an unused Catholic missal.

158. Roberts is one of Johnson's staff secretaries.

we don't know when he can come up and use it *[indistinct]*.

Johnson: Well, I wished we could get somebody that's *not* [busy]. He's the only man I've got here . . . and he's with me from daylight till midnight.

Fortas: Somebody else *[indistinct]*.

Johnson: I don't know when [Milton] Semer's leaving, I don't know how he would be on it; I guess Harry [McPherson] is writing on the speech, I don't know what [Douglass] Cater is doing.[159] I don't know . . . we might get Barefoot Sanders assigned. I think that would be good, and he's a pretty good lawyer . . . from the Justice [Department].[160]

Fortas: Uh-huh. That might be a good—

Johnson: See, Jake's the only person I have here with me. Bill doesn't come anymore, and Marvin [Watson] is up there.[161] I run an office with three people.

Fortas: *[to Moyers]* You think, Bill, do you think [that] Barefoot Sanders could do it? *[to Johnson]* Bill and Jack think he could do it.

Johnson: I think you might call *him* over [and] ask him. We'd tell him we want to *borrow* him [for] a few days . . . maybe get some good person assigned, maybe, from your office down there that could kind of help him, too, that have good taste.[162]

Fortas: Yeah.

Johnson: Well, he's close to Dallas. He's close to these facts, and he knows [Judge] Sarah Hughes very well.

Fortas: Yeah.

Johnson: And he knows the situation, he knows [Irving] Goldberg very well.[163]

[Johnson refers to some problems being generated by Ramsey Clark, his acting attorney general.]

That's my attorney general! I've just concluded our boy hasn't got enough sense to do things except cause us trouble.

I would think, though, that he would let [me] have Barefoot on that, that's the only thing I'm worried about. But maybe if he [Clark] can let Barefoot just come and quietly spend some time on it—

Fortas: Well, he's got something to do. I don't think—

Johnson: I don't know about the propriety [of] gettin' a Justice [Department]

---

159. Semer, a counsel to the president since February 1966, is leaving as of December 31 to return to his law practice. McPherson is special counsel to the president, and Cater is a special assistant.

160. Sanders is the assistant attorney general in charge of the Civil Division.

161. Moyers announced his resignation as the president's press secretary two days ago, effective in a matter of weeks, and is preparing to leave the White House. Watson, a special assistant to the president, has remained in Washington for the holidays.

162. Johnson probably means borrowing someone who is clerking for Justice Fortas or a young lawyer from Fortas's old law firm, Arnold & Porter.

163. Goldberg, a Dallas lawyer, advised Johnson on the swearing-in.

lawyer [to] do it, I guess you have to. And I guess when Jake gets back up there after Christmas . . . but I just don't know what I'd *do* here. He has to talk to everybody, and they just . . . I've had everybody from the governors to Dick Daley to all the newspaper [reporters asking me about it].[164]

[The dicussion momentarily turns to an unrelated issue.]

     What are the *damaging* things to *us* in there? Is it the plane incident in Dallas?

Fortas: Well, the basic dam[aging]—

Johnson: The *outstanding* ones.

Fortas: The *basic* damaging thing is that . . . is that the portrayal of you and, uh, of your friends like Jack, you know, as sort of a bumbling . . . pictured as bumbling *[indistinct]* makes you very *[indistinct]*. That's number one. Number two, there . . . you get a general impression—

Johnson: Jack Valenti or Jack Brooks?

Fortas: Jack *Valenti*.[165]

Johnson: Yeah.

Fortas: You get a general impression, on the basis of specific incidents, of incivility and insensitivity on your part to Mrs. Kennedy. *[indistinct]* For example, that you kept the plane *[Air Force One]* there for an hour just to . . . so you'd get sworn in, and there's a lot of deliberate ambiguity about whether [the] attorney general did or did not tell you to get sworn in then. And it clashes [on one section] he wrote that says the attorney general told you not to . . . which is a damned lie. At one point, they quote Kilduff as referring to the conversation by telephone between you and the attorney general, in which the attorney general said that, and that's why it was *cut*. *[indistinct]* And then things like you—

Johnson: We sure oughta see how Kilduff knew he told me that. I noticed they went back very *anxiously* to determine whether . . . that we kept a recording of that conversation or not.[166]

Fortas: Yeah.

Johnson: Did you see that?

Fortas: Yes, sir.

Johnson: All that? [General Chester] Clifton—[167]

164. Richard Daley is the powerful Democratic mayor of Chicago.

165. Valenti is portrayed as a slick, overly ambitious public relations executive. Manchester, *Death,* 325.

166. The president is referring to the unusual attempt made on December 14, 1963, by General McHugh, probably on the attorney general's behalf, to determine if the conversations between Johnson and Robert Kennedy on November 22 had been recorded. Memo re Telephone Conversation with General McHugh, 14 December 1963, President's Diary—November 22, 1963, Box 2, Special File, LBJL.

167. Major General Clifton was the Army aide to President Kennedy and part of the entourage in Dallas.

Fortas: *[indistinct]* I've seen that . . . [General Godfrey] *McHugh* did that in December [1963].

Johnson: Yeah.

Fortas: *[sounding uncomfortable]* And then there's stuff like, ah . . . Mrs. Kennedy going into the bedroom on the plane, and you were lying on the bed . . . in there, and sprawled across the bedspread, dictating to Marie Fehmer. And, ah . . . demanding that there be photographers and trying to *maneuver* the thing so that Mrs. Kennedy was present at the swearing-in.

It's *all crud* of that kind, really. Then, uh . . . [when] you got back, [you] gave Evelyn Lincoln less than an hour to clear the Oval Office . . . damn lie *[indistinct]*.

Then they say that you had first decided to put it all [on] a Texas commission to investigate the assassination, which so far as I know, is not true.[168] [As far as] I know, [from] my first conversation with *[indistinct]*, you were desperately working with—and I was *helping* you—to prevent a Texas investigation.[169]

Johnson: That is correct.

Fortas: *[chuckles]* Well . . . we went through the tortures of the *damned* to prevent the *damn thing.* And we finally got [Waggoner] Carr up here and had the chief justice go to work on him too.

Johnson: That is correct. . . . Now who would be tellin' 'em *that*?

Fortas: Sir?

Johnson: Who could be telling them that?

Fortas: I don't know. There is a reference in there to [Nicholas] Katzenbach having come over to talk to me. That's the only reference to me that appears, [and] it's basically untrue.

Johnson: Don't you want to talk to Katzenbach about that pretty quick?

Fortas: Well, I will.

Johnson: I sure would, and I'd tell him somethin' *else.* That—

Fortas: I don't want him to know I've *seen* this [the *Look* galleys], though.

Johnson: No, but I would just say that you hear from [Bennett] Cerf or some of 'em the stories, that you['re] involved, that he [Katzenbach] came over to talk to you . . . and that there's some rumor that we didn't want a national commission, that you came in [and] urged it . . . *we* urged it.[170] We went to the top to get the chief justice [to] do it, and we even asked the

---

168. The FBI was always going to investigate the assassination in parallel with a Texas Court of Inquiry before the Warren Commission's establishment.

169. Subsequently, in December 1963, Fortas and Warren had to lean on Texas attorney general Waggoner Carr before he agreed to suspend the Court of Inquiry.

170. Cerf, a publisher at Random House and a television personality, has read the unedited manuscript and was quoted in the press the day before about the allegations in Manchester's book. Associated Press, "LBJ-Kennedys Episode Cited," *Washington Post,* 16 December 1966.

attorney general to *name* people he wanted. [And] he recommended people like Allen Dulles and John McCloy.

   And that there's also an implication that Bobby didn't want us to take the oath, when the implication to *me* was that he thought it [was] better to take it *there.* And that he [Kennedy] would have somebody call me and *give* me the oath—

Fortas: Yes.

Johnson: —and he *did.* And what did Bobby tell him [Katzenbach], when he told him to call and give me the oath? And find out what the *facts* were, he [Katzenbach] usually remembers.

[The conversation touches on the ongoing controversy over whether Robert Kennedy authorized electronic surveillance while attorney general.]

Fortas: Bill tells me, too, that [Arthur] Schlesinger is telling the press and everybody that the White House has a copy of this thing.

Johnson: What of?

Fortas: Of this [Manchester's] text, you know.

Johnson: Of this what?

Fortas: The text of the article.

Johnson: Yeah . . . you mean of the *book*?

Fortas: Well, he's just saying that we have a copy of the galley[s] and the article. *[aside]* Isn't he, [Bill]?

Moyers: Yeah.

Johnson: Oh, of the *Look* articles.

Fortas: Yeah.

Johnson: Yeah, of the book. Yeah. Well—

Fortas: So I think it's *very* important that, ah . . . you haven't seen the damn thing.[171] And Bill saw it and he found it so disgusting that he just wrote Goodwin the letter that he *wrote* him.

Johnson: All right.

Fortas: *[aside to Moyers and Valenti]* [Is] that all right, Bill? Jack? Hmm? Swear to God. Okay, you don't swear.

   [to Johnson] Because I don't think you oughta see the damn thing. Did you send that letter to Mrs. Kennedy?

Johnson: Yes. I wouldn't admit it *there,* though, where you are now. I just wouldn't say anything like that.[172]

Fortas: I have already mentioned it.

Johnson: *[disappointed]* Well, now we got to . . . *[sighs audibly].*

Fortas: You know . . . it came up, necessarily.

---

171. Fortas means that Johnson must appear to be above the fray, and continue to exhibit disinterest in Manchester's work.

172. Fortas is referring to the note he drafted for Johnson that very morning. Johnson doesn't want Moyers and Valenti to know about it, apparently fearing they will leak word of it to others.

Johnson: Yeah, I know. But you read me, don't you?

Fortas: I read you. Yes, sir.

Johnson: *Please,* and thank you.

Fortas: Sure. . . . So would you mind having a call made to Juanita to tell her to turn that stuff over to Barefoot Sanders?

Johnson: Yes, I'll be glad to. What . . . now how do I say "that stuff"?

Fortas: Well, the material that she furnished Bill together with absolutely everything that relates to it.

Johnson: All right. Now one thing, though, she is very insistent on—and I guess with some *merit*—is that most of the stuff we get, we find out our own folks photostated . . . and take it out and keep it. And the Goodwins have run off with a good deal, and [McGeorge] Bundy, I don't know how much *he's* taken out.[173] And each one of 'em are taking it out for their own memoirs, and their own books, and their own things.

And I just say this to you—*only* you—and not wantin' you to repeat it to a *human bein'*. We see a good many evidences of some of this stuff being used [by] men we're tryin' to defend ourselves from *now*.

Fortas: Yes, sir.

Johnson: And we don't think anybody really *consciously* does anything wrong, but my problems are *unconsciously*—

[Johnson complains about the Washington rumor mill.]

Johnson: And so if she [Juanita] and the rest of 'em, practically everybody on the staff, have *grave* doubts about our turnin' this over to anybody except someone *like* you, or someone that's not *copyin'* it all, and then *leakin'* it to somebody. For instance, when they send that to *Bill,* then that becomes known to *Schlesinger* immediately.[174]

Fortas: Um-hmm. Well, I think that she can be told that [the] material is to be made available to Barefoot, and Barefoot oughta work right there.

[approximately five seconds excised]

Johnson: So I will tell her to tell . . . [I] sure wished you could get Clark [Clifford] to look at some of this stuff, too, and get his judgments.

Fortas: Well, I think that's right.

Johnson: He might have somebody in *his* place that could quietly do some of it.[175]

[approximately five seconds excised]

So we might ought *[sic]* to see if there's somebody in . . . I guess. . . . [Is

---

173. Richard Goodwin and Bundy have left the White House staff, and Johnson is concerned they took with them copies of a good number of documents, official and otherwise.

174. Johnson is referring to the fact that after Moyers received the *Look* galleys from Goodwin, Arthur Schlesinger knew about it immediately—almost certainly because Goodwin told him.

175. Johnson means someone in Clifford's Washington law firm.

there] any question of propriety about [a] Justice [Department lawyer] lookin' over this stuff, a Justice lawyer doing it?

Fortas: Oh no, none whatever. No problem of *that* sort.

Johnson: We have a boy named Levinson that's workin' *awfully* hard, Larry Levinson, for [Joe] Califano.[176]

Fortas: Yeah.

Johnson: I don't know anything about his loyalty. . . . Califano thinks he has *unusual* ability as a young man. But that might be a thought. You might want to ask Bill's evaluation of Levinson.

Fortas: Right.

Johnson: He's a Harvard *boy,* and he has done a good deal of briefing.

Fortas: Uh-huh.

Johnson: I believe that Bobby is having his governors jump on me, and he's having his mayors, and he's having his Negroes, and he's having his Catholics . . . and he's having 'em just systematically, one after the other, each day [jump on me]. And I think this [Manchester] book is just—he got rid of the [Rowland] Evans book last month, and he's got this book, and I believe that each one of these things are timed.[177] They got rid of Schlesinger, and they got rid of [Ted] Sorensen, and he told somebody that he had *ten* books coming out in a period of ten months.[178] And [it'd] be ten good ones and ten bad ones: ten good ones on Kennedy, and ten bad ones on Johnson. I don't know whether that's true or not, I haven't counted. But [there are] six or eight of 'em, but he has had Schlesinger, and Sorensen, and Evans, and . . . different ones.

I think, given that's all we *can* do . . . do we have any files or notes that really confirm or deny this stuff *effectively*?

Fortas: On some points. They found a pretty good . . . for example, the airplane logs, if you'll remember, show two telephone conversations from Dallas or the plane *[Air Force One]* between you and the attorney general . . . and so on. Then we have—

Johnson: Now, two [conversations] with Kennedy? Or one with Kennedy, and one with Katzenbach?

Fortas: No. There were two with *Kennedy,* according to the log, and—

Johnson: I thought I had two with Kennedy and one with Katzenbach. But the *book* said that I had *one* with Kennedy and one with Katzenbach.

Fortas: No, the . . . I don't know whether the . . . I think, though, that

---

176. Levinson is a lawyer working in the office of Califano, a special assistant to the president.

177. Johnson is probably referring to the book just published by Evans and Novak, *Exercise of Power.* It is a lucid, detailed, and revealing biography.

178. Both Schlesinger and Sorensen published hagiographies of John Kennedy in 1965. Arthur Schlesinger, Jr., *A Thousand Days: John F. Kennedy in the White House* (Boston: Houghton Mifflin, 1965); Theodore Sorensen, *Kennedy* (New York: Harper & Row, 1965).

Katzenbach became awed in the course of a call from Kennedy to you. That's my recollection. . . .

Johnson: I would sure make 'em bat[ten] that down with the White House. I think we oughta have some good lawyer, too, that's interviewing our Secret Service people, particularly this boy that's with us now, Clint Hill.

Fortas: Yeah. Well, that's what we intend to do, but we think the way to do it best is to do the analysis first.

   Now, the Walter Jenkins notes would probably be extremely valuable as to what went on in the origination of calls from Washington. For example, the logs that we have *here* show that you were talking with Walter and with McGeorge Bundy when the attorney general came on, and that was the time that Katzenbach dictated the oath to Marie Fehmer. [The question is] whether there'd be anything in Walter's notes that would show that.

Johnson: *[hesitantly]* Could you ask him?[179]

Fortas: Mildred [Stegall] has got all those notes in—[180]

Johnson: She *does* have 'em.

Fortas: Yeah.

Johnson: Why, we'll get her when she gets back. She's gonna be here, though, till the first. I guess we oughta get her to locate 'em, huh?

Fortas: Yeah. She ought to locate them, and I don't know whether she can read 'em or not.[181] But if she can't, we'll get Walter to.

Johnson: All right. Okay, I guess what we oughta do is get 'em and get her to *type* 'em up, and send 'em to Barefoot.

Fortas: Fine.

Johnson: All right. Now you want to give some thought to ask[ing] Bill to evaluate Larry Levinson, and ask Joe if he could spare him any on this, or. . . .

Fortas: To work with Barefoot?

Johnson: Yeah.

Fortas: Yes, sir. I'll do that.

Johnson: See if he believes he's that trustworthy. Can you think of anything else?

Fortas: That's it.

Johnson: What is your feeling? Is your feeling still the same about the legitimacy of the lawsuit?

Fortas: Well, having read the manuscript now, my own feeling is that Mrs. Kennedy is genuinely upset about *some* of it. . . . that is very *intimate* with respect to her and the president. And that there's a *kernel* of that in it, and

179. Johnson's relations with his longtime administrative assistant are uncertain given the circumstances of Jenkins's departure in October 1964.

180. Stegall is a staff assistant who worked directly under Jenkins.

181. Jenkins wrote his notes in a shorthand that is not easily decipherable.

that beyond that, the book is a . . . the articles constitute a *plain declaration of war* between the Kennedys' and the Johnsons' [troops]. And that they're trying to go through motions to show that they tried to stop the thing, and [that] it hurts them more than it hurts anybody else. But I think it's a *stupid* thing for them to do because they're going to get into a lot of flak, and before they get through, I think they're gonna get into a lot of flak along the lines of Bill White's piece today. And it will remind them [the press] *again* of Robert Kennedy's reputation as being an arrogant fellow who doesn't really believe in freedom.

I think you're being very wise about this *[indistinct]* . . . it is a rather wise reaction, in my opinion, to the *[indistinct]* attack. That it's *[indistinct]* that to believe that he—

Johnson: Well, do you think this will be extremely damaging to us and the country . . . the effect of the articles, and the comments, and so forth?

Fortas: Yes, sir. And they want to have it damaging to [you], and at the same time they want to say that they wouldn't participate in any dirty pool of that sort. That's their basic strategy—

Johnson: Do you think that—

Fortas: We all . . . that's the way Bill feels about it, too, [and] Jack.
[approximately four seconds excised]

Fortas: And some cabinet member's diary, though, reminded me of that, too. When I read this thing I had to . . . couldn't get any *[indistinct]*.
[aside, to Moyers and Valenti] Did you, Bill? *[indistinct]*
[to Johnson] Did you notice that, sir?

Johnson: No.

Fortas: And there are at least *two* references there from a *[indistinct]* references them specifically. But they are *[indistinct]* and Kenny O'Donnell's *[indistinct]*.

Johnson: The diary is kept, according to [Orville] Freeman—[is kept] by Freeman, and [Stewart] Udall also keeps one.[182]

Fortas: Hmm.

Johnson: You ought to . . . you and Bill oughta look at it from that angle . . . reread those *[indistinct]*.

What does the evidence show about how long she [Jacqueline Kennedy] waited [prior to the swearing-in]? I was under the impression we waited on *her*.[183]

Fortas: No. We just rechecked that today . . . and there was just under half an

---

182. Since 1961, Freeman has been secretary of agriculture, and Udall secretary of the interior. Freeman is a "distinguished" but unidentified diarist in Manchester's book. Manchester, *Death,* 477, 670.

183. Johnson is correct in recalling that the ceremony was delayed for a few minutes, as everyone waited for Mrs. Kennedy to emerge from the stateroom. Manchester, *Death,* 322–23.

hour between the time that she arrived, and the time that the plane [*Air Force One*] took off. You arrived first, then *she* arrived, then the body arrived.

Johnson: How long did the body arrive after she arrived?

Fortas: Just a few minutes. The body came just a couple of minutes after she came, about four or five minutes. Then Judge Hughes came about ten, fifteen minutes later. And the takeoff was about fifty minutes after Mrs. Kennedy came aboard. I had the impression it was the other way, I guess, because of what you told me. But this morning we checked the log [*indistinct*] . . . so she *did* have to wait awhile before Judge Hughes could come and before the plane could take off.

Johnson: Is that gonna react on *us* or on *them*? That the president *shouldn't* be on the plane where the black bag is and where the communications is, and he should have gone on and taken off without takin' the oath?[184]

Fortas: Well, I think that the *thrust* of the book is *very definitely* . . . is a very definite *attempt* . . . the whole thing is to say that you were insistent on taking the oath before the plane took off. That you did this even though it was a terrible thing for this poor woman who was standing there with her bloody *clothes*. That's the net [*indistinct*] of it.

That's what they're trying to get across, and on the reader it will make an impression that I think is to advise us. Because Mrs. Kennedy is portrayed in the book as such a sympathetic character. As a matter of fact, the book is really *disgusting* about Mrs. Kennedy and her husband. [*smirks*] No criticism [*indistinct*], but the book paints it as sort of an *old-fashioned, storybook marriage,* you know, *love* and the kind of thing that happens in the nineteenth century, [a] romantic love story. And he [Manchester] fawns all over them and licks their boots, and the same thing about Bobby. At one point, for example, with the president-elect, his lawyers, including Bobby, can't [*chuckles*] . . . [for] God's sake. . . .

Johnson: Well, God . . . frank—

Fortas: [The point] is that it makes her a very sympathetic character, and the idea of her waiting here in *torment,* or what the book says is [*indistinct*]—

Johnson: And how do we rebut that? By pointing out the necessity of that? Or what?

Fortas: Yeah. The whole thing, it seems to me, hinges on the taking of the oath. And I was telling Jack and Bill this morning that if *I* had been there, if you'd asked me, I would have said that you should not leave the hotel room without taking the oath.

---

184. The "black bag" is actually a briefcase, nicknamed the "Football," carried by a military aide who never leaves the president's side. The briefcase contains various options for nuclear war and special codes enabling the president to positively identify himself to key military commanders. Stephen Schwartz, ed., *Atomic Audit: The Costs and Consequences of U.S. Nuclear Weapons Since 1940* (Washington, D.C.: Brookings Institution Press, 1998), 222.

Johnson: I wasn't in a hotel!

Fortas: I mean the hospital room, without taking the oath. And the reason for it being—[in the] first place, I think [the] vice president becomes president immediately when the president *dies*. But the *symbolism* of the oath-taking is so *tremendous* that it was *essential* that you take the oath *immediately* as president. That's *always* been the case when—

Johnson: Well, that's what everybody has said to me. I've forgotten who it was, somebody [was] talkin' to me a day or two ago, and just said that that has to be done . . . *Eisenhower,* [Dwight] Eisenhower told me. I told him that this was a big problem. He asked me about it. And he just *jumped* up out of his chair and waved his arms and said that, You become president the moment the president is *dead* . . . and you must take the oath as soon as you *can.*

Fortas: Well, that's right.

Johnson: The *reason* I went to the airport [and] didn't take it in the hospital was first, I wanted to be able to *talk* to the attorney general and *get* the oath. And the second thing was, McNamara had always told me that wherever the bag was, that you ought to get in the *air.*

Fortas: Uh-huh.

Johnson: Because *if* you got a warning, that he would never . . . the fact [that] you have the bag there, on the ground, out at the ranch, there's no problem, or wherever you are, if anything happens. He had said in some discussion we'd had—[around the time of the] Bay of Pigs or somewhere—that in his judgment, the thing that anybody ought to do, President Kennedy [or] me or maybe we were talkin' about *[approximately seven seconds excised]* somethin'—

Fortas: Uh-huh.

Johnson: He said that the thing they ought to do is get as *high* in the air as you can because you're [the] least vulnerable *there.* Flying they can't . . . a missile doesn't get you, a plane doesn't get you, you have time to think and you have adequate communications to talk. And so *that* was *why,* I think, we went to the plane, and why . . . after I talked to Irving Goldberg, and he said I oughta get Sarah Hughes, and then he got her out there . . . that we took that oath and then got up . . . left the hospital.[185]

Fortas: Um-hmm. Well, I think to fair-minded people . . . it's clear that you should have taken the oath. It's a . . . this whole buildup *[indistinct].* It may very well be that what Nick says will be. . . . The great importance on this is whether the attorney general told you to do it or not.

---

185. Goldberg, a prominent Dallas attorney active in Democratic politics, was called by Johnson after the president arrived at Love Field. Johnson wanted Goldberg's opinion about administration of the oath and who ought to do it. Manchester, *Death,* 272.

Johnson: What *who* says?
Fortas: Nick Katzenbach.
Johnson: Well, look into that angle of it.
Fortas: Yes, sir.
Johnson: 'Cause I'm convinced that he's *on* that other side every day.
Fortas: Yeah.
Johnson: But maybe he'll be fair.
Fortas: I think he will.

December 20

Tuesday

To Robert Kintner / 7:57 a.m., CST[186]

Kintner is an anomaly on the White House staff. Most of the men who serve Johnson are young and ambitious, with the peak of their careers presumably in front of them. The White House is a stepping-stone on their path to a lucrative or influential position.

By the time he joins the staff in April 1966, Kintner's most illustrious achievements are behind him. He has already served as president of two of the three major broadcasting networks in the nation, and he has carved out an enviable reputation as both a superb executive and promoter of network news. While president of the ABC broadcasting company, he ordered complete television coverage of the Army-McCarthy hearings in 1954, live exposure that was instrumental in bringing Senator Joe McCarthy down. And owing to Kintner, NBC's coverage after the assassination was the most extensive and longest of all the networks at more than seventy hours. Indeed, Lee Harvey Oswald's murder on November 24 was broadcast live only because of Robert Kintner. While the other networks were content to cover only the services in Washington, the NBC executive insisted on live coverage of the transfer of custody in Dallas.[187]

Kintner was brought into the White House to improve the president's flagging public image and presumably the operation of the White House itself. He has a reputation as a tough, inexhaustible executive, and because he has no ax

186. As of the writing of this book, the Johnson Library has released only the assassination-related portion of this conversation.

187. J. Y. Smith, "Robert E. Kintner, Ex-Head of ABC and NBC Radio and TV, Dies," *Washington Post,* 23 December 1980.

to grind, no career to further, no desire for publicity, he speaks with unusual candor.[188] When the controversy over the Manchester book breaks, Johnson naturally turns to Kintner because of his contacts at the most rarefied levels of the media business. His advice on how to handle the matter from a public relations standpoint is bound to be insightful.

A few days earlier Kinter suggested planting an article in either *Time* or *Newsweek* to offset some of the most damaging allegations. But now Kintner is inclined to keep the president above the controversy, seemingly disinterested. Though he is not a lawyer, Kintner believes the lawsuit is basically a ploy, designed so the Kennedys can say "we tried to stop [the book]."[189]

Kintner has quietly contacted Gardner "Mike" Cowles, the founder and publisher of *Look* magazine, about the controversy directly. Cowles is assuring him that the excerpts are now much less objectionable than they used to be, and Kintner tries to get Johnson to understand that Cowles himself bears no ill will toward the president. Publishing the excerpts is strictly a business decision, though it doesn't seem like a particularly good one at the moment. The *New York Times,* among many others, is publishing stories daily about material in the book for free, whereas Cowles paid $665,000 for that privilege.

The most intriguing allegation that Kintner passes along to Johnson is Cowles's conviction that someone in Robert Kennedy's camp is leaking all the pejorative stories about Johnson's behavior contained in Manchester's manuscript. This suggests a high level of calculated duplicity. In the statement Jacqueline Kennedy issued two days before the lawsuit was filed, she criticized the book's "inaccurate and unfair references to other individuals, in contrast with its generous references to all members of the Kennedy family."[190] Propagating these stories while simultaneously trying to disassociate from them has a transparent purpose: to discredit Johnson, even if the allegations are ultimately expunged from the *Look* excerpts or the Harper & Row book. Of all the persons on "the Kennedy goon squad"—which is what *Look*'s executives have taken to calling their adversaries—the adviser most likely to be orchestrating such leaks is Richard Goodwin.[191] He is an inveterate gossip, full of zest and guile. Manchester will later describe him as "tireless, coarse, and shrewd," someone who is betting his future on another Kennedy administration and "willing to do anything" to achieve it.[192] Goodwin served in the Johnson White House until the summer of 1965, and in his letter of resignation he pledged to "never waver" from his "complete and absolute loyalty" to Johnson "because you

188. Dallek, *Flawed Giant,* 298.

189. Kinter to Johnson, letter, 16 December 1966, Manchester File, Box 1, Special File, LBJL.

190. Corry, *Manchester Affair,* 173. Mrs. Kennedy's statement was written by Ted Sorensen.

191. Ibid., 51.

192. Manchester, *Controversy,* 32; "To Help You Keep the Record Straight About That Book," *U.S. News & World Report,* 6 February 1967.

deserve no less."[193] By the fall of 1966, however, Goodwin has, in his own words, "join[ed] the resistance."[194]

It is Goodwin's intention to help bring about a Kennedy restoration as soon as possible, which means not waiting for 1972. Goodwin is exploiting his ties and friendships in both the Kennedy and the Johnson camps to bring this about, but betraying only the incumbent president. Nothing will further Goodwin's goal more than recasting the transfer of power in 1963 to Johnson's disadvantage.

Kintner: [Mike Cowles] will never disclose that I called him, and that the White House has any interest at all, and I believe him . . . unless somebody inside the White House *[indistinct]* using my personal phone.

Ah . . . 95 percent of the unfavorable stuff is out *[five seconds excised]*. On the first issue, the issue about the use of the bedroom . . . Mike thinks [this] has been decreased so that any *alleged* impoliteness, which was very strong, has been very decreased. Bobby Kennedy does not agree that he told you to be sworn in on *Air Force One*.

Johnson: *[long, audible sigh]*

Kintner: On the delay of the plane for the swearing-in . . . it's a difference of *opinion*. Bobby's saying he didn't advocate that. But basically, Mike— whom I trust, and maybe wrongly—says that if you had read—meaning me—the original chapter and what *Look* has changed it to, the difference is between day and night.

Now, he told me that if I wanted to come up to New York secretly, he'd show me the thing and I could bring a copy back.[195]

Johnson: Hmm. What—

Kintner: How do you feel about that?

Johnson: What does he think is damaging in it?

Kintner: Well, he thinks the impression that they tried to give of 10 percent— which was formerly *100* percent—that you weren't as polite to her [Jacqueline Kennedy] as you *should* have been, is *there*. But he thinks 90 percent is cut out. *[five seconds excised]*

Then the other thing he couldn't remember was that the attorney general had been late at the first *cabinet* meeting. Do you remember that incident?

Johnson: No.[196]

193. Goodwin to Johnson, letter, July 1965, Dick Goodwin, Office Files of the President, LBJL.

194. The phrase is taken from a chapter heading in Goodwin's 1988 book, *Remembering America*. It may be significant that the Manchester affair is not mentioned at all in Goodwin's memoir.

195. Of course, Johnson already has access to Moyers's copy, but he is not about to disclose that to Kintner.

196. Johnson has probably never forgotten it.

Kintner: Now I can go up and get the damn thing. He says he won't send it down to me . . . but he'll let me read it.

Johnson: I'd talk to Abe [Fortas] about it, and let's think it over a few days. When does it come out?[197]

Kintner: January 10. It *can't* be stopped.

Johnson: No. Well, I guess the book will be different from the articles, won't they?

Kintner: Yeah, but you see . . . if you affect the articles—and Mike is cooperating here, this is, you know, something he *really* shouldn't do—and I assured him, we weren't after an injunction, or any interest, or any connection . . . that this was Kintner [contacting him] personally. And he said, "Bob, you know me. I love you dearly. I'll tell you anything in the article. You come up and I'll let you read it." He said, "I cut out 90 percent of the unfavorable things to Johnson . . . on that airplane, *Air Force One.*" He said, "That's as far as I could go. The rest of it, I don't think it's important. However, you people may."

Johnson: Uh-huh. Well, I didn't think . . . I thought from what they *leaked* in the paper, it looked like to me it was largely their adjectives. For instance, "he *sprawled* out—

Kintner: That's right.

Johnson: —on the bunk." I didn't *sprawl.* I sat and talked on the *phone.*

Kintner: He changed that to you "dictated to your secretary."

Johnson: And "he *lumbered* out of the room as she came in." Well now, *lumberin'* . . . I don't know . . . I guess that's their way of sayin' I *walked* out. But he didn't *see* me walk out. And he doesn't know whether I *lumbered* or *trotted* or *walked* or anything *else.* But it's the way *they* put it, I think.

Kintner: Well, I think you have a *friend* in Mike, to be frank.

Johnson: Huh?

Kintner: I think you have a friend in Cowles, and I think he's really toned it down.

Johnson: Uh-huh.

Kintner: Now Harper [& Row is] another story.[198]

Johnson: Well, will they have one magazine *line,* and a book with different versions?

Kintner: They could, yeah.

Johnson: Um-hmm . . . hmm.

Kintner: I don't know what the risk is. I'd be happy to go up and get the damn thing . . . 'cause they're gonna win the injunction, I think.

197. Johnson is asking when the first excerpt will be published.

198. Kintner is perhaps reminding Johnson of Harper & Row's reputation as the Kennedys' publisher of choice.

Johnson: Yeah, I would think so. I don't think I would [have you go up]. Let's wait till I come up.[199] I'll see you Sunday or Monday, and I wouldn't tell another human you talked to him.

Kintner: Oh no, no. I haven't told anybody except Abe, who told me to call [you], and Jake [Jacobsen] . . . and frankly I've stayed home [and] used my private telephone. You owe me some telephone calls.

Johnson: That's good, Bob, that's good.

Kintner: I didn't even go through the White House [switchboard].

[The conversation turns to an unrelated topic.]

Johnson: He [Bill Moyers] came to *us,* and *got in* the plane. He was down here at Kennedy's *request.* And Kennedy did not come [to Texas] at *my* request, mind you. That's a *great myth* that he came here to settle things for *me.* He came down here because he wanted to raise a million dollars and try to improve *himself* [politically], and he had been to Massachusetts [and had] done the same thing.[200] I put him off [for] *several* months, and [John] *Connally* put him off several months . . . [we] didn't *want* him to come, told him it was a *mistake* for him to come.

[agitated] And he [Kennedy] finally called Connally—I think maybe on Bill's suggestion—*secretly* to the White House. And didn't tell me anything *about* it. And Connally agreed, if he'd wait two or three months, that he would help him with a [fund-raising] *dinner.*

And he [Kennedy] *didn't* want to [wait], and the dinner was a *failure.* And I came down here [for] a few days and had to call my *personal* friends, long distance, to get them to put up in order for him to even have a *respectable* crowd. But *he* [Kennedy] selected Bill—he and Ken O'Donnell—*to come.* Well then, when the great tragedy came, Bill chartered a plane, came up, got in, and took *charge.*[201]

Kintner: I see.

Johnson: And . . . was very helpful.

[The conversation turns to an unrelated topic.]

Johnson: No, I think they're friendly. He *says* not, though.

Kintner: I don't think the Kennedys are *for* you in any *way.*

Johnson: No, I think that's right.

Kintner: Now one of the things that bothers Mike Cowles is that Bobby is

199. Johnson is at the ranch for the Christmas holiday.

200. Kennedy would have raised approximately $500,000 if the Texas trip had come off as planned ($3 million in 2004 dollars). "As 'The Book' Appears: A Close Look at the Facts," *U.S. News & World Report,* 23 January 1967. Exactly a month prior to the Texas trip, Kennedy raised $600,000 ($3.7 million in 2004 dollars) from a single, mammoth fund-raising dinner in Boston. Tom Wicker, "Kennedy Focuses Upon Goldwater," *New York Times,* 21 October 1963.

201. Moyers was advancing the Austin leg of the Texas trip, including the fund-raising dinner. After the assassination he promptly chartered a private plane to take him to Love Field in Dallas, where he was permitted to board *Air Force One.* Manchester, *Death,* 148, 317–18.

leaking all the material in these articles . . . on the basis that if they do get an injunction, they will be published *anyway.*[202]

Johnson: Yeah.

Kintner: He was very *factual* about it. He said he'd paid, you know, $650,000 on what he felt was a *fair deal.*[203] And I think Mike should get the credit that he had cut down, in his judgment, the derogatory material about you [by] about 90 percent. But now he found himself with (a) a magazine that he'd already *printed,* about maybe to be *enjoined.* But even if it came out, the *New York Times* was getting it *free* every morning.

Johnson: Yeah.

Kintner: I think this is the most terrific power play . . . *I* have ever *seen.*

Johnson: Yes, I think that's right. Well now, what do you think we should do that we're not doin'?

Kintner: I don't think anything. I, as I told you, talked to Abe. And he said to talk to Mike, and Mike . . . told me it was 90 percent cut down. If I'd like to come up, he'd give me the thing. I'd have a serious question of going up and getting it . . . although it's up to you, I'll be happy to do it.

Johnson: No, I think if we got close to it, they would say *we* were editing it, and I don't want to be a censor.

Kintner: Yeah.

Johnson: And I *feel* that . . . they have to live with their own *conscience,* and I read things like *Newsweek* and *Time,* and all this kind of stuff, and I think this is a matter for them [the Kennedys] to live with. I can't change it . . . don't *want* to.

Kintner: Well, I think *[six seconds excised].*

Personally, I would think [that] I would just let it . . . the article come out. And I think you have to [understand]—from Mike's viewpoint—I think it was offered to a lot of magazines, he *bought* it. He did play a part in editing it *down.* He doesn't think it's . . . he thinks it's 90 percent *improved.* I think on the other side, maybe, there's going to be a little more an attitude of just operating the government—to hell with all this personal crap. It's hard to do.

[There is discussion about an unrelated article in the Washington Post.*]*

Johnson: Well, I'll see you about Sunday or Monday, and I hope you have a *good* Christmas, Bob.

Kintner: Well, let me make sure. I told Mike I'd call him back.

Johnson: What I'd do on that, I'd talk to Abe, and I'll talk to him during the day or tomorrow, and then we'll talk about it again.

---

202. Goodwin is the prime suspect here, but whether Robert Kennedy knows (or approves of) everything Goodwin is doing is another question.

203. The actual figure, cited earlier, was $665,000.

The next day Jacqueline Kennedy reaches an out-of-court settlement with *Look* editors. Changes will be made in the four excerpts to be published, affecting approximately 1,600 out of the 60,000-word total. Only passages to which Mrs. Kennedy objects on personal grounds will be changed. In the statement read by Simon Rifkind, Mrs. Kennedy again attempts to distance the Kennedys from "historical inaccuracies and unfair references" that are unfortunately in the book.[204] It is now just a matter of time before an out-of-court agreement is reached with Manchester and Harper & Row.

On this same day the former First Lady responds to Johnson's handwritten note of December 16, saying she is "deeply touched" to have received it. "I am sick at the unhappiness this whole terrible thing has caused everyone," she writes. "[But] the author, and the publishers, always broke their word. . . . At least I made it known that I object—to what he took out—and to what he left in."[205]

December 26

Monday

From Bill Moyers / 10:17 a.m., CST[206]

The White House press secretary is calling Johnson to inform him of an adverse development, though Moyers does not think it is as bad as the president will seem to believe.

The next issue of *Newsweek* magazine contains a story by White House correspondent Charles Roberts purporting to give Johnson's side of the presidential succession story. According to Roberts, it differs sharply from the Kennedys' "evident perception of it" as revealed in the forthcoming book by Manchester.[207] Under ordinary circumstances, the president would probably be pleased to have his side of a story told sympathetically in a prominent publication. That's how the game is played in Washington. But for Johnson, this is no ordinary story to be fought out in the media via selective leaks. The attack by the

204. Corry, *Manchester Affair,* 197, 199.

205. Mrs. Kennedy to Johnson, letter, Wednesday, President Johnson's Statements, Box 3, Special File, LBJL.

206. As of the writing of this book, the Johnson Library has released only the assassination-related portion of this conversation.

207. Associated Press, "LBJ Version on '63 Oath Is Reported," *Washington Post,* 26 December 1966; "Jacqueline Kennedy's 'Victory,' " *Newsweek,* 2 January 1967.

Kennedy forces is existential. It would deny to Johnson the fruits of his labor and ambition, and what he has gained from playing by the rules, however painfully. The unfairness of it cuts Johnson to the bone.

The *Newsweek* story is undoubtedly the product of loose talk, either directly or indirectly, by Johnson men who think they are doing the president a favor by going toe to toe with Manchester's account.[208] The Roberts article alludes to the last abrupt presidential transition, from Franklin Roosevelt to Harry Truman in 1945, in an effusive manner that strongly suggests Jack Valenti was one of Roberts's sources. The language smacks of the kind of embellishment the former advertising executive excels in. Still, it is one thing for friendly columnists, like William White, to come to Johnson's defense primarily of their own accord, as White did in two of his December columns and will do in one January column.[209] But the president is furious about an article that purports to be "his version." Johnson thought he had made it transparently clear to everyone that he does not want to dignify Manchester's allegations by responding to them in kind, at least while he is president.

Much of this unusually long and frequently testy conversation is devoted to the wording of a statement to be issued by George Christian, the stolid Texan who is replacing Moyers as press secretary.[210] Johnson wants a flat denial that challenges both the substance of Roberts's article *and* the accuracy of his reporting. Moyers, however, believes (or knows?) that Roberts's reporting is probably accurate and that Johnson is only courting more trouble with the press by challenging *Newsweek* in this manner, given the president's so-called credibility gap.[211] The depth of Johnson's anger is such that he will not take Moyers's advice. On top of Manchester's charges, the president is sorely disappointed in advisers, current and former, who he believes have violated his confidences.

208. The index to the Daily Diary lists no contacts between the White House, aides to the president, or by the president directly with Charles Roberts after September 20, 1966, until February 24, 1967. Card File Index to Daily Diary, LBJL.

209. William White, "Manchester's Book . . . Comment Becomes a Duty," *Washington Post,* 17 December 1966; "Strange Attacks . . . Johnson Victim of Leaks," *Washington Post,* 22 December 1966; and "A City Indicted . . . Dallas Is Manchester's Chief Target," *Washington Post,* 12 January 1967. While Johnson is remonstrating against leaks by his closest aides, it is possible that he is upset because he wanted to be the only person leaking. The president had several conversations with White in the fall of 1966 as rumors of Manchester's allegations abounded; the president spoke to White on November 3 and 11 and December 14 and 24. None of these conversations were recorded, but it would have been unusual if Johnson had not shared his views with White, a fellow Texan, or at least expressed his appreciation for White's stout defense. Johnson has known White, the winner of a Pulitzer Prize in 1955, ever since the columnist was a congressional correspondent in the 1940s.

210. Moyers will become publisher of *Newsday,* an afternoon newspaper published in Long Island, New York, effective in late January.

211. Just two weeks before, *Newsweek* carried a Roberts column on that very issue. Charles Roberts, "LBJ's Credibility Gap," *Newsweek,* 19 December 1966.

During the conversation, Moyers also undertakes the unenviable duty of reading today's *Washington Post* column by Rowland Evans and Robert Novak to the president, who is at his Texas ranch. If the Roberts story is infuriating, the column is debilitating. Someone in a position to know—and only Abe Fortas, Bill Moyers, and Jack Valenti are privy to the information—must have talked directly or indirectly to the columnists, because the article is too close for comfort. It reports that "close friends" of the president, "including Supreme Court Justice Abe Fortas," are compiling a version of events that will refute Manchester, and that *verbatim transcripts* exist of the president's telephone conversations. About the only facet not exposed by Evans and Novak is the fact that Bill Moyers has the *Look* excerpts and has read them. The columnists may have desisted from reporting this only because of a "non-denial denial" issued a week ago by Moyers.[212]

The Evans and Novak column, coming on top of the *Newsweek* article and Johnson's conversation with Kintner, has a deflating effect on the president. He is beginning to understand that even a talented man like Moyers, whom Johnson looks upon as the son he never had, is no match for the cunning and guile of such Kennedy loyalists as Richard Goodwin. Johnson is under existential attack, and his own advisers are being made fools of, besides acting contrary to his wishes. The Johnson men view the Manchester affair as just another front in the media battle they engage in every day. They do not seem to grasp the insult to Johnson's identity, and very being, as a politician and president.

Surely one of the most interesting statements Johnson makes to his press secretary is to confirm the existence of presidential tape recordings from the administration's very first days. While Moyers is aware of the contemporaneous taping system, and has been for at least two years, until now he has been in the dark as to when it all began.

Moyers: Several things to report. First of all, I got a copy of *Newsweek* and
then I called Chuck Roberts, and he said the following. First of all, he said
that *Newsweek*'s public relations man had put out a [press] release
yesterday saying that this was based upon an *exclusive* interview with you,
and that when [the] *Newsweek* editors heard about it they called that *back,*
because it *wasn't* based on an exclusive interview.

I said, My point, Chuck, is that it *sounds* as if it were. And sure enough,
I've talked to three or four people here this *morning* who say that they've
read *Newsweek,* or read the AP stories of it, and it sounds like *direct
quotes* from the president.

---

212. That Moyers had read portions of Manchester's manuscript was first reported by James Reston on December 18. "I'm not denying that and I'm not confirming it either," Moyers told the Associated Press the next day. James Reston, "Farewell to Camelot," *New York Times,* 18 December 1966; Douglas Robinson, "Calls It 'Cruel and Unjust' to Suggest He Would Dishonor Kennedy," *New York Times,* 19 December 1966.

Do you have a minute to let me read you the pertinent sections from the magazine article?

Johnson: Yes, but I'm not more interested in that as I am as to what he's *done* and *where* he got it and *why* he would be attribut[ing]—

Moyers: He says, quote, "I talked to people to whom the president *talked,* and I'm confident of the information that we received."

Johnson: Well, tell him that's *wrong.* Tell him the president's—

Moyers: I did.

Johnson: I didn't know [General Godfrey] McHugh was *on* the plane.[213]

Moyers: Yeah, that's one story. I said, Chuck, that one story in *itself* is enough to refute it. And then they go on and they keep saying . . . they have a *long* two paragraphs about your memories of the *day* that *Truman* was killed—

Johnson: I've never heard of that—

Moyers: —when *Truman* became president.

Johnson: Of Truman killed?

Moyers: I mean the day when Truman became president, when [Franklin] Roosevelt *died* [in office in April 1945].

Johnson: Well, the only thing I know there, as I told Bill *White* that *night . . .* he wrote a story from Rayburn's office.[214] But none of this stuff that I see in the paper is true.

I think we better write a nice paragraph and say, I've had no interviews on the subject at *all.* And this is completely inaccurate, and untrue, and unfair . . . that I've asked my staff *not* to discuss it. I've asked my *former* associates not to discuss it. And ask 'em to publish it and ask [*Newsweek* owner] Kay [Graham], and just say, This is just *murderin'* us. And you got headlines . . . I read you the headlines, didn't I?

Moyers: Yes, sir.

Johnson: [*reads them anyway*] "LBJ Differs on Kennedy Friction."[215] *That's eight columns!* That's like a *war* story.

Moyers: The *Washington Post* says, "LBJ Version on '63 Oath Is Reported."[216]

Johnson: [*reading*] "LBJ Version Clashes with Book Detail."[217]

[*to Moyers*] They're tryin' to build up the story, you see, by using the

---

213. According to Roberts's *Newsweek* article, there was a confrontation between General McHugh and Johnson as to precisely when *Air Force One* would take off. In fact, according to Manchester, the clash occurred between McHugh and Malcolm Kilduff. Manchester, *Death,* 316.

214. When the news of Roosevelt's death first reached Johnson, he was in the office of House Speaker Sam Rayburn. White, who was covering Congress for the *New York Times* in 1945, wrote a story about Rayburn's reaction to the news based on Johnson's account. "Texan Tells Grief of 'Young Guard,' " *New York Times,* 13 April 1945.

215. Johnson is apparently quoting a Texas newspaper.

216. The headline is from the AP wire service story printed in the *Washington Post,* 26 December 1966.

217. Johnson is quoting another headline from a Texas newspaper.

presidency. The *Dallas [Morning] News* . . . I haven't seen *it* yet, but . . . the *Austin American* didn't use *anything*! But these others do it.

Go ahead now. What does he [Roberts] *say*? He's *talked to* . . . people *who* have talked to the president?

Moyers: Yes, he says, We talked to a number of people—

Johnson: *[reading]* "Johnson's Recollection Reported Differently."

Moyers: That's right.

Johnson: *[still reading]* "*Newsweek* says, LBJ remembers intercepting McHugh, and [concedes], 'I did tell him off.' "

[to Moyers] Now, I never heard of that. I don't remember interceptin' him at all!

[reading] He [Johnson] says, "It [honey] is a word that comes easy [to me] as a Texan. You know, if I [call] some guy's office and he isn't in, I'll say [to] his secretary, 'Honey, have him call me.' "[218]

Moyers: Once when he comes in.

Johnson: Yeah. Now those are their ideas, you see. That's kind of their idea [of] *you-all.*[219]

Moyers: That's right. Well, of course, he [Roberts] won't . . . I said, Chuck, it would help *history* to be right, and if you could tell me where you *got* this? And he said, "Well, I can't do that. I'm not the only one who worked on the story, obviously," he said. "But *we* talked to a *number* of people who had *talked* to the president."

But Mr. President, here's some . . . let me find this one [sentence] . . .

[reading] " 'And I wasn't going to let Mrs. [Jacqueline] Kennedy fly back alone with his body,' he explained to intimates. By Mr. Johnson's *memory,* Robert Kennedy was not *noncommittal.* He *recalls* telephoning Bobby."

[to Johnson] But there's one sentence I wanted to say . . . I wanted to read you, just one minute.

[reading] "The moral Mr. Johnson *seemed to be drawing last week,* without spelling it out, was that no one at the *time* suggested that Truman had shown unseemly haste in promptly taking the presidential oath."

[to Johnson] That is . . . [the article reads] as if you had spent a specific period of your time last *week, talking* to somebody about this. Now, I said to Roberts, I said, this means, Chuck, that the president—who was at the ranch all of last week—would have had to be doing this talking down *there.* And he said, "That's what we understand."

Johnson: Well, that's not true, you see.

---

218. Reportedly, Manchester will write that Johnson inappropriately called Mrs. Kennedy "honey." Manchester, *Death,* 316.

219. Johnson is saying that such gibes reveal the prejudice of Americans from the Northeast toward all Texans and/or southerners, including Moyers.

Moyers: It's just totally fictitious.

Johnson: And I never *heard* of Truman. I've never discussed it with a human.

Moyers: They have two paragraphs in there.

[reading]

> "By coincidence, President Johnson recalls, he and House Speaker
> Sam Rayburn had planned a party for Truman that very day, mainly as
> a morale booster for a man lost in the limbo of the vice presidency.
> 'He doesn't think anybody likes him,' Rayburn told Mr. Johnson. As it
> happened, before LBJ arrived, the guest of honor was suddenly and
> mysteriously summoned to the White House and told to come in the
> front door. What Truman didn't know was that FDR had just died in
> Warm Springs, Georgia. But, as Truman undoubtedly told Rayburn,
> 'they never tell me anything.'
>
> "Rayburn followed Truman to the White House and later filled Mr.
> Johnson in on the scene there: Harry Truman taking charge, thanking
> everyone for arriving so quickly. The oath-taking, administered by
> Chief Justice [Harlan Fiske] Stone, was carried off as soon as Bess
> [and] Margaret Truman arrived. The *moral* Mr. Johnson seemed to be
> drawing last week, without spelling it out, was that no one at the time
> suggested that Truman had shown unseemly haste in promptly taking
> the presidential oath."

Johnson: Well, I'm not drawin' it one way or the other. I *think* that the moment
a president dies . . . the vice president becomes president.

Moyers: Yes, sir.

Johnson: And I have *not* discussed it with anyone to my knowledge. I've never
discussed the Truman *oath-taking* last week, or last *month*! I've talked a
good many times, *following* it [Roosevelt's death], during the years, about
the party that we [were] giving Truman . . . [held] *not because* nobody
liked him. But because Rayburn had heard from an admiral that the
president was dying, and *he* [Rayburn] felt that we should *meet* with
Truman and get to *know* him, and try to be *helpful* to him in case the
problem *[Johnson's voice becomes subdued]* came up.

It was not that nobody liked him. I think *everybody* liked him. I didn't
know anybody that *didn't* like Truman as vice president.

I have said *none* of it, and none of it is *true.* And I don't know what to
do about it under those circumstances. I'm not—

Moyers: George [Christian] will probably be asked [about] it, at his briefing. I
think maybe by then we would . . . we can either do it [one of] two ways:
just say we have no *comment* on it, or second . . . we can do it [one of] two
ways: one, send a telegram and then let George have no comment, or two,
send a telegram to *Newsweek* and let George just use the quote or use the
telegram as his reply to the questions.

Johnson: Well, don't you send a telegram, don't you *open* it then to debate again?

Moyers: Yes, sir. You do . . . no question about it. But Roberts seemed very *disturbed* that we would challenge him so *hard,* and I think he—

Johnson: I think you ought to challenge Kay [Graham], too. Just tell her that we have not been interviewed, that I asked the staff some time ago in *great* confidence not to *speak* on it, not to *debate* it. We've taken the position [that regardless of] whatever the Kennedys wanted, that I took the position when Manchester was selected, that he was a *fraud* [and] I refused to see him.[220]

I've asked my people *not* to see him. And the only ones I know [who did see Manchester] is you and [Lady] Bird, and . . . probably Jack Valenti, who were never under my orders really—didn't pay much attention to 'em—did see him. But I *asked* everybody *not* to, just as I asked 'em not to see Teddy *White.*[221] I think they're [Manchester and White] agents of the people who want to destroy *me.* And I hate for them to use *my* friends to *do* it. But they *do* do it . . . but my friends don't *know* it, and they want [to] be popular, and they just *do* it.

And I don't say it's so much [to be] popular. I don't think my *wife* wants to be popular. But I think she wants to be *accommodating,* would be a good word. And I think in the case of *White,* and I think in the case of *Manchester,* and I think in the case of [Charles] *Bartlett,* and I think in the case of Scotty *Reston,* and I think in the case of Tom *Wicker,* and I think in the case of Chuck *Roberts,* and I think in the case of Peter *Lisagor,* and in the case of Rowland *Evans,* and in the case of those *people,* I *think* that they have people who (a) are *former* associates of mine, or (b) people who know me that I *like,* or (c) . . . people who work for me and want to be accommodating, and feel that they *ought* to.[222]

I think they *use* those to hurt *me* with, and I think that the people don't *recognize* it, don't *realize* it. But I've continuously asked 'em, and I wished you'd *hear* . . . if I could recall for *you,* what I *hear* that my people say, from *you,* to *Jack* [Valenti], to *Buzz* [Horace Busby], to *George* [Christian], to *Walter* [Jenkins] . . . I don't guess Walter's ever said much.

But *all* of 'em *constantly*—somebody coming to me *every* day, and saying that these people say this and that . . . and it's their *impressions* of what happens. And I honestly believe that they feel that they have a right and a duty, first, to defend me. And second, to give their knowledge of [a]

220. See footnote 45.
221. Johnson is presumably talking about White's 1964 edition of *The Making of the President.*
222. James "Scotty" Reston is the *New York Times*'s most influential columnist; Bartlett is a pundit whose syndicated column appears in the *Washington Post;* Wicker is the Washington bureau chief of the *New York Times;* Lisagor is the Washington bureau chief for the *Chicago Daily News.*

situation. And (c) to comment on others . . . and you have no *idea* how troublesome it is, what they *do*. But I have asked 'em all—I told Bob Kintner to ask everybody, he's brought it to my attention three or four times—[I] said nobody on the staff should discuss Manchester in any way.

First thing I heard about it was . . . I understood that there's some [who] felt we oughta put out a *statement*. And Abe [Fortas] called me, and I said, Abe, I don't think we oughta have a statement of *any kind*. Now, if you want to have the facts, then get the facts, and put together *ours* [our version of these stories]. I took every precaution I knew. I asked Marie [Fehmer], and I asked Cliff Carter, and I asked Homer Thornberry to *all* take notes.[223] And I think they *did*. I've never looked at 'em, I've never discussed 'em. But I would try to put those together, and I'd take any questions that the leaks show, in the papers, that are uncomplimentary to me, and try to get the *facts*. And he [Fortas] said that'd be fine.

So that is what's [been] done. Now that's *all* I've done, and I've asked 'em all *not* to discuss the Manchester book. I've told George [Christian] this mornin' to just say that *this* . . . now maybe we oughta change it [and] make it different. I think that you oughta think about it and try to write somethin' that would be one sentence and not get it. . . . But *I'd* say that the president tells me that he has had many requests for an interview in connection with the book and the events it relates to, and he has refused every one. And has asked *all* of his staff to do likewise.

Then I think, if they'd say, Well, does that mean he refused 'em with *Newsweek*? And say, The statement speaks for itself, because it does. You have to give consideration to that.

Moyers: I think I would probably be a little harder on *Newsweek,* a little more . . . *emphatic*.

Johnson: *[reading]* "He [Johnson] said [to Robert Kennedy], 'I hate to *bother* you at a time like this,' to Bobby."

[to Moyers] Now I don't think anything like this; I never thought of a *time* like this. I thought the most important thing in the *world* was to decide who was president of this country at that moment. I was *fearful* that the Communists were tryin' to take us over.

[reading again] " 'I think you should be sworn in there,' *Bobby* said."

[to Moyers] I don't think that Bobby said that at *all*. I don't think Bobby *took* any initiative or any *direction*. I *think* that Bobby agreed . . . that it would be *all right* to be sworn in, and said he wanted to look into it, and [that] he would get back to me, which he did.

223. Johnson is referring to the fact that he specifically asked these three people (his secretary Fehmer, his political aide Carter, and Congressman Thornberry) to start taking notes of key events when they were all huddled together in Parkland Hospital, waiting for news about President Kennedy's condition.

I *think* that after they found out there's no recording—and there may *be* one—I think that they . . . [Godfrey] McHugh went out [to WHCA] and *thought* there was none—and I think *they* have leaked some of this.[224]

[reading] "*Newsweek* said there was an instance when Johnson had to exert authority, according to *Newsweek*'s Chuck Roberts, one of the two [newsmen aboard the plane] . . . [Ken] O'Donnell did it."

[to Moyers] I don't know about that. I didn't know it *[seven seconds excised]*.[225] But I *did* not think that he [O'Donnell] was issuin' orders to countermand mine. But he could have been, I don't know it.

[reading] "LBJ remembers intercepting McHugh."

[to Moyers] I do not. I didn't know he was on the plane, I hardly knew McHugh.

[reading] "Telling him he would tell the pilot when [to] take [off]. '*I did tell him off,*' Johnson conceded."

[to Moyers] I haven't said that to *any* human. I don't think I did [tell McHugh off]. I don't think I had a conversation with him.

[reading] "He agreed that he probably *did* call Mrs. Kennedy, 'honey.' It's a word that comes easy as a Texan. 'You know if I called some guy's office and he isn't in, I'll say to his secretary, "Honey, have him call in." ' "

[to Moyers] Now I don't think that I said that to *anybody* . . . and I don't think I called Mrs. Kennedy "honey." I think that's their *idea of you–all,* and [of] comin' . . . C–O–M–I–N' . . . this stuff they write about Texas. Now Norma Milligan says that she's been workin' on it up *there*.[226] And she says that she's from Oklahoma, and she thinks she understands Texans *better.* So she's been talkin' [to] some people on our staff there. I don't know *who.* Chuck Roberts has been talkin' to some; I don't know *who.* But these are not the facts as I remember them.

And *my* feeling on the Manchester book is [that] the best thing *we* can do . . . is I do not believe that we are equipped—by experience, by tradition, by personality, or financially—to *cope* with this. I just do not believe we know how to handle public relations, and how to handle advertising agencies, and how to handle manuscripts, [and] how to handle book writers. And then I don't believe that we're . . . I just don't think we're equipped for it.

So I think they're gonna write history as they [the Kennedys] want it

224. Johnson is again referring to the effort made on December 14, 1963, by Air Force General McHugh, probably on the attorney general's behalf, to determine if WHCA had recorded the conversations between Johnson and Kennedy on November 22.

225. The excision here may be a reference by Johnson to his perception that O'Donnell was drinking so heavily on the flight back to Washington that his recollections are not likely to be accurate.

226. Norma Milligan is a researcher/reporter in *Newsweek*'s Washington bureau.

written, and as they can *buy it* written. And I think the best way *we* can
write it is to try to refrain from gettin' into an argument, or a fight, or a
knockdown, and go on and do our job every day as best we can. [Even] if
I've just got Marie [Fehmer] doin' it with me. And I *do* that. I stay at *all*
[hours] . . . every hour. And it damn near causes you divorces, and it
almost causes you troubles. We've got everybody callin' around on
different things, and gossip pourin' in—and pipelines of it—because
everybody likes to show that they're close to the president.

And I said to someone the other day that I don't know of but four
people that have left me that I know of that were my people that [were]
brought in after Walter Jenkins was *forced* to leave. He didn't leave of his
own *volition*. But I think that you and Jack [Valenti], and Buzz [Horace
Busby], and George Reedy . . . and I don't believe *any* of 'em did better
before they came in the White House . . . than they did in the White House.
[six seconds excised]

But I think they get different impressions. And I think we just have
to . . . the best thing we can say is as *little* as we can, because you can see
that you are the most truthful, the closest, the ablest, the finest man that's
ever been there. But still, they claim, our press relations are terrible.[227]
Now: if that *is* true . . . then I can't expect 'em to be as good when you're
gone. So the best thing for us to do is just to keep it as limited as we can,
and as little. And my thought would be—and I'm not sure that I'm right,
I'd like for you to think about it—*my* thought would be that George could
say, I've had several requests for interviews with the president or members
of the staff on this question. They have all been declined. The president
has said, has stated, has *refused* to have any interviews on it, and any . . .
purported statements of his are not only inaccurate but untrue.

Now *maybe* that's a little too strong. You had in mind that you'd go a
little stronger than my original one. What did you have in mind?

Moyers: *Newsweek* said, "LBJ's own recollection of" . . . frankly, Mr.
President, if you read this whole piece, it is a *sympathetic piece to you,* and
to your position. But it's based upon *total fabrication.* But it says,
[reading]

"LBJ's own recollections of that fateful day, as he has recounted them
to *friends,* have a touching quality all their *own.* What raced through
his mind when he learned that [the] president was dead was no

227. For about a year—and coinciding almost exactly with Moyers's tenure as press secretary—
the Johnson administration has been plagued by doubt and skepticism about its public pronounce-
ments and explanations, the so-called credibility gap issue. At bottom, it stems from Johnson's
campaigning as the peace candidate in 1964, only to escalate the Vietnam War in 1965. But Moyers has exacerbated the problem because of his tendency to speak too freely on the president's
behalf. Murray Marder, "Credibility Gap: Greater Skepticism Greets Administration Declara-
tions," *Washington Post,* 5 December 1965.

personal thrust for power, but rather the *memory* of the day Harry Truman suddenly inherited the presidency from Franklin Roosevelt more than eighteen years ago."

Johnson: Now that was not true. I don't remember that at *all*. I never thought of it.

Moyers: I never heard you say that.

Johnson: What raced through *my* mind was that, if they had shot our president, driving down there, who would they shoot next? And what was going on in Washington? And when would the missiles be comin'? And *I* thought that it was a *conspiracy,* and I raised that question. And nearly everybody that was *with* me raised it. Go ahead.

Moyers: Well, that's it. So to say that the president's had no interviews doesn't really answer *Newsweek,* because *Newsweek* is saying it *picked this up* from people with whom you have talked.

Johnson: Well, I think nearly everybody *thinks,* though, it's LBJ's interview.

Moyers: Yes. Then it *goes on* to use these words like—

Johnson: It says, "Johnson Differs on Kennedy Friction."

Moyers: Right.

Johnson: "Johnson Version Clashes with Book Details." I don't know my version; I haven't given it. I guess, though, [that] my friends, they do *do* this. Then what would you say?

Moyers: Well, I would say . . . I'd consider putting this in a telegram to Kay Graham, which [would say], *Newsweek*'s account of the president's recollections is not consistent with *any fact* known here.

Johnson: I wouldn't say that 'cause they'll find, in my *statement,* that I said something. We've got to be very *careful.* They have *deliberately* built this credibility [gap issue] by picking up the Communist line on it, and so that any difference I have with Bobby, Bill, [will be exploited].[228] I think this has been carefully constructed through the months to prove that I cannot be believed. So I'm disarmed. And I think where we've got to be *very* careful is that we don't say *anything* that they could *possibly* attribute. [Do] you get my point?

Moyers: Yes. Well, *Newsweek*'s account of the president's recollections is not based on any . . . the president has had no interviews with anyone. The recollections attributed to him in *Newsweek* do not represent the *facts*.

Johnson: Well, why don't we just say "are untrue."

Moyers: All right. *Newsweek*'s account of the president's recollections is untrue.

Johnson: The president has consistently refused to give any interview on this subject. And the statements attributed to him . . . are false.

228. The domestic controversy over Johnson's credibility has been eagerly picked up and magnified by Communist-controlled media worldwide.

Not *all* of 'em are, but some of 'em are. The *McHugh* thing is false; the *"honey"* thing is false; the *Truman* thing is false.

Moyers: All right then. I think I have it here, let me finish taking a note.

[*reading*] "*Newsweek*'s account of the president's recollections is untrue. The president has consistently refused to give any interviews on the subject, and *statements*"—leave out [the word] the—"and *statements* attributed to him in this account are *false.*"

Johnson: Now, does that make us go further, and debate it further? And [keep the issue alive by denying statements] by so-called friends?

The statements attributed to him by so-called friends are false?

Moyers: Well, you know, it all depends on who they *talked* to, Mr. President.

Johnson: "So-called friends and alleged intimates" . . . that's what I'd say, by "so-called friends and alleged intimates."

Moyers: [Statements by] "so-called friends—"

Johnson: "and alleged intimates are *false.*"

Moyers: All right, sir. I think that would do it as far as *Newsweek* [is concerned]. I think we have to ask ourselves whether or not we then want to . . . maybe not release a telegram, but just have George *say*—without mentioning a telegram—just *say* that "I talked to the president about that this morning, and he said that that account is just not *true*. That he has consistently refused to givin' interviews; that he finds the statements attributed to him by so-called friends and alleged intimates to be *false.*"

Johnson: Well, talk to Abe [Fortas] about it—

Moyers: All right, sir.

Johnson: —see what he thinks. I don't want to get in a full *debate* on it. I don't want to *blow up* their story and sell any more of their articles. And you *might* say, as was the *[Washington] Post* story on the A[merican] F[ederation] of L[abor] this week, [the *Newsweek* article is inaccurate].[229]

Moyers: All right.

Johnson: I guess that takes on the *Post* and *Newsweek* always.

Moyers: I called Rowland Evans this morning, Mr. President, but *[seven seconds excised]* because *he* has a very, *I think,* damaging story, but that's to the next point.

[The conversation turns to a discussion about inaccuracies in the Evans and Novak column about the AFL-CIO.]

Johnson: Well, I have no reason why I *shouldn't* [contact Kay Graham to complain about the *Newsweek* article]. I certainly feel that that's my

---

229. On December 21 Evans and Novak published a column in the *Washington Post* alleging deep differences of opinion between Johnson and George Meany, president of the AFL-CIO. Meany subsequently sent the *Post* a blistering letter, stating that the column was false in all its particulars and constituted a "low order of political gossip." George Meany, "A Communication," *Washington Post,* 24 December 1966.

obligation to do it if it's untrue. I think that's the question at issue. Is it untrue? And if it *is* untrue, the people that publish it are responsible, aren't they?

Moyers: Yes, sir.

Johnson: I don't know how I can go to . . . whoever does this on *Newsweek* will say [that] Norma Milligan told George that she'd been working on this. And she's from Oklahoma, and she said that's what she was doin' in Washington. She just come down here. So she and Chuck Roberts wrote the *[Newsweek]* story.

Moyers: Well . . . and there's no question but that they've *talked* to people who *told* them these things. *I'm sure that Roberts and Milligan didn't make it up.* They *talked* to people who *told* them that this is what you *said.* And then they reported that.

I do not believe, Mr. President, that a reporter just *makes this up.* I don't believe *Evans and Novak* make it up. I think they *hear* it, as in the case of the Meany story, from a second-, third-, or even *fourth-hand* source, and then they carry it. And it's their *source* who is *wrong,* and in that extent, the author, or the columnist, or the reporter for not *checking* it with someone who *is* in the know. Just like last week, as I mentioned to you, the *New York Times* and the *Washington Post almost carried* a story about a call *I* was alleged to have made to Arthur Schlesinger, when they *did not even check* with Schlesinger *or* me. And they had a source in New York.

Now, this morning, here's Evans and Novak's column.[230] I'll read it to you in just a minute. And I want to *preface* it by saying, Mr. President, that it doesn't bother me if anyone *disbelieves* me, because I know in my own heart it's true. [But] I have not talked to *anyone* about the subjects mentioned in Evans and Novak this morning. *Not to anyone* except *you.* Not to anyone else in the White House; not to my wife. I called Jack [Valenti] this morning and asked him if *he* had talked to 'em. He said, No, only to Mary Margaret. Well, I haven't even talked to *Judith* about it.[231] But let me read you the column.

[reading]

"Serious Democratic politicians here, both inside and outside the Johnson camp, are alarmed over the political impact of the Manchester book on their party, and consequently, on the 1968 presidential election.

"President Johnson *himself* has displayed no signs of distress to his intimates over the pre-publication of juicy bits and pieces alleged to be in the book, *The Death of a President,* by William Manchester.

230. Evans and Novak, "Pandora's Box," *Washington Post,* 26 December 1966.
231. Mary Margaret and Judith are the respective spouses of Valenti and Moyers.

"And yet these disembodied excerpts put Mr. Johnson in a highly unflattering light in the immediate aftermath of the tragedy at Dallas.

"Showing no concern, the president instead has confided to intimates that 'the ultimate record will be clear.' If those words mean what they *imply,* they mean only one thing: that a massive refutation of the Manchester version, almost *all* of it gathered in interviews with Kennedy intimates, is in the offing.

"One predictable effect of any such refutation would be to heighten the tensions between the Johnson and Kennedy wings of the Democratic Party. Because fairly or not, all the anti-Johnson overtones found in the Manchester book are automatically going to be attributed to allies of the Kennedys who gave the author most of the material. Mr. Johnson himself refused to see Manchester.

"It would be only natural for Johnson allies to strike back at the Manchester book—and hence at the *Kennedys*—with their own version of the traumatic events during those fateful hours after the assassination. Moreover, despite the fact that the White House has told this column that no precise reconstruction of events has even been thought of—"

[to Johnson] Now, that's the note that I had Mary Catherine read Evans when he called on Friday and I refused to talk to him, as I refused last week to talk to *any* reporters.[232] I simply said, Tell him that he is *wrong* . . . that the White House does not have *any* idea of putting together a refutation of the Manchester book.

[reading again]

"Moreover, despite the fact that the White House has told this column that no precise reconstructions have ever *[sic]* been thought of, there are indications that *close* friends of Mr. Johnson, including Supreme Court Justice Abe Fortas, may now be compiling the record.

"For example, in the president's personal files today are notes dictated on the spot, and recollections put down months later, by members of the Johnson official family. A minute-by-minute account of what Mr. Johnson *did,* and of much of what he was heard to *say,* was dictated by Clifford C. Carter, a longtime Johnson intimate, on the flight back to Washington."

[to Johnson] Well, I called Cliff this morning, and he said he *did* talk to Evans last week, but that he didn't tell him anything that he hasn't told anyone else . . . publicly or talked about.

[reading again]

"Jack Valenti, the president's man Friday from the moment of the assassination until he quit the White House earlier this year, was never

232. Mary Catherine [Curry] is Moyers's secretary.

interviewed by author Manchester. But Valenti also has a set of notes giving his version of the new president's conduct from Love Field until late that night in the new president's temporary quarters in the Executive Office Building.

"Valenti took time out in the rush of events the following week to replenish his record. A note written on November 25, for example, recalled that despite the emotional tensions of the moment, Mr. Johnson had reached for a glass of water on the flight back from Dallas with a steady hand."

[to Johnson] I talked to Jack this morning, and he says that he had talked—

Johnson: Now, he's upset.[233] He said that you told him that I had called you and asked you to get a hold of him about this call. I told him I never had *heard* of it, and I hadn't asked you to get a hold of him.

Moyers: No, Mr. President. I told him that you had asked me to call him about the [*Newsweek* article], and talk to different people about the *Newsweek* thing, and see if they talked to him. And I've called a number of people. I had not read this [the Evans and Novak column] at that time, when you talked to me. Then when I came to the office, I read this thing *too* and I just coupled *both* of 'em with Jack. And he said he *didn't* talk to *Newsweek,* but that he had talked to Evans more than a week ago but he didn't tell him *this.*

[reading again]

"Beyond this, reliable politicians now report that verbatim transcripts of telephone and other conversations between the president and others in the post-assassination period have been carefully filed for future use."

Well, that's wrong, because there *are* no verbatim transcripts.

Johnson: Oh no, there are . . . there're a good many.[234]

Moyers: *[puzzled]* I thought . . . all right.

Johnson: *[with tone of satisfaction]* They don't *think* so, but there're a *good* many.

Moyers: I thought that Juanita had said that we didn't have the *equipment* in those days.[235]

Johnson: Well, there're . . . there're *good* many, but. . . .

233. According to the Daily Diary, Johnson last talked with Valenti at 11:33 a.m. on December 25.

234. Johnson is acknowledging the existence of extensive tape recordings since the beginning of his administration.

235. Moyers was aware, by no later than August 1964 and probably earlier, that the president was recording his telephone conversations. The practice was openly mentioned during a Moyers-Johnson conversation about Louisiana governor John McKeithen (D). Johnson and Moyers, conversation, 7 August 1964, LBJL.

Moyers: *[as if Johnson doesn't understand]* Well, he's talking here about [transcripts of conversations] between *you* and other people.

Johnson: Well, there are—

Moyers: All right.

Johnson: —there're a *good* many.

Moyers: *[drops the subject]*

[reading again]

"Although these reports cannot be confirmed, they suggest that ammunition for a counter-attack against the Manchester book—if one is needed—has been stored up for use at any time.

"All of this gives Democrats who aren't principal actors in the drama a distinctly uneasy feeling, and no wonder. If the Manchester book does in fact portray Mr. Johnson in the unflattering hues suggested by the advance publicity, Johnson allies are certain to attack the book's authenticity and produce their own version.

"And that, without question, could start a vicious round of recrimination. Already, for example, some Johnson allies are saying Senator Robert Kennedy of New York advanced the Manchester publication date from post-election 1968 to post-election 1966 to embarrass the president. In fact, the earlier date was picked for only one reason: that Kennedy is completely out of the 1968 presidential picture, but very much in the 1972 picture. If publication were delayed until 1969, he could be charged with using the book to help his political prospects.

"But this kind of charge will continue. And if Johnson intimates do decide that the Manchester book is really harmful to the president, and come up with their own version of what really happened, discord will shake the party to the benefit of the high-flying Republicans."

[to Johnson] Now, when I talked to Evans, he admitted he had talked to nobody in the White House. [He said] that he had talked to *six* people . . . two of whom had told him that Abe Fortas *and* Clark Clifford and *others* might be working on this. They weren't as sure about *Clifford* as they were about *Fortas*. One of them, he [Evans] said, was in New York, and the other one was in Washington. Neither of them, he said, was either working for you or *had* worked for you. He said he talked to *one wife* of a very close friend of yours.[236] And I said, Was this wife the friend of someone who *is* working at the White House, or *has* worked at the White House? He said, "No, it is not." He said, "But I consider the information fairly good."

That's another case [of what I was talking about earlier], six people

236. This description suggests that one of Evans's sources may be Carol Agger, Abe Fortas's wife.

talking to a fella . . . and I'm surprised that they knew what *they* knew. And
I've talked to Ben Bradlee this morning.[237] Here they've got in the
Washington Post a little postscript, which says,
[reading]

"Senator Robert F. Kennedy remains eager to *defuse* his feud with FBI
director J. Edgar Hoover over who authorized the use of electronic
'bugs' in the years that Kennedy served as attorney general.

"*Accordingly,* a Kennedy operative last week discreetly approached
two highly placed White House staff members to elicit their aid in
dampening the controversy. The Johnson men offered their sympathy,
but said the president 'can't control Hoover.' Now the senator is
awaiting fresh charges from Hoover that his former boss [Kennedy]
knew all about the 'bugging.' "[238]

[to Johnson] Well, I told Bradlee . . . I talked to Bradlee for a long time,
and he gave me reason to believe that that had come from [*Post* reporter]
Andy Glass via Dick Goodwin. So I called Goodwin, and Goodwin
admitted that he had talked to Glass last Thursday in New York, and he
said, "Probably I mentioned it. I thought it would be helpful."[239] And I
said, Dick, this is *exactly* what *[six seconds excised]* . . . that Dick, this
is *exactly* what makes it difficult to deal with you, and makes it very
difficult to keep the air clean between the White House and the
senator. Not because the president or the senator are talking, but because
[of] people [reporters] who call *us* [aides to either the president or
senator].

And then I said, You told me you would tell *no* one that you had sent
me a transcript of the *Look* piece. And *I* didn't even tell anybody where I
got it. I didn't even tell the *president* where I got this copy of *Look*
magazine. And I said, But then Arthur Schlesinger tells Jack Valenti that
he knows that we have a copy!

So this is another example of what you were talking about earlier, Mr.
President . . . or what *bothers* you really, is that *these* papers and *these*
reporters use sources that *appear* to know or *do* know, but [that] are second
or third removed from the scene.

Johnson: *[dejectedly]* Well . . . this is your department. You're much more
experienced in it than I am.[240]

---

237. Bradlee, having left *Newsweek* in 1965, is now the managing editor of the *Washington Post.*

238. *Post* Scripts, "LBJ 'Can't Control' Hoover," *Washington Post,* 26 December 1966.

239. This is a typical example of Goodwin's shrewd and manipulative gossiping, to Johnson's detriment. It is not helpful to the president to suggest that Hoover is beyond Johnson's control.

240. Johnson sounds stunned and deflated, as if realizing the full extent of Goodwin's betrayal, and how close aides like Moyers are being played.

Moyers: No, I'm really *not,* Mr. President. I haven't had any . . . you can't control what is uncontrollable. People *[indistinct]*—

Johnson: No, but I mean you've known . . . *I* never did know Goodwin well at all. I hardly *knew* him when he came with us. I never did know Schlesinger well. I never did know even Jack well.[241] He just came in there, and . . . would do it. I *think* that it would be very good if you and Jack, and George, and Buzz, and Cliff would get together, and if y'all wouldn't *talk* to these people . . . either while you're working there with 'em on these discussions, or after you *leave* [the White House staff].

But they *write* these things, or they talk to our people, and so forth. So . . . we just *have* to do that with the press. But the question is, what do we do about *Newsweek* and George, who's briefing right now?

Moyers: Well, I'll call *[indistinct]*—

Johnson: How *simple* can we make it? I would think that I oughta ask him to just not brief for a moment, and [in the meantime] you talk to Abe, and Abe, I imagine, is in Connecticut.

Moyers: No sir, he's in town. I talked to him this morning. I buzzed my secretary and gave her a note, and told her to call George and ask him to hold off briefing until you and I've finished talking. And so that's taken care of. . . .

Johnson: Okay, then *I* would think that you oughta give 'em one sentence and say that, "I've had requests from news magazines and others for interviews with the president and members of the staff about the Manchester book. The president refused to *see* Mr. Manchester, and has refused to give any interviews on this subject, and has asked the staff to do likewise. *I* believe the statements attributed to friends and to alleged intimates are inaccurate and untrue."

Now that's what I would say. What's wrong with that?

Moyers: I think it's fine.

Johnson: I think that [George] Christian saying that [will be okay] . . . it doesn't quote me, but he *ought* to know, you see, by his intimacy with me. *Then* I think it'd be *very* good, if Abe is still there, if you could get Abe to get all y'all together. And *ask* them to please not discuss their experiences in the White House . . . even acknowledging they're there . . . just change the subject.

Moyers: All right.

Johnson: Don't you think that's good with Carter, and with Busby, and with Reedy, and with you, and with Jack?

Moyers: Yes, sir.

---

241. Valenti first met the president in 1957, and in 1960 his public relations advertising agency in Houston got the Kennedy-Johnson campaign account in Texas. He joined the White House staff in November 1963.

Johnson: And see if we can kind of get a little pact on men's honors, and just say now, we don't discuss those things. If we *don't*, I think y'all gonna be *fully* discredited. My judgment is, after a year, or two or three years, you're gonna be almost like Donald Dawson and Harry Vaughn were during that *period,* because they're turning it into something *like* this.[242] And I fully expect to, but I don't think that y'all ought to, and I think you *will,* because *I* told Jack this *morning,* if I *have* to, damn if I won't destroy *everybody* . . . to get the *facts* known. And if people just gonna rear back and say, Well now, *here's my version of it,* I'm defending *him* . . . even with the *best* of intentions, and [then] give somebody like Rowland Evans, or Chuck Roberts, or some of them . . . or Art Buchwald, or those things.[243]

    I want *my* posture to be—and I've *insisted* on this with Abe—that we know what happened, from our own knowledge of what happened. But we'll not let another human know it. I don't want to debate with 'em. I don't think the president of this country at this time ought to. I think it's just *unthinkable* that my whole morning would not be spent on the Vietnam [situation] or anything else, but be spent on this kind of stuff.

Moyers: Yes, sir.

Johnson: And I think that we've had a bunch of traitors, and kids, and things in there that just have brought it about. And I think that *practically* nearly every one of the Kennedy folks have contributed to it. But I think the worst ones are Dick Goodwin, and I wouldn't . . . I think Dick Goodwin *planted* that transcript with you.[244] I think he did it for a *purpose.* You don't believe so, do you?

Moyers: Oh, I think it's quite possible that he did.

Johnson: And I wouldn't *trust* that fella! I just—

Moyers: Mr. President, I don't.

Johnson: I don't believe I'd have any *contact* with him. And I don't know what to *do* about it. *[five seconds excised]*

    [agitated] And I wished *[sic]* you let . . . I'll read you later today, after you've talked [attended] to these other things. You check with Abe—

Moyers: And I'll call you right back.

Johnson: —and then call me right back. And what I would say . . . what do you think we oughta say? Now what's that sentence? Let me get it clear in my mind, so I approve it.

Moyers: All right, sir.

    [reading] "The president has consistently refused to grant any

---

242. Dawson and Vaughn, aides to Harry Truman, are considered two of the least reputable men to have served in the White House in recent memory.

243. Buchwald is a pundit whose column appears in the *Washington Post.*

244. If Goodwin did not plant it, he certainly betrayed a confidence by telling Arthur Schlesinger, Jr., afterward.

interviews to anyone concerning the subjects mentioned in Mr. Manchester's *book*. And he has instructed his *staff* to *also* refrain from any such discussions. *Newsweek*'s account of the president's recollections is untrue. The statement"—

Johnson: All right, go ahead. I would say [that] *Newsweek*'s *account* of the *statements* of *friends* and alleged *intimates* is untrue. So that [if] friends are saying it, they're tellin' [an] untruth, [and] if *Newsweek*'s sayin' it, they're telling an untruth.

Moyers: That is saying that their account of their *statements* is not true, and they may be verbatim *right* . . . I mean they may be *correct* in quoting these people. But it's the statements *attributed* to the president by so-called friends and alleged intimates [that] are false.

Johnson: All right. Okay.

Moyers: I'll call you right back.

From Bill Moyers / 11:46 a.m., CST

Ninety minutes later Moyers is back on the telephone to share Abe Fortas's views on the press statement being prepared in response to the *Newsweek* article. The conversation that ensues is Lyndon Johnson at his angriest.

The president is taken aback to learn that Fortas thinks the *Newsweek* article is, on balance, favorable. Apparently not even Fortas, his most trusted counsel, understands the affront to Johnson's dignity. To stoop to replying to Manchester's allegations is to elevate them and prolong a controversy that Johnson finds excruciating. He cannot comprehend why his advisers do not understand.[245] The result is a display of presidential ire only rarely found on the Johnson recordings.

Moyers, for his part, finally despairs of trying to persuade the president to limit his rebuttal. Being Johnson's press secretary is probably the hardest job in the White House. The president's unhappiness over media coverage is almost congenital.

Moyers: Abe says that we oughta be careful about this because he believes that *most* of it is *good* for our side. He says that—as I read the *Newsweek* thing to him and he's seen it in the papers . . . he says actually, in *his* judgment, [it] makes you look *good,* even if it is *based* upon an inaccurate thing. But

---

245. One notable exception is John Roche, a recent addition to the White House staff. Roche sees "no comment" as the president's best weapon. Johnson should "issue absolute orders that the administration policy is *silence.* Let the Kennedy stockholders fight this one out among themselves." By doing so, Roche is confident that the clan "will erode if not destroy their greatest political asset: the myth of JFK." Roche to Johnson, memo, 23 December 1966, Manchester File, Box 1, Special File, LBJL.

he said that what you *oughta* say is something like this, and I've got it down. Quote, [and] this would be [George] Christian [speaking], "The president has granted no interview to anyone, including Mr. Manchester, and he's asked his staff *also* to refrain from discussing the subject. He has no recollection of saying these things to friends or associates or alleged intimates."

Johnson: No, I think that lays it onto *me*. I don't want to say that at all.

Moyers: *[momentarily speechless]* I went back over this one with him—

Johnson: No.

Moyers: —*Newsweek*'s account of the president's recollections—

Johnson: No, I wouldn't do that at all. I'm against that last sentence there. *[frustrated]* I would just say . . . *oh, hell.* I don't know *why* he [Fortas] would . . . I guess that's his best judgment, though!

Moyers: Yes, sir.

Johnson: The *implication* is that I could have said it without [thinking]. And I never . . . couldn't have done it so, 'cause I don't *know* it.

Moyers: All right. I just had Chuck Roberts on the phone *again,* when you called back. I was just saying to him if you could—

Johnson: *[annoyed] I didn't call back.* Am I calling you now?

Moyers: *[hastens to explain]* No, I called *you,* and you were on the phone.

Johnson: Oh, yeah. I didn't *know* it. *[angry]* I told them the moment you called, to *put you right through.* God-*damn!*

Moyers: That's right . . . and anyway, Roberts was saying, "Well, I *know* that this person *believes* that he heard it from the *president*."

Johnson: *[biting off each word] Well, it's not true!*

Moyers: And that's what I said. I said, Well, Charley—

Johnson: *I* would imagine it's Clark Clifford, or Abe, or somebody that just had these feelings.

Moyers: Abe hasn't talked to Roberts. He told—

Johnson: That don't make any difference, Bill. That's the worst excuse in the world. I would *never* mention that. All you have to do is for me to say somethin' to Lady Bird. You don't have to say it to the *New York Times.* Lady Bird says it to Lynda; Lynda says it to [George] Hamilton; Hamilton says it to Luci; Luci says it to Pat [Nugent]; Pat says it to a football player; a football player says it to his date, and then it gets into [the] *New York Time[s]* as an intimate.[246] I *never* would explain I haven't talked to somebody, 'cause just anybody that hears it, talks it.

Now let's get this last sentence. I would say that . . . have George say, "I will not . . . discuss the *[Moyers begins typing]* various attributions credited to so-called friends and *alleged* intimates, except to say I believe them to be inaccurate and untrue."

---

246. Hamilton, an actor, is dating Lynda Johnson, and Pat Nugent is Luci Johnson's husband.

Now if he can say that without his credibility bein' questioned, without
leavin' the impression that I'm *forcin'* him to do it, that's what I would say.

Moyers: All right. You want him to say that the president has no recollection—

Johnson: *[frustrated]* No. Hell, no!

Moyers: I mean the president *[indistinct]*—

Johnson: *[agitated, almost shouting]* I have a recollection: *it didn't happen!*

Moyers: All right.

Johnson: I think it's a *god-damn lie!* Now that's my *best* judgment, which I'd
bet my *life on!*

[still speaking loudly] I *honestly* don't think *they* thought it happened. I
think this: I have had somebody tell me in the last week that Chuck
Roberts—Jack *Valenti* told me, over the phone—that Chuck Roberts, and
Chuck Bailey, and Peter Lisagor, *all* were really *thinking* that I had been
mistreated.[247] I think what they do is call up some *sap* and tell him that,
you see. *You* know Chuck Bailey doesn't think I'm mistreated. You know
Lisagor doesn't [think so]. If they did, they'd be *happy!* [And that includes
Clark] *Mollenhoff . . .* don't you think so?[248]

Moyers: *[mute]*

Johnson: *I do!* I don't think they're concerned about my bein' mistreated. I
think they'd be the most *happy* people in the world, because I think they
mistreat me the *most!* When I see Chuck Bailey's insinuations and
imputations, and Mollenhoff's, and Lisagor's, I just think . . . so *I* think
that I would just. . . . Read that last sentence I dictated.

Moyers: "I will not discuss the various"—this is George [speaking]—"I will
not discuss the various attributions credited to so-called friends and alleged
intimates, except to say I believe them to be *inaccurate* and *untrue.*" To
that, Mr. President, Abe and I would *add,* The president has granted no
interview to *anyone,* including Mr. Manchester, and he's asked—

Johnson: No, no. I would go on with the first part of your statement.

Moyers: *[exhausted]* All right . . . all right, sir.

Johnson: *[agitated]* I would substitute *this* in *lieu of the fact* that the president
has no recollections, 'cause I *do* have a recollection of not ever sayin' *a
son-of-a-bitchin' word* to [General] McHugh!

Moyers: All right.

Johnson: *[exasperated, almost shouting]* I never said to anybody that *I got
him* [McHugh] *told off.* I never said to anybody that I called her "honey"
because *that was the Texas way!* I don't *believe* that's the Texas way! I
think I would call people honey because . . . if I felt they *were* honey.

247. Bailey is the Washington correspondent for the *Minneapolis Tribune,* a Cowles-owned
newspaper.

248. Mollenhoff is a reporter in the Washington bureau of the *Des Moines Register,* another
Cowles newspaper.

And I might have *very well* said that to Mrs. Kennedy, although I never *felt* that way about her and never *believed it*. I have held her kind of up on a *pedestal* and been very *reserved* with her, as her letters to me will indicate . . . very *proper,* very *appropriate,* very *dignified,* very reserved, as I don't think I called Mrs. [Rose] Kennedy senior *"honey"*! I think that is the creature of someone's *imagination*! So how can I *not recollect it*? When it just didn't *happen*!

    I think "not recollected" *implies* that it *could* have happened and I['ve] not remembered [it], don't you?

Moyers: *[evenly, seeking only to get the president's agreement]* I agree. Well, this is how it would then read, Mr. President. "The president has granted no interview to anyone, including Mr. Manchester"—

Johnson: I would say, "has *refused* to grant any interview." No . . . that's all right, "has granted no interview" . . . that's right.

Moyers: All right. "The president has granted no interview to anyone, including Mr. Manchester, and has asked his staff to refrain from discussing the subject. *I* will not discuss the various attributions credited to so-called friends and alleged intimates, except to say I believe them to be inaccurate and untrue."

Johnson: That's all right.

Moyers: I think that's good. That first part makes it appear that you *really* want to stay out of it. Abe says that's what we oughta give the impression of.

Johnson: That's what we *oughta* do, and I think this meeting of the three of you caused things to kick off.[249] I just don't think you can meet with *anybody.* And it's awful that I *feel* that way, but that is *true.* Now if you, and Jack Valenti, and Abe can't meet without being in a column, I'm damned if I know. Do you?

Moyers: No, sir.

Johnson: Well, just say, except for the grace of God, it might be *me,* and maybe someday it'll be one of y'all. But I can't understand it; *don't* understand it; don't know *why.* But I just *endure* it, and I *have to* for the time allotted me, but I sure don't like it. You call George, though.

Moyers: All right.

The next day leading newspapers, including the *New York Times,* will publish stories about how the White House is disputing both the attribution and the substance of the *Newsweek* account. Just as Moyers fears, the president cannot win the argument. The stories include a statement from *Newsweek*'s editor that he "has confidence in [Roberts] and in the reliability of [his] source."[250]

---

249. Johnson is referring to the December 17 meeting of Fortas, Moyers, and Valenti.

250. "Johnson Aide Disputes *Newsweek* Report of President's Comments on Kennedy Book Controversy," *New York Times,* 27 December 1966.

The battle over the book continues, but now in a somewhat more subterranean manner. The Kennedys leak information to favored reporters designed to cast doubt on Manchester's portrayal of Johnson as boorish and thoughtless, thereby distancing themselves from that depiction. Peter Lisagor, for example, publishes an article in the *Chicago Daily News* about "letters of gratitude" from Mrs. Kennedy to Johnson about his many kindnesses after the assassination. In the opposing camp, whether by design or still against Johnson's wishes, *U.S. News & World Report* begins publishing a series of articles in late December highly favorable to both the president's version of events and his studied refusal to be drawn into the controversy.[251] Columnist William White criticizes Manchester for his portrayal of Dallas, and especially for Manchester's use of the word *tong* to describe Johnson's advisers—tong connoting a criminal gang.[252] Drew Pearson, another columnist favorably inclined to the president, also weighs in with a few sympathetic columns, asserting that the Texas trip occurred at John Kennedy's insistence and showing again how considerate Johnson was of Mrs. Kennedy.[253]

Sooner than anyone imagines, Johnson's public stance of seeming disinterest will be rewarded. Whether because of the lawsuit and the rawness of the effort to control history, or because of how Robert Kennedy is actually portrayed, the senator's "unfavorable" rating will rise and his political stock will suffer a corresponding (if temporary) fall. Alistair Cooke, a longtime British correspondent for *The Guardian,* expresses the view of many observers when he writes that "LBJ emerges with more sense and dignity than anybody, on the plane ride back to Washington, and . . . the Kennedy team seems to have behaved naturally and atrociously."[254]

251. There will be several rebuttals in *U.S. News & World Report.* See "The Book That Has Backfired," 26 December 1966; "Battle over a Book—New Role for Mrs. JFK," 2 January 1967; "Growing Rift of LBJ and Kennedys: Behind the Furor over a Book," 2 January 1967; "As 'the Book' Appears: A Close Look at the Facts," 23 January 1967; "JFK and LBJ: More Untold Stories," 30 January 1967; "To Help You Keep the Record Straight About That Book," 6 February 1967; "In the Hours After Dallas: 'The Book' and the Testimony," 20 February 1967, all in *U.S. News & World Report.* The index to the Daily Diary shows no contact between Johnson and top editors at *U.S. News,* all of whom were well known to the president, so it is not clear who, if anyone, from the White House contributed to the stories. But they were almost certainly written with the cooperation of former or current advisers to the president.

252. William White, "A City Indicted . . . Dallas Is Manchester's Chief Target," *Washington Post,* 12 January 1967; Manchester, *Death,* 88.

253. Drew Pearson, "Fatal Dallas Trip Initiated by JFK," *New Orleans States-Item,* 10 January 1967; "Reveal LBJ Side in Dallas Story," *New Orleans States-Item,* 11 January 1967; "LBJ Considerate of Mrs. Kennedy," *New Orleans States-Item,* 12 January 1967.

254. Alistair Cooke, Book Week, *Washington Post,* 9 April 1967.

In two short years, Johnson's political mandate has evaporated and his ambitious domestic agenda is under attack. The Republican Party has come roaring back after having been read its political obituary in 1964.

In the single biggest upset, and as a possible harbinger of things to come, the GOP won the California gubernatorial race in November 1966. Pat Brown, a prototypical liberal Democrat who governed and believed as Johnson governs and believes, lost his bid for reelection to a political neophyte and former actor named Ronald Reagan, running on a "law and order" platform. The results outside California augur just as well for the Republicans in 1968. Seven other governorships fell to the GOP, including Florida's statehouse, which had not elected a Republican since Reconstruction. The party also gained forty-seven seats in the House of Representatives and three Senate seats. The liberal majority in the Congress is no more, and Johnson will have his hands full getting all the funding he wants for his Great Society programs from the new Congress, though there likely will be less carping about Vietnam.[1]

The bone in the president's throat, though, is not the GOP but his own party—more specifically, the liberals in the Democratic Party. Johnson has lost the support of the party intelligentsia, a crucial segment, and one that has always been frustratingly elusive for him. In the aftermath of Kennedy's assassination, Johnson had bludgeoned the Congress into passing several pieces of legislation that were among liberals' most cherished goals. And once Johnson won a sweeping victory in his own right and still pursued a largely liberal agenda, the party's intelligentsia had nowhere to turn, much less anything to complain about. But the Vietnam War, although supported by a majority of Americans, has provided an opening for blistering criticism. On the domestic front, liberals charge the president with not doing enough to alleviate poverty, discrimination, and the problems of America's inner cities; and insofar as foreign policy is an issue, there is only Vietnam. The once-impregnable Johnson, whose roots were certifiably southern but who governed from the left, is seen as an increasingly vulnerable politician and president.

One barometer sums up the entire situation insofar as Johnson is concerned: the polls that pit the president against Senator Robert Kennedy, the only figure considered a serious obstacle to Johnson's renomination in 1968. As recently as January 1966, Johnson was the two-to-one favorite among rank-and-file Democrats for the presidential nomination, according to the Gallup poll. By January 1967, however, Kennedy leads Johnson by a margin of 48 to 39 percent,

1. Maurice Isserman and Michael Kazin, *America Divided: The Civil War of the 1960s* (New York: Oxford University Press, 2004), 225–26.

as the senator's "star looms larger than ever on the political horizon."[2] No one recognizes better than Johnson, of course, that public opinion is mercurial, and an abrupt decline in Kennedy's popularity because of the Manchester affair will temporarily buoy the president. But the mere idea that he, an incumbent, might face a serious challenge from his own party in 1968 is extraordinarily disheartening. That his putative challenger is Robert Kennedy is infuriating.

January 21

Saturday
From Ramsey Clark / 12 p.m.[3]

Of all the criticisms leveled at the Warren Commission since the summer of 1966, the one that sticks is the panel's seemingly inexplicable decision not to examine closely the autopsy photographs and X-rays. Members of the staff had pressed the chief justice in 1964 for access to these vital records. But after viewing the gruesome photographs, Earl Warren sided with the Kennedys, who were adamant about keeping the autopsy records under lock and key, indeed, under their personal control. The Kennedys were tormented by the thought that if their exclusive custody were ever compromised, morbid curiosity was such that the photographs would eventually be published somewhere.

When Warren made this decision, it effectively left the Commission in the position of relying solely on the testimony and autopsy protocol of the pathologists who conducted the president's postmortem.[4] While less than ideal, that probably would have been satisfactory had the pathologists conducted a letter-perfect autopsy. But it wasn't by the book; far from it. In fact, in accordance with the Kennedys' wishes, the pathologists were denied access to the X-rays and photographs while preparing their findings and as a consequence the

2. George Gallup and Louis Harris, "Two Polls—Has Book Battle Hurt Bobby?" *Washington Post,* 29 January 1967.

3. As of the writing of this book, the Johnson Library has released only the assassination-related portion of this conversation.

4. The three pathologists are Dr. James Humes, a commander in the U.S. Navy Medical Corps, who directed the postmortem; Dr. J. Thornton Boswell, chief of pathology at the Bethesda Naval Medical School, who was Humes's first assistant; and Dr. Pierre Finck, an army lieutenant colonel and (in 1963) a wound ballistics expert at the Armed Forces Institute of Pathology in Washington, who was brought in as a consultant.

autopsy protocol contained errors.[5] Though they were ultimately meaningless, the mere fact that there were errors at all, and that the Warren Commission did not catch and correct them, is now extremely embarrassing—if not damaging— to the panel's presumed integrity.

Last November, the Kennedy family finally yielded possession of the photographs and X-rays to the National Archives.[6] Now Ramsey Clark, the acting attorney general, telephones Johnson to brief him on the latest developments in an effort to put the controversy over Kennedy's postmortem to rest. All three of the pathologists who performed the autopsy have been brought into the National Archives in Washington and asked to affirm that the X-rays are identical to the ones they viewed during the autopsy, and that the photographs (which they are seeing for the first time) conform to their visual memories. The scheme is an effort to repair a broken link in what should have been an official and unassailable chain of custody by the U.S. government, rather than one involving the family of the deceased.

Somewhat to Clark's chagrin, there seems to be a discrepancy between the number and/or kind of photographs in the Archives' possession now, and what Dr. James Humes, the senior pathologist, stated in his testimony before the Warren Commission in March 1964. One photograph of the late president's right chest area seems to be missing.

Clark: We had three pathologists who performed the autopsy on the evening of November 22 come in; we had to bring [Dr. Pierre] Finck in from Vietnam. There're only eight of us, including the three pathologists, [who are] aware of any kind [of meeting]. They went into [the National] Archives last night and sat, [and] they worked till midnight [examining the] autopsy photos and X-rays. They all three seem to have something of a chip on their shoulder. [I] think they'll be . . . [I] think they'll go along with our feeling that they shouldn't *talk*.

Johnson: That they *what*?

Clark: [That] they shouldn't *talk* to anybody, but they're quite *defensive* about the criticism of *them*.

Johnson: Uh-huh.

Clark: They feel that their professional reputations are at stake, and whatnot. They say . . . but we haven't got it tied down in affidavits yet, but we *hope* to have this done by Monday—[we'll] be workin' on 'em today and

5. The X-rays were developed immediately and viewed as needed by the pathologists during the postmortem only. The pathologists were not permitted to see the photographs as they prepared the autopsy protocol. Warren Commission, *Hearings,* 2: 372.

6. Fred Graham, "Autopsy Photos Put in Archives by the Kennedys," *New York Times,* 2 November 1966.

tomorrow here, [and we] may have it done before then. But they're [the affidavits] so *technical* and long, [and] they're [the pathologists] so *reticent* about signin' anything, that it's fairly difficult to work with 'em. But *they* say that the autopsy photos conclusively confirm their judgment as to the bullet that entered the back of the skull, and that it's . . . while not *perfectly* conclusive as to the one in the lower neck, that it's very clear to them that there's nothing in the autopsy photos that contradicts anything that they said.

Now, we've run into one problem last night that we didn't know of . . . [and] that is there may be a photo missing. Dr. [James] Humes, who was [a] commander at the [Bethesda] Naval Hospital at the time—[and who] still is [there], he's a captain now—testified before the Warren Commission that there was one photo made of the highest portion of the right lung.[7] And the other two doctors don't recall that such a photo was made. They do recall discussing the *desirability* of making such a photo, but there *is* no such photo in these exhibits.

It could be contended that *that* photo would be some evidence of the *course* and *direction* of the bullet that entered through the lower part of the neck, and [then] exited. We'll continue to run that down. The only other witness that would have any judgment about it at all would be the [medical] corpsman, naval corpsman, who took the photo, and we haven't talked to him. We're not too sure, until we see what the doctors conclude, [that that's] desirable. But we are left with this one *specific* problem that the doctor—Humes—did testify before the Warren Commission there was such a photo [and] we do not have the photo.

Johnson: [Or that] it wasn't delivered to you.

Clark: [Or that] it was not delivered to me. But we—that's very clear. Another part that is of concern to me, and it's not tied down yet either, is Dr. [George] Burkley's part.[8] You remember, I talked to him [last] November the eighth, when we were down at the [LBJ] Ranch . . . after I talked with you about it.[9] We haven't discussed it since, but he gets *very* emotional on the subject if I start cornering him about it. He says that he knew where the autopsy photos were all the time, that they were in his possession. Now this is not . . . he's not entirely clear about it. The possession will become an issue in a significant way that it had not been until, in our judgment, until last night because of the missing photo . . . the *said* missing photo . . . this contradiction as to whether there was any photo [at all]. *[indistinct]*

7. Warren Commission, *Hearings,* 2:363.

8. Dr. Burkley has been the White House physician since the Kennedy administration.

9. Clark was visiting President Johnson at the ranch that day. Daily Diary, 8 November 1966, LBJL.

Johnson: Hm-hmm. . . . Well, they weren't actually *in* his possession, were they?

Clark: He said that they were actually in his possession in that he [had] seen them and had them in his safe in [the] EOB . . . [an] office sort of thing over in [the] EOB. That he later released them to Mrs. [Evelyn] Lincoln.[10] *[indistinct]* . . . which I am . . . I think I *know* was prepared by Bob Kennedy. I [don't] think that Dr. Burkley knew what he had. I [don't] think he'd ever been in . . . that he'd ever examined them.

But . . . I'll tell you [what] the real problem is, when you start talkin' with him about it, what he says is that it's just outrageous that *anybody* would want to look at those photos, the personal property of a dead president and his family. It's just a horrible thing to talk about [and] think about. People shouldn't *do* that. And if you try to explain the real problem to him, why he just . . . he just don't *[indistinct]* at all.

His inventory coincides with what we had . . . the inventory that we got, the material that was delivered to *us,* by a Kennedy [family] representative, Burke Marshall, and Angela Novello.[11] So that would indicate that between his letter, and what we received November 1, [that] everything is *there,* therefore if there was another photo, it would have been before they delivered it to Mrs. Lincoln.

Johnson: Okay.

Clark: I don't really think he had actual possession. I think he may have had some . . . he had constructive possession part of that time. But we have evidence that the material was given to him *before* this, [and] was in [the National] Archives *longer* than this. And nobody at [the] Archives knew it was there.

Johnson: Hmm.

Clark: Mrs. Lincoln has storage space, including some security vaults, because she was working over there on the president's papers and all, and that would be . . . [the] presidential library, and, of course, security files. [Mrs.] Lincoln had the key . . . of course, it was a complete surprise *[indistinct]*.

Johnson: Okay, I'll talk to you later about it.

---

10. Mrs. Lincoln was President Kennedy's personal secretary.

11. Marshall, an assistant attorney general in Robert Kennedy's Justice Department, is now the Kennedy family lawyer in matters relating to the late president. Angela Novello is Robert Kennedy's personal secretary.

January 25

Wednesday
From Nicholas Katzenbach / 7:45 p.m.

In 1964, when President Johnson had to select Robert Kennedy's successor, he promoted Deputy Attorney General Nicholas Katzenbach with some reluctance. A keen student of presidential history, Johnson knew that more attorneys general had gotten more presidents in serious trouble than any other group of people, including the Congress. This was the very reason why President Kennedy appointed his brother to be the nation's top law enforcement officer, and Johnson also wanted someone who was intensely loyal. He was not at all sure that Katzenbach was that man, although he certainly recognized that Katzenbach had done a remarkable job dealing with the southern barons in the Senate on civil rights issues.

In Katzenbach's first two years as attorney general, Johnson never once regretted his decision. The forty-four-year-old Katzenbach was impeccable in his "expeditious devotion" to Johnson's interests and the law, and also proved an able administrator of the Justice Department.[12] By the summer of 1966, however, after a bruising battle with J. Edgar Hoover over the legal authority for conducting electronic surveillance, Katzenbach believed his usefulness as attorney general was over. He expressed a desire to become involved in foreign policy, and the president accommodated him when a suitable opening occurred.[13] In September 1966 Katzenbach stepped down from his cabinet post to become undersecretary of state, then the number-two job in the State Department. For the president there was a purpose to be served, too. Katzenbach's stock with his former boss, Robert Kennedy, remained just as high as it was with the president, and Johnson hoped that Katzenbach's new role would help deflect criticism from that particular quarter.

The relationship between Johnson and Katzenbach, which began as a shotgun marriage, is now close enough for the president to let loose with almost

12. Johnson with Moyers and Bundy, conversation, 4 November 1964, 9:56 a.m., LBJL.

13. Katzenbach will reveal the primary reason for his voluntary demotion during a Senate hearing in 1975. The "bitter" dispute persuaded Katzenbach that he "could no longer effectively serve as attorney general because of Mr. Hoover's obvious resentment." Church Committee, *Hearings: Federal Bureau of Investigation,* 94th Cong., 1st Sess. (Washington, D.C.: U.S. Government Printing Office, 1976), 6:218; Athan Theoharis and John Cox, *The Boss: J. Edgar Hoover and the Great American Inquisition* (Philadelphia: Temple University Press, 1988), 378–95.

anything that is bothering him. With respect to the Manchester book controversy, Katzenbach is in a unique position: while he cannot speak to what happened aboard *Air Force One,* few people played a more central role in the events of November 22. It was Katzenbach who dictated the oath of office so that it could be administered to Johnson, and he is fully cognizant of all the pressures and considerations involved in the swearing-in, a dispute that is at the center of the book, albeit undeservedly.

Initially, the two men discuss a variety of subjects, including a new consular convention with the Soviet Union under consideration by Congress. It would permit Moscow to enlarge its diplomatic outposts in the United States, and since so many Soviet consular officials are in fact KGB agents, the new agreement is not a popular one. But soon Johnson is lamenting what Senator Richard Russell calls the "warfare in our own party." And then the president turns to what's *really* eating at him: the *Look* magazine serialization of Manchester's book. The first of what will be four installments has just been published and is a sensation.[14] Notwithstanding Mike Cowles's fears about being scooped, the extensive press coverage has served only to whet the public appetite. The *Look* issues will sell out the moment they hit the newsstands.[15]

In a stunning reversal of fortune though, publication seems to hurt the Kennedys and not Johnson. As late as December, it was thought that Manchester's portrait of Johnson, as allegedly "boorish, rude, and lacking in respect for the martyred president," would damage the president's reputation and perhaps even his chances for renomination in 1968.[16] Yet the latest public opinion polls are showing dramatic (albeit temporary) declines in public approval for Robert and Jacqueline Kennedy, the first blemish on the Kennedy escutcheon since November 1963. In public relations terms, Johnson has won the "battle of the book" because of the Kennedys' striking ham-handedness. John Connally, among many others, believes Johnson's "gentlemanly attitude" toward the whole thing has carried the day, and John Roche advises that continued "absolute silence" is essential.[17]

14. Johnson is aware of the major editing changes in the first *Look* installment, having read an analysis prepared by Hayes Redmon. Redmon to Moyers, memo, 11 January 1967, Manchester File, Box 1, Special Files, LBJL.

15. The excerpts appear in *Look* magazine in the issues dated 24 January, 7 February, 21 February, and 7 March 1967. The first installment covers events leading up to November 22; the second narrates the events of November 22 up until the official announcement of the president's death; the third tells the story of the swearing-in and ends with the arrival of *Air Force One* in Washington; the fourth covers events from the postmortem in Bethesda to the president's burial on November 25. Meanwhile a settlement of Mrs. Kennedy's suit against Harper & Row and Manchester was reached on January 16, clearing the way for publication of the book on April 7.

16. Jerry Landauer, "The Manchester Book Could Hurt Johnson's 1968 Reelection Chance," *Wall Street Journal,* 20 December 1966.

17. George Christian to Johnson, memo, 13 January 1967, and Roche to Johnson, memo, 23 January 1967, both in Manchester File, Box 1, Special File, LBJL.

While the Manchester affair is a rare stumble by the Kennedys, Johnson is still steaming over his depiction by the author, and with reason. *The Death of a President* will sell 1.3 million hardcover copies, and an estimated 70 million Americans will read at least one of the four *Look* excerpts; 54 million read all four.[18]

[The two men have been discussing the split in the Democratic Party].

Johnson: . . . and if you've seen the new Gallup [poll], it just—I mean the new Harris [poll]—it just reverses 'em.[19] God, it's *murderin'* Bobby and Jackie both.

Katzenbach: I know it.

Johnson: It just *murders* 'em on this thing, and . . . these damn lies in there, Nick, it's just things that I never heard of. *[increasingly agitated]* It was just the most *awful* thing *that I ever heard of!*

> *[mockingly] My* insistin' that Kennedy put up a deer head and forcin' that poor man to go huntin'. Hell, he not only killed one deer, he insisted on killin' the second one, [it] took two hours, and then, by God, he insisted on killin' one for Torby O'Donnell![20] And we just worked so hard . . . it took *three* hours and I finally gave up, and said, Mr. President, we just can't do it.

> *I* didn't force him to come to Texas. Hell, he wanted to come out there *himself* . . . called up, and he *came.* He didn't bring Mrs. Kennedy and he may have told her . . . that he didn't want her to come because he brought some other people.[21] *[bitter laugh]*

> But it's a helluva note to go with it. I'm not gonna say a *word.* I'm just gonna keep my counsel and try to endure it. But it's a *vicious, mean, dirty, low-down stuff* about all this damn business of the. . . .

> [In] one place they say I slumped, [and] had a vapor inhaler and wouldn't take any leadership.[22] And the next day I was so arrogant I was

18. Dexter Filkins, "Ailing Churchill Biographer Says He Can't Finish Trilogy," *New York Times,* 14 August 2001; William Manchester, *Controversy and Other Essays in Journalism, 1950–1975* (Boston: Little, Brown, 1976), 63.

19. The percentages of last November, which showed Robert Kennedy to be the leading choice of rank-and-file Democrats for the 1968 nomination, have now almost exactly reversed after the Manchester controversy. George Gallup and Louis Harris, "Two Polls—Has Book Battle Hurt Bobby?" *Washington Post,* 29 January 1967.

20. On November 17, 1960, the president-elect and vice president–elect went on an eight-hour deer hunt at the LBJ Ranch. Their party included Ken O'Donnell, and Representative Torbert Macdonald (D-Massachusetts), Kennedy's Harvard roommate and closest friend in Congress. Johnson is so agitated he is conflating names.

21. Johnson may be making a veiled reference to President Kennedy's extramarital affairs.

22. Johnson is referring to Manchester's description of him upon arriving at Parkland Hospital. Johnson "stood with his broad shoulders braced against a blank wall, sniffing from a vapor inhaler that he always carried. . . ." William Manchester, *The Death of a President: November 20–November 25, 1963* (New York: Harper & Row, 1967), 229–30.

bossin' everything! And the *thought* that I oughta go to a plane that didn't have the bag, and didn't have the communications—by God, after this terrible thing had happened—is *inconceivable* to me.[23]

Katzenbach: I think Manchester's just *sick.* I think that's . . . [a simple fact].

[Johnson alludes to the situation in Vietnam before returning to the subject of the Kennedys and what Katzenbach might do to stop Democrats' internecine warfare.]

Johnson: We haven't got any cinch on winnin' out there [in Vietnam] at all. It's just the *opposite,* I'm afraid. And I just think that we . . . I don't think Rusk can do it, and McNamara can do it, or I can do it. I think maybe you're *fresh* enough, and *objective* enough, and *judicious* enough, and *honest* enough, [and] *sincere* enough . . . [a] friend of *all concerned.* You don't have to be a traitor to anybody. You just have to be *good,* and do what's *right.* But somebody's gonna have to divide up the pie here, and say now—I never make a critical word of *any* Kennedy, at *any* time. I'm just not gonna *do* it! I'm not gonna say it. I'm dodgin' [the issue]. I've taken these damn books and these things . . . and now John *Connally's* writin' one.[24] What he's gonna say, God [only] knows.

But I know one thing you can truthfully say: [that] Kennedy insisted for two years that he come [to Texas] and make five money-raisin' speeches. And he [Connally] finally told him, in my presence, [he] said, Mr. President, they gonna think all the Kennedys want out of Texas is *money.* He hadn't been down here, and [Connally] said, I'd suggest you make one money-raisin' speech, and whatever else you do, you do totally nonpolitical. And he told him [President Kennedy] that in the spring—[in] April [1963]—and he told him that in June. And then 'cause I wouldn't encourage it, by God, he [President Kennedy] called him [Connally] up and wouldn't let me know he was *callin'* him! And he [Connally] came up here and had a *secret* meetin' with him [President Kennedy], and I [only] found out about it 'cause he asked Bill Moyers to advance it. And he [President Kennedy] *told* John, the reason he didn't tell me [was that] the vice president's not enthusiastic. So . . . we go through all *that* kind of stuff.

[facetiously] But even if we *had've* made the *tragic* mistake of forcing this poor man to put up a deer head here, along with his fish. . . . I don't know who forced him to put up the fish in the Fish Room that he caught on

23. As noted earlier, the military aide carrying this briefcase is the president's constant companion, so Johnson is (typically) speaking for effect here.

24. In direct contradiction of Manchester's explanation—that Kennedy went to Texas only to settle down quarrelsome Democrats—Connally is writing an article for *Life* magazine that will be featured on its cover. John Connally, "Why Kennedy Went to Texas," *Life,* 24 November 1967.

his honeymoon . . . but I damn sure didn't force him to put up *anything*![25] And it's just a manufactured lie.

[sarcastically] [A] poor little deer, he saw it in his eye and he just couldn't shoot it.[26] Well, hell . . . he wasn't within 250 yards of it.[27] He shot it, and he jumped up, and *hurrah*! [It went] right on the fender of the car, so he could kill another one. And we had to stay out there an hour or two later till he killed a *second* one. Most of 'em [ranchers] got a rule, they won't let you kill but one [deer]. But he was the president and the law says you can kill two, and we wanted him to have whatever he *wanted*. But there [was] nobody [who] forced this man to do a damn *thing*. He wouldn't [have] been competent to be president if he . . . I think it's a greatest desecration of his memory that an *impotent* vice president could *force* this strong man to do a goddamn *thing*!

Katzenbach: I [think it's] ridiculous. . . .

[They resume discussing the consular convention and pending ambassadorial nominations.]

January 26

Thursday

To Ramsey Clark / 6:29 p.m.

During a ten-minute conversation that covers a wide range of matters, including the consular convention, the acting attorney general brings the president up to date on the autopsy controversy.

Clark: Are you where you can talk there?
Johnson: Yes. Sure.

---

25. Manchester writes that Kennedy was "inwardly appalled" by the mounted deer head and put up the trophy only after repeated inquiries from Johnson. Manchester, *Death,* 119.

26. According to Manchester, the "memory of the creature's death had been haunting" to Kennedy. Ibid. In his first draft, Manchester opened the book with the deer-hunting scene, but then agreed to move it to a less conspicuous place. Jeff Shesol, *Mutual Contempt: Lyndon Johnson, Robert Kennedy, and the Feud That Defined a Decade* (New York: W. W. Norton, 1997), 355.

27. According to a 1961 letter concerning the hunt, Kennedy was 327 paces, or approximately 272 yards, away from the deer he shot. Jenkins to Kellum, letter, 30 May 1961, Manchester Book—Hayes Redmon, Box 2, Special File, LBJL.

Clark: I think we have the three pathologists and the photographer signed up now on the autopsy review. And their conclusion is that the autopsy photos and X-rays conclusively support the autopsy report rendered by them to the Warren Commission.

We were not able to tie down the question of the missing photo *entirely,* but we feel much better about it. And we've got *three* of the four signed to an affidavit that says these are all of the photos that they took, and they don't believe anybody else took any others. There is this unfortunate reference in the Warren Commission *Report* by Dr. Humes to a picture that just *does not exist,* as far as we know.[28] [We] are checking further to see where the pictures were at all times, but from every indication, that was an error at the *time.* It puts Dr. Humes in kind of an awkward spot, though.
[Clark turns to an unrelated subject.]

February 20

Monday
To Ramsey Clark / 9:40 a.m.[29]

President Johnson is calling the acting attorney general because of an astonishing story published in the *New Orleans States-Item* on Friday afternoon. The Orleans Parish district attorney, Jim Garrison, has "launched an intensive investigation into the circumstances surrounding the assassination of President John F. Kennedy," according to the copyrighted article.[30]

On January 23 *States-Item* crime reporter Jack Dempsey briefly alluded to the probe in his regular "On the Police Beat" column, but it attracted virtually no attention then. Charles Ward, an assistant DA in Garrison's office, confirmed to Dempsey that an investigation had been launched but simultaneously down-

28. Clark means in Dr. Humes's testimony before the Warren Commission. See footnote 7.

29. As of the writing of this book, the Johnson Library has released only the assassination-related portion of this conversation.

30. Jack Dempsey, Rosemary James, and David Snyder, "DA Here Launches Full JFK Death 'Plot' Probe," *New Orleans States-Item,* 17 February 1967. This may not have been the first conversation between Johnson and Clark about Garrison, as they spoke on Saturday morning, the day after the *States-Item* story appeared. But neither that conversation, nor ones with Abe Fortas on the mornings of February 18 and February 20, were tape recorded. Daily Diary, 18 and 20 February 1967, LBJL.

played the matter, stressing that it was entirely routine given something as important as a presidential murder. And Ward suggested that the probe was not going to go much further, for "he did not place much faith in the implications raised thus far."[31] But a month later, when Dempsey and other *States-Item* reporters check rumors about the probe, they find Garrison's investigators have spent more than $8,000 following a trail that has already taken them, since late November, to Dallas, Houston, Chicago, Miami, Washington, D.C., and San Francisco.[32]

After nine months of criticism of the *Warren Report* in new books and in the press, amid calls for a new investigation and a dramatic decline of public confidence in the Commission's findings, the other shoe has finally dropped.[33] Disbelief has gone beyond being a cottage industry, the realm of so-called assassination buffs who cannot accept the Warren Commission's verdict.[34] For the first time since the publication of the *Warren Report* in September 1964, a duly constituted law enforcement official has instigated a reexamination of the panel's work on the grounds that there was a conspiracy. And although his legal reach is limited, Garrison has subpoena power over the jurisdiction in which he claims the conspiracy was hatched.

The forty-five-year-old Garrison is considered a responsible, reform-minded prosecutor, with a decided flair for publicity. Flamboyant (though not by Louisiana standards), he is politically ambitious, like most district attorneys, and is said to be eyeing either the statehouse or the U.S. Senate seat held by Allen Ellender, who is nearing retirement at age seventy-six.[35] As the "fighting DA" for Orleans Parish since 1962, Garrison has attracted much favorable (and national) attention for his cleanup of rampant vice and crime in the city's old French Quarter.[36] His crusading efforts even resulted in a landmark legal ruling after eight city judges tried to cut off some of his funding. When Garrison suggested their joint decision raised "interesting questions about racketeering influences," the judges promptly (and successfully) sued him for character defamation, and the case went all the way to the U.S. Supreme Court before

31. Jack Dempsey, "On the Police Beat: Hit-Run Culprit Is Buggy Driver," *New Orleans States-Item,* 23 January 1967.

32. The expense figure is $46,200 in 2004 dollars. Dempsey, James, and Snyder, "DA Here Launches Full JFK Death 'Plot' Probe."

33. In November 1966 *Life* magazine published an influential article that called for a new inquiry, and in January 1967 the *Saturday Evening Post* followed suit.

34. This moniker will become prevalent once it appears in a *New Yorker* article. Calvin Trillin, "The Buffs," *The New Yorker,* 10 June 1967.

35. Jack Wardlaw, "Closeup: The New Orleans DA," *New York Post,* 23 February 1967; "Flashy Prosecutor: Jim Garrison," *New York Times,* 25 February 1967.

36. The widely read *Saturday Evening Post* published a flattering story about Garrison four years earlier. James Phelan, "To Old New Orleans: The Vice Man Cometh," *Saturday Evening Post,* 8 June 1963.

Garrison's conviction was overturned in October 1964.[37] In a city notorious for its deeply embedded graft and corruption, Garrison is untainted by scandal; indeed, his lean good looks make him seem like the prosecutor ordered up by central casting. Lately, like most big-city district attorneys, Garrison seemed to have his hands full keeping a lid on the city's burgeoning crime rates, 1966 having been dubbed the "year of the criminal" in New Orleans because of record-shattering increases in felonies.[38] His interest in the Kennedy assassination seems to have come out of nowhere.

At this point that is about as much as is known about the New Orleans DA, save for the fact that like most public officials, he is accorded the presumption of being responsible. There is little on record (aside from the 1964 Supreme Court case) to suggest that the telegenic prosecutor is also a cunning demagogue, the likes of whom have not been seen since the days of Joe McCarthy. Thus the almost universal response to Garrison, both in and outside New Orleans, will be that *he must have something.* Most people cannot believe that a prosecutor would otherwise dare reopen the crime of the century—so much so that by the time the president calls Ramsey Clark, New Orleans is in the process of becoming a media maelstrom, exceeded (in recent memory) only by the frenzy that engulfed Dallas in November 1963.

Besides the presumption of legitimacy accorded a public official, there is another reason why the news from New Orleans is not simply dismissed out of hand. If there was a conspiracy in 1963, it is not inconceivable that events in or persons associated with New Orleans had something to do with it. The city figured into the FBI's and the Warren Commission's investigation because Lee Harvey Oswald, who was born there in 1939, resided there twice: first as a teenager in the mid-1950s, and then, most importantly, from late April until late September 1963, just before his trip to Mexico City.[39]

Still, Clark is already discomfited by one "nutty" aspect of the story, namely the rumor that Garrison is allegedly linking Johnson with the conspiracy. As fantastic as this rumor sounds, its source is credible. It comes via Representative Hale Boggs, whose district encompasses much of New Orleans, putting him in a position to know whereof he speaks. Boggs, of course, was also on the Warren Commission, which puts him in a bit of a dilemma. Whereas he might be inclined to speak out against Garrison (whom he apparently dislikes) and denounce the DA's probe, it is risky to attack a prosecutor who shares the same

37. L. J. Vidacovich, " 'Fighting D.A.' of New Orleans Winning Lone Crusade," *Washington Post,* 13 December 1964. Ultimately, the Warren Court deems Garrison's remark provocative, but not so reckless as to be legally defamatory.

38. Allan Katz, "More Police Key to Curbing Crime, Experts Agree," *New Orleans States-Item,* 27 December 1966.

39. Oswald, twenty-four years old when he died, had spent more of his life in New Orleans (eight years all told) than in any other place.

jurisdiction. To Clark, any allegation about Johnson's involvement is an early indicator that Garrison might be deranged.

It perhaps comes as a surprise to Clark that Johnson treats the whole matter with considerable equanimity, not even swearing or muttering to himself when Clark brings up Boggs's story. The president's reaction is in marked contrast to his response last October when the insinuation first surfaced. As it turns out, the news from New Orleans is far from the wildest story making the rounds. Johnson asks Clark if he has heard about an even more fantastic rumor in Washington, one that was conveyed personally to the president by syndicated columnist Drew Pearson, considered something of a renegade by his Washington peers.[40] The story, which Johnson heard a month earlier, is that after the 1961 Bay of Pigs debacle the CIA sent men into Cuba to assassinate Fidel Castro, who then retaliated. And as if the implications of that weren't staggering enough, Pearson also says that Robert Kennedy concocted the plots against Castro, as they occurred in the days when he was "riding herd" on the agency for his brother.[41]

Little wonder that Johnson receives the news from New Orleans with such restraint. He professes to Clark that he finds Pearson's story "incredible," but he also must think about being cautious and discreet. It is political dynamite for Johnson to spread, or be associated with spreading, an allegation so potentially damaging to Robert Kennedy. The president probably believes that if Garrison is on to anything at all in New Orleans, it may be strands from the Pearson story, which does lead back to Washington. Perhaps the New Orleans DA is confused, for the time being, over some false or misleading information, and is therefore mistaken about to which Washington doorstep the trail supposedly leads. Certainly, Johnson is not personally worried about anything that might come of either the Garrison or the Pearson developments, should one, the other, or even both prove accurate.[42]

40. With 50 million readers nationwide in 600 newspapers, Pearson is one of the most influential muckrakers in journalism, having excelled in the form since 1932. Everyone reads Pearson's "Washington Merry-Go-Round" column because Pearson and Jack Anderson, his partner, consistently break important stories. But the *Washington Post* purposefully relegates the column to the comics page rather than printing it opposite its editorial page. "The column was both a boon, for its scoops and its investigative reporting, and a bane, for its feuds and its often sloppy and tendentious reporting," a *Post* historian will explain. Chalmers Roberts, *The Washington Post: The First 100 Years* (Boston: Houghton Mifflin, 1977), 244. According to Anderson, however, he and Pearson regard being next to the comics in the *Post* as a badge of honor. Alden Whitman, "Watchdog of Virtue," *New York Times,* 2 September 1969; Jack Anderson, *Peace, War, and Politics: An Eyewitness Account* (New York: Forge, 1999), 334.

41. Pearson first learned about the story on January 13 from Washington attorney Edward Morgan and told President Johnson about it three days later, with Morgan's consent. Pearson Diary, 13 and 16 January 1967, Box 2, Pearson Papers and Daily Diary, 16 January 1967; both LBJL.

42. In sharp contrast, Robert Kennedy is *very* concerned about what Garrison is up to and where the trail might lead. He will ask his preferred investigator, Walter Sheridan, now working for NBC, to examine Garrison's charges. Kennedy will also ask his press secretary, Frank

As always when faced with a ticklish politico-legal problem, Johnson consults Justice Abe Fortas first, and does not even try to hide this fact from Clark. Johnson's suggestion about what to do is essentially Fortas's considered advice with respect to the Garrison and Pearson developments. Watch them both carefully . . . start a file . . . don't interfere . . . see how they play out.

Clark: . . . [patience] with him. I talked to Deke [DeLoach] further about it yesterday.[43] He was gonna have a report over for me . . . or have the report in by nine, I should have it over fairly shortly, I guess.

I *think* that what he [Jim Garrison] is workin' on must be the associations that Oswald had in the three or four months that he was down there [in New Orleans] in '62 [and] '63. I doubt . . . I think it'd just be *incredible* if he [Garrison] had anything that went beyond that. I think this *subject* is so volatile and emotional, though, that it could get confused and obscured.

[uncomfortably and hesitantly] I had heard that Hale Boggs was sayin' [that] he—Garrison—was sayin' that . . . or privately around town [was saying] that it [the assassination] could be traced back [to you] . . . or that you could be found *in* it some place, which . . . I can't believe he's been *sayin'* that. The bureau says they haven't heard *any* such thing, and they['ve] got lots of eyes and ears.[44]

'Course, that was a [credible] fella like Hale Boggs. But Hale gets pretty emotional about people that he really doesn't *like,* and people who have fought him and been against him, and I would be more inclined to attribute it to *that.* Either that, or this guy Garrison [is] *just completely off his rocker.*

Johnson: Who did Hale tell this to?

Clark: *[somewhat in disbelief]* Apparently Marvin [Watson].[45]

Johnson: *[aside to Watson]* [Did] Hale tell you that—Hale Boggs—that this fella [Garrison, this] district attorney down there, said that this is traced to me or somethin'?

Watson: Privately he [Garrison] was usin' your name as having known about it

Mankiewicz, to follow developments closely. And he will contact Edwin Guthman, his former press secretary who is now the national editor at the *Los Angeles Times,* to ask a personal favor. "Bobby wanted to know everything. He was very curious," Guthman will later recall. "I put five reporters on it." Evan Thomas, *Robert Kennedy: His Life* (New York: Simon & Schuster, 2000), 333–34.

43. DeLoach is the FBI's liaison to the White House.

44. Clark is referring to the bureau's use of informants, who fill FBI file drawers with reams of useful and useless information. It is not clear whether Clark knows this, but the bureau became aware of Garrison's rumored investigation in early February, shortly after it was first revealed in the *States-Item.*

45. Watson, a special assistant to the president, is the White House liaison to the FBI.

[the assassination]. I said [to Boggs], Will you give this information to
Barefoot Sanders?[46] Ramsey was out of town, this was Saturday night. He
[Boggs] said, I sure will. So I asked the operator to get Barefoot and
Ramsey together, and they *did.*

Johnson: *[to Clark]* Yeah, I don't know about it. They don't ever let me *in* on
it, Marvin and Jake [Jacobsen] over here, so you have to call me direct.[47]

Clark: Well—

Johnson: They just think this stuff's for *them.*

Clark: Such *nutty* things that . . . it's awfully explosive but. . . . The *press,*
really, has quite a jaundiced eye about it . . . and about Garrison, so far.[48]
I had several press interviews out in Des Moines [on] Saturday evening
and afternoon, and the thrust of their questions is, What kind of nut *is*
this?[49]

Johnson: Two things, I think. You *know* [there's] this story going around about
the CIA and their tryin' to get . . . sendin' in the folks to get [Fidel] Castro.

Clark: To assassinate Castro.

Johnson: Have you got that full story laid out in front of you, and [do you]
know what it is? Has anybody ever told you all the story?

Clark: No.

Johnson: I think you oughta have that. I don't . . . it's *incredible.* I don't
believe there's a thing in the world to it, and I don't think we oughta
seriously consider it. But I think you oughta know about it.

Clark: Who would I get it from?

Johnson: I've had it from three or four [sources]. I've forgotten who's come in
here. I'll have to check it.

Clark: Does the bureau have it?

Johnson: No, I don't think so. You might ask 'em. *Pearson*—Drew Pearson—
came [in] and gave it to me. [Pearson] said [Edward] Morgan told him . . .
[Morgan is James] Hoffa's lawyer.[50] He [Morgan] says that they have a
man [John Rosselli] that was involved, that was brought in to the CIA,
with a number of others, and instructed by the CIA and the attorney

46. Sanders is an assistant attorney general in charge of the Justice Department's Civil Division.

47. Jacobsen is a special counsel to the president.

48. Perhaps the press is privately skeptical, but Garrison is getting a lot of attention.

49. Clark was in Iowa on Saturday to address a Drake University Law School alumni dinner.

50. Though he does not have the reputation of, say, Edward Bennett Williams, to Washington insiders Morgan is known as one of the toughest, shrewdest, and best-connected criminal attorneys in town. He is particularly well plugged into the FBI, having joined the bureau in 1940 and risen to the rank of chief inspector before striking out on his own as a lawyer in 1947. Morgan has also served as a counsel to three congressional investigations, including the 1946 congressional investigation into the Pearl Harbor attack, and a 1950 Senate investigation into Communist penetration of the State Department. During the latter Morgan became enmeshed in a bitter feud with Senator Joe McCarthy (R-Wisconsin), who accused Morgan of being a skilled "whitewasher" of embarrassing secrets. "E. P. Morgan to Enforce Price Curbs," *Washington Post,* 18 February 1951.

general [Robert Kennedy] to assassinate Castro after the Bay of Pigs [in 1961].[51]

Clark: *[uncomfortably]* I've heard that . . . you know, I've heard that *much*. I just haven't heard [any] names, and places, and . . .

Johnson: Well, let's see who it is . . . let's see. I think it would be, [it would] look very bad on us if we'd had it reported to us a number of times and we just didn't pay any [attention]—just *laughed* . . . if this is true.

He [Morgan] says that his [client's] limitation—let's check it and see if [the statute of] limitation[s] *does* run out in November . . . they say that the limitation runs out in November.[52] I don't know about this conspiracy, or how much—how many years [the statute of limitations runs]—

Clark: [It'd] be six years, all right, which would be November probably. But it [the statute of limitations would] not [run out] for a *concealed* situation.

Johnson: Well, that's what I'd *think*. But anyway, he [Pearson] says in November he's [Rosselli's] going to tell it. And that—

Clark: Mr. Pearson is [going to publish the story?]

Johnson: No. This individual [Rosselli].[53]

Clark: This individual?

Johnson: Yeah. And these lawyers [Morgan, for one] have it. There's just *all kinds* of things that come to me every day. I don't pay any *attention* to 'em, but *maybe* I was a little worried this mornin' because one of my lawyer friends told me I oughta call you and talk to you about it.[54] So [that] you'll have a *file* that protects *you,* that you just don't look like they report these things to us and we just throw 'em overboard and say, Well, we don't like 'em and it['s] not what we wanna hear, so we're not gonna do anything about it.

But anyway, [the story is] that following this, Castro said—they [the plotters] had these pills, and they're supposed to take 'em when they [Castro's regime] caught 'em, and they didn't get to take their pills—so he [Castro] tortured 'em. And they told him all about it, and who was present and why they did it. So he [Castro] said, Okay. We'll just take

51. Johnson does not know the identity of Morgan's client, but he is John Rosselli, a member of the Cosa Nostra, the Italian-dominated criminal syndicate known popularly as the Mafia. Rosselli's name will not surface publicly until 1971, when Jack Anderson publishes it.

52. Morgan has apparently told Rosselli that the statute of limitations is six years for conspiring to kill someone *if* the plot fails. Rosselli, therefore, cannot be prosecuted after November 1967 for plotting Castro's demise. Of course, since the conspiracy was instigated by the CIA, Rosselli could conceivably claim he had U.S. government sanction. But as a mobster, he probably does not trust the government.

53. Pearson's diary suggests he fully intends to publish the story once the statute of limitations has expired and he has heard Rosselli's complete story. Pearson Diary, 13 January 1967, Box 2, Pearson Papers, LBJL.

54. Johnson talked to Fortas about an hour ago; the conversation was not recorded, as noted earlier.

care of that. So then he called [Lee Harvey] Oswald and a group in, and told them to . . . about this meetin', and go set it up and get the *job* done.

Clark: Uh-hmm.

Johnson: Now that's their story. And I talked to *Abe* [Fortas] about it first, and he just said, Well, it's so incredible that . . . he'd do it.[55] Then they also claim that y'all have tapped his lawyers'—Hoffa's lawyers'—telephones and haven't admitted that yet, and that they gonna have to explode that.[56] That . . . [a] man can't talk to his preacher [or] confess to his priest, or talk to his wife, or talk to his doctor or lawyer without the *bugs* around him, and *that's* terrible. Well anyway, so much for *that* part of it.

Now here's what I *called* about. I just think that if you haven't *heard* that, maybe you oughta put yourself in a position to either hear Pearson or whoever's circulatin' it. There've been two or three here circulatin' it to me, and Pearson was just *one* of 'em. But I've forgotten who the others *are*.[57] They were *reputable* people, or they wouldn't [have] gotten in *here*.

Clark: Pearson was in last week.

Johnson: Who?

Clark: I said Pearson was in to see me last week and sat here for thirty [or] forty minutes [and] never mentioned anything about it.

Johnson: Well, he came to see me . . . came to see me in the [Executive] Mansion, oh, I'd say a month ago.[58] And there was *before* that one or two others, but I can't remember *who*. They were *responsible* people. But it sounded just so [incredible]. . . just like your tellin' me that Lady Bird was taking *dope*. I just wouldn't pay much attention to it. If I'm seein' her every day, I just don't believe that that was *involved*.

55. Johnson called Fortas at 8 p.m. on January 16, six and one-half hours after his hour-long meeting with Pearson, and the president then met privately with Fortas in the Executive Mansion early on the morning of January 17 for seventy-five minutes. Daily Diary Index, 16–17 January 1967, LBJL. There is no documentation to corroborate that Johnson and Fortas talked about the Pearson story on either day, but it seems very likely. It's not clear whether Fortas, according to Johnson, finds it incredible that Robert Kennedy directed assassination plots against Castro, or that Castro dared retaliate.

56. In 1964 Teamsters Union president Jimmy Hoffa was convicted in Chattanooga of jury-tampering and received an eight-year sentence. As of 1967, he has yet to spend a day in prison. His lawyers are appealing the conviction, alleging, among other things, that the Justice Department acquired information illegally from FBI bugs and wiretaps before and during the trial. The appeal will be denied, and Hoffa will begin serving his sentence in March—ten years after the federal government began pursuing him. Victor Navasky, *Kennedy Justice* (New York: Atheneum, 1971), 491.

57. Pearson is the only person known to have told Johnson about assassination plots directed against Castro. But in his March 2 conversation with John Connally, Johnson will again suggest that he heard the same story from someone in addition to Pearson.

58. The date was January 16, and the off-the-record meeting lasted from 12:30 to 1:30 p.m. In his diary Pearson wrote that "I told the president about Ed Morgan's law client. . . . Lyndon listened carefully and made no comment. There wasn't much he could say." Daily Diary, 16 January 1967; Pearson Diary, 16 January 1967, Box 2, Pearson Papers; both LBJL.

Anyway, I'll try to think of the other names and give 'em to you. He's the only one I can remember now, and I don't credit it . . . I credit it 99 [and] 99[/100] percent *untrue*. But that's somethin' I think we oughta *know* has been reported, and y'all oughta do what you think oughta be done to protect yourself.

On this New Orleans thing: I'm told that what I oughta say to you is [for you] to ask the FBI . . . to immediately take notice of all these statements, review 'em very carefully—*evaluate* them—ask their local people without quote "without *interfering* with the local investigation," or without obstructin' it . . . "interfering or obstruction."[59] They say be *sure* to get you a careful sentence in there, so it won't look like that . . . they can't say that you came along and wanted to *cover up* somethin' . . . busted 'em up. And *notify* the FBI to—without interfering or obstructin' the local thing—to follow it very carefully, and to report to you *anything* that is material or of any value.

Clark: Well, I've done that—

Johnson: By memo?

Clark: —since Friday. No, [I] just called Deke.

Johnson: I wonder, though, if you shouldn't do that [write a memo]. Abe says that it's so *delicate* and *touchy* that he thinks I ought to ask the attorney general . . . he said [J. Edgar] Hoover nearly said that—

Clark: I can confirm it, even by memo, and—

Johnson: That's what I would do.

Clark: —catch an earlier date, but it's really out of line with the practice and, therefore, would seem a little extraordinary. I don't think—and also, as *I* saw the strategy, we wanted to keep completely out of the public eye because we'd just escalate it . . . give Garrison a chance to lay it on *us,* [and] focus attention on the problem, if we . . . [if] people see us . . . in what appears to be a very interested posture.

Johnson: Well, I'm not tryin' to make *anything* public. I'm just tryin' to think about a president sittin' here, and seeing it on nationwide television—

Clark: Uh-hmm.

Johnson: —Sunday and Monday, and saying that *here is* other accomplices. Here's accomplices, here's [our] other evidence, here's so-and-so . . . and bein' totally *immune* to it and unaware and *uninterested* in it.

Clark: Uh-hmm.

Johnson: And *I* would think that what you oughta do is—[and] you can be your own judge about it—but I would think what you oughta do is either write or call Deke, and take notes on what you say to him, and say the president has seen this on television and read of it. And he says to tell you,

59. Again, Johnson is apparently taking his legal cues and precise language from Justice Fortas.

without interfering or obstructin' in any way the local investigation, to be *sure* . . . that if there's anything *to* this or any *scintilla* of evidence that should be considered, that you be sure that it's presented to me.

I don't know that that would—that's not a press release. I think that his [Hoover's] local people there [in New Orleans are] watchin' it anyway, probably. But I think that would show that you weren't tryin' to [interfere] . . . [or that] you were totally uninterested in pursuin' it.

Clark: No, I did that . . . I did everything that you've said last week, except I didn't mention *your* name in it. And I can do that, and I didn't document it, but I can do that [easily].

Johnson: Well, maybe you don't need to do either; you be the judge. I'm just tellin' you what Abe told me *he* thought we oughta do.

Clark: Well, it can't hurt.

Johnson: This had a pretty good run this mornin' on NBC.[60]

Clark: [It] can't hurt and it could be important, so . . . I'll do it.

February 22

Wednesday

From Ramsey Clark / 6:40 p.m.

The day after its February 17 scoop, the *New Orleans States-Item* published another copyrighted story about Garrison's investigation. This time the newspaper introduced its readers to one of the targets in the probe, a forty-eight-year-old man named David Ferrie, who could not have been more colorful if he had stepped out of a Mardi Gras parade. Over the next four days Ferrie became nationally notorious as one of the central figures in what Garrison's office calls "definite" evidence of an assassination plot.[61]

Ferrie sought out a *States-Item* reporter because he felt hounded by Garrison and feared that the district attorney might railroad him.[62] "Supposedly I have been pegged as the getaway pilot in an elaborate plot to kill [President]

---

60. Johnson is probably referring to the morning *Today* show on NBC, which apparently treated the news from New Orleans as credible.

61. Rosemary James and David Snyder, " 'Definite' JFK Death Plot in N.O., DA Aide Quoted," *New Orleans States-Item,* 18 February 1967; Neil Sanders, "Ferrie's Is 10th Mystery Death," *New Orleans States-Item,* 23 February 1967.

62. George Lardner, "Ferrie Last Seen 'In Good Spirits,' " *New Orleans States-Item,* 23 February 1967.

Kennedy," Ferrie told the *States-Item*.[63] He denied knowing Lee Harvey Oswald in 1963, although Ferrie had been affiliated with the local Civil Air Patrol in 1955 when Oswald, then fifteen years old, briefly attended some meetings as a cadet.[64] Ferrie freely admitted to the reporter having been investigated in 1963 by both the Secret Service and the FBI but insisted he had nothing to hide.[65] His story checked out in every respect, but Ferrie, who also listed himself in the New Orleans telephone directory as a psychologist, nonetheless seemed odd and a bit shady. A former pilot for Eastern Air Lines, he was cashiered in 1961 after being arrested on a morals charge involving young boys—Ferrie is a homosexual—and his unusual habits and appearance don't help matters.[66] He lives in squalor and also suffers from a rare skin condition called alopecia universalis, which leaves him hairless, even where his eyebrows should be.[67] He compensates by wearing a crude homemade wig and false eyebrows that are a rust-colored shade of red.[68]

Garrison initially reacted to Ferrie's self-exposure by announcing that arrests were imminent and that "convictions would be obtained."[69] Then he quickly retrenched, throwing a cloak of secrecy around the investigation and claiming that "premature publicity" was obstructing the probe and that no arrests would be made "for months." When newsmen asked why he wasn't willing to turn to the federal government for help, Garrison responded, "What? And wait three years?"[70]

About seven hours before this conversation between the president and Clark, Ferrie was found dead in his squalid apartment, having suffered a fatal brain aneurysm. It stemmed from a congenital condition, according to the Orleans Parish coroner.[71] But Jim Garrison is insisting that Ferrie's death is a suicide if not a murder. At a news conference hastily called four hours after the

63. James and Snyder, " 'Definite' JFK Death Plot in N.O."; Patricia Lambert, *False Witness: The Real Story of Jim Garrison's Investigation and Oliver Stone's Film* JFK (New York: M. Evans, 1998), 47, 55.

64. Lambert, *False Witness,* 28. The Civil Air Patrol, established in December 1941, is a volunteer civilian auxiliary to the USAF that assists local and federal agencies on search-and-rescue missions and border patrols.

65. Ferrie's activities were also investigated by the Texas Rangers (state police), the Houston Police Department, and the New Orleans Police Department in addition to the federal agencies. Lambert, *False Witness,* 29.

66. Ibid., 61.

67. Ibid., 24.

68. David Snyder, "Sick Ferrie Felt World Was Unjust," *New Orleans States-Item,* 23 February 1967.

69. Jack Wardlaw, "Flamboyant Jim Garrison: What's Behind the Furor in New Orleans," *National Observer,* 27 February 1967.

70. "Tighter 'Plot' Case Secrecy Sought by DA," *New Orleans States-Item,* 21 February 1967.

71. Lambert, *False Witness,* 60.

discovery of Ferrie's body, Garrison said, "The apparent suicide of David Ferrie ends the life of a man who, in my judgment, was one of history's most important individuals. Evidence developed by our office had long since confirmed that he was involved in events culminating in the assassination of President Kennedy."[72]

For Clark, who was inclined to think Garrison a poseur from the outset, the DA's behavior now is confirmation of that initial reaction. He points out to Johnson that after Ferrie talked to newspapermen to complain about Garrison's "witch hunt," Garrison went to some lengths to suggest Ferrie was peripheral to the conspiracy. Now the DA is abruptly reversing himself, claiming that Ferrie was under constant surveillance and on the verge of being arrested.[73] The fact that Garrison's investigation has not moved beyond a man already cleared years ago—first by the New Orleans police, then by the FBI, the Secret Service, and the Warren Commission—also suggests to Clark that Garrison is blowing hot air.

Johnson, for his part, no longer seems to think that Garrison is pursuing some angle of the Drew Pearson story. He does make one suggestion to Clark that is interesting, though. He tells the acting attorney general to contact Russell Long, the garrulous junior senator from Louisiana with a drinking problem, and warn him away from the case. Long is in the Senate leadership, having succeeded Hubert Humphrey as the majority whip in 1965. And Johnson probably knows that Long has always believed that there was a second gunman in Dealey Plaza, the *Warren Report* notwithstanding, and that President Kennedy was in fact the victim of a conspiracy. Long was the most prominent U.S. senator to have called for a reopening of the federal government's investigation once attacks on the *Warren Report* began to mount in the fall of 1966.[74]

What Johnson does not know is the pivotal role Long played in instigating Garrison's probe in the first place. Once they found themselves seated together on the same airplane headed for New York in November 1966, Long and Garrison naturally began discussing a principal topic of the day: criticism of the Warren Commission as the third anniversary of the assassination approached. The senator mesmerized Garrison with a long litany of his doubts about the *Warren Report*, including his belief that Oswald was the fall guy and at most a decoy in Dealey Plaza.[75] Although he had his own doubts, too, Garrison was genuinely taken aback to hear that such a powerful person in Washington, the second-

72. "Murder Ruled Out in Ferrie Death," *New Orleans States-Item,* 23 February 1967.

73. George Lardner, "JFK 'Plot' Figure in New Orleans: His Own Story," *New York World Journal Tribune,* 23 February 1967. In fact, there was no intent to arrest Ferrie. Lambert, *False Witness,* 65.

74. "Second Person Aided Oswald, Long Asserts," *New Orleans States-Item,* 22 November 1966.

75. James Autry, "The Garrison Investigation," *New Orleans* 1 (April 1967). In all likelihood, Long's suspicions were influenced by the fact that his own father, Senator Huey Long (D-Louisiana), was assassinated in 1935.

ranking Democrat in the U.S. Senate, entertained such misgivings.[76] Upon his return to New Orleans in November, the district attorney immediately launched his reinvestigation.

Clark: The [FBI] special agent in charge down there . . . it took him several hours *[indistinct]*. [He] says that they are quite convinced the death [of Ferrie] was by natural causes, that it was a small cerebral hemorrhage, a burst blood vessel in the brain. The only part of the autopsy that's not complete is the toxicology, and it'll take two to three days to complete that. Ferrie had *come to* the bureau [FBI's field office in New Orleans on] Saturday . . . this is a recap[itulation]. Let me give you a full recap on the Ferrie thing.

The FBI interviewed Ferrie in November of '63 because he had known Oswald in New Orleans . . . he [Ferrie] was a commercial pilot. And there was some allegation at the time that he may have flown Oswald *to* Dallas. *All* the evidence at that time indicated that that did not *happen* . . . that the plane that he [Ferrie] had was just not suited for the purpose.[77] That any idea the plane would've been used to take Oswald to *Cuba* after the [assassination] . . . after he did this was just not a real possibility. In addition to that, of course, Oswald had *left* New Orleans and *gone* to Dallas long before President Kennedy's trip was *known* of. So there just doesn't seem to be anything there.

Ferrie denied it all, quite vociferously. He talked . . . he called the bureau [on] Saturday, [and] said that he was quite a sick man and he was just *disgusted* with Garrison, he was going to *sue* him for slander.[78] That he [Garrison] was talkin' about him, and that he [Ferrie] just didn't know anything about *any* of this, as he had told them. And [Ferrie] wanted to know how . . . what the bureau could do to help him with this *nut!*

Garrison has apparently said that Ferrie wasn't involved . . . that he's checked it out [and] his plane wasn't suitable. That while he [Ferrie] may have been a part of *discussions,* he wasn't one of the people that he [Garrison] was referring to. So *fortunately,* unless he [Garrison] tries to change, he's apparently cut himself off from using *Ferrie* as his way out of what I think is his predicament. Ferrie was a homosexual and he had a *long* list of arrests. And there's an eleven-year-old boy [who was] with him

76. Robert Mann, *Legacy to Power: Senator Russell Long of Louisiana* (New York: Paragon House, 1992), 254–55.

77. When New Orleans detectives examined Ferrie's airplane at New Orleans airport in November 1963, they found it was not in flyable condition. It had flat tires and instruments were missing. Nor had Ferrie rented any aircraft. Associated Press, "No Ferrie Link with Oswald, Warren Told," *New Orleans States-Item,* 23 February 1967.

78. Clark is revealing that Ferrie, after telling reporters his side of the story, also went to the FBI's New Orleans field office seeking federal help.

when he was discovered, but they don't have any evidence of foul play.[79] It's all pretty . . . a pretty *sordid* mess.

I've been tryin' to figure *some* way . . . I'd given a . . . kind of a backgrounder to some press people *yesterday,* sayin' that I thought Garrison had the clear responsibility to report *anything* that he had to the Secret Service and the FBI *immediately.* That I couldn't imagine *any* half-responsible district attorney in the country, in a situation *vaguely* comparable to this, not *immediately* reporting it to them as being a matter of national concern [and] responsibility. Of course, we weren't going to do anything to interfere with his investigation.

The SAC down there [in New Orleans] just can't talk with him.[80] There's no . . . they just . . . he just has no confidence in Garrison. He's afraid that Garrison would try to *use* him. Deke [DeLoach] feels quite strongly that it'd be a mistake to *push* it. I'm sure that if . . . I had thought at one time of either callin' him or writin' him *myself.* But [I'm] afraid he [Garrison] would use that to try to *escalate* the thing. *[indistinct]* go away.

There are people concerned about it. Scotty Reston called me about an hour ago . . . [and I] told him off the record that we didn't . . . [that] the FBI was watchin' it as closely as they *could.*[81] From every indication . . . every piece of evidence that *we* had indicate[d that] highly erratic people were involved . . . [and that there's no] factual basis to support *any* of it.

That's . . . that's what we have on Ferrie. He sure took a bad time to die.

Johnson: *[chuckles]* I would . . . well, I'll *call* you back. I'm going—

Clark: One other thing: Garrison's claimin' that this [Ferrie's death] is obviously suicide.

Johnson: I'll give you a ring. I have a meeting on this . . . CIA thing now.[82] I will have. I'll give you a ring after I get out of that [and] we'll . . . *probably*

---

79. Ferrie was found unclothed and dead in his bed by the youth, who claimed he didn't know Ferrie and "just happened to wander in." Sanders, "Ferrie's Is 10th Mystery Death."

80. SAC is an acronym for "special agent in charge," the FBI's title for the head of a field office.

81. Reston will eschew writing anything about Garrison's allegations in his Washington column, and in all likelihood influences the *New York Times* coverage of the controversy after his conversation with Clark.

82. The president is about to meet with McNamara, Rusk, Katzenbach, and White House staffers Douglass Cater and George Christian to discuss an intense controversy that has erupted over covert CIA subsidies to a whole range of private organizations, including student, labor, educational, legal, professional, and business organizations. The subsidies, some of them dating back to the early 1950s, were instituted to counter Moscow's support of similar, ostensibly independent groups that were in fact tools for anti-American propaganda. The covert CIA funding was first revealed by *Ramparts* magazine in mid-February and has sparked a firestorm of controversy. Daily Diary, 22 February 1967, LBJL, and Michael Warner, "Sophisticated Spies: CIA's Links to Liberal Anti-communists, 1949–1967," *International Journal of Intelligence and Counterintelligence* 9, no. 4 (Winter 1996–97).

get together in the mornin'. But I have some ideas. I think that somebody oughta talk to [Senator] Russell [Long] up on the Hill . . . and give him just what you've told me about this whole picture, so he doesn't get involved with a wild statement.

Clark: Russell Long?

Johnson: Yeah.

Clark: Well, that's . . . that sure . . . if that would be effective, we sure oughta do it, because [we've] gotten in too far already.

Johnson: *Much* too far . . . they oughta know it.

Clark: Yeah. I [can] get right to that, I'll do—

Johnson: I'd just do it now. [I'd] just say [to Senator Long], if you can run by here, or if I can run see you, I think I oughta discuss some of these things. And I would make him [Long] come by there quietly, or run by his apartment. Because he just . . . shoots from the hip and doesn't know what he's talkin' about. I think [if] it'd be on just background, you'll get a little better [result]. Okay.

Clark: Fine, sir.

Johnson: I'll call you probably in the mornin'. Maybe you might come by before I get over from the [Executive] Mansion where we don't get interrupted.[83]

March 2

Thursday

From John Connally / 9:22 p.m.

Unbeknownst to the outside world, after David Ferrie's death several of Jim Garrison's top aides have begged him to drop his faltering investigation, which they see as going nowhere fast. Ferrie's sudden demise is a golden opportunity, they tell the Orleans Parish district attorney, because it provides a perfect excuse. With his alleged "chief witness" dead, Garrison can credibly argue that the investigation cannot continue. "Are you crazy?" Garrison responds. "Don't you realize that we are on the verge of solving one of the crimes of the century?"[84]

83. Johnson will meet with Clark for more than two hours the following afternoon. Daily Diary, 23 February 1967, LBJL.

84. This extraordinary confrontation between Garrison and his top aides will remain a secret for sixteen years. Dean Baquet, "Assistants Begged DA to Drop Case," *New Orleans Times-Picayune,* 20 November 1983.

On March 1 Garrison stuns New Orleans—and several lawyers and investigators in his own office—by ordering the arrest of Clay Shaw, the retired managing director of the International Trade Mart. It is roughly akin to New York's district attorney arresting Robert Moses for conspiring to assassinate President Kennedy. Shaw's Trade Mart, *the* architectural landmark in the city's skyline, is responsible for vastly increasing the attractiveness of New Orleans as a shipping port and has been imitated by trade-minded cities around the world. Apart from Shaw's deserved reputation as one of the city's most esteemed and civic-minded businessmen, he is best known locally for pioneering the postwar renovation of the historic French Quarter, and for being a respected amateur playwright who can claim Tennessee Williams as a friend. The fifty-four-year-old Shaw has never been linked, much less investigated, in connection with the assassination of President Kennedy, and the city is dumbstruck by the news. Still, and although New Orleans has seen more than its share of colorful public officials engaged in dubious acts, the benefit of the doubt falls to Garrison. Few people, outside Shaw's circle of acquaintances and his lawyers, believe that a district attorney would be *so* reckless and irresponsible as to arrest a man without substantial evidence. Again the refrain is heard: Garrison *must have something.*

These events unfold as Texas governor John Connally is on a promotional visit to New York. The wounded survivor of the Dallas motorcade is publicizing the next world's fair, which is scheduled to open in San Antonio in April 1968. While Connally is bent on generating attention for the Texas exposition, New York reporters only want to ask him about the startling news of an actual arrest.[85] One New York radio news outlet—WINS, recently converted to a 24/7 news format—is particularly eager to make a mark for itself and tries to beat all other outlets, even the wire services, with the latest developments. WINS cites reports from the DA's office almost verbatim, using "an unimpeachable source," most likely Garrison himself.[86] The feverish reporting eventually gets to Connally, who has always concurred with the findings of the Warren Commission despite his well-publicized differences over the "single bullet theory." His certitude shaken, now the governor doesn't know what to think. Late Thursday evening he decides to talk to the president.

Connally probably expects the president to be intrigued for two reasons. The governor knows that there is often a conspiratorial bent to Johnson's thinking. In addition, the story Connally is hearing casts Robert Kennedy in a very

85. John Devlin, "San Antonio World's Fair in '68 Announced Here by Connally," *New York Times,* 3 March 1967.

86. Edward Cocke (UPI), "JFK Plot Thickens: Radio Report Links Assassination to Castro Team," *Boston Globe,* 3 March 1967. According to WINS reporter Doug Edelson, who is quoted in the UPI account in the *Globe,* "One thing is certain. At least one man in this country believes every detail I've just related. That man is District Attorney Jim Garrison."

damaging light. But Johnson has developed a jaundiced attitude about Garrison's allegations *and* assassination plots supposedly directed against Castro during the Kennedy administration.[87] With respect to the former, the FBI has firmly convinced the president that Garrison is a charlatan and that nothing he says merits serious attention. Meanwhile, Abe Fortas has pointed out to Johnson just how full of holes the Drew Pearson story seems to be upon close inspection.

A week before, the Garrison probe and Pearson story tended to reinforce each other in Johnson's mind. Now the FBI's discrediting of Garrison, along with Fortas's doubts, incline him to think that the Castro retaliation story is just as wild and fanciful as anything coming out of New Orleans.

Johnson: [I'm] fine, Johnny.

Connally: I'm sorry to bother you. Can you listen to me for about five minutes?

Johnson: Sure.

Connally: All day today I have been interviewed up here . . . they're continually breaking stories on this *conspiracy* thing . . . based on what this fella, this DA in New Orleans talks about, [this DA] named Garrison.

I have just been interviewed *again.* And of course, I just simply say that I know *nothing* about it. But a newsman named Paul Smith has just been here to interview me again. They have a long story on the radio tonight, over WINS, a news radio station here in New York.[88] Charley Payne is the [WINS] general manager. He's been talkin' to me off and on all day and tryin' to keep me posted on it.[89] They [WINS] supposedly have a story from a man who saw the files in Garrison's office . . . he is the DA in New Orleans. I don't have the *whole* story, but here's what they say.

That Garrison has information that would prove that there were *four* assassination [teams] . . . *assassins* in the United States, sent here by [Fidel] Castro, or Castro's people. [Sent] not by Castro himself, but one of his lieutenants. One team was picked up in New York . . . but *did* not . . . was picked up and interviewed by the FBI and the Secret Service, but did not reveal a great deal of information which was *available.*

One of the teams was composed of Lee Harvey Oswald; this fella

87. Before talking with Connally, Johnson has conversations with Ramsey Clark (at 10 a.m.) and with Senator Richard Russell (3:04 p.m.) that are not recorded. These may concern Garrison and, if so, probably deepen Johnson's skepticism toward the New Orleans DA. Daily Diary, 2 March 1967, LBJL.

88. WINS, part of the Westinghouse broadcasting chain, became the first New York radio station (and second in the nation) to switch to an all-news, all-the-time format in April 1965. As such it is a respected media outlet whose influence extends beyond New York. "Radio Station in New York to Broadcast News Only," *Wall Street Journal,* 19 March 1965.

89. Advertisement, "Group W Area Vice Presidents and General Managers," *New York Times,* 5 March 1967.

[Clay] Shaw, that has just been arrested in New Orleans yesterday; and the [deceased] man [named David] Ferrie; plus one *other* man. They were teams of four. And there were two *other* teams that I know nothing about.

WINS Radio has had some reporters, according to the media here, in *Cuba* . . . working on various angles of this thing for the past [few] days. They also have a team of reporters *in* New Orleans *with* Garrison. In Cuba they found, according—[and] this is *very* confidential, and *all* of this is not goin' on the air . . . *at all*.[90] But in Cuba . . . and the two reporters that they had there were working from different angles and came together with *exactly* the same story.

The story—that they're *not* going to publish—is that after the [1962] missile crisis, President Kennedy and [Nikita] Khrushchev had made a deal to leave Castro in power. But about six months after the missile crisis was *over*, the CIA was *instructed* to assassinate Castro . . . and sent teams into Cuba. Some of 'em were captured and tortured, and Castro and his people—and I assume Che Guevara—heard the whole story.[91] The information they have here, which they're *not* gonna run, is that President Kennedy did *not* [put] the order to the CIA, but that some *other* person extremely close to President Kennedy *did*. They did not name the man . . . but the inference was very clear. The *inference* was . . . that it was his *brother* [who] ordered the CIA to send a team into Cuba to assassinate Castro. Then one of Castro's *lieutenants,* as a reprisal measure, sent four teams in[to] the United States to assassinate President Kennedy. [And] that Lee Harvey Oswald *was* [one of the] members of the team operating out of New Orleans.

Now this is the story that they *think* they have. This is the information that was given to me tonight, less than an hour ago, by a reporter named Paul Smith, who came here to [instruct] Charley Payne, whom I knew in Texas. [Payne was] a radio man down there, and he's now the general manager of WINS.

I thought this would be of interest to you. I know nothing more about it than that, but I thought you oughta know that.

Johnson: Good. This is confidential, too. We've *had* that story on about three occasions. The people here say that there's no basis for it.

Connally: Hmm.

---

90. Connally seems to be referring to the fact that WINS will report only half the story the governor says the radio station has. WINS will broadcast the claim that President Kennedy was "murdered by a group of plotters directed from Cuba," but will refrain from reporting that these plotters were sent in retaliation for U.S. plots on Castro's life. Cocke, "JFK Plot Thickens."

91. Major Ernesto "Che" Guevara, an Argentine Communist, helped lead the 1959 Cuban revolution and then became deputy premier under Castro. But there is a great mystery as to his whereabouts now; he has not been seen in public for two years. Barnard Collier, "Growing Evidence Puts Guevara in South America," *New York Times,* 9 July 1967.

Johnson: I have had some . . . I've given a lot of thought to it. First, one of
   [Jimmy] *Hoffa's* lawyers went to one of our mutual friends—
Connally: Yeah.
Johnson: —and asked him to come and relay that *to* us . . . just about like you
   have related it.[92] [A] week or two passed, and then *Pearson* came to me,
   Drew Pearson—
Connally: Yeah.
Johnson: —[and he] told me that the lawyer, Edward Morgan here [in
   Washington], had told him the same thing and said that they would
   plead . . . they would tell all the story after November, when the [statute
   of] limitation[s] ran [out]. I don't know . . . our lawyer [Ramsey Clark]
   said they couldn't believe that there's any [statute of] limitation[s] on a
   [concealed] conspiracy, but . . . [Then] I talked to another one or two of
   our *good* lawyers that I have recognized—
Connally: Yes, sir.[93]
Johnson: —[who's] pretty high-placed, a few months ago—
Connally: Yes, sir.
Johnson: He evaluated [it] pretty carefully and said that it was ridiculous.
   With this CIA thing breaking and the thing turning, as it did, in
   reconstructing the requests that were made of me back there, at the
   [beginning], right after I became president, I have talked to some more
   [people] about it, and I've got the a[ttorney] g[eneral] coming down to see
   me tomorrow night . . . to spend a weekend with me.[94] I thought I'd go
   over it with him *again* just so that they could . . . so [J. Edgar] Hoover and
   'em could watch it very *carefully*.

92. It is not clear who this "mutual friend" is.

93. Connally seems to understand that Johnson, while preferring not to name him, means Abe Fortas. When the Johnson Library releases the WH series of 1967 recordings, they may shed more light on the president's discussions of this sensitive matter with Fortas.

94. Johnson is leaving early the next morning to spend the weekend in Texas. Clark, whose nomination has just been confirmed by the Senate, will not join the presidential entourage at the LBJ Ranch for an unknown reason. Daily Diary, 3–6 March 1967, LBJL. Again, the "CIA thing" the president is referring to is the controversy over covert CIA financing of nongovernmental organizations both in the United States and abroad. By "requests made of me," Johnson is probably referring to the decision he made after November 22 about whether to continue covert subversion of Castro's regime, and in particular U.S. support for a military coup d'état. See Memorandum of Meeting with President Johnson, Subject: Cuba, 19 December 1963, in U.S. Department of State, *Foreign Relations of the United States, 1961–1963: Cuban Missile Crisis and Aftermath* (Washington, D.C.: U.S. Government Printing Office, 1996), 11: 904. Following the assassination, President Johnson incrementally but steadily moved away from the Kennedy policy of actively fomenting the violent overthrow of Castro's regime. Joseph Califano, *Inside: A Public and Private Life* (New York: Public Affairs, 2004), 126. Prior to joining the White House staff in 1965, Califano was general counsel of the army and, as such, a member of the Interdepartmental Coordinating Committee on Cuban Affairs, an ad hoc interagency group that oversaw most (but not the ultra-sensitive) aspects of the covert war on Cuba in 1963–64.

They say that . . . there's not anything *to* the Garrison story, [at] least
Hoover says so, as near as he can *tell*. He says that they interviewed
[David] Ferrie, and they interviewed this other fella [Dean Andrews], very
carefully and closely.[95] And the fella [Andrews] claims that he got a *call*
from Oswald, but they [the FBI] can't find any record of it.[96] And the
doctor that had him [Andrews] under surveillance said that he wasn't in a
position to *talk* on November the twenty-third, and [that] he [was] under
very heavy sedation.

And that the [Clay] Shaw thing is a phony, and that Ferrie died of
natural causes, and that *that* was a phony. But that—some of these *same*
sources that were preventin' . . . tryin' to involve this *jail* thing . . . have
been feeding stuff to Garrison as they did *here*.[97]

I don't know whether there's any basis for it or not. I noticed even
Larry—Larry Blackmon, yesterday, was in to see me on another
matter—and he started makin' a big pitch about this *other* situation.[98]
So I don't know how much of it is being fed out through their network
and through their channels, and how much of it anybody would know.
It's pretty *hard* to see *how* . . . we would know directly . . . what
Castro *did*.

Connally: Yeah.

Johnson: The story varies a good deal. If you go to lookin' at it [hard], as
Abe said, Who is it that's *seen* Castro? Or heard from Castro? Or *knows*
Castro . . . that's [in a position to] . . . [who] could be . . . *confirming* all
this? [Fortas said] that we just *hear* that this is what he *did*, but nobody
points to how we *hear* it.[99]

95. Andrews is a colorful New Orleans character: five foot seven and 240 pounds, he is a
bona fide lawyer and simultaneously an opportunist looking to make a name for himself. In
November 1963, while hospitalized for pneumonia, Andrews claimed to have received a mysterious call from a man asking him to represent the accused assassin. The FBI thoroughly investigated
and determined that Andrews was simply seeking some of the notoriety that any counsel for
Oswald was sure to receive; the lead, like the contemporaneous investigation of David Ferrie,
proved to have no bearing on the president's assassination. Four years later, however, it is this kind
of meaningless shard that Garrison has the power to exploit.

96. Andrews did not claim the call was from Oswald directly, but from a man Andrews identified as Clay Bertrand. By December 1963, Andrews all but admitted the call was a publicity hoax
and Bertrand a "figment of his imagination." Lambert, *False Witness,* 35.

97. Johnson seems to be suggesting that the same lawyer who fed Drew Pearson the story
about assassination plots against Castro has been in contact with Garrison.

98. A real estate developer from Fort Worth, Blackmon is president of the National Home
Builders Association and active in political fund-raising in Texas. John Willmann, "Texas Builder
Rumored Choice for Agency Post," *Washington Post,* 8 December 1965.

99. Fortas, with his characteristic astuteness, has pointed out a flaw in the Rosselli/Morgan
allegation. Rosselli's knowledge of CIA plots against Castro may be firsthand, but his claim that
Castro retaliated is based on hearsay and speculation.

Connally: Yeah.

Johnson: So we will look into it, and I appreciate very much your callin' me, and I'll try to bear this in mind. I may have you talk to the other fella when you get back home, just for a minute, because I think that it's somethin' we *have* to be *aware of* and *watch,* without gettin'—[100]

Connally: Caught either way. He [Payne] made me *promise*—

Johnson: —caught either way. [Robert Kennedy] talked today to stop the bombing, and had a pretty good crowd.[101] [Mike] Mansfield complimented him, and [J. William] Fulbright did, and [so did] a good many [other senators]. And you got a very *persuasive* speech to the public that wants peace and all that kind of stuff. He [Kennedy] said if we just stop [bombing] for a *week* and set a day certain, and tell 'em, and then if it didn't [work], go *on* [bombing].

Well, we've done that three times. We just finished [the] Tet period, we gave 'em a week and they didn't stop.[102] They just loaded 50,000 tons of cargo down there. But they voted on it [the bombing] in the House on an amendment offered to stop the bombing, and they only got seventeen votes.[103]

Connally: Ah-ha.

Johnson: It was three hundred and somethin' to seventeen. So I'm gonna leave here in a little bit, soon as I get through with the Congress—I've had my last reception—and go home. When are you goin' home?

Connally: I'm goin' tomorrow.

Johnson: Okay, well . . . I'll talk to you. You goin' to the ranch or Austin?

Connally: I'm goin' to Austin.

Johnson: Hm-hmm. Okay, well—

Connally: I'll talk to you down there. I just thought [that] since this was out in the communications—

100. It is not clear whether Johnson is suggesting that Connally talk to Fortas, or to Clark.

101. Hedrick Smith, "Kennedy Asks Suspension of U.S. Raid on North; Administration Unmoved," *New York Times,* 3 March 1967. Kennedy's forty-five-minute address is the latest in a series of widening breaches between the president and the senator over the conduct of the war. As James Reston observes, Kennedy wants to entice the North Vietnamese to the negotiating table via a bombing halt. Meanwhile, he is engaged in a "verbal bombing of the White House." James Reston, "Washington: On De-Escalating the Johnson-Kennedy War," *New York Times,* 3 March 1967.

102. Tet is when the new year is traditionally celebrated in Vietnam.

103. That morning the House of Representatives took up a bill authorizing supplemental funds for Vietnam. Representative George Brown (D-California), one of the very first opponents of the war, offered a nonbinding amendment stating that "none of the funds authorized . . . shall be used to carry out military operations in or over North Vietnam." The Brown amendment was defeated by a vote of 372 to 18. U.S. Senate, Committee on Foreign Relations, *The U.S. Government and the Vietnam War: Executive and Legislative Roles and Relationships, 1961–1964* (Washington, D.C.: U.S. Government Printing Office, 1984), 2: 598–99.

Johnson: Yeah . . . yeah, I think that's *right*. I think that's *good* . . . and I think it's right. I think—

Connally: I don't know how . . . I don't know what either. I thought [this] might tie in with somethin' you knew, and I don't *want* to know anything. I don't *need* to know it, but I just wanted [you to know what's goin' on]—

Johnson: Well . . . no . . . I've told you *all* I know. That's all *we* know. And the FBI thinks that both Ferrie and Shaw are frauds—I mean, that *Garrison* is usin' 'em as a fraud, that they have interviewed both of 'em at great length.[104]

Connally: Yeah.

Johnson: They have heard these things, and they interviewed 'em back in [1963–64], for the Warren Commission. They do not give any credit to it, but we can't ever be *sure,* and we just want to keep watchin' and so on [and] so forth.

Connally: Okay, sir. I'm sorry to disturb you.

Johnson: Thank you, Johnny.

Connally: All right. 'Bye.

104. Johnson's assertion is only partially correct. While the FBI thoroughly examined the allegation involving Ferrie, Clay Shaw was *never* investigated in connection with the assassination. The president is probably just repeating the error Ramsey Clark made during an impromptu press conference held earlier in the day. Inundated by questions about Shaw's arrest, Clark mistakenly answered that Shaw had also been investigated by the FBI in November–December 1963 and then cleared. Clark's misstatement will go uncorrected for three months. Robert Semple, "Clark Discounts a Shaw Conspiracy," *New York Times,* 3 March 1967; Lambert, *False Witness,* 81–82, 306–07; George Lardner, "Justice Admits Error in Shaw-Bertrand Tie," *Washington Post,* 3 June 1967.

Epilogue

The Kennedy assassination is apparently not a topic of conversation in the remaining telephone recordings made by President Johnson up until his last days in office.[1] There may be several reasons for this absence, but the primary reason seems to be Johnson's taping habits. There is a steep decline in the number of conversations recorded during 1966 and 1967 in comparison with 1963 and 1964, when the taping was at its zenith. The pace of recording will pick up again in 1968, either because it is an especially eventful year or because Johnson becomes more concentrated on creating a historical record. But no one really knows, because the president is not known to have ever explained why he recorded extensively during certain periods and very little at other times.

Despite this void, the assassination of John Kennedy never ceases to be an issue for Lyndon Johnson, both for the balance of his administration and afterwards. Some of the most dramatic developments since November 1963 will occur in the weeks and months just ahead.

For much of 1967 New Orleans DA Jim Garrison will hold the nation in thrall with bogus claims of having cracked the conspiracy behind November 22. The legitimacy conferred by elective office gives Garrison a license for audacious mendacity, and he exploits this privilege (and the Zeitgeist) to the hilt, as did Joe McCarthy. Owing to a clever piece of Soviet KGB disinformation planted in a Communist Italian newspaper, Garrison is duped into believing that businessman Clay Shaw has a secret life as a "[CIA] man . . . trying to bring Fascism back to Italy."[2] And on the basis of this deception, Garrison will feverishly construct a vast government conspiracy. Shaw's 1969 trial will prove a debacle—a jury declares him not guilty after deliberating all of fifty-four minutes—but Garrison wins the psychological war despite losing the legal bat-

1. This finding of the Johnson Library is based on its initial review of the tape recordings for the selective K series release. As noted earlier, it is possible that some assassination-related recordings were overlooked in the initial survey and will surface as the Library continues to process all the recordings for the exhaustive White House series. As of the writing of this book, the WH series has been processed through July 1966, while the K series consists of selected recordings from November 22, 1963, to March 28, 1967.

2. Jim Garrison, *On the Trail of the Assassins: My Investigation and Prosecution of the Murder of President Kennedy* (New York: Sheridan Square Press, 1988), 87; Max Holland, "The Power of Disinformation: The Lie That Linked CIA to the Kennedy Assassination," *Studies in Intelligence,* Fall/Winter 2001.

tle. Prior to Garrison's intervention, not even the Warren Commission's worst domestic critics claimed the federal government was actually *complicit* in the assassination. Garrison will be more responsible than anyone (apart from the KGB) for spawning the insidious lie that the CIA was responsible for President Kennedy's murder and the 1963 "coup d'état."[3]

Garrison's abuse of prosecutorial discretion will have few rivals in the annals of American jurisprudence. But in truth, the very public spectacle in New Orleans from 1967 to 1969 pales next to the private drama that absorbs the president during this same period. It will grip Johnson well into his restless retirement.

On March 3, 1967—the day after Johnson's conversation with John Connally—Drew Pearson's associate Jack Anderson breaks the story of the plots against Castro. The forty-four-year-old Anderson, who started out as one of Pearson's legmen in 1947, is the muckraking columnist's heir apparent, halfway between employee and full partner.[4] Pearson told the president he would not be publishing the allegation until November at the earliest, but he gave that assurance in January, before Garrison arrived on the scene.[5] The day of Clay Shaw's arrest, Pearson is accompanying Earl Warren on a goodwill tour of five Andean countries in South America. Anderson thus takes it upon himself to devote the entire March 3 column to the Castro story lest the "Washington Merry-Go-Round" get scooped completely.[6]

"President Johnson is sitting on a political H-bomb," begins the column, "an unconfirmed report that Senator Robert Kennedy may have approved an assassination plot [against Castro] which then possibly backfired against his late brother." The column is sensational, yet so thinly sourced—it literally admits the story is a rumor—the *Washington Post* and *New York Post* spike the column and refuse to publish it. But hundreds of other subscribing papers nationwide do. Anderson rushes into print because he fears being beat by Jim Garrison. The column observes that this very allegation "may have started New Orleans' flamboyant District Attorney Jim Garrison on his investigation of the Kennedy assassination, but insiders believe he is following the wrong trails."[7]

3. Garrison, *Trail,* 277. In 1991, Oliver Stone's *JFK* will painstakingly replicate Garrison's fable, thus giving it the distinction of being the only American feature film produced during the Cold War to have, as its very axis, a lie manufactured in the KGB's disinformation factories. Max Holland, "The Demon in Jim Garrison," *Wilson Quarterly,* Spring 2001; "How Moscow Undermined the Warren Commission," *Washington Post,* 22 November 2003.

4. Susan Sheehan, "The Anderson Strategy," *New York Times,* 13 August 1972.

5. November is presumably when John Rosselli can no longer be charged with conspiring to kill Castro because the statute of limitations will have run out.

6. Warren and Pearson are traveling aboard *Air Force One* to Bolivia, Chile, Peru, Ecuador, and Colombia. "We never conceded the field if there was a sliver of a chance that we could scoop the competition," Anderson will write in his memoir. Jack Anderson, *Peace, War, and Politics* (New York: Forge, 1999), 82–83.

7. Drew Pearson and Jack Anderson, "A Rumor Persists About Assassination," *San Francisco Chronicle,* 3 March 1967. Although not all papers subscribing to the column make the distinction,

Drew Pearson hears plenty about the dramatic developments back home, even in the Andes. Wherever the chief justice holds a press conference the *Warren Report* and Garrison's arrest of Shaw top the list of questions—indeed, they are the only subjects newsmen want to ask Warren about.[8] The questioning is so relentless and the skepticism so intense that the chief justice, who steadfastly refuses to comment publicly on the assassination back home, feels compelled to come to the defense of the Commission bearing his name.[9]

Pearson does not apparently learn about his March 3 column, however, until he returns home in mid-month. And then he is none too pleased with his associate's decision. "It was a poor story in the first place, and violated a confidence in the second place," notes Pearson in his diary. "Finally it reflected on Bobby Kennedy without actually pinning the goods on him."[10] Pearson even thinks the *Washington Post* and *New York Post* were right not to run the column. Yet he is not so displeased that he will publish a retraction. In mid-March Pearson talks with Edward Morgan, who tells him that he recently ran into his client in Las Vegas. The mobster approached Morgan clutching a clipping of Anderson's column and was "most indignant." His client, Morgan now says, will not cooperate in advancing the story any further.[11]

The seemingly premature March 3 column has other repercussions as well. After reading it in the *States-Item,* Jim Garrison contacts Jack Anderson and invites him down to New Orleans. Pearson agrees to foot the bill, "to see what the score is."[12] Anderson visits in early April, shortly after a three-judge panel declares there is probable cause to put Shaw on trial. The Orleans Parish DA will completely flummox the junior muckraking columnist. Anderson leaves Louisiana "very much impressed" with the DA and believing "there is some authenticity to Garrison's claims," though he promises not to write a word about them for the time being.[13]

---

the byline reads "Today's column is by Jack Anderson." On March 7 the *Washington Post* will publish a short follow-up item in the Pearson/Anderson column that hints at a connection between Garrison's New Orleans probe and rumors of a 1963 CIA plot against Castro. Pearson and Anderson, "Castro Counterplot," *Washington Post,* 7 March 1967.

8. Marquis Childs, "Exploiting Profits from a Tragedy," *Washington Post*, 15 March 1967; Pearson Diary, 3 March 1967, Box 2, Pearson Papers, LBJL.

9. United Press International, "Warren Satisfied with Conclusions in Kennedy Report," *New York Times,* 4 March 1967.

10. Pearson Diary, 20 March 1967, Box 2, Pearson Papers, LBJL.

11. Ibid.

12. Ibid., 21 March 1967.

13. Garrison's absurd explanation to Anderson is that Clay Shaw, David Ferrie, and Jack Ruby were part of a homosexual ring recruited by the CIA to kill Castro. This trio then picked Lee Harvey Oswald to commit the assassination, but when Oswald proved unable to get a visa to enter Cuba, the conspirators "turned around and decided to assassinate Kennedy . . . us[ing] Oswald as the patsy." Ibid., 24 March 1967; DeLoach to Tolson, memorandum, 4 April 1967, Record 157-10006-10270, JFK, NARA. In his 1999 memoir, Anderson will claim that he found Garrison unpersuasive in April 1967, but that was not the case. Anderson, *Politics,* 112.

The most profound reaction to the column, however, is the official one. Spurred by the first appearance of the rumor in print, Ramsey Clark finally does what Johnson suggested he do during their conversation on February 20: the attorney general asks the FBI what it knows about the allegations. On March 6 the FBI prepares what is surely one of the most astonishing memorandums in the bureau's history. The caption itself is enough to set hearts palpitating at the CIA: "Central Intelligence Agency's Intentions to Send Hoodlums to Cuba to Assassinate Castro."[14] The FBI knows far less than it thinks about the totality of the covert operation, but unlike the Pearson/Anderson column, the bureau's information is hard and fast on three vital questions. The CIA did try to have Castro assassinated from 1961 to 1962 and possibly into 1963; the agency engaged members of the criminal syndicate in the United States in this effort; and Attorney General Robert Kennedy knew about the plots, and Cosa Nostra involvement, contemporaneously. Before receiving this confirmation, President Johnson dismissed the rumor as being no more credible than the suggestion that Lady Bird was "taking dope." Now he must grapple with the implications of this stunning revelation, and what, if anything, he should do about it.[15]

One of his first impulses is to talk to Chief Justice Earl Warren. When Pearson and Warren return from South America, the president invites them to visit the Oval Office on March 13 at 7 p.m., ostensibly to talk about their goodwill trip. Before Pearson arrives, the president meets privately with the chief justice for forty minutes, with only Marvin Watson, the White House staffer who handles liaison with the FBI, in attendance.[16] Little is known about this pre-meeting meeting (although much can be inferred from a similar conversation Warren has with Pearson eight days later). The chief justice has known about the Morgan/Rosselli allegation for two months, since January, when Pearson told him three days after telling President Johnson.[17] But until he steps into the Oval Office, Warren does not know that the fantastic is also true. The chief justice's rock-solid belief in his own report must have been shaken, at least

14. Wannall to Sullivan, memo, 6 March 1967, Kissinger/Scowcroft Files, GRFL.

15. At Johnson's insistence, the FBI is asked to interview attorney Edward Morgan to learn everything he knows and to try to get him to divulge the name of his client John Rosselli. But Morgan is one of the last lawyers in Washington who might be intimidated by two FBI agents asking questions. He is not about to give any additional information without getting complete immunity for his client in return. Morgan promises to contact the FBI "if he discovered any way to reveal the full details of this matter." Memorandum re Assassination of President John Fitzgerald Kennedy, 21 March 1967, Record 157-10005-10347, JFK, NARA.

16. Daily Diary, 13 March 1967, LBJL.

17. Pearson told Warren on January 19, after having received permission from Rosselli's attorney Edward Morgan. The "chief justice was decidedly skeptical," wrote Pearson in his diary. Warren argued that "if Castro had been operating through Oswald, he would have had more people involved; it would not have been a one-man job." Pearson Diary, Box 2, 19 January 1967, Pearson Papers, LBJL.

momentarily, by the revelation.[18] Ultimately, however, Warren concludes that while Castro may have wanted to kill President Kennedy, and may even have sent teams to the United States for that purpose, Oswald did not act under the control or at the behest of the Cuban leader.[19]

The president's meeting with Warren has two consequences. The chief justice, besides being a persuasive advocate, is very conversant with the damning evidence against Oswald and believes him guilty beyond a reasonable doubt. Johnson's confidence in that part of the *Warren Report* is probably bolstered; indeed, the president may even come to understand, for the first time, that John Connally's dissent from the single bullet theory is specious, seemingly plausible but in fact impossible. Yet the conclusion that Oswald acted alone in Dealey Plaza, of course, doesn't rule out a conspiracy. And now there is more reason than ever to believe that Fidel Castro instigated the plot, not for some vague purpose of getting even after the missile crisis, but in retaliation for assassination attempts on his life. The president, perhaps with Warren's encouragement, is determined to get the rest of the story from the CIA, the agency harboring the secrets.

On March 22 Johnson asks Richard Helms, the CIA's liaison to the Warren Commission in 1964 and DCI since June 1966, to prepare a full report on the allegations in the Pearson column. It is not known whether the president divulges to Helms that he already knows from the FBI there is a kernel of truth to the story, or whether Johnson pretends to find the claim outlandish, secretly intending to test Helms's candor about such a sensitive matter. In either case, Johnson does not ask "idly or in passing. . . . But ask[s] directly, formally, and explicitly, in a tone and manner which [do] not admit of evasion."[20]

The president is the one person outside the agency whose need to know is

18. Pearson's notes from when he is present on March 13 make no mention of the March 3 column, the *Warren Report,* or even the headline-making antics of Jim Garrison, who is acting more like a carnival barker than a district attorney in pursuit of a serious matter. Instead, according to Pearson, the president treats his guests to an earful about the Manchester book and how Robert Kennedy has tried to deny Johnson's legitimacy "every step of the way," including making Johnson "stay over in [his] old [EOB] office" after the assassination. Any serious discussion about what to do in light of the FBI confirmation seems to have occurred when Warren and Johnson met privately. Pearson Diary, 13 March 1967, Box 2; and Pearson, typewritten notes, 13 March 1967, Chief Justice Earl Warren #1, G246, 3 of 3; both Pearson Papers, LBJL.

19. Eight days after his meeting with Johnson, Warren tells Pearson that he is prepared to believe that Castro wanted to kill the president, and may even have sent some teams to do it. But "we know Lee Oswald killed Kennedy, and I am satisfied that there is no evidence that anyone else did." Pearson Diary, 21 March 1967, Box 2, Pearson Papers, LBJL.

20. Thomas Powers, *The Man Who Kept the Secrets: Richard Helms and the CIA* (New York: Alfred A. Knopf, 1979), 120–22. For good measure, Johnson also asks about CIA involvement in the assassinations of Ngo Dinh Diem and Rafael Trujillo, the two leaders who sparked his 1963–64 remarks about "divine retribution."

self-defined, and Helms has no alternative but to come back with a specific and complete answer. In some sense, though, Helms's exact response is superfluous. Johnson's mind is already made up on the basis of the FBI's confirmation alone. In early April, the president says as much to Marvin Watson, who immediately passes the observation on to Deke DeLoach.[21] A day later, on April 5, Johnson repeats his conclusion to Drew Pearson, who is probably relieved to learn that he and Anderson are no longer out on a limb. "We think there's something to . . . that old man Morgan['s] information," the president tells Pearson. "There were some attempts to assassinate Castro through the Cosa Nostra, and they point to your friends in the Justice Department." Pearson immediately corrects Johnson. "You mean one friend in the Justice Department," he says, meaning Robert Kennedy.[22]

In early May, Helms requests a private meeting with Johnson to present the results of the investigation conducted by the CIA's inspector general (IG).[23] The May 10 meeting commences at 5:55 p.m. and lasts almost an hour. Again, almost none of the details from this meeting are known, but undoubtedly Helms is mortified by the presence of George Christian.[24] Johnson's press secretary often takes notes when the president has a private meeting with a reporter, and that may be the reason for his presence now. Helms probably pleads with Johnson not to have anything written down of what he is about to say, because the first rule in keeping secrets is "Nothing on paper." The IG report flouts that rule with a vengeance, but there is only one copy of the draft report and Helms has no intention of ever allowing it out of the CIA. He hasn't even brought it with him to the meeting; his oral briefing will be based on some handwritten notes he's jotted down, plus his own knowledge as deputy director for plans from 1962 onward. Johnson seems to have assented, because there are no extant notes of the meeting. Yet Christian is present throughout, probably because the president wants a witness to what he is about to hear with his own ears.

It is an easy matter for Helms to dispense with the Diem and Trujillo assas-

21. Associated Press, "LBJ Reportedly Suspected CIA Link in JFK's Death," *Washington Post*, 13 December 1977; Powers, *Man Who Kept the Secrets*, 157.

22. Pearson Diary, 5 April 1967, Box 2, Pearson Papers, LBJL. On May 6 Pearson will inform Warren of the confirmation from the president. "Imagine appointing a man like John McCone in a position where he can make decisions like that!" exclaims Warren. Yet the assassination plots involving mobsters began well before McCone became DCI, and were kept secret from him. Church Committee, *Alleged Assassination Plots Involving Foreign Leaders*, 94th Cong., 1st Sess. (Washington, D.C.: U.S. Government Printing Office, 1975), 99.

23. Daily Diary, 10 May 1967, LBJL.

24. If Helms was less than thrilled about the press secretary's presence, he never let on. If Christian did write a memo of the conversation, it is not among his papers at the LBJL. Nor did Christian talk about the meeting in his oral history on deposit at the Library. It was taken over five occasions from 1968 to 1971, years before the significance of the May 10 meeting became known. George Christian Oral History, LBJL.

sinations. The CIA was not responsible for either death, Helms tells Johnson. Castro, ironically, is another matter. And so eight years before it becomes public knowledge, the president learns that CIA plots to assassinate Castro date back to August 1960, to the Eisenhower administration, as plans for what became the Bay of Pigs invasion reached their final stages. Castro was supposed to be dead, in fact, by the time the exiles landed. In 1960–61 it seemed clever to arrange the assassination via members of the criminal syndicate, or at least it seemed so to Richard Bissell, then the CIA's deputy director for plans. The mobsters, presumably, were just as anxious as the U.S. government to get rid of Castro, and if something went wrong, it would be difficult to link a compromised, Cosa Nostra–style plot with official Washington. Now, though, the CIA is vulnerable to blackmail.

The more interesting part, at least to Johnson's mind, is what Helms tells him next. After the Bay of Pigs debacle, rather than draw back the Kennedy administration redoubled the effort. The injunction to the CIA was simple: *get rid of Castro and Castro's regime* via any possible means, short of another invasion. The ill-advised alliance with Cosa Nostra members persisted until 1962, coming to an end only because the mobsters were never able to deliver on their promises. (Indeed, Helms thinks the mobsters may have been stringing the CIA along from the outset, and in this judgment he is not alone.) Still, efforts to decapitate the regime in one violent swoop continued well into 1963. One of them was in the works at the very time of President Kennedy's assassination.[25]

If Johnson asked the CIA director under whose direction the CIA acted, Helms would have told the president that Robert Kennedy "personally managed the operation" to assassinate Castro.[26] Then again, Johnson may not have bothered to ask the question if he thought he already knew the answer. In addition to the FBI confirmation, and what Edward Morgan has asserted about the former attorney general's central role, it is common knowledge within the White House that President Kennedy made his brother the driving force behind the clandestine effort to overthrow Castro after the Bay of Pigs. As one administration official will describe the post–April 1961 effort, from "inside accounts of the

25. The extent to which Helms briefed Johnson about efforts up until November 1963 to remove Castro is uncertain. In his testimony before various congressional committees in the 1970s, Helms will adamantly draw a distinction between attempts to eliminate Castro via political action in late 1963, however violent, and the outright assassination plots involving mobsters and other schemes from 1961 to the spring of 1963. Whether this is a distinction without a difference is a debatable issue. Church Committee, *Alleged Assassination Plots,* 179.

26. The quote is taken from what Helms will personally tell Secretary of State Henry Kissinger in 1975 after allegations of CIA wrongdoing surface in the press. The presumption is that Helms, if asked, would have told President Johnson the same thing in 1967. Kissinger and Ford, memorandum of conversation, 4 January 1975, Kissinger/Scowcroft Files, GRFL.

pressure he was putting on the CIA to 'get Castro,' [Robert Kennedy] seemed like a wild man who was out-CIAing the CIA."[27]

Johnson's response to Helms's briefing is rather laconic, perhaps surprisingly so. Helms is quite familiar with the president's conspiratorial turn of mind, for he, too, heard Johnson opine openly, on December 19, 1963, that Kennedy's assassination was an act of retribution for the murder of Diem, possibly not even "divine."[28] Helms probably hastens to remind the president that the CIA, FBI, and Warren Commission all looked long and hard for a connection between Oswald and the Cuban government, but came up empty-handed. There is no evidence Oswald was controlled by or acting on behalf of any foreign power. Yet persuading Johnson of that now is a futile exercise, as Helms is probably the first to realize. The president is utterly convinced that "something more than" Oswald acting alone was involved in Kennedy's assassination, and that something involves Castro's Cuba.[29]

One of the tantalizing yet unanswerable questions is what effect, if any, Johnson's knowledge has on Robert Kennedy's decision to run in 1968. In keeping with the Kabuki-like nature of Washington politics, where the media are often the chosen vehicle for not-so-veiled messages, the New York senator probably considers Drew Pearson's March 3 column a shot across his bow, as Pearson is known to be on very friendly terms with the president. For all Kennedy knows, *Johnson* is the source of the story rather than the other way around, and the column is a harbinger of things to come should Kennedy decide to challenge the president.[30] Kennedy's response to the Pearson column, insofar

27. Harris Wofford, *Of Kennedys and Kings: Making Sense of the Sixties* (Pittsburgh, Penn.: University of Pittsburgh Press, 1992), 386.

28. Powers, *Man Who Kept the Secrets,* 121, 157.

29. Ibid., 157. In 1975, Helms will recall that "the first time I ever heard such a theory as that enunciated was in a very peculiar way by President Johnson." Church Committee, *Final Report: The Investigation of the Assassination of President John F. Kennedy,* 94th Cong., 2nd Sess. (Washington, D.C.: U.S. Government Printing Office, 1976), 5: 71.

30. There is no indication that Johnson urged Pearson/Anderson to publish what appeared on March 3. According to the president's Daily Diary, which is usually reliable, he had no contact with Pearson from February 15 to March 12, nor with Anderson directly. Moreover, Johnson's conversation with John Connally on March 2 belies the suggestion that he was egging the columnists on, and Pearson's diary also rules the president out of the matter. For a contrary view, see Evan Thomas, *Robert Kennedy: His Life* (New York: Simon & Schuster, 2000), 336, 464. *After* the March 3 column appears, press secretary George Christian, who is under standing orders to help Pearson in "every way," makes sure Pearson and Anderson are made aware of a February 28 news article that lends more (albeit superficial) credence to the notion of a retaliatory conspiracy hatched in Cuba. The article appeared in *El Tiempo,* a Spanish-language newspaper published in New York. Kenneth Thompson, ed., *The Johnson Presidency: Twenty Intimate Perspectives of Lyndon B. Johnson* (Lanham, Md.: University Press of America, 1986), 120; and Memorandum for Marvin Watson, 7 March 1967, with attached note, "George Christian reports he did what he was supposed to do on this," Cuba and Related Matters, Office Files of Mildred Stegall, LBJL.

as it is known, is to hurriedly search his files for any pertinent information.[31] He also arranges to have lunch on March 4 with Richard Helms, who probably assures him that the president hasn't asked the CIA director anything yet—and if and when Johnson does, Helms will fight to protect his agency from damaging disclosures.[32] There is, in fact, a complete convergence of interests between the CIA and Robert Kennedy over the "get Castro" operation and the need for continued secrecy about it.

Certainly any attempt to publicize the truth is fraught with risks for Johnson. There would be a ferocious counterattack from Kennedy partisans, and Johnson might be left unable to "prove" an allegation that would be perceived as monstrous. Then again, a sitting president could hardly ignore the price the CIA and the United States would pay for admitting that it tried to instigate in Havana what happened in Dallas, and until he bows out on March 31, 1968, Johnson fully expects to run for and serve another term. The final, incalculable factor is Johnson's residual loyalty to John Kennedy and the office of the presidency. Johnson believes, and with good reason, that he has always kept faith with the 1960 political partnership forged in Los Angeles. As much as he might be tempted to derail Robert Kennedy's ambition by publicizing the story, Johnson has to realize that President Kennedy's reputation will be sullied, too, along with the office itself. The president is, in one historian's words, "trapped between two Kennedys. He [can] not openly attack Robert without implicitly attacking John."[33]

Still, the threat of disclosure looms. In this respect, the timing of Senator Kennedy's announcement that he fully intends to back Johnson's presumed bid for reelection seems premature, if not curious. On March 2, as noted during the president's conversation with John Connally that day, Kennedy makes his break with administration policy over Vietnam official via a dramatic address on the Senate floor. The next day the Pearson/Anderson column appears, and two weeks later Kennedy pledges to support Johnson in 1968, calling him "an outstanding president."[34] Indeed, throughout the spring of 1967, the senator speaks more warmly of Johnson than he ever has in public. At a fund-raising dinner in New York on June 3, Kennedy introduces Johnson to the audience, noting that the president "won the greatest popular victory in modern times [in 1964], and with our help he will do so again in 1968." He also credits Johnson for having "never failed to spend [his popularity] in the pursuit of his beliefs or

31. Thomas, *Kennedy,* 336.

32. Ibid.

33. Paul Henggeler, *In His Steps: Lyndon Johnson and the Kennedy Mystique* (Chicago: Ivan R. Dee, 1991), 218.

34. "He has been an outstanding president and I look forward to campaigning for him in 1968," said Kennedy during an impromptu news conference. Richard Reeves, "Kennedy Will Aid Johnson in 1968," *New York Times,* 18 March 1967.

in the interests of his country."[35] Privately, the senator resents his own words and Arthur Schlesinger, Jr., chides him for the favorable comments. "They seemed out of character," observes Schlesinger, "and that is one thing you must never be."[36]

By the fall the pre-Manchester polling numbers have reasserted themselves, and Johnson is again on the political defensive, as liberal Democrats search for a champion to lead a "Dump Johnson" movement. Uncharacteristically, Kennedy vacillates when repeatedly importuned to challenge Johnson, disappointing and even infuriating some of his closest aides and supporters. They cannot understand his putting party above principle when the moral choice is ostensibly so stark, and when Kennedy's hatred of Johnson is just as obsessive as Johnson's disdain for Kennedy. "I have never seen RFK so torn about anything," observes Arthur Schlesinger, Jr., in December 1967.[37] Kennedy knows the resources of the president's office, though, and expresses concern about what a desperate incumbent might do. There is some talk among Kennedy aides about blackmail, and no one is more concerned than Angela Novello, the senator's devoted secretary, who knows more of Robert Kennedy's secrets than anyone. As she will recall in 1969,

> I wanted Bob in the White House so badly, but I didn't want him to run in '68 because I was afraid of what certain people in high places would do. . . . I was afraid LBJ would . . . you know how vindictive he is! That if Bob threw in his hat . . . that worried me.[38]

As late as January 1968 Kennedy is still categorically asserting he will not oppose Johnson "under any foreseeable circumstances."[39] Ultimately, however, the senator backs into the race on March 16 after the 1968 Tet offensive ostensibly changes the political calculus. The uprising seems to belie Johnson's claim of genuine progress in Vietnam and propels Senator Eugene McCarthy to an unexpectedly large percentage of the vote in the New Hampshire Democratic primary in early March. McCarthy's showing enables Robert Kennedy to plausibly claim his challenge to Johnson is not "personal," but stems from the split in the Democratic Party.[40]

---

35. Richard Witkin, "Johnson, in City, Vows to Maintain Peace in Mideast," *New York Times*, 4 June 1967.

36. Henggeler, *In His Steps,* 223; Arthur Schlesinger, Jr., *Robert Kennedy and His Times* (Boston: Houghton Mifflin, 1978), 776.

37. Schlesinger, *Robert Kennedy,* 835, 837, 839–40.

38. Thomas, *Kennedy,* 355.

39. David Broder, "RFK Won't Oppose LBJ Renomination," *Washington Post*, 31 January 1968.

40. David Broder, "Kennedy Is Considering Race Against Johnson," *Washington Post,* 14 March 1968.

Because of what Johnson knows, he undoubtedly reads a *Washington Post* story datelined March 25 quite differently than almost everyone else in official Washington. Robert Kennedy, by putting himself on the frequently unscripted campaign trail, is unavoidably exposing himself to questions about a subject he has scrupulously and successfully dodged for years, namely, the controversy over the *Warren Report*. On his first campaign swing through California, the senator finds he cannot duck college students demanding to know where he stands, try as he might to ignore a barrage of questions. Finally, in "apparent discomfort," Kennedy coldly tells the shouting students, "Your manners overwhelm me. Go ahead . . . ask your question." No, he would not reopen the investigation, Kennedy says. "I stand by the [*Warren*] *Report*."[41] After reading this article, if not well before, Lyndon Johnson surely realizes how wrong he was to ever believe that Kennedy fomented criticism of the Warren Commission. No one has a greater stake in keeping the issue absolutely devoid of controversy.

But now that the one thing Johnson has feared most from the first day of his presidency—Robert Kennedy seeking to reclaim the office in the name of his brother—has actually come to pass, it is the last straw.[42] On March 31 Johnson declares he is not a candidate for renomination. In the next several weeks, the president will play a role in leaking a story that is profoundly embarrassing to Kennedy's candidacy, namely, the then–attorney general's role in the 1963 wiretap on the telephone of the Reverend Martin Luther King, Jr.[43] Yet Johnson says nary a word to advance the story about the assassination plots against Castro.

There is little doubt that the Cuba secret weighs heavily on the president though. A revealing barometer is his gut reaction to the news that Robert Kennedy has been mortally wounded shortly after midnight, California time, on June 5. The president is awakened almost immediately and will not be able to

41. "5000 Greet Kennedy in Watts Area," *Washington Post*, 26 March 1968; Associated Press, "Questions to Kennedy on Assassin," *The Times* (London), 26 March 1968. Besides stating his opposition to a reinvestigation, Kennedy deflects calls to open immediately the Warren Commission's records at the National Archives. They should be opened at the "appropriate time," which means not for decades.

42. The "American people, swayed by the magic of the name, were dancing in the streets," Johnson will later tell biographer Doris Kearns. "The whole situation was unbearable for me. After thirty-seven years of public service, I deserved something more. . . ." Doris Kearns, *Lyndon Johnson and the American Dream* (New York: Harper & Row, 1976), 343.

43. Apart from his role in the plots against Castro, nothing is potentially more embarrassing to Kennedy's presidential campaign than the wiretap placed on the telephone of Dr. King. On May 25, 1968, a few weeks after King's assassination, in the midst of the Oregon primary, and just before the all-important California primary, the Pearson/Anderson column publishes a story claiming that Robert Kennedy ordered the wiretap in 1963. With good reason, the Kennedy campaign presumes this leak is Johnson's handiwork. Fred Graham, "Drew Pearson Says Robert Kennedy Ordered Wiretap on Phone of Dr. King," *New York Times*, 25 May 1968; Thomas, *Kennedy*, 378–79.

sleep the rest of the night.[44] In between telephone calls to Clark Clifford, Ramsey Clark, J. Edgar Hoover, and Secret Service chief James Rowley, Johnson begins doodling on a memo left over from the previous day.[45] With the identity of Robert Kennedy's assailant unknown in the wee hours, Johnson wonders if Fidel Castro has decided that his retaliation isn't complete until both Kennedy brothers are dead. Johnson scratches out a few disjointed words: "Costra [sic] Nostra . . . Ed Morgan . . . send in to get Castro . . . planning."[46] By late morning it is apparent that the assassin, Sirhan Sirhan, is a disturbed loner with no apparent ties to Cuba and probably no political motivation whatsoever. Johnson drops his initial thought of another Cuba-instigated conspiracy against a Kennedy.[47]

In the months and years to come, Johnson will be deeply ambivalent. He will be torn between his loyalty to John Kennedy, the man who helped Johnson overcome his regional handicap, and his antipathy toward Kennedy's brother, the man who did more than anyone to deny Johnson his legitimacy. In October 1968, shortly before his retirement begins, Johnson volunteers a piece of information to veteran newsman Howard K. Smith, whom he deeply respects. "I'll tell you something [about Kennedy's murder] that will rock you," says the soon-to-be former president during the Oval Office interview. "Kennedy was trying to get to Castro, but Castro got to him first." Smith begs Johnson for details. "I was rocked all right," Smith will later recall, ". . . [but Johnson] refused, saying it will all come out one day." The president is obviously worn down by the bitterness of his years in office, and the newsman is left wondering if he has just witnessed a last bit of Johnson blarney.[48]

In political exile Johnson continues to seesaw between discretion and aching for the truth to come out, explosive though it is. In September 1969 Johnson is interviewed for a series of programs about his presidency that are to be

44. "There was an air of unreality about the whole thing—a nightmare quality," observes Mrs. Johnson in her diary. "It couldn't be true. We must have dreamed it. It had all happened before." Lady Bird Johnson, *A White House Diary* (New York: Holt, Rinehart and Winston, 1970), 679–81.

45. When they are processed for release, these conversations, some of which were recorded, may confirm that Johnson initially suspected Cuban involvement in Robert Kennedy's assassination. Daily Diary, 5 June 1968, LBJL.

46. Notes written 5 June 1968 on memo dated 4 June 1968, June 1968 (1 of 3), Box 30, Handwriting File, LBJL.

47. In his Robert Kennedy biography, Evan Thomas suggests (on the basis of these handwritten notes) that Johnson is toying with the idea of reviving the Castro story on June 4, the day Kennedy wins the California primary and appears headed for the Democratic nomination. But the notes, while written on a memo dated June 4, were clearly identified by the secretary who collected them as being from "June 5, 1968 a.m.," that is, *after* Kennedy has been mortally wounded. They probably indicate Johnson's initial thoughts about who might be responsible for the attack on the senator rather than an effort to cast aspersions on Kennedy. Thomas, *Kennedy*, 392.

48. "Johnson Is Quoted on Kennedy Death," *New York Times,* 25 June 1976. Johnson will make a nearly identical remark to White House aide Joe Califano around the same time. Joseph Califano, *Inside: A Public and Private Life* (New York: PublicAffairs, 2004), 126.

broadcast in three installments over CBS in 1970. As they discuss the violent 1963 transition, anchorman Walter Cronkite asks Johnson whether he is satisfied that there was no foreign conspiracy. "I can't honestly say that I've ever been completely relieved of the fact that there might have been international connections," replies Johnson. Cronkite pushes a little harder and asks whether Johnson's lingering suspicions involve Cuba. "Oh, I don't think we ought to discuss the suspicions because there's not any hard evidence that would lead me to the conclusion that Oswald was directed by a foreign government."[49] Three weeks before it is aired, Johnson has second thoughts and insists that this exchange be cut out entirely, on grounds of "national security." After a tense internal dispute, CBS reluctantly obliges and removes all references to the *Warren Report*. But the story leaks out anyway that Johnson "expressed fundamental doubts about the Warren Commission's conclusion" during the Cronkite interview.[50]

While Johnson's remarks are interpreted as a knock against the very panel he created, he doesn't intend them as such. At every opportunity he reiterates his confidence in the competence, ability, and honesty of the Warren Commission members. During a December 1972 dinner with the chief justice and Mrs. Warren, Johnson goes out of his way to praise Warren's leadership of the panel: "Chief, of all the things you have done for your country, the most important was your work with the Commission on the assassination of President Kennedy."[51] Whether he realizes it or not, Johnson's views are indistinguishable from those of Senator Richard Russell. Knowing full well the intensity of the Kennedys' effort to overthrow Castro in 1962 and 1963, Russell steadfastly refused to sign a Commission report that ruled out a conspiracy hatched by or in Cuba.[52]

Of course, Johnson always has at his disposal a perfect and powerful vehicle for telling the rawest of truths about his tenure: his presidential memoir, which is under contract to Holt, Rinehart and Winston, a prominent New York publisher. But he will choose not to use his November 1971 book, *The Vantage Point,* to tell this story, or many others for that matter. Though painstakingly researched and fully documented, the memoir will be a stilted and predictable read, drained of its vital juices, and treated as such by the critics. Consequently, Johnson's most revealing statement will be published six months after his death

49. Murray Illson, "Johnson in '69 Suspected Foreign Ties with Oswald," *New York Times,* 26 April 1975.

50. Christopher Lydon, "Johnson TV Interview Abridged at His Request," *New York Times,* 29 April 1970; Ronald Kessler, "LBJ Cuts Remarks on JFK Death," *Washington Post,* 28 April 1970.

51. Earl Warren, *The Memoirs of Earl Warren* (Garden City, N.Y.: Doubleday, 1977), 358.

52. This was the other of the two "*dis*-sents" that Russell insisted upon before he would sign the *Warren Report.* Johnson and Russell, conversation, 18 September 1964, LBJL. Consequently, and contrary to the widespread perception, the *Warren Report* did not rule out a conspiracy. The compromise agreed upon stated that on the basis of the *evidence before it,* Oswald was not part of a conspiracy, foreign or domestic, to assassinate President Kennedy. *Warren Report,* 21.

in January 1973; it was uttered during a June 1971 conversation that he knows will be published posthumously if it is ever published at all.[53]

The conversation occurs two months after Johnson's memoir is finished, while he is presumably reading the galley proofs. Johnson receives Leo Janos, one of his former speechwriters and now the Houston bureau chief for *Time* magazine, at the Johnson Library in Austin. Together with *Life* editor Thomas Griffith, Janos is there to discuss serialization of Johnson's memoirs in *Life* prior to the book's publication in November. "It was a charm session, to get [Time-Life] interested," Janos will later recall.[54] Apart from this encounter, the former president is virtually a media recluse. He routinely refuses all requests for interviews on any subject.

Though completely unplanned, the conversation occurs at a propitious time. After a nearly four-year hiatus, columnist Jack Anderson (Drew Pearson having died in 1969) has breathed new life into his 1967 scoop about CIA plots to assassinate Fidel Castro in the early 1960s. Relentless prodding of Edward Morgan finally resulted in a meeting with Morgan's mysterious client and, eventually, in permission to publish John Rosselli's name as the CIA's underworld contact. No one followed up Anderson's three columns in January/February, but at least now they were being published by the *Washington Post*.[55] Another factor contributing to Johnson's expansive mood is the *New York Times*'s publication, three days earlier, of what will come to be known as the "Pentagon Papers." There is much to talk about, in other words, when Janos and Griffith arrive on June 16, and Johnson will not disappoint his guests.

Over a cup of coffee after lunch, Griffith raises the subject of President Kennedy's assassination. Perhaps Griffith has the now-famous deleted Cronkite segment in mind, or is wondering about the recent Anderson columns. Confident that his guests will obey the ground rules—all his remarks, Johnson says, are off the record—the president not only restates what was deleted from the CBS broadcast but goes further than he ever has before as to the details.[56] "I never believed Oswald acted alone, although I can accept that he pulled the trigger," says Johnson. And though he cannot prove it, he is convinced President

53. Johnson will also reiterate his belief in a Cuban plot during a 1972 interview with syndicated columnist Marianne Means, who writes for the conservative Hearst newspaper chain. Oswald was "either under the influence or the orders" of Fidel Castro when he committed the act, avers the former president. Once more, however, Johnson effectively retracts what he has just declared. He swears Means to secrecy and she will not disclose the remarks until April 1975. Marianne Means, "LBJ Linked Castro to JFK Death," *News Tribune* (Woodbridge, N.J.), 22 April 1975; Illson, "Johnson in '69 Suspected Foreign Ties."

54. Author's interview with Leo Janos, 23 March 2004. Time-Life eventually declines to serialize the memoir, and excerpts will be published in the *Washington Post* and other newspapers.

55. Jack Anderson, "6 Attempts to Kill Castro Laid to CIA," *Washington Post*, 18 January 1971; "Castro Plot Raises Ugly Questions," *Washington Post*, 19 January 1971; "Castro Stalker Worked for the CIA," *Washington Post*, 23 February 1971; Anderson, *Politics*, 107.

56. Johnson to Janos, letter, 14 July 1971, Post-Presidential Subject File, Box 361, LBJL.

Kennedy was slain in retaliation for CIA efforts to assassinate Castro. After he assumed office, says Johnson, he found "we had been operating a damned Murder Inc. in the Caribbean."[57]

When it is published two years later, in an elegiac piece about Johnson's last years, the declaration provokes only a ripple of attention. The mythology around JFK does not leave room for it, for one, and Johnson's well-known penchant for exaggeration—his tendency to speak for effect—works against him. With conspiracy theories about the assassination a cottage industry, the fact that Johnson believed in one of them is interesting, but only mildly so. It is easy to discount the views of a president whose term gave rise to the phrase "credibility gap." Besides, the American public seems to want no part of Lyndon Johnson owing to his divisive five years in office—none of his regrets, reminiscences, or revelations. And neither do Democrats. Johnson was more or less told to stay away from the 1972 national convention, a stunning rebuke to the man who occupied the White House just four years before.

Johnson's remark is dismissed until 1975, when a series of unpredictable events unfold, ignited by the Watergate break-in. A season of inquiry forms in Washington because of that unprecedented scandal, and eventually it envelops the heretofore sacrosanct CIA. When the allegations of agency wrongdoing surface, they fall on the desk of Gerald Ford, the first man ever appointed, rather than elected, to the presidency. He is also one of the three surviving members of the Warren Commission. And precisely because of that service, Ford is genuinely shocked when he learns the truth about one of those misdeeds, especially Richard Helms's explanation that Robert Kennedy "personally managed the operation" to assassinate Castro.[58] The president finds the secret about the assassination plots "too large" and troubling to bear, as Thomas Powers will later write. On January 16, 1975, two weeks after being briefed, President Ford inexplicably blurts out a reference to presidentially sanctioned assassination plots during a White House luncheon with the publisher and top editors from the *New York Times*. The instant he blunders, Ford hastens to add that the disclosure is off the record. But in five weeks the story will be broken by reporter Daniel Schorr on the *CBS Evening News*.[59]

In the congressional investigation that ensues, there is a sudden groundswell of thinking in Johnson's direction. In October 1975 Senator Richard Schweiker (R-Pennsylvania), a member of the Senate select committee investigating the CIA, and particularly its performance in the wake of the 1963

57. Leo Janos, "The Last Days of the President: LBJ in Retirement," *The Atlantic Monthly*, July 1973; United Press International, "LBJ Theory of JFK Slaying Told," *New York Times*, 17 June 1973.

58. Kissinger and Ford, memorandum of conversation, 4 January 1975, Kissinger/Scowcroft Files, GRFL.

59. Powers, *Man Who Kept the Secrets*, 290–91.

assassination, confidently predicts that the oft-maligned *Warren Report* is finished. "I think the Warren Commission *Report* is like a house of cards," Schweiker tells a news conference. "It's going to collapse."[60] Normally mild-mannered, Schweiker is woefully underinformed and foolishly overconfident. At least one member of the Commission, Allen Dulles, appreciated the full context at the time, and possibly Richard Russell did as well, for little escaped him. Collectively, the Warren Commission might not have known about contemporaneous American-hatched plots to kill Castro. But it certainly examined Oswald's links to Cuba as carefully and minutely as possible—indeed, as if it *did* know.

Lyndon Johnson was not wrong to jump to his conclusion about a link between Castro and Lee Harvey Oswald, and may charitably be forgiven for doing so. Ultimately, he was mistaken. Notwithstanding what Washington was trying to accomplish in Havana, Oswald did not work for any secret service "larger than the power centers in the privacy of his mind," as Norman Mailer will later put it.[61]

Johnson's opinion on who stood behind Oswald is not, in any case, what is most significant about his attempts at post-presidential revelation. Rather, and somewhat awkwardly, he was trying to draw attention to what was, from his vantage point, the central story of his years in office: the mutiny of liberal Democrats against his unexpected ascension to office and their unfair treatment of him. During the four years that remained to him after leaving the White House, he was deeply conflicted about releasing information that would tarnish Presidents Kennedy and Eisenhower. But Johnson obviously hoped the truth would eventually surface one way or another, and perhaps redress history's verdict on his own presidency.

60. "Schweiker Predicts Collapse of *Warren Report* on Kennedy," *New York Times,* 16 October 1975.

61. Norman Mailer, *Oswald's Tale: An American Mystery* (New York: Random House, 1995), 352.

Acknowledgments

I owe my first debt to Jean Holke, who has believed in and supported my work from the beginning. After the Lyndon Baines Johnson Library released the first assassination-related conversations in 1993 and 1994, the so-called K series, Jean agreed to transcribe the tapes anew once it became clear that the contemporary transcripts prepared by the president's secretarial pool were only fair approximations of what had been recorded. Jean, a retired legal secretary, is a tireless and interested worker, and my first introduction to the nuances of the tape recordings came about because of her efforts. The first drafts of most of the the K series recordings (November–December 1963, January–February and September 1964, December 1966, and January–March 1967) are her work—in other words, the bulk of the transcripts contained in this book. I cannot thank Jean sufficiently for her labors. Every author ought to be so lucky.

My agent, Elaine Markson, has been the soul of patience for as long as I have called myself a writer, sticking with me despite so many detours we've both lost count. I am grateful that she is still open to new ideas and recognized immediately the intrinsic value of a separate book that would fully exploit and explain Johnson's tape recordings pertaining to the assassination. The same holds true for Jonathan Segal, my editor at Knopf. Though he is anxious to publish what will be my primary contribution to the literature on the assassination, a forthcoming history of the Warren Commission, Jon nonetheless realized that a book utilizing the presidential recordings could stand by itself as a worthwhile publication. This book has also benefited from Jon's exacting editing. While many of the conversations must be included in any book that purports to present Lyndon Johnson's assassination-related conversations, a large number fall into a gray area. Jon helped sculpt the book and sharpen the commentary, so that while it may not be an exhaustive treatment, it is comprehensive and representative. Jon's assistant, Ida Giragossian, helped me navigate a multitude of editorial tasks.

Virtually any book that dares to add to the voluminous literature on the assassination faces an uphill climb. I am more grateful than normal, therefore, for the recognition and generous support received from the J. Anthony Lukas Prize Project sponsored jointly by the Columbia University Graduate School of Journalism and the Nieman Foundation at Harvard University. In 2001 I received the Lukas Work-in-Progress award for my book on the Warren Commission. There could be no greater mark of validation than that prize, and it arrived at a serendipitous juncture. This volume is intimately linked to that effort, and I trust that Linda Healey and Arthur Gelb, the trustees of the Lukas Prize Project, and Nancy Hicks Maynard, Thomas Powers, and Rebecca Sinkler, the judges who granted me the award, will not object to having two books emerge from my receipt of a Lukas Prize rather than just the one promised.

This book could not exist without the work of the Lyndon B. Johnson Library in Austin, Texas. Harry Middleton, the retired director, deserves a special accolade for arranging to make the tapes available decades earlier than anticipated. This book exploits not only conversations released under the provisions of the 1992 John F. Kennedy Records Collection Act but several that would not be available save for Mr. Middleton's efforts. Mrs. Claudia (Lady Bird) Johnson is equally deserving of praise for recognizing how useful and fascinating it would be to hear history being made with the "bark off."

The archivists at the Library always responded to my requests for information promptly and with unfailing grace, even when the question appeared trivial. In particular I should like to thank senior archivists Claudia Anderson and Regina Greenwell for their exceptional patience, cooperation, and thoughtful suggestions. Archivists Laura Harmon, Barbara Constable, Sarah Haldeman, Renee Gravois, Will Clements, and Mary Knill, along with Linda Seelke, recently retired from the Library, Tina Houston, the Library's assistant director, and Betty Sue Flowers, the director since 2002, also facilitated my use of the Johnson Library holdings. Philip Scott, the audiovisual archivist, deserves thanks for patiently explaining the complicated provenance of the *Air Force One* tapes from November 22. The Lyndon Baines Johnson Foundation awarded me a Moody Grant in the winter of 2004 so that I could fashion my annotations from primary records, and I am grateful to the foundation's Grants Review Committee, its director, Larry Temple, and its assistant director, Larry Reed.

Second only to the archivists at the Johnson Library are the people who maintain the John F. Kennedy Assassination Records Collection at the National Archives in College Park, Maryland. Steven Tilley, Martha Wagner Murphy, Matt Fulgham, and James Mathis have been invaluable guides to using the collection and unstinting in their efforts to answer an endless list of questions and requests. The next most important research facility for making sense of the Warren Commission is the Richard B. Russell Library in Athens, Georgia. Sheryl Vogt, the director, was unflagging in her efforts to help me research historical minutiae. A residential fellowship in 1998 from the John Nicholas Brown Center for the Study of American Civilization in Providence, Rhode Island, enabled me to research pertinent holdings at the John F. Kennedy Library in Boston. Joyce Botelho, then director of the center, and Professor James Patterson were instrumental in arranging that fellowship. Without Richard Baker, director of the U.S. Senate Historical Office, I would not have been able to make sense of Johnson's fleeting references to events that occurred during his years in the Senate and as vice president. At the Georgetown University Library, Nick Brazzi kindly helped me recover an obscure taped interview of George Ball from the Michael Amrine Papers. David Horrocks of the Gerald R. Ford Library was a knowledgeable and willing guide to critical documents from the Ford presidency. Gary Mack, archivist for the Sixth Floor Museum in Dallas, was a reliable expert on where to find obscure facts, that is, if he did not already know them. I have also made use of the following archival collections: Hale Boggs Papers at Tulane University (with the help of Kevin Fontenot); John Sherman Cooper Papers at the University of Kentucky (with the assistance of Jeff Suchanek); Allen Dulles Papers at Princeton University (aided by Ben Primer); John McCloy Papers at Amherst College (assisted by Daria D'Arienzo); and the Earl Warren Papers at the Library of Congress. These collections were instrumental in helping me understand the context of the recordings, although their full value will be reflected more in the book to come.

Several colleagues aided me in annotating complicated subjects accurately yet succinctly. Professor David Barrett took time from his own forthcoming book on congressional oversight of the intelligence community in the 1940s and 1950s to help me with that arcane subject, especially as it influenced formation of the Warren Commission. Patricia Lambert graciously read the parts of the manuscript having to do with the Jim Garrison fiasco in 1967, a subject that almost defies simple explanation. Paul Hoch has been a vigilant critic and supporter of my work, as well as an invaluable guide to the thicket of books, articles, and arguments about the assassination. Priscilla Johnson McMillan was a thoughtful sounding board on the William Manchester affair, in addition to being a staunch ally and offering the wisest counsel one could hope for.

I am also indebted to several editors who have leaned against the wind and published my related articles over the years, thus enabling my work to continue and sharpening my analysis. They include Elsa Dixler and Art Winslow, former literary editors at *The Nation* magazine, and Victor Navasky, currently the editorial director; Richard Snow, editor of *American Heritage*; Ben Franklin, editor of *The Washington Spectator*; Stanley Kutler, former editor of *Reviews in American History*; Robert Wilson, editor of *Preservation*; Glenna Whitley, senior editor of *Dallas* magazine; Mark Kramer, editor of the *Journal of Cold War Studies*; Steve Lagerfeld, editor of *The Wilson Quarterly*; Errol Laborde, editor of *New Orleans* magazine; Barbara Pace, editor of *Studies in Intelligence*; Fred Hiatt, editorial page editor of the *Washington Post*; and finally, Cullen Murphy, managing editor of *The Atlantic*, and Amy Meeker, a senior editor there.

Robert Dallek generously shared all the Johnson tape recordings he purchased after completing his two-volume biography of the president. Dr. Erin Mahan, a historian at the U.S. Department of State, has been an invaluable colleague for several years now. Professor Anna Nelson at American University and Dr. William Joyce of Pennsylvania State University have been steadfast in their support of my work on the history involved in the assassination, despite a pace that appeared to be glacial at times. On the Kennedy and Johnson presidencies, and the peculiarities of a tapes-based narrative, I benefited from exchanges with professors Frank Gavin at the University of Texas and Jon Rosenberg at Hunter College, CUNY. Vanderbilt professor Tom Schwartz's detailed knowledge of the Johnson years was especially helpful in the latter stages. Tarek Masoud, a doctoral candidate at Yale University, generously took the time to research the Abe Fortas papers for answers to questions that could only be settled there. I also gained perspective from the collegial advice of William Burr, Richard Drake, Alfred Goldberg, Dan Guttman, Samuel Halpern, Mark Hulbert, John McAdams, Robert Mann, Katherine Meyer, Jeffery Paine, Sam Papich, Jay Peterzell, Herbert Romerstein, Robert Schrepf, Jay Tolson, Howard Willens, Andy Winiarczyk, and the late Scott Breckinridge.

Martel Electronics of Yorba Linda, California, made practical suggestions that enabled me to enhance the sound quality of the tape recordings, thus making the transcriptions more accurate. Wendy Margolis was a patient guide to the intricacies of a new word processing program, and Benjamin Healy proved an expert checker of fact. For their hospitality and counsel along the way, I would like to thank Donna Harsch, and especially Jason Berry, Darwin Payne, and Michele Stanush. They made working in New Orleans, Dallas, and Austin, respectively, comfortable and thus rewarding. The Hotel Lawrence was my favorite place to stay in downtown Dallas.

The encouragement from my family has been vital, naturally. I cannot write that they didn't wonder sometimes, but my parents, Bernhard and Dora, and my sister, Laja, seldom questioned me. My wife, Tamar, and daughter, Nora, are my balm and ballast. Absent Tamar's forbearance and encouragement, this book would not have been written.

Index

A NOTE ON THE TYPE

The text of this book was set in a typeface called Times New Roman, designed by Stanley Morison for The Times (London), and introduced by that newspaper in 1932.

Among typographers and designers of the twentieth century, Stanley Morison was a strong forming influence, as typographical adviser to the Monotype Corporation of London, as a director of two distinguished English publishing houses, and as a writer of sensibility, erudition, and keen practical sense.

In 1930 Morison wrote: "Type design moves at the pace of the most conservative reader. The good type-designer therefore realizes that, for a new fount to be successful, it has to be so good that only very few recognize its novelty. If readers do not notice the consummate reticence and rare discipline of a new type, it is probably a good letter." It is now generally recognized that in the creation of Times Roman, Morison successfully met the qualifications of his theoretical doctrine.

Composed by Creative Graphics,
Allentown, Pennsylvania
Printed and bound by Berryville Graphics,
Berryville, Virginia
Designed by Virginia Tan

Max Holland has worked as a journalist in Washington, D.C., for more than twenty years. From 1982 to 1986 he wrote a column for *The Nation* magazine, and he remains a contributing editor at *The Nation* and *The Wilson Quarterly*. From 1998 to 2003 he was also a research fellow at the Miller Center of Public Affairs, University of Virginia. He has received several prizes, including fellowships from the Guggenheim Foundation, the National Endowment for the Humanities, and the Woodrow Wilson International Center for Scholars. He is the author of *When the Machine Stopped: A Cautionary Tale from Industrial America*, and *The CEO Goes to Washington: Negotiating the Halls of Power*. In 2001, he won the J. Anthony Lukas Work-in-Progress Award, jointly given by the Columbia University Graduate School of Journalism and Harvard University's Nieman Foundation, for his research on a narrative history of the Warren Commission. That same year he received a Studies in Intelligence Award from the Central Intelligence Agency, becoming the first author working outside the U.S. government to be so honored. He lives in Silver Spring, Maryland.